Principles of Inductive Rural Sociology

T. LYNN SMITH
University of Florida

PAUL E. ZOPF, Jr.
Guilford College

 F. A. DAVIS COMPANY, Philadelphia

Principles of Inductive Rural Sociology

Dedicated to the Memory of Pitirim A. Sorokin
Great Master of Inductive Rural Sociology

PREFACE

This book was written for college and university students engaged in the study of rural life; but it is also addressed to all workers who are engaged in activities designed to increase the welfare of the people on the land, and especially to those public servants who are responsible for planning, guiding, and carrying out agricultural policies in various parts of the world. In that connection its very existence and especially its international dimension are justified in considerable measure by two facts: (1) that even now at least two thirds of the world's people derive their living from agriculture and closely related activities; and (2) that the great bulk of this agriculture is conducted under such sociocultural conditions that it generates dismally low levels of living.

The decades since World War II have seen the multiplication of detailed analytical studies of this and that part of the sociology of rural life, but even at present synthesis is lagging far behind analysis. The general objective of this volume has been to give due consideration to all scientific approaches that bear upon the field and to assemble from the most reliable sources pertinent facts, significant tested hypotheses, and inductively derived theoretical generalizations relative to the social relations among those who make up rural populations. In this way it is hoped that the present work will contribute to systematization in the examination of the basic sociological principles relating to rural life.

Since 1945, the development of a science of rural society has been pushed forward vigorously. It has not been easy to incorporate all of the more significant new contributions, even in summary form. But the reader, seeking the significance of the term "inductive" in the title of the book, is assured that a serious examination has been made of large numbers of recent research findings in the several specialized areas of the sociology of rural life. He also may be sure that the same applies to publications in the broader realms of sociology. The pertinent conclusions and principles derived from these studies have been woven together to the best of the authors' abilities in the pages of this book. These findings include those drawn from studies made in all sections of the United States and also from the voluminous works now available, many of them by American sociologists, of rural life and labor in all parts of the world.

T. Lynn Smith acknowledges once more the assistance given by his wife, sons, and many other persons in the preparation of his earlier volumes (including the various editions of *The Sociology of Rural Life* and *Brazil: People and Institutions, Rural Sociology: A Trend Report,* and *Colombia: Social Structure and the Process of Development*), which have been drawn upon for the materials used in this book; he also desires to thank his present research assistant, Blaine Stevenson, who has helped substantially with this work.

Paul Zopf acknowledges his substantial debt to many people. Foremost is that owed to the senior author—friend and former teacher, T. Lynn Smith—for inspiration and instruction in the study of rural life and for the viewpoint that sees rural sociology as an integral part of general sociology. Gratitude also is due many people at Guilford College, where he has been privileged to participate in the excitement of inquiry of many kinds for more than a decade. In particular, his colleagues William Burris, Jerry Godard, Grimsley Hobbs, E. Daryl Kent, and David Stafford helped provide the atmosphere and the encouragement which made it possible for him to carry out his part of the total task of bringing the volume to completion. Students at Guilford College have made much the same contribution to the work, especially as they have reacted to various hypotheses, analyses, and statements of sociological principles as their instructor has seen them. Finally, inestimable gratitude is due his wife and son for generating encouragement, domestic accord, and patience, but mostly for being who they are.

T. Lynn Smith
Paul E. Zopf, Jr.

CONTENTS

5 CONCLUSION 489

PART ONE

INTRODUCTION

Chapter 1 outlines the features of science in general, presents the essentials of the scientific method, states the nature of sociology, explains the relationships of rural sociology to the general science of society, and gives some of the more important stages and milestones in the development of the sociology of rural life. It also sets forth a number of the recent trends in the study of rural society and emphasizes the need for more efforts at synthesis in the field of rural sociology. The second chapter, "The Country and the City," presents the particular ways in which the rural cultural environment and social organization differ from the urban—the factors that make society, culture, and people in the country different from those in the city.

1
THE SCIENTIFIC STUDY OF RURAL SOCIETY

This volume is the result of an endeavor to assemble in one textbook the essential facts and basic principles that have been secured through the application of the scientific method to the study of rural societies in their various aspects. Its authors have tried to keep constantly before themselves a broad perspective of the origins and development of rural societies in all parts of the world. Therefore, they hope that their interpretations and conclusions are soundly based upon the situations in various "underdeveloped" parts of the world as well as on those among people considered more "advanced."

SCIENCE

Science is a term used to denote an organized body of knowledge, including both fact and theory. It is a species of theoretical knowledge, and as such it differs from all applied skills and practical wisdom. Science is the accumulation, arranged in a systematic manner, of facts and principles that have been derived from the application of the scientific method. The word also is used as a collective noun to embrace the various sciences such as physics, chemistry, geology, and astronomy; on the other hand, it may refer to one of these separately. To the extent that the scientific method is applied to the study of human relationships, the resulting body of fact and inference entitles sociology and the various social sciences to be classed with the other sciences. Because of this it is desirable to consider, first, the principal characteristics of science itself, and, second, the essentials of the scientific method.

3

Science possesses certain characteristics in common with other species of knowledge such as philosophy and history, but it differs from them in fundamental ways. All sound knowledge is dependent upon critical discrimination—the ability to get at the naked facts and not to be misled by mere appearances, generally accepted ideas, or one's own desires. Generality and system are also essential to all science. Science seeks to discover order in nature, to ascertain common and repeated characteristics. For science, the most important facts are those that occur many times, those that are constant or repeated in time or space. For this reason, science is concerned with types and classes and with general principles or uniformities. The unique is of little scientific value; individual objects or particular events are of interest merely as specimens.

The most fundamental characteristic of science, and the one that most clearly differentiates it from philosophy, is empirical verification. Sensory stimuli are all-important in scientific endeavor, and science begins with observation. It does not end there. After the mind has reflected upon its observations, it tends to run forward into the unknown, to penetrate the realm of supposition. Propositions are developed that may be true, but in science all hypotheses and explanations must be thoroughly checked by further observation. Mere internal consistency is not a sufficient test of scientific validity. A well-disciplined scientific mind is one capable of formulating significant hypotheses. For scientific purposes hypotheses that cannot be tested are useless, regardless of how consistent they may be with other hypotheses. In philosophy, on the other hand, the chief criterion of usefulness and value is that a hypothesis or proposition be consistent with previous assertions. Unlike philosophy, science insists that all hypotheses be tested empirically, and it retains only those that are confirmed by further observation. So in common with other species of theoretical knowledge, science is based upon critical discrimination, generality, and system. Unlike other systems of knowledge, science is interested in the ordinary, usual, and commonplace and demands the empirical verification of all hypotheses.

THE SCIENTIFIC METHOD

The mental activities used in the acquisition of scientific knowledge are of two main types: (1) *observation;* and (2) *inference.* The essence of the scientific method consists in skill in securing unbiased, pertinent observations and accuracy in making logical and meaningful inferences from these observations. Observation is the operation of perceiving objects and occurrences, their features, and their existing inter-relationships. It is also the conscious comprehension of experiences of the mind. Inference is the development of conclusions within the framework of others already formulated and either grounded in observation or posited tentatively for additional evaluation and testing. Observation is of two types: (1) *bare observation* of uncontrolled phenomena; and (2) *experiment*. Bare observation is so commonplace that its basic importance in scientific endeavors is frequently overlooked. In sharp contrast to the neglect of bare observation in many of the sciences, experiment has been so useful in setting the stage for fruitful observation that it is frequently asserted to be all-important. In addition to experimentation, or the control of extraneous factors so that only one circumstance is varied at a time, there are many other aids to observation. The astronomer has his telescope, the botanist his microscope, and the chemist his test tubes and retorts. In the social sciences, where experiment is rarely possible, the carefully designed schedule and the well-kept record have proved useful aids to observation.

Inference, too, may be divided into two chief types, namely, *induction* and *deduction*. Induction is the process of ascertaining some general uniformity or regularity among the phenomena under observation. It consists of reasoning from the particular to the general. It is the process by which a general conclusion is reached through the observation of the specific facts. Deductive reasoning consists in applying general conclusions expressed in concepts to particular classes or cases. It involves postulating attributes of the specific from a knowledge of the general. Both induction and deduction are indispensable elements of the scientific method. Induction plays a useful role in the formulation of hypotheses or generalizations concerning uniformities or principles that may be valid; in inductive reasoning the individual cases suggest broader generalizations, which *may* be true. Deduction then comes into play to see what consequences would follow if the induction were valid. If the hypothesis itself is of significance, and if some of these results or consequences can pass empirical tests, then the hypothesis is a good one, and the testing of it will contribute to human knowledge. Thus, through induction comes hypothesis, and through deduction the stage is set for testing the hypothesis. The testing of significant and meaningful hypotheses is important in the advance of scientific knowledge. The great scientist can conceive the important hypotheses, and can then devise ways of testing them with empirical data. The good hypothesis permits, through the application of deduction, the inference of consequences that may be tested empirically; it does not conflict with any established uniformity, and the consequences inferred from it do not conflict with the phenomena.

Observations and inferences are of very little value or meaning unless arranged in an orderly system. For this reason, *classification* and *description* are of importance in the scientific method. Observations or sensory experiences, are so diverse that we avoid chaos by trying to find some logical arrangement of them. Classification was one of the earliest and simplest ways of determining order in nature; it remains one of the most important. The human mind has a tendency to note similarities among different things, and this process constitutes a beginning in classification. Things possessing common attributes are placed together in a class and given a name. Language would be impossible without names, for every common name denotes a class of objects. At present, many groupings seem superficial indeed, and will not do for scientific purposes. In some cases, such as with the nouns "community," "culture," "social class," and "institution," one is likely to find the dictionary so loaded with multifarious meanings of the terms that it may be difficult to discover any that are sociologically valid and pertinent. Nevertheless, popular classification in language is the usual starting point for scientific classification.

Of necessity, classification for scientific purposes must be more exact than that for practical purposes. For classification to be of value in the study of a particular phenomenon, all the things that evidence that phenomenon must be brought into one category and then arranged in a series according to the degree to which they exhibit it. In classification, the rules of logical division must be kept in mind. Thus, there must be: (1) only one basis for division, so that the subclasses are mutually exclusive; (2) an exhaustive division, with each step being proximate; and (3) appropriateness in the entire division and each of its segments.

Description is also of primary importance in the scientific method. When objects or traits are recognized as constituting a class, the next scientific task is to name and describe the group. The description may consist of a mere statement giving the easily recognized parts, qualities, and processes. Very frequently in scientific classifications, however, the predicating of attributes is not sufficient; exact quantitative measures are essential. Some sciences have developed elaborate systems of nomenclature and terminology as means of obtaining short but adequate descriptions. Most of the social sciences, and particularly economics and sociology, rely greatly upon statistical devices as convenient and quantitative ways of describing their data. Description of a class necessarily involves enumerating the most important attributes of the class, i.e., those most likely to be correlated with the remaining characteristics. It also involves consideration of differences. In sociology, the *frequency table* is of fundamental importance for summarizing and showing the outstanding characteristics of mass data. Measures of the average— whether the arithmetic average (*mean*), the most frequent value (*mode*), or the middle value (*median*)—are of great value in sensing the magnitude of the typical class member. The *standard deviation* or σ is of great assistance in visualizing the extent to which the series is clustered about or departs from the average of the group.

It should be apparent that definition is closely associated with classification, being largely the statement of the principles involved in the particular classification. An object or thing is adequately defined when it is (1) referred to its proper class, and (2) differentiated, through the enumeration of its unique characteristics, from the remainder of the objects in that class.

The scientific roles of perspective and insight also need some clarification. To see clearly the position and relative importance of phenomena in time and space is to have perspective. To understand the relationship among facts, to evaluate properly the results and importance of the various relevant factors, is to have insight. Perspective and insight are the indelible marks of the educated person. Both probably come through intense practice and experience in grappling with carefully selected sensory impressions. Rigidly focused observations, however, and especially those in which the attention is directed for the purpose of interrogating nature concerning the validity of a specific hypothesis, are the warp and woof of the learning process.

SOCIOLOGY AND RURAL SOCIOLOGY

Difficult as it is to define the field of sociology as a whole, it is even harder to set forth the nature and limits of the field of rural sociology. As has been remarked, there are almost as many definitions of sociology as there are sociologists; a similar observation probably has even greater validity in the case of rural sociology. The pragmatic approach, which would define sociology as what sociologists do, fails completely with respect to rural sociology. Rural sociologists, like other scientists, do not cease their pursuit of knowledge about a specific topic or problem when the line of investigation they are pursuing leads across disciplinary boundaries into another field of knowledge. Neither do they stop in their efforts to understand a matter merely because the next logical steps involve the study of urban situations and the use of urban data.

As a simple working definition of rural sociology, we use the following: Rural sociology, the sociology of rural life, is the systematized body of knowledge that has resulted from the application of the scientific method to the study of rural society, its organization and structure, its processes, its basic social systems, and its changes.

As is stressed in Chapter 2, it is not easy to draw a satisfactory distinction between the rural and urban portions of society. Actually, society is not divided into two sharply differentiated portions, one urban and the other rural. Instead it is comparable to a spectrum in which the elements clearly identifiable as rural are found in an undiluted form at the one extreme, and those most indisputably urban at the other, with the two gradually changing in relative importance as one moves across the spectrum. Thus, from the standpoint of the size of the community, the relative importance of agricultural and pastoral activities, the degree of social differentiation, or any of the other important criteria that may be used to distinguish between rural and urban, the rural features become less and the urban more important as one passes from the single farmstead to the cluster of farm homes at a crossroads, to the farmers' hamlet, to the agricultural village, to the trade-center village, to the town, to the small city, to the large city, and to the great metropolitan center. Furthermore, into this continuum must be fitted the varying degrees of urbanization or rurality, represented by the more remote portions of the metropolitan area, the various situations that make up what is known as the rural-urban fringe, and many other combinations of the rural and urban patterns of living. Thus, rural and urban are not merely the two parts of a simple dichotomy but, rather, segments on a scale in which the smallest, most remote settlements of agriculturists, herders, and collectors figure at one extreme, and the largest, most diversified and most complex centers of manufacturing, transportation, and commerce are located at the other. The vast majority of communities are neither purely rural nor purely urban, but combine rural and urban features in varying porportions.

Backgrounds

Rural sociology was a large and integral part of the general subject when, in the last 2 decades of the nineteenth century, courses in sociology appeared almost simultaneously in scores of American colleges and universities. This was particularly true at the University of Chicago, where George E. Vincent[1] and Charles R. Henderson laid much of the groundwork which

[1] Vincent's role seems to have been overlooked by those who have written on the development of rural sociology, perhaps because his writing in the field was cut short by his rapid advancement to the presidency of the University of Minnesota and then to that of the Rockefeller Foundation. Nevertheless, he was responsible for the prominence with which the study of rural social phenomena figures in *An Introduction to the Study of Society,* the first textbook on sociology to be published in the United States. Later, when he was elected president of the American Sociological Society (1916), he organized the annual meeting of that professional organization around the theme "The Sociology of Rural Life" and took as the topic for his presidential address "Countryside and Nation." In 1917, too, when president of the Rockefeller Foundation, he was one of a group of nine leaders who made themselves into the Committee on Country Life, which was responsible for the organization of the American Country Life Association.

led in 1892 to the organization of the Department of Sociology, and at Columbia University, where Franklin H. Giddings, from his chair in the Faculty of Political Science, began to interest graduate students in the sociological study of rural communities.

In a considerable measure, however, the development of rural sociology, and perhaps of general sociology as well, arose from the humanitarian philosophy that was a potent force in the United States during the closing decades of the nineteenth century. With the exhaustion of the supply of unoccupied new land, the passing of the frontier, and the growing pains of an industrial civilization, there developed an acute awareness that all was not well in the United States and particularly in rural America. The decline of the open-country church and the depopulation (or "folk depletion," in the terminology of Edward Alsworth Ross) of the rural portions of New England and other parts of the Northeast were among the facts that stimulated a humanitarian interest in rural life. Such an interest, characterized by a strong desire to do something to improve life in the country, had become widespread by about 1900. It was especially apparent among the clergymen of the time. An immediate effect of their activity was the establishment of courses in rural social problems at the University of Chicago, the University of Michigan, Michigan State College, and the University of North Dakota. To the clergymen and other humanists of the time must also be credited the creation of the atmosphere that led President Theodore Roosevelt to appoint his famous Commission on Country Life. The hearings conducted, the meetings promoted, and the report published by the Commission and the activities they gave rise to were responsible in large measure for the development of rural sociological research and teaching in the United States.

The Commission itself was appointed in 1908. The occasion was a visit to this country, and a call upon the President, by the noted Irish author and reformer, Sir Horace Plunkett. Roosevelt was quick to see the need and to grasp the opportunity. In fact, his enthusiasm led him to propose to Congress that the "Department of Agriculture . . . should become in fact a Department of Country Life." Roosevelt persuaded a noted naturalist, Professor Liberty Hyde Bailey of Cornell University, to head the Commission, and Henry Wallace, Kenyon L. Butterfield, Gifford Pinchot, Walter H. Page, Charles S. Barrett, and William A. Beard to serve as members. Of the group, Butterfield definitely deserved to be classified as a rural sociologist. In his letter of appointment, the President stressed: "Agriculture is not the whole of country life. The great rural interests are human interests, and good crops are of little value to the farmer unless they open the door to a good kind of life on the farm."

The famous *Report of the Country Life Commission,* published in 1909, called for better living on the farms and recommended three measures for promoting the desired objective: (1) "taking stock of country life . . . an exhaustive study or survey of all the conditions that surround the business of farming and the people who live in the country"; (2) nationalized extension work; and (3) "a campaign for rural progress. We urge the holding of local, state and even national conferences on rural progress, designed to unite the interests of education, organization and religion into one forward movement for the rebuilding of country life."

In line with these recommendations, the next decade was one of great ferment—often more or less aimless—in hundreds of groups and associations whose members were motivated by a desire to bring about a genuine improvement in the rural life of the nation. Many of the first steps in the development of rural sociology as a discipline were taken before 1920; the years between 1909 and 1920 must be thought of as the period of the general social survey. In an attempt to follow through the recommendations of the Commission on Country Life, during these years hundreds of rural life conferences were held throughout the nation, and thousands of rural social surveys were attempted. In the survey movement Warren H. Wilson, a Ph.D. in sociology under Giddings at Columbia, was largely responsible, as director of Town and Country Surveys for the Presbyterian Church in the United States, for the conduct and publication between 1912 and 1916 of sixteen "Church and Community Surveys" covering seventeen counties in twelve different states. Another clergyman, Charles Otis Gill of the Congregational Church, and his cousin, Gifford Pinchot, made detailed studies of every church in two counties, one in the state of New York and the other in Vermont, and wrote *The Country Church: Decline of Influence and Remedy* as a report on their studies.

The activities of Wilson and Gill, accompanied by numerous less well-oriented endeavors by ministers in other denominations, eventually led to a formidable undertaking by the survey department of the Town and Country Division of the Interchurch World Movement. In the years immediately following World War I, this organization undertook a study of rural life in the United States on a scale unparalleled before or since. As Morse and Brunner have recounted the facts in the introduction to their *The Town and Country Church in the United States,* the survey was organized in every state in the union, in charge of a paid, full-time director. "About three-fourths of these supervisors were clergymen, all of whom had been country ministers at one time or another. . . . The rest . . . were laymen who were, almost without exception professors of rural sociology or economics at educational institutions . . . ." The first duty of each state director was to organize his state, that is, to secure young ministers to become directors of the survey in each county and to get others to serve as assistants. Nearly 8,000 persons, of whom over 1,000 were laymen, contributed their time. When the Interchurch World Movement collapsed, the survey was operating in over 2,400 counties. The salvaging of some of the results of this endeavor was one of the big accomplishments of the Institute of Social and Religious Research, which was organized in 1921.

The Country Life Movement and the American Country Life Association are also to be reckoned with in giving the background out of which rural sociology developed. In the early stages, the entire set of surveys and rural life conferences came to be known as the Country Life Movement. However, the rise of the Conservation Movement, also largely stimulated by the *Report of the Country Life Commission,* offered a channel through which much of the energy was directed; the doctrine that the economic factor was predominant, that if the farm family had an adequate income all other rural problems would take care of themselves, was accepted by many interested in rural betterment.

The Rise and Development of Rural Sociology

The genesis of rural sociology occurred in the decades immediately preceding 1920. As already indicated, rural sociology was an important, integral part of sociology in general when the new subject made its way into college and university curricula near the turn of the century. Courses in rural sociology and rural social problems were among the first ways in which differentiation appeared in the offerings in sociology. The preparation of course outlines and reading lists laid the basis for what later became the first texts and other general works in the field. Before 1920, though, it is possible to single out several developments that can be considered as the first steps in the growth of a genuine rural sociological literature. The first of these was the completion of doctoral dissertations at Columbia University by James M. Williams, Warren H. Wilson, and Newell L. Sims; these were done under the direction of Franklin H. Giddings and involved the study of specific rural communities. The second was the election of George E. Vincent as president of the American Sociological Society and, as a consequence, the selection of "The Sociology of Rural Life" as the theme of the eleventh annual meeting of that organization, in 1916. The third was the publication of the first rural sociology textbooks, Gillette's *Constructive Rural Sociology,* in 1913, and Vogt's *Introduction to Rural Sociology* in 1917. Furthermore, the first rural sociological paper to be presented before the

American Sociological Society was one entitled "Rural Life and the Family," given by Kenyon L. Butterfield at the third annual meeting in 1908. In 1912, J. P. Lichtenberger of the University of Pennsylvania solicited and edited a set of papers for a special "Country Life" issue of the *Annals*.

Probably the most important event before 1920 was Charles J. Galpin's study of *The Social Anatomy of an Agricultural Community* and its publication, in 1915, as a bulletin of the Wisconsin Agricultural Experiment Station. This study demonstrated that the American farmer was not a "man without a community," defined the rural community in clear and objective terms, and described a method whereby its limits could be delineated. Largely as a result of this research, Galpin was called to Washington in 1919, when his friend and superior at the University of Wisconsin, Dr. Henry C. Taylor, went to the U.S. Department of Agriculture to organize and head the Bureau of Agricultural Economics. There, Galpin began the work that led to the establishment of the Division of Farm Population and Rural Life.

A decade of progress followed in the years 1920 to 1929. This period was the one in which substantial form was given to the emerging field of rural sociology. Galpin, from his position as chief of the Division of Farm Population and Rural Life, adopted the policy of using a major portion of his budget for cooperative projects with sociologists throughout the nation interested in rural life. The University of Wisconsin and Cornell University appear to have been the chief beneficiaries of this policy, although sociologists at other state institutions, at private universities such as Tulane and Brigham Young, and at least one college for Negroes, also received some assistance. The studies completed under these arrangements form a substantial part of the publications until about 1932. Also of importance was Galpin's demonstration of the need for and interest in data concerning the farm population of the United States, leading in 1930 to the use of the rural-farm category as a basic component of the tabulations of population census data.

The work of Edmund deS. Brunner during this decade also deserves mention. Brunner was largely responsible for salvaging parts of the surveys undertaken by the Interchurch World Movement and for organizing the supplementary work needed to make the most of those materials. Through the establishment of the Institute of Social and Religious Research, of which he became director, his major efforts were focused upon rural sociology, and he acquired the experience needed to plan, finance, and conduct the original survey of 140 agricultural villages. As the decade closed he had already developed most of the plans for the 1930 resurvey of the same communities, which, combined with the second resurvey in 1936, completed the most comprehensive study of rural social change that has been made.

The passage of the Purnell Act by Congress, a measure of paramount importance in the history of rural sociological research, came in 1925. Since the exact provisions of this law have been widely misunderstood by those who have not examined its wording and studied the hearings that led to its adoption, it seems advisable to offer a few words of clarification. There is nothing in the Act which specifies that Purnell funds *shall* be used by the agricultural experiment stations for the support of rural sociological research. It is merely permissive. The provisions of the Purnell Act, through which each state receives $50,000 annually for research purposes, made it possible for any director of an agricultural experiment station who desired to abide by the spirit as well as the letter of the law to use substantial sums for the support of rural sociological research in his state. As a result, many of the stations soon began to have rural sociologists on their staffs and developed substantial programs of rural sociological research. To this factor is to be attributed much of the credit for the national and international recognition of rural sociology achieved by men working at such institutions as Cornell University, the University of Wisconsin, the University of Minnesota, Michigan State University, Louisiana State University, North Carolina State University, Washington State University, the University of Missouri, and the University of Kentucky.

Another significant development during this short period of rapid progress was the beginning of the work on levels and standards of living. Pioneers were E. L. Kirkpatrick, first at Cornell University and later in the Division of Farm Population and Rural Life in the U.S. Department of Agriculture, and Carle C. Zimmerman at the University of Minnesota.

Finally, the decade 1920 to 1929 was the one in which efforts at synthesis got under way in earnest. This difficult work began on a small scale with the preparation of Gillette's book *Rural Sociology*. It was advanced considerably when, in 1926, Taylor published the first edition of his *Rural Sociology,* and with the apearance of the first edition of Sim's *Elements of Rural Sociology* in 1928. The culmination came in 1929 with the publication of *Principles of Rural-Urban Sociology* by Sorokin and Zimmerman, followed within a few years by the appearance of the three volumes of *A Systematic Source Book in Rural Sociology* by Sorokin, Zimmerman, and Galpin. The work of preparing these books brought to bear upon the field of rural sociology, in a long concerted effort, Sorokin's ingenuity and vast knowledge of European society and sociology, and Zimmerman's genius, determination, drive, and mastery of developments on the American scene. Rarely have such extraordinarily able representatives of two such diverse currents of thought been brought together to work intensively for a period of five or six years. The result was the finest synthesis of the field of rural sociology ever achieved.

The period of maturation occupied the years 1930 to 1945. At first, the difficult work of synthesis was the outstanding feature, and the appearance of *A Systematic Source Book in Rural Sociology* was the chief event. This was ably supplemented by Brunner and associates with their resurvey of 140 agricultural villages and its expansion by Brunner and Kolb into *Rural Social Trends* (1933). In this form, the study was one of the monographs prepared as a basis for the report of the Committee on Recent Social Trends appointed by President Herbert Hoover. A considerably revised edition of Taylor's *Rural Sociology* appeared the same year, a reworked version of Sim's *Elements of Rural Sociology* in 1934, and Kolb and Brunner's *A Study of Rural Society* in 1935. Then five years elapsed, during which an expanding corps of rural sociologists devoted themselves to intensive research on an unprecedented scale, before the results of other sustained efforts at synthesis appeared in print. In 1940, though, Landis's *Rural Life in Process* and Smith's *The Sociology of Rural Life* presented the results of two new and somewhat different attempts at sketching the overall plan of the discipline. Two years later, *Rural Sociology and Rural Social Organization* set forth the results of Sanderson's lifetime of effort in the general work of synthesis. Within special fields, during this period, Sanderson's *The Rural Community* (1932), Zimmerman's *Consumption and Standards of Living* (1936), and Sanderson and Polson's *Rural Community Organization* (1939) were significant syntheses.

The outstanding feature of the period under consideration, however, at least in immediate effects, was the activity of rural sociologists in connection with President Franklin D. Roosevelt's New Deal. Harry Hopkins had hardly set in motion (1933) the efforts of the federal government to pour relief funds into the states before members of Congress and others began asking sharp questions as to who was receiving the funds and what relation, if any, there was between need and aid. Hastily, a few rural sociologists were called to Washington and asked to help supply the answers. The cooperation of various rural sociologists at the state agricultural experiment stations was asked for and promised. It was not easy, however, to organize the necessary surveys on the scale required, and considerable confusion resulted. Finally, Dwight Sanderson was asked to take over as Coordinator of Rural Research for the federal agency, and to perfect an organization that could secure and analyze the necessary facts. Sanderson wisely relied upon rural sociologists located in the various states and, where possible, upon the members of the staffs of the agricultural experiment stations. In about half

14

the states a rural sociologist was given the title of State Director of Rural Research and a per diem allowance for travel. Relief funds were authorized for enumerators and clerical assistants. These state organizations then undertook two types of research activities: (1) execution, in the selected areas, of plans made at the national level; and (2) the conduct of approved and relevant projects which were locally designed. Hundreds of publications resulted from these efforts.

In the meanwhile, some rural sociologists, and Carl C. Taylor in particular, had been intensively engaged in the work of the Subsistence Homesteads Division of the Interior Department. Eventually, after various interdepartmental shifts and changes, Taylor was posted to the Department of Agriculture as chief both of the Division of Farm Population and Rural Life and of the Division of Social Research of the Resettlement Administration (later the Farm Security Administration). This was accompanied by a greatly expanded program of rural sociological research on the part of the federal government, with some of its personnel stationed in various regional and state offices.

In summary, it can be said that very few, if any, rural sociologists worked through the years between Franklin D. Roosevelt's first inauguration and the attack upon Pearl Harbor without being involved personally in the administrative and research activities of the Federal Emergency Relief Administration (or Works Project Administration), the Resettlement Administration (or Farm Security Administration), or the Division of Farm Population and Rural Life, Department of Agriculture. Most carried on such activities in addition to their regular duties on the teaching and research staffs of the various colleges and universities. The net result was to bring rural sociology to maturity much earlier than otherwise would have been the case.

Two other closely related developments during this period which greatly influenced the development of rural sociology as a scientific discipline were the founding of the journal *Rural Sociology* in 1936 and the organization of the Rural Sociological Society in 1937.

A final development in this period was a substantial beginning of professional work abroad by some of the more experienced rural sociologists. This was the beginning of a type of activity that, following World War II, became a principal endeavor of many outstanding men in the field.

As is generally the case in the growth of new lines of endeavor, the start was slow and unspectacular. Shortly after 1920, E. C. Branson recorded his observations of rural society in Europe in a small volume entitled *Farm Life Abroad*. In 1931, Terpenning, in his *Village and Open-Country Neighborhoods,* published the results of a systematic study, during the preceding years, of village patterns of settlement in European countries and their contrasts with the pattern prevailing in the United States. Carle C. Zimmerman spent the year 1930-1931 in Siam, making the systematic study of rural social organization and levels and standards of living which formed the basis for his volume *Siam: Rural Economic Survey.* In 1934, Zimmerman was a member of the commission sent to Cuba by the Foreign Policy Association, and the results of his studies of rural family living formed a substantial part of the commission's report on *Problems of the New Cuba.* This seems to have been the first concrete step in the development of rural sociological interest in the area of Latin American studies. In 1935, Zimmerman, accompanied by T. Lynn Smith, made a reconnaissance trip in Mexico; Zimmerman in 1936 and Smith in 1938 returned to Mexico for additional observation. In 1939, assisted by a Julius Rosenwald Foundation fellowship, Smith extended his observations to South America, briefly visiting all the countries of that continent.

Late in the fall of 1941, shortly before the attack upon Pearl Harbor, the Department of State decided to send three experienced rural sociologists, Carl C. Taylor, Nathan L. Whetten, and T. Lynn Smith, to the embassies in Buenos Aires, Mexico City, and Rio de Janeiro, for the purpose of making systematic studies of rural life and rural society in Argentina, Mexico, and Brazil. The observations made and studies undertaken in connection with these missions eventually resulted in the publication of Smith's *Brazil: People and Institutions* in 1946, 1954, and 1963, Taylor's *Rural Life in Argentina* in 1948, and Whetten's *Rural Mexico* also in 1948. In 1945, Lowry Nelson was given a comparable assignment in Cuba and made the studies on which his book *Rural Cuba* is based. All four of these assignments were arranged by the State Department in cooperation with the Office of Foreign Agricultural Relations of the Department of Agriculture. Early in the 1940's, Charles P. Loomis, then with the Division of Farm Population and Rural Life, went to Peru, El Salvador, and Mexico for studies of the rural problem. In 1944, shortly after he returned from this work, Loomis, along with Olen E. Leonard, transferred from the Division of Farm Population and Rural Life to the Office of Foreign Agricultural Relations, and they there began the series of activities that gained them prominence in Latin American area studies as well as in rural sociology.

Shortly after he returned from Brazil in 1943, T. Lynn Smith was sent by the Department of State to Colombia, as adviser to the Colombian government on the problem of colonization (subdivision of estates) and settlement, with the additional duty of studying and reporting upon the cultural setting for agricultural extension activities in Colombia and El Salvador. Approximately half of his time was spent on this work during the next three years. Then, as the period under consideration drew to a close, he was given another assignment to Brazil. There he did additional work in Goiás, and was sent as a member of a two-man United States–Brazil team to make a reconnaissance study of the São Francisco Valley in connection with proposals for developing the power potentials of the Paulo Afonso falls and the agricultural possibilities of the valley.

During the closing years of this period, George W. Hill went to Venezuela to work in the government's Institute of Immigration and Colonization; as the end of hostilities in Europe approached, Charles P. Loomis was sent there, and Irwin T. Sanders was given an overseas assignment by the State Department which eventually led to a special study of a Balkan village. In addition, there were the experiences in all theaters of war of rural sociologists who were in the armed services—experiences that ultimately led some of them into professional and rural sociological activities abroad. Thus, as the postwar era approached, the stage had been set for American rural sociologists to apply the technical knowledge of their field in all parts of the world, and the work in and on Latin America was already quite advanced.

Postwar Developments And Trends

Many important developments in rural sociology have taken place since World War II, and present trends promise many more in the near future. In addition, the influence of factors not yet clearly perceived may bring about changes as sudden and as important as those of the 1930s.

Probably the most important overall development has been the concentration of work in rural sociology at the agricultural colleges, and especially in the agricultural experiment stations. Before the passage of the Purnell Act in 1925, relatively little rural sociological research was done at these stations. Further, it is probable that the courses offered by the agricultural colleges ran a very poor second to those in church-related and private institutions of higher learning. In fact, nearly all the research undertaken at the stations was on projects financed in part by the Division of Farm Population and Rural Life in the Department of Agriculture because of Dr. Galpin's interests and policies. Even after the Purnell Act was passed, a full decade elapsed before rural sociological research became well established at some of the institutions that today have the strongest programs. During the formative years, and in those of rapid growth and development as well, the research at the agricultural experiment stations and the courses at the agricultural colleges had by no means a monopoly in the field.

Since 1945, however, it has been different. The bulletins, circulars, memoirs, and other publications issued by the agricultural experiment stations constitute the great bulk of rural sociological literature. The articles prepared for *Rural Sociology* are, for the most part, written by people at the colleges and universities in which the agricultural experiment stations are located. Also, in very large measure, the rural sociologists who have pioneered the work in other countries are those who are, or were at the time they began such activities, associated with the agricultural experiment stations.

Even the research activities of various federal agencies withered after 1945, so that in recent years the accomplishments of the rural sociological personnel remaining in the Department of Agriculture make a poor showing compared to the achievements between 1935 and 1945. This is true despite the high quality of work of those now employed by the federal agencies. The dismemberment of the Bureau of Agricultural Economics and the severe budgetary curtailment of the activities formerly embodied in the Division of Farm Population and Rural Life were, of course, the changes bringing about the decline of rural sociological work in the federal departments. With the federal agencies doing little sociological research, the concentration of activities at the agricultural experiment stations became even more pronounced.

These changes in the organization of rural sociological activities have been paralleled by radical changes in the attention given to various portions of the content of rural sociology. Certain parts of it, once at the core of interest and activity, have been largely neglected since 1945, others have maintained much of their former relative importance, and there have been rapid strides taken in the development of a few new phases of the discipline. Each of these is briefly commented upon in turn.

The rural church, the rural home and family, and standards and levels of living appear to be the three areas of research most largely neglected in recent years. Since Brunner completed the second resurvey of the 140 agricultural villages in 1936, no comprehensive sociological study of the rural church situation has been undertaken in the United States. Furthermore, on the state level, nearly all the most adequate studies were undertaken before 1950; relatively little has been done since. Few studies of the rural family have been made since midcentury. The situation is similar with respect to levels and standards of living. Ever since an agreement was reached among the various federal agencies that the Bureau of Home Economics and not the Bureau of Agricultural Economics should do budgetary research on farm-family living, this part of rural sociology has suffered. The prohibition in Washington carried over into the states. However, through the construction of scales and indexes for measuring variations in levels and standards, rural sociologists seem to be developing approaches that may in the future produce significant knowledge and understanding in this important area.

Studies of rural social organization (including the community and the neighborhood), population, social stratification, man-land relationships, social participation, and social change seem to be receiving about as much attention as they did before 1946, although several of them badly need comprehensive and systematic study.

At least five new or relatively new fields of study were, on the other hand, developed rapidly by rural sociologists in the years after the War: health and medical services; the diffusion of agricultural practices; aging and retirement; suburbanization; and rural society in other lands. Since 1945, the nation's rural sociologists have made major contributions by applying, to the study of health, medical services, and hospital planning, the knowledge of population materials and analysis, and of community delineation, that they had acquired. The impetus in these fields seems likely to continue.

Since 1945, too, rural sociologists have set about investigating the nature of the social process by which new agricultural information and techniques reach, and are applied by, the farmers for whom they are intended. The accomplishments here are already substantial. Since it combines a challenging theoretical aspect with a promise of results of great practical value, this is a logical type of work for the staff members of the agricultural experiment stations, and it may be expected to expand in the years immediately ahead.

Rural sociologists have not remained entirely aloof from the challenges to research and action posed by the recent rapid aging of the population of the United States. Some of them have pioneered in the study of aging and retirement—a logical development, since their knowledge of demographic and survey techniques enable them to get the answers to some pressing questions with a minimum waste of time and effort. During the 1970s, as the problem in many rural areas becomes even more acute, studies in this aspect of rural sociology are likely to increase in number and improve in quality.

The problems of the rural-urban fringe and, indeed, the entire subject of suburbanization, is another new field in which rural sociologists are leading the way. This particular combination of the rural and urban ways of living is increasing rapidly in the United States. In it there may even be much of the general pattern of living for the future. Rural sociologists in more and more states are likely to be challenged by opportunities for studies in this field during the next decade.

Finally, the remarkable amount of work rural sociologists have done in other countries since 1945 requires special emphasis. This is perhaps the most significant development in rural sociology during the postwar period. Hundreds of professionally trained rural sociologists have had one or more assignments in Latin America, Africa, Asia, and other parts of the world. They have worked, many of them year after year, in about 100 separate and distinct nations. Some of the older and more experienced members of the group have worked in as many as ten countries located on several continents. Research has been their major activity, although many have helped to administer official or philanthropic projects, and a few have served as advisers to the governments of other countries. Some, but not many, have taught. Many publications have resulted from such activities, including much of the most substantial work in rural sociology to be published in this period. In addition, since much of the activity is fairly recent, the books and articles based on work abroad which will appear during the next ten years probably will greatly outnumber those published since 1946. If properly used, they can contribute much to teaching and general writing in the field of rural sociology, and, indeed, to the enrichment of sociological literature in general.

In conclusion, it seems necessary to add a few words about the present need for synthesis in the field of rural sociology. From 1930 on, analysis has greatly outstripped synthesis. Since the third volume of *A Systematic Source Book in Rural Sociology* by Sorokin, Zimmerman, and Galpin appeared in 1932, the results of hundreds, if not thousands, of research endeavors have appeared in print; however, attempts to systematize and organize the items of knowledge contained in them have been modest. The most substantial contributions have been made in Sanderson's *Rural Sociology and Rural Social Organization,* Landis's *Rural Life in Process,* Nelson's *Rural Sociology,* Taylor and associates' *Rural Life in the United States,* Loomis and Beegle's *Rural Social Systems,* and Smith's *The Sociology of Rural Life.* But none of these—nor all of them taken together—is adequate, and none of them has appeared after 1955. A great effort to systematize the results of the research that has been done in rural sociology is the greatest need of the discipline. (For one appraisal of the state of rural sociology, see Ref. 163.)

Additional Readings

1. ANDERSON, C. ARNOLD, "Trends in Rural Sociology," in Robert K. Merton, Leonard Broom, and Leonard S. Cottrell, Jr. (eds.), *Sociology Today*, New York: Harper & Row, 1959, chapter 16.

2. BEALER, ROBERT C., and FREDERICK C. FLIEGEL, "A Reconsideration of Social Change in Rural Sociology," in James H. Copp (ed.), *Our Changing Rural Society: Perspectives and Trends*, Ames: Iowa State University Press, 1964, chapter 9.

3. BERTRAND, ALVIN L., "Introduction," in Alvin L. Bertrand (ed.), *Rural Sociology*, New York: McGraw-Hill Book Company, Inc., 1958, chapter 1.

4. BRUNNER, EDMUND deS., *The Growth of a Science*, New York: Harper & Brothers, 1957.

5. COPP, JAMES H., "The Future of Rural Sociology in an Industrialized Society," in James H. Copp (ed.), *Our Changing Rural Society: Perspectives and Trends*, Ames: Iowa State University Press, 1964, chapter 11.

6. HOFSTEE, E. W., "Rural Sociology in Europe," *Rural Sociology*, Vol. 28, No. 4 (December, 1963), pp. 329–341.

7. LARSON, OLAF F., "Income and Welfare of Rural People—Agricultural Research Significant to Public Policy, Public Welfare, and Community Improvement," *Rural Sociology*, Vol. 30, No. 4 (December, 1965), pp. 452–461.

8. NELSON, LOWRY, "George Edgar Vincent: Rural Social Scientist," *Rural Sociology*, Vol. 31, No. 4 (December, 1966), pp. 478–482.

9. NELSON, LOWRY, "The Rise of Rural Sociology Abroad: The Pre-Purnell Period," *Rural Sociology*, Vol. 30, No. 4 (December, 1965), pp. 407–427.

10. NELSON, LOWRY, *Rural Sociology: Its Origin and Growth in the United States*, Minneapolis: University of Minnesota Press, 1969.

11. ROGERS, EVERETT M., *Social Change in Rural Society*, New York: Appleton-Century-Crofts, Inc., 1960, chapter 2.

12. SLOCUM, WALTER L., *Agricultural Sociology*, New York: Harper & Brothers, 1962, chapter 1.

13. SMITH, T. LYNN, *Rural Sociology: A Trend Report and Bibliography*, published as *Current Sociology*, Vol. VI, No. 1, Paris: UNESCO, 1957.

14. SMITH, T. LYNN, *Studies of Latin American Societies*, New York: Doubleday & Co., Inc., 1970, selections 1 and 2.

15. TAYLOR, CARL C., "The Development of Rural Sociology Abroad," *Rural Sociology*, Vol. 30, No. 4 (December, 1965), pp. 462–473.

2

THE COUNTRY AND THE CITY

Nothing seems more apparent than the contrast between the city and the country. However, one who attempts to set forth the specific differences between the city and the country, to distinguish accurately between rural and urban, is immediately confronted with some serious difficulties, obstacles that are not readily perceptible. Even in scholarly treatises it has usually been thought enough to use a simple dichotomy—the rural and the urban, the country and the city—as though these two were readily distinguishable and mutually exclusive categories. This is the practice followed in the official population statistics of most countries. Regardless of the basis selected for the differentiation, usually some inconsistency or weakness in the scheme will appear if it is subjected to analysis. Consider, for example, size of community, the criterion most frequently used and the basis used by the United States Census Bureau in differentiating rural from urban. In America, incorporated centers range in size from hamlets with fewer than 100 inhabitants to great metropolitan centers with millions of residents. Is a village rural or urban? How shall a town be classed as it grows and develops? When does a given center cease to be a village and become a town or city? Similar questions might be raised about any other attempt to distinguish between rural and urban on the basis of a single characteristic. Is a manufacturing center with 2,000 inhabitants as rural as an agricultural trade center of 3,000 population? or an Asiatic village community in which 5,000 farm people reside? or a Mexican city of 20,000 population, most of whom are engaged in agriculture?

To go further, let us suppose that the enjoyment of administrative and governmental functions or titles is the basis for distinguishing urban centers from rural territory, as is the case in many countries. Is the sleepy little agricultural village of less than 1,000 inhabitants, although the seat of a local governmental unit, more entitled to be classed as urban than a bustling mining or manufacturing center several times larger which lacks such administrative functions? Is a decadent old town necessarily entitled to be considered a city today, even though it is in possession of a charter from some medieval monarch attesting to the fact that the rank of "city" had once been conferred upon it?

The distinctions made on a basis such as the size of the community, legal incorporation or the lack of it, the possession of a charter or title conferred by some long-dead king, may be quite inadequate for sociological purposes. What may be very useful statistically may leave a great deal to be desired from the standpoint of deeper sociological analysis. The nine differences between the rural and urban portions of society that we consider to be of greatest significance are discussed in this chapter. They are based to a considerable extent upon the excellent analysis by P. A. Sorokin and Carle C. Zimmerman in (Ref. 477, pp. 13–58).

OCCUPATION

Among all the differences which have been noted between the rural and urban portions of society, the occupational difference seems to have the most fundamental importance. Agricultural, pastoral, and the collecting enterprises are the bases of the rural economy; "farmer," "cultivator," "agriculturist," and "countryman" are almost synonymous.

One of the fundamental characteristics of farming is that those who engage in it deal with living, growing things, either plants or animals, or both. This is in sharp contrast with urban occupations, which determine that those following such callings shall handle lifeless or mechanical things and instruments. The nature of agriculture also prescribes that the farmer shall work in a natural environment, with the fresh air and sunshine of the open country and also the changing seasons and weather, instead of in the artificial environment of the city, where the heat of the summer, the cold of the winter, and the dryness and dampness of the weather are all moderated by man's ingenuity.

The foregoing should not be interpreted to mean that there are not important variations within the agricultural occupation. Size of the farm business, system of agriculture, type of farming, and many other factors contribute to make farmers differ from one another. Let us consider type of farming, for example. Although, as compared with urban occupations, farm tasks are multitudinous, with each farmer performing a wide variety of them, some specialization takes place. In the United States the cotton belt, the wheat belt, the corn belt, and so on, involve different kinds of farming. They in turn are fundamentally different from dairy, truck, tobacco, and fruit farming. Ranching is still different, as are other highly specialized enterprises such as growing rice or sugar cane. Similarly, in Brazil, or Colombia, or Mexico, the activities of people in the coffee-producing areas differ sharply from those who live in the cotton zone, the pastoral districts, and other types of farming areas. Indeed, throughout the world as a whole, the types of crops grown determine differences in labor and specialization.

Within the general agricultural occupation, each of these types of farming gives rise to distinct rhythms of daily, weekly, monthly, and seasonal activities. The dairy farmer must be on the job at specified hours every day of the week, year in and year out, although he may have a great deal of leisure at other hours of the day. Other types of farming, such as wheat growing, are characterized by peak loads of labor at certain seasons; almost continuous work day and night during the harvest may be followed by long periods of relative inactivity. Such a distribution of working periods exerts a profound influence upon the personalities of the individuals concerned.

The amount and nature of the rewards from the various types of farming also make for fundamental differences among farmers. It is one thing to count on the small, steady, frequent, and relatively sure amounts received by the dairy farmer and quite another to gamble on the small fortune to be made or the great losses to be incurred in the large-scale commercial production of crops like watermelons or potatoes. A slight variation in temperature is of little consequence to the producer of corn and hogs; it may be the difference between success and failure to the citrus grower or the coffee producer.

In general, the care of livestock calls for skills and aptitudes different from those involved in the growing of plants. General farming calls for a fusion of the two. All the variations make for special activities, distinctive family time budgets, and different attitudes toward the work. Each in turn serves as a mold in which the personalities of the participants are formed.

It must be stressed, however, that the nature of the agricultural and pastoral occupations is the basis upon which all valid distinctions between rural and urban are founded.

SIZE OF COMMUNITY

The limitations or conditions imposed by the agricultural life in turn give rise to other fundamental features of rural life, aspects that are frequently seized upon as the elementary and distinctive traits of rurality. For example, the nature of farming demands a considerable area of land per person, a fact that makes large rural communities almost impossible and brings about a low density of population. In other words, the size of the community and the density of population are both directly dependent upon the nature of the agricultural occupation. For convenience these two, and especially the size of the community, are frequently taken as the bases for distinguishing between the rural and urban portions of a society. Small community and rural community, and urban center and large community, become nearly synonymous. In statistical compilations, size of community has come to be the criterion of rurality most frequently used. This is the practice followed in the censuses taken by various countries, including the United States, where all incorporated centers with 2,500 or more inhabitants are now classed as urban. This criterion has proved useful only because the nature of agriculture makes large communities of farmers almost impossible.

DENSITY OF POPULATION

Low density of population is another feature of rural society that is a condition of the nature of agriculture and is frequently accepted as the basic difference between the rural and urban modes of living. Since a considerable area is necessary for successful farming—whether growing plants, grazing livestock, or both—agriculture inevitably results in a low density. It is obvious that the farmer must reside either on or near the land he tills; this requirement effectively prevents large aggregations of rural people. This is true of even the most densely populated agricultural countries. If it were otherwise, no land would be left on which to grow crops or graze livestock. Even the most intensive agricultural systems fail to bring about a density of population remotely approaching that of the spacious suburbs, which constitute the residential areas for the elite classes of urban centers in the United States. Far more striking are the contrasts of the open country with the apartment-house, tenement, and slum districts of modern cities.

These differences in the density of population color many important features of rural and urban life. For the city person, high density means, on the one hand, congestion, noise, lack of privacy, high rents, difficulty in parking, unclean air, constant exposure to disease, psychological isolation, nervous strains, and numerous other disadvantageous environmental influences. But, on the other hand, it also means numerous social contacts, availability of all conceivable specialists and services, opportunity to specialize, possibility of selecting associates, freedom from the inquisitiveness and gossip of primary group members, superior schools, well-supported churches, opportunity for cultural advantages, availability of modern household conveniences, safe water supply, greater variety in diet, and so on.

For people in the country, the low density of population has many advantages. It offers the opportunity for quiet and solitude. It means that fresh air is abundant, air not contaminated by having been breathed over and over again, saturated by soot and smoke, and thoroughly mixed with fumes from vehicular exhausts. Low density of population is favorable to an abundance of grass, trees, flowers, birds, and other natural beauties. It is also favorable to intimate social relationships, those forms of social interaction possible only in small primary groups, which shield the farmer from psychosocial isolation, and it frees the countryman from the city's noise, frictions, and nervous strain. However, the low density of population also has its negative aspects. It means, to some extent, geographical isolation—although this is rapidly being overcome in much of the world by improved transporation and communication. It also means constant exposure to the prying eyes and wagging tongues of neighborhood gossips. A small population cannot support up-to-date schools with good teachers; the consolidation of rural schools has severe disadvantages, and local dependence upon national agencies for school aid seems to result in serious deficiencies. The same limitations are true of churches. Where population is sparse, cultural advantages are rare and expensive, and modern conveniences are scarce and costly. The most skillful professional men seek the thickly populated districts for the advantages they offer. Both city and country have strong points and weak points; all in all, density of population works effectively to make life in either area vastly different from that in the other.

Density of population is also related to the number of social contacts. Some urban groups, notably the white-collar workers, constantly deal with other human beings. These individuals are thus placed under tremendous mental strain; often people come to be regarded as pawns to be manipulated for personal ends, rather than as friends and neighbors, or even as enemies, as is more generally the case in the country.

ENVIRONMENT

That agriculture is the primary occupation of the rural population has been indicated. Two other important rural characteristics, namely, small communities and low density of population, also have been identified. Although size of community and density of population are commonly used as the basic criteria for differentiating rural from urban, analytical thinking reveals that

27

both are dependent upon *occupation,* which is the primary factor. The primacy of the agricultural occupation limits rural life in many ways and determines many of the channels in which the processes of rural life must move. By determining the nature of the environmental influences amid which rural people must live, agriculture wields an all-important influence upon all aspects of rural life; environmental factors of various kinds, operating upon organic bases, give rise to all behavior patterns of humanity.

The concept of environment is itself so broad that it must be broken down into its constituent elements before it can serve any specific purpose of sociological analysis. We stress the roles of: (1) the physical or inorganic environments; (2) the biological or organic environments; and (3) the sociocultural environments.

The physical environments include all physiographic factors—soil, climate, inorganic resources, natural forces such as winds and tides, combustion, radiation, and gravity. Attention has already been directed to the fact that the rural person is directly exposed to these forces, while the urbanite's cultural surroundings place a thick manmade shield between him and nature in the raw.

The second class, the biological environments, embraces all microorganisms, insects, parasites, undomesticated plants and animals, together with the relationships between these, both ecological and symbiotic.

The sociocultural environments may be subdivided into three categories: (a) the physiosocial, (b) the biosocial, and (c) the psychosocial. The physiosocial comprises those portions of our material culture the objective expressions of which are constructed from inorganic materials, i.e., tools, weapons, vehicles, machines, roads, etc. The biosocial may be either nonhuman or human. Domesticated plants and animals used by man which are derived from organic sources make up the nonhuman portion; the human part consists of human beings in their service relationships to one another. The third part of the sociocultural environment, the psychosocial, is the inner behavior (attitudes, ideas, desires, values, etc.) of the human population. Customs, folkways, mores, and external symbols, such as language, make up the outward expressions of this category.

Owing to the nature of the agricultural occupation, the farmer lives in an environment radically different from that of the urbanite. First, great importance should be attached to the fact that practically all aspects of rural life are conditioned directly by the physical environment. Most agricultural activities necessitate outdoor work. This means that the farmer is directly exposed to the weather. He basks in the beneficial influences of abundant sunlight, pure air, and fresh breezes. He is in direct contact with nature in all its friendly aspects. On the other hand, he lacks the protective physio-cultural environment—exemplified by steam heat, air conditioning, and paving—which stands between the urbanite and the inclemencies of the weather; he is also in direct contact with the less friendly side of nature.

Agriculture is merely the process of encouraging or directing the creative forces of nature. For this reason, the rural person is more influenced by the organic environment than is the city person. Much of this environment is benign, and it should be stressed that the farmer, who deals constantly with living things, usually sees the organic aspect as a friend to man. Dirt, or soil, is the basis for his livelihood. The same is not so true of one who lives in the city. Shut off from the bulk of natural phenomena, to him the organic environment may be displayed through the medium of contaminated milk or water, or through the spread of a contagious disease. To a far greater extent than the countryman, the urbanite sees only the menacing aspects of the organic environment. For him dirt and bacteria become almost synonymous. That his life, too, is dependent upon the workings of natural organic forces is seldom called to his attention.

There are likewise great differences in the sociocultural environments of rural and urban people. The physiosocial environment (the material culture) of the city greatly exceeds that of the country in quantity as well as in complexity. Buildings, machines, pavement, and other manmade things are the bases from which the city is constructed. The richest accomplishments of the country in these respects pale before the overwhelming display of the city.

The biosocial environment of the country also differs from that of the urban area. In no respect is this made more striking than by contrasting the seething mass of humanity in the city—composed of all races and nationalities—with the dispersed but more homogeneous group of any particular rural district.

Later, considerable attention will be directed to analyzing the nature of the psychosocial aspects of rural society. Here it is sufficient to state that in this respect, too, the urban environment is much more complex than the rural.

SOCIAL DIFFERENTIATION

The social differentiation of the rural world differs in several fundamental respects from that of the urban. In the first place, the city's social groups are more numerous and complex than those of the country. This difference is intimately associated with the differing origins of rural and urban populations. Until well along in the twentieth century, few if any of the world's cities produced enough children to offset the number of residents who died. Even since 1950, or the period in which urban places in all parts of the earth have mushroomed, the bulk of the increase of population is due to the movement of people from the rural districts to cities and towns, and, to a lesser extent, to the natural increase of the urban population and the pronounced tendency of immigrants to establish themselves in urban areas. As a consequence of these migrations, the city numbers among its inhabitants members of many races—those of long-term residence in the society being most heavily represented, of course, but the population including a sprinkling of peoples from all corners of the earth. Culturally, too, the city reflects all religious, political, occupational, educational, national, and linguistic groups. The urbanite lives amid this tremendous diversity, constantly in contact with people having widely divergent ideas, beliefs, mores, languages, economic positions, occupations, religious traditions, morals, etc.; this is particularly true of those who live in the cities of the United States. The Urbanism Committee of the National Resources Committee has said (Ref. 303, p. 10):

Never before in the history of the world have great groups of people so diverse in social backgrounds been thrown together into such close contact as in the cities of America. The typical American city, therefore, does not consist of a homogeneous body of citizens, but of human beings, with the most diverse cultural backgrounds, often speaking different languages, following a great variety of customs, habituated to different modes and standards of living, and sharing only in varying degrees the tastes, the beliefs, and the ideals of their native fellow city dwellers. In short, far from presenting a picture of a single unified body of human beings, the American city is a motley of peoples and cultures forming a mosaic of little worlds which in part blend with one another, but in part and for a time, remain segregated or come into conflict with one another.

In spite of all its heterogeneity and complexity, the city possesses a high degree of integration and coordination. Through division of labor and specialization, all parts have become mutually interdependent. The downtown business area, the industrial, wholesale, shipping, and storage districts, the slums, the middle-class residential portions, the better residential sections, and even the suburban fringes are all part of a functioning whole. The city is a genuine social system, not a mere agglomeration of ethnic, cultural, and social components.

The situation is strikingly different in the country. Social differentiation has not proceeded as far as it has in the cities. Rural districts are essentially homogeneous, even in countries such as the United States, India, or Brazil—in each of which the tremendous rural area embraces almost all the racial and cultural groups that are found in the cities. The reason is an essential difference between the social structures of rural and urban districts. Rural society may be said to be segmented; it does not function as an integral unit. Instead it is made up of thousands of small, relatively independent and unrelated entities—families, neighborhoods, and communities. Unlike the situation in urban communities, the actual portion of rural society with which a given individual or family comes in contact exhibits little heterogeneity. The farmer's contacts are mainly with other farmers, who in turn are the sons of farmers. His associates generally are also members of his own religious group, neighbors of much the same economic and educational attainments, persons whose mores, traditional beliefs, language, and general behavior patterns are very similar to his own. The countryman's contacts are mostly with those who live nearby. It matters little that elsewhere in the nation there are other farmers with radically different cultural traits and behavior patterns. For practical purposes, the important thing is that each segment of rural society is highly homogeneous, or very slightly differentiated.

But, as we have pointed out, rural society does not function as a unit. It lacks the integration of the more highly differentiated urban society. Such unity as it has is based mainly on similarities and not on the mutual interdependence brought about by specialization. As a consequence, it is very difficult to secure concerted action on the part of the rural population. Rural society remains the product of numerous small, relatively independent and unrelated segments.

SOCIAL STRATIFICATION

The principles of class and caste operate differently in rural societies from the way they work in urban groupings. There seem to be at least four major differences between the social pyramids of rural and urban areas. (1) Social classes are fewer in rural society than in urban society, although rural society is far from classless. (2) The extremes of the social pyramid are not so far apart in rural societies as in urban. (3) The range of social classes is not only smaller in rural society but rural classes tend to be intermediate or "middle classes." The rural social pyramid as a whole neither sinks so low nor rises so high as the urban pyramid. Despite the servile or semi-servile status of rural workers in many places, rural society in general lacks the extremes of wealth and poverty, of authority and disfranchisement, of privilege and lack of privilege to be found in the city. (4) The caste principle is not so rigid in urban as in rural societies. Although there are more classes, their membership is not so fixed. Movement from one class to another is easier than in rural society, where intimate social contacts make one's antecedents well known to all members of the community and cause one's position to be more largely determined by the status of his immediate ancestors than is the case in the city.

SOCIAL MOBILITY

Despite great variation within the agricultural group, rural people as a whole are less mobile than the members of urban groups. This applies to shiftings on a horizontal plane from one social group to another, and to vertical changes both up and down from one social class to another. It applies equally well to culture traits and population, and is true both in a highly mobile society like that in the United States and also in the longer-established and less mobile societies of Europe and Asia.

That there is more horizontal mobility, shifting from one social group to another, in the city than in the country is reflected in a number of ways. For example, despite the "rural exodus," farm children more frequently inherit their fathers' occupation than is the case in other groups; farmers are primarily sons of farmers, but members of urban occupations are recruited from many occupational groups other than their own. Another important aspect of horizontal mobility is the shifting from one family group to another, reflected in the fact that broken homes are far more prevalent in the city than in the country. Still another is that between religious groups.

Intensive vertical social mobility—the passing up and down from class to class of individuals and culture traits, such as is present in cities—is unthinkable in rural society. So also is the great social insecurity resulting from excessive mobility. Six principal factors seem to be responsible for this: (1) Churches, army headquarters, political headquarters, parliaments, universities—most of the important institutions that serve as channels of vertical circulation, the ladders for ascending and descending the social scale—are concentrated in the cities. To use these avenues for social climbing, one must leave the country and go to the city. Furthermore, while the country may have social ladders of its own, those who climb them attain a particular position in the rural world but are not thereby guaranteed a position of comparable importance in the urban milieu. The reverse is more likely to occur. (2) Since social stratification is not so great in rural districts, country people have less chance to rise or fall from class to class. (3) Differential fertility, which results in the dying out of the urban upper classes, leaves vacancies in the top positions of the social pyramid and thus serves as a vacuum which creates a vertical current. This factor operates very little or not at all in rural areas, where differential fertility is not so great or is entirely lacking. (4) Parents and children are dissimilar in their biological and psychosocial traits, and this condition is more pronounced in the city's heterogeneous population than in the country's more homogeneous one. Since children who lack capacities as great as those of their parents frequently are unable to maintain themselves at the level to which they were born, and children possessing greater abilities than those of their parents are likely to ascend to a higher social level, this becomes an important factor in vertical mobility. (5) Every change of social or cultural environment fosters vertical mobility. Sociocultural changes are particularly great in urban districts. (6) The caste principle seems to be stronger in rural than in urban areas. Where inheritance counts in determining social status, the mobility from one class to another will be decreased.

SOCIAL INTERACTION

The rural system of social interaction differs from that of the city. The number of social contacts is, of course, much greater in the city than in the country. The nature of urban occupations makes it necessary for the urban dweller to encounter hundreds of people each day. Recreation, too, in the city must be found where others are present; solitude is practically impossible. Within the home, which is hardly separated from the dwellings of others, the newspaper, the telephone, radio, and television bring a multitude of secondary contacts.

The situation is quite different in rural areas. Even today, unless the farmer lives on a trunk highway, visitors except peddlers and salesmen are rare enough to be a treat. In many of the more isolated farm sections, strangers are a curiosity and may be the object of considerable suspicion. Only at church, at farm gatherings, or at the movies in the nearest village does the farmer meet with large groups—and these are assemblies of neighbors for the most part. Shopping expeditions to towns and cities are major occasions for mingling in crowds. The bulk of the farmer's contacts is with members of his family and with immediate neighbors. In many ways, the general store is the most important rural social center, and its informal contacts loom large in the rural system of social interaction. The farmer's secondary contacts, through the same devices as the city man's, are increasing greatly but are still far less numerous than those of the urbanite. On the whole, the farmer has relatively few social contacts.

There are important qualitative differences between the rural and urban systems of social interaction: (1) The area of contact of the rural person is narrower and more limited than that of the urban person. The people and institutions with which the farmer is in contact are located in a relatively small area; those of the urbanite are much more widely disseminated and may be scattered throughout the world. (2) The total number of contacts by the ruralite in his relatively small social world is much less than is that of the urbanite in his comparatively large social milieu. (3) Rural contacts are largely personal in nature, whereas urban contacts tend toward the impersonal. The city man knows very little about the thousands of people he sees or meets in the course of a day's work; the majority of them he may never see again. All is very different in rural society. The personality of each individual is well known to everyone in the neighborhood. All forms of social interaction in rural communities are greatly affected by this intimate acquaintanceship. The social contacts are intimate, personal, and tend to be lasting. (4) Of the total number of social contacts, a large proportion of the farmer's are those of a permanent, strong, and durable nature; the bulk of the city person's are casual, superficial, and short-lived. (5) Because of those differences the rural system of social interaction is less differentiated and complex, less plastic and at the same time less superficial, less standardized, and less mechanical than the urban system.

SOCIAL SOLIDARITY

Finally, there is a basic difference in the social solidarity or cohesion of rural and urban societies. The forces making for unity in the two are quite different. The rural world has a unity based on similarities—the union which results from common traits, objectives, and sameness of experience. In essence it is established upon very informal and noncontractual relationships. Urban solidarity, on the other hand, is a type of unity based on differences, dissimilarities that arise from the division of labor, specialization, and the mutual interdependence of dissimilar parts. This type of solidarity is founded upon strictly formal and contractual types of relationships.

Additional Readings

1. BERTRAND, ALVIN L., "The Nature of Rural-Urban Differentials," in Alvin L. Bertrand (ed.), *Rural Sociology,* New York: McGraw-Hill Book Company, Inc., 1958, chapter 3.

2. FUGUITT, GLENN V., "The City and the Countryside," *Rural Sociology,* Vol. 28, No. 3 (September, 1963), pp. 246–261.

3. HATHAWAY, DALE E., J. ALLAN BEEGLE, and W. KEITH BRYANT, *People of Rural America* (A 1960 Census Monograph), Washington: Government Printing Office, 1968, chapter I.

4. ROGERS, EVERETT M., *Social Change in Rural Society,* New York: Appleton-Century-Crofts, Inc., 1960, chapters 3 and 4.

5. SOROKIN, PITIRIM A., and CARLE C. ZIMMERMAN, *Principles of Rural-Urban Sociology,* New York: Henry Holt & Company, 1929, chapter II.

6. SOROKIN, PITIRIM A., CARLE C. ZIMMERMAN, and CHARLES J. GALPIN, *A Systematic Source Book in Rural Sociology,* Minneapolis: University of Minnesota Press, 1930, Vol. I, chapter IV.

7. TAYLOR, CARL C., "The Evolution of American Rural Society," in Carl C. Taylor and others, *Rural Life in the United States,* New York: Alfred A. Knopf, 1949, chapter II.

8. TAYLOR, LEE, and ARTHUR R. JONES, JR., *Rural Life and Urbanized Society,* New York: Oxford University Press, 1964, chapter 3.

9. WILLIAMS, ROBIN M., JR., "American Society in Transition: Trends and Emerging Developments in Social and Cultural Systems," in James H. Copp (ed.), *Our Changing Rural Society: Perspectives and Trends,* Ames: Iowa State University Press, 1964, chapter 1.

PART TWO
THE RURAL POPULATION

The study of rural population is one of the most advanced phases of the entire field of rural sociology. For this reason it deserves careful treatment, and Part Two contains two chapters, which sketch many of the salient points about rural population. Chapter 3 includes information about the number and distribution of the rural inhabitants in a large number of the world's countries, an analysis of the importance of the rural population, and a detailed exposition of the composition of rural populations in general. Knowledge concerning the important vital processes, the rate of reproduction, and the rapidity with which people die also is outlined in this chapter. Chapter 4 includes a treatment of the spatial movements of the rural population, especially the highly important rural-to-urban migration, and the various factors, forces, media, and consequences involved. This chapter also analyzes the movement of people into frontier areas, inter-regional migration, the movement from farm to farm, and nomadism, especially the type that involves migratory agricultural laborers. Finally, it sets forth some information about the selectivity of migration.

3

SIZE, DISTRIBUTION, and CHARACTERISTICS OF THE RURAL POPULATION

In a treatise on the sociology of rural life, it is essential to give a prominent place to a discussion of the rural population, because any thoroughgoing understanding of rural society and rural life is largely dependent upon knowledge of the characteristics of rural people themselves. It is known that rural people differ from the general population in many ways but, as a rule, no great stress is placed on this knowledge, even though the differentiating characteristics may be precisely the factors that would do most to facilitate an understanding of the principal phenomena of rural life. For example, it is frequently asserted that rural society is complacent, that it lacks dynamics, that it is content to follow traditional ways—in short, that rural folk are ultraconservative. Perhaps this is true; if so, it seems important to note that in most societies, especially those in which the agrarian way of life predominates, elderly people occupy positions of relative importance. People of advanced age are more numerous in the rural than in the general population, and, despite a few exceptions, aged people tend to be conservative. But even this point should not be stressed as much as a second one, namely, that in rural society elderly people retain control of the farm property much longer, and they continue to direct actively the affairs of the community to a much larger extent than is true of urban people in the same age groups. This tends to be true whether the elderly actually live on the farms or in small towns and villages nearby. All of this is important if one would really understand rural life and the ways in which it differs from urban life (see Ref. 424).

The unwillingness of the rural portions of a society to change the traditional ways of doing things is also widely recognized. It frequently forms the basis for urban disparagements of rural life and is no small factor in preserving plantation systems, minifundia, primitive systems of agriculture, chaotic ways of dividing land and assigning titles, and many other conditions sorely in need of effective change in broad areas of the world. Here again, the demographic basis of the phenomena should not be overlooked. Note that the rural population is composed more largely of native elements than is the general population; these groups tend to preserve the native culture. Conversely, foreign-born elements and those which come from distant portions of the same society will always be concentrated in the cities, and these groups introduce a diversity of cultural features and tend to bring about change. Thus, a much greater part of rural New Yorkers are the sons and daughters of people born in the state of New York than is true of the population of New York City; rural Europeans, Africans, Asians, Latin Americans, and others are more generally the sons and daughters of people born in the respective nations, and even the particular communities, in which they reside than are the people who make their homes in the cities of these societies. The rural population contains large portions of those particular ethnic elements that have given the culture of a society its particular mold or cast. The traditional ways of doing things, the accepted national folkways and mores, are very largely the creations of rural folk and their ancestors. They represent the cultural heritage into which rural people have been born and in which they have been reared. The most intimate associations and sentiments of rural people are firmly bound up with the traditional culture patterns. Urban people, on the other hand, generally are more cosmopolitan, less limited in their perspectives to the cultural horizon of any single national group. In view of this fact, it is not surprising that country people insist on preserving the cultural values of the group much more than do city people. Since these cultural values belong to the rural folk, quite naturally they have a stronger appeal to the rural population than to the urban. These are but a few examples of the importance of including in a study of rural life an analysis of the makeup of the rural population.

THE NUMBER, DISTRIBUTION, AND IMPORTANCE OF THE RURAL POPULATION

There can be no doubt that the bulk of the world's population is rural and derives its livelihood from agricultural or pastoral pursuits. Merely the overwhelmingly rural nature of both China and India would make that statement true even though all other parts of the earth were far more urban than they are. However, it is not easy to determine, even approximately, the numbers of rural people in the various countries. In some areas of the globe, such as wide sections of Asia and Africa, there have been few or no efforts to conduct complete and reliable censuses of population and, even where efforts have been made, as in China in 1953, underenumeration and other inadvertent distortions make the data of limited value. In many other areas where censuses have been taken, little attention has been paid to any rural and urban classification of the inhabitants. Further, even where a rural-urban division of the population has been made, there has been little uniformity in the criteria employed in establishing the two residence categories or even in the tabulations completed. Some countries, such as the United States and France, have relied heavily upon *size* of the community, as measured by the number of inhabitants, as the basis for separating the population into the rural and urban categories. Others, including Canada, Scotland, Sweden, and the Soviet Union, have depended to a much greater extent on the nature of the title or charter a place has received from the central government in determining whether its people were rural or urban. For these reasons, the rural and urban percentages reported for one country may be difficult or impossible to compare fairly with those for another.

The need for comparable data with respect to the rural and urban populations of the various countries of the earth is one of the things to which the population commission of the United Nations early gave attention. As a result, several issues of its monumental *Demographic Yearbook,* published annually since 1948, contain comprehensive tabulations by residence with brief indications of the criteria employed in the various countries for separating the urban residents from the rural. In order that the essential materials may be readily available for study and comparison, a summary of some of the more important items from the United Nations compilations is presented in Table 1. However, these data are available even now for only half of all existing nations and territories; they do not provide a complete view of the number and distribution of the world's rural people or of their proportional significance in each country. For example, while enumerations and estimates have been made for India, thereby allowing it to be included in the compilations, none is available for mainland China, thus forcing it to be excluded. The published materials do contain, however, the distinction by residence for about two billion of the world's people. Of these, roughly 63 per cent are classified as rural. Furthermore, rural people make up the majority of the population in over 70 per cent of the nations and territories listed in Table 1. Considering that the ones that are not represented are

41

TABLE 1

The absolute and relative importance of the rural population of each country
for which data are available

Region and country	Year	Total population	Rural population	Per cent rural
Africa				
Algeria	1960	10,205,000	6,891,000	67.5
Angola	1960	4,830,449	4,317,906	89.4
Congo, Democratic Republic	1955–57	12,768,705	9,916,437	77.7
Gambia	1963	315,486	287,677	91.2
Ghana	1960	6,726,820	5,175,460	76.9
Guinea				
African Population	1955	2,570,219	2,357,400	91.7
Kenya				
African Population	1962	8,365,942	7,924,203	94.7
Non-African Population	1962	270,321	41,115	15.2
Mauritius	1962	681,619	364,759	53.5
Morocco	1960	11,626,232	8,214,561	70.7
Northern Rhodesia				
Non-African Population	1961	84,380	14,400	17.1
Nyasaland				
Non-African Population	1961	20,890	9,580	45.9
Senegal	1961	3,109,840	2,404,040	77.3
Seychelles	1960	41,425	30,921	74.6
South Africa	1960	16,002,797	8,521,669	53.3
South West Africa	1960	526,004	402,648	76.5
Southern Rhodesia				
African Population	1962	3,618,150	2,963,610	81.9
Non-African Population	1961	239,310	61,620	25.7
Sudan	1956	10,262,536	9,408,663	91.7
Swaziland	1956	237,041	230,993	97.4
Togo	1958–60	1,439,800	1,305,130	90.6
Tunisia	1956	3,783,169	2,435,685	64.4
Uganda	1959	6,536,616	6,220,627	95.2
United Arab Republic	1960	25,984,101	16,120,398	62.0
United Republic of Tanzania	1957–58	9,087,577	8,644,218	95.1
Zambia				
African Population	1963	3,409,110	2,741,000	80.4
America, North				
Antigua	1960	54,060	32,664	60.4
Barbados	1960	232,333	220,881	95.1
Bermuda	1960	2,671	0	0
British Honduras	1960	90,019	41,615	46.2

The absolute and relative importance of the rural population of each country
for which data are available

Region and country	Year	Total population	Rural population	Per cent rural
Canada	1961	18,238,247	5,537,857	30.4
Canal Zone	1960	42,122	28,693	68.1
Cayman Islands	1960	7,622	7,622	100.0
Costa Rica	1963	1,325,155	868,577	65.5
Dominica	1960	59,863	44,451	74.3
Dominican Republic	1960	3,013,525	2,095,544	69.5
El Salvador	1961	2,511,330	1,531,330	61.0
Honduras	1961	1,884,765	1,446,947	76.8
Jamaica	1960	1,609,814	1,134,313	70.5
Martinique	1961	292,594	170,655	58.3
Mexico	1960	34,923,129	17,218,011	49.3
Netherlands Antilles	1960	135,715	41,582	30.6
Nicaragua	1963	1,536,240	909,220	59.2
Panama	1960	1,075,541	629,328	58.5
Puerto Rico	1960	2,349,544	1,312,268	55.9
St. Kitts—Nevis and Anguilla	1960	56,693	41,114	72.5
St. Pierre and Miquelon	1962	4,990	703	14.1
Turks and Caicos Islands	1960	5,716	5,716	100.0
United States	1960	179,323,175	54,041,888	30.1
Virgin Islands	1960	32,099	14,082	43.9
America, South				
Brazil	1960	70,967,185	38,976,247	54.9
Guyana	1960	560,406	397,945	71.0
Chile	1960	7,375,200	2,472,700	33.5
Ecuador	1962	4,581,476	2,964,892	64.7
French Guiana	1961	33,535	11,901	33.1
Peru	1961	9,747,000	5,076,600	52.1
Uruguay	1963	2,592,600	460,600	17.8
Venezuela	1961	7,523,999	2,445,375	32.5
Asia				
Bahrain	1959	143,135	49,416	34.5
Brunei	1960	83,877	47,347	56.4
Cambodia	1958	4,740,000	4,132,000	87.2
Ceylon	1963	10,624,507	9,038,454	85.1
Cyprus	1960	573,566	367,583	64.1
Federation of Malaya	1957	6,278,758	3,599,085	57.3
Hong Kong	1961	3,133,131	700,225	22.3
India	1961	438,271,500	359,435,607	82.0
Indonesia	1961	96,318,829	81,960,457	85.1
Iran	1956	18,954,704	13,001,141	68.6

The absolute and relative importance of the rural population of each country for which data are available

Region and country	Year	Total population	Rural population	Per cent rural
Iraq	1957	6,339,960	3,853,517	60.8
Israel	1961	2,179,491	481,575	22.1
Japan	1960	93,347,200	52,540,400	56.3
Jordan	1961	1,706,226	957,935	56.1
Korea, Republic of	1960	24,989,241	17,992,495	72.0
Mongolia	1963	1,018,800	603,500	59.2
Nepal	1961	9,387,661	9,123,633	97.2
North Borneo				
Sabah	1960	454,421	386,747	85.1
Sarawak	1960	744,529	632,772	85.0
Pakistan	1961	90,282,674	78,027,944	86.4
Philippines	1960	27,087,685	18,985,209	70.1
Sikkim	1961	162,189	155,341	95.8
Singapore	1957	1,445,929	533,586	36.9
Syria	1960	4,353,451	2,668,496	61.3
Thailand	1960	26,257,916	21,479,268	81.8
Turkey	1960	27,754,820	20,447,004	73.7
Vietnam, North	1960	15,916,955	14,398,201	90.5
Europe				
Albania	1955	1,391,499	1,008,330	72.5
Austria	1961	7,073,807	3,538,247	50.1
Bulgaria	1956	7,613,709	5,057,638	66.4
Channel Islands	1961	47,099	31,295	66.4
Czechoslovakia	1961	13,745,577	7,206,565	52.4
Denmark	1960	4,585,256	1,187,920	25.9
Finland	1960	4,446,222	1,959,485	44.1
France	1962	46,456,260	17,174,200	37.0
Gibralter	1961	24,502	0	0
Greece	1961	8,388,600	3,657,200	43.6
Hungary	1960	9,961,044	6,002,637	60.3
Ireland	1961	2,818,341	1,519,194	53.9
Isle of Man	1961	48,150	21,513	44.7
Italy	1961	50,623,569	26,454,849	52.3
Luxembourg	1960	314,889	119,059	37.8
Malta and Gozo	1957	319,620	115,622	36.2
Monaco	1961	22,297	0	0
Netherlands	1960	11,461,964	2,288,426	20.0
Norway	1960	3,591,234	1,538,600	42.8
Poland	1960	28,798,680	15,192,380	52.8
Portugal	1960	8,889,392	6,881,219	77.4
Romania	1956	17,489,450	12,015,186	68.7

The absolute and relative importance of the rural population of each country for which data are available

Region and country	Year	Total population	Rural population	Per cent rural
Sweden	1960	7,495,316	2,041,692	27.2
Switzerland	1960	5,429,061	2,644,075	48.7
United Kingdom				
England and Wales	1961	46,071,604	9,233,162	20.0
Northern Ireland	1961	1,425,042	655,041	46.0
Scotland	1961	5,179,344	1,533,356	29.6
Yugoslavia	1961	18,549,291	13,307,607	71.7
Oceania				
Australia	1961	10,508,186	1,872,180	17.8
Fiji Islands	1956	345,737	282,428	81.7
New Zealand	1961	2,414,984	872,768	36.1
Tonga	1961	65,620	65,620	100.0
Western Samoa	1961	114,427	92,728	81.0
U.S.S.R.	1959	208,826,650	108,848,955	52.1

Compiled and computed from data in United Nations, Demographic Yearbook, 1962, pp. 304–315, Table 10; 1963, pp. 162–230, Table 5; and 1964, pp. 648–664, Table 27.

generally more rural than the average, in reality far in excess of two thirds of the 3.5 billion people who inhabit the planet derive their livelihoods from some form of agriculture or stockraising. As imperfect as these indicators may be, they certainly are sufficient to demonstrate that most of mankind depends directly upon the soil for survival and functions within various sociocultural settings which reflect that basic fact. This condition of rurality alone is sufficient to refute the often-heard contention that the study of rural life is no longer worthwhile and that attention might better be directed to an examination of urban life. Even if this were warranted in a few highly urbanized nations such as Australia, Canada, Japan, and the United States, it certainly cannot be justified for most of the societies of man, even in an age of rapid urban growth.

A fairly comprehensive portrayal of the distribution of the world's urban people, and therefore of its rural folk, may be obtained by using other, more complete materials which the United Nations now publishes each year. For about 90 per cent of all nations and territories, the world body publishes annually the numbers of people living in capital cities of all sizes, in other centers of 100,000 or more, and, when they exist, in densely settled "urban agglomerations," which consist of large cities and their densely settled peripheries. The people who live outside such concentrations are not, of course, solely the rural group; in the United States, in 1960, for example, all urban people were 69.9 per cent of the total whereas those in the centers under consideration were only 57.8 per cent. Furthermore, the materials are subject to other minor limitations. But at the moment these data alone make it possible to distinguish populations on any residence basis whatsoever in virtually all of the world's sovereign countries and in a great majority of the territories and possessions. Also, there is greater uniformity in these data than can be found in other materials separating rural and urban, simply because in the former the United Nations itself applies certain uniform definitions and makes its own estimates when other figures are unavailable, whereas in the latter each of the countries has the prerogative to devise its own criteria of "rural" and "urban" and to gather and evaluate its own data accordingly. By including capitals, the material on cities possesses the advantage of being available for at least the urban center which is the principal one in almost every society. Therefore, in practice, the materials apply to some urban centers possessing as few as 6,000 persons and to others containing as many as ten million inhabitants.

Employing the materials described above, Figure 1 has been prepared

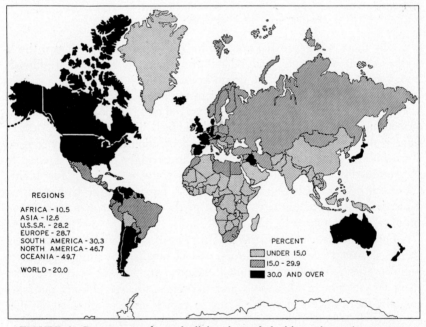

REGIONS

AFRICA - 10.5
ASIA - 12.6
U.S.S.R. - 28.2
EUROPE - 28.7
SOUTH AMERICA - 30.3
NORTH AMERICA - 46.7
OCEANIA - 49.7

WORLD - 20.0

PERCENT

UNDER 15.0
15.0 - 29.9
30.0 AND OVER

FIGURE 1. Percentages of people living in capital cities, other urban centers with 100,000 or more, and urban agglomerations, each nation and territory.

showing for nearly all nations and most territories the percentages of people living in the capital cities, in other centers of 100,000 or more, and wherever possible those in the urban agglomerations. Three groups of societies may be distinguished. First, those whose total populations contain relatively high proportions (30 per cent or more) of city dwellers. There are fewer than 30 of these and they are concentrated in North America above the Rio Grande, the extremities of South America, northwestern Europe, Japan, and Oceania (largely Australia and New Zealand). In general, these are societies in which industrial growth has proceeded far and in which urbanization is a long-term phenomenon. To be sure, there are large numbers of rural people in these places, but their proportions are not so great that an agrarian way of life can be said to dominate entire countries in this group. Moreover, in most of these societies, agriculture and stockraising are carried on in a manner that tends to produce substantial middle classes of farm people rather than vast hordes of poverty-stricken agricultural laborers and infinitesimally small, wealthy, landowning elites. Many of the countries have these groups, of course, but the extremes do not tend to pervade totally the relationships between man and the land.

Second, the nations and territories that contain moderate proportions (15 to 29.9 per cent) of persons living in the kinds of cities under consideration. These cover relatively broad areas and include Mexico and parts of the Caribbean, the central portion of South America, North and South Africa, eastern Europe, sections of the Near East and the Middle East, and the vast Soviet Union. There are nearly 100 of these societies. Some of them have recently become industrially important, and many are just now witnessing significant reductions in the relative importance of agriculture and the agrarian way of life. This is certainly the case in Mexico, Brazil, and a few other countries of Latin America. Much the same might be said of South Africa, the Soviet Union, parts of eastern Europe, and the Scandinavian countries. In all of these, agriculture and rural life remain highly significant elements of national life but tend to occupy less important roles, whereas urbanization and industrialization are becoming far more significant. Furthermore, in many such places, "agrarian reform" is a major element, which implies that agriculture itself is receiving a rational and critical evaluation with a view to improving production and enhancing the social relationships between man and the land. In some cases, considerable headway has been made in the basic rebuilding of rural life; in many others the bulk of fruitful change is yet to take place. In a number of instances these nations have begun recently to make rapid strides away from extreme rurality and toward a higher degree of urbanization. Still other societies in this intermediate group are those whose balance between rural and urban people has changed comparatively little but which became urbanized or at least non-agricultural early in their histories. Several countries in the Middle East and a few in North Africa, where agriculture always has been limited severely by lack of moisture, may be placed in this category.

Third and finally, the nations and territories that have small relative shares (less than 15 per cent) of their people living in capital cities, those of 100,000 or more, and urban agglomerations. There are also almost 100 of these. However, despite the fact that their distribution is fairly wide, they certainly represent a smaller share of the world's countries than was the case only a decade or two ago. In the western hemisphere, only Bolivia in South America, three of the countries of Central America, and sparsely inhabited Greenland fall into this category. In the eastern hemisphere, India and China, of course, are the most significant of these slightly urbanized nations. In addition, nearly all the rest of Asia and practically all of Africa south of the Sahara must be placed in this group. These societies, many of which have become independent or have endured disruptive political revolutions in the years since World War II, are the truly agrarian portions of the globe. In most, agriculture and its ramifications provide the principal sociocultural matrix within which national life goes on. Moreover, a large number of these places also must be styled as "underdeveloped"; in no small measure this unenviable status arises from the fact that agriculture, as it is carried on, tends to be antiquated, underproductive, and wasteful of time and human energy. As a result, these are countries whose levels of living tend to be comparatively low and whose people often exhibit a restlessness that flares periodically into serious violence. The great revolution in China and the desolation in Vietnam are merely two examples of the kinds of national traumas that may occur.

In general, then, belts of truly rural people cover virtually all of Asia and Africa. Sections in which rurality is yielding in importance while urbanization is gaining significantly are found in parts of Latin America, eastern Europe and Scandinavia, the Near East and Middle East, and North and South Africa. The more limited regions in which urbanization is a major fact of life and rurality a far less significant one embrace much of North America and some of South America, western Europe, the two great nations in Oceania, and Japan.

The Importance of the Rural Population

The rural population is of fundamental importance for a number of reasons: It comprises the bulk of the inhabitants in most societies, reaching 90 per cent or more in some; even in highly industrialized nations, such as the United States, it may make up one third or more of the total.

In virtually all countries, the rural people make inordinately large contributions to the national population for the future. Historically, they have been the source from which the depleted human resources of the urban centers were replenished. They have been especially significant in this respect where immigration was greatly restricted, often being the major source of urban growth. Even now, in many societies where urban populations do reproduce themselves, the rural districts continue to be heavy contributors of new urban residents, often excessively so.

The institutions maintained by the rural population, especially the family and church, are those in which much of the oncoming population of the nation is nourished and through which it acquires membership in the larger society.

Except in those unfortunate societies where agricultural laborers make up the bulk of rural people, the farming population constitutes an immense national balance wheel. It serves as the stabilizing influence necessary to keep the rapidly changing social life of the cities from precipitating disorders, strikes, revolutions, and other upheavals to a greater extent than is now the case. The rural citizenry, if strong and intelligent and if related to the land in a manner it considers to be equitable and productive, is one important guarantee that these will less often come to their most extreme stages, perhaps to the point where civilization itself may be destroyed. Even in places where the agitation for change is great among rural people, the actual alteration that takes place tends to be less traumatic, its participants less volatile and revolutionary, than among those who would bring about change in the urban centers.

In times of national peril, the rural population of middle-class status constitutes a reservoir of national patriotism and manpower. It comprises a citizenry largely unaffected by disruptive philosophies, which flourish amid the heterogeneous ethnic and cultural mixture that is the city, and which frequently come to be the greatest deterrent to international peace.

The deep-seated resistance to change characteristic of rural culture acts to preserve many distinctively national cultural traits and complexes which might otherwise be lost in the city's tendency to create and to embrace the new. In the eternal conflict between the forces of institutionalization and those of change, rural society is almost always aligned on the side of the former.

In the rural enterprises of farming as they are conducted by middle-class people, the opportunity remains to combine the skills of entrepreneur, manager, and laborer in one individual. This gives rise to a well-developed type of personality, a citizen fully attuned to the interests of all classes in the society and capable of participating in the democratic process with the least possible class discrimination. Moreover, even in societies where the great bulk of the farmers belong to the lower class and possess few of these attributes, effective efforts to reform and rebuild rural life must seek to multiply the number and enhance the position of middleclass farm operators.

COMPOSITION OF THE RURAL POPULATION

The composition of any population consists in its characteristics: the age profile, the balance between the sexes, race and national origin, marital condition, levels of education, types of occupation, and religious affiliation. There are, of course, fundamental differences in the make-up of rural and urban populations along the lines of these various characteristics, but often the variations are not well known. Even with an awareness of the differences, these differences seldom receive the attention they deserve in the formation of public policies which involve rural folk or urban residents separately, or both together. For example, the fact that the country has a disproportionately large share of children, many of whom will spend their adult lives in the city, seldom receives adequate attention in the financing of public schools, especially in those great agrarian regions of the world where local rural government is forced by central government to remain so weak that it is incapable of establishing and maintaining proper schools. Therefore, the present section of this chapter deals with some of the salient features of the composition of rural populations.

The data upon which the general observations must be based leave a great deal to be desired, both in completeness and in accuracy. Nevertheless, those that are available in the various editions of the *Demographic Yearbook* are the best to be had and may be used to illustrate several points. In particular, the materials that have been published separately for rural and urban populations contain cross-classifications by age and sex, and, while the data are affected by the inconsistent criteria of "rural" and "urban" employed by the various countries, they do provide the principal documentation of the conclusions which follow.

Age Composition

The individual's age is his most important characteristic, because the way he thinks and behaves and the needs he has are closely related to the number of years he has lived. Age also has a bearing on such diverse matters as his marital status, the role he plays in the society of which he is a part, his tendency to move or to stay in one place, and his chances for parenthood and even for survival. In addition, the age profile is a fundamental feature of the whole society and, of course, separately of its rural and urban portions. An "old" population, for example, with an extremely high proportion of people aged 65 and over has quite different problems than a "young" population with a superabundance of children under 15. The former must concern itself with matters of retirement and medical-care programs for the aged, while the latter should (but generally doesn't) invest heavily in education and child-welfare services. In both cases, a vital factor is the proportion of persons in the "productive" age ranges (15 to 64) who must finance the various programs and services. Thus, social planning in either rural or urban areas must account directly for age variations as well as for social characteristics that are likely to be associated with age.

The principal ways in which the makeup of the rural population differs from that of the urban may be summarized as follows: (1) The rural population usually includes relatively large proportions of children; (2) the rural population has a comparatively low percentage of its people in the ages 15 to 44, i.e., the years of life in which there is an especially heavy migration of farm people into cities; and (3) the rural group in most societies contains a disproportionately large share of persons above the age of 45. The city, on the other hand, has a scarcity of children, a high percentage of people in the young adult ages, a moderate percentage of those aged 45 to 64, and relatively few people aged 65 and over. In the last case, though, not only do many of the aged tend to concentrate on farms but they also appear with great relative frequency in villages, small towns, and some types of suburban areas. In a few societies, of which the United States is one, they now are appearing in metropolitan centers in much greater proportions.

These variations are illustrated in Figure 2. The four societies whose age profiles are shown are different in many respects, and their populations range from those with very high percentages of rural folk, in India, to those with high percentages of urban residents, in France, Japan, and the United States. Nevertheless, in each of the four societies, even in India where the national age norms are shaped almost entirely by the rural profile, children are abundant in farming districts but scarcer in cities; young adults are found with greater relative frequency in cities than on farms; and persons aged 45 and over tend to remain on farms or in small towns and villages to a greater degree than they appear in cities. Taking the 1960 population of the United States as an example, children under 15 make up 32.4 per cent of the rural-farm group but only 30.1 per cent of the urban; persons from 15 to 44 constitute only 34.9 per cent of the rural-farm but 40.1 per

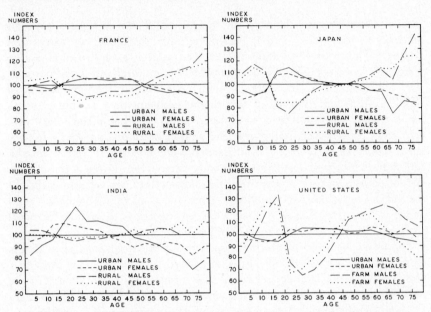

FIGURE 2. Index numbers showing the relative importance of each age group in the rural and urban populations of France, India, Japan, and the United States, by sex. (For the United States, only the urban and rural-farm populations are included.)

cent of the urban; those from 45 to 64 comprise 23.3 per cent of the rural-farm and 20.8 per cent of the urban; and those 65 and over comprise 9.3 per cent of the rural-farm and 9.1 per cent of the urban. The close similarity of the rural-farm and urban populations in the relative abundance of the aged is a condition peculiar to the United States because of the relatively large proportion of elderly farm widows who migrate to cities in the United States.

From an economic standpoint, the chief significance of these data is this: Rural areas with low proportions of their populations in the productive ages (15 to 64) must care for high proportions of dependent persons, i.e., the very young and, to a lesser extent, the very old. From an educational standpoint, the importance is that an excessive burden is placed upon the few adults to provide facilities for large numbers of children, many of whom are to migrate and spend their productive years in urban centers. From an institutional point of view, the significance is that there will be a scarcity of energetic young adults to assume leadership in community, civic, and religious affairs. Furthermore, the traditional conservatism of the country may be enhanced greatly by its age composition as well as by its particular distribution of ownership of real property.

52

The differences in the age composition of rural and urban populations seem to be the result of several factors. First, the differential birth rates of country and city give the rural districts their excessive proportion of children. Second, there is generally a strong movement of able-bodied young persons from the farms to the cities. Part of this arises out of the specialization and division of labor in cities, which creates varied economic, educational, political, and other opportunities that attract young and vigorous persons from the country. Thus the agencies that induce country people into city life concentrate their efforts upon young adults. Third, if the rural person is to migrate to the city it must be while he is young, energetic, and capable of making adjustments, and before residence in the country has developed ties such as family obligations, sentimental attachments, community responsibilities, deep-rooted habits, property ownership, and acceptance of the rural way of life. After the age of 25 or 30, relatively few persons leave the country for the city. Fourth, in societies where the scattered-farmsteads pattern of settlement prevails, after people attain the age of 45 or 50, a great many of them, especially the widows of farmers, take up residence in villages or small towns near the farms. Finally, many persons in the older age groups who have spent the productive years of their lives in the cities move to the country or to small towns to spend the twilight of life. For some, such a transfer represents the attainment of a lifelong objective; for others, this landward migration represents an attempt to make slender resources go as far as possible in a place where living costs are low, after their earning power has been seriously curtailed or terminated entirely. But in either case this reflux of elderly people toward the land helps swell the numbers of the aged in the villages and the open country. Combined with the greater expectation of life in the rural districts of many countries, it accounts for the high proportion of oldsters in most rural populations.

Perhaps the social significance of these various conditions is demonstrated most clearly by comparisons such as the following: Broadly speaking, persons of less than 15 years of age and those who are 65 or over are dependent upon those aged 15 to 64. Therefore, the ratio of dependents to contributors is an important index of the variations in socioeconomic conditions which are closely associated with differences in the age profile. Generally, in most parts of the world, the ratio of dependents to contributors is significantly higher in the rural districts than it is in the cities. For example, in 1960, the urban population of Japan contained only 50 persons in these dependent ages for every 100 aged 15–64; in the rural population, the corresponding number was 68 per 100. In India, in 1961, the figures for the urban and rural populations were 71 and 81, respectively. These differences by residence result from the fact that the farming areas of most societies have far more than their *pro rata* shares of children, although the elderly also help to swell the heavy support burden that rural workers must carry. When the higher dependency ratio is combined with the fact that incomes in the farming districts are usually considerably lower on the average than are those in cities, the world's rural producers clearly are at a distinct disadvantage in providing a reasonably adequate level of living for themselves and the dependent population.

Sex Composition

Whether an individual is male or female ranks as his second most significant characteristic, preceded in importance only by age. Thus, the relative percentages of males and females in the rural and urban segments of society have great influence upon the sociocultural conditions of each. When males greatly outnumber females, or vice versa, the unequal sex ratio reacts in a significant manner upon the rates of marriage, birth, death, and so on. It also affects the tempo of practically all social activities. Scarcity of women is largely responsible for the unique characteristics and reckless abandon of life on a frontier, in mining or lumber camps, and in steel towns. On the other hand, the lack of men is felt keenly in textile centers or in those where office functions supply a significant proportion of the jobs. Some residential cities are overcrowded with women; and in many rural villages, women, especially widows, are the principal element in the population.

Significant variations in the ratios of the sexes exist between the rural and urban populations. Generally, males outnumber females on the farms, while women are more numerous than men in the cities. Agriculture is largely a man's occupation, a fact reflected in the high proportion of males in rural populations. On the other hand, residential cities and industrial and commercial centers, other than those in which heavy industries such as steel are concentrated, number large proportions of females among their inhabitants. Some data, calculated from the materials for a few of the countries which report residence by age and sex, will bring this point out clearly.

In the United States as a whole, in 1960, there were about 97 males for each 100 females; in the urban portion of the population the ratio was 94; and in the rural-farm portion it was 107. In Costa Rica, in 1963, there were about 99 males for each 100 females in the total population but in the urban segment the number was 89 and in the rural part it was a much higher 107. Even in France, where females outnumber males in both residential segments of the population, in 1962, the sex ratio for the nation was 95, that for the urban population was 92, and for the rural group, 99. The analysis might be continued indefinitely, but in each case where censuses are sufficiently reliable to enable accurate conclusions, and where special circumstances (as in India where males outnumber females in both the villages and the cities) do not alter the general condition, the rural districts contain larger than average shares of males and the cities contain disproportionately high percentages of women. The disparity tends to be the greatest, of course, in the young adult years and in old age.

Several factors directly affect the sex ratio. At least one of them arises in large part from the sociocultural differences between rural and urban living. In the first place, in most parts of the world the sex ratio at birth is well above 100, often close to 105. However, the death rate at virtually all ages is higher among males than among females, and this condition eventually makes itself felt in the form of a sex ratio which is lower at each successive age level, irrespective of residence. Especially among older people, differential mortality tends to decimate the male population, and aged widows come to outnumber aged widowers by a wide margin. The survival potential of women is greater, of course, in those societies that have learned to control effectively the various maladies associated with pregnancy and childbirth. In societies where existence is especially difficult for women and where life expectancy for both sexes is relatively short, the population tends to be characterized by high proportions of children, among whom males predominate. So important is this situation in India, for example, that in 1961 overall sex ratios were well above 100 for both rural and urban segments of the population.

Secondly, long-range migration, which takes people across national boundaries, and especially from one continent to another, tends to be more selective of males than females, so that immigrant populations usually have comparatively large proportions of men. For example, in the United States in 1930 (the year in which the foreign-born population was the largest), the native-white population had a sex ratio of 101, but the foreign-born white group had one of 116. In cities, the native whites exhibited a ratio of 96 and the foreign-born whites one of 112. In the rural-farm population, native whites produced a ratio of 112, but the foreign-born whites generated an extremely high one of 140, despite the fact that the foreign-born farm population was small compared to that of the cities. Thus, in both rural and urban areas, populations that have undertaken international migration greatly abound in males, especially those in the relatively young adult years. Conversely, those societies that lose large numbers of people through international migration may find themselves with superabundances of women and may embody sociocultural conditions that reflect that fact.

Finally, in relatively short-distance migrations, including the movement of people from farms to cities within their own societies, females, especially those aged 18 to 25, appear in disproportionately large numbers. As these young women move from rural to urban areas, the flow may be so great that the sex ratios are significantly higher for rural populations in the young adult years than they are for urban groups of comparable ages. So great has this movement been in the United States and a few other highly urbanized nations, that the levels of *fertility* in rural-farm areas actually have been reduced substantially. In many extremely rural countries, such as India, this selectivity of migration has yet to make its major effects felt, but as the rate of urbanization accelerates in such places, selectivity by sex certainly may be expected to widen the residential disparity in the proportions of males and females. In some other societies, such as the United States, when the great wave of rural-to-urban migration has passed, the tendency is for the balance between the sexes to become more even among farm and urban populations.

Race and Nativity

Of all the traits that distinguish one population from another, race and nativity are among the most obvious and important. Race, a biological concept, is based upon physical traits, such as texture of the hair, cephalic index, skin pigmentation, and so forth, whereas national origins, although somewhat correlated with race, are an index of the cultural heritage of a people, of the background of folkways, mores, and other customs characterizing particular groups. Sometimes, as in the United States census, for example, a classification is used which is a mixture of the two, making it necessary to consider them together.

Rural areas might well be styled as the homes of the long-established racial and ethnic groups in a society; whereas the cities generally are the places of residence of those who have arrived recently. R. Livi, an Italian scholar, has formulated a principle that seems adequate to explain virtually all the known facts on the subject (see Ref. 477, pp. 106–107 and 113). Two things need to be kept in mind to grasp his explanation: (1) that hereditary biological factors are of sole importance in determining race; and (2) that urban populations are heterogeneous and recruited from far-distant places, while rural populations are homogeneous and recruited mainly from the immediate vicinity. Therefore, in a country, or even a section of a country, where the long-established population is white, as it is in the nine states that make up the region known as the Northeast in the United States, the proportion of nonwhites in the city's hodgepodge population will exceed that of the rural area's homogeneous group. Conversely, in places where the native population is Negro, as in most of sub-Sahara Africa, the urban population, which includes many foreign elements, will contain an abnormally large share of whites, as compared with the rural group, which is recruited mainly from the native Negroid stock. Thus, in the northeastern United States, where whites are the native population, in 1960, 77.7 per cent of the members of this race were in the urban population, 20.0 per cent in the rural-nonfarm, and 2.3 per cent in the rural-farm segment; whereas among Negroes, who have arrived in the Northeast relatively recently, 95.6 per cent were living in the cities, only 4.1 per cent in the rural-nonfarm areas, and a mere 0.2 per cent on farms. In the South, of course, both Negroes and whites long were primarily rural people, and, in that region, members of the two races are found with about the same relative frequency in the cities and on the farms. In Kenya, where Negroes are the long-established population and whites are a come-lately group, the latter are proportionately more abundant than the former in the cities, and they are found with far less relative frequency in the rural districts. Thus, in 1962, 84.8 per cent of the whites of Kenya lived in cities and 15.2 per cent lived in the rural areas; whereas only 5.3 per cent of the native Negroes lived in urban centers and the remaining 94.7 per cent lived in the rural areas. With regard to race, the one uniform difference by residence is the greater variability and higher proportions in the urban population of races which have just recently arrived and the greater degree of homogeneity and comparatively high percentages of the native groups in the rural population.

The fact that the "native" elements in a population constitute high proportions of the rural people, while "foreign" elements are concentrated in the cities is well illustrated by the case of the United States. In 1930, when the foreign-born white population was at its maximum (13,336,407), 80.3 per cent lived in cities, 11.6 per cent in rural-nonfarm territory, and only 8.1 per cent on farms. The proportions of the foreign-born were highest in the most industrialized and urbanized section of the country—the Northeast—and lowest in the most rural region—the South. In fact, the latter has received but an infinitesimally small share of the tremendous influx of foreign-born people who have migrated to the United States in the last century, although there are fairly sizeable numbers of Spanish-speaking people in Texas and Florida. Furthermore, not only are foreign elements much scarcer in the rural population than in the urban, but those foreign-born who do reside on farms generally have been in the United States longer and have had more time to become acculturated than the foreign-born residents of the cities. In fact, some of the most recent arrivals (Cubans, Hungarians, and other "refugees") are located almost exclusively in the large cities of the nation.

The fact that foreign-born persons are concentrated in the cities of their adopted countries must be taken into account if rural-urban comparisons of many other social characteristics are to be made. For instance, the foreign-born usually have a distinctive age and sex distribution, males generally being very heavily represented, children practically unrepresented, and so on. Among other things, in countries where the foreign-born population is substantial, its concentration in cities means that large numbers of foreign-born males at the marriageable ages are to be found in urban centers, because such long-distance migrants are predominantly males. For example, the sex ratio for the nearly one million people who migrated to Australia during 1960 through 1965, inclusive, was 111; that for the four million who went to the Federal Republic of Germany during these years was 225. Were it not for the presence of men from other countries, urban sex ratios in the receiving countries would be much lower than they are because large numbers of native young women gravitate to the cities from the country. Thus, the factors involved in migration and the selectivity of migration operate in such a manner that large numbers of native females are thrown into immediate proximity to the unmarried immigrant males. At the same time, they are removed from practically all social contacts with the native males in the rural districts. The result is a great excess of females in the city and a scarcity of women in the country. Consequently, the dynamics of population movements may operate in a manner that gives the male of foreign birth a comparative advantage over his native-born farm rival in securing a mate from among the native women. The immigrant woman also is placed in a very keen competitive situation with regard to attentions from men. Most of these dynamics were very much in evidence in the United States just a few decades ago, and they continue to be of great importance in such places as Brazil, Australia, West Germany, and others which receive many immigrants. In any event, it is certain that the concentration of foreigners in the cities and their relative scarcity in the country is fraught with much social significance for the nations involved.

Occupational Status

It goes without saying that agriculture, stockraising, and, to a lesser extent, forestry and a few other minor pursuits provide the jobs and the occupational status for the majority of rural people. However, not all rural workers engage in these endeavors, nor do all urban workers refrain from agricultural employment. Moreover, when occupation is considered at the world level, the sizeable share of the world's farming enterprises which provides inadequate levels of living is a fundamental fact, which directly affects two thirds or more of the earth's people. The related fourfold need to move some people out of low-status agriculture, to raise the levels of those who continue to farm, to train many who prefer to seek other jobs, and then to make those other jobs available, constitutes a formidable set of social problems intricately interwoven with rural occupational patterns. Finally, it is difficult to overestimate the socioeconomic significance of the facts that most of the jobs being performed in the world at the moment are in some way associated with the use of land and that agricultural employment provides not merely jobs but an encompassing way of life. Moreover, the implications for social change stagger the imagination, when one considers that rapidly increasing numbers of the world's rural job holders are impelled to seek urban employment and will swell the ranks of both the employed and the unemployed in the cities of their respective societies.

In addition to the differences in kinds of occupations that rural and urban people are likely to follow, there are several other variations that appear in the overall occupational situation. In the first place, the composition of the labor force varies considerably by residence. For example, males aged 14 to 24 and those aged 50 and beyond are especially heavily represented in the rural labor forces of many societies, whereas those aged 25 to 49 are particularly abundant in the urban forces. However, upon reaching 65, a great many urban workers are able to retire, but farm men are more apt to continue working until they die, largely because the agricultural occupation is simply one part of a total way of life, which one does not abandon with the same facility that one leaves an industrial job. Urban women of most ages have higher rates of involvement in the labor force than do those in farming districts, for, as suggested above, agriculture is typically a man's occupation. However, this apparent under-representation of rural women is somewhat artificial, because much of the work they do on farms does not qualify them for inclusion in the official statistics. In addition, the potential female labor force in many farming areas is greatly reduced by the large migration of young women to cities, where they do find jobs. Consequently, as a society urbanizes, its total labor force comes to include larger proportions of women.

In the second place, where reliable official statistics are available, rates of unemployment are greater among urban workers than they are among the rural group. However, these materials generally give little or no indication of the extent of "underemployment" (miniscule return for time and effort invested) in either residence group. In reality, this is a most serious matter in farming areas throughout the world, being more prevalent there than it is in cities. Underemployment may arise from a number of conditions. For example, it is a serious problem in areas where systems of agriculture are so primitive and unproductive that the return for the time and labor invested by the worker is slight by any standard. It exists widely in places where the farms are small but where all the members of the family engage in agricultural production. Here again, the return for the aggregate amount of time and labor invested is minimal. Underemployment also occurs in places where peak seasons of planting and harvest are interspersed with long periods of inactivity on the part of agricultural workers. These various forms of underemployment are most likely to appear in places where the proportion of farm laborers is large and that of farm owner-operators is small. It is especially typical of areas that are given over predominantly to large landed estates and the kinds of agriculture in which they generally engage.

In the third place, proportions of workers in the various classes, such as "self-employed," "wage and salary workers," and so on, vary considerably by residence. Rural people are far less likely than urban workers to labor for regular wages or to be governmental employees, but they are far more inclined to be self-employed or to be unpaid family workers. Farming, especially that carried on in places where the family-sized unit is widespread, creates a comparatively high proportion of workers who own, rent, or otherwise operate farms as independent businesses. This may even be true in parts of the world where tiny minifundia are under the more or less autonomous control of the families that reside on them. The unpaid family worker, of course, is a logical component of farming, because families as units become infinitely more involved in their agricultural enterprises than the families of urban workers can ever be in the kinds of jobs which are common in cities. The number of urban businesses in which family members actually do take an active part, receiving few or no actual wages, is insignificant when compared to the vast number of farms of all sizes in which all members of given families participate.

In the fourth place, although most rural workers do engage in agricultural and pastoral pursuits, by no means are all of them so employed. Conversely, despite the fact that most urban workers are engaged in nonagricultural occupations, a fair proportion of them is involved in farm work. For example, in the United States in 1960, there were about 4.7 million employed workers living in rural-farm areas, but only 60 per cent were engaged in agriculture and related pursuits. The remainder were involved in manufacturing (12 per cent) and a variety of other industries which could scarcely be placed in the categories of agriculture, livestock raising, and forestry. At the same time, however, there were nearly 4.3 million workers employed in agriculture throughout the nation and although 66 per cent of them lived in rural-farm areas, another 22 per cent inhabited rural-nonfarm areas, and a rather surprising 12 per cent lived in cities. Manufacturing, predominantly an urban occupation, employed about 17.5 million people in

1960, 76 per cent of whom lived in cities. But another 21 per cent resided in rural-nonfarm areas and 3 per cent lived on farms. Thus, rural residence certainly is no guarantee that a worker will be engaged in agriculture or related activities any more than residence in a city ensures that he will not make his livelihood from such activities. Of course, where urban jobs are infrequently available to farm folk and rural residence is avoided by urban workers, as is the case in many other nations, there may be a greater tendency for the rural population and the farming population to be the same, but even so, many variations on the general theme may be found.

THE VITAL PROCESSES

Birth and death (the vital processes) and marriage make up the three great crises in the lives of individuals. From the standpoint of society, the fertility, the mortality, and the marital condition of the population are among the most important items in a system of national bookkeeping. It is not surprising that the collection of demographic data concerning the vital processes began at a very early date. The English pattern of registration, from which practices in the United States have been derived, dates back to 1538, the time of Henry VIII, when the clergy were charged with the responsibility of making weekly records of all baptisms, marriages, and deaths, and were also made responsible for the care of the register in each of the parishes. Marriage can best be indexed with data on marital condition, given in a later chapter. In this section are discussed the questions of human fertility and mortality.

Fertility: Rates of Reproduction

Several indexes might be used to measure the levels of fertility but in this volume the one employed is the *fertility ratio,* which is the number of children aged 0 to 4 per 100 women aged 15 to 44. This is obviously well controlled by age and is not distorted by variations in the sex ratio. In addition, it is based upon actual census enumerations, which in most societies are likely to be more dependable than are the registrations of births. The data necessary to compute the fertility ratio also are available for a comparatively large number of countries and are cross-classified by rural and urban residence far more frequently and more satisfactorily than are the registration materials. There are, though, some disadvantages associated with the use of the fertility ratio. For example, a concentration or scarcity of women in one or a few of the 5-year age ranges between 15 and 44 may produce some distortion;

these two conditions actually are characteristic of many urban and rural populations, respectively, with women aged 20 to 29 being superabundant in cities but inordinately scarce on farms. Furthermore, the data on which the fertility ratio is based are available only after each census, and the use of children aged 0 to 4 means that an additional time lag is added to that already present in census materials. But, all things considered, the fertility ratio is still the most reliable index of reproduction in most of the countries that need to be taken into account.

Rural people generally have had relatively high levels of fertility, as compared with urban people, generating the demographic truism that the country is the producer of population, the city the consumer. This was the case when the new science of "political arithmetic" gave us our first glimpse of rural-urban differentials in fertility in England in the middle of the seventeenth century (cf. Ref. 605, pp. 52–56), and in most societies it has remained generally valid since that time. Only in a few societies since World War II have the fertility levels of rural and urban people tended to converge. In the United States in 1960, for example, the fertility ratios for the urban and rural-farm populations were 54 and 58, respectively, whereas only 10 years earlier the comparable figures were 44 and 60, producing a much wider difference. This move toward greater similarity is due, in part, to the fact that urban areas have received inordinately large shares of females in the most fertile years. Furthermore, the comparatively high birth rates that now obtain in many cities are often those found among people with recent farm backgrounds, comparatively little schooling, and relatively low levels of living. Despite these fairly rare cases of convergence, the general rule throughout the world is a wide disparity between the rates of reproduction of farm and city populations. This contention is supported by the materials in Table 2, in which are presented the fertility ratios for 28 selected countries scattered throughout the seven major regions of the earth.

Based upon an examination of fertility ratios for these and other societies, a number of observations may be made concerning the fertility differentials between rural and urban populations. Most of them can be illustrated conveniently by materials for the United States, given in Table 3. First, as we have indicated, with few exceptions rural people reproduce at substantially higher rates than do urban populations. Second, this differential tends to change as degrees of rurality and urbanization change. Thus, when extremely rural areas are contrasted with highly urbanized places, the differential is the greatest; when the sociocultural variations between the two are minor, the differential is least in evidence. Third, the distance rural people live from urban centers is positively correlated with their levels of reproduction. So significant is the influence large cities exert over the outlying countryside,

TABLE 2

Fertility ratios in selected countries, by residence

Region and country	Year	Total population	Urban population	Rural population
Africa				
Ghana	1960	88.6	81.6	90.8
Morocco	1960	89.9	75.8	96.3
South Africa	1960	70.2	58.8	80.1
South West Africa	1960	74.4	62.0	77.8
United Arab Republic	1960	77.9	77.2	78.3
America, North				
Canada	1961	60.6	55.6	74.8
Costa Rica	1963	94.8	73.8	112.4
Nicaragua	1963	88.9	77.3	98.2
Puerto Rico	1960	73.6	59.2	86.5
United States	1960	56.3	54.1	62.1 [a]
America, South				
Guyana	1960	89.8	69.3	99.7
Chile	1960	68.3	60.2	91.7
Ecuador	1962	81.9	73.9	86.8
Peru	1961	79.7	70.2	89.3
Uruguay	1963	44.2	41.7	58.1
Asia				
India	1961	71.9	66.6	73.0
Israel	1961	61.2	54.0	88.0
Japan	1960	34.5	31.3	41.1
Korea, Republic of	1960	86.6	72.5	93.0
Turkey	1960	76.2	58.5	82.5
Europe				
France	1962	37.0	34.4	42.2
Greece	1961	41.0	33.1	49.9
Poland	1960	54.4	46.0	63.7
Portugal	1960	45.1	31.3	49.9
Sweden	1960	33.7	32.6	37.3
Oceania				
Australia	1961	52.8	49.3	71.5
New Zealand	1961	62.7	52.8	81.4
U.S.S.R. [b]	1959	69.5	57.6	82.0

[a] Includes rural-nonfarm and rural-farm inhabitants.
[b] Children 0–4 per 100 Women Aged 15–49.
Sources: United Nations, Demographic Yearbook, 1963, pp. 162–230, Table 5; 1964, pp. 648–664, Table 27; and 1965, pp. 230–240, Table 8.

TABLE 3

Fertility ratios by size of place and color, United States, 1960

Size of Place	Total	Whites	Nonwhites
All urban	54.1	52.5	64.7
Urbanized areas	53.7	52.1	63.5
Central cities	51.3	48.5	63.1
Urban fringes	57.1	56.7	65.9
Other urban	55.5	54.0	70.6
10,000 or more	54.7	53.1	68.7
2,500 to 10,000	56.6	55.0	73.4
All rural	62.1	59.7	84.0
Rural-nonfarm	63.4	61.3	83.0
Rural-farm	58.0	54.2	86.2

Compiled and computed from data in U.S. Bureau of the Census, U.S. Census of Population: 1960, General Population Characteristics, United States Summary, Final Report PC(1)-1B (1961), pp. 148–152, Table 46; General Social and Economic Characteristics, United States Summary, Final Report PC(1)-1C (1962), pp. 199–200, Table 65.

that rural folk who live relatively close to such centers have lower levels of reproduction than do those who live at greater distances. Moreover, in most societies rates of reproduction tend to decrease steadily and evenly as the proximity to large cities increases. Fourth, the fertility rate decreases as the size of community increases, so that levels of reproduction generally are lower in villages of 1,000 to 2,499 than they are in the open country; they are lower in towns of 2,500 to 9,999 than they are in the smaller villages; and so on, until the lowest rates are found in the central core of the very largest metropolitan centers. Fifth, rural-urban differentials in birth rates exist no matter which racial groups are under consideration, although within each residence category the reproductive behavior of the races on the whole may be quite different. For example, in the United States the fertility ratios of whites living in cities are lower than those of whites living on farms, and those of urban Negroes are lower than those of Negroes in the farming districts. But by the same token, urban whites as a group reproduce at lower rates than urban Negroes, and farm whites generally reproduce at lower rates than farm Negroes. However, in places where there are distinct class differences between racial groups, mortality levels for the less-privileged group may be so much higher and rates of immigration so much lower than those for the dominant group that no real difference in net growth rates may occur. In some places, so greatly may high death rates and low immigration rates offset high birth rates that, proportionately, the lower-status group actually may become a smaller share of the total population. These are precisely the conditions that caused the Negro population of the United States to decline from about 19 per cent of the total in 1790 to around 10 per cent in 1960.

The materials in Table 2 suggest that no matter what the range of socio-cultural conditions, populations throughout the world exhibit the rural-urban fertility differential described above. This relationship may be altered, but scarcely ever is it reversed by the relative degrees of rurality and urbanization of a nation, by the prevalence of political stability or chaos, by the predominance of agriculture or industry in the national economy, by high or low levels of living, or even by the fact that fertility rates may be very high or very low for total populations. Fertility differences are one of the fundamental variations that set the rural world apart from the urban. Moreover, the differences may be even more exaggerated in many places than the data imply, for when censuses embody serious deficiencies, the underenumeration of rural children is likely to be one of them.

Several elements seem to be responsible for the tendency of rural folk to reproduce at higher rates than do urban people. Sorokin, Zimmerman, and Galpin attribute this condition to a series of factors, including religion and the traditional mores which, in a large number of countries, have long encouraged comparatively high levels of reproduction, much after the manner of the Judaic-Christian injunction to "multiply and replenish the earth." This positive view of human reproduction is certainly consistent with the philosophies and attitudes characteristic of the agrarian way of life. According to these authors, cities have freed themselves to a considerable extent of such attitudes, while the country has not.

Family organization is also cited as an important factor. Among rural groups, familisim has been the principal form of social organization, and the family still retains much of its strength in the country. In sharp contrast to the familistic nature of rural society, which encourages the production of children, is the highly individualistic life of the cities, where the person and his interests are given first consideration. The economic factor is also important, because of the greater expense of bearing and rearing children in the city, and also because children contribute far more to the economic support of the rural family than of the city family. Less competition of other wants in the rural districts, the lower mobility of the population, the lower density of population, earlier marriage on the average, and less use of birth control are also listed as factors to explain why the country population is more prolific than is the urban population (Ref. 478, Vol. 3, pp. 141–144).

Mortality: Rates of Death

Mortality is the second of the vital processes, although generally it is less significant than fertility in producing population change. However, on a national basis, it is usually more instrumental in this respect than is migration, which along with births and deaths, constitute the three primary factors that can alter population size. One should stress that the recent huge upsurge in the population of the world is due almost entirely to a precipitous decline in the death rate, particularly of infants and other young children, unaccompanied by any significant change in the birth rate. In addition, the materials on this subject, especially those on the causes of death, provide valuable insight into the general well-being of the various groups in a population. Most of what we know about health levels, for example, is inference from mortality data. Thus, it is possible to acquire considerable understanding of the socioeconomic conditions of a group whose chief causes of death are the contagious and deficiency diseases and whose infant mortality rates are comparatively high. Such a population, exemplified by many of the world's huge rural groups, will have a far different level of living than one whose major causes of death are heart disease, cancer, cirrhosis of the liver, and other so-called "degenerative" illnesses characteristic of advanced age and thus found prominently in a population with a relatively long expectation of life.

Despite the importance of the subject of mortality, the relevant data present a number of difficulties: (1) For many sections of the world, there are no distinctions made on the basis of residence in the published data. As a result, even the 1966 *Demographic Yearbook,* which is devoted largely to the subject of mortality, contains no separate tabulations of the data for rural and urban groups. (2) Although the registrations of deaths are more complete in most places than are those of births, underregistration, especially in the rural areas, still creates considerable distortion in the data. (3) Even where residence distinctions are drawn, deaths sometimes are reported according to place of occurrence rather than place of residence of the individual. Therefore, urban centers containing large hospitals frequently seem to have higher death rates and rural areas lower rates than they actually do. For these and other reasons, although many of the observations that follow apply to rural and urban differences generally, they are based principally upon conditions in the United States, for which rural-urban distinctions are available. Even so, however, the mortality statistics for the rural population of the nation are not distinguished according to farm and nonfarm status.

The two best indexes that can be used to measure mortality without becoming involved in distortions created by various population characteristics, are death rates that are age- and sex-specific and the life expectation table. The one chosen to illustrate the general principle for the present volume is the infant mortality rate, which is the number of deaths of children aged 0 to 1 per 1,000 live births. This index is especially closely related to socioeconomic status, because it reflects the levels of prenatal and postnatal care received by mothers and infants. Therefore, particularly wide variations occur on a racial basis in the United States, while some lesser ones occur within each race between the rural and urban segments of the population. For example, in 1960, urban whites and urban nonwhites had infant mortality rates of 23.2 and 40.9, respectively; whereas rural whites had one of 22.4 and rural nonwhites one of 48.5. Thus, while the nation's white infants living in cities have a slightly lower survival rate than do those living in the rural districts, the reverse is true for nonwhites. This arises, of course, from variations in social status, with rural Negroes receiving a particularly paltry share of the medical and sanitation benefits the society as a whole has to offer. A similar relationship between mortality and race may be found in other parts of the world where different racial groups tend on the whole to occupy different levels in the class system. For example, T. Lynn Smith discovered a like differential by race in Brazil, where infant mortality rates are highest for the darkest skinned inhabitants, decreasing for the lighter, "which is approximately the same as moving from the higher to the lower social and economic strata" (Ref. 444, pp. 117–118).

Not only do infant mortality rates vary from the rural to the urban categories within each racial group, but they also are different for cities of various sizes (see Table 4). Nevertheless, whites have somewhat higher infant mortality levels in cities of most sizes than in rural areas, whereas nonwhites have lower rates in virtually all sizes of cities than they do in rural areas. In any case, the rural Negro in the United States, and the agricultural laborer anywhere else in the world, has an especially high mortality rate and thus, a record of poor health and related conditions associated with mortality. It should be borne in mind, though, that part of this disadvantage may be explained as a result of the under-registration of births among rural laborers, which artificially inflates their infant mortality rate.

In general, then, overall levels of mortality tend to be at least somewhat lower in rural areas than they are in cities unless wide status differentials or other factors generate exceptions. In seeking reasons for this greater survival potential of rural folk, there is little reason to suppose that the causes are to be found in any innate biological factors differentiating the rural from the urban population. Neither will economic factors or the prevalence of medical care or hygienic facilities be of any assistance, for their operation is all in favor of the urban groups. Death controls are generally used earlier and more effectively in cities than they are in the farming districts, as is demonstrated by the situation among nonwhites in the United States. Furthermore, the size of the birth rate, which has a high positive correlation with that of the death rate, would by itself make the mortality of the country outstrip that of the city. For these reasons, in explaining the lower mortality of the country

TABLE 4

Number of deaths of children under one year of age per 1,000
live births, by residence and color, United States, 1960

Residence Category	Total	Whites	Nonwhites
United States total	26.0	22.9	43.2
Urban places	26.3	23.2	40.9
1,000,000 or more	27.7	22.9	39.7
500,000 to 1,000,000	29.0	24.8	38.5
250,000 to 500,000	28.1	24.8	38.4
100,000 to 250,000	26.8	23.5	40.7
50,000 to 100,000	24.4	22.6	37.7
25,000 to 50,000	23.9	21.8	44.3
10,000 to 25,000	24.5	22.3	47.7
2,500 to 10,000	26.6	24.3	48.8
Rural Areas	25.7	22.4	48.5

Compiled from U.S. Department of Health, Education and Welfare, Vital Statistics of the United
States: 1960, *Vol. II,* Mortality, *Part B, Section 9, pp. 60–77, Table 9–2.*

it is necessary to seek in the rural world other factors strong enough not only
to account for the observed differences in rural and urban mortality, but also
to offset the effects of the influences mentioned above, which operate in a
manner favoring low mortality in urban areas. Sorokin and Zimmerman
gave this problem careful consideration and enumerated the following important factors in the situation: (1) low density of population in the country,
which is especially important in connection with mortality from infectious
diseases; (2) greater integrity of the rural family, and especially the influence
of the maternal care of the child exercised in the rural family; (3) the outdoor
work of the rural population, which enables rural people to secure an abundance of fresh air and sunshine and plenty of physical exercise in the performance of farm tasks; (4) the lower level of anxieties associated with rural
life; and (5) the better adaptation of the human organism to the rural
surroundings in which it has evolved, as contrasted with the artificial
environment of the city, to which the human species is a relative stranger
(Ref. 477, p. 204).

There are variations in the principal causes of death between rural and
urban people in many parts of the world, but unfortunately the materials
necessary to examine these accurately and in detail are not to be had. However, while it is unwise to generalize too broadly from those for the United
States, some patterns that can be observed for rural and urban people in this
society do carry over into others. Suffice it to say that urban people are
somewhat more likely to succumb to tuberculosis, syphilis and other venereal

diseases, cancer, diabetes mellitus, heart disease, most kinds of circulatory problems, ulcers, cirrhosis of the liver, nephritis, and a few others. Rural people, on the other hand, are more likely to fall victim to a variety of unspecified infectious illnesses, influenza and pneumonia, gastritis, congenital malformations, accidents of various kinds, especially those involving machinery and livestock, several deficiency diseases, and some others. In the United States, heart disease and related illnesses account for over half of all deaths in both groups, and cancer for roughly another 16 per cent in cities and 14 per cent in rural areas. Furthermore, the relative importance of the many causes of death varies so greatly by age, sex, socioeconomic status, and other conditions that the unavailability of these cross-classification factors by residence makes further analysis of causes unfruitful.

Additional Readings

1. BOGUE, DONALD J., and CALVIN L. BEALE, "Recent Population Trends in the United States and Their Causes," in James H. Copp (ed.), *Our Changing Rural Society: Perspectives and Trends,* Ames: Iowa State University Press, 1964, chapter 3.

2. HATHAWAY, DALE E., J. ALLAN BEEGLE, and W. KEITH BRYANT, *People of Rural America* (A 1960 Census Monograph), Washington: Government Printing Office, 1968, chapters II–V, VII, and X.

3. HO, PING-TI, *Studies on the Population of China, 1368–1953,* Cambridge, Mass.: Harvard University Press, 1959, chapters VI, VII, and VIII.

4. PRICE, PAUL H., "The Rural Population," in Alvin L. Bertrand (ed.), *Rural Sociology,* New York: McGraw-Hill Book Company, Inc., 1958, chapter 5.

5. SAUNDERS, JOHN V. D., *The People of Ecuador: A Demographic Analysis,* Gainesville: University of Florida Press, 1961.

6. SLOCUM, WALTER L., *Agricultural Sociology,* New York: Harper & Brothers, 1962, chapters 2 and 5.

7. SMITH, T. LYNN, *Studies of Latin American Societies,* New York: Doubleday & Co., Inc., 1970, selections 3–6.

8. SMITH, T. LYNN, and HOMER L. HITT, *The People of Louisiana,* Baton Rouge: Louisiana State University Press, 1952, chapters 4, 5, 6, 7, 11, and 12.

9. SMITH, T. LYNN, and DOUGLAS G. MARSHALL, *Our Aging Population—The United States and Wisconsin,* Wisconsin's Population Series No. 5, Madison: University of Wisconsin, 1963.

10. SMITH, T. LYNN, and PAUL E. ZOPF, JR., *Fundamentals of Population Study* (second ed.), Philadelphia: F. A. Davis Company, 1970, chapter 4.

11. TAEUBER, CONRAD, and IRENE B. TAEUBER, *The Changing Population of the United States,* New York: John Wiley & Sons, Inc., 1958, chapter 6.

12. TAYLOR, LEE, and ARTHUR R. JONES, JR., *Rural Life and Urbanized Society,* New York: Oxford University Press, 1964, chapters 4 and 5.

13. ZOPF, PAUL E., JR., *North Carolina: A Demographic Profile,* Chapel Hill: University of North Carolina Population Center, 1967, chapter VIII.

4
INTERNAL MIGRATION

Migration, or the movement of people from one place to another, is of great social significance. This is especially true of present-day migrations. In pre-agricultural times, for the most part, migrations were by groups, and the movement from one place to another did not bring about the wholesale disruption of social relationships. However, among people who are sedentary—a condition first brought about largely by permanent attachment to parcels of agricultural land—the shifting of residence from one locality to another means the disruption of all social ties. This is especially true, of course, when single individuals rather than whole families migrate from their places of birth to other areas.

Most advanced peoples and cultures take for granted permanent residence and a settled mode of living. It should not be forgotten, however, that there are other modes of life than the sedentary, and that they have played important roles in world history. The student of rural society can learn much from the fascinating study of nomadic and pastoral societies and the great migrations of ancient times, when surges of barbarians poured into the areas where the sedentary habits of the people had induced great advancements in culture or civilization. The repeated overrunning of the highly developed cultures of the "Fertile Crescent" between the Tigris and Euphrates rivers by the more barbaric tribes from the deserts has a peculiar interest for the North American because of its intricate relation to our own cultural heritage. Old Testament accounts tell much about the subjugation of the settled agricultural Canaanites in the western portion of the Fertile Crescent by the Hebrews, then a group of primitive nomads who followed a pastoral life, driving their flocks from one oasis to another. A thousand years later, the

Roman Empire was overrun by barbarians from the north, and chronicles of this mass migration still hold a prominent place in the literature of the people. With the emergence of national states and a rather general adoption of fixed abodes, the nature of migration changed, but it did not lose its importance as one of the significant forces in social life. During feudal times, and in the period when large landed estates of various kinds were established in many parts of the world, members of the landowning elite and laborers alike became rather firmly anchored to the land. Social organization, the relationships between people, and the relatively slow rate of social change reflected that fact. With the coming of large-scale industrialization and urbanization, however, great tides of migration again resumed, as unprecedented numbers of people began to leave sedentary agriculture to seek the advantages of urban living. In recent decades, agricultural laborers in particular have left the land *en masse* throughout the world, but they also have been joined by farm people of all other kinds. As a result, most modern societies are highly fluid, and those that have not yet reached this state promise to do so in the future.

TYPES OF INTERNAL MIGRATION

The subject of migration is large, and its many subdivisions are not of equal concern for present purposes. For example, emigration and immigration, as elements of social change at the international level, are large questions calling for specialized treatment by themselves, although they generally are beyond the scope of this volume. However, internal migration, or the movement that takes place within national states, is of primary concern to one who would understand rural life and its relationships with urban life. It is unfortunate, though, that the data on this subject are often among the most incomplete of all demographic materials. Nevertheless, for present purposes, five phases of migration seem to be especially significant and deserve treatment within the limitations imposed by the materials that are available: (1) the interchange of population between rural and urban areas, including both the highly significant movement from farms to cities and the smaller back-to-the-land migration; (2) the pushing forward of various land frontiers, usually by persons intending to become involved principally in agricultural or pastoral pursuits; (3) interregional migrations, and especially the migratory currents that carry populations to and from the rural regions; (4) farm-to-farm movements; and (5) the constant stream of migratory agricultural laborers and other nomads flowing in many well-defined currents from place to place within their respective societies. We shall discuss only these five aspects in this chapter, although in their ramifications they involve many other phases of the general subject.

RURAL-URBAN MIGRATION

Migration from the farms to the cities is probably an indispensable concomitant of urban life. As suggested in the preceding chapter, it is a fundamental factor making for the growth of virtually all cities and enabling most of them to replace the residents who die or move away. In fact, it usually is far more important than natural increase in making for urban growth. This form of movement is an ancient phenomenon, but not until the nineteenth century in Western Europe and North America did it reach massive proportions. In fact, since that time, so great has been the migration and so significant its sociocultural implications, that the societies in which it has occurred on a large scale have been changed in many basic ways. These have included drastic alterations in occupational patterns and the size of communities, and in the social categories of differentiation, stratification, mobility, interaction, solidarity or cohesion, and control. As a result, this form of migration has precipitated basic realignments among the various groups in Western societies in particular, and has helped to change fundamentally the cultural environment within which those groups function.

In the years since World War II, the rural-to-urban migration has come to affect significantly virtually all societies, even those whose urban centers have comparatively little to offer the migrants from the farms in the way of jobs, housing, status, and so on. It even goes on apace in countries containing vast amounts of sparsely settled territory in which efficient, productive agriculture might well be carried on if the social relations between man and the land were adjusted to make such basic activities possible. As it is, though, vast numbers of people in both developed and underdeveloped countries feel that their greater advantage lies in the city rather than on the land; these swell the ranks of the rural-to-urban migrants in unprecedented numbers. Rapidly rising aspirations of disadvantaged people throughout the earth seem to be the basis of changes in thought patterns which have assumed truly revolutionary proportions. The flight from the land is one of the major manifestations of this drastic departure from the fatalism of the past. Certainly the movement is the most significant of the several types of internal migration; and while there is also some movement of people from the cities to the farms, it is by far the smaller of the two currents of rural-urban migration.

The Extent of Rural-Urban Migration

Adequate statistical materials that deal directly with rural-urban movement and the other types of internal migration under consideration are difficult to find. In fact, much of what is known about migration actually results from manipulations of data on births and deaths and on the numbers of people involved in base populations, resulting in the inference that measured population changes that cannot be attributed to the two vital processes must be the result of migration. Even in the United States, where population data are often highly informative, there are comparatively few data that make it possible to contend *directly* with migration, and especially with the places of origin of migrants. Much the same is true of other societies, as reflected in the fact that even now the United Nations is able to report nothing on internal migration, let alone to refine the subject according to the subdivisions suggested above.

On the basis of present information concerning migration it is probably valid to generalize somewhat as follows concerning the rural-urban exchange of population. In normal times, such as the years immediately preceding World War I, when remuneration in agriculture and that in industry are fairly well balanced, the cityward flow of population carries away the excess natural increase from the rural areas, leaving just about enough to maintain the populations of the various rural areas, taking enough to make up the vital deficit in the cities and to bring about urban growth. In abnormal times, when rural areas are greatly disadvantaged, such as the 1920's in the United States, for instance, the appeal of the cities' high industrial wages combines with other lures to attract all the country's natural increase of population and to cut into its reserves as well. In such periods, urban growth and rural depopulation go hand in hand. On the other hand, in times of great disorder, distress, upheaval, famine, or disease, people flee the cities. In such periods, great alarm is felt for the future of the city; security seems to be found only on the land. In the United States, for example, this type of movement occurred during the depth of the great depression in the years 1931 to 1933, a development that was checked only by strenuous governmental efforts through the Civil Works Administration, the Federal Emergency Relief Administration, and other agencies.

To interpret properly the rural-urban exchange of population, several well-established facts and principles should be kept in mind and related to one another. In the first place, it is necessary to recall that, as suggested in the preceding chapter, the natural increase of population (excess of births over deaths) is almost always lower in the cities than in the rural areas; that it probably increases in direct proportion to the distance from the urban center and that it reaches its maximum in the most rural areas, where the forces of urban influence strike last of all, and then only weakly. Thus, the more remote the area from urban centers, the greater the surplus of population over replacement needs. Second, it should be remembered that part of the city's replacements and much of its growth are due to migration, primarily from the rural areas and to a lesser extent from abroad. Finally, we should remember several principles of migration. Formulated by Ravenstein after careful studies in Great Britain, the Continent, and America, and supported by subsequent studies done by many others, these principles or "laws" have considerable significance. With some slight changes in the phrasing, several of these principles most useful in interpreting rural-urban movements of population are as follows: (1) Most migrants move only a short distance; (2) the process of absorption is like this: inhabitants of the immediately surrounding area flock to the city, creating gaps in the rural population, which are filled by persons from more remote districts, which removal in turn creates other gaps, until the attractive force of the city makes itself felt, step by step, in the most remote corners of the society; (3) each main current of migration sets up a compensating countercurrent, and the process of dispersion is the reverse of the process of absorption; and (4) long-distance migrants go immediately to great centers of trade and industry. (See Ref. 373). Figure 3 illustrates the process of absorption and dispersion.

To generalize again: In normal times, migration and differential natural increase of population seem to combine in the following manner: Natural

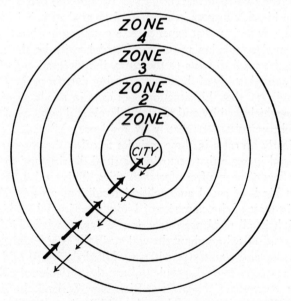

FIGURE 3. Chart illustrating the process of absorption and dispersion of rural-urban migrants.

increase resembles a huge saucer, with the city, a "dead sea" area, at the center; the most remote and isolated sections, the areas of high natural increase, make up the rim. Migration is like a giant steam shovel, reaching out to the outermost limits, cutting down population increase to replacement levels, leveling off the rate of growth in the rural districts, and heaping population up in the cities of the middle. Here it either is "consumed" or contributes to urban growth. During periods of prosperity, in spite of the rapid reproduction of the people in poor land areas, the population of such sections does not mount. Movement out of the areas is large, movement into them slight if any. To change the figure: In normal times, isolated sections are on the giving end of the migratory current, the cities on the receiving end. In times of distress, all is changed. Migration from the rural areas is immediately blocked; movement into them either commences or becomes more intense; the damming up of youth in these remote areas, supplemented by the backwash from the cities, causes the population to mount at a dizzy pace.

There are some materials that make it possible to illustrate the extent of rural-urban migration. One approach involves an examination of the changes in the rural and urban populations of a large number of countries, using what is known about birth and death rates to assess the relative importance of migration in the two residence categories. Because the excess of births over deaths is considerably greater in most rural areas than it is in cities, as discussed above, any society that experiences a greater growth rate of its urban than of its rural population must be affected heavily by the migration of people from the rural districts to the cities, if immigration from abroad is minor. A thorough study of these factors, using data from the *Demographic Yearbook,* indicates that this situation does exist in nearly all of the world's countries for which fertility and mortality levels and patterns of growth and decline can be calculated separately by residence. Migration to the cities, therefore, clearly operates in these societies to offset the comparatively high rates of natural increase that occur in the rural districts and to bring about the massive flow of people from farms to cities. This tends to be the case no matter what kinds of social and political conditions prevail. For example, it is found in most of the countries of Latin America, where birth rates are relatively high in all residence categories; in Japan, where birth rates have plunged dramatically throughout the nation; in the Soviet Union, where vast numbers of city and country people were killed during World War II; in India, where poverty compels people to leave the agricultural villages for the cities; and in Australia, Canada, Costa Rica, New Zealand, the United States, and much of Western Europe, where the middle class nature of a good deal of the farming makes it comparatively attractive, both as an occupation and as a way of life.

Generally, then, migration from the country to the city continues steadily throughout the world. So great is its magnitude, and so powerful are the influences that have generated it, that the flow has become nearly inexorable and, on the whole, practically irreversible. It shows some signs of decreasing in such countries as the United States, where the farm population is a relatively small minority, but even there the migration still goes on. There is a countermovement, to be sure, but it represents a small fraction of the vast numbers of those who have left the farm for the city. Furthermore, where there is a significant movement of people from the cities to the rural areas, the latter tend to be suburbs, small towns and villages, and other rural-nonfarm places. The basic fact is that agriculture is losing people in unprecedented numbers in practically all parts of the world; and in the countries where the flow is just now beginning in a massive way, its major sociocultural consequences are yet to be felt. India, China, Latin America, Africa, and other areas stand on the verge of a rural-to-urban migration that will make previous movements in those places seem modest by comparison. Concomitantly, it is certain to produce problems that now also are minor by comparison.

The second approach to an examination of rural-urban migration is based on an analysis of the net results of movement to and from large urban centers and that to and from the most highly rural districts. We use the United States as an example. The Bureau of the Census now computes net migration gains and losses for all of the nation's Standard Metropolitan Statistical Areas—those large urban agglomerations that cover one or more counties and contain one or in some cases more large cities. The latter are assumed to influence almost totally the socioeconomic conditions of the counties within which they are located. Many of the Standard Metropolitan Statistical Areas do contain rural people, including some farm people, but these are few as compared with the urban group, and their interests and activities usually are greatly affected by the presence of the urban center. In addition, net gains and losses through migration are known for all counties in the United States, including those that have no urban people whatsoever. Therefore, it is possible to compare the gain-loss patterns of the Standard Metropolitan Statistical Areas with those of the almost 1,000 counties that lack urban inhabitants. Obviously, the Standard Metropolitan Statistical Areas do not account for all of the nation's urban people, but they do contain approximately four fifths of the urban total. Therefore, they are by far the most inclusive urban units in the society and their gains and losses reflect the principal changes in the nation's city population. By the same token, the counties that lack urban people do not contain all of the nation's rural folk, but changes in their populations certainly reflect migratory losses from the most rural districts.

During the time that the appropriate records have been kept, all Standard Metropolitan Statistical Areas taken together have experienced substantial net gains through migration. In the period from 1950 to 1960, for example, the net increase by this means was almost nine million people, or nearly 10 per cent. Furthermore, on an individual basis, the vast majority of these metropolitan units also gain more people by migration than they lose in this way. Some do lose, however; they tend to be located in states that fall into two classes: (1) those that contain the nation's older urban agglomerations, which send many people to outlying suburban areas and to other sections of the country; and (2) those that are more rural than most and whose cities lack the kind and number of jobs and other advantages that would attract people from the rural areas. On the whole, then, migration to the largest cities and their immediate environs goes on relatively rapidly, despite the fact that the rural-farm population is comparatively small and has probably already experienced a peak in the number of people who will leave for urban centers. In this connection it should be borne in mind, of course, that many of those who migrate to the metropolitan centers also come from other cities and from the rural-nonfarm portion of society.

Opposing the net migration gains experienced by the metropolitan units are the net losses borne by the rural counties. For example, from 1950 to 1960, these highly rural sections, taken together, sustained a net loss loss of almost two million people, or about 20 per cent. These counties are scattered widely throughout the country, but, as expected, they tend to be concentrated in the South, the Midwest, and other typically agricultural portions of the nation. Thus, the exchanges of people by migration continue to be instrumental in bringing about the redistribution of population, swelling the ranks of the metropolitan group, among whom natural increase is relatively low, and diminishing the size of the farm segment, whose rates of natural increase are comparatively high.

Even though the rural-to-urban migration is beginning to "mature" in the United States, Western Europe, and a few other areas, and to involve a smaller share of the total populations in these places, in other parts of the world the movement is just now getting underway or is approaching its peak. For example, in many "underdeveloped" nations, cities have an almost magnetic attraction for vast hordes of farm people, especially those who are agricultural laborers with few or no rights to the land. Extensive studies by T. Lynn Smith suggest that this is the case in much of Latin America. In Brazil, Colombia, Mexico, Venezuela, and many other nations, farm folk in large numbers are flocking into national capitals, the principal cities of states and provinces, the seats of municipios and other minor civil divisions, and urban centers of all sizes, no matter what their political or administrative status (Ref. 452, pp. 53–70). Some of these migrants come directly from the farming districts, and others arrive from small towns and cities, leaving places that are then filled by persons leaving the most rural areas. But no matter what the pattern of succession, much of Latin America is characterized by a great influx of new urban residents recruited from the rural districts, where the birth rates often are extremely high. Moreover, the flow is helping to precipitate the vast social transformation that is going on in the area. There may be no other single factor more vital in bringing about new patterns of accommodation or adjustment, redefinitions of social roles, reappraisals of patterns of stratification, increased demands upon existing social institutions, significant alterations in the forms of social interaction, and other changes. This Latin American pattern is being repeated in much of Asia, Africa, and other major sections of the globe with no less than revolutionary impact.

Factors, Forces, and Media

Mass migrations of people from rural districts to cities throughout the world, but especially in the so-called "underdeveloped" countries, are intertwined with a vast network of factors, forces, and media. Generally, these may be grouped into two categories: (1) the significant social and cultural changes that have generated the movement and have been instrumental in the development of the urban centers that receive the migrants; and (2) the host of conditions that motivate individuals to leave the farms and seek a different life in the cities.

The great improvements in transportation that have been made in the twentieth century are first among the changes that have been instrumental in bringing about rural-to-urban migration. These innovations have enabled many people to cross national boundaries as immigrants, but they have allowed infinitely more people to move about within their own societies, most often from the farms to the cities. Recently, the development of roads, the manufacture and importation of motor vehicles, the greater ability to service these vehicles and to repair the roads and rails over which they travel, have all contributed strongly to a condition in which those persons who wish to move can do so by some mechanical means. Improvements in means of communication also contribute to the migration, largely because they make it possible for rural people to learn about life beyond the confines of their areas. In many cases, this new knowledge provides a powerful incentive to leave the farms and seek improved opportunities in the cities.

The growth of systems of education, although it is in its early stages in many parts of the world, is a second factor helping to pave the way for massive internal migration. In the main, a significant attitude change is involved, for no longer do masses of people accept widespread illiteracy and the problems that accompany it as inevitable. In turn, this attitude change is reflected in migration in two ways. In the first place, almost everywhere educational facilities in urban centers are superior to those in the rural districts; rural people often migrate in pursuit of improved education, sometimes for themselves, but much more often for their children. In the second place, as levels of education slowly rise, they are accompanied by a more acute awareness of the problems of remaining on the land, the real and imagined attractions of the cities, the possibility of acquiring non-agricultural jobs, and a host of other conditions. For many, the awareness leads to action, and one of the courses that action frequently takes is flight from the land.

Contacts between societies also play a significant part in bringing about migration from the farms to the cities. This is particularly true when disadvantaged people in the "underdeveloped" parts of the world come together with representatives of predominantly middle-class societies. The contacts bring about the knowledge that middle-class standards, the growth of urban-oriented industry, equitable man-land relationships, and other factors have resulted in high levels of living. In many such cases of contact, the growth of industry and the proliferation of urban jobs seem more promising than does the significant reform of man-land relationships. Therefore, in pursuit of the higher levels of living that seem to be common in the industrialized Western nations, many in Latin America, Africa, and elsewhere join in the flight from agriculture to become part of the urban populations of their respective societies. The contacts between societies, of course, may take the form of actual physical encounters of the representatives of two cultures, but far more frequently they occur simply because vast numbers of people throughout the world are exposed to the mass media, which portray the more enviable socioeconomic conditions. Radio, television, and newspapers are highly instrumental in this respect, although the presence of middle-class foreigners among lower-class nationals in a society also may have considerable effect. Representatives of the Peace Corps, the Alliance for Progress, UNESCO, and so on, may be important in this respect in some areas.

The "revolt of the masses" —the eventual dawning of discontent with the system of large landed estates, the two-class pattern of social stratification that it spawns, and the inevitable poverty that it generates—is also a major force paving the way for mass migrations from the rural districts. Perhaps no social institution is as inflexible as the large landed estate, and, for many of the laborers who are its ultimate victims, hope for change lies not in any basic rebuilding of the system but in departure from it. Therefore, in parts of the world such as Latin America, coloni, sharecroppers, and agricultural laborers of other kinds are deserting *latifundia, haciendas,* and other large holdings in numbers that would have astounded their parents and grandparents. The fatalistic resignation to the life of a field hand on land that can never be owned except by a wealthy *patrón* is passing rapidly, and one of the symptoms of its demise is the wholesale migration to cities of lower-class farm folk. Of course, the modest skills of the laborer place him in a poor position in the competition for urban jobs, but for many, this stark reality is insufficient to overcome the aspirations that propel farm people toward large cities.

Labor legislation and social welfare provisions are coming into being in many parts of the globe, but almost without exception, these gains benefit the urban worker much more than the rural laborer. As a result, any wish that the rural family may have to participate in these new fruits of social concern and legislation stands a better chance of being implemented in the city than on the farm. Also, though the wide dissemination and acceptance of agricultural techniques and practices may encounter countless barriers and be painfully slow, word of the advantages to be found in the cities often spreads like wildfire. Again, this situation is well illustrated by the conditions in many of the Latin American countries, where copious legislation has been enacted and promulgated, providing for minimum wages, maximum hours, and other advantages for the workers. These operate almost always to the benefit of urban people, and the rural worker who wishes to share in the enacted benefits becomes well aware that his opportunities to do so will be far greater in the city than they are on the land. This factor too helps to bring about an acceleration in the pace of rural-to-urban migration.

The rapid growth of industry, tied almost invariably to urbanization, also is helping to draw people from the country into the cities. In many societies where the population is mostly rural, the conviction has arisen among the power factions that the principal means of gaining stature in the modern world is to develop industry as rapidly as possible. As a result, industries of various kinds are springing up in places that long were rural in most respects, culminating in the expansion and proliferation of cities that attract large numbers of those who would work in these industries. Parts of Africa, for example, are attempting to make the great leap from colonial status into the second half of the twentieth century, and that seems to imply to many leaders that industrialization should have high priority. The goal of this endeavor is the production of a gross national product sufficiently large to finance education, welfare programs, development of many kinds, and the solution of a host of deep-seated and complex social problems. One actual result, partly inadvertent, is the wholesale swarming of people from the countryside into the industrial and commercial centers who produce as they go a host of new social problems.

Internal violence in some countries has caused large numbers of rural people to seek the comparative safety of the cities of their respective societies. Nowhere has this been more apparent than in Vietnam, where large numbers of inhabitants of the rural villages have flocked in desperation to Saigon and other large cities in an effort to find maximum protection. In other countries, where the violence has no particular political dimensions but is perpetrated by roving bandits and malcontents, large numbers of people also have left the isolated hinterlands for the relative protection afforded by the cities. In some cases, as in Colombia for example, both kinds of violence have racked the countryside, producing major movements of people from the farms and villages to Bogotá, Medellín, and other large cities.

Changes in the function of cities in many countries have made them more attractive to the would-be migrants from the rural districts. The changes have been particularly significant in this respect in areas that long were dominated by a colonial pattern of existence. These places include much of Latin America, where Spanish and Portuguese colonial patterns persisted long after the independent republics were established early in the nineteenth century. They also involve large sections of Africa where the British, the Belgians, the French, and others exercised direct colonial control until after World War II; and they embrace India and much of Southeast Asia, where some of these same powers maintained themselves in a dominant position until the middle of the twentieth century. In the case of colonial possessions, many of the cities that were established early and that grew considerably in size were merely administrative, military, and residential centers, designed and located so as to contribute to the consolidation of empire. Even in Latin America, where little territory was under colonial control after 1825, the central governments of the various republics tended to maintain many outlying cities as the administrative centers of vast territories.

Not until the twentieth century in such large places as Buenos Aires, Havana, Montevideo, Rio de Janeiro, and others did trade and commerce come to be principal functions, eventually overshadowing the former tendency to specialize in administration. Since about 1920, many cities in Latin America have become highly important centers for manufacturing and for a wide variety of other industries. Included in this group are Bogotá, Lima, Medellín, Mexico City, Monterrey, Pôrto Alegre, Santiago, and São Paulo. Thus, cities in Latin America and elsewhere have become highly diversified and have grown into important centers for a wide variety of functions. As a result, they now offer rural people attractions that cities never possessed as administrative and political enclaves. In addition, of course, as cities have changed in character and have come to provide jobs and other opportunities that were virtually unknown a few decades ago, the means of transportation also have improved greatly, thus providing rural people with the facilities to migrate to the cities.

The conditions that have provided incentives for individuals to leave the farms for the cities also must be taken into account. In the parts of the world where the large landed estate long has dominated the rural scene and where agricultural laborers are legion, several of these conditions are especially effective in impelling individuals and their families to migrate to the cities. Some of these influences are: (1) reports of the advantages in the city sent by earlier migrants to friends and relatives who continue to live in the rural districts; (2) the tendency for the best, often the only, secondary and higher educational facilities to be located in the cities rather than in the farming areas; (3) the recruitment by many upper-class families of urban house servants and grounds keepers from among the rural population, frequently from among those who labor on the family's large rural estate; (4) widespread efforts on the part of various corporations to bring workers from the farms to the cities in order to labor in construction projects and other kinds of enterprises; (5) the temptation among young women in the rural districts to accept at face value the attractions of urban living described by young men with whom they may come into contact; and (6) descriptions of the virtues of urban living that are presented to rural people by a great variety of persons, including transportation workers who pass through the rural districts, schoolteachers who have been reared and trained in cities but whose jobs take them into the countrysides, friends and relatives of rural folk who return from the city periodically to visit with their comrades and kinsmen, and many others who form a human link between the city and the outlying rural areas. It is obvious from this enumeration of the media which help to precipitate rural-to-urban migration, that a great deal of the motivation to move is supplied through

83

various kinds of personal interaction between the city dwellers or visitors, who know the city well, and the rural folk, to whom it is merely an illusion. There is, perhaps, no better illustration of the importance of word of mouth and personal influence in bringing about the wide and rapid dissemination of an idea or practice.

Effects of Rural-Urban Migration

The analysis of the factors and forces that precipitate rural-urban migration should not blind one to the fact that the movement also has profound consequences. The first of these, of course, is the almost fantastic growth of towns and cities that is taking place at present throughout the world. As mentioned above, the excess of births over deaths clearly is a less important factor in urban growth than is the migration of rural people into the cities. In fact, in most societies, rural-to-urban migration accounts for a much larger share of the total increase of urban populations than do natural increase and foreign immigration combined. In turn, the high growth rate of existing cities and the proliferation of new ones have profound effects upon the sociocultural matrix of all except the world's most isolated and tradition-oriented societies.

The second effect of migration to the cities is the creation of a vast and complicated network of social problems, some of which have existed for centuries but are becoming more oppressive, and others of which have sprung up only recently. Moreover, in the heterogeneous mixture of the city, the various problems are more closely interwoven, the consensus that would bring about their clear definition and aid in their solution is more difficult to achieve, and the implementation of solutions that may be found is more difficult than it ever was in the rural districts. In part, this change arises from the fact that the social problems that have long existed in rural areas affected smaller numbers of people and frequently were accepted as inevitable, whereas in the cities large numbers are involved and there is a higher degree of unwillingness to endure various social maladies. As a consequence of this impatience, born of the drive to transform higher standards of living into higher levels of living, social action of many kinds is a major contemporary element in cities everywhere. Problems related to crime and delinquency, intergroup contacts, housing, congestion, health and sanitation, jobs, traffic, and so on are commonplace. So great is the pressure that they impose upon the political leadership in many societies that the comment is often heard that cessation and even reversal of the rural-to-urban migration would indeed be a blessing. In fact, in some sections of the globe, there are shortages of workers in the rural districts, although mechanization of agriculture is increasingly capable of dealing with this problem. Unless societies are willing to enact severely restrictive legislation that would bring a halt to the movement from farms to cities, the flow will not stop or be reversed. Consequently, the reality facing most of the world's cities is one of working out patterns of accommodation that will enable the long-time city populations and the new arrivals from the country to coexist in a reasonably productive manner and to realize at least a major share of their respective aspirations. Changes in social institutions and in the cultural environment necessary to make possible this accommodation on the scale of the actual migration, form one of the paramount challenges facing mankind.

A third effect of the exchange of people between the rural areas and the cities is homogenization, or the gradual breaking down of the differentials that long have separated rural and urban populations. This process, discussed later, brings about the mixing of cultural, ethnic, religious, racial, and other elements in society in such a way that the isolated, easily distinguished pockets of people that once characterized most societies are less in evidence. This effect is produced in large part by the same influences that persuade individuals to move from rural to urban areas. Thus, the attractiveness of certain institutions, visitations between earlier migrants to the cities and persons who remain behind on the farms, and other influences discussed above are highly significant in bringing about homogenization. Actually, the process has two dimensions: (1) the physical movement of rural people to the cities, followed by continued contacts between persons in both residence groups; and (2) the diffusion of social and cultural elements from the cities to the farming areas, partly by word of mouth, partly by example, and partly by means of various mass media. In addition, homogenization itself, by bringing together people of highly diverse origins and backgrounds, greatly increases the number of possible combinations of social and cultural traits, so that the accumulation of these and the rate and diversity of innovation are greatly enhanced.

Fourth and finally, the movement of people from farms to cities helps to bring about increases in levels and standards of living. That is, life in the urban centers, although often harsh and frustrating, on the whole presents the migrants with more in the way of material comforts than were to be had in the rural countryside. Furthermore, urban living tends to increase the numbers of things and services that are defined as necessities. If even a portion of these can be obtained, the level of living is likely to rise above that in the farming areas, where needs were felt to be fewer and where many of them were met insufficiently or not at all. As the level of living rises among urban people, the standard or aspiration also rises, and the city family soon finds itself involved in the constant process of delineating new and higher goals toward which it wishes to move. This orientation to achievement, generally created in the cities, also finds its way back to the rural districts, where it impels additional people to leave farming and migrate to urban centers. In particular, the aspirations are expressed in terms of better educational facilities, better jobs, improved housing, higher income, and advanced social status. Even in places where social systems permit them to be obtained by relatively few migrants, the *possibility* that they can be achieved is sufficient to increase the already heavy movement of people from the farms to the cities.

PUSHING FORWARD OF THE FRONTIER

All other forms of internal migration pale in significance when compared with the rural-urban movement. Yet, at various times in many sections of the globe, the expansion of populations into areas that previously were uninhabited has assumed massive proportions. The migratory movement involved in the opening of a frontier is, of course, well known to people in both Americas. The process of settling a new land caused swarms of people to spread from the Atlantic to the Pacific in what is now the United States. The same kind of movement is going on even now in Canada with the push to populate the western sections of the country, in Alaska, and in many sections of Latin America.

For example, increasing numbers of Brazilians of the old stocks and new immigrants are pushing inland from the sea, partly as the result of a planned national effort to reduce the population pressure on the narrow strip of land along the Atlantic coast. Substantial numbers of Colombians are moving down from the Andes mountains and spreading out onto the low plains at their base, occupying in many cases lands that once were the rich farming districts of their Indian ancestors but fell exclusively into pastoral use during the colonial period. In Peru, Argentina, Ecuador, and many other countries of Latin America, similar frontiers are expanding into sparsely inhabited or even virgin territory. In Oceania, Australia continues its efforts to open new northern lands for agricultural pioneers; the conquest there includes efforts to provide sufficient water to facilitate commercial agriculture and stockraising and to support life itself. Finally, fragmentary evidence suggests that the search for living space, for various raw materials, and for land on which to produce food has prompted both the Soviet Union and China to settle new areas, creating the frontier type of migration even into regions where the climate is inhospitable.

Statistics on this matter, of course, are virtually nonexistent for most portions of the world where it is occurring, but there seem to be certain characteristics that are part of the movement in many of those areas. First, when the movement is not thoroughly regulated according to some rational plan, the location of the frontier tends to shift as one area becomes settled and another beckons. In Brazil, for example, where much of this kind of migration is going on, in the 1930's it took the form of pioneering in the forests of western São Paulo; a few years later it involved settlement in the jungles of north-central Maranhão and the Rio Doce Valley in Minas Gerais; and at present it continues as colonization in the virgin areas of western São Paulo, northern Paraná, southern Mato Grosso, and central Goiás (Ref. 444, pp. 157–159). Second, the migration often involves whole families. Sometimes these include the members of three generations, at other times only two. In the movement to cities, there is a great tendency for young unmarried adults to predominate, but in the opening of the frontier, families are found more frequently. Third, when unmarried migrants only are taken into account, the opening of the frontier involves a relatively high proportion of young men, whereas the reverse is true for the movement from the farms to the cities. As mentioned before, this division lends quite different characteristics to each of the migrant populations and to the areas that receive them. Fourth, in many places where frontiers are being opened, the migrants wish to become owner-operators of their own relatively small farms, and they direct their efforts accordingly. In some areas, land grants and sales and leases enable migrant families to control adequate family-sized farms, either immediately upon settling or after a specified period of time has passed and certain conditions are fulfilled. In other places, holdings are modest in size. Unless the society clearly prohibits the establishment of such units, however, the family-sized farm seems to be the ultimate goal of a large share of the migrants. Finally, no matter what their aspirations to landownership, those who open the frontier come in large numbers from the lower class. As has been the case for many generations throughout the world, a substantial share of the people who blaze new trails and establish themselves in previously uninhabited areas comes from among those to whom the society has provided few of its benefits. Therefore, the group that populates a frontier generally is a heterogeneous mixture of landless families who aspire to landownership, nonconformists who have been relatively unsuccessful within the confines of traditional society, exploiters who sense opportunities of various kinds in the relatively unstructured and, frequently, lawless conditions of a new area, and others whose circumstances in the traditional society have been tenuous at best.

In some parts of the world, such as Australia, where colonization and settlement are proceeding according to a deliberate plan, there actually is developing an important group of middle-class owner-operators of family-sized farms. In some other places, the frontier simply provides the opportunity for new large landed estates to be established; such a development ordinarily is accompanied by the importation of agricultural laborers and the tendency to create rather rapidly an extension of the two-class system of social stratification that usually exists elsewhere in the same society. In yet other areas, those of the communist bloc in particular, settlement is planned and rigidly regulated in such a way that state farms are established, generating for the people who are brought in to work upon them most of the same problems that accompany the entrenchment of the large landed estate in its other forms. Eventually, of course, all types of movement into frontier areas will come to a halt when virgin areas are no more, but at the moment, in some societies, it is of considerable importance as a form of internal migration.

INTERREGIONAL MIGRATION

The examples of migration from one region to another are legion, but most of them have in common the fact that the migrants are engaged in the search for better socioeconomic conditions. When expectations rise beyond their ability to be met in a given area, or when existing circumstances deteriorate to the point where desperation becomes widespread, vast numbers of people may be disposed to migrate to other places. Such movement goes on when periodic droughts force people to flee the Sertão in the northeastern corner of Brazil, the interior of Australia, the Great Plains of the United States, the Russian Steppes, and other regions, and to seek the relative safety of other, more hospitable areas. It occurs also when large numbers of people in many different societies become dissatisfied with prevailing systems of stratification, with restrictive relations of man to the land, and with a host of other unfavorable conditions. It also takes place when political pressures or deeply rooted social traditions place certain groups at a perennial disadvantage in a particular region that has long been their home. Often these various types of interregional migration take on important rural-to-urban characteristics.

Some of the salient features of movement between regions can be made clear by the use of two examples. The first of these involves the transfer of large numbers of people to the farms in the state of São Paulo, Brazil (for an analysis of this movement, see Ref. 444, pp. 172–184). The second deals with the movement of Negroes from region to region in the United States, generally from rural areas in the South to urban centers elsewhere. In the case of São Paulo, the migration has been composed predominantly of agricultural workers brought into the state to assist in the production of coffee, sugar, and cotton. Many of these migrants have come from the arid states of northwestern Brazil; a large share has arrived from neighboring Minas Gerais; and most of the remainder have moved from Bahia, Alãgoas, Pernambuco, and other states near the coast. With a few temporary interruptions, the movement has gone on since the turn of the present century. It has assumed some of the characteristics of migration to a frontier, in that many of the migrants have settled in the western part of the state upon land newly opened for cotton growing and general farming. As a result, unlike the movement between regions in other parts of Brazil or elsewhere in the world, this migration has not been predominantly a flow of people from farms to cities. Thus, not only is it an interregional movement with a number of features of the opening of a frontier, but it also has the attributes of a farm-to-farm shift. Foreign immigrants have been a small part of the total group, but in the main the migrants have come from a variety of older farming districts in Brazil into the newly established ones of São Paulo.

The characteristics of the migrants are worthy of note. First, in contrast with most of the migratory currents in the United States, a relatively large number of children is involved. Second, because the migration is a comparatively long-distance one, and because farms, rather than cities, are the destinations of most of the people, men, rather than women, tend to predominate. In fact, despite the large influx of children and the tendency for a comparatively large number of families to make the move, males are almost twice as numerous as females in this migration. The frontier characteristics also contribute to this situation. Third, a very high proportion of families is involved in the migration to São Paulo. This condition, unusual in long-distance mass migrations, results in part from the fact that the natural environment in the areas from which the migrants come often is so harsh that whole families, representing several generations, are driven to seek better conditions. Also, the involvement of families bespeaks the high degree of unity that exists in the Brazilian domestic unit, no matter what the family's class level or the ages of its members. As a result, the movement greatly resembles the flight from the American "Dust Bowl," which groups of kinsmen deserted in search of better circumstances. Fourth, there tends to be a unity-producing "consciousness of kind" among the migrants, transcending families and bringing about the formation of larger social groups. The fact of close association during the many days or even weeks of travel is partly responsible for this kind of solidarity, as is the mutuality of the adventure, the anxiety over the unknown that lies ahead, the tightly organized rural neighborhoods and small communities from which the migrants come, and the significance of the extended family. Fifth, a higher proportion of dark-skinned Brazilians is involved in the migration than is to be found already living in the state of São Paulo. This is important in helping to bring about a more equitable distribution of the various racial groups that make up the population. Finally, one of the most limiting characteristics of the migrants as a whole is the fact that as many as three fourths of the total are unable to read and write—a condition that certainly limits the levels of success to which they may aspire in their new homes unless steps are taken to change the situation significantly.

Brazil, of course, either has experienced or is experiencing now other currents of migration, including the movement of many people *from* the state of São Paulo to Paraná, Goiás, and other states. For present purposes, however, the heavy migration to São Paulo serves as an adequate example of migration from one region to another.

The second significant interregional movement—that of Negroes from the South to other sections of the United States since 1910—has some features in common with the one just described, but it also differs in many fundamental ways. Most important, this migration has significant rural-to-urban features, for though most of the migrants labored in agriculture during their residence in the South, very few of them have entered farming in the Northeast, the areas around the Great Lakes, California, and the other regions to which they have moved. This large regional shift of Negroes has involved at least five separate stages (for an analysis of this movement, see Ref. 457, pp. 155–173).

First, in the period before World War I, Negroes were concentrated almost exclusively in the South, and the vast majority of them worked in agriculture, usually as laborers. In fact, so great was this concentration that in 1910, over 83 per cent of the nearly 10 million Negroes in the country lived in Alabama, Arkansas, Florida, Georgia, Kentucky, Louisiana, Mississippi, North Carolina, South Carolina, Tennessee, Texas, and Virginia. In the main, these descendants of slaves knew and could avail themselves of no other life than that of lower-class workers on the plantations.

Second, in the period during and after World War I, large numbers of southern Negroes left the region and moved into northern cities, especially Chicago, New York, Philadelphia, Detroit, Cleveland, St. Louis, Baltimore, Washington, Pittsburgh, Cincinnati, and Columbus (Ohio). Most of them were rural people, but during this period some also left southern cities for those in other parts of the nation. Those who migrated were encouraged to do so, of course, by the fact that industrial prosperity coupled with agricultural depression followed World War I and also by the perennial fact of racial segregation in the South. When depression struck the entire economy in the 1930's, the movement slowed down considerably as Negroes and whites alike clung to the meager security that the land provided, but with the recovery and the growing investment in a defense program in 1938 and 1939, it resumed. The migrants continued to go almost exclusively to urban centers, generally the same ones that had been the earlier large recipients.

Third, during the time that Negroes were leaving the South in unprecedented numbers, others also were moving about within the region, principally from the farms to the cities. In fact, this movement was already well under way by the time Negroes first began to move to cities in other regions; and during the depression years it continued at a greater pace than did the interregional shift. Its eventual magnitude is reflected in the fact that by 1960, over five and a half million, or nearly a third of all Negroes in the nation, lived in towns and cities in the 12 southern states listed above. Another large share, of course, was living in rural-nonfarm areas, which also signifies the rather rapid decline of agriculture as a way of life for the southern Negro.

Fourth, the period of World War II witnessed a continuation of Negro migration from the South, but it also saw a significant change in direction. That is, large numbers moved to the states of the Pacific coast, especially California, in order to help fill the demand for labor in the wartime industries located there. To be sure, some Negroes had found their way westward in earlier decades, but the migration to this region went on in earnest only after Japan attacked Pearl Harbor. Even after the war had ended, the flow to this region continued, and it is going on at the present time. Again, this was rural-to-urban movement almost exclusively, the principal recipient being Los Angeles, which had 334,763 Negroes in 1960, followed by Oakland, San Francisco, and San Diego. Other cities in California, Oregon, and Washington also acquired fairly sizeable numbers of Negroes as a result of this change in the direction of the migration.

Finally, the movement of Negroes continues to bring about redistribution within the South. Mainly, the urban and rural-nonfarm populations are increasing at the expense of the rural-farm group. In fact, so great has been the decrease of the latter in every state in the South, that between 1920 and 1960, Negroes in this category declined from almost five million to less than one and a half million. What is more, the period from 1950 to 1960 witnessed by far the greatest rate of migration of the four decades under consideration. In addition, there has been considerable redistribution of the Negro farm population within the southern region. In 1920, for example, the states with the largest Negro farm populations were, in descending order, Georgia, South Carolina, Mississippi, Alabama, North Carolina, and Texas; but in 1960, the largest groups were to be found in Mississippi, North Carolina, South Carolina, Georgia, Alabama, and Virginia, in the order named.

The movement of Negroes out of the South cannot continue indefinitely at the same rate, but, nevertheless, there is still a large number of young Negroes who eventually will follow the example of their predecessors and migrate to other regions.

FARM-TO-FARM MIGRATION

Not all significant rural migrations involve the crossing of state lines or the passing from farm to city or from city to farm. In a multitude of societies practicing many different kinds of agriculture and employing various ways of relating man to the land, large numbers of people move annually from farm to farm. In places where the adequate family-sized farm has been institutionalized, on a widespread scale, the average owner-operator tends to remain on his farm for a comparatively long period of time, adding to its size and increasing its value. Under these conditions, much of the farm-to-farm movement that does occur takes place among younger men and their wives and children who are in the process of ascending the agricultural ladder. The older adolescent may leave the parental farm and seek employment on another place as a wage hand, only to leave that situation after a few years to become the renter of a farm, and finally to shift onto a holding that he himself has purchased or inherited. Thus, in these middle-class areas, while an individual climbing the agricultural ladder is in the tenant class, he is more mobile than when he becomes an owner. This pattern gives rise to a definite age cycle of migration, but it also confines the movements within a limited area.

In areas where the large landed estate dominates rural life and where a middle class of farmers is small or nonexistent, migration among the land-owners may be slight, unless, of course, any particular ones remove to urban centers and leave the farm operations largely in the hands of managers. The laborers, however, have a tendency to change farm residence frequently, unless they are prevented from doing so by indebtedness, law, peonage, custom and tradition, or other factors. During the heyday of the share-cropping system in the United States, for example, the laborers were a highly mobile group, some of them remaining on one plantation for a single season and shifting to another the next season. Much of this migration was inherent in the nature of sharecropping arrangements: the customary "contracts," usually verbal, worked so greatly to the advantage of the planter that the sharecropper was impelled frequently to seek new and better terms. The massive movement among these people suggests, though, that most geographical changes brought about little actual betterment and that the illusion of being able to improve upon the contractual arrangements by moving from plantation to plantation was rarely transformed into reality. Although few remnants of sharecropping remain in the United States, the type of movement that it generates still occurs widely in parts of the world where large proportions of the agriculturists are laborers or low-status tenants of various kinds. The excessive movement of people that goes on is one of the social corollaries of large-scale agriculture that do most to emphasize the social and economic wastes inherent in the concentration of landownership. In some places, the restlessness, the despair, and the chronic fruitless mobility of these disadvantaged agricultural folk is being transformed into demands for change and even into a considerable amount of violence.

Leaving most of the categories of laborers aside, there still is an inverse relationship between tenure status and rates of farm-to-farm migration. Among the operators, persons who are full owners of their farms move less frequently on the average than do part owners; part owners move less often than managers; and managers move less often than renters. Within the class of renters, a like relationship holds: Those who pay cash rents move less frequently than the ones who pay a fixed amount of produce; the latter, less often than share renters who pay a percentage of the crop; and so on down to sharecroppers and others in the laborer category, where, on the average, the highest degree of movement takes place. In general, then, the nature of the rights that agriculturists have to the land is highly significant in producing particular rates of movement from one farm to another. Stable rights, which permit the exercise of suitable management techniques and encourage a high level of investment in land, buildings, equipment, and so on, are associated with a comparatively low rate of movement from farm to farm. Conversely, the lack of rights to the soil, or even those tenuous rights that are associated with sharecropping and low-status tenancy is reflected in much greater mobility. Under these conditions, farm-to-farm movement produces little improvement for agricultural families.

The association between farm ownership and low rates of farm-to-farm migration often is found even where the units are very small. For example, in that portion of the United States popularly designated as "Appalachia," there is very little of this kind of migration. In these mountainous areas, the typical farm is operator-owned, but it also is too small and its terrain often too rugged to be mechanized successfully or even to provide a reasonably adequate level of living. Therefore, it confers relatively low socioeconomic status. Yet most of the holdings are occupied by white owners who rarely migrate from one farm to another. There is movement, of course, but it is largely of the rural-to-urban type, in which young adults move from these small places into urban centers. This tendency to avoid farm-to-farm migration, despite the comparatively low social status of these farm folk, exists because of tradition, the long-time family ownership of a particular farm, and the unwillingness to jeopardize a meager but known existence for an unknown situation.

In some places, including a number of the countries of Latin America, a type of annual migration from one "farm" to another results from the nature of fire agriculture. This destructive system is practiced by millions of peasants in Brazil, Bolivia, and other countries. Each family that employs this system annually chops down a small patch of forest, often on a steep slope; allows the vegetation to dry; burns the smaller residue and permits the larger stumps and trunks to remain; and finally plants its few seeds or tubers in the soft, ash-covered soil. Little or no cultivation is done during the growing season, and by the time the meager crop is ready to harvest, the patch again has become covered with new vegetation. The process is repeated annually, creating the seasonal shift of large numbers of families as they go through the wasteful and time-consuming process of felling, burning, planting, harvesting, and moving. Generally, this kind of migration, which could be considered a type of nomadism, lacks any clear direction and sets up no important, identifiable currents. It usually involves quite short distances, often has the characteristics of temporary "squatting," in which legal ownership of the land is ignored, and ordinarily turns the migrants themselves into a most unstable group. These people generally lack personal possessions of any consequence, to say nothing of farm buildings and equipment, and, although they remain within a general locality, customarily they also enjoy no significant degree of integration into a community. The peasant who functions within this kind of situation rarely exhibits a standard of living that would lead him to improve his level of living; and he ordinarily possesses few of the skills that would make improvement possible, no matter what his intentions.

Finally, in many sections of the world, large-scale farming and sharecropping also seem to set up a current of migration from the plantations, which usually monopolize the good lands, to small farms in the poorest sections, and then back to the plantations. This retreat to the hills and other land poorly suited to agriculture has occurred in parts of the United States, in Colombia, and in a number of other societies, although in many cases some of those displaced from the plantations do not return but remain on the small, underproductive farms in the poorer regions.

NOMADISM

Few countries are without nomads, people who shift from place to place, lacking any permanent residence, making their livelihoods from various kinds of agriculture and stockraising. In some countries, there are those who tend wandering herds of livestock, usually moving from place to place according to a discernible pattern, which is generally related to the availability of pasture and water at various seasons of the year. In others there are the practitioners of fire agriculture, discussed previously. In many societies, there are the migratory agricultural laborers who literally follow the crops, also along identifiable routes; and it is these who are of principal concern in this section. Finally, there are workers who are transported into other countries during peak planting and harvesting seasons in order to fill the temporary demand for large numbers of field hands. Such was the case, for example, with Mexican laborers who until 1965 were brought into California, Texas, and other parts of the Southwest to work in various kinds of vegetables, small fruits, and other crops. It also is true of the "off-shore" laborers (from Barbados and other islands in the West Indies) who are imported for work in Florida and other states on the Atlantic seaboard. However, in practically all cases when persons fall into the category of migratory agricultural laborers, their occupational status is the lowest and their material condition the least enviable of any group in the society. When this position is combined with minority group membership, the composite social status is generally the lowest imaginable. For instance, in the United States, the low socioeconomic status of the Negro who is an unskilled migratory agricultural laborer is exceeded only by that of the "wetback" Mexican peon whose illegal entrance to the Southwest prevents him from taking advantage of the meager protections the law offers to his fellows who have a right to be in this country.

In the United States, migratory workers number about a half million, although this figure does not account for other family members who certainly swell the total affected by the socioeconomic conditions involved. This rural proletariat alone makes possible the seeming "efficiency" of certain large agricultural operations and accounts for the most serious relief problems of many towns and cities. Taylor suggests that the number has remained constant for several years (Ref. 518, p. 55), but the tendency for the group to persist is due to certain changes in our methods of agriculture. In the South, the decline of the system of sharecropping is intimately linked to the sustained demand for workers from off the plantations; and, throughout the United States, the growing tendency to seasonality in the need for farm help preserves the large group of migratory agricultural laborers.

Several kinds of crops are involved in this phenomenon, and each of them, because of its own particular requirements, tends to generate a particular stream of migration. These are as follows: (1) The wheat belt migration, which, from 1900 until the 1920's, saw the movement of large numbers of workers to Texas in June, and from there northward to the Dakotas and even Canada. Some workers followed the entire route, others from local areas participated in harvests in their own regions. At present, the mechanization of wheat production has made this flow largely of historical interest. (2) The cotton belt migration, which is confined principally to its western portion, especially Arizona, California, New Mexico, and western Texas, largely because sharecropping persisted so long and stubbornly in the "Deep South" that no other system requiring the lavish use of labor became widespread before the 1950's. (3) The movement in areas where small fruits and vegetables are grown. Such crops as strawberries, grapes, beans, tomatoes, and others require careful handpicking and have generated a great deal of migration northward from the Gulf of Mexico to Lake Michigan, with stops in Florida, Louisiana, central Arkansas, Kentucky, Illinois, Michigan, and New York. Many of these people also participate in the harvest of tree fruits and vegetables along the way, and some eventually fan out toward the Northwest and the fruit-growing sections of Washington and Oregon. (4) The movement of sugar workers. Including those who harvest both beets and cane, this group is highly localized; workers harvesting cane in Louisiana are drawn from the immediate vicinity, laborers cultivating and harvesting sugar beets in the Mountain States and the Middle West are recruited in their general areas, and so on. "Following the crop" is hardly possible in sugar production. (5) The migration to and within California following fruit and truck crops. In fact, much of the nation's migratory labor population now is confined to California and to the other states of the west coast because of the nature of farming in that area. The Imperial Valley of California is perhaps the single most important area insofar as the recruitment of migratory agricultural laborers is concerned.

Of all the migrations of rural people, the shifting of migratory laborers from one seasonal crop to another is fraught with the most serious social consequences. Earnings are low and sporadic, exploitation is frequent, expenditures for transportation are high, and there is little possibility of accumulating any reserve to tide the workers and their families over periods of unemployment or adversity. Housing of such workers is mostly a makeshift affair, with little or no care given to sanitation. Attachment to or participation in the activities of social institutions such as churches and schools is almost out of the question for the migrant laborer or the members of his family. Even the whites are not accepted by the communities in which they work temporarily, and workers of other races and of foreign birth find still greater discrimination. A system of agriculture based on migratory labor breeds the most demoralizing social results that can be contemplated.

SELECTIVITY OF MIGRATION

There are certain ways in which those who migrate differ from those who do not. Obviously, the differences depend in great measure upon the type of migration under consideration. For example, there are distinguishing sets of characteristics among those who leave the farms for the cities, those who follow the crops from place to place, those who participate in the opening of a frontier, those who shift about from one farm to another, and so on. In seeking to identify the characteristics of various kinds of migrants and to speak intelligently to the question of selectivity, one encounters a considerable amount of speculation, especially over the issue of whether those who migrate are somehow "better" or "worse" than those who do not. This line of reasoning is largely unrewarding, but there are several characteristics that are associated with the several kinds of migration.

First, there are certain kinds of selectivity by age. Basically, migration that is not forced and in which individual motivations are involved is concentrated among young adults. This is particularly true, of course, among those who move from farms to cities in most societies, the peak tendency to migrate coming between the ages of 18 and 25. Much the same can be said about international migration. In that case, though, such groups as Jewish refugees from Nazi Germany, Arab refugees from Israel, Cuban exiles who fled Castro's regime, Hungarian "Freedom Fighters," and others would not fit this pattern—persons of all ages were found in large numbers in these and similar kinds of movements. Migration is much more common, however, among older adolescents and young adults than it is among people in any other age group. Noteworthy, however, is the rather heavy migration in the United States of persons who have passed their sixty-fifth birthdays. In particular, this group seems disposed to move in at least two major currents: (1) to the typical "retirement" areas in Florida, California, Arizona, and a few other places; and (2) from the farms of the nation to nearby small towns and villages and sometimes even to larger cities.

Second, migration is selective in many cases according to sex. Again, the particular form that the selectivity takes depends strongly upon the kind of migration involved and also upon age. In general, if the moves are of long distance, such as the shift of persons to São Paulo state from many distant parts of Brazil or the movement of Negroes from the southern United States to cities in the North, in California, and elsewhere, males tend to predominate. If, on the other hand, the migration is of comparatively short distance, as it is when persons move into cities from the nearby countrysides, females tend to outnumber males. As a result, of course, the farms are left with

97

disproportionately large numbers of males, despite the fact that death rates among them are higher than those among females, no matter what the residential situation. It must be stressed, though, that very high proportions of both males and females aged 18 to 25 migrate from the farms to the cities, no matter which of the two groups is the larger.

Third, at least in the United States, Brazil, the Soviet Union, and other societies where various racial and ethnic groups are important in the population, these may figure in the several kinds of migration under consideration. As mentioned before, the rural-to-urban movement in the United States has had as one of its major components the shift of Negroes out of the South and into other parts of the nation. So great has been this movement that the Negro population is becoming urban at a greater rate than is the white, and Negroes migrate between states proportionately more often than does the white group. Ultimately, as levels of education, job opportunities, and other conditions become more alike among the races, such differentials can be expected to disappear, but, at least for the present, the Negro population of the United States, impelled by motives that it was not previously permitted to develop and by opportunities that did not exist earlier, is a highly mobile one.

Finally, the relationships between other kinds of characteristics and rates of migration are not sufficiently known to enable many accurate conclusions to be drawn. In some cases, there is a certain selectivity according to marital status; in others, religious affiliation is important; and, in still others, levels of education may play a part. The work necessary to deal definitively with these matters remains to be done.

Additional Readings

1. BAALI, FUAD, *Relation of the People to the Land in Southern Iraq*, Gainesville: University of Florida Press, 1966, chapter 8.

2. BANKS, VERA J., CALVIN L. BEALE, and GLADYS K. BOWLES, *Farm Population—Estimates for 1910–62*, Washington: Economic Research Service, 1963.

3. BEALE, CALVIN L., "Rural Depopulation in the United States: Some Demographic Consequences of Agricultural Adjustments," *Demography*, Vol. 1, No. 1 (1964), pp. 264–272.

4. HAMILTON, C. HORACE, "Educational Selectivity of Migrants from Farm to Urban and to Other Nonfarm Communities," in Mildred B. Kantor (ed.), *Mobility and Mental Health*, New York: Charles C Thomas, 1965, chapter 7.

5. HAMILTON, C. HORACE, "Population Pressures and other Factors Affecting Net Rural-Urban Migration," *Social Forces*, Vol. 30, No. 2, December, 1951, pp. 209–215.

6. RAMSEY, CHARLES E., and WALFRED A. ANDERSON, *Some Problems in the Regional Study of Migration*, Cornell Department of Rural Sociology Bulletin No. 53, Ithaca: Cornell University, 1959.

7. RAMSEY, CHARLES E., ALLAN D. ORMAN, and LOWRY NELSON, *Migration in Minnesota, 1940–50*, Minnesota AES Bulletin No. 422, St. Paul: University of Minnesota, 1954.

8. SMITH, T. LYNN, *Brazil: People and Institutions* (third ed.), Baton Rouge: Louisiana State University Press, 1963, chapter IX.

9. SMITH, T. LYNN, *Latin American Population Studies*, Gainesville: University of Florida Press, 1960, chapter 4.

10. SMITH, T. LYNN, *Studies of Latin American Societies*, New York: Doubleday & Co., Inc., 1970, selection 7.

11. SMITH, T. LYNN, and PAUL E. ZOPF, JR., *Fundamentals of Population Study* (second ed.). Philadelphia: F. A. Davis Company, 1970, chapters 19 and 20.

12. SOROKIN, PITIRIM A., CARLE C. ZIMMERMAN, and CHARLES J. GALPIN, *A Systematic Source Book in Rural Sociology*, Minneapolis: University of Minnesota Press, 1932, Vol. III, chapter XXII.

13. TAEUBER, CONRAD, and IRENE B. TAEUBER, *The Changing Population of the United States*, New York: John Wiley & Sons, Inc., 1958, chapter 5.

14. TARVER, JAMES D., and CALVIN L. BEALE, "Population Trends of Southern Nonmetropolitan Towns, 1950 to 1960," *Rural Sociology*, Vol. 33, No. 1 (March, 1968), pp. 19–29.

15. WHETTEN, NATHAN L., and ROBERT G. BURNIGHT, "Internal Migration in Mexico," *Rural Sociology*, Vol. 21, No. 2 (June, 1956), pp. 140–151.

16. ZOPF, PAUL E., JR., *North Carolina: A Demographic Profile*, Chapel Hill: University of North Carolina Population Center, 1967, chapter XII.

SOCIAL ECOLOGY, ORGANIZATION and STRUCTURE IN RURAL SOCIETY

"Social organization" is used in this book to refer to the structural aspects or the form of rural society. Next to population, this is the most highly developed portion of the sociology of rural life. Part Three falls logically into three divisions: (1) relations of the people to the land; (2) relations of person to person; and (3) the institutional aspects. The five important relationships between the population and the land are as follows: (1) the manner in which the people are distributed on the land, or form of settlement; (2) the way in which the land is divided for purposes of surveying and recording; (3) the nature of property rights in the land; (4) the distribution of ownership and control of the land; and (5) the ways of extracting a living from the soil, designated in this volume as the "systems of agriculture." Two aspects of personal relationships are analyzed: the discussion of social differentiation sets forth the nature of the social units or groupings in rural society; and that of social stratification describes the class and caste elements in rural social organization. Finally, Part Three concludes with a discussion of the functioning of the more fundamental social groups—the family, educational agencies, the church, and political bodies—and of the established institutional forms through which they work.

5
FORM OF SETTLEMENT

The manner in which the rural population is arranged on the land is one of the most important aspects of rural social organization. The terms "form of settlement," "type of settlement," and "settlement patterns" are used by various authors to refer to the spatial relationships of farm dwellings to one another and to the cultivated land. The nature of the agricultural process requires that each farmer have a relatively large acreage; this requirement inevitably makes the density of an agricultural population slight. Therefore, in the location of farm residences, a choice must be made between placing the homes near one another and at a distance from the fields, or placing the dwellings amid the fields and away from one another. If the first alternative is chosen, one mode of settlement, with its social consequences, arises; if the second is selected, the arrangement and the effects are quite different.

Like other aspects of the cultural heritage, a form of settlement, once established, becomes the "natural" pattern and is accepted as a matter of course. To the average American, for example, the "natural" type of settlement is one in which the homes of the farm families are scattered over the landscape, each in the midst of the fields cultivated by the operator, and all at some distance from one another. In other words, dispersed settlement patterns are common and nucleated patterns rare in the rural United States. Agricultural villages exist, of course, but, from early times, most of these have been merely trade and service centers for the farm population. They are not genuine farm villages. In them live professional and business classes, laborers, many retired farmers, and many widows. Only to a minor degree do they serve as locations for homes of farmers. Throughout most of the world, however, the hamlet or village with the homes of farmers grouped together in clusters is most common. Surrounding the village at some distance are the lands tilled by the farmers whose homes make up the villages. Most of the landscape is devoid of farm buildings.

There must be some pattern of settlement, but diverse circumstances cause the patterns to differ. Unquestionably, however, the manner in which the population is spaced on the land is a conditioning factor that vitally affects all other aspects of social organization and the social processes. It is also one of the most persistent elements of the cultural heritage. Innovations and changes in established forms of settlement can be made only in the face of great resistance. That old, durable settlements should perpetuate traditional patterns is to be expected and should not be disquieting to those who attempt to understand rural life or those who intend to bring about significant agricultural development. Every effort should be made in the establishment of new colonies, even in so-called experimental settlements, not to allow cultural inertia to result in the unconscious transfer of the customary pattern of settlement to the new communities. A comparative study of the advantages and disadvantages of each of the various possibilities is the sound approach in social planning. Some of the great colonizers of the past, such as William Penn and Lord Selkirk, realized the importance of this rational and deliberate selection of the right type of settlement pattern. They even experimented on a considerable scale with various possibilities. Today, if social planning in and for rural areas is to amount to more than pure verbosity, it must start with the types or patterns of settlement that might be used in the most effective way in the areas undergoing reconstruction and colonization.

TYPES OF SETTLEMENT

The possibilities offered in the distribution of the farm population on the land are definitely limited. In fact, all the existing forms of settlement may be grouped into three principal types.

The Village Form of Settlement

From the standpoint of the number of people affected throughout the world, the village form of settlement is by far the most important. In Africa (Fig. 4) and in Europe, Asia, and much of Latin America (Fig. 5), it is the principal mode of settling on the land. It is not unknown in the United States, although relatively rare. In this type of settlement, the homes of the farmers are grouped together to form a village or hamlet, leaving the cultivated fields, pastures, and woodlands in the surrounding area quite devoid of

FIGURE 4. Village type of settlement used by the natives of Senegal, Africa. From *Vollstandige Völkergallerie,* Meissen, F. W. Goedsche, n.d., II Abtheilung.

dwellings, except for the "crop-watching cottages" found in some countries. In a generalized picture, such a settlement usually consists of five parts: (1) Forming the core is the village proper, made up of the homes, barns, and other farm buildings; (2) nearest the village are small garden plots; (3) more remote are the cultivated lands; (4) sometimes competing with the cultivated plots for land adjacent to the village and sometimes beyond the arable lands are pastures; and (5) most remote from the village, at the outer limits of the community's domain, usually are to be found waste-lands and woods. Where density of population is not great, there may be an indeterminate area between communities, and the property of one village may shade indiscriminately into that of another. The essential element in the village pattern is the clustering of farm homes in a village and the separation of the dwellings from the fields, which lie about the core of the settlement.

The village nucleus itself shows a great many variations. In Europe, for example, there are pronounced differences between the settlements established by the Germans and those made by the Slavs. The genuine German village was merely a compact group of homes arranged with no definite plan.

FIGURE 5. Village settlement in Peru, surrounded by fields on the remnants of the old Inca terraces. Courtesy of M. Kuczynski-Godard.

FIGURE 6. German village of the *Runddörfer* type and the surrounding fields. Courtesy of Plan und Karte, G.m.b.H., through Katharina Elisseieff.

FIGURE 7. German village of the *Strassendörfer* type and the adjacent fields. Courtesy of Plan und Karte, G.m.b.H., through Katherina Elisseieff.

Slavic villages, on the other hand, were constructed in a distinctive and orderly fashion. They are of two principal types, "round" villages (*Runddörfer*) and "long" villages (*Strassendörfer*). (See Figs. 6 and 7 for examples of these types.) The distinctive culture patterns carried by each ethnic group and given material expression in the type of village constructed have helped scholars to understand the migrations of the various stocks in prehistoric times.

Village settlements in the United States are no less distinctive in character. A feature of the New England "plantations" was the village common, or green, at the center of the settlement. In the Southwest, the Spanish colonizers were first concerned with the location of the plaza, which in the inland towns was a rectangle in the center of the pueblo, and in the river or coastal locations was placed facing the waterfront. The Mormon settlements in the Rocky Mountain region conformed closely to the plan for the "City of Zion" that was formulated as early as 1833. The essential elements of the Mormon plan called for a rectangle 1 mile square to be divided into blocks of 10 acres; these were then cut into half-acre lots, allowing 20 houses to the block; streets were 8 rods wide and ran north-south and east-west. (Fig. 8).

FIGURE 8. The village pattern of settlement—a typical Mormon village from the air. Photo by the Western Division Laboratory of the Agricultural Adjustment Division.

Single Farmsteads

In sharp contrast with village patterns of settlement is that in which each farm home is located among the fields worked by the family. Whereas the village settlement is characterized by close and intimate contact between the homes of the farmers, in the scattered mode of settlement the homes of the farmers are widely separated from one another (Fig. 9). Just as the village pattern of settlement makes the relationships between the family and the land remote and intermittent, scattered farmsteads make for close and constant contacts between the family and the land, but more distant relations with other farm families.

There are varying degrees of remoteness between the dwellings under a system of single farmsteads. If density of population is slight and holdings are large, the houses will be more dispersed than in areas of denser population and smaller farms. Cultural and natural factors also affect the dispersion of the homesteads. If situations are chosen in valleys, and the surrounding ridges are used for boundaries, as was true in the early trans-Appalachian settlements, each farm home will be nearer to the center of the holding and further from neighbors. The more nearly square are the tracts of land, other

FIGURE 9. The scattered-farmsteads type of settlement—the Iowa design for farming, from the air. Photo by The Register and Tribune Company of Des Moines, Iowa.

things being equal, the more difficult it is for farmers to construct their homes near to one another. The checkerboard pattern of land division that prevails in the United States, if combined with the scattered-farmsteads type of settlement, nears the maximum possible in isolation of farm homes. In Brazil, Colombia, and many other countries, however, the use of metes and bounds in dividing the land also has brought about extreme dispersion of farm homes.

The Line Village

If some common base of departure is employed in laying out the land, if the length of the holdings is great in comparison with the width, and if the farm families rather consistently locate their dwellings at the same end of their ribbonlike farms, a considerable aggregation of dwellings can occur without sacrificing residence on the farmsteads. Such a settlement has the appearance of a long, one-streeted village winding its way across the landscape (Figs. 10, 11). It has often been classed with villages proper, in which the farmers live apart from the land, in the group of nucleated settlements. The fact that, under such a pattern, farmers live on their lands is sufficient

FIGURE 10. Bayou Lafourche from the air. Note the extensive line village settlements. Observe the plantation with its nucleated settlement in the lower right-hand corner. Photo by the Davis Aerial Photographic Service, Houma, Louisiana.

reason, however, to differentiate it from other agglomerated types and to place it in a separate category.

Two highly rationalized varieties of the line-village pattern of settlement deserve special mention. One of these has been used by native Brazilians and Japanese immigrants alike in parts of the state of São Paulo, Brazil (Fig. 12). Note that the riverfront system of land division used gives all farms access to the stream; that the road encircles the valley in which such a settlement is located; and that the line-village arrangement of the houses, all on the land as well as on the road, results in fairly compact settlement. The second type has been used to some extent in the modern colonization of an ancient land— in the laying-out of some of the new agricultural communities the Jews have built in modern-day Israel (Fig. 13). In this case, the farms and homes all front on a circular street, and the wedge-shaped holdings become wider as their depth increases. Were it not for the fact that each of the farm homes is located on the tract of land that makes up the farm, this compact arrangement would properly be classified in the true-village category rather than as one of the varieties of the line-village type of settlement.

Line-village settlements are common throughout the world, apparently in many cases arising spontaneously along the banks of rivers. This mode of arranging the population on the land early became set in the cultural patterns

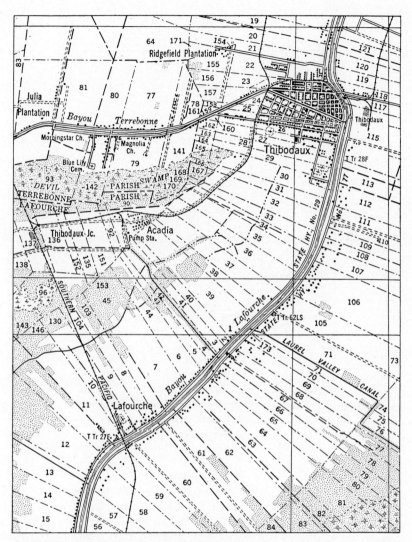

FIGURE 11. The line village settlement pattern—map of a portion of Lafourche Parish, Louisiana, showing the riverfront land division and the typical arrangement of farm homes.

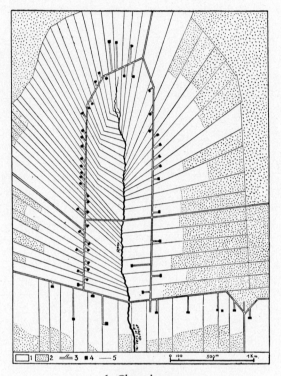

1. Cleared area.
2. Worked area.
3. Road.
4. House.
5. Property line.

FIGURE 12. Plan of a modified form of the line village settlement pattern used by Japanese colonists in the state of São Paulo, Brazil. Reproduced by courtesy of the author and publisher, from Pierre Monbeig, *Pionniers et Planteurs de São Paulo,* Paris: Librairie Armand Colin, 1952, p. 211.

FIGURE 13. The settlement of Nahalal, Israel in its early years of existence, depicting a highly rationalized settlement of the line-village type. Courtesy United Israel Appeal.

of the French, who carried it to many countries, including parts of Canada and the United States. Interestingly enough, the line village seems to have developed independently in south Brazil and has come to be the dominant settlement pattern in the important small-farming areas of that country.

ADVANTAGES AND DISADVANTAGES OF THE VARIOUS SETTLEMENT PATTERNS

The comparative desirability of the various patterns of settlement is greatly dependent upon the point of view. If economy is important, and especially if the farm-management aspects are the primary elements considered, the village pattern is highly undesirable. Village residence makes the proper care of livestock a great problem. To keep horses and cattle in the village, which is usually done, entails the transportation of feed to the village and of the manure back to the fields. To secure pasture, the stock must be driven out from the village and back again daily. If they are kept in the fields, someone must go frequently to see that feed and water are available, for work stock and cattle cannot be left to themselves several miles from the dwelling for any great length of time. In any case much time is lost driving to and from the fields. Under the village pattern of settlement, it also is more difficult to use byproducts from the farming enterprise for the feeding of chickens, pigs, and other farm animals.

There is also the matter of fragmentation of holdings into several separate tracts, which are often scattered throughout a fairly wide area. This is an almost inevitable concomitant of the village type of settlement. The ancient Hebrews, the Russians, and others arrested the development of extremes along this line with legal provisions for community ownership of land, periodic redistribution of holdings, and other steps. Private property in land and a system of inheritance that does not provide for transmitting landed properties intact to one heir bring about a rapid pulverization of landholdings. For example, in Newton, Massachusetts, on May 1, 1635, the holdings of one John White consisted of the following elements: (1) two small tracts of about three rods each in "cowyard row." On one of these was located his dwelling, farm buildings, and garden; (2) three separate tracts in "old field," one containing two and one-half acres, and two of one acre and one rod each; (3) one acre on "long marsh hill" and another tract of three acres in "long marsh"; 13½ acres in the "neck of land"; 11 acres in the "great marsh"; and one acre in "ox marsh" (cf. Ref. 327, pp. 449–451). In the Mormon villages of the present day, fragmentation continues as a source of inconvenience and vexation to the inhabitants. In the village of Ephraim, for example, Nelson discovered the extreme case of a man with a farm of 12 pieces, no two of which were adjacent (cf. Ref. 314, p. 11, and Ref. 313, p. 28).

Acute as the problem is in the village studied by Nelson, it is minor in comparison with the situation in the older countries of Europe, where farms of 10 or 20 hectares often are subdivided into scores of separate plots (see Fig. 14). For example, in Spain, and especially in the northwestern quarter of the country, fragmentation of agricultural holdings is severe. In the nation as a whole there is an average of 17 separate tracts per farm, but the figure is much higher in the provinces of the northwest, such as the average of 84 tracts per farm in Soria. Moreover, the fragments are parts of farms that would be quite small even if all the bits were contiguous. The condition in northwestern Spain seems to have been brought about principally by three factors. In the first place, much of the region never came under the domination of the Moors; this has meant that those Moslem conquerors were in no position to erase the older patterns of land division and control that existed there. Furthermore, the southern part of the nation, completely wrested from the Moors by 1492, became an area of large consolidated holdings that were granted to many of the military chiefs who helped to expel the Moslem invaders, with the result that much of the fragmentation, which might have

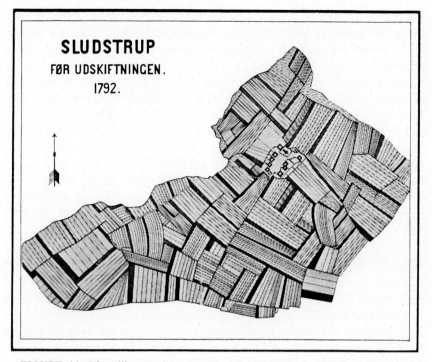

FIGURE 14. The village settlement pattern is often accompanied by fragmentation of holdings. The shaded strips represent the fragments of the farm of an operator living in the hamlet of Sludstrup, Denmark, as they were in 1792. Reproduced from Ref. 38.

continued there, was swept away. Secondly, the deliberate tendency during the late medieval period to bring about equality by rotating the control of the land in a district and by subdividing it annually according to the number of citizens was especially significant in bringing about fragmentation at an early date. Finally, the subdivision of large holdings by inheritance was most effective in producing the splintering effect in the space of a few generations.

Fragmented holdings, which often accompany the village pattern of settlement, may present a few advantages. They may help to diffuse the interests of a family throughout the community, spread the risks associated with farming, and allow agriculturists to have access to a wide variety of soil types. However, most of the effects are disadvantageous. Fragmented holdings render mechanized farming virtually impossible, with the result that large numbers of Spain's agricultural families are unable at present to relinquish primitive systems of agriculture in favor of those that are more efficient.

Fragmentation also makes it impossible for the agriculturists to use modern methods of scientific farming, creates a tremendous waste of time and energy as the farmer travels from one tract to another, and, in some cases, almost prevents him from visiting certain of the separate tracts at all. Moreover, as the farm people travel from plot to plot, they not only trespass on the lands of others but simply get in each other's way. The phenomenon also makes it nearly impossible to combine agriculture and stockraising economically; and it wastes great amounts of land that must be devoted to paths, fences, hedgerows, and other divisions between the fields. Often, it produces a condition in which some plots cannot be irrigated. Finally, fragmentation of individually owned holdings makes it extremely difficult for governments to exercise the right of eminent domain in order to obtain land on which to carry out various projects of public interest and need (cf. Ref. 448, pp. 140–149).

Portugal, too, suffers from the problems produced by fragmented agricultural holdings. In that country, the 853,568 farms, which average only 12.9 acres in size, are subdivided into an average of six tracts per farm (see Ref. 459, pp. 319–343). Obviously, this condition is a tremendous impediment to social and economic progress in the nation. It has passed far beyond the stage in which it might be advantageous in distributing the risks of farming or in diffusing the interests of the family throughout the community. In fact, fragmentation ranks with illiteracy and the extremely small size of the farms themselves as one of the principal social problems with which Portugal is confronted.

Even if fragmentation of holdings is not a problem in particular countries, for farm management the village system obviously is greatly inferior to both the line village and the single-farmsteads type of settlement. Undoubtedly, this is the factor that has caused the diffusion of the single-farmsteads pattern of settlement throughout the world as one of the direct results of the employment of North American agricultural engineers as technical experts in various foreign countries.

If one approaches the question of settlement patterns from the standpoint of social efficiency, however, the advantages of the village system are readily apparent. Close and intimate contacts with neighbors, proximity to social institutions, availability of playmates for children, ease of mutual aid, and, in brief, a rich social life are made possible when the homes of farmers are congregated in the true village community. The case for the village type of settlement has never been stated better than it was set forth by Timothy Dwight more than a century and a half ago:

It is a remarkable fact that New England was colonized in a manner widely different from that which prevailed in the other British colonies. All the ancient, and a great part of the modern townships, were settled in what may be called the village manner; the inhabitants having originally planted themselves in small towns. In many other parts of this country the planters have almost universally fixed themselves on their several farms, each placing his house where his own conscience dictated. In this manner, it is evident the farmer can more advantageously manage his own property, can oversee it more readily, and labour on it with fewer interruptions, than when it is dispersed in fields at some distance from each other.

But scattered plantations are subject to many serious disadvantages. Neither schools nor churches can, without difficulty, be either built by the planters or supported. The children must be too remote from the school, and the families from the church, not to discourage all strenuous efforts to provide these interesting accommodations. Whenever it is proposed to erect either of them, the thought that one's self, and one's family, are too distant from the spot to derive any material benefit, will check the feeble relentings of avarice, the more liberal dispositions of frugality, and even the noble designs of a generous disposition. Should all the first difficulties be overcome, trifling infirmities, foul weather, and the ill state of roads, will prevent a regular attendance. But the family, or the children, who do not go with some good degree of regularity to the church or the school, will in the end scarcely go at all. The education of the one, and the religion of both, will therefore in many cases be prevented.

At the same time, persons who live on scattered plantations are in a great measure cut off from that daily intercourse which softens and polishes man. When we live at a distance from every neighbour, a call demands an effort, and a visit becomes a formal enterprise. A family thus situated, must in a great measure be confined to its own little circle of domestic objects, and wrought insensibly into an insulated character. At the sight of a stranger the children, having been unaccustomed to such an object, are abashed, and the parents awkward and uneasy. That which generally gives pain will be regarded with apprehension, and repeated only from necessity. Social intercourse, therefore, exercised too little to begin to be pleasant, will be considered as an incumbrance; and the affections which cherish it, and which it cherishes and refines in its turn, will either sleep or expire. The gentle and pleasing manners, naturally growing out of it, can never be formed here. On the contrary, that rough and forbidding deportment, which springs from intercourse with oxen and horses, or with those who converse only to make bargains about oxen and horses, a rustic sheepishness, or a more awkward and provoking impudence, take possession of the man, and manifest their dominion in his conduct. The state of the manners, and that of the mind, are mutually causes and effects. The mind, like the manners, will be distant, rough, forbidding, gross, solitary, and universally disagreeable. A nation, planted in this manner, can scarcely be more than half civilized; and to refinement of character and life must necessarily be a stranger.

In such settlements schools are accordingly few and solitary; and a great multitude of the inhabitants, of both sexes, are unable either to write or read. Churches are still more rare; and the number of persons is usually not small, who have hardly ever been present either at a prayer or a sermon. Unaccustomed to objects of this nature, they neither wish for them, nor know what they are. The preachers whom they hear are, at the same time, very frequently uneducated itinerants, started into the desk by the spirit of propagandism; recommended by nothing but enthusiasm and zeal; unable to teach, and often even to learn. In such a situation, what can the character and manners become, unless such as have been described?

A New-Englander, passing through such settlements, is irresistibly struck with a wide difference between their inhabitants and those of his own country. The scene is changed at once. That intelligence and sociality, that softness and refinement, which prevail among even the plain people of New England, disappear. That repulsive character, which, as Lord Kaimes has remarked, is an original feature of savage man; intelligence bounded by the farm, the market, and the road which leads to it; affections so rarely moved as scarcely to be capable of being moved at all, unless when aroused to resentment; conversation confined to the properties and price of a horse, or the sale of a load of wheat; ignorance, at fifty years of age, of what is familiarly known by every New-England school-boy; wonder, excited by mere homespun things, because they are novelties; a stagnant indifference about other things, equally common, and of high importance, because they are unknown; an entire vacancy of sentiment, and a sterility of mind, out of which sentiment can never spring; all spread over a great proportion of the inhabitants, make him feel as if he were transported to a distant climate, and as if he were travelling in a foreign country.

New England presents a direct contrast to this picture. Almost the whole country is covered with villages; and every village has its church and its suit of schools. Nearly every child, even those of beggars and blacks in considerable numbers, can read, write, and keep accounts. Every child is carried to the church from the cradle, nor leaves the church but for the grave. All the people are neighbours; social beings; converse; feel; sympathize; mingle minds; cherish sentiments; and are subejcts of at least some degree of refinement. More than six hundred youths, natives of New England, are always in the colleges erected here. In almost every village are found literary men, and social libraries. A great number of men also, not liberally educated, addict themselves to reading, and acquire extensive information. Of all these advantages the mode of settlement has been one, and, it is believed, a powerful cause. (Ref. 109, Vol. 1, pp. 300–302.)

Thus, much depends upon the point of view. In a relatively self-sufficient economy, the choice between villages and isolated farmsteads, if made in a rational manner, would involve weighing the social advantages of the village against the farm-management advantages of the scattered farmsteads. However, as society becomes more complex, and its members more interdependent, and as organic solidarity comes to overshadow that of the mechanistic type, the significance of other economic factors is greatly increased. These factors are all those involved in relationships, communication, and exchange with the larger society. Today electricity, paved roads, telephones, radios, television sets, daily access to fresh food, transportation for school children, and other amenities have become basic necessities of life. Thus, in addition to the economics of farm management, the costs of transportation and communication with the outside world must be considered. Great indeed must be the economies of farm management to pay for the vastly increased expenditures for paved roads, automobiles, gasoline, school buses, electric and telephone lines, and so on, necessitated by the single-farmsteads pattern of settlement.

Fortunately, the choice is not limited to two settlement types. The line-village type of settlement offers a convenient way of attaining most of the social advantages of compact settlement without sacrificing the farm-management advantages that come from residence on the land. Such a pattern of settlement also offers great economies in the provision of all the avenues for contact with the larger society—good roads, electric lines, minimum distances for school buses, and so forth. Without doubt, in many farming regions, including rural North America, the line-village type of settlement would prove an economic and social boon to a large part of the rural farm population.

It is difficult to change the fundamental pattern of settlement, once it has been established, even in those rare cases in which cultural inertia is overcome through popular education to the extent that the mass of the people are aware that possibilities other than the traditional pattern exist. It is a cumbersome task to move farm buildings from one site to another; and the inconvenience of such transfers is probably a small matter compared with the difficulties inherent in rearranging the boundaries of lands. One who suggests that changes are desirable and possible is likely to be considered an extreme visionary. Nevertheless, if it is possible to make the farm population aware of the advantages and disadvantages of the several types of settlement, we believe that thorough changes could be brought about in the course of a half century or so, even in places where the same form of settlement has persisted for centuries.

Much might be accomplished through careful planning of farmers' roads. In places where the rectangular system of dividing the land results in sections and parcels of sections that are square, the placement of roads around each section causes the greatest possible economic costs to fall upon the population that must support such a project. This condition exists in virtually all of the United States settled after 1787. Such a situation both encourages and is fostered by the use of the scattered-farmsteads pattern of settlement, whereas with either the true village or the line-village form of settlement it would not be necessary to build a road around every section of land. The paving of a farm road makes the land next to the pavement more desirable than comparable land not adjacent to the highway. When a new paved road passes through a farming territory, there is a tendency for farm dwellings, barns, and other buildings to appear next to it. Part of this is due to the fact that old buildings back in the fields are gradually being destroyed and replaced by new ones located on the highway. Part of it also is due to the moving of farm buildings out to the road from the fields in which they previously were located. If roads were placed no nearer to each other than two miles, the mileage of projected roads in the United States, for example, would be reduced by approximately two thirds, even though the rectangular system of surveys would continue in use.

If the placement of roads were as described above, there would be a gradual change in the basic pattern of settlement owing to the farmers' tendency to locate their buildings along the highway. The fundamental change would come about in the following way: Farms do not remain of a given size year after year; some are growing, others diminishing in extent. Farm estates are constantly being accumulated by some operators, only to be divided later among the heirs. Consider the simple case of dividing equally between two heirs one half section, 320 acres of land, a situation often found in the United States. In the past each recipient has been satisfied to have his 160 acres in a square, a quarter section. Now suppose a paved road passes along the end but not the side of the original holding. With this new factor in the situation, the chances are excellent that each would desire his 160-acre allotment to front on the highway. Instead of quarter sections, each would seek a plot consisting of four "forties" laid end to end; the farm would be four times as deep as it was wide. Therefore, in subdividing lands of any size the road would be a factor of genuine significance demanding consideration. Because of this, careful planning of roads in rural districts would in all probability change settlement patterns in two or three generations. Moreover, changes caused by the careful planning of roads in the manner just discussed can be brought about in settled areas with far less upheaval and fewer infringements upon individual freedom and choice than would be generated by virtually any other means. Obviously, road planning would influence settlement patterns even more easily in parts of the world where colonization and permanent settlement are yet to take place, or where resettlement is projected. Already, along the highways radiating out from many large cities throughout the world, where the rural population is increasing, this factor is fostering settlements of the line-village type.

EXAMPLES OF THE THREE SETTLEMENT PATTERNS

Actual cases of the three basic forms of settlement are found in great numbers throughout the world. However, the United States alone contains a rich sampling of all three types, along with many minor variations of each; probably, more is known about settlement patterns in this country than in most others. Therefore, a reasonably representative view of actual settlement types can be obtained by examination of those that occur in various sections of the United States. In the main, of course, although the settlers tried out almost every possible way of arranging the population on the land, creating the present accumulation of the different forms, the single farmstead has been and remains the principal American pattern of settlement. Nevertheless, true-village patterns have played their part in the colonization of the country, and the least common of the three, the line-village settlements, certainly have been important in a few selected areas.

Village Settlements

Cultural influences are so potent as social determinants that, almost inevitably, the first English colonists transferred the traditional English village form of settlement to the New World. In New England, practically all the early settlements were established according to the village pattern. With virtually no modification, group settlement, or the "swarming" of established communities, carried the village pattern of settlement throughout New England and to some extent into New York and New Jersey as well. The settlement types were so little changed from the villages of England, and the villages of England from those of Germany, that the New England village of Puritan days was an almost exact replica of the German village in the time of Tacitus. The location, general appearance, and composition of these villages of New England have been set forth concisely by Timothy Dwight as follows:

New England villages . . . are built in the following manner.

The local situation is pitched on as a place in itself desirable; as a place, where life may be passed through more pleasantly than in most others; as a place, not where trade compels, but where happiness invites to settle. Accordingly the position of these towns is usually beautiful. The mode of settlement is such as greatly to enhance the pleasure intended. The body of inhabitants is composed of farmers; and farmers nowhere, within my knowledge, of a superior character for intelligence and good manners. . . .

To this character of the inhabitants the manner of locating and building these towns is happily suited. The town-plat is originally distributed into lots, containing from two to ten acres. In a convenient spot, on each of these, a house is erected at the bottom of the courtyard (often nearly enclosed); and is furnished universally with a barn, and other convenient outbuildings. Near the house there is always a garden, replenished with culinary vegetables, flowers, and fruits, and very often, also, prettily enclosed. The lot, on which the house stands, universally styled the home lot, is almost of course a meadow, richly cultivated, covered during the pleasant season with verdure, and containing generally a thrifty orchard. It is hardly necessary to observe, that these appendages spread a singular cheerfulness and beauty over a New England village, or that they contribute largely to render a house a delightful residence. (Ref. 109, Vol. 2, p. 317.)

Very early there arose among some of the inhabitants of New England a desire to leave the village and establish homes on the land. Innovations in this field were not welcomed, and, in fact, various decrees and regulations were written and enforced with the intent of preserving the early village form of settlement. Some of the colonial settlements also found it necessary to restrict the establishment of new plantations so as to avoid the proliferation of scattered farmsteads, which, the local church and secular authorities felt, made for inadequate protection and social interaction.

Thus, cultural forces, supplemented by law, enabled the village type of settlement to maintain its importance in the older parts of New England for more than 200 years. As late as 1820, Timothy Dwight, the president of Yale University, gave the following indignant reply to Volney's assertion that scattered farmsteads were frequently to be found in New England: ". . . The representation of M. Volney is merely a flight of the imagination. It will appear also that a great part of the ancient settlements in New England, instead of being scattered farmhouses, are composed chiefly of villages. . . ." (Ref. 109, Vol. 4, p. 207.) Dwight, who had traveled on horseback through practically every township in New England, undoubtedly had good evidence to support his contention. In his notes concerning a township he nearly always mentioned the mode of settlement. Such entries as the following are numerous throughout the four volumes of his work:

The town [Deerfield] is built on an elevation, spreading out from the foot of the mountain. The principal street, on which stand three-fourths of the houses, runs from north to south. The buildings are generally neat; and exhibit everywhere a tidy, thrifty appearance. The inhabitants are generally farmers, and of the first class in this country. (Ref. 109, Vol. 2, pp. 54–55.)

Immediately above Watertown lies South-Farms; the southern parish of Litchfield . . . the houses good farmers' dwellings, of which a little village is formed around the church. (Ref. 109, Vol. 2, p. 351.)

Pomfret contains a pretty village, lying partly on this road, and partly on the Norwich road, which joins it at right angles. The inhabitants are principally a collection of sober, industrious farmers. (Ref. 109, Vol. 3, p. 127.)

Milford . . . was purchased by the Rev. Peter Prudden and others, principally from Wethersfield, in 1639. Forty-four planters settled themselves here immediately; but they found the Indians so numerous, that they surrounded the town plat, nearly a mile square, with a strong palisade. (Ref. 109, Vol. 3, p. 501.)

A few of the settlements such Old Hadley, Old Deerfield, and Sunderland, Massachusetts, have preserved their patterns largely intact until the present day.

In New York, where the original settlers were Dutch, single farmsteads constituted the prevailing pattern of settlement. Neither on the large estates nor in the areas of small farms was the village type of early importance. Later on, comparisons of the lot of the Dutch settlers with that of the English in New England convinced the authorities, including Stuyvesant, of the superiority of the village form of settlement. They imposed considerable pressure on the settlers to remold the settlement pattern in such a way that the true village became its central feature. For example, when the settlers of Pavonia petitioned for special favors in other matters, Stuyvesant granted their requests on the condition that they concentrate their homes into a village. However, such efforts were successful only to a minor degree; although a few settlements of the village type persisted for many years, the bulk of the state was colonized with single farmsteads. New York also served as a powerful center in diffusing the scattered-farmsteads type of settlement westward.

Under the influence of Penn, much experimentation with settlement patterns took place in Pennsylvania, but those of the village form prevailed in the beginning. Penn himself described the type of settlement used in the colony as follows:

We do settle in the way of Townships or Villages, each of which contains 5,000 acres, in square, and at least Ten Families; the regulation of the Country being a family to each five hundred Acres. . . .

Our Townships lie square; generally the Village in the Center; the Houses either opposit, or else opposit to the middle, betwixt two houses over the way, for near neighborhood. (Ref. 339, p. 263.)

In the Middle Colonies of New Jersey and Delaware, early efforts were devoted to establishing the village form of settlement. Much the same was the case in Maryland. Jamestown, the first settlement in Virginia, was of the village type; and later, when a modified form of the manorial system became the dominant institution of Virginia, one of the characteristic features of each plantation was a slave "village" or "quarters" for the Negroes. The slave village was the Negro's world. Miss Bremer observed these villages in the Carolinas and Georgia and outlined their essential characteristics as follows:

I range about in the neighborhood, through the rice fields and Negro villages, which amuses me greatly. The slave villages consist of small, white-washed wooden houses, for the most part built in two rows, forming a street, each house standing detached in its little yard or garden, and generally with two or three trees about it. (Ref. 48, pp. 288–289.)

Mrs. Leigh gave a more detailed description:

At the rear of the house about twelve yards, is what is called the colony, where are situated the kitchen, servants' sitting-room and bedrooms, the laundry and dairy, and in a corner of the yard is a turkey-house, full of prime Christmas fowl. Behind the colony is Settlement No. 1, where the coloured people (I believe this also is the correct term) reside. It consists of an avenue of orange trees, on each side of which are rows of wooden houses, and at the end of which, facing the avenue, is what was the old hospital, but which is half of it the church and the other half the residence of our English labourers, eight in number. (Ref. 242, pp. 243–244.)

Throughout the South, wherever the planter class settled, the three-way association between large landholdings, good land, and the Negro supported the ante-bellum plantation with its village form of settlement. Even the planters concentrated their homes to a considerable extent into towns and villages, from which they commuted to their plantations at distances of 10, 15, and even 30 miles. A case in point is the sugar-producing sections of south Louisiana, where the plantation system has retained the nucleated settlement pattern until the present (Fig. 15). Settlements of freeholders,

FIGURE 15. A Louisiana sugar-cane plantation, showing the mill, the homes of the planter and his skilled employees, the "quarters," and the surrounding fields. Photo by Davis Aerial Photographic Service, Houma, Louisiana.

arranged on the village plan, also were attempted in North Carolina, South Carolina, and Georgia, although the plantation and the dispersed-farm-steads settlements eventually gained the upper hand.

Cultural heritage is persistent. Even though the practice of squatting had spread the isolated farmstead throughout the back settlements from Maine to Georgia, attempts were made to develop village settlements beyond the Alleghenies. A clear case of this attempt was the first settlement (Manchester) in the Virginia Military District, established by General Massie from Kentucky. Massie gave notice of his intentions to the settlers of Kentucky in the winter of 1790, offering to the first 25 families to join him a donation of one in-lot and one out-lot of 100 acres on condition that they would settle in the village he proposed to establish. Instead of 25, 30 families accompanied him; and by the middle of March, 1791, the village was planted and surrounded with strong pickets.

More usual in the settlement of the western country, however, was a combination of the village and the scattered-farmsteads types of settlement. Each settler located a cabin on his claim, but he also assisted others in the construction of a fort or station into which all the families in a neighborhood could retire in time of danger. Monette describes the typical fort or station as follows:

. . . A station, in most cases, was constructed for the protection of a large number of families, as a safe retreat in time of danger. It consisted of an inclosure of cabins, stockades, and block-houses, embracing about two acres or more, in the shape of a parallelogram or square; the inclosure being formed generally by cabins on two sides and by stockades on two sides. A large station sometimes presented three sides inclosed with cabins, the windows and doors all on the inner side. The outside wall of the cabin was generally ten or twelve feet high, without external openings, and perfectly bulletproof, with the roof sloping downward to the inside. The cabins otherwise were finished in the usual manner, for the residence of families. The gate or entrance was a strong puncheon door between the parallel walls of adjoining cabins, and protected by a platform and sentry-box above. The remainder of the inclosure was completed by strong palisades set in the ground, with their sharpened points standing ten feet above ground. The whole inclosure, cabins and stockades, was provided with port-holes for defensive firing. In time of danger the gate was closed, and securely barricaded each day at sunset. During the day, if no immediate danger threatened, the inmates dispersed to their several homes or employments, until nightfall again approached. (Ref. 298, Vol. 2, pp. 12–13.)

One interesting feature of the settlement of the West is the part played by various communistic or cooperative colonies. There have been many of these, and all have used the village pattern in the establishment of their settlements. The Shakers, New Harmony, the Amana colony, the "Little

Landers," Bishop Hill, New Llano—wherever one of these "social experiments" has been tried, the village mode of settlement has been used.

Greatly influenced by these communistic and socialistic attempts, especially those of Owen, and also strongly motivated by the ideal of founding in America the New Jerusalem, were the Latter-Day Saints, or Mormons, under the leadership of Joseph Smith. In Ohio, Missouri, Illinois, and later on in the Great Basin, settlements were established by this group according to the village pattern. Today, in Utah, Idaho, Arizona, Wyoming, Montana, Colorado, New Mexico, Nevada, Montana, and in Alberta, Canada, and Chihuahua, Mexico, are to be found village communities in which several hundred thousand of these people live. For many years, the origin of this particular variety of the village community was attributed to borrowing from New England or to the need for protection. Actually this settlement form is a cultural complex whose origins are to be found in the communistic "United Order" doctrines of Mormonism and the repeated efforts of the Latter-Day Saints to build the New Jerusalem on this continent. (cf. Ref. 308.)

With the penetration of Spanish culture into what is now the United States, another variety of village settlement came into this country. This element has been especially important in the Southwest. Many present cities, such as Los Angeles, San Jose, and San Francisco in California, and El Paso and San Antonio in Texas, were established according to the village pattern of settlement either as missions or as colonial municipalities. In much of Texas, New Mexico, Arizona, California, and in southern Colorado, the village pattern thus introduced continues to exert an important influence upon the behavior of the rural inhabitants of the region. In fact, life in these village settlements in the southwestern United States still bears strong resemblances to that in similar settlements in Mexico, Peru, and some of the other Spanish American countries (Figs. 16, 17).

Finally, before leaving the examples of village settlements, we should mention two recent developments impelling toward compact settlements for farming people. One of these is the rise of "suitcase farming" in the Great Plains. A person living in a city such as Denver may go, for a few weeks during the planting season, to eastern Colorado or western Kansas, and, with the use of a tractor and other equipment, prepare the soil and plant a crop. Then he will return to his home in the city until the harvest season, when another short visit to the fields is sufficient to gather the grain. The use of tractors and combines may make these visits extremely brief. The net result is town or city residences for many persons engaged in agricutural production. A similar phenomenon is to be observed in western fruit-growing sections. With the assistance of the automobile, many owners of

FIGURE 16. Portion of the village nucleus—village type of settlement, Peru.

FIGURE 17. Village type of settlement—village center and surrounding terraced fields in Peru.

orchards are enabled to live in a town or city and commute to and from the orchards when necessary. These developments, particularly important at the present time in the western states, may eventually come to have an important bearing on the settlement patterns of the United States. Already there are substantial areas in the nation in which significant proportions of the farm operators do not live on the land.

The Line Village

Line villages are known throughout the world, although they are far less common than are nucleated villages as a means of arranging the rural population on the land. Their origins seem to lie in peculiar geographic features that combine with cultural needs and practices in such a way as to place a premium upon river frontages, alluvial fans at the foot of sharp escarpments, intervals along beds of streams that flow through narrow mountain valleys, "dry points" along ancient dunes and levees of a marshy region, and so on.

For the most part the line-village form of settlement in the United States is the result of French cultural influences. From early times, the line village has been an important settlement form in France. Well established by the ninth century was the practice of dividing land into rectangles 30 rods wide by 720 rods long, known as the *mansus regalis*. This division was widely associated with line villages in the Frankish realm. The diffusion of this pattern seems to have followed the fortunes of the Carolingians (751–987). Soon it was known and used in Holland, where both marsh and moor *Hufen* were surveyed in this manner, and where the practice was also adopted in forest settlements, or *Waldhufen*. Dutch migrants seem to have carried the pattern to Germany, where it was widely used in the colonization of Weser, Holstein, Mecklenberg, and Brandenberg. Later, it played a most important role in the spread of German cultural influences to the East.

French colonists also brought the pattern to America, where it was widely used in Canada and in Louisiana. The line-village form of settlement was used in the other French settlements throughout the New World also. At Old Kaskaskia, Prairie du Rocher, Cahokia, and Prairie du Chien on the Upper Mississippi; in and about St. Louis, Fort Chartres, St. Genevieve, and St. Charles, Missouri; Vincennes, Indiana; Green Bay, Wisconsin; and Detroit, Michigan, are still to be found traces of the old French line villages and riverfront land division in the land system.

Line villages in the United States, however, have not been due entirely to French influences. Grouped settlements approximating the line village have appeared in several parts of the United States quite independent of

French cultural contacts. For example, Dwight, (Ref. 109, Vol. 4, p. 26) in his travels through New York, passed through several villages that comprised "long continued lines of farm houses, distant from each other an eighth, a fourth, a half, and sometimes three-quarters of a mile." Even in Connecticut and elsewhere he found line-village settlements, as did other writers. The unequal desirability of the lands located in the intervals along the rivers, and on the terraces above them may have played a part in giving rise to this form of settlement in New England. In general, these villages were established in the years following 1713, when land speculators obtained large tracts and offered inducements to the first settlers to establish residence on their holdings. The proprietors usually laid out the townships beforehand into long, narrow strips from 30 to 120 acres in size, and the resulting settlements were necessarily of a line-village type. In North Carolina, 10 families of Moravians who moved from New England and located in Wachovia laid out their farms of 200 acres each so as to form a line village. In South Carolina, in the Marion District, the settlers built their homes immediately on the river in close proximity to one another for convenience of transportation, social interaction, and better protection.

Single Farmsteads

The typical settlement in the United States is composed of isolated farmsteads. The dispersed form of settlement is more important here than in any other country, although it also occurs widely in Brazil and some other areas. Probably because of its significance in the United States, there is a tendency among American scholars to regard this pattern as the most advanced, and as one that has developed through a series of stages from other less progressive modes of settlement. Scattered farmsteads are an old phenomenon, however, and ethnocentric attitudes are not sufficient to make them an excusively North American condition.

Scattered farmsteads have existed in America from early times. In and about Boston, for example, many of the "old planters" did not live within the limits of the village settlements later established, and were not always on friendly terms with the residents of the Massachusetts villages. In spite of strong pressure from the religious community, centrifugal forces were always operating to bring about dispersion of homes. The operation of some of these forces at Watertown is reported as early as 1631 (Ref. 208, pp. 63–64), where there were "pleasant Springs, and small Rivulets running like veins throughout her Body, which hath caused her inhabitants to scatter in such a manner, that their Sabbath-Assemblies prove very thin if the season favour not. . . ."

After 1713, when the General Court had ceased to guide settlement and the establishment of new communities was in the hands of land speculators, the line village came into use; but it was a transitional form, and, during the last part of the colonial period, new settlements were definitely of the scattered-farmsteads type. In the report of his travels through the western and northern portions of New England, Dwight repeatedly mentioned the scattered nature of the settlements and commented (Ref. 109, Vol. 4, p. 3) upon the "usual inconveniences, both moral and physical, of such settlements."

In New York, despite the efforts of the authorities to the contrary, the isolated-farm pattern of settlement prevailed, both on the manors and in the areas of small holdings. At the time of Dwight's visits, only scattered farmsteads were to be observed. Moreover, throughout all the back settlements from Maine to Georgia, scattered farmsteads became the prevailing mode of settlement and, with the exceptions noted in the discussion of village and line-village settlements, came to blanket all the United States. In fact, probably no development in American agriculture has been more significant than the transition from the early pattern of village settlement to the typical American isolated farm of the present day. Had America been covered with village communities of the pattern established in the original colonies and preserved in full force for generations, the cultural landscape of the nation would be very different, the characteristics and problems of the farming communities quite unlike those that we know. One can search hundreds of historical treatises and documents, however, without finding any real attempt to answer questions as to why and how this transition occurred.

In the preceding pages, it has been shown that village settlements were the established modes of locating on the land in early New England, in Pennsylvania and the other Middle Colonies, and in the first settlements of Virginia, South Carolina, and Georgia, and that the ante-bellum plantations throughout the richer portions of the South were arranged in this manner. The English form of settlement was envied by the Dutch in New York, who attempted to copy it. As late as 1820, its virtues in New England were highly extolled by the president of Yale University. In some parts of New England it persists to this day. Why was this pattern of settlement abandoned in favor of single farmsteads as the tide of settlement left the seaboard and forged its way to the Pacific? Did not the village settlement pattern have every advantage and stand every chance of blanketing rural America?

Old cultural forms persist unless great disturbing forces intervene. Consider the factors asserted to be responsible for the variations in settlement types: Was the physical environment responsible? What was there in the physical environment of western and upper New England and the western portions of the other colonies that caused the village to give way to single farmsteads in those areas? The need for protection is frequently cited as a factor making for compact village settlements. Why, then, did the colonists who settled among the peaceful and even helpful Indians of New England use the village pattern, while their descendants and the later immigrants resorted to the single farmstead when they moved among the savage Iroquois and later the Sioux? What about the soils? The isolated-farm type of settlement that came into being in the back portions of the original colonies spread from the Atlantic to the Pacific and came to be the method of settling on soils of almost every conceivable type. Can the availability of water, wood, pasture, and so on adequately explain why village settlements gave way to scattered farmsteads, and why, with few exceptions, these were allowed to prevail throughout the United States?

An explanation of the transition from the village form of settlement to one based on single farmsteads must necessarily be very tentative. Nevertheless, some of the conditions that were associated with the process may be enumerated. First was the difficulty of caring for livestock in the village. For example, Bradford's first complaints about the dispersion of homesteads during the early days of Plymouth specify the cause as the increase of the livestock. Second was the decrease of religious homogeneity and solidarity which originally had helped to keep the settlers together in villages and in close proximity to their churches. Third was the shift from governmental to proprietorial responsibility for organizing new settlements. The governmental authorities had proceeded on the principle of intensive settlement— one township or group of townships being granted at a time, with settlement well under way before "swarming" to new clusters was permitted. When governmental traffic in lands was replaced by private speculation, which often attained wild and unrealistic dimensions, no such control was exerted, the scattered-farmsteads pattern found free reign, and group settlement declined. Fourth was the creation in the new frontier environment of a personality type not afraid of the wilderness and equipped to cope with its hardships. Fifth was the practice of "squatting" on unoccupied land, especially that which was abundant in the West. Clearly, the only way in which a man could hope to hold the land which he had claimed extralegally was to establish himself and his family directly upon it—a condition which almost inevitably resulted in the scattered-farmsteads pattern of settlement. Sixth, and finally, was the establishment of isolated farms as a type of defense measure. That is, those entrenched in power in the older settlements near the eastern coast offered lands to newcomers on the condition of actual settlement and habitation for 10 months out of the year, in order to erect a barrier between themselves and the Indians.

PATTERNS NOT YET DETERMINED

In some large parts of the world, such as the great heart of South America, the settlement pattern is yet to be established. In these places, small numbers of squatters, nomads, or others of a temporary kind may be found, but they have not yet produced stable settlements or clearly identifiable settlement patterns. In part, these are public lands that have never been alienated; in part, they are great private holdings, or latifundia, that remain almost totally unconquered and unused. Which of the settlement patterns actually will be employed when these lands are occupied remains to be seen, but the basic fact is that they present the opportunity for rational and deliberate settlement. It is relatively difficult, though not impossible, to change a pattern once it has been institutionalized and used for generations; it should be far easier to plan carefully and economically for settlement of unpatented or uninhabited lands. As mentioned above, probably the most efficient form that might be used is some variation of the line village, which combines the advantages of residence on the farm land with those that arise from grouped settlement.

However, in great areas where the problems of health and sanitation are the determining factors in the success of new settlements, the village arrangement may be preferable. During at least the early years of a new colony, the herculean tasks of protecting the colonists from the attacks after nightfall of plagues of fever-bearing mosquitoes and of safeguarding supplies of water for domestic purposes are greatly reduced if the dwellings are grouped compactly into villages or hamlets. Especially in connection with projects for the settlement of the Great Amazon Basin, the village pattern of settlement should be given the most careful consideration.

Additional Readings

1. DYER, WILLIAM G., "Development of a Mormon Line Community," *Rural Sociology*, Vol. 21, No. 2 (June, 1956), pp. 181–182.

2. FALS-BORDA, ORLANDO, "Fragmentation of Holdings in Boyacá, Colombia," *Rural Sociology*, Vol. 21, No. 2 (June, 1956), pp. 158–163.

3. NELSON, LOWRY, *The Mormon Village: A Pattern and Technique of Land Settlement*, Salt Lake City: University of Utah Press, 1952.

4. NELSON, LOWRY, *Rural Sociology* (second ed.), New York: American Book Company, 1955, chapter 4.

5. SLOCUM, WALTER L., *Agricultural Sociology*, New York: Harper & Brothers, 1962, chapters 6 and 7.

6. SMITH, T. LYNN, *Brazil: People and Institutions* (third ed.), Baton Rouge: Louisiana State University Press, 1963, chapters XI and XVI.

7. SMITH, T. LYNN, *Colombia: Social Structure and the Process of Development*, Gainesville: University of Florida Press, 1967, chapter 7.

8. SMITH, T. LYNN, "Fragmentation of Agricultural Holdings in Spain," *Rural Sociology*, Vol. 24, No. 2 (June, 1959), pp. 140–149.

9. SOROKIN, PITIRIM A., CARLE C. ZIMMERMAN, and CHARLES J. GALPIN, *A Systematic Source Book in Rural Sociology*, Minneapolis: University of Minnesota Press, 1930, Vol. I, chapter V.

10. TAYLOR, LEE, *Rural-Urban Problems*, Belmont, Calif.: Dickenson Publishing Company, Inc., 1968, chapter 5.

11. TAYLOR, LEE, and ARTHUR R. JONES, JR., *Rural Life and Urbanized Society*, New York: Oxford University Press, 1964, chapter 8.

6
LAND DIVISION, LAND SURVEYS, and LAND TITLES

Wherever the institution of private property in land prevails, the ways of making the physical divisions of the land among the proprietors, surveying the boundaries that separate the holdings of one owner from those of another, and the ways of preparing and recording titles or deeds are among the most important of the institutions that govern the relations of man to the land. The three are so intimately interlinked that they must almost be thought of as comprising one single feature of the land system.

THE SOCIAL SIGNIFICANCE OF LAND DIVISION

The manner in which lands are divided is one of the most all-pervasive determinants in rural life. Stable farm life is made easier when the boundaries of the holdings are easily determined, well known, and subject to a minimum of litigation. At all times, systems of surveying farm lands and of recording the titles to these lands are of great social significance to the individual farm family. In case of legal question, surveying and recording frequently have been of overwhelming importance. Whenever a society has adopted both agricultural life and the trait of private property in land, the manner in which the lands are divided among the population has become of paramount importance.

Geographers have demonstrated very clearly the effects of the division of land upon the cultural landscape, but it should be insisted that the importance of land division is much greater in the social than in the geographic sphere.

Almost every aspect of the social system is affected by the mode of land division used. Consider the effect upon communication and transportation: Roads, highways, utility lines, fences, hedges, and terraces are a few of the devices whose location and direction are affected by the manner in which the lands are subdivided. Or again, consider the effects upon the legal aspects of agriculture and rural life: Only a definite, determinate, and permanent system of surveying makes possible a simple, accurate, and efficient recording of titles, easy transfer of property rights, and quick and certain resurveys of disputed boundaries. In these and many other ways a determinate mode of dividing lands makes for harmonious personal relationships and contributes to the smooth, efficient operation of private and governmental controls.

Endless unproductive and destructive litigation accompanies the lack of such a system. For example, the original North American colonies were without an orderly pattern of land division. Europe passed on a haphazard form of land division that had come down from earliest times; although in some respects it had been sufficient for the static types of social organization of early Europe. Through the centuries, the metes and bounds of these indeterminate and indefinite systems had become crystallized in the minds of the peasants; so invariable were conditions that only occasional quarrels over the removal of landmarks troubled the small village communities. Most of the early American settlements were subject to some regulation as to locations, but this was lacking in system and regularity. In the westward surge of settlement, however, especially in the illegal squatting on unoccupied lands and particularly in the settlement of the trans-Appalachian counties, all semblance of order disappeared. Throughout the Appalachian valleys and westward to the 1785 fringe of settlement, haphazard surveys and freedom of location resulted in great confusion, ceaseless litigation, and finally in thousands of devastated hopes.

The adoption in 1785 of the checkerboard system of land surveys overcame most of the difficulties due to faulty surveying and recording, and introduced a system almost perfect for these purposes. But the checkerboard pattern of surveys, adopted to facilitate the ready sale of public land, brought about other social consequences hardly of less importance. Today the typical American farm family is greatly isolated from its neighbors, forced to pay high taxes to obtain such modern necessities as roads and public utilities, and barred from many social contacts with other families and with social institutions, all because the checkerboard pattern of surveys, coupled with scattered settlement, has proved to be socially and economically shortsighted and inefficient.

In broad areas of the world, systems of surveying and giving title to the land remain faulty, if, in fact, they may correctly be thought of as being "systematic" at all. For example, Brazil and Colombia, in which the situation is representative of that in much of Latin America and even in "developing" nations in many other places, are plagued by very expensive and inefficient ways of surveying, dividing, and deeding the land. These two countries inherited their methods from their respective Portuguese and Spanish antecedents; at many points, the two countries have never been able to improve upon them. In recent years, however, Brazil has developed highly rational methods of allocating lands that never before have been deeded and of subdividing large landed estates. Colombia has taken some steps in this direction, but there the practice of settlement of people on scattered farmsteads creates problems similar to those produced in the United States and parts of Canada when the checkerboard system of surveys was introduced. In most parts of the world, though, the village pattern of settlement is prevalent; the type and degree of social interaction and community and neighborhood organization are virtually unaffected when this superior system of surveying is used. In any case, most countries that undertake to improve their systems of land division face the twofold task of instituting a suitable new system for allocating unused lands or subdividing large holdings and undoing the debilitating effects of an existing system usually inherited from the Old World.

TYPES OF LAND DIVISION

Man's ingenuity has created numerous modes of dividing the lands among the population. For convenience they may be grouped into three principal types: (1) metes and bounds using impermanent objects as markers; (2) riverfront systems wherein the point of departure is relatively stable; and (3) rectangular patterns founded upon astronomical observations. In addition, several other varieties of land division may be placed together in a miscellaneous category.

Metes and Bounds

Men have not always sensed the importance of system when they have settled on land and divided it among the respective families. In most instances, even in modern times, practically no orderly system has been followed. This has been especially the case in virgin areas, where the supply of land seemed inexhaustible and men came to think they were entitled to plenty of good land whenever they wanted it. For this reason, the history of the United States is filled with instances of almost complete freedom of location. Thousands of individuals and communities have seated themselves upon lands, established claims, and outlined boundaries without making the slightest pretense to system or order.

In North America, before the American Revolution, each colony disposed of lands in its own way. The southern colonies particularly, where individual settlement was the rule, allowed almost complete freedom of location. The settler was permitted to establish his land warrants upon any unappropriated soil. The surveys were supposed to be made by public surveyors, but many of these men were inexperienced, and there were countless opportunities for error. Furthermore, records were poorly kept. Individual initiative played an important role. Anyone could select unappropriated land and have the county surveyor lay it off under his own direction. He was not required to consider the situation of other properties or their relation to his own. This indeterminate nature of the system produced great overlapping and endless litigation and allowed some men to obtain monopolies of the best lands.

New England gradually evolved a system of surveying townships, many of which were 6 miles square; but even there, where the village pattern of settlement was general, many communities established the limits of their claims through a system of metes and bounds. However, group settlement reduced the irregularity within the community, made for compactness, and placed the responsibility for accurate surveys upon the entire community.

Irregularity of holdings, indefiniteness of boundaries, and confusion of land titles probably reached their maximum in the trans-Appalachian settlements. Among the pioneers, no one was more adept at squatting on unoccupied government or private land than were the German and Scotch-Irish immigrants who settled the frontiers. The Ulstermen, particularly, settled on any unoccupied land as they pleased and were in constant trouble with the state governments as well as with the Indians. In many of these cases the shape of the tracts claimed has been governed by the objective of securing the most desirable lands. Therefore, such plots were extremely variable in shape, and their boundaries were based upon the positions of indefinite natural objects such as trees, stones, mountains or hills, watercourses, and so on. Such metes and bounds produce the greatest irregularity of holdings, not to mention the fact that they foster clouded titles, misunderstandings and conflict, and untold legal proceedings. The following example is typical of thousands of surveys in the years before 1785:

Surveyed for Ann Garrett, 130 acres of land on part of Military Warrent No. 5901, on Upper Twin Creek, a branch of Paint Creek.

Beginning at two beeches, west corner of Abraham Shepherd's survey No. 4710; thence N. 73° E. 170 poles, crossing the creek to a poplar, east corner to said survey;

thence N. 89° W. 93 poles to two beeches; thence S. 55° W. 40 poles to a sugar tree, hornbeam, and white oak; thence West 110 poles, crossing the creek at 95 poles to two buckeyes and an elm. (Ref. 340, pp. 22–23.)

Figure 18 is a map of a rather typical farm surveyed according to metes and bounds.

Persons whose lands adjoined usually selected the division lines between their holdings long before any surveys were actually made. Tops of ridges and watercourses were most often relied upon as guides, and buildings generally were placed in low-lying areas so that produce, firewood and timbers, animals, and other farm products might move downhill to the house. As a consequence of such practices holdings often were extremely irregular, entirely unrelated to each other, and part of no system. Frequently —in Kentucky, for example—the entries that were made in the land office were so vague and inaccurate that later settlers were unable to determine the location and extent of the patented lands, and overlapping or "shingle" titles resulted. Once established, such confusion and the resultant legal contests can be eliminated only with the greatest difficulty.

Inaccuracies introduced by the use of poor instruments, by careless sur-

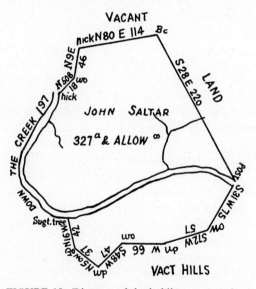

FIGURE 18. Diagram of the holdings surveyed to John Salter on May 22, 1776, and returned to the surveyor-general of Pennsylvania, showing the usual manner of marking the limits of a patent. After Ref. 99, p. 472.

veyors, and by the presence of tremendous natural handicaps tended to make the situation even more confusing. Moreover, in many places, poor records of the grants were kept; various early practices allowed such things as shifts of registered titles to new lands if those originally claimed were found to belong to someone else. In many such cases, of course, the land was claimed, but the appropriate changes in title certificates never were made.

Metes and bounds and riverfront patterns of location vied with each other in early America. Because of group settlements in New England, which did much to regulate the outline of holdings within the community, surveys in that area exhibited more regularity than did those in the South, where almost complete individual freedom of location prevailed. However, the riverfront pattern played a significant part in the history of southern settlement. Metes and bounds and freedom of arrangement on the land attained their greatest importance in the peopling of the Appalachian valleys and the territories west of the mountains, south of the Ohio, and east of the Mississippi. Throughout much of this area, the shingle titles thus created long disturbed the economic and social development of the settlements.

Indeterminate boundaries resulting from the metes and bounds system also lend themselves well to various types of swindles and rascality. The history of land claims throughout the New World is replete with examples of grantees who set about improving their holdings, only to find themselves dispossessed by prior grant holders after their homes had been built and their farms established. This situation was common in California, for example, where the vague Spanish grants, delineated by natural boundaries, often were taken away from one grantee by another who had a prior claim. Perhaps the most famous case was that of Daniel Boone who, as an elderly man, was dispossessed of the homestead that he had established in Kentucky and forced to make a belated new start in the West.

The defects that stem from metes bounds systems continue to plague many of the world's "developing" nations. They result from the fact that land surveys executed by this method are indefinite, indeterminate, and impermanent, and the titles that are registered as a result are unreliable. It could not be otherwise when the boundaries of landholdings depend upon references that can shift position or disappear entirely, and which, at best, are approximate rather than exact. Riverbeds dry up, and new ones are cut; trees die, and others of the same species come into being near by; rocks and other "permanent" objects are moved or broken up by temperature changes and various endeavors of man; and even mountain ridges, hills, and valley centers are affected by erosion, landslides, and farming practices. In every case, the use of such objects is open to variations in sighting and interpretation by succeeding generations of surveyors, causing once-exact property lines to become vague. The situation may be complicated even further by defining one landholding merely by stating that it adjoins another, with the absurd result that each is described by the boundary of the other. Finally, in some parts of the New World the effect of metes and bounds is compounded by the fact that while some of the boundaries may have been vaguely described, often others were not indicated.

The use of metes and bounds has produced many intensely critical contemporary problems. In fact, the uses to which land is now put make exactitude far more necessary than did many early ones. Intensive farming and the high value of a great deal of agricultural property demand proper systems of land division to a far greater degree than do extensive farming, various types of communal efforts to use the soil, or pasturing. The booming interest in mineral rights and the very large amounts of money involved in exploitation of oil and other resources call for precision in dividing land and assigning titles. The high premium which may be placed on a few yards of land in or near a thriving metropolis tolerates none of the indeterminate placement of property lines that arises when metes and bounds are used. However, the fact that most civil court cases in many countries involve land disputes is evidence that the debilitating legacy of the early indeterminate systems of land division is very much part of the modern scene.

Riverfront Patterns

In many parts of the world the riverfront, the seacoast, or the lakeshore has served as a basis for systems of land surveys. Such a practice makes surveys and titles significantly more definite and determinate than do metes and bounds. In West Florida, during the period of English domination, for example, it is reported that the governor was instructed to grant each settler proportional parts of the most desirable and the least desirable land, to limit the breadth of the holding to one third of its length, and to see that the length extended not along the banks of any stream, but inland from the waterway. This second system may well be styled the *riverfront pattern*.

Many former colonial parts of the world were settled while water routes were all-important for purposes of transportation and communication. In those early days, streams were an aid to social interaction rather than a factor contributing to social isolation. In the southern colonies of the present United States, and throughout Central and South America, locations on the banks of navigable streams were valued highly. As late as the end of the seventeenth century, practically all land grants in Virginia were situated upon the larger rivers. In laying off the estates, the surveyors adopted the bank of the stream as a base and ran their lines at right angles to the river for a distance of one mile. Patents were arranged side by side in the same manner so that the holdings made up a series of parallelograms fronting on the river and extending into the interior for the necessary distance. This arrangement brought considerable regularity and system into the distribution of lands, and from the standpoint of surveying and recording of titles it represented a marked improvement over the use of metes and bounds.

Even with the river front as a base, many irregularities appeared. Some of these were, of course, introduced by the meanderings of the streams. Others resulted from the inaccuracy of instruments. Useless acreages were often left out of account entirely. Not uncommonly, side lines were lengthened or shortened to correspond to natural phenomena. Finally, the difficulties of surveying and general carelessness added much to the irregularity of the pattern.

In New England, which attained the greatest regularity of landholdings, many surveys were made largely according to the riverfront pattern; but this system owes its greatest development in America to the French, and, for this reason, it was most prevalent in areas settled by them. Riverfronts were highly valued, and a frontage of 5 arpents (roughly 950 feet) commonly accompanied a depth of 40, making holdings eight times as long as they were wide. In both Canada and Louisiana, this riverfront type was used as a basic system of surveys; and this pattern, established so early, persists to affect the social activities of the present-day population. The French left an indelible stamp upon the American land system at every place they settled in the great West: at Detroit; on Green Bay; around Vincennes, Indiana; in the neighborhood of Kaskaskia, Illinois; in and about St. Louis, Missouri; and elsewhere. (See Fig. 19 for an example of French riverfront surveys).

Although most of those who settled the New World were little concerned with the system of surveys, the selection of the riverfront as a base did much to bring order and system into the manner of dividing lands among the settlers. Freedom of location under such a system was considerably restricted, holdings were much more determinate, and, on the whole, boundaries were much more permanent. It is true, to be sure, that the course of a river is not fixed in the sense that the position of a star is stable. Sudden changes in the courses of rivers have disorganized land titles and caused endless litigation. Most rivers are gradually changing their courses; this deviation has sometimes been a fruitful source of confusion. On the whole, however, the adoption of a river as the base of departure for surveys is vastly superior to the selection of trees, which may soon disappear; stones, which may be moved; or even divides, which may be difficult to locate exactly. When

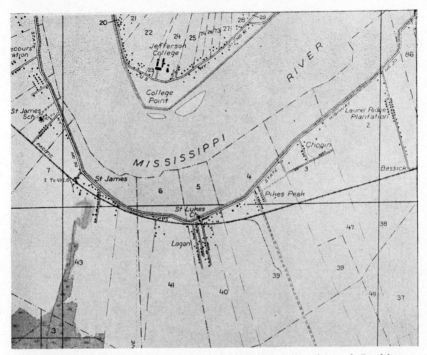

FIGURE 19. Map of a selected area on the Mississippi river in south Louisiana. Note the outlines of the French concessions granted according to a riverfront system of dividing lands, and the official rectangular system that has been superimposed. Observe how changes in the bed of the river have disrupted the old surveys. The arrangement of homes on the sugar-cane plantations, in the "lanes," and in line villages may also be seen.

watercourses become the determining factor in land surveys, as they did in many of the colonies, it represents a decided advance over the indeterminate system of metes and bounds.

The riverfront pattern of land surveys has been perfected in the small farming areas of south Brazil. The system in general use in these prosperous rural communities permits the farmer to live on his land without sacrificing the social and economic advantages of being near to neighbors; at the same time, the farms and roads are laid out in a manner that is best adapted to the topography of the area. This system is a modified version of that so characteristic of French settlements throughout the world (Fig. 20). In the earlier Brazilian colonies, such as the settlement of Germans at Blumenau in Santa Catarina, the river was taken as the base of the surveys; roads were cut to follow the streams; and holdings rectangular in shape, except for the

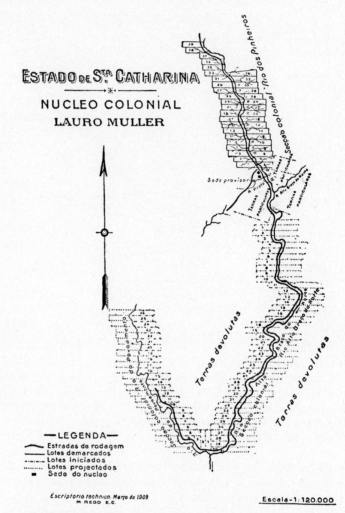

FIGURE 20. System of land division used in the early Brazilian colonization projects. Reproduced from *Relatorio, Servio de Povomento em 1908*, Rio de Janeiro: Imprensa Nacional, 1909, p. 123.

end fronting on the water, were laid off. Most of the plots were 110 meters wide and 1,100 meters deep. In other colonies, the dimensions of the allotments varied, but the principle of slight width in comparison with the depth of the farm was always followed.

From the very first, the system of land division used in these colonial sections of Brazil possessed one distinct advantage over comparable systems in France, Canada, and the United States. Meanders in the streams did not lead to the use of nonparallel lines for bounding the sides of the holdings, so that the width of the holding was uniform throughout its length. In the early Brazilian colonies, the rear boundaries of the contiguous concessions made up a jagged line which created serious problems in the settlement of the lands back from the rivers and also prevented the fullest adaptation of settlement patterns to topographical features. More experience in allocating lands brought improved practices, and at present, the systems used in dividing the land produce boundaries which are reasonably definite, determinate, and permanent. New lands are carefully surveyed, and streams and ridges are identified and mapped. Long, narrow landholdings then are laid out, with a watercourse as one of the end boundaries and a natural divide or a road as the other. The system adapts well to natural features; each farmer has waterfront, bottom land, and hillside, but none is able to obtain a monopoly on the best lands, leaving the poorest for later arrivals. The logical form of settlement under these conditions is, of course, the line village, complete with its social and economic advantages.

A variation of the riverfront type of land division is the one that lacks a watercourse but uses a road as a boundary. This method is not as desirable as that which depends upon immovable celestial points of orientation, for even roads may be destroyed and relocated, but it is a great improvement over the system of metes and bounds. In some respects it is superior even to the riverfront system, for the relocation of a road is a deliberate action, and any variations that may result are more capable of precise measurement and registration. Road-based boundaries may change, but usually not in the same gradual, capricious manner whereby a river meanders and shifts its bed. When roads are used in this way, the line village is effective as the principal form of settlement.

Rectangular Systems

For purposes of surveying and recording, the ultimate in simplicity of land division is attained when all survey lines run parallel or at right angles to one another and the lands are divided into uniform rectangles. The surveys are most determinate and the divisions most permanent when they are based upon astronomical observations and are independent of surface references. The official land system of the United States, called for convenience the "checkerboard pattern," meets these conditions exceedingly well. From the standpoint of surveying and recording, it represents the acme of simplicity, determinateness, and permanency, and no more adequate mode of land division has been devised. It provides definite bounds, free from overlapping claims; insures against loss of landmarks, since each point may be redetermined with great accuracy; and, of great importance, it renders possible the simplest and most effective kind of deed.

The background of the rectangular system of the United States is fairly well known. It came into existence at the birth of the public domain, when the states ceded their western lands to the United States. The system is largely the work of Thomas Jefferson. The bill that created this pattern of land surveys was reported from a Congressional committee (Jefferson, chairman) on May 7, 1784. As first drawn, the bill provided that lands should be divided into townships 10 miles square and subdivided into 100 sections of 640 acres each. It was debated; amended at the insistence of the New Englanders, to make the townships 6 miles square, or 23,040 acres, with 36 sections of 640 acres each; and passed on May 20, 1785. An important provision of the new law forbade the sale of unsurveyed public lands. The first surveys made according to the new national system were in the territory northwest of the Ohio River in the range of townships in the state of Ohio that adjoin the state of Pennsylvania.

The American checkerboard system of land surveys uses the principal meridians as the bases of the divisions. Starting from these measurements of longitude and latitude, the lands are first surveyed into rectangular townships, one block of which, extending north and south, is called a "range." Then the townships are subdivided into the sections which make up the smallest unit whose outer boundaries are required by law to be surveyed. However, the law created imaginary lines which formed four squares, or quarter sections, of 160 acres each. Each of these was in turn broken down into four squares of 40 acres per square. Any surveyor in the various states and territories, assisted by the field notes from the original survey, could lay out the definite lines of a subdivision if they were required. Moreover, this process could be repeated an endless number of times on the same land without shifts in boundaries taking place as a result, should resurveys become necessary. Figure 21 shows a typical section of such checkerboard surveys.

As mentioned before, the ordinance of 1785 required that public lands be surveyed according to the checkerboard pattern before they could be patented. Accordingly, this pattern of survey has been used in all parts of the United States settled after that date, except those later territorial acquisitions where lands had previously been laid off in some other manner by the Spanish, the French, and others. With minor exceptions, the system has been spread over the entire states of Ohio, Indiana, Illinois, Michigan, Alabama, Mississippi, Arkansas, Missouri, Iowa, Wisconsin, Minnesota,

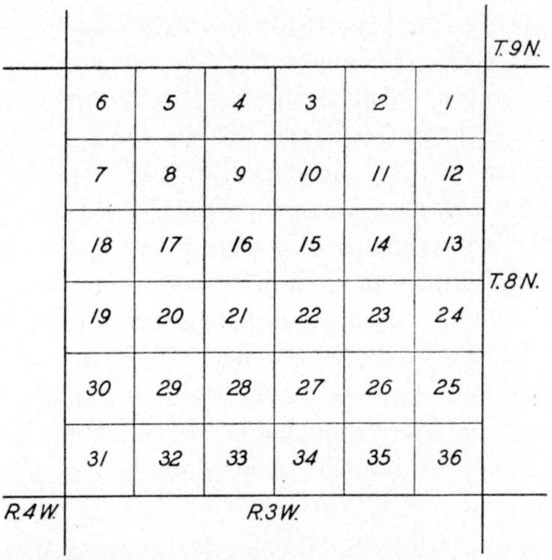

6	5	4	3	2	1
7	8	9	10	11	12
18	17	16	15	14	13
19	20	21	22	23	24
30	29	28	27	26	25
31	32	33	34	35	36

FIGURE 21. The official checkerboard pattern of land division in the United States. Note the arrangement of the 36 sections in the township.

North Dakota, South Dakota, Nebraska, Kansas, Oklahoma, Colorado, Wyoming, Montana, Idaho, Utah, Arizona, Nevada, Washington, and Oregon. It has also been used in parts of California, New Mexico, Texas, Louisiana, and Florida. The areas embraced in these 30 states constitute the great bulk of the land in the nation, every variety of climate, temperature, and rainfall, and topographic variations from the swamp and plain to the most rugged mountain ranges on the continent.

The influences of the American system of land surveys have not been confined to the United States. The land system of Canada was patterned upon that of the United States, but contains some slight modifications. In a few parts of Japan, American agricultural experts were responsible for the introduction of a miniature checkerboard pattern of surveys. Colombia, Brazil, and certain other Latin American countries have made some use of a rectangular system similar to that of the United States. In total, however, much of the land division which has occurred throughout the world has not had the advantage of this system or of any of its better variations, and as a result, vast acreages are not clearly laid out, accurately described, or dependably registered and titled.

Miscellaneous Forms

In addition to the three types of land division discussed in the preceding pages, there are several other varieties deserving of mention. The first

147

of these is probably purely theoretical. It was proposed some years ago by Dr. E. Deville as a way of modifying the rectangular system used in Canada so as to permit farm homes to be grouped together in small hamlets without sacrificing residence on the land (Fig. 22). According to this plan, 12 farms of 160 acres each would constitute one hexagonal township. The idea involved in this proposal, with its wedgelike farms, is not too different from that used in laying out some of the new Jewish colonies in Israel, in which farm homes and other buildings are located on a circular road, with farm lands radiating away from the road. Within the circle formed by the road and the line village are the various services, agencies, and institutions required by the members of the community. The resultant locality group enjoys not only the advantages of having farm families live on their land, but also ease of social contact and economy of operation.

The circular mode of dividing the land employed in Cuba during the colonial period was unique. Apparently, each cattle rancher was allowed to describe his grant as the land lying within a certain radius of his headquarters (Fig. 23). Today, hundreds of these old boundaries still survive,

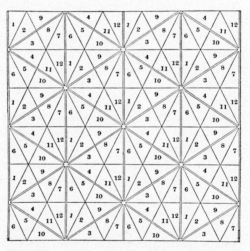

FIGURE 22. Diagram of a hexagonal system of laying out a township with twelve farms, of 160 acres each, radiating from the center. From a design by Dr. E. Deville, in Thomas Adams, *Rural Planning and Development,* Ottawa: Commission of Conservation, 1917, facing p. 259.

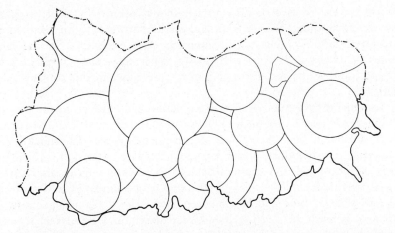

FIGURE 23. Plan of a part of the terminio municipal de Mantua, Cuba, showing circular surveys and other property lines. After a map in the "Atlas" of the *Censo de la Republica de Cuba,* 1943.

although they have since been overlaid by the metes and bounds pattern so commonly employed in Spanish America and have been subject to great modification by the socialistic principles under which Cuba now functions. The obvious problems that these circular *mercedes* produced center on disputed ownership of land where the circles overlap and in the interstitial areas created by this type of land division.

CORRELATIVES OF THE VARIOUS SYSTEMS OF LAND DIVISION

The evolution of land systems throughout the world has employed almost every possibility in the manner of dividing lands among the population. For instance, in America, indeterminate location and haphazard surveys were widely used in the group settlements of New England as well as in the individualistic settlements of the middle and southern colonies. On the frontier, among the trans-Appalachian settlements, indeterminacy ran riot. The riverfront pattern, in various degrees of intensity, or with frontages varying from one fortieth to one third of their depth, has been widely scattered in the United States. In the French and Spanish colonies, especially French Canada, Louisiana, and Texas, this was the prevailing mode of dividing lands. In 1785 a thoroughly determinate rectangular system was adopted and became a national pattern for subdividing public lands.

What are the relative merits and weaknesses of these various systems? How should we judge the efficiency and merit of any system for subdividing agricultural lands? How can weaknesses, once established in the land system, be overcome? And particularly, what immediate steps may be taken to improve the American pattern for use either in this country or in others?

Two general principles relative to equitable and efficient modes of subdividing lands may be set forth. (1) For purposes of surveying and recording, it is essential that the system of surveys be simple, determinate, and permanent. It should be based not upon surface references, which are relatively short-lived and changeable, but upon astronomical observations. It must provide for quick, easy redetermination of boundaries, and above all make possible a short and simple deed. (2) Unless the village form of settlement is used, the social welfare of the agricultural population requires that the holdings be considerably less in width than in length—the principle of the long-lot survey. Only this provision allows the individual families to have close neighbors. Unless landholdings are relatively narrow as compared to their length, it becomes impossible for farmers to avoid having excessive distances between their houses. This circumstance in turn makes prohibitive the cost of securing roads, telephones, electricity, school buses, and many of the other advantages of modern living. The extent to which this long-lot principle is followed determines how close together farmers are allowed to arrange their homes.

Judged by these standards, metes and bounds location has little to recommend it as a system of land division. It fails entirely to meet the first condition, since it makes surveying and recording as difficult as possible, is based upon short-lived references, and generally gives rise to endless quarrels, lawsuits, and social conflict. Such a haphazard system is absolutely unsatisfactory from the standpoint of governmental controls. Usually evolved under conditions where possession is all-important, this system has seldom been associated with any kind of group settlement. Highly individualistic in background, it appears never to have given rise to line villages. By and large, it has been almost as ruthless in isolating farm houses from one another as the checkerboard rectangular system. Indeed, metes and bounds location, after the initial advantage of allowing each person to gerrymander his claim to include any unoccupied land he desires, appears to have only one thing in its favor: It possesses the doubtful advantage of allowing farmers located in hilly districts to arrange their fields and build their homes so that everything "comes downhill to the house."

The riverfront pattern of land division meets our first condition much better than metes and bounds location, but not nearly so well as a rectangular system. In any given case, the amount of uniformity in the riverfront pattern is dependent upon the nature of the river, lakefront, or coast upon which it is based. Of course, the limits of holdings defined on one side by the bank of the stream and running back inland a specified distance are much more fixed and easily determined or resurveyed than those patents whose boundaries are marked with trees, stones, and other perishable and readily movable features of the landscape. To the extent that the shores of the lake or stream remain fixed, the system offers determinateness and permanency. However, it is well known that rivers are constantly cutting away from the bank on the outside of curves and building up sandbars on the inside. In the course of time this makes for confusion. Occasionally a river suddenly changes its course. Where such a stream is the base for land surveys, this shift causes great confusion in the land titles. In all, the riverfront pattern is vastly inferior to rectangular patterns for the purposes of surveying and recording.

It is, however, in relation to the second condition that the riverfront system of land division has its greatest advantage. The conservation of river frontages seems to have been a major determination wherever this pattern has been used. It has usually been specified that holdings may not lie with the long side on the river, and frequently the amount of frontage granted has been relatively small compared to the length of the holding. Out of these conditions has been developed the close association that exists between the riverfront pattern of land division and the line-village form of settlement; the line village makes for ready contact between farm families and economical provision of such modern conveniences as roads, telephones, electricity, and so on. In the colonies of the southern United States, where freedom of location was somewhat limited by regulation of the amount of river frontage that could accompany a given acreage, the relationship between this form of settlement and the manner of dividing lands was in a rudimentary form. Closer was the association in the Spanish settlements such as those of southern Texas. The system reached perfection in the French settlements of Canada and Louisiana and in Lord Selkirk's colonies on the Red River of the North.

The checkerboard rectangular survey that has been used in the land system of the United States is one of the simplest, most determinate, and most permanent ways of dividing lands ever devised. From the standpoint of surveying and recording, it approaches perfection. However, from the standpoint of the social and economic welfare of the population on the land, it creates as many problems as does any other way of dividing lands. Combined with the isolated or scattered-farmsteads type of settlement, the checkerboard system has greatly handicapped the rural population of the

United States for more than century and a half. It produces great physical and social isolation, increases the cost of supplying utilities and other services and of building roads, hinders participation by farm families in various institutions, and multiplies the difficulty of purchasing supplies and marketing crops.

The social inefficiency of the dominant mode of dividing American farm lands is the more to be regretted because it is possible to have a system just as simple, just as determinate, and just as permanent as the checkerboard pattern without setting obstacles in the way of social contacts among the population and making the cost of roads, electricity, and other services prohibitive. Use of rectangles instead of squares would make practicable the formation of line village settlements without detracting at all from the system for surveying and recording purposes. Moreover, this change would provide farm families with the advantages of living on their land and avoid the disadvantages.

For illustrative purposes consider two areas in which 160-acre farms are arranged as in Figures 24 and 25. In the first, farms are uniform quarter sections; in the second, they consist of rectangles 1 mile long and one quarter of a mile wide. In the area using rectangles, 1 mile of road would reach as many homes as would 4 miles in the area divided into squares. Similar saving in lines for electricity and telephones would be attained. In every respect, making the width of holdings only one fourth of their length

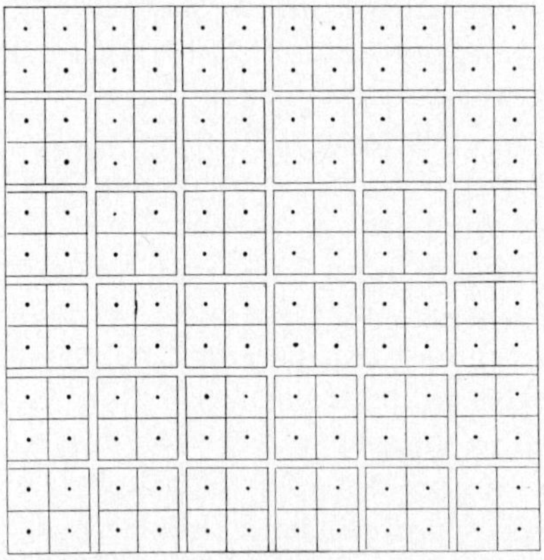

FIGURE 24. A township divided into 144 tracts of 160 acres each, illustrating the extreme dispersion of farm homes resulting from the checkerboard pattern of land division.

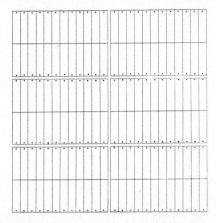

FIGURE 25. A township divided into 144 tracts of 160 acres each, illustrating the grouping of farm homes made possible by a slight revision in the customary pattern of land division.

would contribute to the social and economic welfare of the population. Even from the standpoint of technical agriculture and farm management such a system probably has more advantages than disadvantages.

Some years ago, in connection with his work in South America, T. Lynn Smith proposed a similar system for use in the vast unsettled portions of Colombia and Brazil. This system provides for laying off an entire country into square degrees by projecting all the degrees of latitude and longitude across its territory. Each of the squares formed in this manner is numbered on a base map. The actual survey lines would be run as needed, only a little in advance of actual settlement, so as to avoid resurveys after prolonged nonuse of the land. In the surveys, each square degree would be divided into square sections and lots, as in Figure 26. The lots, including 100 hectares or 247 acres, would frequently be small enough for family-sized farms without further subdivision, but the plan allows for dividing each of them into 25-hectare tracts if it is deemed advisable. To deed a given acreage of land according to this system, it is necessary to indicate only the parcel, lot, section, square, and degree involved.

In the third century B. C. the Egyptians already were using a comparable manner of dividing their lands (Fig. 27). This system, nearly 2,300 years old, has not yet been used to great advantage in vast portions of the modern world and is scarcely even considered in many parts where new land is still available for surveying, division, and settlement.

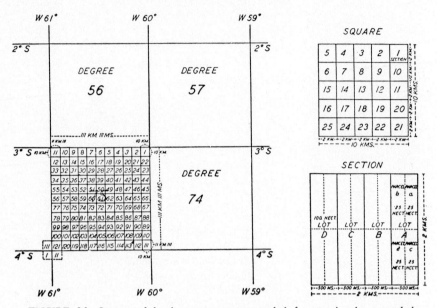

FIGURE 26. System of land surveys recommended for use in the unsettled parts of South America. Reproduced from Ref. 444.

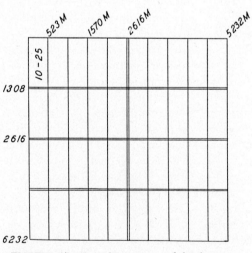

FIGURE 27. Egyptian system of land surveys of the third century B.C. After Ref. 419.

Even in areas where the checkerboard system exists, as it does in most of the United States, the pattern could be changed in a few generations into a "long-lot" system if two principles were followed: (1) regulation of inheritance in such a way that a property received by heirs would conform as much as possible to the long-lot system; and (2) placement of roads and utility lines along every second section line so that deep rectangles rather than squares would be serviced, to encourage farm people to locate their buildings in such a way as to create some form of the line village.

SOME FEATURES OF A SUITABLE SYSTEM OF LAND DIVISION

Some countries contain lands that have not yet been assigned and settled, which presents the opportunity for the development of ideal systems of land division and title registration. Many of them also contain lands now privately owned as large estates, which may revert to public control and become available for colonization and settlement. There the opportunity also is great for use of a rational system of land division embodying simplicity, permanence, and definite and determinate boundaries. Because of these chances to avoid the mistakes of the past, new systems of surveying, dividing, and assigning the lands should meet a number of ideal conditions, all included in a set of enforceable laws which is appropriate for the particular society involved. The system and its various provisions must:

1. Distinguish between land that is available for settlement and that which needs to be reserved by government, either for specific public purposes, such as forest preserves, or for subsequent adjudication.
2. Require the use of existing lines of latitude and longitude in order to make astronomical points of orientation the basis of the survey system.
3. Establish appropriate sizes for the rectangular plots that are to be laid out and for the smaller units into which they will be subdivided.
4. Guarantee that these holdings will be not square but several times longer than wide.
5. Identify various classes of adjudicable land according to potential use, so that no person or group of landholders will be able to obtain monopolies on the best land, leaving the poorest for others.
6. State unequivocally the minimum dimensions of a property which may be held by an individual farm family, and prevent the subsequent fragmentation of that holding into smaller parcels.
7. Provide for the acquisition of additional properties by a landholder only when they are adjacent to his original holding in order to avoid having the total farm composed of noncontiguous pieces.

8. Restrict the number of parcels of land available to any one farm family in order to avoid monopolistic consolidation of holdings or the restoration of large landed estates.

9. Allow the granting of provisional titles to land, but make receipt of an unrestricted title contingent upon certain conditions regarding the use and improvement of the land, erection of buildings and fences, and residence on the land for specified periods of time annually. A clear deed should be obtained after a given number of years, or the property should be forfeited on the assumption that the current holder will not meet the minimum conditions.

10. Prevent illegal squatting on land that has been withheld from settlement for public purposes and on any other to which the individual does not have either a provisional or clear title, and provide for the exclusion of such persons when they do appear.

11. Require examination of existing individual claims which are below minimum size or which are in the public domain in order to impose certain standards for use and improvement and a time limit for annexing sufficient land to meet the minimum size requirements.

12. Provide for the clear and unequivocal identification of land parcels and of original title holders as well as of all subsequent holders who come into being when property is transferred. Extensive mapping is necessary in this situation.

13. Encourage the extension of financial credit to persons who comply with the provisions in order to facilitate improvement of the land and to make adherence to the ideals as attractive as possible.

14. Provide for the nullification of such earlier legal encumbrances on the land as would make a system of this kind impractical.

15. Require roads and utility lines to be established in such a way as to avoid the checkerboard pattern and the scattered-farmsteads settlements which are associated with it.

16. Guarantee the availability of sufficient funds and the appointment of adequate personnel at all levels to ensure the actual implementation of the ideal provisions.

Such a land-division system would be simple, definite, determinate, and permanent. It would avoid the problems of the checkerboard pattern, as well as those engendered by haphazard ways of assigning and settling the land. The system would prevent monopoly of the best lands and of scarce resources located on them, and would in no way force the latecomers or the less affluent to accept nothing but poor tracts. Limitations on total size and the number of parcels available to a given holder are an absolute necessity, as are the requirements which prevent the fragmentation of holdings and the creation of tiny minifundia. Perhaps above all, this system would avoid dependence upon metes and bounds as a system of surveying and dividing the land and should minimize legal entanglements arising from questions of ownership.

Additional Readings

1. BAALI, FUAD, *Relation of the People to the Land in Southern Iraq,* Gainesville: University of Florida Press, 1966, chapter 3.

2. FALS-BORDA, ORLANDO, *Peasant Society in the Colombian Andes,* Gainesville: University of Florida Press, 1955, pp. 68–70.

3. LEONARD, OLEN E., "Land Division and Titles," in Alvin L. Bertrand (ed.), *Rural Sociology,* New York: McGraw-Hill Book Company, 1958, chapter 11.

4. LEONARD, OLEN E., *The Role of the Land Grant in the Social Organization and Social Processes of a Spanish-American Village in New Mexico,* Ann Arbor: Edwards Brothers, Inc., 1948, chapter 5.

5. NELSON, LOWRY, *Rural Cuba,* Minneapolis: University of Minnesota Press, 1950, chapter 6.

6. SMITH, T. LYNN, *Brazil: People and Institutions* (third ed.), Baton Rouge: Louisiana State University Press, 1963, chapter XII.

7. SMITH, T. LYNN, *Colombia: Social Structure and the Process of Development,* Gainesville: University of Florida Press, 1967, chapter 4.

8. SMITH, T. LYNN, "Colonization and Settlement in Colombia," *Rural Sociology,* Vol. 12, No. 2 (June, 1947), pp. 128–139.

7
LAND TENURE

Land tenure refers to the rights that people have in the land, that is, to their legal privileges to use, cultivate, dispose of, and even exploit specified portions of the earth's surface. Tenure is, therefore, a social relationship between human beings and the land; it is reflected in a broad array of social regulations regarding the use of the soil. In turn, tenure is closely associated with other relationships between man and the land, such as the size of agricultural holdings, class and caste systems, planes of existence and aspirations for improvement, changes in status, and systems of agriculture. However, the close tie between tenure and other social relationships does not justify considering them identical.

Practically every society has placed some restrictions upon the use of land. Provisions regulating the use of land and for governing the associations between those who own and control it and those who do not are part of the earliest literature known to mankind. A study of the early law codes reveals that much attention was given to matters relating to the employment of land. One of the earliest codes, and one that served as a pattern for many that followed, is that of Hammurabi, written some four thousand years ago. It was prepared at a time when agriculturists lived within the town walls and went out to cultivate the surrounding areas; its rules concerning several of the social relationships between people and the land are explicit. No less than 17 of its 247 sections pertain to the use of the soil, and of these at least 13 (numbers 42–47, 52, and 60–65) deal with land tenure, defining specifically the accepted relationships of the landlord and the tenant. However, both in the codes and in present laws, observers might complain that the regulations favor the interests of the land-lord as opposed to those of the tenant.

Although the Hebrew culture was nomadic, provisions governing land tenure are of considerable importance in their ancient regulations. Even more important are the statutes regulating land property rights that are found in the law codes of the Hindus, the Chinese, and other ancient peoples. Thus the problems of land tenure are as old as is civilization based upon agriculture.

Land problems are also very pressing in the modern world. After World War I, almost every nation was troubled by problems of land tenure. The "Green Rising" in Europe brought fundamental changes in the land systems of nearly every country of central Europe and the Near East. The cry of "land for the peasants" was one of the most powerful stimuli in the early phases of the Russian Revolution. At this time, Germany and Italy made sweeping changes in their tenure systems; reforms in Spain made up one stage in the development of the Spanish Civil War. Agrarian reform is the core of the recent Mexican Revolution; fundamental changes in the land system are being attempted in Brazil, Chile, Colombia, and other Latin American countries. Programs designed to bring about a wider distribution of landownership in Europe and Asia also are much in evidence. Finally, vast maladjustments in land systems were partly responsible for communist revolutions in China and Cuba, and they form part of the many problems that afflict Vietnam.

The United States has never faced questions of land tenure in the serious manner that has been forced upon other countries. Because of the seemingly inexhaustible supply of good lands, this nation long was able to postpone many fundamental questions of land tenure and the distribution of land property rights. This is not to say that no attention has been given to such problems. The ceding of state lands to the federal government created the bond that did most to bring about a strong union among the original states; the revenue from the sale of these lands paid for the operation of the governmental machinery, and the ready outlet to the West quieted most of the difficulties in the East. Prompted by riots and bloodshed, the new government early evolved a system or lack of it, whereby settlers could get possession of unoccupied lands. Customary procedures for obtaining land without leave eventually came to be thoroughly legalized in the homestead laws. Furthermore, with additional good land available, the question of landgrabbing by the privileged, large grants to railroads, and similar situations did not come in for great consideration, or at least they did not lead to fundamental reforms.

The subject of land tenure involves two basic considerations: (1) the nature of land property rights that exist in a society and the manner in which they have come into being; and (2) the classification of those who participate in the process of agriculture according to tenure. The latter also involves the social statuses of persons in the several tenure classes and their places in the system of social stratification.

SYSTEMS OF PROPERTY RIGHTS AND THEIR EVOLUTION

Many systems of land tenure are functioning in the world at present, but they tend to fall into two major classes: (1) those that have developed in communist countries and are variations of state ownership and control; and (2) those that have come into being in the remainder of the world and vest the rights to the land in individuals under various systems of private ownership and control. The first of these systems at present is relatively inflexible and has demonstrated neither great efficiency in agricultural production nor any important tendency to evolve into other forms. Therefore, although the system demonstrates considerable "staying power" in some countries, it clearly is a variation of the large landed estate, in which ownership and control reside with the state and the mass of the agriculturists are landless laborers. It offers little or nothing as a means of reforming total agricultural systems so as to give farm people effective control over the land that they work and to place each of them in the positions of manager, entrepreneur, and laborer.

In the second system of tenure, that based upon private ownership of land, there are great variations in the ways lands are held, the period for which they are secure, and the types of rights that governments reserve for themselves. The individual's property rights in land may be said to reach their maximum in a system of ownership in *fee simple,* or virtually absolute right to use and dispose of the land. This form is the one toward which most of the world has moved in the several centuries since the decline of feudalism. At the other end of the scale is serfdom, under which the person's only right in the land is the security he obtains because of the fact that he cannot be parted from it. Between the two there are many shades of difference. Furthermore, in addition to tenure rights there is the absence of such rights. A substantial portion of the population of the world, servile and semi-servile agricultural laborers, lacks any property rights whatsoever in the land. In most places where this is the case, land is still held as private property, but by a small landed elite rather than by the great mass of people who gain a livelihood from agriculture. The existence of these large groups of landless workers, comprising perhaps half of the world's total population, is eloquent testimony to the fact that widespread fee-simple ownership neither developed rapidly nor became a universal cultural feature, even in major portions of the Western World. Obviously, the existence of fee-simple ownership is no guarantee that the mass of agricultural people will benefit appreciably from its provisions.

Many systems of property rights have come into being throughout the world, but in all of them, the land originally belonged, in theory, to the political unity possessing sovereignty, whether that sovereignty was manifested in a king, an oligarchy, the citizens of a democracy, or some other entity. The conditions or qualifications imposed in granting lands to subjects or citizens are many. For example, at the time of the discovery of America, the feudal system was still in full practice in England. Under feudalism the king allocated land to his trusted followers in return for specific services, especially those of a military nature. This practice is known as *knight-service*. The knightly lord of the manor, in turn, let out portions of his estate to various serfs and tenants in exchange for services rendered and portions of the crops and livestock produced. Usually the common people were bound to the land, and the services and obligations they owed to the lord were legion and specified in minute detail. Before the attempted colonization of America became successful, a bitter struggle brought about the substitution of *socage* for knight-service. In the former, lands were held by a fixed and determined service not of a military nature and not subject to variation at the will of the sovereign. The charter given by Elizabeth to Sir Walter Raleigh in 1584 granted him and his heirs and assigns the right to dispose of lands in fee simple (i.e., pure inheritance, free of conditions or limits on alienation). This step was a tremendous one toward liberation of landholding.

Although there were many attempts to transfer the feudal system to America, only socage tenure was established, and even this was usually only a form. By the ordinance of 1787, the first general legislation by Congress on the subject of real property, all the leading features of feudalism were specifically repealed. This ordinance made the individual absolutely independent of the state and the sole owner of his land, and abolished any vestige of serfdom. It provided for the establishment of thousands of independent holdings out of the public domain. Thus in the United States it became a fundamental maxim that the state is the source of the title to land. Therefore, all titles, to be valid, must derive from the grants made by or under the authority of England, Sweden, Holland, France, Spain, Russia, Mexico, the colonies, the federal government, or (in some cases) the governments of the several states. All treaties defining boundaries, purchases, and cessions, or relating to territory now in the United States, specifically guard individual property rights in the land. The one right retained by government is that of eminent domain.

In nearly all of Spanish America, too, many of the inhibiting effects of Spain's system of property rights were prevented from doing serious damage. Largely because of the chaotic and restrictive feudalistic tenure forms found in the mother country, the Council of the Indies, which was organized to administer the Spanish possessions in the New World, determined to grant fee-simple titles without debilitating encumbrances. Land had to be used for 4 years before a final, unrestricted title was granted, but this restriction was intended to guarantee development of the holdings, not to attach to the titles conditions for service or payment.

In other parts of the world, the evolution of tenure forms toward fee-simple ownership has been slower and less complete than it was in the United States and most of Spanish America. There have been some changes, to be sure, but even those that occurred in many of the countries of Europe, the heartland of ancient feudalism, have been more difficult and inclined to take place in a fragmentary rather than a sweeping manner. In the Arabic world, and in sub-Sahara Africa, there have been some currents of change making for the emergence of fee-simple forms of land control in preference to other types of restricted tenure, but the changes often have been harsh and even violent, frequently involving a forced transition from tribal tenure to that based upon individual ownership. Even so, in many parts of the globe where the trend is toward fee-simple ownership, this is no guarantee that ownership will be widely or equitably distributed among the people who actually till the soil. In many places, fee-simple ownership has accrued to a handful of landed gentry, forcing the mass of agricultural workers into the statuses of landless tenants and agricultural laborers of various kinds.

TENURE CLASSES

For many purposes it is necessary to classify the agricultural population according to tenure; but the lack of data and the confusion in terminology make such an endeavor on a world-wide basis a very difficult task. Much of the difficulty arises from such problems as semantic inconsistencies when language barriers are crossed, the lack of adequate censuses of agriculture needed to supply basic data, imprecise and unclear definitions of such terms as "renter," "tenant," "farm," and "farmer," and the frequent reluctance of social scientists to undertake this exceedingly complicated and often unrewarding kind of investigation. Perhaps one of the greatest handicaps is the inadequate distinction made between persons who own agricultural land and those who actually participate in one capacity or another in the process of agricultural production. For example, in areas where absentee owners, owner-operators, renters, tenants, and sharecroppers all are grouped into the single category of "operators," that designation becomes worse than meaningless. In places where a "farm" or "agricultural establishment" includes everything from the very tiny subsistence plot used by an agricultural laborer to a vast plantation or an immense "ranch" or "hacienda," developing a reliable and valid classification of the tenure statuses of the agricultural population is virtually impossible. As a result, it often becomes necessary to abandon any thought of using designations and classes that would make it possible to analyze tenure on a world-wide scale, and to use those that are peculiar to one country or a small group of countries.

Farm Operators and Farm Laborers

Despite the many problems associated with dividing agricultural populations into tenure groupings, some such classification must be developed if this important topic is to be analyzed at all. Therefore, because the relative importance of the numbers of farm operators and farm laborers in a given society is the best single indicator of the tenure situation and of the overall circumstances of the agricultural population, the classification is based on these two broad categories. In developing such a classification, several factors must be taken into account. In the first place, we must know how many families are headed by members who depend directly upon agriculture for a livelihood. In addition to the families of farm operators and farm laborers who live on the land, this category should embrace all those headed by agriculturists who do not live on their farms. In order to do this it must include those who live in a nearby town or city and commute daily to their farms on a daily basis, those who stay temporarily on their farms during planting and harvesting, those absentee owners whose wealth is still derived from agriculture or from pasturing, and others.

In the second place, it is necessary to ascertain not only the proportions of *individuals* who are ranked as operators or as laborers, which is the manner in which most agricultural censuses present these important facts, but the percentages of *families* which fall into these respective groups because of the tenure statuses of their heads. These data reflect much more accurately the proportions of the total population affected by the sociocultural conditions associated with each of the two tenure groups under consideration.

Finally, it is perhaps most essential to know much more about these several matters for the category of farm laborers. The published materials pertaining to these persons are likely to be far less informative than are the ones concerning operators, making the social and cultural significance of laborers in agricultural populations even more obscure than is that of persons in the various groups of operators. This deficiency is especially marked in many of the societies where the large landed estate prevails and where laborers are usually an overwhelming majority of the agricultural population. Under such conditions as these, comparatively few farm people are likely to embody the combined patterns of thought and behavior or orientations of the entrepreneur and the manager. Furthermore, the widespread lack among the laborers of the skills, authority, responsibility, involvement, and incentive that are learned in managing a farm produces a cultural heritage that causes succeeding generations to think and behave only as laborers having the meanest status. The low levels and standards of living created by this kind of condition become very debilitating and deeply entrenched in the network of social relationships and in the cultural environment. The system also is very costly to the society involved, for if the agriculturists do not have a wide variety of managerial skills, then the highly variable nature of farming, changing with the seasons and with many other conditions, finds them without the versatility necessary to improve agricultural life. Therefore, whenever laborers are superabundant in the agricultural population, there is little reason to expect them to have the adaptability, the wide range of skills, the knowledge, the interest, and the incentive necessary to increase agricultural production, conserve the soil, and produce and use the many techniques and tools that successful farming or ranching requires.

Major Classes of Farm Operators

The basic forms of tenure, as mentioned above, are those of operators and laborers. Farm operators are the ones who run the farm businesses. They are the entrepreneurs. They make the actual decisions in operating the farm or the ranch, including decisions regarding the crops to be planted, the time for cultivation, fertilization, and irrigation, and similar matters relative to the production of plants and animals. Obviously, the *owner-operator,* the entrepreneur or manager who has title to the land he uses, is of primary importance as the first member of this large group.

A second category of operators is composed of *farm managers* who are employed for the job of running farm enterprises that they do not own. Absentee landlords, whether persons, banks, insurance companies, or groups of heirs, use the services of such specialists. However, when managers or administrators are employed, it is usually on comparatively large holdings, not infrequently large landed estates which help to perpetuate two-class systems of stratification throughout the world. These estates may monopolize vast acreages of the best land and often are owned by absentees who rarely visit their holdings. They are, of course, the antithesis of the family-sized farm. Under these conditions, the existence of a relatively large proportion of managers among the farm operators in a particular area may be associated with severely limited opportunities for the majority of the agricultural population.

The members of a third major class of operators—the *renters*—do not own land but pay in one way or another for the use of farmsteads. Within the broad renter category are several specific types. The *cash renter*, in return for a particular sum of money, is entitled to the use of the land for a given period of time. The landlord frequently makes certain reservations as to how the land shall be used, and these are ordinarily recorded in the lease; but usually such a tenant exchanges cash for the right to use and manage a specified piece of land as he wishes, becoming, in effect, the temporary owner of that land and assuming the full risk of profit or loss. The *standing renter* is one who pays a fixed amount of produce (bales of cotton, tons of sugar cane, bags of rice, and so on) for the use of the land. Usually his lease differs from the cash tenant's primarily in the kind of payment, but it is obvious that the landlord assumes part of the risk. That is, his rent varies with the price of the product. Finally, the *share renter* or *tenant* is the entrepreneur who secures the right to the use of the land in return for a specified share of the crop. Under a share-renting arrangement there is the greatest division of risks of production and chances of profit or loss between the landlord and the renter. The landlord shares the chances inherent in both price fluctuations and crop failure; and frequently the respective spheres of responsibility of landlord and tenant are unclear in this type of arrangement. This form of tenure should be distinguished carefully from that of the *sharecropper,* who is actually a laborer receiving a part of the crop as his reward for the physical toil which he makes available to the owner. He is in no sense a farm operator and has few of the skills and responsibilities which go along with the functions of management and investment. In fact, so low is the status of this agriculturist that in societies where there is a concept which designates him, the implication almost always is highly depreciative.

Major Classes of Farm Laborers

The great majority of the world's people are, at the moment, in the unenviable category of agricultural laborers. Fundamentally, these are persons who derive their livings from farming or pasturing, but who have no rights in the land except perhaps the nominal one to use a tiny fragment of someone else's holding on which to grow a few subsistence crops. They are without permanent or stable rights to use even that bit of land as they see fit, to transfer it, or otherwise to treat it as their own possession. In virtually every case, they are forced by their lowly status to ignore the fundamental functions of the investor and the manager and to offer in a wasteful and inefficient way the only means of production that they have—labor. But despite the fact that servile and semiservile agricultural laborers are plentiful around the globe, the results of efforts to identify and classify them have been confusing and often misleading. We do not yet know the number, the location, and the degree of persistence of this vast category of workers. Moreover, while the bulk of them appears in many types of classifications as "free," many of them are, in fact, held in bondage by tradition, their relationships with the land and the landowners, their low levels of living, their lack of skills and aptitudes, and their persistent tendency to rear succeeding generations in precisely the same debilitating traditions with which they themselves are bound. In effect, they are tenaciously held by the systems of which they are part. These systems may include the pattern of traditional large landed estates held in fee simple, that of "state" and "collective" farms in the communist parts of the world, the one which confines agricultural workers to hopelessly tiny *minifundia,* or that which gives rise to a significant group of migrant agricultural laborers who follow the harvest of crops in some parts of the earth where farming is highly mechanized. In any event, our methods of classification do not yet accurately reflect the basic fact that most of the world's people are agricultural laborers in extremely low socioeconomic positions.

Those in the first major class of present-day agricultural laborers, having the lowest social status, are not unlike the *coloni* of the latter days of the Roman Empire. In fact, so greatly do many of the world's agriculturists resemble these early antecedents that the term is a suitable one for classifying great numbers of people throughout the modern world. The coloni of ancient, medieval, and modern times generally have been allotted the use of tiny fragments of the earth's surface upon which to grow a few crops in return for their expenditure of labor for the owners of the land. While this system is one of near bondage, often involving transfer of workers with the bulk of them appear in many types of classifications as "free," many of them immobilized in their positions for a lifetime, it also contains the rudiments of its own change. That is, the land allotted to the individual colonus may be infinitesimally small, but the use of it does enable him to develop a few of the managerial skills which are characteristic of farm people functioning under more equitable forms of land tenure. Therefore, it is no mere coincidence that in many parts of the globe where this system has prevailed, there is now the widespread cry for agrarian reform, often expressed as the demand for more suitable tenure arrangements. In the long run, the highly restrictive system that generated the status of colonus was also the one that helped to give him the hunger for the broader exercise of the few managerial skills that he was forced to develop. This factor has been partially responsible for precipitating the growing unrest among those of the status of colonus now found in many parts of the earth.

The second group of agricultural laborers, generally ranking significantly above the coloni in the status attached to their tenure, are those known as *sharecroppers* in the southern United States and by various other semiderogatory names elsewhere in the world. These workers ordinarily receive a share of the crop in payment for their labors, although the manual tasks which they perform may be no more useful to personal development than are those performed by the even more lowly coloni. Nevertheless, the term sharecropper in the United States usually implies considerably more personal freedom than does that of colonus in many other societies, although the material levels of living may be nearly identical in both cases. Usually, the sharecropper also enjoys the opportunity to use a small plot of land and often a shack on the plantation on which he works. He tends, however, to be only temporarily attached to a given landholding or landlord, principally because the verbal arrangement under which he commits his services frequently is no more than an annual one; and when a new cropping season approaches he often makes his informal "contract" with the owner or manager of another plantation. Much of this turnover takes place because of certain disadvantages for the sharecropper, which are built into the system. First, this laborer lacks most of the skills, the education, and the unencumbered access to land that would enable him to develop an efficient, profitable agricultural enterprise. The entire system of which he is a part lacks any features that would remedy this situation. Second, because his efforts are almost certain to produce a poor return and, therefore, a low level of living for himself and his family, the sharecropper is likely to become discontented quickly with the particular arrangement that he has made with a landowner. Third, this discontent provides him with the motivation to seek better arrangements in the form of a new contract; but because neither the overall system nor his role in it has changed, the worker's abilities and freedom of operation have improved little, and as a result he is prone to invest a lifetime in drifting from one plantation to another. Therefore, the sharecropper population of the southern United States was highly fluid. In other parts of the earth where a counterpart of this laborer is to be found, tradition, family ties, the stifling of incentive, low standards of living, indebtedness to the landowner, and other restrictive features tend to make for much less movement in this category of laborers, although immobility should not be taken as evidence of more productive tenure arrangements for the persons involved.

Sharecropping as a means of paying wages to a laborer is a one-sided arrangement, favoring the well-educated, sophisticated landowner and placing the laborer of humble means, minimal education, and virtually non-existent political power almost always at a disadvantage. It is fundamentally an exploitative system in which the landowner extracts the best possible terms from the laborer, and the worker, in turn, extracts from the soil the maximum crop which can be produced with a minimum input of any means of production except labor. Moreover, by advancing credit to the sharecropper before and during the growing season and by keeping the financial account of this indebtedness, the plantation owner often is able to obtain far more than his fair share of the crop, part of it ostensibly as payment for indebtedness incurred. However, because of just this type of highly commercialized interest on the part of the owner, the sharecropper is no longer as profitable nor as reliable as is new, mechanized equipment. Consequently, he is rapidly disappearing from some agricultural areas. In many cases, displaced sharecroppers and their families, beset by their various deficiencies and debilities, have poured in large numbers into urban centers in search of industrial jobs. Ironically, the same high degree of mechanization and even automation that is coming to pervade more plantation agriculture has already eliminated large numbers of jobs for the unskilled in urban industries, putting the displaced sharecropper at an almost impossible disadvantage in finding employment that will return a level of living even as high as the one he had experienced under the sharecropping system.

The third major group of agricultural laborers is that of the *wage hands*. This category is a diverse one, containing those who are more or less permanent workers, at least to the extent that they are employed on a monthly or annual basis; those who are much less permanent in their laboring capacity; and the ones who live on the farms on which they work and those who live elsewhere. All of these wage hands taken together generally have somewhat higher status than the sharecroppers and the coloni beneath them, although none of the three groups achieves a level of living which remotely approaches that of most of the people in the various operator categories.

In addition to the laborers named, there is the whole group of people who are members of the agriculturists' families, but who receive no formal wage. They, of course, may range all the way from the older children of the owner-operator of a family-sized farm, participating in the efficient and satisfying business of farming while learning the many skills of management and entrepreneurship, to those who are the ragged offspring of migratory laborers and who gain little from life except the mean heritage of the nomadic agricultural laborer. The fact that none of these people receives a wage is clearly not sufficient to place them in the same category. It is far more enlightening to classify families according to the tenure status of the head than to classify individuals.

Another group of lowly wage hands who are difficult to classify effectively is that of migratory agricultural laborers, who follow the harvest. In the United States, for example, many of these landless wanderers begin the season harvesting winter vegetables in the Florida Everglades, follow the crops into other parts of the South, fan out into the orchard and cropping parts of the Great Lakes and of Washington and Oregon, and finally migrate back to Florida and Texas for the winter growing season and the spring harvest. Their socioeconomic situations are exceedingly tenuous, the types of arrangements under which they work are unpredictable and exploitative and designed for the benefit of landowners and their representatives, and the legal and other protections of society which they can expect are absolutely minimal. They are, literally, people without community ties and without the benefits which could be supplied by sedentary existence, even in places where their statuses might remain low. Furthermore, when the position of agricultural migrant is combined with minority-group membership, the lowest status of all results; and that status tends to persist generation after generation, afflicting not only the persons themselves but the segments of the societies through which they move. In most societies, the unskilled laborer occupies a mean position; among that group, the agricultural worker is the most unfortunate; and within that category, the combination of the status of migrant with minority-group membership produces a condition that is very close to involuntary servitude. Such a condition makes for very low levels and standards of living, which tend to become self-perpetuating, producing a group of nomads who have virtually no property except that which they wear and drive and, even worse, who come to expect nothing more.

A Classification of Tenure Statuses

The several categories of agriculturists discussed above may be used to construct a classification of tenure statuses in which the people who have the highest position stand at the top, and those suffering the lowest possible circumstances, at the bottom. These several tenure groups represent a continuum of decreasing rights to the land upon which the agriculturists labor, and may be ranked as follows:

A. Farm operators
   1. Owners
   2. Managers or administrators

3. Renters
   a. Cash
   b. Standing
   c. Share
B. Farm laborers
   1. Wage hands
   2. Sharecroppers
   3. Coloni

SOCIAL AND ECONOMIC CORRELATIVES OF LAND TENURE

The socioeconomic circumstances which are attached to the tenure status of the owner-operator on the one hand and of the agricultural laborer on the other represent widely separated extremes. The owner-operator is generally in a position to develop his human potentialities to the maximum in the agricultural setting, particularly if he is part of a family-sized farm system of agriculture. The laborer, conversely, suffers from most of the disadvantages which a society has to offer and is able to pursue successfully very few of the many possible lines of human endeavor. The two groups of people are poles apart and the comparative chances which life offers to each of them differ in many obvious ways.

But the conditions surrounding the tenure status of "tenant" are not so clear cut. Therefore, we can learn much about the nature and desirability of farm tenancy as a system of land tenure by evaluating the social and economic conditions associated with it either as cause or as effect. Tenancy, for example, may be closely related to the types of farming which prevail in given areas. Those that require large investments and do not yield quick results tend to be associated with owner-operatorship, whereas annual crops, easily marketed and requiring relatively little capital investment, are grown extensively by tenants.

Another important association is that between tenancy and high land values. From the economic point of view the farmer's expenditures for land must compete with his expenditures for work stock, equipment, and other operating needs. If much of a man's capital is tied up in land, he may have inadequate funds with which to provide suitable power sources, implements, and supplies, and as a consequence farm operations may suffer. Therefore, in some areas there is a close relationship between the extent of farm tenancy and the degree to which farming is commercialized; where tenancy is highest, the average value of farms is highest, because farm operators are least able to acquire property or are least willing to render themselves "land poor" by tying up the greater part of their capital in expensive real estate. This relationship between tenancy and land values holds, of course, only in areas where "tenant" is synonymous with "renter," and not in places where share-croppers and several other types of farm laborers are indiscriminately mixed in with tenants.

When leases are for a short time, as in the United States, tenancy is associated with rapid depletion of the fertility of the soil. The tenant's interests are best served if he mines as much as possible from the landlord's farm during his brief stay, while returning an absolute minimum to it. To plant soil-building crops or to allow land to lie fallow in order to accumulate moisture is for the tenant to sacrifice his own welfare for that of his successor. To practice contour plowing and strip cropping is a burden and not a benefit to the tenant with a short lease. He may serve his immediate interests much better by plowing across terraces than along them. Fertilizers cannot be used profitably unless their contributions can be harvested during the period of the lease; and soil-building organic fertilizers are of no use whatsoever under these conditions. In brief, the system of farming practiced under a short-term lease is one of the significant causes of rapid soil erosion, breakdown of soil structure, and loss of much of its fertility.

For the sociologist, one of the most important associations is that between farm tenancy and poor, ill-kept homes and farm buildings. Where tenancy is high, semipermanent and movable farm property is poor. The tenant who makes improvements on the landlord's farm runs the risk of having his rent raised thereby. This penalty upon industry and initiative might be removed, of course, if the landlord could be required to reduce rent, extend the lease on the original terms, or otherwise grant concessions to the renter who produces improvements, but the negligible political influence of the tenants makes the enactment and enforcement of the necessary legislation highly improbable.

Where leases are of the short-term variety, inadequately supported and poorly attended social institutions are one of the results, often because the tax base is insufficient. The children of farm tenants are enrolled in the schools in smaller proportions than are the children of owners, and their attendance is more sporadic. The tenant's children frequently must change schools in the middle of the term, and often find themselves the victims of various kinds of discriminations within the system. Where tenancy is high, the rural church suffers in membership and attendance; tenants rarely participate in civic and governmental affairs. In short, tenancy is closely associated with poorly attended and ill-equipped social and civic institutions and agencies.

To generalize about the conditions that are produced by tenancy is difficult, because the tenure systems of modern nations differ radically from one another and are not easily comparable. Perhaps the Danish and English systems best illustrate the extremes. Denmark has directed its efforts to reform the tenure situation toward building a nation of farm owners and has practically eliminated farm tenancy. In England, on the other hand, long-continued thought and effort have gone into the development of a leasing system that enables the landed proprietors to retain control of the land and at the same time gives the tenants enough privileges and security to promote good farming practices. Therefore, tenancy cannot be considered an unmitigated evil simply because it is not ownership. A system might be evolved in other parts of the world in which tenancy could become a secure and rewarding way of engaging in agricultural production. In fact, it may even become a necessary form of tenure in some areas if land prices become sufficiently high that the cultivator who wants to develop a productive, efficient farm, capable of providing him with a reasonable level of living, cannot afford to tie up the great bulk of his capital in the purchase of land.

Various legal protections and safeguards should be built into an adequate relationship between landlord and tenant and provide for leases that are formal and written rather than vague and verbal, and that can be terminated only after proper notice has been given by either party. The guarantees should stipulate that the tenant be compensated rather than penalized by the owner for improvements agreed upon by both and that those of a removable nature can actually be removed by the tenant at the expiration of the lease. Furthermore, the lease should motivate the tenant to conserve the soil and other property of the owner and to eliminate wasteful procedures during the period of the contract. In addition, the provisions should demand the keeping of adequate records whenever outlays have been made for which compensation will be expected. If, after a period of an initial lease (usually one year), the arrangement is terminated by either party without good cause, there should be legal recourse for losses sustained as a result. For periods when unfavorable climatic, market, or other uncontrollable circumstances exist, provisions should make it unnecessary for either party to assume a disproportionate share of the loss resulting from the situation. In most cases, safeguards should restrict the degree to which the tenant can be held liable for rental payments when such conditions occur. Certain minimum standards for housing, sanitation facilities, and other necessities of life need to be set and enforced. Finally, some mechanism needs to be established which will make for impartial and equitable mediation and even arbitration between landlord and tenant when the differences between them develop to the point where the two are unable to resolve the problem.

Under safeguards such as those listed above, farm tenancy can produce virtually the same favorable conditions engendered by ownership, and in many cases may even be superior to the latter if it avoids the necessity for the farmer to invest most of his resources in landownership. In fact, even now many of the ills which are ordinarily attributed to tenancy are in reality the results of large-scale agriculture, the concentration of landownership and management, and the types of tenant-landlord arrangements which often prevail; they do not arise from the mere fact of tenancy itself.

LAND TENURE AND RURAL DEVELOPMENT

By its very nature land tenure is intimately associated with levels of living in agricultural areas and, as a result, is closely related to needs for comprehensive rural development. However, land tenure plays a dual role in this respect: in areas where particular types of land tenure prevail, they are the *cause* of a multitude of other social features associated with the well-being of agricultural people; but in those same areas, the extant forms of land tenure also are the *effect* of other antecedent conditions. In both cases, land tenure is simply one part of a complex network of socioeconomic conditions found on the rural scene, being a fragment of the various prevailing ways of life of the agriculturists, the social systems within which they function, and the non-empirical values which underlie these social systems. Consequently, land tenure, like all other single elements of agricultural existence that may be isolated for purposes of analysis, must be looked upon as both cause and effect and as a part of a much larger whole.

By the same token, it is impractical to consider rural development unless its various components are viewed as interwoven, and unless those who would promulgate development are willing and prepared to contend with a vast fabric of interrelationships, problems, and consequences of social change, and not with only one or a few of its threads. Generally, unilateral efforts to make farm owners of laborers, to introduce a few modern agricultural implements into a primitive system of agriculture, to strengthen social institutions in rural communities which are themselves weak, to instill aspirations to middle-class status in farm people whose social systems will not permit this to be translated into reality, or to engage in many other activities in isolation from the overall framework do not constitute agricultural or rural development. A regrettable number of well-intentioned "technical assistance" programs has failed because of this very shortcoming.

Actually, progressive changes in the tenure status of individuals in areas given over to the family-sized farm system of agricultural organization come close to being an ideal model for improvements in this aspect of rural life.

In such places the *agricultural ladder* or the series of steps whereby an individual progresses from a young family worker to an older full owner of his own farm has operated effectively to ensure a high degree of vertical mobility. In family-sized farm areas, the social pyramid is relatively low and flat, social classes are few, caste is unimportant, and a majority of the population occupies successively the various social strata in the pyramid, culminating in a group of individuals who are effective managers, entrepreneurs, and workers on their own family-sized farms. Under these conditions, which were well exemplified by the situation in the midwestern United States around the turn of the present century, the young farmer on his way to ownership began work as an unpaid laborer on the home farm, where he remained until the age of 18 or so; then he probably hired out to neighboring farmers for a cash wage. After a brief interval in this category, the second rung of the agricultural ladder, the young farmer had sufficient savings to purchase work stock and equipment and advanced to the third rung of the ladder, the tenant or independent-renter stage. Eventually, farm ownership was attained by all but a few. In addition, it was perfectly possible for persons to descend in the social scale, and this often happened. The entire process de-emphasized ascribed social status, and greatly encouraged the highly dynamic achieved type.

These successive improvements in the tenure positions of specific individuals are peculiar to areas where the family-sized farm dominates, and are virtually nonexistent in those where the large landholding and accompanying *minifundia* prevail. Under the latter conditions, any appreciable operation of the agricultural ladder would quickly dissolve the large estates and place the former laborers on farms of their own. This movement obviously is entirely alien to the areas in which the large landed estate and its accompanying forms of land tenure hold sway. Nevertheless, the fact that the agricultural ladder generally does not function in places where the large estate predominates should not be taken as a rationalization for avoiding efforts to make the ladder more operable. In the final analysis, the parts of the world where the need is greatest for such a fluid situation as this are those which are in danger of falling into the anarchy of much more violent changes precipitated by the persistent inflexibility of social systems in the face of rising standards of living among the laboring classes. Under the threat of such dire consequences, the need for development of *total* agricultural situations and of tenure arrangements in the process is imperative.

Significant agricultural development probably involves three fundamental changes in land-tenure arrangements around the world. In the first place, vast numbers of laborers who choose to remain in agriculture need to move into the status of the owner-operator if they are to develop their full potentialities as agriculturists and even as human beings. Second, other groups of laborers living in areas where land values are high and where ownership of land would consume all of their resources should be brought into the ranks of renters who have clear-cut, stable, and long-term rights to use given pieces of land and whose improvements and efforts to produce will be suitably rewarded rather than penalized. This type of tenure may also be a compromise in some areas in which there is little chance of subdividing large landed estates but where landowners might be brought into the position of offering equitable rental arrangements to some agriculturists. Under these conditions, a stable and secure renter might well become the independent entrepreneur, manager, and worker who is capable of functioning in an efficient and rewarding manner. This system of tenure, of course, is acknowledged to be less desirable than that involving high proportions of owner-operators. In the third place, owner-operators, renters, and other agriculturists should experience considerable increases in their rights to use the land in many parts of the globe.

It should be made abundantly clear that efforts to raise the levels of living of agricultural laborers while they continue to be laborers are shortsighted and do not constitute fundamental agricultural development. Even though the coloni of Latin America, the migratory laborers of the United States, and the sharecroppers and their equivalents throughout the world do, in fact, desperately need increases in their levels of living, the answer to their collective plight does not properly reside there. Rather, when the total agricultural systems of which they are parts allow them to become stable and secure operators of farms to which they have long-term or permanent rights, agricultural development will have proceeded to a significant point. It will be nearly complete when all of the other necessary changes which are closely related to tenure status have actually taken place for the vast majority of the agriculturists in the areas in question.

Additional Readings

1. BAALI, FUAD, *Relation of the People to the Land in Southern Iraq,* Gainesville: University of Florida Press, 1966, chapters 4 and 7.

2. BERTRAND, ALVIN L., "Land-Tenure Systems and Problems," in Alvin L. Bertrand (ed.), *Rural Sociology,* New York: McGraw-Hill Book Company, 1958, chapter 12.

3. CRIST, RAYMOND E., *Land for the Fellahin: Land Tenure and Land Use in the Near East,* New York: Robert Schalkenbach Foundation, 1961.

4. FORD, THOMAS R., *Man and Land in Peru,* Gainesville: University of Florida Press, 1955, chapter 4.

5. HARRIS, MARSHALL, *Origin of the Land Tenure System in the United States,* Ames: Iowa State University Press, 1953.

6. NELSON, LOWRY, *Rural Sociology* (second ed.), New York: American Book Company, 1955, chapter 13.

7. PARSONS, KENNETH H., RAYMOND J. PENN, and PHILIP M. RAUP (eds.), *Land Tenure: Proceedings of the International Conference on Land Tenure and Related Problems in World Agriculture Held at Madison, Wisconsin, 1951,* Madison: University of Wisconsin Press, 1956.

8. RAPER, ARTHUR F., and CARL C. TAYLOR, "Landowners and Tenants," in Carl C. Taylor and others, *Rural Life in the United States,* New York: Alfred A. Knopf, 1949, chapter XV.

9. SAUNDERS, JOHN V. D., "Man-Land Relations in Ecuador," *Rural Sociology,* Vol. 26, No. 1 (March, 1961), pp. 57–69.

10. SCHULMAN, SAM, "The Colono System in Latin America," *Rural Sociology,* Vol. 20, No. 1 (March, 1955), pp. 34–40.

11. SMITH, T. LYNN, *Brazil: People and Institutions* (third ed.), Baton Rouge: Louisiana State University Press, 1963, chapter XIII.

12. SMITH, T. LYNN, *Colombia: Social Structure and the Process of Development,* Gainesville: University of Florida Press, 1967, chapter 3.

13. TAYLOR, CARL C., *Rural Life in Argentina,* Baton Rouge: Louisiana State University Press, 1948, chapter VIII.

14. TAYLOR, CARL C., and others, *India's Roots of Democracy: A Sociological Analysis of Rural India's Experience in Planned Development Since Independence,* New Delhi: Orient Longmans, 1965.

8

SIZE OF HOLDINGS AND SIZE OF FARMS

The extent to which the ownership and control of the land is concentrated in a few hands or widely distributed among those who live from farming is probably the most important single determinant of the welfare of the people on the land. Wherever there is widespread distribution of landownership one also observes (1) the strongest propulsions to steady work and the maximum of thrift; (2) the highest average levels and standards of living; (3) the least development of social stratification, the fewest class distinctions, the relative absence of caste, and very little class conflict and class struggle; (4) a high degree of vertical social mobility so that the individual comes nearest to occupying the social position commensurate with his effort and natural abilities; (5) general intelligence that is at a high level and a minimum in range; and (6) a rural population having well-rounded and highly developed personalities.

The opposite of this system, the concentration of control in the hands of a few and reduction of the masses of the population to the category of landless agricultural workers, appears to result in (1) a very low average level of living, and an equally low standard, although the members of the landowning elite may live in fantastic luxury; (2) tremendous class distinctions between the favored few at the apex of the social pyramid and the toiling masses who lack any rights to the soil; (3) relatively little vertical social mobility, because caste is strong and because the chasm which separates the upper classes from the masses is so great that the offspring of those of low estate, even those of rare ability find it almost impossible to ascend in the social scale; (4) low average intelligence, because the great attainments of the select members of the small upper class are far more than offset by the meager development of the personal qualities of those who belong to the lower strata; (5) people skilled only in the performance, under the closest of supervision, of a limited number of manual tasks, and unable to carry on the self-directed activities involved in managerial and entrepreneurial work; (6) personal contacts characterized by the features of domination-subordination, order-and-obey relationships; and (7) a society that stresses routine, regulation, and order rather than innovation, progress, and change.

Where large-scale agriculture prevails, the vast majority of those involved are nothing more than laborers whose total potential as human beings remains undeveloped and who are subject to all of the disabilities mentioned before. On the other hand, where landownership and control are widely distributed among those who make up the rural population, such problems are of little consequence. Middle-class social status is the rule, arising not from the accident of birth, but from the individual's own abilities and efforts to succeed. Such a condition is a quite logical part of the pattern of social relationships associated with family-sized farms. Within this relatively large middle class, individuals move up and down to levels fairly commensurate with their talents and effort. The farmer in such a system is a laborer, as is the one working on the large estate he does not own. However, unlike the serf, the peon, the sharecropper, or even the wage hand, he is also an entre- preneur and the manager of his own farming affairs. In these capacities he is constantly motivated to seek efficient, economical methods and he lacks any predisposition to preserve wasteful routine or a debilitating status quo. Where owner-operators of family-sized farms are typical, average levels of living and of intelligence are likely to be very high. There is little in the social relationships of these persons that would bring some under the domina- tion of others; genuine leadership is common, but operates among a com- munity of farmers who have no reason to fear each other or to acquiesce to principles and procedures with which they disagree.

THE DISTINCTION BETWEEN SIZE OF ESTATES AND SIZE OF FARMS

In parts of the world where those who own the land farm it themselves, the farms and estates usually are found to be identical units. However, in many areas the bulk of the best land is in large holdings, whereas the operating units are of moderate size or even very small. For example, in Great Britain the huge estates of the nobility and the landed gentry traditionally have been subdivided for purposes of agricultural operations into farms operated by tenants. Increasingly, these may be thought of as family-sized units. Only at the yeoman level, where the holdings have been of about two or three hundred acres, are the sizes of the properties generally equivalent to the sizes of the farms.

A prominent feature of society in the Near East and on through India and Pakistan is the immense estates of potentates, which are tilled by tenants who must pay rack rents for the small subsistence farms they are permitted to cultivate. Under these conditions there is no resemblance between the huge "estate" and the tiny, tenant-operated "farm." In these parts of the world "land reform" or "land tenure reform" designate efforts to improve the lot of the cultivators and to change the relationships of man to the land. In some places, including the Philippines, one of the principal measures in reform programs is the outlawing of farm tenancy in recognition of the fact that the operating farm is merely a tiny fragment of the owned estate.

In the Americas, the landholding is usually the equivalent of the farm. In Latin America the large *estancias, haciendas, fundos, fazendas,* and so on almost always are managed as single operating units. In fact, in many parts of the region the concept of farm is totally lacking, and in others the distinction between farm and estate is extremely vague. Except in Argentina, where large numbers of farm tenants produce wheat, corn, flax, and other crops, and in a few other areas where speculators may briefly rent portions of the haciendas in order to produce one cash crop, little of the land held in large estates is tilled in smaller operating units or farms. The great grazing estates, the huge sugar-cane plantations, the vast coffee establishments, and others are usually operated as single units. Each may contain a multitude of peasant families who are afforded the utilization of tiny parcels of land for their own subsistence, or the estate may operate far below its potential level of production, but these conditions do not belie the fact that the landholding and the operating unit are one and the same. The tenant, working a few hundred acres as an independent and identifiable farm within a huge estate still is rare; the peasant, working as a laborer within the whole social complex of the estate is commonplace. This high degree of correspondence between farm and landholding in Latin America may result from the fact that the large estates long were withheld from cultivation and allowed to function as inefficient but integral pastoral units.

In the United States, too, the estate is essentially the same thing as the farm. It is both the landholding and the operating unit. In the lifetime of the typical owner-operator, the total land owned at any given time is used in the farm business. At some time additional land may be added to the farming unit by renting, but this is not general, and if other parcels of land are purchased both the size of the holding and the size of the farm increase simultaneously. Moreover, some of the apparent departures from the general tendency for the estate and the operating unit to be the same actually are part of it. The southern cotton plantation, for example, is no exception to the rule, since the late and unlamented system of sharecropping was in social and legal fact a method of paying wages for labor and not of leasing plots of land to small tenant operators. Nor are the numerous farms that are acquired and held by banks, insurance companies, religious organizations, and other corporations an exception to the rule under consideration. One never thinks of or refers to the estate of the X National Bank, nor the large holding of the Y Insurance Company. Rarely are the several farms owned by one of these agencies contiguous, and almost never are two or more of them operated as a single farm business by the professional farm managers who are placed in charge of them. Likewise in some of the Rocky Mountain states, such as Colorado and New Mexico, the oil millionaires who are consolidating thousands of small farms and ranches into a few large "spreads" on which they amuse themselves by playing the roles of "cattlemen," would never consider any kind of arrangement that would not keep their newly consolidated ranches inviolate as large individual units. All the territory they succeed in bringing inside their fences is from that time on part of a new little "cattle kingdom." Only occasionally may one of the members of the families of small farmers or ranchers who formerly owned and used the land find work as one of a small number of poorly paid "cowboys" who come to be the only permanent residents of once thickly populated districts.

CLASSIFICATION OF LANDHOLDINGS

The classification of agricultural holdings is difficult, especially if we try to develop categories applicable to many different societies. The size of a farm is not easy to determine, because the elements of production are all variable and may be combined with one another in smaller or larger proportions. Perhaps the most frequently used criterion is the area of the holdings, and with the present level of knowledge, it is probably the most practical alternative. Yet, the use of land area as the basic factor in classifying the holdings is brought into question by great variations in the quality and productivity of the land. Differences in rainfall, in the structure and native fertility of the soil, in the length of the growing season, in the prevalence of plants and animals, in diseases and pests, and in a multitude of other factors make area alone an imperfect measure. For example, in any of the arid sections of the world a few acres, well irrigated, represent a far more valuable and productive holding than do many hundreds of acres of exactly the same kind of land to which water cannot be brought. In those humid sections where rainfall is great, the value of a given amount of land varies tremendously according to the control that is exercised over water, including both irrigation and drainage, and the extent to which the more serious crop pests and diseases are controlled. For these and other reasons, a measure of area is a very unsatisfactory means of classification. Holdings vary from the small plot of land controlled and used by the part-time farmer and his family to supply part of the foodstuffs they consume to the extensive holdings of the land baron whose subjects may number hundreds or thousands. Some agricultural families are entirely landless, others have tiny parcels of land which are insufficient to support them adequately, still others have portions well adjusted to their capacities, and a few own and control acreages that greatly exceed their own needs and on which they use the labor of the landless classes.

Other criteria might be used to classify holdings. One of these is the number of workers on the properties under consideration; but then the question of productivity per worker becomes problematical. For example, five members of a middle-class farm family in Iowa, using sophisticated agricultural machinery and techniques on 320 acres make up a vastly different farming enterprise from five members of a peasant family, working as laborers with the most primitive tools and methods on a few acres of a large estate in any of the plantation areas of the world. Clearly, there is an exceedingly wide gap between the productivity per person in each of these situations. Moreover, before the number of workers per farm becomes a useful criterion for separating the holdings, it will be necessary to possess data that will employ some sort of "full-time equivalent" to account for the many workers who are engaged in farming only on a part-time basis. Of course, even then the matter of "underproductive" workers will continue to present problems in the efforts to classify the holdings.

In some cases, the units of power per farm—number of horses, mules, tractors, and so on—are taken as the basis for classifying agricultural holdings. Here the obvious problem is one of comparing some farms employing tractors to do the work with others using animal power and even with those depending only upon human muscle and endurance. Valid cross-cultural comparisons cannot be made under these circumstances.

Eventually, the gross value of farm production may become a more useful criterion for classification. In areas where farming is highly commercialized, the amount of cash sales already serves in this capacity. It is of little value, however, in places where farming is of the subsistence or self-sufficient type and where practically nothing is sold. Even in the most remote of the world's subsistence-agriculture areas, however, demands are increasing for various kinds of industrial products; and there is only one way for farm people to obtain these desired items—grow enough cash crops to return sufficient income to enable them to make the desired purchases. Therefore, at some future time the gross sales per farm may become a more valid criterion for purposes of classification of farms, at least those which are commercial.

The essential distinction for classification seems to be one that separates the farming unit in which the operator and the members of his family supply the capital, execute the managerial functions, and perform the greater part of the manual labor required for the farm tasks, from the one in which the labor supplied by the operator and his family is only incidental, operations surpass the single-family scale, and a force of laborers is maintained to perform the manual work on the farm. With this distinction in mind, area is probably the most feasible basis of classification available at present. For purposes of analysis, landholdings may be divided into the following four categories: (1) tiny subsistence tracts of farm laborers; (2) *minifundia;* (3) family-sized farms; and (4) large holdings.

Subsistence Tracts of Laborers

The tiny patches operated by agricultural laborers actually are so infinitesimal and supply such a small fraction of the needs of the families involved that they cannot be considered farms. They are little more than token bits of land afforded the workers on huge plantations in order that they might erect crude homes and raise a few subsistence items. Sometimes the patches are owned; more often their use is granted to the laborers, while title remains with the owner of the large holding of which they are fragments, but in nearly every case they are part of an overall complex of social relationships that bind workers to the estate and to virtual serfdom within its boundaries. Rather than providing the operators of such tracts with a small advantage, these patches are so tiny that no family can expect to farm independently the one it uses, and it is with little choice that the members turn to laboring jobs on the large plantation in order to survive. The small patches increase the degree of servility and dependence, and are not the first step toward greater control over land or increased independence in farming. Unfortunately, a vast proportion of the world's agriculturists exist under the circumstances associated with these tiny subsistence plots. The social status of their operators can be nothing other than that of manual laborer under the uncompromising eye of the landowner and his overseers. For the sociologist, the inclusion of these patches as "farms" in the official statistics of some countries is highly misleading.

Minifundia or Small Peasant Holdings

Minifundia also are small agricultural holdings, but are sufficiently large to be the main support of the people who live and work upon them. They shade imperceptibly into the tiny tracts operated by farm laborers which were discussed in the preceding section. In many cases the two are nearly indistinguishable; yet the minifundia, often only an acre or two in size, can support a family at the pitifully low level of existence to which the members have become accustomed if they work at other jobs, usually as laborers on large estates. As a rule of thumb, an agricultural property falls into the *minifundia* class if one or more members of the family must work at other jobs in addition to their endeavors on the agricultural plot in order to provide a bare creature existence and to hold the line against starvation. Such a unit in no way resembles the highly commercialized venture that may be designated as a family-sized farm and that provides a middle-class level of living. The facts that families operate the minifundia and that subsistence crops are grown certainly are not sufficient for inclusion of these holdings within the category of the family-sized farms.

The term *minifundia* comes from the Andean countries of South America, where it is applied to the hundreds of thousands of tiny farms which blanket the mountainsides of Ecuador, Colombia, Venezuela, and others. It is well known that many of the Latin American countries suffer severely from the blighting effects of the *hacienda* system, that involving large estates, but it often passes unnoticed that several of the countries are plagued with the Siamese twin of the hacienda, the extremely small farms which deserve the name minifundia. In fact, so regularly do the two go together that they may be thought of as comprising an overall socioeconomic system which includes the lives of landowners and laborers alike and dominates rural life.

Wherever persons once lived as serfs, as they did in wide areas of Europe, Asia, and Latin America, minifundia are found in large numbers. In those sections they have become a type of permanent limbo between legal servility from which the laborers have been permitted to escape and respectable levels of living to which they have not been able to ascend. In many places, minifundia are the points of anchorage to the landscape of a class of peasants who are bound inextricably by an unofficial master-and-man relationship with the owners of large estates, which they have little hope of changing or leaving. Life on the tiny holding, whether as owner, renter, squatter, or plantation laborer, is an austere form of accommodation to this manner of bondage; yet, because of rising aspirations and growing discontent with such an arrangement, it cannot be expected to endure indefinitely. The whole arrangement came into being principally because the best lands, level, fertile, and capable of supporting a large agricultural population at reasonably high levels of living, were long ago consolidated into the large estates on which the peasants now labor.

The world contains literally millions of these small holdings and almost countless millions of people who live out their lives within the dual confines of minifundia and haciendas. Among this group, however, expectations are rising, frustrations are increasing, and the impetus for change is becoming less capable of containment. These conditions are accompanied by increases in both the number and areas of distribution of the minifundia. Many of those who once rose slightly from serfdom to peasantry and became the operators of minifundia now are dissatisfied with the latter status and are demanding yet other advances in their levels of living and their opportunities. In addition, the soil in many agricultural parts of the world has eroded, the natural fertility has been dissipated, and the number of acres necessary to support a family adequately has increased so that farms that once were reasonably adequate have fallen into the minifundia class. In some cases, larger farms have been subdivided by inheritance to such an extent that the remnants, too, must be placed in the minifundia class. Most important, better techniques and machines, which make it possible for a family to cultivate larger and larger amounts of land, also make many small, formerly adequate holdings much too diminutive to rank as anything except minifundia. The last situation has occurred commonly in the United States in such sections as the Appalachian Mountains, the Ozarks, and other "hill" sections of the South. In these cases, the levels of living which can be derived from the small farms simply are not commensurate with the higher standards of their occupants. Many holdings which once were in the category of family-sized farms have fallen into the minifundia class in this way. It is this situation, limited in distribution and counterbalanced by the enlargement and growth in number of adequate family-sized farms, which has given rise to the popular misconception in the United States that the family-sized farm is a moribund institution that soon will pass from the rural scene.

Family-Sized Farms

The family-sized farm is one on which each farm family has sufficient land to occupy its members fully at agricultural or pastoral pursuits, but not enough territory to necessitate the steady employment of a great deal of supplementary labor. If labor is employed, it is of the "farm hand" type and not the great mass of manual workers who perform most of the farm tasks by hand under the watchful eye of an overseer or driver. Tractors, motor trucks, combines, and all other modern machinery and equipment might well add to the production per member without destroying the family-sized farm concept; but similarly increased production attained by adding laboring forces from outside the family would just as certainly cause a given farming unit to fall outside the category.

Farms which properly belong in the family-sized class may vary considerably in acreage for several reasons: individuals differ in their ability to make use of the land; the amounts of capital available for investment vary substantially from one agricultural entrepreneur to another; the systems of agriculture that prevail in some areas allow farm families to operate much larger acreages than do those common in others; the productivity of the land in some places is different from that in others; and the families of some agriculturists may have more members than those of others, thereby altering the amount of labor that can be thrown into farming. Nevertheless, there are some universal features of the genuine family-sized farm. In order to qualify for inclusion in this category, a given farming unit must draw from among family members, including the head of the household, for the great bulk of its labor. It also must call forth from the family a substantial capital investment and must tax to the utmost their inventiveness and ingenuity as managers. Moreover, the family-sized farm provides those who manage and operate it with a level of living consistent with the standard of living in the area in which it is located. Any holding so small or unproductive that it forces a family into circumstances that are defined locally as "poor" belongs in the minifundia class. One that allows a family to live within a very small wealthy elite clearly falls into the group of large estates. The fact that each of these extreme types of holdings may be owned, operated, or controlled by a single family is not sufficient to place either one in the class of family-sized farms. Finally, any farm that deserves the description family-sized must be under the exclusive control of a family. It may be owned, as is usually the case, which certainly seems to be ideal; or in some instances it may be rented under equitable, long term arrangements; but the control of the unit and the basic decisions in its operation must reside with the family members themselves.

The designation of a farm as family-sized does not depend upon the degree to which it is a self-sufficient "subsistence" holding or a "commercialized" operation. The crucial factor is that the farm be of such size that the entire expense, planning, operation, and control, and most of the labor are the responsibility of a single farm family. The farm that has grown in size and value because the owner-operator family has been able to use efficient machinery in production should not be assumed to have moved out of the family-sized class. For example, in Iowa, many holdings have been enlarged and the production per acre has increased greatly, but they continue to be controlled and operated solely by the members of single families using highly mechanized methods and sophisticated techniques to increase the return on their labor. The fact that the production of such farms includes a high proportion of cash crops and few subsistence items does not take them out of the category under consideration. Conversely, the landholding on which one family has come to reside and work but over which they have no real control and which is merely a small portion of a large estate where the members also work as laborers should not be construed as having entered into the family-sized category, even though virtually all of what the family eats and wears is grown on the place.

The family-sized farm has long been the American ideal. It is generally thought to be the design of American agriculture. Historically, the small holder of the North is representative of the operator of the family-sized unit, as contrasted with the large Tory landholders, many of whom were forced to flee the country at the close of the Revolution; and in the South the hill farms have exemplified the family-sized holdings as opposed to the large estates of the more level terrain. The expulsion of the northern Tories and the subdivision of much of their land; the practice of squatting, eventually legalized through the Homestead Acts; and the influx of land-hungry peasants from Europe firmly fixed a family-sized farm pattern in much of the northern and western parts of the nation. (See Fig. 28.) In the South, however, many of the large proprietors were patriots, and the Revolution had little effect upon the distribution of the ownership of the land. Later on, land speculation and land grabbing, the institution of slavery, and the more rapid spread of settlement firmly established a system of large-scale agriculture upon the good land areas of the region. In the Southwest, too, the Spanish practice of allocating large grants of land resulted in a distribution of ownership different from the family-sized farm pattern. In general, the family-sized type of landholding and all that it implies have pervaded agriculture and rural life in New England, the Midwest, the area around the Great Lakes, and certain portions of the Southeast and the Southwest. In each section, there has been a direct correlation between the importance of the owner-operator and the strength of the family-sized farm system.

The family-sized farm exists in a few other parts of the world and is only now appearing in yet others. (See Fig. 29.) Many of the small units on which rather primitive systems of agriculture are employed bear little resemblance to the much larger and highly efficient units found in sections of the United States, Canada, and a few other areas, but even within the United States, the small holdings in the hills of the South, contrasting markedly with the plantations of the lowlands and the deltas, are genuine family-sized operations. They and many other such diminutive operations throughout the

FIGURE 28. The family-sized farmstead of a middle-class Vermont farm family. Photo by Marion Post Wolcott in the Farm Security Administration Collection at the Library of Congress.

world, however, are too small to be efficient in this mechanized era; these farms should be enlarged so that improved systems of agriculture may provide the owner-operator families with middle-class levels of living. The development of agriculture and the improvement of rural life are a formidable challenge for those who would restructure rural life throughout the world. If the agricultural situation is reformed to the extent that landless laborers become the proprietors of small parcels of land, eventually it may become necessary to encourage some small holders to leave agriculture and others to consolidate the holdings into larger family-sized farms to use improved technology in the most efficient possible way. Otherwise, the smaller farms, once a great improvement over the situation in which all but a handful of the agricultural population were laborers, may become minifundia, operating inefficiently and providing the owner families with low levels of living. Such a condition would largely defeat the basic intent of establishing independent landownership by families.

FIGURE 29. Small family-sized farms in the Colombian highlands. Courtesy of the Office of Foreign Agricultural Relations, U.S. Department of Agriculture.

Large Holdings

This term refers to the situation in which the ownership and operation of the land is in the hands of a few, while the majority of the rural people, usually large in number on any one holding, are forced to work on the estates of the elite. It also relates to the circumstance in which the proprietors of the estates perform none of the labor although they may be managers. In many cases, the owners of the land leave even the management to someone else and live in cities. Aside from the large number of uneducated, unorganized, and unskilled lower-class laborers and the failure of the proprietors to engage in any manual work—factors which produce certain common social effects discussed below—large holdings throughout the world are extremely diverse. They are exemplified by cotton plantations in the Mississippi Delta, rice plantations in South Carolina, sugar-cane plantations in Louisiana and in much of the Caribbean area, coffee *fazendas* in Brazil, cattle *estancias* in Argentina, tea estates in Ceylon, rubber plantations in Indonesia, and many others (Figs. 30, 31, and 32). They also include the various types of "communes," "collectives," and "state farms" of the communist countries (Fig. 33). Usually vast acreages are encompassed within each of the holdings, but the category also includes units of only a few hundred acres on which the essen-

FIGURE 30. A large cotton plantation in the southern United States. From a Library of Congress copy of a Currier & Ives print of a painting by W. A. Walker, 1884.

191

FIGURE 31. A sugar-cane plantation in Peru, from the air.

FIGURE 32. The central portion of a large landed estate in East Prussia. Courtesy of Plan und Karte, G.m.b.H., through Katherina Elisseieff.

FIGURE 33. The lavish use of labor on one variety of the large landed estate—a People's Commune in one of the communist countries. Photo courtesy of *Foreign Agriculture*.

tial work is done by peasants or laborers rather than by the proprietor or any members of his family. Therefore, one can find an almost infinite variety of sizes and types of large, landed estates.

One helpful subdivision of the group of huge holdings is that which has come into general use in much of Latin America. It includes on the one hand the *haciendas, fazendas, estancias, fundos,* and other estates on which the land is used in a reasonably productive manner, and on the other hand the *latifundia,* which are poorly used or entirely unused. The latter are symbols of inherited wealth even though they may produce little or nothing. They are havens for capital which remains otherwise uninvested and unavailable for more useful purposes in the "developing" areas in which they are usually found. Many of the most vociferous demands for agrarian reform are being directed at the large unused holdings: They preserve the two-class system and prevent the masses of people in predominantly agricultural societies from having any control over the land, and, in fact, their dormancy has institutionalized the nonuse of the land by anyone in any manner. Obviously, they do nothing to raise the levels of living of the vast majority of the people, nor to help bring them more in line with the rising standards of living or aspirations now found in these societies. It is frequently difficult to distinguish latifundia from estates that are somewhat productive, for the social conditions they produce are often identical, but the conceptual separation is useful in

193

that it allows an additional step in the task of classification of the many kinds of holdings.

Large-scale productive agriculture is in reality the use of the factory system in growing plants and animals. Concentration of landownership, centralized control of the large force of laborers, specialization in single crops ("monoculture"), rigid supervision, and division of labor among the workers are some elements of the system. Its essentials are probably best shown by the extent of supervision of the laborers by those in charge of the plantation. The former are allowed virtually no opportunity for innovation and are discouraged, often brutally, from departing from the established routine. Agricultural tasks and even life itself are greatly regimented, the details of production are routine and inflexible, labor is performed in a segmented manner, and both landlord and laborer are effectively prevented from developing the traits that result when the agriculturist is simultaneously a capitalist, a manager, and a worker. The *laborer* does not even remotely resemble the middle-class *farmer* from those parts of the world where the family-sized farm is the predominant way of organizing agricultural production and rural life.

SOCIAL EFFECTS OF FAMILY-SIZED FARMS VERSUS THOSE OF LARGE AGRICULTURAL UNITS

The effects of large-scale agriculture are apparent in the many social problems that infest a region in which there is concentration of landownership. There, the qualities by which the rural people may be identified are molded by the debasement of the great masses and the artificial elevation of small elites. Few have the opportunities to develop the psychosocial equipment that makes for ingenuity, efficiency, and relatively high levels of living. As Alfred H. Stone has said (Ref. 486, p. 11), there is "something inherently vicious in the whole [plantation] system and methods, from an economic standpoint—from the beginning to the present time." In contrast with these areas of large holdings, those devoted to family-sized farms, even though frequently far inferior in soil and other natural conditions, stand out clearly. Where the rural social system associated with these smaller holdings is prevalent, the personalities of those who farm the land and their social groups and human contacts are characterized by none of the master-man relationships, the penalties imposed upon innovation, or the premium placed upon routine and tedium by which the large estate is plagued. Furthermore, there is little of the inevitable poverty which results when tiny subsistence tracts or minifundia are common. The family-sized farms on which owner-operators invest money, labor, and managerial skills and techniques produce middle-class *farmers* rather than lower-class *peons,* and *sharecroppers.* Moreover, if the family-sized farms are of sizes suited to the best of mechanization and other production techniques available at any given time, and if the man-land relationships are such that farms can grow in size when new technology and techniques increase production per man-hour, the area in which they predominate will almost certainly have a high average level of living with little in the way of poor and wealthy extremes. In short, the family-sized units avoid most of the problems that arise when a landowning elite is found in combination with a mass of landless laborers, or even when the farms are owned by those who work them but are too small to allow efficient production with modern machinery and techniques.

Two Great Rural Social Systems

As mentioned before, the size of agricultural holdings is closely associated with a broad array of sociocultural elements. Very different sets of these elements develop into full-blown social systems corresponding to the size of landholdings in agricultural areas. These great systems—those based upon the large estate and upon the family-sized farm—give rise to characteristic social forms, functions, and processes (Fig. 34).

Before the industrial and urban developments in the nineteenth century the history of civilization consists largely of the conditions and events associated with these two great, all-embracing rural social systems. The large holding was, the principal basis of social organization in ancient times, throughout the medieval period, and, in most parts of the "civilized" world, until recently. In Latin America, for example, not only is it the traditional unit, but is the one that presently is having broken the grip in which it has held the societies and economies during the entire colonial epoch and that of national independence as well. Its antithesis, the family-sized farm, is the institution that was proved so effective in the nineteenth and twentieth centuries in bringing forth the great abundance of food and raw materials, in developing abilities and capacities, and in elevating to unprecedented heights the levels of living in northwestern Europe, Canada, most of the United States, and a few other parts of the world. The high degree to which human history is an account of slavery, serfdom, peonage, and various other kinds of servile or semiservile labor is due almost entirely to the age-old dominant position of the huge landed estate and the social system based upon it. In contrast, any development of a democratic or republican type of political and administrative organization has been closely associated with the emergence and growth of a rural social system based on family-sized farms.

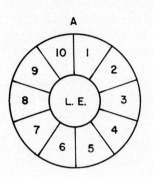

A. BASED UPON LARGE ESTATES

1 HIGH DEGREE OF SOCIAL STRATIFICATION
2 LITTLE VERTICAL SOCIAL MOBILITY
3 CASTE IS AN IMPORTANT FACTOR
4 LOW AVERAGE INTELLIGENCE
5 RESTRICTED DEVELOPMENT OF PERSONALITY
6 "ORDER-OBEY" PERSONAL RELATIONS
7 ROUTINE ALL-IMPORTANT
8 MANUAL LABOR IS DEGRADING
9 LOW LEVELS AND STANDARDS OF LIVING
10 LITTLE INCENTIVE TO WORK AND SAVE

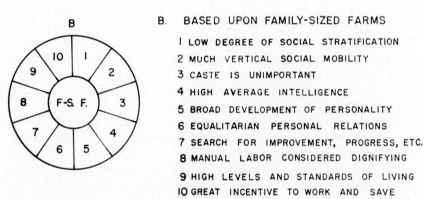

B. BASED UPON FAMILY-SIZED FARMS

1 LOW DEGREE OF SOCIAL STRATIFICATION
2 MUCH VERTICAL SOCIAL MOBILITY
3 CASTE IS UNIMPORTANT
4 HIGH AVERAGE INTELLIGENCE
5 BROAD DEVELOPMENT OF PERSONALITY
6 EQUALITARIAN PERSONAL RELATIONS
7 SEARCH FOR IMPROVEMENT, PROGRESS, ETC.
8 MANUAL LABOR CONSIDERED DIGNIFYING
9 HIGH LEVELS AND STANDARDS OF LIVING
10 GREAT INCENTIVE TO WORK AND SAVE

FIGURE 34. Societal features associated with the two great rural social systems.

One or the other of these two rural social systems is the universe that determines the patterns and developments of life of those who live and work in rural areas. Therefore, it seems advisable to offer a summary of the contrasts in the ways in which the two all-embracing rural social systems operate.

Social stratification tends to be extreme wherever a few large proprietors have a monopoly in ownership and control of the land. Then society quickly comes to be divided into a small aristocracy at the top of any social scale, and a great mass of workers who exist at a mere creature level at the bottom.

It matters little whether the landed gentry dominate the laborers by some kind of rack rent, or whether the workers are clearly and unambiguously peasants. In either case, a few families occupy the apex of the social order, possess all of the economic, political, and social power, and insist upon an ostentatious display of domination in their dealings with all persons of inferior status. In both cases, there are few persons who fall into any kind of middle class in the broad range between the exalted positions of the elite and the debased situations of the landless workers.

Entirely different is the class structure which is generated wherever substantial family-sized farms dominate the rural scene. In such regions, families headed by farmers of true middle-class status are in the vast majority, so that social stratification is slight, and that which is present consists almost entirely of differences within the middle class. Aristocratic elements are absent, and even the richest of the families appear ludicrous in any attempts they may make to imitate the ways of those of upper-class status elsewhere in the society. At the same time such a society produces very few persons who will pass their lives as wage hands, peons, sharecroppers, or any other category of landless agricultural workers. Definitely, the rural social system that is brought into being and perpetuated by the family-sized farm has no place for a large hereditary class of rural laborers.

Vertical social mobility in the society in which the ownership and control of the land is concentrated in the hands of a few powerful proprietors is quite different from that in the society that features widespread distribution among the heads of families who work the soil. Mobility is also closely related to the class system, for both the prevailing type of social stratification and the pattern of mobility are generated by the same great force that forms the heart of the system. Vertical social mobility in the social system integrated about the large landed estate is practically nil. The elite families at the apex of the social scale are able to maintain even their least capable members in the small upper stratum, whereas those born of low estate cannot even hope to attain places in the small group of highly situated persons. In the two-class system, there are no levels to which they could aspire in the immense vertical distance that separates the toiling masses from the oligarchy or aristocracy.

Entirely different is the degree of movement up and down in the socio-economic scale in the rural social system which develops wherever family-sized farms are allowed to multiply and flourish. It is true, as pointed out elsewhere, that social stratification in this case is limited largely to the small gradations which occur within the middle class. Even so, however, the movement of some persons to higher positions within the middle class, and the sinking of others to levels lower than those they once occupied, goes on briskly. One farmer, by putting forth extra effort, exercising thrift, taking advantage of opportunities for more formal training, and learning through experience, may better his position and that of his family. Every now and then he adds to the size of his farm, improves his land and buildings, betters his drains and fences, adds to his equipment and livestock, increases the comfort and attractiveness of his home, and elevates his level of living. While this progress is taking place, another farmer in the same locality may be inclined to avoid work and neglect management problems, to allow his land and equipment to deteriorate, to spend money freely on items considered locally to be inappropriate, and so on. Such a person may find it difficult to maintain his status in the social scale. Gradually, or even suddenly, he may lose the ownership of his land, be unable to maintain his accustomed level of living, sink in the estimation of his fellows in the neighborhood and community, or, in a word, fall sharply in rank, power, and prestige. Thus, even though the distances involved are short ones, there is considerable vertical mobility in the social system that is functionally related to family-sized farms.

Caste elements are especially variable from one of the great rural social systems to the other. From what has already been said with respect to social stratification, it follows as a necessary corollary that the two-class system and the lack of vertical social mobility that are generated by the large estate will make caste (or the inheritance of social position) a striking feature of this social system, whereas relatively free vertical movement among the various layers of the middle class will reduce caste to a position of little or no consequence in the family-sized farm system. This sharp difference is given further emphasis by the close association that has existed throughout the entire historical period in many parts of the world between the social system based on the large landed estate and slavery, serfdom, peonage, and a wide variety of other forms of servile and semiservile labor.

Levels of intelligence are also greatly affected by the sociocultural conditions amid which one lives in either of the rural social systems. The role of the agricultural laborer, even where he is not a slave, serf, or peon, contributes little to the realization of most of the potentials of the human being. In the one rural social system, those in the small, elite upper class develop to a point near the maximum the features of the intelligent man or woman, but the high scores of this small minority do very little to offset the pitifully low standing of the immense majority of the population who are only slightly removed from the mere creature level. Very much higher is the average for those in the other system, who, as operators of family-sized farms, must master a wide variety of skills and techniques, mental as well as physical.

On any comprehensive intelligence test that may be devised, the scores by those in the social system based upon family-sized farms should prove to be vastly superior to those for the population enmeshed in the one in which the large estate is the moving force.

Personality development in the system of large estates is strongly conditioned by the fact that, except for the few members of the elite, the inhabitants of the rural zones are concerned only with one of the three basic economic functions, i.e., that of the one who supplies the manual labor. They are born in the huts and hovels of the workers and they grow and develop (to the extent that they develop at all) in these same rude shelters; from very early ages they perform routine tasks required in agricultural and pastoral activities. Unceasingly they are subject to the orders and control of those who administer the big estates and of the various overseers, straw-bosses, or drivers who are charged with handling the labor. They rarely have any opportunity to develop those personality traits that pertain to the all-important function of management, nor those involving thrift, investment, and the use of capital. In other words they pass their entire lives repeating endlessly a limited number of manual tasks that once were the work of slaves and that most readily can be made those of animals and machines.

Strikingly different from all this are the thousands of activities contributing to the development of personality of one born into the farm family in a middle-class society. From their earliest moments, the children in such families are acquiring a fund of knowledge in a broad range of experiences that have to do with the successful performance of managerial activities, the acquisition and employment of capital, and the most efficient use of their own manual labor. After they reach the age of adolescence, a substantial part of their own waking hours must be devoted to all three of these basic economic functions. By the time they reach adulthood, these persons proudly carry most if not all of the responsibility for their own well-being and that of their families. From the qualitative standpoint as well as the quantitative, the human abilities are developed to a degree that is far nearer the potential than is the case in the rural social system based on large estates. It must be stressed that the motivations in the system are those generated by the person himself, for he is under the supervision of no overseer of any type except the head of the household.

Personal relationships in a plantation system, on the one hand, and in a family-sized farm system, on the other, are intimately related to the factors already discussed as cause and effect. Most striking, of course, are the differences between the pattern of superordination and subordination which arises and prevails wherever the large landed estate has been permitted to exercise its influence and the predominantly equalitarian contacts between man and man that are produced by a fairly equitable distribution of rights to the land among the heads of agricultural households. Even the phenomenon of leadership has little in common in the two social systems, for it is inaccurate to use such a term to designate the domination which is characteristic of the one, whereas it specifically applies to the activities in the other through which one person seeks to secure the support and direct the thought and actions of others of approximately his own social status.

Established routine versus the search for progress is a fundamental dichotomy between the two rural social systems under consideration. It is practically impossible to find adequate exercise of managerial details coupled with the failure to develop the human capacities of those in the lower socioeconomic class in rural societies where large estates are dominant. Therefore, stultifying routine at a rudimentary level comes to represent the social value *par excellence* in such places. Indeed, except in the minority of cases, most of which are plantation ventures using foreign capital, the huge rural establishment is almost certain to resort to monoculture of one type or another, because such activities hold at an almost irreducible minimum the number and complexity of the tasks which slaves, serfs, peons, sharecroppers, and other laborers must perform, and which the owners, bailiffs stewards, strawbosses, managers, overseers, drivers, and gang leaders must be sure are performed in exactly the prescribed manner. In this social system, which generally produces a single crop using traditional methods, the worker who for any reason, including that of increased efficiency, departs from the prescribed procedures is in grave danger of severe reprimand or even corporal punishment, and there is small likelihood that he will receive a reward of any kind. The "best" worker is the one who performs, hour after hour and day after day, from one end of the year to another, and under the watchful eye of the labor boss, a few simple physical tasks in exactly the manner that has been demonstrated to him. In this social system, such routine and the low esteem in which labor and those who perform it are held forestall even the first steps in the improvement of agricultural methods. In fact, any innovation may be considered and treated as deviant behavior!

All of these factors are decidedly different where family-sized farms have generated the prevailing rural social system. In this situation, the head of each family of cultivators performs simultaneously all three of the basic economic functions: He builds up his own modest amounts of wealth and invests them in land and operating capital; he and the members of his family participate actively in the performance of various farm tasks, if indeed they are not solely responsible for supplying the labor used on the farm; and, above all, he spends most of his waking hours throughout his lifetime engaged in various aspects of the managerial function. The mere fact that the one who plans and directs the farm enterprises also is the one who must perform the labor involved serves as a strong, unceasing stimulus to the search for less laborious, more effective, and more productive ways of tilling the soil, controlling weeds and pests, making the harvest, and transporting things on the farm and from the storehouse to the market. In such a system no overseer or driver can prevent the adoption of any improved practice. Such a system was, in the final analysis, responsible for the fact that practically all of the revolutionary agricultural implements and machines were perfected by or for middle-class farmers in a very few parts of the earth.

The attitude toward manual labor   and those who perform it in the system of large estates is one of great depreciation, which serves as a serious obstacle to progress and development. It could hardly be otherwise in a civilization in which, throughout all history and in all parts of the earth, there has been a close association between those large rural properties and servile labor of various types. The cause-and-effect relationship involved makes it inevitable that manual labor, or the primary function of the slave, the serf, or the peon, will become the symbol of lowly position in life. Furthermore, if perchance the workers belong to a different racial or ethnic stock from that of the masters, physical characteristics also tend to become indicative of mean stations in society. Under these conditions it may be practically impossible to eradicate the association between the depreciative connotations of work with the hands and certain physiological features such as skin color and texture of the hair.

Where family-sized farms give a middle-class framework to society, the attitude toward manual labor is entirely different. In the social system of such a society work with the hands is considered meritorious, uplifting, and dignifying, and any stigma involved is upon the one who, unless physically unable to take part in work activities, may attempt to avoid his share of the physical labor. The middle-class farmer takes pride in his prowess as a worker and from their most tender years he teaches his children to do the same.

Levels of living,   on the average, are vastly different in the two rural social systems. In the one whose whole being is causally linked to the plantation or other large estate, the consumption of goods and services per family unit is extremely low; whereas, when family-sized farms find anything like a favorable environment in which to grow and develop, the average per family is much higher. In the former, the aristocratic display of wealth and luxury on the part of the masters is like a drop in the sea in contributing to the general average; while in the latter, the lack of a landed aristocracy has only an imperceptible influence upon the general state of well-being of the masses who till the soil. In this case, the plane of living is always relatively high, and frequently high on the absolute basis as well.

Habits of regular work and thrift are the last we shall mention of the basic components of the two sharply contrasting rural social systems. Weak indeed are the propulsions to steady work in the system generated by large landed estates and the two-class system of social stratification which accompanies it; and strong and exacting are such stimuli wherever the general way of life is determined by family-sized farms. Deserving of every emphasis possible is the fact that in the former the agricultural population must be composed almost entirely of peons or other menial types, even if they are not actually slaves, serfs, or of some other servile status. Under such circumstances the individual best serves his own interests by avoiding in every way possible any expenditure of his own energy for the purpose of advancing the affairs of the estate or plantation. Similarly, since he has no reason to expect or even hope that either he or his children can ascend in the social scale, any attempt to save would be highly irrational. If these conditions did not prevail, the upward vertical mobility of those in the lower class would destroy in a single generation the system of large landed properties.

In no way do the behavior patterns of the farmers of family-sized farms contrast more sharply with those of plantation peons than in this matter of propulsions to regular work and saving. Day and night the operator of a substantial farm is preoccupied with problems connected with the management of his land, the improvement of his fences and drains, the upkeep of his buildings, the care of his livestock and machinery, the condition of his soil and crops, and so on. From daybreak until long after night his hours are filled with strenuous mental and physical activities for which it seems the days and weeks are never long enough. Impinging upon him from every direction are stimuli calling for greater effort rather than the invention of ways and means of deceiving some driver or overseer. The goal of enlarging and improving his farm leads him to maximum efforts to save and accumulate capital. Even within the family budget the many expenditures in the cost of living must face the keenest competition from those for operation of the farm. Furthermore, almost always he is driven by the aspiration that each of his children should occupy a position in the social scale that is higher than his own, and he tries in every way to bring this about by formal schooling, enlargement of the farm, improvement of farm practices, and so on. In brief, the stimulus to steady, hard work and regular, substantial saving reaches its maximum in the rural social system generated by family-sized farms and their middle-class owners.

Size of Farms and the Mechanization of Agriculture

Mechanization favors the development of the medium-sized agricultural units or family-sized farms. The great majority of the marvelous machines, implements, and techniques which now can do so much to ease the burdens of farm work and increase the productivity of agriculturists throughout the world are closely adjusted to the needs and activities of the operators of family-sized farms and were developed in areas where these farms predominate. Tractors, modern plows, cultivators, combines and harvesters, wagons, motor trucks, milking machines, cream separators, pumps, corn-pickers, mowing machines, hayloaders, potato diggers, potato sorters, and hundreds of other important machines are carefully adjusted to the needs of agricultural units in which a man and the members of his family do the bulk of the work. Even the combines for harvesting grains require relatively few hands, but in this case, because of costs and other factors, until the present it has been rather common for these to be owned by specialists who do custom work for the farmers of an area.

The explanation of this association between type of farm and mechanization is that many of the machines and implements were invented and perfected by or for the operators of family-sized farms in northwestern Europe and parts of the United States and Canada. Indeed, it is difficult to conceive of accomplishments such as those of John Deere or Cyrus H. McCormick being made in regions dominated by the large estates and their twin, the minifundia. If any of these inventors had been the owner of a magnificent plantation, a large hacienda, a splendid estancia, or an extensive fundo, today his name would not figure in any list of the forerunners of mechanized agriculture. As the proprietor of an immense tract of land and with a position at the top of the social pyramid, his interests would have been directed almost exclusively to the fields of finance, politics, literature, administration, diplomacy, and so on. Hence it is almost impossible to think of him as devoting interminable hours and days experimenting with broken saw blades and other pieces of rusty metal in an attempt to construct agricultural implements that would reduce the burden of his own labor, and that of his neighbors, in the indispensable work of the farm. Or if any one of them had been born in the hut of one of the peons on such a large estate, or even in an area blanketed with minifundia, probably he would have passed his days repeating endlessly, under the vigilant eyes of some majordomo or overseer, the rudimentary and routine tasks demanded of him and his fellows.

However, the order-and-obey system of personal relationships that prevails on the plantation or other large agricultural unit is not the only thing that minimizes its contributions to the invention and perfection of agricultural implements and machinery. Although they are rare, there actually have been cases in which the landed gentry of a given country interested themselves in the improvement of agriculture in general and the development of better tools and equipment in particular. One of the most striking examples is represented by the country squires of England during the eighteenth and nineteenth centuries. Britain's rural gentry of the period, and also their fellows in the British colonies, were highly motivated to build up the soil, improve the livestock, enrich the variety of crops, better the crop combinations and rotations, and make all other innovations that offered promise of increasing the productivity of their lands. Indeed, to the extent that was permitted by social and recreational activities called for by their traditional pattern of life, they were remarkably effective in establishing the bases of modern agriculture. To their work we owe in large part our modern breeds of draft and saddle horses, vastly improved types of beef and dairy cattle, and modern varieties of hogs, sheep, and poultry. They worked out the basic systems of crop rotation; they tried out ways of improving the soil through liming, marling, and drainage. In spite of all this, however, the nature of the master-man and man-land relationships in a system of large-scale agricultural operations kept them from the invention and perfection of agricultural machinery.

Consider, in this connection, the critically important case of Jethro Tull and his horse-hoeing drill. Tull was a Berkshire squire who owned and operated a farm called "Prosperous," although apparently it brought him little prosperity. He gained immortality through a book entitled *New Horse-hoeing Husbandry* (1731). Early in the eighteenth century, this perceptive rural gentleman invented the first machine ever used for drilling grain, and began the writing that did so much to revolutionize agriculture. Because his work was far in advance of his time, his ideas were ridiculed, and his suggestions and recommendations stoutly opposed. The significant point, however, is what happened on Prosperous, the farm he himself was operating. P. H. Ditchfield, noted British scholar, who has informed us on the subject, says about Tull: "His greatest trials resulted from the opposition of his own labourers, and he complained bitterly about them, because they thought that these new inventions would undermine labour; these men deliberately broke his machines, and refused to obey his orders." (Ref. 98, p. 230.)

Fortunately for the world, in this case the direct action of workers who were threatened with technological unemployment did not permanently deprive mankind of the benefits of inventive genius. Tull's principles and mechanical designs had been published, a fact that probably saved them from the oblivion that has been the end of thousands of other progressive discoveries. Although his book received scant attention in England, it was eagerly received in France, where it was translated three separate times and became the basis for a famed work on agriculture by M. de Hamel du Monceau of the Royal Academy of Science in Paris. Largely as a result of the favorable reception on the Continent, Scottish farmers adopted Tull's recommendations for the cultivation of turnips; and finally, through this roundabout course, an event tinged with irony to the extreme, Squire Tull's horse-hoeing husbandry made its way from Scotland to its place of birth in Berkshire. (Ref. 98, p. 230). In more recent times, the introduction into England of the mowers and grain harvesters that had been developed in the family-sized farming districts of the United States was strenuously opposed by the laborers employed by Britain's famed yeoman farmers. For example, Mr. Price of Alstone bought a mower, but he was "obliged to bring the machine home every night and lock it up. When they went to the fields in the morning they would find pieces of iron bars driven into the ground among the grass." Moreover, one of the first binders used "was set on fire at a village near Tewkesbury" (Ref. 582, p. 107).

In summary, the revolutionary development of agricultural machines and implements in the course of the last hundred years is due above all to the ceaseless quest by the operators of family-sized farms for labor-saving devices for their own farms and those of their neighbors. Furthermore, the fact that the greater part of the agricultural machinery available at present is adapted for use on family-sized farms is of tremendous importance for future agricultural development. It should cause the best-advised private and governmental agencies throughout the world to give preference to such agricultural units in their various projects and programs. In everything related to the mechanization of agriculture, it seems certain that the family-sized farms will retain their advantage for many years to come.

SITUATION AND TRENDS

During the last century, various factors have been chipping away at the entrenched position of the large landed estate; and in the decades ahead, the forces promoting a transition to family-sized farms are likely to be even more potent than they are at present. Nevertheless, at the present time the great bulk of the world's farm people are living either as laborers on large, privately-owned estates or on communist state farms and collectives, or as the operators of excessively small minifundia. Large numbers of the world's cultivators are tenants paying rack rents. In all these cases, the positions occupied, knowledge and skills possessed, facilities available, and control allowed the families involved make it impossible for them to do much more than meet their minimum creature needs. In some places, conditions do not provide even those bare necessities. Those who are the owner-operators of family-sized farms, enjoying the favorable features of the upper middle class into which most such persons fall, even now are in a very small minority of the world's agriculturists.

Historically, substantial family-sized farms in the hands of owner-operators appeared and increased rapidly in number in the United States only after 1830, when developments allowed them to push into the Ohio and Mississippi valleys from parts of New York, Pennsylvania, Maryland, and Virginia. The growth of this institution and the rural social system of which it is the central feature are unparalleled as instruments making for the well-being of the agricultural population. This important development has never received the attention that it deserves. As early as the 1890's, however, the keenly perceptive Colombian observer, Salvador Camacho Roldán, recognized that placing land in the hands of the cultivators in parcels of sufficient acreage that they might be designated as family-sized farms was the principal cause of the enviable development of the United States. The succinct generalizations of this discerning visitor deserve careful attention. A few of the most pertinent comments he addressed to his fellows among the large landholding classes in Latin America are as follows:

Among the causes of the prosperity of Anglo-Saxon America I consider the principal one to be the system adopted from the beginning for the distribution of the public lands in small allotments, which put within reach of the worker this primary element of all riches, the first condition of independence and of personal dignity among men, and the indispensable basis of political equality, without which republican forms are a fraud. This system and the institution of the Homestead Law, which established the cultivation of the land by the worker as the only way of acquiring the ownership of land and which assured its possession by the family, has given an enormous stimulus to labor to the proletarian classes; it has completely changed the conditions of the ancient social organization, which placed the land in the hands of a few privileged persons; it has established imperishable bases for democracy; it has founded upon general participation the most perfect cooperation between those involved; it has cheapened the price of the means of subsistence; it has been a powerful attraction to immigrants from other countries; it has given the incentive for the construction of a vast net of railways; it has sustained the demand for domestically manufactured goods; and it has created in all parts new articles for international trade.

Indeed, what, if not the hunger to acquire the ownership of land, has attracted this enormous current of American and European migrants to populate the solitudes of the West and to found these new and powerful States in the Valley of the Mississippi? What, if not the demand created by the extremely numerous and well-to-do *farmers* of these new regions, supports and sustains New England's mills for manufacturing textiles of cotton and wool, machinery, and agricultural implements? Who, if not these four or five million small owners, collect in their harvests these hundreds of millions of loads of corn and wheat and fatten each year these forty million hogs, and care for and milk these sixteen million milk cows, the products that make up two thirds of the food of the American people and two thirds of the articles exported? And where, if not in the Mississippi Valley, among these virile cultivators of the soil, were first organized the hundreds of regiments of volunteers who, under the command of Grant, Sherman, and Thomas, gave the stroke of death to the slave-holding Confederacy at Mill Springs, Fort Donaldson, Vicksburg, Pittsburg Landing, Chattanooga, and Nashville? Is not the aspiration to become owner of a small piece of land, to become free of the *rack-rent,* of the ever-increasing rent of the already monopolized lands of Europe, the principal thing which leads English, Irish, and German cultivators to abandon their homes in numbers of more than half a million per year in search of security and dignity in the American prairies? Is not the competition of millions of those who sell the foodstuffs that which, by lowering the prices of these, makes life easy, cheap, and abundant in these regions?

The large mass of owners of small farms, established principally in the West, today dominates the elections in this Republic and maintains the equilibrium between the semi-feudal ideas of the large proprietors of the South, the aristocratic tastes of the wealthy owners of the factories in New England, and the magnates of speculation in the central States of New York, Pennsylvania, and New Jersey.

Thus, it is in the United States that one can best study the change that the nineteenth century is beginning to bring about in the conditions of the collective life of the people. The ancient world was the kingdom of privilege, of the shameful exploitation of the multitudes in favor of the few, of the luxury of the aristocrats amidst the destitution and misery of the masses. In the French Revolution there arose, alongside the nobility and the clergy, the Third Estate, into whose composition entered the manufacturers, the merchants, those in the liberal professions, and the scholars and writers: at the present time the Fourth Estate is already surging forward in the form of the body of artisans and laborers who have received the right to vote in elections. In the United States, in 1880, of nine million of those who cultivated the soil, nearly five million were landowners and barely four million were agricultural wage hands. In this shines forth, therefore, the aurora of the redemption of the oppressed. Those who were previously slaves hitched to the ball and chain, later serfs of the glebe, and still later sharecroppers, have already begun to be the owners of the land which they water with the sweat of their brows. And this transformation is not as a result of the blood of martyrs, nor by means of a violent convulsion of the social structure with a promise of order and peace, but through the slow and sure action, peaceful but victorious, of the best type of human social organization.

Of all the grandeurs that I had the opportunity to see during my rapid trip through the heart of that country, none appeared to me so great as this social fact, because the independence, the liberty, and the equality of men does not consist in mere words written as a promise in the political constitutions, but in true and tangible facts which place men on the road to redemption. (In Ref. 442, pp. 80–83.)

Some other parts of the world also have witnessed the development of family-sized farms or of holdings which at least resemble them in many ways. In Australia and New Zealand such establishments appeared, except that they tended to be considerably larger than those in the United States and Canada. In Denmark after 1850, dairying and the production of bacon hogs for the markets of Great Britain gave rise to large numbers of flourishing family-sized farming units.

In Great Britain, too, the twentieth century has seen a remarkable transition from a system of agricultural organization in which a yeoman farmer specialized exclusively in the management of a farm of about 300 acres, one on which from five to fifteen laborers performed the manual labor, to a pattern in which the operators themselves do substantial amounts of the work. The activities of the farmer himself through the period from about the time of the American Revolution to the beginning of the first world war are well described in the following paragraph:

The farmer . . . (the man with three hundred acres or so, his own property) did not work so hard as his wife—in terms of actual manual labour he did no work at all. He looked after his farm, and controlled his labour, he went to market and fairs, he knew the value of what he had to sell, and he was a good judge of the sheep, cattle and horses which he had from time to time to buy, but of actual work on the farm he never did a stroke; why should he when he could get all the hard work done for him at the rate of two shillings or half a crown a day, and for some part of those years for eight shillings a week. Such a farmer could not afford to work, it was only a waste of his time. (Ref. 612, p. 35.)

This way of life of Britain's substantial members of the rural middle class was largely brought to an end by the train of circumstances generated by World War I. Primary in importance among these, of course, was the general mobilization of the farmers' sons and the younger members of the agricultural labor force, their long service in the armed forces, and their decimation during the four years of war.

The war robbed us of a generation, of all the best and flower of it, and the effect has been that instead of the son treading in his father's steps, and presently taking his place, it is now the case of the grandson having to succeed the grandfather—a nation of old men who can't forget old times, old practices, and the young, very young, men who have no patience with these outworn views, and no experience of their own. (Ref. 612, p. 128.)

With this thrust toward radical change, together with the mechanization of agriculture and the "dole," the years since 1920 have been ones in which many of Britain's farms have been transformed into those truly belonging in the family-sized category. Not only did machines take the place of workers, but the costly and efficient pieces of equipment came to be run by the farm operators themselves. The second factor, the "dole," had two important results: (1) It was very effective in reducing the available supply of cheap agricultural laborers, thus forcing the grandsons of the old yeomen to do much of the farm work themselves; and (2) it was the forerunner of a similar change on a large scale that has taken place in the United States since 1933 and the coming of the New Deal of Franklin D. Roosevelt. As the welfare rolls provided places of refuge for unskilled and slightly productive workers, the laborer no longer had to accept menial jobs in agriculture, domestic service, or any other industry; the yeoman farmers of Great Britain, like the planters of the southern United States, no longer could lavishly use labor in agriculture. In this way, in the England of the 1920's and 1930's, just as in states such as Louisiana and Alabama in the 1940's and 1950's, relief and welfare programs did much to help transform the small plantations and the one-time farms of the yeoman into family-sized units.

Finally, other parts of Europe also witnessed reforms that brought into existence variations of the family-sized farm. In such countries as Czechoslovakia, Romania, and Hungary, the "Green Rising" precipitated the subdivision of many large estates into units similar to those we call family-sized farms. In some cases, they more nearly resembled the yeoman holdings in Britain than they did the genuine family-sized units in the United States, but certainly they represented a significant step away from the domination of large estates and their many socioeconomic problems.

Since World War II, agrarian reforms in some areas have brought some peasants closer to being operators of family-sized units. In many of these cases, the cultivators have been able to move up into the lower middle class. Such substantial agrarian reform programs have been carried out in Japan, Taiwan, the Philippines, Italy, Egypt, and Venezuela. In Mexico, a "reform of the reform" has created more family-sized establishments. Furthermore, some areas that are now being developed effectively for the first time are benefiting from deliberate colonization or resettlement programs that emphasize the family-sized unit. These are well represented by many private and public projects in Argentina, Uruguay, and Brazil.

Agrarian reforms in the communist-dominated nations, however, usually maintain the bulk of the rural people as agricultural laborers. The completeness of this change varies from country to country. For example, such collectivization was completed long ago in the Soviet Union and continues to be the prevalent situation; it is the nearly universal state of the rural population in mainland China; and lately it has become the condition of those who till the soil in Cuba. On the other hand, although collectivization was begun in such "satellite" countries as Poland, East Germany, Czechoslovakia, Yugoslavia, Bulgaria, and Romania, it was not accomplished in a wholesale manner and exists side by side with small peasant holdings of various kinds.

In many parts of the non-communist world, the trends seem to indicate an increase, albeit slow, in the proportional significance of the family-sized farm. However, many who would accept the evidence of this development also are entranced with the idea that in the United States, the family-sized farm is fading in importance and that it will soon be replaced by huge agricultural units, each employing a large number of highly specialized workers. This interpretation of the trends with respect to this all-important feature of rural social and economic organization is most commonly expressed in such notions as "the family farm has disappeared," or "the family-sized farm no longer is of any importance in the United States." There is no evidence to support this idea in the statistical data from censuses of agriculture or in the facts to be observed in rural districts.

The companion stereotype which seems to prevail about the organization of agriculture in the United States appears to be one in which the huge agricultural unit, manned by armies of hired workers and equipped with great numbers of machines, dominates the rural scene. California's great "factories in the field," Montana's "bonanza farms," huge commercialized plantations in the South, great counterparts of the "King Ranch" in Texas, and the like are thought to have replaced the traditional farms that were adapted to the amounts of capital, management, and labor that could be supplied by a man, his wife, their children, and in some cases, a few other near relatives, plus such "hired help" as might be needed in seasons of peak labor requirements.

The available evidence supports neither the contention that the family-sized farm is disappearing nor that which portrays the huge holding as the dominant unit in American agriculture. It is true that since 1945 the number of farms in the United States has decreased and the volume of production and sales per farm has increased. However, according to Radoje Nikolitch, of the United States Department of Agriculture,

Three observations demonstrate the error of identifying the postwar changes in number, production, and size of farms with the concentration of farm production in large non-family businesses: First, the very small units account for most of the net decrease in number of farms. Second, farm production, land, and other resources are concentrating not in a smaller number of large farming organizations, but in a rapidly expanding number of adequate farms. Finally, the number of farms and farm production are increasing more rapidly among adequate family farms than among larger-than-family farms. (Ref. 317, p. 84.)

Mechanization has made the family-sized farm in the United States increasingly efficient and has actually made it possible for such units to become an even more significant part of American agriculture than they were a few decades ago. If mechanization were inconsistent with the continuing predominance of the family-sized farm, these units would became a smaller proportion of the total agricultural holdings. They also would contribute less to the total of farm sales. The evidence indicates the contrary:

In 1949 there were 17 family farms for each larger-than-family farm. In 1964, that ratio increased to 26 family farms for each larger-than-family farm. For every $100 of sales by larger-than-family farms in 1949, family farms marketed $195. In 1964, for every $100 of sales by larger-than-family farms, family farms sold $275 worth of farm products.

In 1949, the adequate family farms (those with $10,000 or more of sales) accounted for 7 percent of all farms and for 23 percent of total farm marketings. In 1964, they accounted for 26 percent of all farms and for 54 percent of all farm marketings.

This rapid expansion of adequate family farms is evidence that the traditional independence of American farmers is not endangered by any concentration of farm production in a few "farming factories" or in large corporate businesses in agriculture.

Family farms are getting fewer and bigger, but there is no indication of their replacement by larger-than-family farms. (Ref. 317, p. 89.)

There is considerable evidence that efficiency of agricultural production does not increase indefinitely as the size of the farm increases. In an analysis of several studies of the influence of farm size upon efficiency of production, J. Patrick Madden found that operations on one- and two-man units could be fully mechanized and made to realize all the economies of larger size and that, in fact, extremely large units tended to encounter substantial inefficiencies engendered by problems of management and the handling of large numbers of workers (Ref. 267, especially p. ii). The vast bulk of agricultural machinery is, after all, geared to the family-sized farm and would be expected to perform most effectively under those conditions. The optimum size of holding for efficiency varies with the type of crop and other conditions, but it is important that the family-sized farm of moderate proportions can approach the maximum in economical operation. It need not be incorporated into a huge estate in order to be efficient, and it need not remain a small nineteenth-century subsistence operation in order to fall into the family-sized class. Efficiency, expansion of size and income, and the characteristics of the genuine family-sized farm all are thoroughly compatible features and all continue to be viable parts of American agriculture. No factors have been identified that might cause all this to change in the future.

Additional Readings

1. BAALI, FUAD, *Relation of the People to the Land in Southern Iraq,* Gainesville: University of Florida Press, 1960, chapters 5 and 6.

2. BAALI, FUAD, "Relationships of Man to the Land in Iraq," *Rural Sociology,* Vol. 31, No. 2 (June 1966), pp. 171–182.

3. CARROLL, THOMAS F., "The Land Reform Issue in Latin America," in Albert O. Hirschman (ed.), *Latin American Issues,* New York: The Twentieth Century Fund, 1961, pp. 161–201.

4. FORD, THOMAS R., *Man and Land in Peru,* Gainesville: University of Florida Press, 1955, chapter 3.

5. JOHNSON, CHARLES S., *Shadow of the Plantation,* Chicago: University of Chicago Press, 1934.

6. LOOMIS, CHARLES P., JULIO O. MORALES, and RALPH H. ALLEE, "Study of the Strategy of Change on Large Estates and Small Farms in Latin America," in Charles P. Loomis and others (eds.), *Turrialba: Social Systems and the Introduction of Change,* Glencoe, Ill.: The Free Press, 1953, chapter 14.

7. McBRIDE, GEORGE M., *Chile: Land and Society,* New York: American Geographic Society, 1936.

8. NELSON, LOWRY, *Rural Cuba,* Minneapolis: University of Minnesota Press, 1950, chapter 5.

9. SMITH, T. LYNN (ed), *Agrarian Reform in Latin America,* New York: Alfred A. Knopf, 1965.

10. SMITH, T. LYNN, *Brazil: People and Institutions* (third ed.), Baton Rouge: Louisiana State University Press, 1963, chapter 14.

11. SMITH, T. LYNN, *Colombia: Social Structure and the Process of Development,* Gainesville: University of Florida Press, 1967, chapters 2 and 6.

12. SMITH, T. LYNN, *The Process of Rural Development in Latin America,* Gainesville: University of Florida Press, 1967, chapters 2 and 3.

13. SMITH, T. LYNN, *Studies of Latin American Societies,* New York: Doubleday & Co., Inc., 1970, selections 14 and 19.

14. WHETTEN, NATHAN L., *Rural Mexico,* Chicago: University of Chicago Press, 1948, chapters 4 and 5.

9

SYSTEMS OF AGRICULTURE

The functionally integrated set of ideas, culture traits, skills, techniques, practices, prejudices, and habits used by the members of a given society in agriculture constitutes another of the basic relationships between man and the land. As were those discussed in the preceding chapters, this part of the social order also is highly institutionalized. Among most of the world's agriculturists, accepted methods are standardized on the local or community level; the value systems of the community are usually oriented to the preservation of the existing ways of cooperating with nature. This fundamental part of the cultural heritage and social organization of a given people is called its *system of agriculture*. This term was chosen in order to stress the complexity, systematic arrangement, and organic unity of the cultural complex in action.

The system of agriculture must be defined broadly enough to include all of the lore, practical skills, and scientific knowledge about agriculture, stock raising, and farm transportation. Thus, that of a primitive community may have as central elements the digging stick used by the women of the tribe and a set of religious or magical practices designed to promote fertility; that of the most modern farming community may involve a highly intricate combination of tested practices assembled from many parts of the world, well-established scientific principles, and mechanical and other engineering skills that were inconceivable when the operator of one of the farms was a boy in the same locality.

Historically, the acquisition of the fund of knowledge that enables the modern farmer to multiply the gifts of nature, to bring forth plants and animal products in abundance, is mankind's greatest accomplishment. Only to the extent that mastery over the natural processes multiplied the amount of food and fiber that one man could produce were human energies available for the other activities that have brought us to the space age. The present geographic distribution of various systems of agriculture is probably the most reliable indicator of the basic reasons for the tremendous differences in levels and standards of living to be found throughout the world. One of the principal political, social, and economic tasks confronting the human race in the second half of the twentieth century is to bring the agricultural systems in the "backward" or "underdeveloped" countries nearer to the high levels already achieved in many parts of the United States, Canada, northwestern Europe, Australia, and New Zealand. For many years to come, efforts to improve the basic agricultural systems in many parts of the world are likely to be one of the chief ways of attacking the hunger, poverty, misery, and disease that are the lot of most of mankind.

AGRICULTURAL SYSTEMS AND LEVELS OF LIVING

One who travels throughout the world, even in a cursory manner, is certain to observe that standards and levels of living vary greatly from one place to another. In most of Asia, for example, he will note that the lot of the common man is almost inconceivably low. In Europe, he will find that the peoples of the northwestern countries enjoy much larger amounts of goods and services than do those of the southern and southeastern parts of the continent. In the New World, he will soon see that the plane of living in the United States and Canada is much above that in Latin America. In the United States itself, he will see that, on the average, the level of living of those north of the Ohio is higher than that of the people who live south of it; and in Brazil, which occupies half of the South American continent, he will find that people living in the southern states of Rio Grande do Sul, Santa Catarina, Paraná, and São Paulo have much higher levels and standards of living than do those in the more northerly sections of that large country.

Naturally, since these differences have been evident to many people, a great many explanations of the phenomenon have been advanced. The one that has enjoyed by far the most popularity is, of course, that which attributes the basic reason for the differences to heredity or racial features. According to this line of reasoning, the level of living enjoyed by a given people is fairly indicative of its inherent capacities. Certain peoples have high levels of living because they are "superior," and those who have low levels of living must, therefore, be "inferior." More recently, industrialization has been seized upon by many as the principal cause or explanation of the variations. Overlooking almost entirely the fact that such differences existed long before the industrial revolution, this argument attributes high levels of living to a high development of industrialization, and low levels to the lack of it. We accept neither of these explanations as the important ones, and advance the truly cultural hypothesis that differences in the systems of agriculture practiced by various peoples are the real key to an understanding of the ways in which the widely varying levels and standards of living were generated and perpetuated.

The analysis of the level of living among any people may be resolved into a consideration of the following three factors: (1) the quantity and quality of the natural resources available for exploitation by man; (2) the output per worker; and (3) the manner of distributing the results of the productive process among those who have had a part in it.

Natural resources in and of themselves are of no importance until man's cultural heritage has reached a stage that enables them to be used. For all we know, certain groups of Eskimos in the Arctic regions, Indians in the heart of South America, or tribes in Assam may be occupying lands rich in ores yielding uranium. If left to themselves, there is small possibility that such groups would ever develop their cultures to the point at which these treasures would form a significant part of the natural resources actually used. The great iron resources of Venezuela or Brazil were of no consequence to the natives whom the Portuguese, Spaniards, French, Dutch, and English encountered along the shores of the New World. The cultural heritages of those Indians did not include a knowledge of iron and how to obtain and use it, although their need for such a metal was very great. They were as avid in borrowing it from the white men to make sharp and durable points for their arrows and spears as are modern industrialists in developing the mines, building the railroads and ports, and establishing the smelters that are essential before those natural resources can add to the sinews of contemporary civilization. Any inventory of natural resources is almost impossible to make because man's developing cultural heritage constantly is changing the facts of life with respect to what is and what is not to be included as a resource.

The output per worker is a more serious matter for those interested in the levels and standards of living in any part of the world. It is precisely here that the agricultural system in use has such a tremendous bearing upon the living conditions of mankind. In such countries as Argentina, Brazil, the United States, and Soviet Russia, the pressure of population upon resources is much less than in China, India, and most of Europe, but in all the productivity per worker is largely determined by the extent to which labor is used in the process of production. If human labor is expended lavishly, that is, if it is combined with relatively small inputs of capital and management, the output per man can only be small. It cannot compare favorably with the production per man-hour in a place where each person makes considerable use of tools, or power machinery in his work.

If, as had long been true throughout the southern part of the United States, the average farm worker uses relatively little power and equipment, and even if the hand tools that are employed are crude and ill-adapted to the tasks to be performed, production per man is certain to be low. Until the basic system of agriculture is improved, levels of living can hardly be expected to rise substantially. They certainly will not rival those in parts of the nation in which hand tools are seldom depended upon and the tools in use are much more highly perfected, and especially where generous inputs of power and expensive farm machinery are combined with the labor of the average farmer. If, as is the case throughout large parts of the American tropics, those of Africa, and those of the western Pacific, man's only aids in his struggle with nature are the ax and fire, the output per worker is bound to be small. Or if, as is generally true throughout the densely inhabited parts of Asia, hoe culture is the rule, supplemented here and there by a few poorly designed, crudely manufactured, and awkwardly drawn farm implements, the production of a few bushels of rice may require the expenditure of tremendous amounts of human time and energy. In all these cases, the problem of production is fundamental, and until there is a greater return per worker, the average levels and standards of living must remain low. On the other hand, where a system of agriculture prevails in which each worker makes use of plenty of land, efficient tools and implements, and large amounts of power—where capital is combined liberally with labor—there results a much greater rate of production per worker. Under such circumstances, given anything approaching an equitable system of distribution, the levels and standards of living can be very high.

The role of management also is of fundamental importance. If each person engaged in farming is a thinking, deciding, acting agent, performing for himself the managerial functions of the agricultural enterprise (as is the case on the typical farm in the midwestern part of the United States or on those that blanket northwestern Europe), the rural level of living is thereby greatly increased. It puts to shame the situation in the areas of large estates, such as the Indonesian plantations, plantations in the southern United States, Spanish-American *haciendas,* Brazilian *fazendas*, and other types of large estates in all parts of the earth. Where the men who perform the manual labor also participate actively and intelligently in the management of the enterprises, tremendous amounts of human energy are not knowingly and needlessly wasted in the production process. Such a combination of skills in the same person also greatly simplifies the equitable distribution of the product. These facts, plus the additional one that the worker receives a return for managerial activities, and interest on his investment, in addition to his laborer's wage, do much to insure a relatively high level of living. On the other hand, in all types of large-scale agricultural activities there is a tendency for managerial activities to be used sparingly, and labor lavishly, so that large amounts of human energy go for naught. The laborers, who are the breadwinners for almost all of the families, can at best receive no more than the meager return attributable to their own poorly used labor; and as a rule, the nature of the distribution process in areas dominated by the large estate makes it impossible for most of the farmers to obtain more than the minimum necessary to meet their bare creature needs. In those countries where the absence of a general property tax permits the greatest monopolization of rural real estate, capital is tied up in land, and the misery of the people associated with large estates reaches its maximum. In these cases, a most inefficient combination of the economic factors of production, along with the failure of the mass of the workers to receive any return for managerial activities, makes it inevitable that the level and standard of living will be very low.

A CLASSIFICATION OF AGRICULTURAL SYSTEMS

One frequently hears that the farmer today can care for 750 acres as easily as George Washington's father could cultivate 50. Allowing for a very broad margin of error in the estimates, the point still is clear. The improvements in man's systems of agriculture have been tremendous. With much reason one might maintain that only by means of such improvements was it possible for energy and thought to be devoted to nonagricultural activities; and that in the last analysis the development of science and philosophy, of commerce and industry, and of what we know as modern civilization was made possible only through the discovery and application of better agricultural techniques.

There is little need of elaborating in detail the proposition that historically and geographically, the variations in systems of agriculture are very great. It is well to mention, however, that some five thousand years ago, the peoples of Egypt and Mesopotamia already had systems of tillage vastly superior to those used in many parts of the world in the early years of the space age. By the time the Sumerians and Egyptians had perfected writing, they had rather highly developed systems of agriculture. They made abundant use of the plow, wheeled vehicles, hitching apparatus, draft animals, and irrigation in producing and transporting the food crops on which their civilizations depended. It may be that the agricultural arts never attained any substantially higher level until hundreds of years after Columbus sailed to the New World.

Geographically one can easily encounter the most diverse systems of agriculture, from the most simple to the most complex. Properly classified, these may even suggest the lines of cultural evolution through which man increased his control over nature, or cooperation with her, before recorded history began. From this point of view each of the distinct systems of agriculture described below may be thought of as a stage in the history of civilization; however, it should not be assumed that any given people passed through all these stages in sequence.

T. Lynn Smith has classified the various systems of agriculture into the following six types: (1) riverbank; (2) fire agriculture; (3) hoe culture; (4) rudimentary plow culture; (5) advanced plow culture; and (6) mechanized farming. Each of these will be described and discussed in turn.

Riverbank Plantings

Because this is the simplest and presumably the first system of agriculture, we shall begin by raising a few specific questions about the transition from a collecting society to one based on agriculture. In spite of all that has been written on the subject, the early phases of man's life as an agriculturist seem neither entirely clear nor entirely unknown. Precisely what was involved in the transition to an agricultural stage of existence from the collecting economy that is generally presumed to have preceded it? How were pastoral activities related to the two? Is it fair to assume, as most writers seem to have done, that agriculture began with tillage by means of the primitive digging stick or a crude hoe?

The first farming probably was only a slight transition from the collecting stage that preceded it, and no doubt, woman was the first agriculturist. It seems likely that she first interfered in the processes of nature by thinning out competing plants from among those wild ones from which she had come to expect a gift of seeds or tubers. This practice alone hardly could be classed as farming. However, when she got and applied the idea of taking some of the seeds and depositing them in a spot where they could sprout, take root, and grow, she had begun her long history as an agriculturist. The fact that one crop season probably followed immediately upon the other, so that it was not too great a strain to forgo the pleasures of consumption, may have been an important factor in the transition. The soft, mellow loam deposits left on its banks by a receding stream probably were among the first places she selected for her plantings. At least, primitive peoples learned very early that merely by saving seeds and pressing them into such spongy surfaces with the foot they could greatly multiply the gifts of nature. In any case, such a system of farming seems to be the simplest possible, since no tools are needed, not even the digging stick.

This elementary system of agriculture, which we call the riverbank type, is still widely used throughout the great Amazon Basin in South America, and in much of the Orinoco Valley as well. In those areas alone, hundreds of thousands of persons are largely dependent upon this simple process for their daily bread. It may still be used in other parts of the world, although documentation is lacking. Furthermore, there is at least some reason for supposing that the early development and perfection of agricultural methods in the valleys of the Nile, the Tigris, and the Euphrates were facilitated by the advantages these locations offered for these first beginnings of agriculture.

Where the riverbank type of agriculture prevails, transportation on the farm is limited to the back or head of woman herself, and transportation to the market, if it exists at all, is by water or by foot.

Fire Agriculture

Possibly, at least in some places, tillage with the digging stick or the hoe may have developed directly out of the favored situation in which nature's rivers did a thorough job of preparing beds for seeds. It is even possible that the first combination of agricultural and stockraising enterprises was one in which, as the river's waters receded, animals were used to tread the broadcast seeds into the muddy surface of the land. In many parts of the earth, however, another system of agriculture developed, one that is still employed by millions of people. This is the method to which we have given the name *fire agriculture*.

Soft, pliable portions of land are also left where a fire has encountered the highly concentrated, dried results of centuries of abundant plant growth. Such a newly burned-over area in a virgin forest lacks the many weeds that might compete with the crop. Hence, it is merely a step from the point where mankind depends upon nature's rivers to prepare the soil for the seeds to that in which fire may be relied upon for the same purpose. Tremendous areas in Central and South America, Africa, Asia, and Oceania are still occupied by peoples who have not passed beyond this elementary and destructive stage of agricultural existence. The word "destructive" is used advisedly, because in this method of production, annually a section of virgin forest or second growth that has been standing for decades must be destroyed.

Fire agriculture is a complex of agricultural practices in which the preparation of the soil for planting consists of clearing out the undergrowth from a patch of forest with a cutlass or machete, felling the larger trees with an ax, permitting the tangled mass of fallen timber and brush to dry for a while, and then firing the entire lot. This part of the process is performed during the dry season, so that when the rains begin there is a tract of cleared and spongy surface awaiting the seeds (Figs. 35, 36, 37). In many areas, no tools whatsoever are used in the planting process, the openings for the seeds being made by a few strokes of the big toe, and the loose soil filled in on top of them by a sidewise movement of the foot. Elsewhere, a digging stick or even a crude hoe may be used to open and fill the small holes in which the seeds are deposited. No hoeing or other cultivation is performed while the crop is growing, although competing shoots and suckers are sometimes cut away with a cutlass or machete. Frequently, some of the unburned limbs and branches are used to construct a rude fence about the

FIGURE 35. Fire agriculture as practiced in Pará, Brazil. Fallen timber ready for the fire.

FIGURE 36. Fire agriculture as practiced in São Paulo, Brazil, showing rice stubble and shocks among the burned timber.

clearing in order to keep animals out of the growing crops. Two or even three crops may be grown in quick succession, after which the land is abandoned to grow up to second growth, while the farmer repeats the process in another part of the forest.

In the parts of the world in which fire agriculture remains the standard means of producing food crops, farm and farm-to-market transportation have hardly advanced to the point at which the wheel and animal traction help relieve men and women of their burdens. Human beings themselves are the principal beasts of burden, atlhough those living near the waterways may make use of boats and canoes for transporting products over the longer distances. The use of pack animals also may be an integral part of this system of agriculture.

Fire agriculture, of course, requires tremendous inputs of human labor for the production of a few pecks of corn or beans or a small heap of tubers or roots. However, throughout the equatorial portions of the earth's surface it continues to be the sole reliance of millions of people for extracting a living from the soil.

221

FIGURE 37. The transition from fire agriculture to hoe culture in Brazil—land on which rice was produced a few years previously by the system of fire agriculture is now planted to young coffee trees, which will be cultivated with the hoe. Courtesy of Herbert K. Ferguson.

Hoe Culture

Once it has been established through trial and error that soft, spongy surfaces are favorable to the growth of seeds, the stage has been set for man to take another basic step in the evolution of his agricultural systems. Men and women of many tribes throughout the world hit upon the idea of using sharp sticks for stirring the soil. Possibly the idea of such tillage first came from the use of sticks in the collection of tubers, but the use of the digging stick is not a complicated development. In some cases, only hand grips were depended upon, while among many peoples the sticks selected and shaped were ones with which the foot, as well as the hand, could be used in the application of human energy to prepare the seedbed or take a harvest of root crops or tubers (Figs. 38, 39). Once such tillage was established, only the principle of fertilization was needed to make possible a permanent agriculture and a sedentary life.

From the digging stick came the hoe, which continues to be the chief implement used by most of the world's agriculturists. This development

FIGURE 38. The highly developed digging stick employed by the Indians of the Andean countries. After Guaman Poma, a Peruvian artist and writer of the sixteenth century, as reproduced in Bulletin 143 of the Bureau of American Ethnology, 1946, II, pp. 213–214.

involved the fastening of a blade of bone or other sharp and durable material to the base of the digging stick and then substituting a pull for a thrust in its manipulation. This fundamental invention was probably made independently over and over again by peoples separated geographically and historically. In any case, hoe culture rivals elementary plow culture, with which it also competes for dominance as the world's most widely used system of agriculture. In the opening decades of the space age, hundreds of millions of the world's agriculturists know and use no less energy-consuming methods of extracting a living from the soil than hoe culture (Fig. 40). Their ways of getting products from the soil are vastly inferior to those the Egyptians were using at the dawn of history.

In those sections of the world where hoe culture remains supreme, the sickle is the principal device used in harvesting grain crops. There, too, transportation on the farm and the movement of products from farm to market require the expenditure of maximum human effort. Men and women

223

FIGURE 39. Modern Peruvians using the digging stick portrayed in Figure 38. Courtesy of M. Kuczynski-Godard.

FIGURE 40. Cleaning weeds from a field of rice in Colombia, illustrating the lavish use of labor on large estates that rely upon hoe culture. Courtesy of Kenneth Wernimont.

themselves continue to be the chief beasts of burden, although pack animals or small watercraft may be used to a limited extent.

Rudimentary Plow Culture

Before man had perfected an alphabet that enabled him to make written records, he had developed and widely diffused a rudimentary plow for use in tilling the soil. Quite probably, the same inventive peoples were responsible for both, although the actual origins are obscured by the darkness of prehistoric times. The first plow probably was merely a digging stick so selected or so fashioned that two persons could cooperate in its manipulation, one pulling and the other pushing; or it may have been an adaptation of the hoe. By about 4000 B. C., however, the crude wooden plow, having a metal point, and drawn by oxen, had already become the chief reliance of agricultural peoples in Egypt, Mesopotamia, and probably several of the other cradles of civilization. These early plows, like their present counterparts in many parts of the world, were highly inefficient. They merely rooted and tore the soil instead of lightly cutting and neatly turning it. The fact that animal traction was used to pull the instrument was a revolutionary achievement, even though to hold the implement itself and to manage the oxen required the participation of several persons in the process. Lumbering oxen, with their jerky movements, cannot be hitched efficiently to modern turning plows, and their use in combination with the old rooting variety is even less satisfactory.

Rarely, if ever, were horses hitched to the rudimentary plows of the ancient world, and the same is true in the second half of the twentieth century. Throughout most of Asia, southern and eastern Europe, and many of the Spanish American countries, the crude wooden plows commonly used are drawn either by oxen (Fig. 41) or, in the more humid parts of Asia, by the water buffalo. In the ancient civilizations and the Mediterranean ones that succeeded them, the possession and use of horses was limited largely to members of the upper classes. They were used extensively by members of the elite for riding and for hitching (with breast strap only) to chariots, especially in activities connected with war, but they were far beyond the reach of the menial classes who tilled the soil.

Rudimentary plow culture, and the crudely hitched and inefficient animal traction associated with it, form the agricultural system still used by the majority of the earth's agriculturists. Its preeminent position in China and India alone would be sufficient to make this generalization valid, but the statement is reinforced by the importance of this elementary mode of tilling the soil in parts of Oceania, southern and eastern Europe, and much of Latin America.

FIGURE 41. The central elements of rudimentary plow culture as practiced in Colombia. Photo U.S. Department of Agriculture.

The methods of harvesting the crops and threshing them also remain essentially the same in this system of agriculture as they were, as shown by the earliest written records, in ancient Egypt and Mesopotamia. Then as now, the wheat, rice, and other grains from which man makes bread were harvested by hand with the sickle. Then as now, they were threshed merely by grasping a handful of straw and beating the heads upon the ground, by the flail, or by driving animals over the straw spread out on the threshing floor.

Transportation on the farm and from farm to market made somewhat less rigorous demands upon human energy in the stage of rudimentary plow culture than in the stages that preceded it. The use of the wheel seems to be an integral part of this complex. By the time man's material culture had advanced to the point at which he was able to use draft animals to pull a crude plow, he also seems to have attained a knowledge of the wheel and its use in a rude cart. Hence, the two-wheeled cart drawn by oxen is widely used today by the world's agriculturists. Slow, crude, and inefficient as it is, nevertheless its development and use has done much to relieve men and women from primary roles as beasts of burden (Fig. 42).

FIGURE 42. Brazilian oxcart. From a drawing by Percy Lau, courtesy of the Instituto Brasileiro de Geografia e Estatistica.

Advanced Plow Culture

Before mankind could advance beyond the level of rudimentary plow culture, several fundamental conditions all had to be met at the same time and place. Northwestern Europe was the scene of the early basic inventions and discoveries involved in this change, although many of the more revolutionary improvements eventually were made in the United States. Let us consider briefly what was required for the development of an agricultural system markedly superior to those of the Egyptians, the Greeks and Romans, and most of mankind today.

In the first place, a better source of farm power than that provided by the ox or the water buffalo was necessary. An animal with a smoother gait was needed so that the force could be applied more evenly and steadily. The horse was admirably fitted for this role, but for him actually to perform it, his use had to spread into regions where he was not owned solely by the upper class. This condition was fulfilled among the Germanic tribes of northwestern Europe, who were in contact with but not entirely dominated by the Romans. Eventually, after the use of horses as draft animals became established, types highly adapted to heavy farm work were bred, also in this part of Europe. These, of course, differed tremendously from the horses the Romans had used for their chariots, or the Arabian breeds, famed for their speed and smooth-riding qualities, used by the pastoral peoples of western Asia.

Secondly, the basic improvement of the system of agriculture required the perfection of hitching equipment to secure more efficient application of the animal power expended. Equipment adapted to the physique of the horse was especially needed, so that horses could be used to pull farm implements and vehicles. The old harnesses used by the Egyptians, Greeks, and Romans for hitching horses to their chariots definitely were inadequate. They depended upon the breast strap; and harnessed in this manner, any horse that threw his full weight forward in order to pull a heavy load would quickly have his wind cut off. Therefore, the perfection of a horse collar was of critical importance. We have not been able to determine fully the history of the invention and perfection of this fundamental device, but certainly its more important applications took place in northwestern Europe. Possibly the hitching of horses to sleighs and sleds furnished the idea that resulted in the lucky improvisation, but that cannot as yet be definitely established. In any case, the perfection of a collar that made possible the use of horses as draft animals gave the countries of northwestern Europe, and the new ones such as the United States, Canada, Australia, New Zealand, and South Africa, which received their cultural heritages from them, tremendous advantage over other areas of the world in the production and transportation of basic agricultural commodities. As suggested before, this initial advantage and its cumulative effects do much to explain current differences in levels and standards of living throughout the world.

The invention and perfection of a turning plow was a third development prerequisite to the emergence of a system of agriculture vastly improved over the ancient plow culture practiced by the Egyptians and their successors. This development, too, came about in northwestern Europe, and its beginnings seem to have come in Roman times. The attachment of two wheels to the beam of the plow first took much of the burden of holding the instrument from the plowman. By the fifteenth century, this plow had acquired a moldboard (of wood) and was coming to resemble a modern implement.

It is hardly an accident that the English colonies in North America and the independent nation that they became were the location in which many fundamental developments took place in the use of the horse as a draft animal, the further improvement of harnesses and hitching equipment, and the perfection of the turning plow. The shortage of labor for hire; the frontier society, with its stimulation to change and adjustment; and the self-direction and individual responsibility of the farmers helped create a social situation in which the search for the new and the better became a thing of great necessity and merit.

By the time the United States became an independent nation, the evolution of the plow was near the stage at which metal could be used for some of the parts other than the point. Thomas Jefferson worked out the mathematics of the turning plow; and the first steel plow that would turn the prairie soils of the midwestern states was made by John Deere in 1837 from the blade of an old sawmill. (Fig 43). These accomplishments are only two of the more important ones that came out of a feverish half-century of effort in this country to improve agricultural implements, an epoch that opened shortly after the United States had adopted its Constitution and resumed the activities of peacetime. Others that might be mentioned include the development of early types of reapers and mowing machines, crude threshing machines, and grain drills and corn planters.

The fundamental improvements mentioned above were accompanied or quickly succeeded by others. The second half of the nineteenth century saw the perfection of the mowing machine and the development of the mechanical binder as an integral part of the grain harvester (Fig 44). All

FIGURE 43. Replica of the steel turning plow made by John Deere in 1837. Photo courtesy of the J. I. Case Company.

229

FIGURE 44. Grain harvest in the United States around 1890, near the acme of advanced plow culture. Photo courtesy of the International Harvester Company.

along the agricultural front in the United States and Canada, aided by the exchange of ideas and machines among the American countries, those of western Europe, and Australia and New Zealand, headway was made in the perfection of a highly efficient system of agriculture. By the opening of the twentieth century, in the areas where the work of advancing agricultural technology had been pursued most assiduously, advanced plow culture with animal traction had nearly reached its acme of excellence. Henceforth, most of the improvements made concerned the substitution of mechanical power for draft animals.

As exemplified by the practices in the midwestern and far western parts of the United States and other areas in which agricultural methods were most advanced at the opening of the twentieth century, the major features of advanced plow culture may be summarized as follows:

1. The basic instrument used in tillage was the sulky steel plow. It was mathematically designed to cut and turn, rather than to root and tear, as its predecessors had done. Finely balanced and adjustable, it could be drawn with a minimum of effort by the three or four horses commonly used for the purpose.

2. Along with the plow went a host of other pieces of horse- or mule-drawn equipment, the exact ones used depending upon the crops grown in the locality. Among these are the mowing machine, the reaper with its mechanical binder, the corn planter, a wide

variety of grain drills, the cotton planter, tooth and disk harrows, and cultivators of many kinds for the tillage of row crops.

3. Well-established breeds of horses were developed specifically for draft purposes and trained to perform many types of work (Fig. 45).

4. Harnesses and hitching equipment included the all-important horse collar, cleverly designed and skillfully made and adjusted to get the most efficient use of horsepower in pulling wagons, plows, and other farm vehicles and implements.

5. The development of highly perfected four-wheeled farm wagons (Fig. 46) enabled transportation on the farm and to the market to keep pace in efficiency with the tremendous advances that had been made in preparing the seedbed, planting the crop, cultivating, and harvesting.

6. Threshing machines, cotton gins, potato sorters, hay derricks and balers, and many other types of equipment were used in cleaning the crops and preparing them for storage or for the market. Many of these devices were powered by animal traction,

FIGURE 45. The basic complex (horses as draft animals, well-balanced hitching equipment, the horse collar, and the steel turning plow) that helped raise the levels of living of American farmers to among the highest in the world. Photo courtesy of the J. I. Case Company.

FIGURE 46. This combination (horses as draft animals, horse collars, harness, and the four-wheeled wagon) played a fundamental role in the development and maintenance of the American level of living. Photo courtesy of the U.S. Department of Agriculture.

and some by steam engines. All of them greatly multiplied the strength of men's arms for the tasks of producing and processing the food, feed, and fiber upon which twentieth-century civilization relies.

By 1910, the advanced plow culture system of agriculture had largely attained its zenith of development in certain parts of the United States; the spectacular improvements to come were to be largely in terms of the mechanization of agricultural production. Between then and 1920, the use of horses and mules as sources of farm power reached its maximum and began to decline, whereas the number of tractors on farms began to rise at a dizzy pace. The situation varied widely from one part of the nation to another, however, and these differences should not be passed by without comment. Whereas the farmers of the corn belt and those in the western parts of the country had developed the use of draft animals and agricultural machinery to a high degree, the planters and other farm operators in the South continued to rely heavily upon hoe culture and, at best, an elementary form of plow culture. At a time when the average farm worker in the heart of the corn belt could unite his labor with that of three or four horses and make use of several hundred dollars' worth of implements and machinery, his fellow in the South had very little power and equipment to assist in making and gathering a crop. As the mechanization of American agriculture approached, the advanced plow culture of the midwestern and western states might be symbolized by the picture of a farmer with a team of four or more horses hitched to a sulky plow, a grain harvester, or a combine. In the South, on the other hand, the more appropriate imagery would be that of a man with one mule hitched to a simple walking plow, although even that would be a somewhat optimistic view of the system of agriculture then in general use throughout the region.

Mechanized Farming

In the second half of the twentieth century, agriculture in the more advanced sections of the United States, Canada, and a few other areas should be classed as mechanized farming. In this system of agriculture, the ordinary farm family makes use of a tremendous number of the most refined products of modern science and engineering. Light, large, finely adjusted implements powered by tractors are the core elements in this complex (Fig. 47). Brute force ranks low, mechanical and managerial skills high, among the qualities making for success on the part of the farm operator in the mechanized system of agriculture. In this most advanced stage of agricultural production, the efforts of a few hundred thousand farmers contribute more toward

233

FIGURE 47. Highly mechanized agriculture—simultaneous seeding and fertilization. Photo courtesy of the J. I. Case Company.

feeding and clothing the world's population than do those of many millions of the toiling masses who know no system of agriculture other than an antiquated hoe culture or rudimentary plow culture.

In large part, the farm implements used in mechanized farming are merely improved versions of those of advanced plow culture. They are larger, geared to higher speeds, subject to finer adjustments, and made of lighter and more durable metals. Many of the machines or instruments are adapted to much more specialized functions than were their predecessors; and some of them, such as the cotton picker and sugar-cane harvester, perform operations for which the older, multipurpose contraptions were completely unsuited. In addition, such machines as the flame cultivator are based on entirely different principles of weed control, and the use of the airplane for dusting purposes is a radical depature from earlier methods of spreading insecticides (Figs. 48–52).

In all probability mechanized farming is still only in its beginning stages, and two decades from now, when it may be more highly perfected, the implements and machines in use may make the most advanced ones used at present seem antiquated indeed. It may only then be possible for us to

FIGURE 48. Highly mechanized agriculture—airplane dusting a Surinam rice paddy to control insects. Photo courtesy of *Foreign Agriculture*.

see clearly the principal identifying characteristics of mechanized farming. Even so, mechanization is becoming the chief hope of those attempting to bring about agricultural development in many parts of the earth.

FIGURE 49. Highly mechanized agriculture—simultaneous preparation of seedbed and planting. Photo courtesy of the Ford Motor Company.

FIGURE 50. Self-propelled picker at work harvesting cotton. Photo courtesy of John Deere and Company.

FIGURE 51. Self-propelled combine harvesting grain in the western United States. Photo courtesy of the Ford Motor Company.

FIGURE 52. The use of complex machines—harvesting, cleaning, and loading corn. Note that only two men are needed to operate all the costly and effective equipment. Photo courtesy of John Deere and Company.

Additional Readings

1. BERTRAND, ALVIN L., *Agricultural Mechanization and Social Change in Rural Louisiana,* Louisiana AES Bulletin No. 458, Baton Rouge: Louisiana State University, 1951.

2. BERTRAND, ALVIN L., "Social Patterns and Systems of Farming," in Alvin L. Bertrand (ed.), *Rural Sociology,* New York: McGraw-Hill Book Company, Inc., 1958, chapter 13.

3. HATHAWAY, DALE E., J. ALLAN BEEGLE, and W. KEITH BRYANT, *People of Rural America* (A 1960 Census Monograph), Washington: Government Printing Office, 1968, chapters VIII and IX.

4. PEDERSEN, HARALD A., "Mechanized Agriculture and the Farm Laborer," *Rural Sociology,* Vol. 19, No. 2 (June, 1954), pp. 143–151.

5. PEDERSEN, HARALD A., and ARTHUR F. RAPER, *The Cotton Plantation in Transition,* Mississippi AES Bulletin No. 508, State College: Mississippi State University, 1954.

6. RAMSEY, CHARLES E., and JENARO COLLAZO, "Some Problems of Cross-cultural Measurement," *Rural Sociology,* Vol. 25, No. 1 (March, 1960), pp. 91–106.

7. RYAN, BRYCE, "The Agricultural Systems of Ceylon," *Rural Sociology,* Vol. 20, No. 1 (March, 1955), pp. 16–24.

8. SHARP, EMMIT K., and CHARLES E. RAMSEY, "Criteria of Item Selection in Level of Living Scales," *Rural Sociology,* Vol. 28, No. 2 (June, 1963), pp. 146–164.

9. SKRABANEK, ROBERT L., "Commercial Farming in the United States," *Rural Sociology,* Vol. 19, No. 2 (June, 1954), pp. 136–142.

10. SMITH, T. LYNN, "Agricultural Systems and Standards of Living," *Inter-American Economic Affairs,* Vol. III (1949), pp. 15–28.

11. SMITH, T. LYNN, *Brazil: People and Institutions* (third ed.), Baton Rouge: Louisiana State University Press, 1963, chapters X and XV.

12. SMITH, T. LYNN, *Colombia: Social Structure and the Process of Development,* Gainesville: University of Florida Press, 1967, chapter 5.

13. SMITH, T. LYNN, *The Process of Rural Development in Latin America,* Gainesville: University of Florida Press, 1967, chapter 4.

14. SMITH, T. LYNN, *Studies of Latin American Societies,* New York: Doubleday & Co., Inc., 1970, selection 17.

15. WAYLAND, SLOAN R., *Social Patterns of Farming,* New York: Columbia University Seminar on Rural Life, 1956.

10

SOCIAL DIFFERENTIATION

Social groups, or the forms of human association, are the units of which society is constructed; and the study of social differentiation, or the nature and development of social groups, is of primary importance in the study of society. Together with the study of social interaction, or the processes and activities of social groups, it makes up the central core of sociology. Recognition of the importance of the social group as the primary determinant of personality is now widespread. In essence, an individual's personality is a reflection of the groups to which he belongs. The associations of which one is a member serve as the molds in which his personality is shaped. In a very basic way, one's social position mirrors his family status, his citizenship and nationality orientations, his religious group, his occupational category, and all his other associational ties. It is also impossible to determine an individual's status in society without knowing his involvement in particular groups, the relation of these groups to each other within a given society, and the relation of this society to others.

NATURE OF THE SOCIAL GROUP

Definitions of the social group are legion, although many authors make extensive use of the term without specifically defining it. An adequate definition of social group, it seems to us, must use at least three elements: (1) plurality of persons or social beings; (2) social interaction between these individuals; and (3) social solidarity or cohesion, sometimes designated the "we-feeling" among the members. The concept of plurality or combination is inherent in all groups, social or otherwise; it needs no expansion here.

Almost all sociologists agree that in order to have a genuine social group, interaction is indispensable. If this element is lacking, the term designates a mere statistical entity, such as a group of persons of the same age, and does not refer to a real, functioning unity. This point deserves elaboration. The social process is one of interaction, mutual awareness, stimulation and response. Individuals isolated on separate islands could never constitute a real social group. In the social process, each member of the group is aware of the other members and is influenced by them; his reactions are not what they would be if he were alone. In turn, he serves as a stimulus to others. For this reason, the behavior of the group is considerably different from the sum total of the behavior of the various individuals taken separately. Such a statement is not intended to maintain the possibility of a group mind, but merely to emphasize that a number of persons, by mutually conditioning one another's behavior, give rise to a product different from one created by the same individuals when they are not interacting with one another.

It is also important to note that plurality and interaction by themselves are not sufficient to bring about a social group. For example, soldiers of opposing armies in hand-to-hand combat certainly cannot be termed a social group, although they exhibit much social interaction, mutual awareness, and response to stimuli. They lack the genuine unity or cohesion between the interacting individuals, i.e., social solidarity, or "we-feeling," that is essential before a social group can be said to exist. Hence, it is pertinent to inquire how this unity or solidarity is attained.

Emile Durkheim, the famous French sociologist, has produced one of the most penetrating analyses of this phenomenon. He rightly distinguished two types of social cohesion among members of various groups, one type arising out of similarities among the members (like attracts like), which he designated *mechanistic* solidarity, and a second type dependent upon division of labor, specialization, and the resulting interdependence of parts, which he styled *organic* solidarity (Ref. 430, pp. 129–132 *et passim*). According to Durkheim, simple, primitive groups owe their unity almost entirely to such a high degree of homogeneity that one member of a primitive tribe comes near being a duplicate of every other person in the group. As social differentiation proceeds, and division of labor and function takes place, unity based on similarities is gradually replaced by solidarity growing out of the mutual interdependence of parts, each of which by itself lacks self-sufficiency.

Durkheim demonstrated the importance of his classification by correlating the type of social solidarity with other social characteristics. His analysis of the fundamental nature of crime and punishment is especially illuminating. Thus he shows that in a society in which mechanistic solidarity is strong (such societies are exemplified by primitive peoples and many small, isolated rural communities), everyone sees reflected in his own personality all the essential characteristics of the group. For this reason, in such a society, great stress is placed upon conformity. Departures from the traditional mores are dealt with severely; and an offense against one member is an offense against the entire group. Restrictions are many so that violations are numerous; and these meet with immediate and passionate repression and punishment.

On the other hand, says Durkheim, when organic solidarity (that based upon division of labor) is at the basis of social cohesion, the nature of crime is quite different. An offense against one is not an abuse that affects all. Some persons in society can play the role of mere interested spectators. In extreme cases, organic solidarity may cause law enforcement to become a contest between the offenders and the officers of the law, with a considerable part of the population acting only as bystanders.

Sorokin, Zimmerman, and Galpin have carried on the analysis of mechanistic group solidarity in much more detail. They set forth (Ref. 478, Vol. 1, pp. 307–308) a list of 14 traits of similarity that, according to them, are efficient in developing solidarity or cohesion among the members of a social group. The "efficient" ties or bonds in their list follow:

1. Kinship and community of blood (real or assumed [totemic])
2. Marriage
3. Similarity in religious and magical beliefs and rites
4. Similarity in native language and mores
5. Common possession and utilization of land
6. Territorial proximity
7. Common responsibility
8. Community of occupational interests
9. Community of economic interests
10. Subjection to the same lord
11. Attachment to the same social institution or social agency
12. Common defense
13. Mutual aid
14. Living, experiencing, and acting together

According to Sorokin, Zimmerman, and Galpin, at least one of these ties must be operating before a real social group is possible. They further classify social groups on the basis of the number of common social bonds possessed, styling those groups united by only one tie *elementary*, those possessing two or more efficient social ties as *cumulative*. These authors also demonstrate that the traits may cluster in varying degrees, that some groups are united by almost all of them, others by only a few. Cumulation of social bonds was naturally great in many primitive communities of early times, and is also common among the simpler of contemporary societies. Many rural communities have retained large numbers of their cumulative characteristics, particularly in those countries where the village form of settlement prevails. In several such instances, the locality bond is reinforced by so many other ties that it is valid to refer to these as cumulative communities. Urban groupings, on the other hand, tend to be elementary in nature. They are largely associations with specific purposes: functional associations, or interest groups. As social differentiation proceeds, the cumulative groupings tend gradually to disappear and to be replaced with these interest groupings or functional associations. Even in rural societies with the scattered-farmsteads pattern of settlement, cumulative groupings become very weak.

But despite their interesting and important analysis, Sorokin, Zimmerman, and Galpin neglect the important role played by specialization and the division of labor and the resulting mutual interdependence of individuals. Organic solidarity, or cohesion arising from the lack of self-sufficiency of the individual, plays an equally important role with mechanistic solidarity as a basis for social groupings. In fact, organic solidarity is the basis of the marriage group—neither man nor woman alone being sufficient to perform the all-important function of reproduction—and is thus indispensable in the family, the most fundamental of all the groups. Because it is present in the family, the importance of organic solidarity is great in the rural as well as in the urban portions of society. To a considerable extent the decrease in mechanistic solidarity has been offset by an increase in organic solidarity of the rural group. This is further complicated by the fact that in real social groups, the two forms of solidarity are not always easily distinguishable.

Thus, in summary, the concept social group seems to involve at least three elements: (1) plurality of persons or social beings; (2) social interaction among these individuals; and (3) social solidarity among the members, a unity that may be achieved as the result of bonds of similarity or as a result of the interdependence arising from specialization and division of labor in all the social spheres from the biological to the economic. As society has proceeded from its more simple primitive stages to its highly complex urban and metropolitan expressions, mechanistic solidarity has become less important and organic solidarity more important in the cohesion of its social groupings. Nowhere is this more apparent than in the vast urbanization now under way throughout the world.

PRIMARY AND SECONDARY GROUPS

Scholars have developed numerous classifications of social groups; but for many purposes the work of Charles H. Cooley is of paramount importance. Cooley was basically interested in the means by which the offspring of human parents acquire their personalities. He early stressed the important social role of the *primary* group, primary in the sense that it was the source of the individual's personality traits. By definition this is a form of relationship "characterized by intimate face-to-face association and cooperation." It is best represented by the family, the neighborhood, and the peer group. According to Cooley, human nature is largely determined by means of the social contacts obtained through membership in these three primary groups (Ref. 79, pp. 23–26).

To accompany Cooley's category of primary groups, other sociologists have completed a dichotomy of ideal types by designating groups lacking in face-to-face relationships as *secondary*, or derivative. These two categories represent one of the most fundamental classifications in sociology. As will be shown later, primary groups are of overwhelming importance in rural society, but relatively of much less significance in cities.

THE NATURE AND IMPORTANCE OF LOCALITY GROUPS

Another important basis for classifying groups is that of the territory or area occupied by the members. In addition to the family, which is the smallest social grouping whose interests and activities converge in a definite locale, human societies are always segmented into neighborhood and community groups. Each of these three occupies a definite part of the earth's surface and is an area of human association; and together they comprise the fundamental cells of which the nation and the total society are built. Even though the larger society may disintegrate, the smaller locality groups remain. Thus, locality groups form another important category of associational types that is of particular importance in the study of rural society. Locality groups are characterized by having uppermost the factor of territorial proximity. Like the family and other primary groups, they are forms of association; but unlike other groups, they have the territorial basis as a fundamental constituent. Within the category, three important types of groups may be distinguished: neighborhoods, communities, and states or nations. In the sociology of rural life, the roles of the neighborhoods and communities are of basic importance, although it should not be forgotten that the rural segment is an indispensable part of any nation.

THE NEIGHBORHOOD

Neighborhoods are the smallest locality groups. They are small clusters of families. Such groupings are present to some extent in cities, but they are of fundamental importance in rural districts. The neighborhood has been well defined as the next group beyond the family that has sociological significance. Literally, it occupies the area within which neighboring, i.e., mutual aid, is extended or takes place among families. Small localities in which country people live and interact with one another frequently, and in an intimate manner, are neighborhoods. Within the territorial limits of the neighborhood, primary group relationships find their first expression outside the family.

In parts of the world where the rural milieu predominates, neighborhoods may be the fundamental areas of association for rural people, who constitute the great bulk of the population. Such neighborhoods may approach economic self-sufficiency. The families in some of these neighborhoods possess so many traits in common that they constitute a cumulative social group of a high order of cohesion. Frequently, the families of a neighborhood are all related to one another. Differentiation along economic, religious, occupational, and educational lines is often so slight as to be negligible. The folkways, mores, and traditional morals attain a high degree of homogeneity.

Revolutionary changes in these patterns are under way throughout the earth, but in many places, neighborhoods still persist and are of great variety. In most places, it still is difficult for a family to be successful on the farm without the mutual aid of neighbors, even though, in the present-day organization of rural life in many highly developed areas, the function of neighborhoods has atrophied considerably from its earlier dominant position. Though neighborhood awareness has weakened, however, neighborhoods have not all disappeared.

Perhaps the best examples of neighborhoods are to be found where geographic barriers tend to isolate small numbers of people. Remote mountain valleys, coves, and tiny islands often provide the physical setting in which the best examples of neighborhoods are produced. Neighborhoods also have developed and persisted, however, without the presence of any marked physical barriers; for in general, the social organization of farm settlements usually has been oriented to the neighborhood. The families tributary to a local institution such as an open-country church, a crossroads store, a village market, a one-room school, or an associational organization often constitute genuine neighborhoods. Enough other activities may be attached to such an institution or facility to make it of the utmost importance to the families in the vicinity (Fig. 53).

In highly industrialized parts of the world, the neighborhood still survives, but in a somewhat changed and weakened position compared with that it enjoys in more rural areas. In the latter the neighborhood still retains a

FIGURE 53. A village in the Colombian Andes.

considerable part of its vitality, drawn in large measure from self-sufficiency, attachment to home and family, simplicity of manners, and emphasis upon kinship, friendship, and visiting. As mentioned before, such neighborhoods often continue to be centered around a rural church, a one-room school, or other facility. This may be the case if the village pattern of settlement prevails, as is the case in most of Europe, parts of Spanish America, and nearly all of Asia, or even if the scattered-farmsteads pattern is the rule, as in Brazil, Canada, Colombia, and the United States. Of course, the most rural portions of the world furnish a large variety of neighborhood types. Thus, while a high degree of homogeneity may prevail within local rural neighborhoods, substantial heterogeneity is likely to exist between them, even within the same society.

Many factors have contributed to keeping these small neighborhood groups in a place of fundamental importance. Among these, the lack of facilities for communication is important. Retarded educational systems also have been influential. Many other, more obscure factors are involved. For example, because of the persistence of primitive modes of travel in many areas, various local needs must be served at the neighborhood level if they are served at all. Attachment to small, widely distributed institutions for meeting some important needs does its part to assist in keeping locality groups small; and the neighborhood still performs a vital function in the social organization of rural life for the bulk of the world's agriculturists.

THE COMMUNITY

Communities also are locality groups. In general, they are larger than neighborhoods, although in some cases, it may be difficult to distinguish between the two. Communities also are more self-sufficient than neighborhoods. Today the neighborhood seems to be waning and the community waxing as the most important unit in the organization of rural life. This, as much as any other factor, has produced renewed interest in "community development." For example, in the so-called developing sections of the earth, the study of specific rural communities and their changes has played a major role in awakening and promoting interest in the modern pragmatic and empirical sociology. These studies are the ones that have most to offer those persons in charge of community development projects in Latin America, Africa, and India and other parts of Asia.

Nature and Definition of the Community

Because of the great variety of concepts denoted as community, even by some of those engaged in community development programs, it is of utmost importance that an acceptable definition of this basic term be in the mind of any serious student of the subject. We sketch certain generally accepted propositions pertinent to the subject as follows. In the first place, the rural community is one of the "natural areas" with which the sociologist deals. Each rural community has a specific physical expression; it is a small but definite part of the earth's surface. Even though its boundaries do not figure on the geographer's maps, they are indelibly stamped upon the minds of the local inhabitants. Indeed, they are the limits that determine effectively the area of social participation, mutual awareness, and collective action of many types. Hence, one should think of a community as a specific part of world, national, or state territory in which the residents realize that they are in the same situation and thereby are impelled to efforts for the welfare of the group above those brought forth in response to family and neighborhood responsibilities and obligations.

In the second place, the rural community is also a social group and, as such, is an area of social interaction. It is, of course, one member of a general category of locality groups; but it differs in some fundamental ways from other important locality groups such as the family and neighborhood. To begin with, it is larger than either of these, and indeed, it may encompass hundreds of families and a dozen neighborhoods. Whereas the family and the neighborhood are the basic examples of primary groups, the community may include persons and families who are unknown to each other and between whom contacts are of a secondary nature or even lacking. In fact, some of the families and neighborhoods that help to constitute the community unit may be openly hostile to one another. It follows, of course, that the persons comprising a specific rural community may be highly diverse in their social characteristics, and highly individualistic in many of their activities. They may have very little in common with one another except the fact that they all reside in one specific fragment of territory, depend upon its institutions and agencies for the satisfaction of their basic needs, and participate for better or worse in the vicissitudes of its existence.

In the third place, a substantial array of locality groups cannot be placed accurately in the neighborhood or community categories. These groups are clearly distinguishable, they occupy an identifiable area, and they exhibit interaction and awareness of membership on the part of the persons concerned; yet they fall into no categories that have been adequately identified or defined. Even the terms "semicommunity," "partial community," and "incomplete community" are not sufficient to bring about proper definition and classification of such groups. At present they must be thought of as intermediate members of the series that extends from the rural neighborhood at one end to the huge metropolitan community at the other; but their existence and proliferation make the task of community study even more difficult, especially in light of the fact that even the extremes of the continuum are often grossly misunderstood.

In the fourth place, the community as a genuine social group differs fundamentally from other entities having territorial bases such as counties, towns, or cities. A person may be a *resident* of a community, or of any one of the other three; but most residents are *citizens* of their counties, towns, or cities, whereas they are *members* of their communities.

Finally, the features of the genuine community are best described in MacIver's definition. He states (Ref. 266, pp. 9–10): "Any circle of people who live together, who belong together, so that they share, not this or that particular interest, but a whole set of interests wide enough and complete enough to include their lives, is a community."

Structural Types of the Rural Community

Because of the current importance of community development programs in many parts of the world, it is well to emphasize the various structural types of the rural community. This is the case particularly because, consciously or unconsciously, everyone engaged in colonization and resettlement programs must determine the structural type of the community in which the lives of the colonists or settlers are to be encompassed. The greater the extent to which this can attain the rational and informed plane at which such matters are handled in the settlement programs of Israel, the better the colonization and settlement projects are likely to be in Latin America, Africa, and Asia.

From the structural point of view the rural communities of the world may be grouped into two large types: (1) what may be designated as the village structural type; and (2) the service-center–farmsteads type. The first of these includes all those cases in which the community is made up of one or more villages or hamlets in which the agricultural families reside and that also contain the edifices in which are located mercantile establishments, schools, churches, the offices of professional men, and other institutions and services used by members of the community. The second includes all cases in which the homes of the farm families are dispersed amid the fields, pastures, and woodlands used by the members of the community, most of the farm residences being at some distance from the village or town that serves the commercial, ceremonial, recreational, and other social and economic needs of those belonging to the particular locality group.

Obviously, the structural type of community depends in a large measure upon the settlement pattern that is in use in the society or portion of the society of which it forms a part. Nevertheless, it would be erroneous to consider the settlement pattern synonymous with the structural type of the community. The former has a much more limited meaning than the latter. It refers merely to the spatial relationships of the farmers' homes to one another and the spatial relationships of the homes to the lands that are used for fields and pastures. But this should not lead to the confusion of identifying the structural types of the rural community with the more simple and limited features involved in mere settlement types.

For the most part, the village structural type of rural community prevails wherever the village pattern of settlement is in use. This pattern of settlement is characterized by the fact that all or most of the farmers of the community live in homes that are located in one or more villages or hamlets and in close proximity to the churches, schools, commercial establishments, offices of professional men, banks, newspapers, and other services available in the community. The members of the farm families commute daily to the various parcels of land scattered throughout the community's territory. It is importat to note that the line village of the circular type, such as is found in some of the settlements in Israel, also represents the village structural type of rural community, even though in these cases, the more customary village pattern of settlement is not employed. In these Israeli settlements, it is essential to stress that the home of each farm family is located on the land it uses (similar to the situation in the scattered-farmsteads type of settlement), thus vitiating any thought that they might be classified as village types of settlement.

It is also important to distinguish two subtypes of the village structural type of rural community. In many parts of the world, the pattern is one in which all of the services available in the community, and practically all the homes of the families making up the community, are located in a single village or town. Many of these are so small and also so slightly differentiated that often it is difficult to see exactly how the locality group that qualifies as a community is different from a neighborhood. This is to say that the personal relationships are frequent, close, and intimate, everyone knows everyone else well, face-to-face social contacts are the rule, and social differentiation is developed only to a slight degree. At the other extreme, however, many of these agricultural communities are very large. There are many cases in which population centers having as many as 5,000 or even 10,000 inhabitants are almost exclusively residential centers for agricultural families that gain a livelihood by cultivating the land within a radius of 10, 15, or even 20 miles of the center. In many of these, of course, the nucleus of the community is so large and the tributary area is so extensive that effective combinations of living and farming arrangements become extremely complicated. When farmers must commute daily between their residences in a population center and their fields and pastures in the surrounding area, the point of diminishing returns is quickly reached with respect to the distance through which it is socially and economically feasible to carry on such commuting. As a result, it may be impossible to make use of this structural type of the rural community, for in order to get the size needed for the maintenance of adequate social and economic institutions, it may be necessary to have a community that includes too much territory to enable crop and livestock enterprises to be handled effectively.

Fortunately, however, the second subtype of this structural pattern provides a relatively easy way out of the dilemma. This subtype is in fairly common use in the Orient, and it recently has been deliberately established in some sections of Israel. This subtype of the village structural pattern is one in which a large, central village is used as the location for all the institutions and services needed by the residents of a modern community, and in which the other portions of the community consist of a number of satellite villages (Fig. 54). The latter serve largely as residential centers for farm families, but they also contain a few such essential institutions as churches or chapels, elementary schools, and general stores. Because of the success with which this adaptation of the village structural pattern has been used in Israel, it deserves serious consideration by those in charge of coloniza-

FIGURE 54. The center of a large rurban community in Peru.

tion and other agrarian reform programs in other parts of the world. It also offers a way in which many already densely populated sections of the world in which the small village units seem to be one of the chief obstacles to progress may adjust to the larger and more diversified community patterns that seem to be required for satisfactory living in the second half of the twentieth century. Difficult as the changes involved may be, they certainly are small in comparison with the almost impossible task of changing completely the traditional systems of many areas.

The service-center-farmsteads structural type of rural community is the one commonly found in such countries as Canada, the United States, Argentina, and Brazil. In all cases it consists of two sharply differentiated parts: (1) a nucleus of considerable size, which is essentially a commercial, ceremonial, institutional, and recreational center, and only to a limited extent a location for the homes of those who engage directly in agricultural and stockraising enterprises; and (2) a large surrounding zone of open country, of considerable size, made up of the farms and homes of agricultural families who depend upon the social and economic services available in the nucleus. Where this type of community is found, it is not unusual for many of the schools, churches, stores, processing plants, and other institutions that serve the agricultural population to be located in the open country; and this is especially the case in those sections of the world in which the line-village pattern of settlement is the manner employed for arranging the farm families on the land. In all cases, though, most of the institutions and services are located in the village or town that serves as the nucleus of this structural type of the rural community.

The degree to which the open-country portion of such a community is integrated with the trade and service center depends, of course, upon a considerable number of factors, of which the stage of social differentiation is by no means the least important. Before good roads and rapid means of transportation, such as the automobile, come into general use in the rural sections of a country, the farm families in the area surrounding a small trade and transportation center may be almost exclusively dependent upon it for all the goods and services not directly available to them in the open-country districts in which they live. Later on, their loyalties, attachments, and patronage may be divided among a considerable number of centers of varying sizes, degrees of social differentiation, and distances from the farm in question.

RURAL COMMUNITY DEVELOPMENT

There is much confusion throughout the world as to the meaning of the term "community"; and a high proportion of the so-called community studies of recent years deals with what should be designated "societies in miniature" rather than with the fundamental features of the social group deserving the name "community." In many cases, attention simply has been centered on selected sociocultural phenomena as they happen to exist in particular small geographical areas. Frequently, any serious efforts to delineate community boundaries, to study the structure, functions, processes, and differentiating features of this group, or to comprehend its relationships with other locality groups are totally lacking. Furthermore, the wide variety of community types found throughout the world and the changes occurring rapidly within them greatly complicate even the most careful attempts to investigate this vital topic. However, even the multiplicity of vaguely conceived and imprecisely expressed ideas relating to the concept of community is dwarfed by the chaotic condition of all that has to do with the expression "community development" or the equally ambiguous "community organization." Community development may denote anything from the organization of rural educational institutions to measures designed to locate, delineate, and analyze specific locality groups with intent to strengthen the functions and increase the cohesion of the communities involved. Most frequently found, though, probably is the assumption that community development consists of organizing welfare activities or local self-help efforts. All of these activities are badly needed in most of the developing rural societies. Ordinarily, these societies are the ones in which the two-class system of social stratification has prevailed for centuries. They are the nations in which the masses of the rural people are either agricultural laborers or, at most, the owners or renters of very small plots of relatively poor land. Many of them are the countries in which hoe culture and the still more primitive system of felling and burning are the principal ways of getting products from the soil. Finally, they are the societies in which there is no local *self*-government, and in which all local government often is ineffectual because the minor units are merely administrative subdivisions of the central national structure.

It hardly improves the situation to designate everything intended to accomplish changes as community development. In this text, this expression is intended to denote the process of increasing the role and functions, the strength and vitality, the self-sufficiency, and the general adequacy of locality groups properly classified as communities, be they rural, rurban, urban, or metropolitan.

Causes of Arrested Community Development

The impediments to community development in various parts of the world need to be identified and measured by those working in the discipline of sociology. In doing this they are in a position to assist materially persons who are responsible for planning programs that will overcome the effects of such barriers and make possible the development of strong, virile communities throughout the earth. Therefore, it is useful to examine some of the principal causes of weak community organization or arrested community development. As is the case with most social and economic equations, the causal situation is extremely complex. Many factors are almost inextricably bound together in the causative complexes that are responsible for retarded community development in Africa, Asia, Latin America, the United States, and other parts of the world. Nevertheless, almost without exception, in areas in which the rural community is weak, certain features will be found; and it is well to single out several of them.

First is the concentration of ownership and control of the land in a few hands, and the consequent reduction of the masses of the people to the status of agricultural laborers. Where a favored few own and control the bulk of the best lands, as is true in several parts of the United States and in many other portions of the world, much of the population is held in positions at the bottom of the social scale. They are deprived of any opportunity to exercise the managerial and proprietorial functions, and at best, they can receive no more than the meager rewards attributed to their poorly used toil. They also are unable to transmit to their children any attitudes, aptitudes, and skills other than those involved in the routine performance, under the watchful eye of an overseer, of a few types of manual labor. Despite occasional exceptions, the concentration in a few hands of the ownership and control of the land means that the bulk of the population is reduced to a level of mere creature existence, and anything resembling a strong and satisfactory community life is absolutely impossible.

A second factor, closely related to the concentration of landownership as a cause of arrested community development, is the lack of control by the people of the community themselves of the basic forces on which their well-being is dependent. The system of large estates is part and parcel of this lack of control, especially when the landlords are absentees. In many parts of the globe, much of the land is owned by a few people residing in state and national capitals or other cities. Most of these landlords visit their estates only at rare intervals. Although they secure the bulk of all that is produced within the community, over and above that required to meet the bare creature needs of the workers, they make very small contributions to the support of community institutions and agencies. Because of the power that these owners exercise at the national and state levels, the people who live in the community largely lack control over their own destinies, chiefly because the small landowning group has a stranglehold upon the political and administrative life of the nation. They see to it that there are national and state prohibitions to prevent the people in the local unit of government from levying any significant tax upon the land, or otherwise establishing any effective means whereby significant proportions of the energy expended and products produced locally are pooled for the support of schools, the building of roads and bridges, the provision of health services, and so forth. Land becomes an asylum for capital, social pressures fail to insure its economic use, and the workers and their families exist in poverty, ignorance, misery, poor health, and hunger. Even the church languishes in the community whose lands are held by a few absentee owners.

A third factor in weak community devolopment is certainly the lack of schools and other educational institutions. Irrespective of the cause, unless it possesses adequate facilities, freely available to all children, in which they may acquire the basic elements of a general education and considerable training and drill in vocational subjects, no rural community can advance very far or become very strong. Also essential for the fullest development is a rich set of extension services, library facilities, visual aids, and the other means to assist the adult members of the community to keep abreast of current knowledge about technical agriculture, homemaking, and community living.

A fourth principal cause of retarded community development is the ineffective and inefficient ways in which the bulk of the world's farmers are attempting to wrest a living from the soil. Even at present, at least half of the world's agriculturists are dependent upon methods of farming that are less effective than those being employed by the Egyptians at the dawn of history. Wherever man's principal aids in his struggle with nature consist only of the ax and fire, of the hoe, or even of the crude wooden plow drawn by the lumbering ox, the factors of production are being combined in a highly inefficient manner. Labor, which is the very life blood of human beings, is being expended with abandon, and management and capital sparingly, in the production process. Production per man inevitably is very low. Under such circumstances, the members of the rural community can never produce enough to enable them to attain a standard and level of living that are anything except very low. In many cases, too, the standard and level of living within the community are still further depressed because of the fact that of the little actually produced, a large share goes to the owner of the land, who is not infrequently an absentee landlord.

Finally, many rural communities make a poor showing due to the simple fact that the area in which they are located is overpopulated. Therefore, with the existing state of knowledge of what constitutes resources and how they may be used, there are more people on the land than it can maintain at anything like a desirable level of living. Even though labor is wasted with abandon, there is still much unemployment and underemployment of the rural workers. In the most extreme cases, it seems that greater community lethargy could scarcely have come into being.

Locating and Identifying the Community

Before a specific community can be developed, the first logical step is to find and identify that particular locality group. Precise information is needed about the community itself, its principal features, and the location of the boundaries that separate it from other community groupings. This type of work has been a major concern from about 1910 until the present of those interested in the sociology of rural life. Nevertheless, such work, further refined so that it would be clear in each case whether the level of social integration at which the work was being done was that of the rural community, the rurban community, the urban community, or the metropolitan community, respectively, must be the first step in all well-planned programs of community development.

Identification of the community also should include an examination of the factors making for solidarity in the integrated relationships that comprise this locality group. Depending upon the part of the world under consideration, community cohesion may center primarily on various economic functions, ceremonial activities, administrative or local governmental efforts, or educational endeavors. In any given case, of course, when one of these sets of factors tends to prevail in creating and preserving community unity, the others, although subordinate, may also be present.

The economic functions of trade, commerce, marketing, processing of farm products, transportation, and related activities have provided much of the cohesiveness found in the rural community in the United States. In the scattered-farmsteads pattern of settlement that characterizes most of the rural portions of the country, the small population center that has formed the core of the community has been given over largely to these economic activities, drawing to itself the farm families living in the outlying countryside. In many other societies, the economic functions are greatly limited; a weekly market often is the only way in which they show much influence in producing and maintaining solidarity. However, in such nations, the economic factor is tending to increase in importance and to rival the administrative or ceremonial function as an element making for social cohesion among the community members (Fig. 55).

In many portions of the world, the social solidarity of the rural community derives in large part from ceremonial or religious interests. Mexico seems to be a case in point, although during much of the twentieth century, the church in that country has been formally restricted in its activities. In rural Mexico, the principal religious buildings and functions are located in the towns and villages that are the seats of *municipios*, or countylike units, and that generally form the nuclei of rural communities. Any chapels that may exist in other parts of the community generally are subordinated to the principal church and usually supply only a minor portion of the total religious needs of the members of the community. In contrast, the relatively autonomous open-country church in the United States has tended to be a rallying point in the rural neighborhood and to enhance the social solidarity of that grouping; but it has not been particularly effective in promoting cohesion of the community as a locality group. As a result, the religious and ceremonial activities in the United States have been far

255

FIGURE 55. Market day in a rurban community center in Peru.

less influential than economic factors in producing rural community solidarity.

In most parts of Latin America and many other areas as well, local governments, generally operating as subdivisions of the central government rather than as autonomous, locally controlled units, usually dominate approximately the same territory as that over which a given local church exercises influence. As a result, though the prevalent form of allocation of power may not make for community solidarity, neither does it tend to produce a large number of small, politically autonomous partial communities or fragments of communities as is often the case in the United States. In the latter country, large numbers of these administratively independent local governmental units fail to comprise the societal cells that we have designated as communities. Furthermore, a wide variety of other types of districts established in the United States, such as conservation districts, tax districts, and others, has been created with little or no regard for natural communities or other locality groups. As a result, the functions to which they are related rarely are elements making for community solidarity.

Finally, the rural school may serve as a factor producing social cohesion in locality groups of various types. In the United States, the small, rural elementary school has tended to be a neighborhood affair and to foster unity within that grouping. At the same time, however, larger secondary schools have been located in the trade and service centers that are the nuclei of genuine rural communities in the United States and, as such, have helped to promote social solidarity in those integrated and functioning clusters of people. In many other parts of the world, the school at any level has been so rare as to provide no important basis for solidarity of any degree, either in the neighborhood or the community. Even those schools that have developed in the centers of some larger communities in the so-called developing nations are such recent arrivals or are so few and far between and so unavailable to the lower strata of the population that they, too, are ineffective in generating social cohesion at the community level.

Community Scorecards

A method of evaluating communities must be developed to determine the nature and to measure the extent of desired and directed social changes actually taking place. Community scorecards are one device that may serve in this capacity. Only by a comparison of the situation at a given time and the assessment of the amount of change toward established goals can we be sure that a process of development actually is going on. The sociologist is the one equipped to study such changes in those locality groups that we designate as communities. This study involves, of course, the construction, standardization, and application of scales and other measuring devices that can be used to ascertain the score or standing of a given locality group at one point in time; and then, by later repetition of the tests, the extent to which changes have or have not taken place. Two or more applications of such a community examination, with careful analysis of the scores, are necessary in order to determine on an objective basis the nature, direction, and amount of change or development.

T. Lynn Smith has set forth certain fundamental propositions directly and closely related to the strength or weakness of a specific community; it would be a simple matter to construct and apply a community scorecard based on them. This, by successive applications, could supply a basis for determining the score or standing of various communities at a given date, and the nature and direction of change in one or more communities between the time of the first application and one or more subsequent points in time. The propositions are as follows:

1. A rural community is strong when all its inhabitants have had their human capacities and abilities developed to levels approximating their potentialities. In the

fundamental rural industry of farming, this state is most nearly attained when each person who gains a livelihood from agriculture is able to perform simultaneously all three of the basic economic functions, i.e., those of laborer, manager, and capitalist, with a skill approaching that which he might acquire under the most favorable circumstances.

Dexterity in the use of tools, implements, equipment, and machinery and the ability to maintain, train, pack, harness, hitch, and direct animals are essential to the efficient performance of the labor on which the agricultural or other rural mode of existence is based. In the strong rural community, all the members are exercising these skills to the utmost; overpopulation or underemployment, outmoded tools and equipment, and servitude to established routines of work and a host of other factors do not dissipate human energy and destroy the efficiency of labor in the productive process. Man is endowed with an original nature that enables him to acquire a vast range of managerial and entrepreneurial skills. These peculiarly human abilities become central features in the specific personality. In the strong rural community, they are being exercised by all the heads of households, and children are being reared who expect to perform them as a matter of course. Finally, the average person is capable of developing to a considerable extent all the attitudes and behavior patterns of the proprietor. Thrift, saving, the postponement of the pleasure of immediate consumption in the hope of securing greater satisfactions later on, and all the other features that lead to the accumulation and exercise of property rights, are possessed to a high degree by the average person in thousands of rural communities in many parts of the world. When the rural community is strong, the personality of the ordinary citizen is highly developed in the performance of the managerial and proprietorial functions, as well as in the execution of the essential manual labor, which he considers to be honorable and uplifting. In such a community, the masses of the people are not denied the privilege of developing fully all three of these fundamental features of personality by the nature of the class system, the manner in which the ownership and control of the land are distributed, absentee landlordship, the lack of opportunities for vocational and other types of education, and the dead weight of custom.

2. A rural community is strong when all of its inhabitants are enjoying levels and standards of living that are high, based on the potentialities of the area in which they live. This state is, of course, highly dependent upon factors discussed in connection with the preceding proposition. In addition to these, however, certain others should be mentioned. These include a population that is not in excess of the "carrying capacity" of the area, ways of extracting a living from the soil that husband human toil while making generous inputs of capital and management, the freedom and intellectual stimulation that produce high aspirations on the part of the ordinary citizens, and an abundance of technical and scientific information readily available to the members of the average farm family.

3. A rural community is strong when its institutions are organized and functioning in a manner that provides the fullest satisfaction of the needs of its members, insures that the oncoming generation will develop full and well-rounded personalities, and has the effective agencies needed to provide for the care of those who are unable to

care for themselves. The virile community also must possess a strong family organization, functioning effectively as a welfare agency and basic educational institution. In addition, it should have a school system and a set of welfare services that will bear comparison with the best in any other rural or urban society. Fortunately, since the basic ingredients needed for the organization of educational and welfare services are not elements proffered from the outside, but rather arise from the effective pooling and management of local efforts, with adequate care and guidance they are readily available to any rural community in any part of the world.

Basic Decisions in Community Development

Before much progress can be made in the area of community development, several fundamental questions need to be confronted and several decisions made. These questions are closely related to precisely what is intended by the term "community development," the kinds of communities within which development should take place, the relative ease or difficulty with which such development may be financed, and the relationships between change in a given community and that occurring in the total society. Therefore, at least four decisions must be made if planning for community development is to be realistic and effective.

First, it must be decided whether the efforts at community development actually are those designed to increase the effectiveness of the locality group that is a genuine community or whether they are merely relatively uncoordinated efforts to engage in rural welfare activities, to improve some of the technical aspects of farming, to foster self-help programs, and so forth. At best, these latter endeavors may improve somewhat the various aspects of community life, but they generally lack the overall perspective and integration needed to help create more useful and functional communities as such.

Second, assuming that proposed efforts actually are those designed to strengthen the community, the types of communities that should be made the focus of development need to be determined. The decision must be made to develop strictly rural communities, rurban communities, small urban communities, or those of some other type. In this connection, it becomes crucial to understand the patterns and directions of social change already under way and to identify as many currents as possible within it in order to avoid programs of "development" that may quickly be invalidated or subverted by countercurrents of change already in progress. For example, it would be folly to organize developmental activities around the small, highly isolated, self-sufficient rural community in a developing nation where burgeoning improvements in transportation and communication would soon decrease the isolation of such groups to the vanishing point, while greatly enhancing the social importance of much larger community centers that exercise influence over a far wider territory.

Third, whether or not the local governmental unit has and can exercise the power to levy taxes may be one of the most important factors in deciding whether it or some other body must undertake to carry on an effective program of community development. In many parts of the world, local governments lack the power to impose taxes that can be used at the local level. Under these conditions, the needs for community services may so hopelessly outdistance the ability of the community to finance them that either developmental plans will fail or the efforts must be taken up by some other body able to finance the proposed programs. When the only agency able to engage in such activities is the central government, the attendant red tape is likely to become so debilitating that little actual development takes place.

Finally, some judgement must be made as to the types of social cohesion that will be fostered as the community develops. In some places it will be necessary to develop a community in which similarity of thought and behavior and relative homogeneity give rise to that type of social solidarity designated as "mechanistic." This attempt will call for one type of planning. In many more places, it will be vital to develop larger communities in which the growing interdependence of dissimilar parts and more highly specialized persons, few of whom are able to function with any great measure of self-sufficiency, create the organic type of social cohesion. This development will call for quite different types of programs. It seems likely, given the patterns of social change under way in the world at present, that the latter type of situation is more likely to be involved than the former.

LEVELS OF INTEGRATION

There are in existence at least a dozen genuine social groups that may be considered locality groups; and at least half appear as rural entities. The many groups involved include those that range in size and complexity from a small cluster of families in a given neighborhood, at the one extreme, to the great metropolitan community at the other. As yet, however, we have only two concepts—neighborhood and the community—to apply to the 10 or 12 unknowns in the tremendous range that is involved. Just a little larger and more complex than the neighborhood, there is, of course, a locality group whose members are integrated with the services of a small hamlet at the crossroads. Its population is too diverse, its members are not sufficiently in contact with one another, and those residing in the locality are much too involved in several smaller and mutually exclusive circles for this entity to qualify as a primary group. Therefore, it is not entitled to be called a neighborhood; on the other hand, neither does it qualify as a community. The institutions and services provided in the hamlet or in other sections of the locality are far too limited in range and too restricted in number, and the inhabitants of the locality are too strongly attached to other larger and more distant population centers for the satisfaction of the bulk of their social and economic needs for it to be designated even as a partial or incomplete community. It is merely an X_3 in a series in which the farm family is X_1, the neighborhood is X_2, and the great metropolitan community is X_n. What may be called the rural community, the social grouping that deserves to be designated as the rurban community, and the locality group which properly could be designated as an urban community are three other X's in this scale. Perhaps they might more accurately be thought of as three additional levels of integration. They probably would correspond to X_6, X_7, and X_8, respectively, in the series. This designation is made deliberately, for as social differentiation proceeds, the tendency is for the loyalty and attachments of the individual farm family to be divided among a number of population centers at varying distances from its home, and it is by no means uncommon for a given farm family to be integrated into a rural community at one level and into a rurban, urban, or even metropolitan community at another. In any case, because we have as yet only the term "community" to apply to such a wide diversity of locality groups, it is essential that modifying adjectives be used with the utmost care and thought. In order to distinguish between a rural community, a rurban community, and an urban community, we suggest the following:

The *rural* community category should include all those locality groups, large enough and complete enough to qualify as communities, in which the trade and service center constituting the nucleus of the community definitely is directly dependent in all essential respects upon the trade and patronage of the farmers who live in the open-country part of the community. Thus, agricultural activities are the dominating ones in the rural community.

The *rurban* community category should include all those locality groups that qualify as communities in which the relative importance of the urban features of the nucleus are approximately equal to those of the agricultural activities of the open-country part of the locality. In the rurban community, the agricultural interests of the group are approximately in balance with commerce, transportation, manufacturing, and other nonagricultural activities.

Finally, the *urban* category should include all those integral locality groupings (and not merely the portions within the corporate limits of the urban centers) in which the farmers who live in the open-country districts surrounding the cities definitely have their social and economic life intertwined to a considerable degree with that of the people who live within the urban center. In the urban community, though, agricultural interests definitely do not dominate community affairs, as is the case in the rural community; nor are they even approximately in balance with the nonagricultural interests of the locality groupings, as is the situation in the rurban community. The needs and wishes of the people in the farming area of any urban community play a secondary role, or little or no role at all, in the determination of community policies and activities. When they form a part of an urban community, the farmers in the zone surrounding the nucleus are largely dependent on their personal relationships with those who manage certain mercantile establishments, those who direct the activities of specific institutions, and so on, for the services they need. They personally are able to do little or nothing to influence directly the various community services and agencies as such.

Within a given country at a given time, of course, there is a wide variation from one part to another in the degree to which the society is in the neighborhood, the rural community, or some other stage of social organization. In a particular society, at the same time that the locality groupings of all sizes, from the individual farm family to the urban community, are being integrated thoroughly into a great metropolitan community such as New York or London, Rio de Janeiro or Buenos Aires, or Moscow or Delhi, there are other sections of the same nation in which the rural community is still the dominant locality group, and still others in which rurban communities represent the maximum level of social integration. In fact, in the more remote and isolated sections of the country, the neighborhood may actually continue to be the fundamental locality grouping. All of this will necessitate a great deal of study before the science of sociology actually will be well prepared to play the role that it should in the entire process of community development.

Additional Readings

1. BERTRAND, ALVIN L., "Rural Locality Groups: Changing Patterns, Change Factors, and Implications," *Rural Sociology,* Vol. 19, No. 2 (June, 1954), pp. 174–179.

2. ENSMINGER, DOUGLAS, "Rural Neighborhoods and Communities," in Carl C. Taylor and others, *Rural Life in the United States,* New York: Alfred A. Knopf, 1949, chapter IV.

3. FORD, THOMAS R., and WILLIS A. SUTTON, "The Impact of Change on Rural Communities and Fringe Areas: Review of a Decade's Research," in James H. Copp (ed.), *Our Changing Rural Society: Perspectives and Trends,* Ames: Iowa State University Press, 1964, chapter 6.

4. HALPERN, JOEL M., *The Changing Village Community,* Englewood Cliffs, N. J.: Prentice-Hall, Inc., 1967.

5. NELSON, BARDIN H., "Neighborhood and Community Organization and Trends," and "Community Development Programs," in Alvin L. Betrand (ed.), *Rural Sociology,* New York: McGraw-Hill Book Company, Inc., 1958, chapters 6 and 7, respectively.

6. NELSON, LOWRY, *Rural Cuba,* Minneapolis: University of Minnesota Press, 1950, chapter IV.

7. NELSON, LOWRY, CHARLES E. RAMSEY, and COOLIE VERNER, *Community Structure and Change,* New York: The Macmillan Company, 1960.

8. ROGERS, EVERETT M., *Social Change in Rural Society,* New York: Appleton-Century-Crofts, Inc., 1960, chapter 6.

9. SANDERS, IRWIN T., "Community Development Programs in Sociological Perspective," in James H. Copp (ed.), *Our Changing Rural Society: Perspectives and Trends,* Ames: Iowa State University Press, 1964, chapter 10 .

10. SLOCUM, WALTER L., *Agricultural Sociology,* New York: Harper & Brothers, 1962, chapters 19 and 25.

11. SMITH, T. LYNN, *Brazil: People and Institutions* (third ed.), Baton Rouge: Louisiana State University Press, 1963, chapter XVII.

12. SMITH, T. LYNN, *Colombia: Social Structure and the Process of Development,* Gainesville: University of Florida Press, 1967, chapter 8.

13. SMITH, T. LYNN, *The Process of Rural Development in Latin America,* Gainesville: University of Florida Press, 1967, chapters 5 and 6.

14. SMITH, T. LYNN, *Studies of Latin American Societies,* New York: Doubleday & Co., Inc., 1970, selections 8, 9, 11, 20, and 21.

15. SOROKIN, PITIRIM A., CARLE C. ZIMMERMAN, and CHARLES J. GALPIN, *A Systematic Source Book in Rural Sociology,* Minneapolis: University of Minnesota Press, 1930, Vol. I, chapter VI.

16. ZIMMERMAN, CARLE C., *The Changing Community,* New York: Harper & Brothers, 1938.

11
SOCIAL STRATIFICATION

Although the terms "class" and "caste" are used frequently in sociological literature, their connotations are by no means universally agreed upon. It is certain, however, that there is in existence no Utopian society in which class lines are entirely obliterated; every society is stratified to some extent. Some members of every society enjoy more rights and privileges, consume more goods and services, and acquire more duties and obligations than other members of the same society. Society is divided into layers, some of which occupy a higher position than do others. Therefore, the study of human society inevitably involves a consideration of social stratification.

THE CONCEPT OF SOCIAL CLASS

It is rather generally accepted practice to refer to the layers or strata found in society as social classes. Inequalities in wealth and income, therefore, are evidences of economic stratification; the existence of social ranks within a group, some members enjoying more authority and prestige, more honors and titles than others, is a proof of sociopolitical stratification; and a situation in which some occupations are preferred to others, in which some types of work are considered more honorable, dignified, and uplifting than others, and in which those engaging in some activities have authority over those employed at other tasks is a demonstration of occupational stratification. As it is often used, the term "class" is no more than the designation for a number of individuals in the same society whose economic, occupational, and political statuses are closely similar.

265

Social class, as the term is used in this text, has a very specific meaning. In the first place, it does denote a number of persons, in a given society, whose economic, occupational, and sociopolitical levels are closely similar. In the second place, these individuals also must recognize that they have a social and economic status similar to that of their fellows; they must be conscious of the fact that the fortunes of all those on their level are inextricably bound together, and thereby be impelled to identify with those on a comparable social plane. The second part of this definition is intended to indicate that there is no social class, regardless of similarities in levels of living, felt needs, and ambitions, unless a "consciousness of kind," a group solidarity has been established.

In order to arrive at such a concept of social class, one must, of course, be cognizant of the fact that all societies are divided into various economic levels, occupational layers, and degrees of social prestige and political power and influence, and that elements of a class identity are involved in each case. The varying amounts of wealth and income enjoyed or received by different people are very closely related to the occupations they follow. They also are closely associated with the amount of respect persons command from their fellows and the extent to which they are privileged to exercise power and authority in political and other social affairs. The three scales are not perfectly correlated: A few occupations, such as those of clergyman or college professor, carry considerable social prestige and influence, even though the monetary rewards generally are rather meager; an old aristocracy may maintain its position at the top of the hierarchy for several generations after the bulk of its wealth and income has disappeared; and it may take a long while for the newly rich to be accepted into the "four hundred" or its equivalent in any given society.

In addition to the designation *social class,* there are several other terms which should be understood. As suggested above, *social stratification* is the condition in which those who have the characteristics of given classes in common fall into the various layers, ranks, levels, or strata. These layers, arranged in such a way that vertically they form a graded hierarchy, comprise the *class structure* of the society. Within this structure, the position that any particular individual occupies is termed his *social status.* If the status is determined solely by the accident of birth into a particular social situation and there is little or no opportunity for that position to change, *ascribed* status is found to be highly significant and elements of *caste* generally are seen to characterize the society in question. On the other hand, if the individual is born into a society that expects him as he grows and matures to improve his position in comparison with that of his parents and if the necessary social mechanisms, such as education, are provided to make this possible, then heavy emphasis is placed upon *achieved* or *acquired* status and the elements of caste are virtually absent. Finally, a *class system* is the most encompassing of the concepts for it includes all of the features which are common to systems in general. From the sociological point of view, these are especially forms, functions, and processes. The class system, of course, is unlike other systems, in that it provides for the gradation of society into various socioeconomic and sociopolitical levels, the placement of individuals within these levels, the interrelationships among those who occupy the several layers, and the infinite numbers of social roles or parts which individuals are expected to play as occupants of the various strata.

CHARACTERISTICS OF THE VARIOUS SOCIAL CLASSES

The "consciousness of kind" indicated above is an indispensable characteristic, which must be present before any given group of people may legitimately be designated as a social class. In agricultural areas throughout the world, much of the social solidarity that prevails within the upper, middle, and lower classes, respectively, arises from the extent to which the representatives of each layer concern themselves with the three economic functions, namely, the possession and investment of capital, the exercise of managerial responsibilities, and the expenditure of labor. It is these three functions that are associated with the separation of agriculturists in the world's societies into the various classes or strata.

Where landowning elites are found, in conjunction with large estates or plantations, the members of the small upper class are usually only capitalists or investors, and frequently not very proficient ones at that; in extreme cases even that function is denied to the drones who may control much of the wealth and income of a society. At most they give only cursory thought to the managerial activities associated with their holdings and they avoid in every possible way even the slightest participation in any of the laboring tasks involved. There are a few exceptions, however, the most notable being the British landowning gentry, who do engage in many cases in managerial functions. Moreover, they generally reside on their properties as contrasted with the absentee landlords who comprise the upper class in many other regions of large holdings. Yet, in common with members of the agricultural upper classes in other sections of the globe, they engage in none of the manual tasks that must be done on their estates. These are left to the laboring classes, although in areas where the landowners themselves are involved in farm management the workers frequently are spared much of the abuse to which

267

their fellows are subject in places where the agricultural and pastoral operations are a matter of slight importance to the proprietors and are left in the hands of some kind of overseers, managers, or administrators.

In areas with large estates, the inevitable antithesis of the small upper class is the large lower class of persons who toil on the land. Under these circumstances, members of the two layers are separated by a vast social chasm, and there is usually little in the way of a middle class which would serve to mitigate the debilities and abuses created by a two-class system and by the lack of vertical social mobility that goes with it. Thus, it is the status of laborer, involving no participation in any of the entrepreneurial functions and virtually none in managerial duties, that generates the characteristics of those in the lower strata in the two-class situation. Toil with the hands, the indelible mark of inferior status in this type of social organization, becomes the one that creates among their members the recognition of common interests and the bond of unity. It is the essence of their "consciousness of kind." It may be, of course, that the managerial function is not effectively carried out by anyone on the large estates, including those who ostensibly are charged with "managing," and under such conditions the laborer, working a few acres, may develop some rudimentary managerial techniqes and talents, but these are of little importance in creating the sense of solidarity and identity among the workers; labor continues to be the essence of their being. The overall organization of the estate system, the lack of preparation and training for managerial duties on the part of the serfs, sharecroppers, peons, and other menial types, and the tendency for underproduction, inefficiency, and traditional routine to become institutionalized, rarely allow members of the lower class to identify with any status except that of the laborer. Moreover, the workers become quite adept at "getting by" with as little effort as possible; proficiency at evasion becomes an inevitable feature of their sense of values. It is to their advantage to devise ways and means of avoiding work and to perform that which they cannot avoid in as superficial a manner as possible. To the extent that they are guided by self-interest, their preoccupation must be with placating an overseer or manager in such a way as to avoid punishment, not with increased proficiency, improved methods, or change. All of these elements become parts of the solidarity which unites the laborers and gives them common bonds with others of their kind throughout the world.

Members of the genuine middle class of agriculturists are versatile with respect to all three of the economic functions under consideration. Usually operating on units we have described as "family-sized," these farmers save and invest small amounts of their own capital, which they husband carefully and efficiently (see Fig. 56). Unlike the wealth of the upper classes, these savings will not support any elaborate ostentation or any great display of con-

FIGURE 56. Dwelling of a middle-class farm family on a family-sized farm in Wisconsin. Photo courtesy of the Soil Conservation Service.

spicuous consumption. The interest earned by such capital is merely one of the three sources of the income from which the middle-class family derives its total support. In addition to performing the role of the investor on a limited scale, the middle class is also the managerial group *par excellence*. Much of the responsibility for the planning and the execution of the details in all economic activities connected with farming is in the hands of its members. They expend considerable effort in such duties so as to maximize the return on their investment of time, money, and labor. But neither the fact that they are investors of capital nor their managerial responsibilities causes persons of the middle class to neglect and depreciate the skills involved in performance of any and all of the multifarious tasks involved in successful farming. As a class they do not consider manual labor demeaning; but they do seek in every way possible means of reducing the amount of labor necessary to perform any particular job, so that the energy saved might be devoted to other important tasks. Such inventive entrepreneurs are constantly recombining these three vital factors of production so that the maximum returns are realized from whatever must be invested in the total farming endeavor.

By no stretch of the imagination can these middle-class capitalists be thought of as possessing a feeling of kinship with the landowning upper classes who are neither managers nor laborers. Neither have they a sense of unity with lower-class laborers who are permitted access to no other position within their societies, even though the middle-class farmer also generally toils from sunup to sunset. At the very most, they consider the status of manual laborer acceptable only when it is that of the young man who will occupy such a position for a few short years while he strives toward the eventual operatorship of his own farm. A lifetime spent at nothing except agricultural labor is unthinkable among persons of this class. But they do have a very strong "consciousness of kind" with other members of the middle class of agriculturists who guard carefully the small investments they have built up, who assume individual responsibility and self-direction in most of their occupational activities, and who esteem the dignity of human labor. This sense of identification with others at the same level frequently makes for a higher degree of solidarity than is to be found in the lower-class laboring segment or even in the upper-class landowning group.

Class differences almost always become associated with the caste element, although the two are not clearly divisible. To the extent that free social circulation between the layers of the class structure is hindered by factors not directly related to the capacities of the individual members and the energies exerted by them, the class system partakes of caste characteristics. When readily distinguishable features, such as the color of the skin, come to be associated with class membership because of conquest, an old system of slavery, or other means, the caste features are especially likely to become strong and difficult to eradicate. This produces little overt upheaval in a static society, where most people accept the estate to which they were born and are permitted to receive few if any stimuli encouraging them to seek a higher one, but it is fraught with serious consequences in terms of personal frustration and social conflict in a mobile society, such as the United States, in which the channels of social ascension—educational institutions, the military, property ownership, and others—are open to persons who possess the physical characteristics which were once characteristic of those in a servile group. Then the scrambling of class and caste relationships may bring untold suffering and misery to millions of human beings even though they are making tremendous progress from the standpoints of material well-being, health, and levels of living. As the so-called "underdeveloped" nations are swept into the maelstrom of the modern world and partake of rising aspirations, the shattering of old patterns and the crumbling of hoary attitudes are likely to generate a chaotic situation in the relationships of class and caste.

In addition to the nature of the several social classes just considered, two other matters should be kept in mind by those who deal with the class system in any part of the world. The first of these is the fact that it is necessary to make a distinction between an *intermediate* social level and a *genuine* middle class. There are always various gradations in the economic, occupational, and sociopolitical statuses, even, for example, among the laborers on a sugar-cane plantation, where they all may be characterized as belonging in the lower social class; or among the farmers in a district monopolized by family-sized farming units, where all certainly are members of the middle class. The failure to distinguish what is merely a stratum intermediate between two others from a true middle class is responsible, of course, for much of the tremendous variation one finds between the estimates of two or more writers relative to the importance of the upper, middle, and lower social classes in a given society.

The second basic consideration that should be kept in mind by those who attempt to study and describe any society is that there is absolutely no reason for one to expect to find representations of all of the social levels or layers in the population of any given locality, state, or nation. Geologists certainly do not count upon finding examples of all of the earth's strata in any one specific location, and there is no more reason why the sociologist should assume that he will discover all of the social classes in a given place at any particular time. Indeed, in the family-sized farming districts of the midwestern part of the United States, all of the major socioeconomic levels are subsumed under one genuine middle class; members of the upper and lower classes are conspicuously absent. In many other societies, especially those in which a system of large estates has dominated the social, economic, and political aspects of rural life, the traditional pattern is a two-class system in which there is a small stratum of elite families at the apex of the social scale and a large mass of impoverished, uneducated, unskilled, and only slightly productive workers at the base of it. Such societies often contain little or nothing in the way of middle-class farm families to help fill the broad void that exists between the upper and lower extremes of their two-class systems, that is, between the small layer of the elite and the huge masses of servile or semi-servile workers.

CLASS SYSTEMS OF CONTEMPORARY AGRICULTURAL SOCIETIES

Actual class structures throughout the earth are exceedingly complex, exhibiting an almost endless variety of combinations of the ideal types of classes. The real situations are little studied, and in the present state of knowledge it is doubtful if any thoroughgoing analysis or classification is possible. It is fairly certain that there are upper, middle, and lower or disadvantaged groups scattered throughout the spectrum of the world's agriculture. It should be recognized, however, that in many societies these shade gradually into each other and that there are many lesser social layers within each of the three major ones. Moreover, as previously noted, there is absolutely no reason to expect all three of the principal social classes to be found in any particular farming district. In fact, it is uncommon for the rural portions of the most societies to contain representatives of all three strata; and it is quite usual for them to embody examples of one- and two-class patterns of stratification. For instance, a single layer of middle-class operators of family-sized farms is the rule in the "corn belt" of the United States, while the widely separated and sharply defined levels of a two-class situation prevail in the plantation South and other areas of large agricultural holdings. The latter situation probably resembles most closely the majority of the world's agricultural societies, although this does not mean that they are uniform or contain similar proportions of people in the various classes.

In general, farm laborers, including virtually all of the world's peons, sharecroppers, and coloni, make up the bulk of the lower agricultural classes and account for the majority of the earth's agriculturists. Among the lower classes the hierarchy would, no doubt, have the migratory agricultural workers, those who follow the crops and have no fixed residence and no established status, at the bottom of the scale; sharecroppers and coloni probably occupy at most times and in most places the middle stratum; and the wage hands and peasant proprietors or renters of small tracts rank at the top of these disadvantaged groups. The middle classes, most numerous in those portions of the earth given over exclusively to the family-sized farm system, are made up of farm operators, both owners and renters. In these cases, a family's position is determined about as much by stability, permanence, and dependability as by the ownership of land. The upper agricultural classes consist almost entirely of large landholders, and only where a system of large estates long has been dominant is a genuine elite likely to exist. Such a hereditary upper class in the rural portions of the world may be found on the traditional plantations, on the large estates which have passed intact through many generations of the same family, on the magnificent ranches which long have run huge herds or flocks of livestock, and on other variations of the large holding.

In all these cases a word of caution is necessary: The past history of a family as well as its present economic circumstances must be taken into account in determining social status. The "dead hand of the past" holds some families that have suffered severe economic reverses at a level quite inconsistent with their present economic circumstances; likewise, it makes it difficult or even impossible for the newcomers, the upstarts, and the climbers to attain the social positions commensurate with their financial resources. A family's social status frequently is more closely correlated with its economic status of a quarter of a century in the past than with that of the present. As indicated above, permanence, stability, and dependability are important factors in establishing the social status of a rural family. In a society where family-sized farms prevail, the renter who moves frequently soon comes to rank at the base of the social pyramid with the farm laborers who also shift about frequently; while the renter who remains on a farm decade after decade may attain a position similar to that of the landowners who are likewise strongly attached to specific tracts of land.

Major portions of the earth's surface are given over to agricultural societies that serve as specific examples of the general types of class systems under consideration. The two-class system, with a small elite at the apex, a large mass of laborers at the bottom, and few persons who comprise a genuine middle layer, has been the traditional pattern in much of the world. In such places as England and sections of Brazil, the two-class situation involves a true landed gentry who reside on their holdings; but in most places the landowners are absentees, preferring to reside in large cities and to leave the operations of their great estates in the hands of stewards or managers. The latter circumstance, along with the social conditions it generates, is typical of most of the Near East, the Far East, and Spanish America.

One variety of the single-class system is that which is found in areas of northwestern Europe, the United States, and Canada that have been given over to the owner-operatorship of family-sized farms. In these places, a genuine middle class is the rule and the most extreme levels of the structure generally are found to be the upper and lower portions of that middle class. In some areas of the United States, especially the South, large holdings have been the rule and have given rise to the two-class situation; but even in that general region there have been many operators of small family-sized farms who probably fall into the lower portion of the middle class. These are the people who live on the "hill" farms of the Ozarks, the Appalachians, and a few other sections. Likewise, much the same is true in parts of Colombia, where small farms in the hands of owner-operators are scattered over the mountainous terrain of the cordilleras. Finally, a somewhat similar one-class pattern seems to exist in many sections of Southeast Asia and Oceania, where the inhabitants fall into the upper segment of the lower class and the lower portion of the middle class, to comprise a stratum that is homogeneous in many ways.

In a few places, an example of which is Haiti, there are relatively large numbers of agriculturists who own and operate very tiny subsistence tracts but who are not the subjects of large landholders, for none is to be found in these few sections. Those in Haiti were liquidated in the "agrarian reform" that accompanied the French Revolution, and the descendants of the freedmen have never been subjected by new masters. Therefore, the stratification system that predominates among these autonomous operators is a one-class pattern, but by no stretch of the imagination is it a middle-class situation. The holdings are too small, the systems of agriculture are far too antiquated, and the levels of living are too low to make such areas anything but those of lower-class agriculturists. Nonetheless, they are another example of the single-class situation.

While it is comparatively rare, a three-class system occasionally may be found in a given agricultural area. Such is the situation in Louisiana, where plantation areas contain the landowning elite and the laboring lower class that make up the two-class pattern characteristic of the most fertile districts of the South. There, also, the hilly regions contain the small farmers, who fall into the bottom of the middle class. The latter are joined by the descendants of the Arcadians, living in the southern part of the state, who also properly are classified as belonging to the lower stratum of the middle class. Finally, the upper portion of the middle class is represented reasonably well by the operators of adequate family-sized farms in the southwestern or "prairie" part of Louisiana, where the production of rice is combined with the raising of beef cattle in much the same manner that corn, beef cattle, and hogs make up the core of agricultural production in the midwestern part of the United States. In total, then, the pattern of social stratification in rural Louisiana as a whole is accurately portrayed by a pyramid in which the upper class, two segments of the middle class, and the relatively large lower class all are represented.

The class structure of the total farm population of the United States is a composite of a multitude of more limited ones which vary widely from region to region, state to state, and county to county. At the county level especially, there often is sufficient homogeneity so that some highly distinctive patterns of stratification appear. Such places tend to generate one-class and two-class systems rather than three-layer patterns. In order to show a few of the widely different local patterns that make up the national class structure of the farm population, it is necessary to re-emphasize that the distinctions between the three major classes are based upon the extent to which the three principal economic functions are performed by the members. In turn, it seems essential to subdivide the large middle class, which contains more than two thirds of the nation's farm people, into its upper, middle, and lower components on the basis of the economic standing of the members. (For the data and procedures upon which these separations are based, see Ref. 463.) When this is done, the stratification pattern of the nation's farm people as a whole appears as in Figure 57. Five of the typical variations found in various counties throughout the United States are shown in Figures 57 and 58. They include the following:

A two-class system in which the vast majority of the farm personnel are laborers working on huge corporation farms is illustrated by the case of Imperial County, California. Our procedures, worked out for application to all counties in the nation and limited by the kinds of data available for such units, attribute those in Imperial County who manage the farms and super-vise the activities of the workers to the upper class. Obviously, they belong with those who make up the middle sectors, despite the fact that their duties are merely extensions of the activities of the large corporate entities that own the farms and provide the operating capital. Nevertheless, their placement in the stratification system cannot obscure the highly significant fact that the class structure consists essentially of two parts: (1) the very large lower stratum of workers; and (2) several proportionately small higher social layers composed of those who manage the farms. This structure also is well repre-sented in Palm Beach County, Florida, and other sections of the country where the extremely large, highly commercialized farm holds sway, and the class system is made up of a large proportion of laborers and a relative hand-ful of others who are responsible for management of the operations. Some-thing similar is found in such places as Dutchess County, New York, where over half of the agriculturists are in the lower class. In that county, however, a three-class system is generated by large corporation dairy farms, which employ many laborers and a few middle-class managers, and by a small number of large landed proprietors, a rural gentry who are upper class in every sense of the term.

Another two-class system prevails in the cotton plantation sections of the South as represented by Tunica County, Mississippi. There, lower-class laborers comprise over three quarters of the farm people, the managers and overseers make up a small middle stratum, and the plantation owners con-stitute the tiny elite at the summit of local and state society. A similar pattern exists in other plantation sections of the South, especially where the crop is either cotton or sugar cane.

A one-class system, in which the bulk of the farm people fall into the top stratum of the middle class, is typified by the pattern in Shelby County, Iowa. There the highly mechanized substantial family-sized farm dominates agri-culture, and rare indeed are those who must be classed merely as laborers occupying the lowest stratum of society. Uncommon also or entirely lacking are persons who belong to an upper class. The pattern is repeated in other

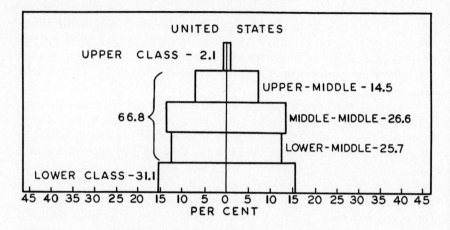

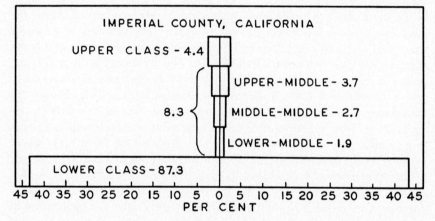

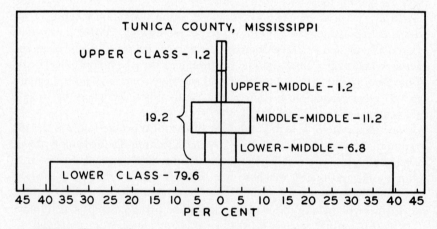

FIGURE 57. Stratification patterns of the farm populations of the United States, Imperial County, California, and Tunica County, Mississippi.

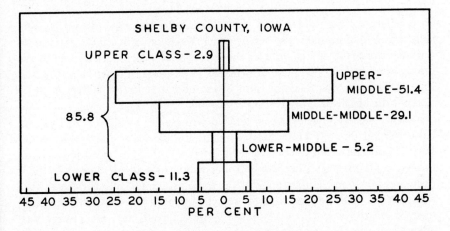

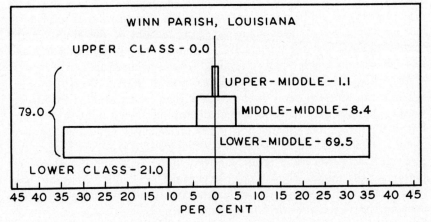

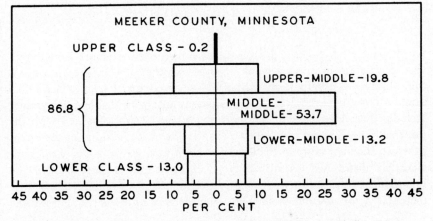

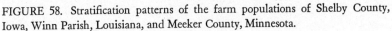

FIGURE 58. Stratification patterns of the farm populations of Shelby County, Iowa, Winn Parish, Louisiana, and Meeker County, Minnesota.

areas where the highly successful corn, beef cattle, hog type of farming prevails, but it is dominant also where other kinds of agricultural or pastoral activities are conducted as part of the rural social system tied closely to the family-sized farm of adequate dimensions. It appears in other Iowa counties such as Kossuth, Ida, Grundy, and Sioux, and it is found widely in other states of the Midwest and several other regions.

Another variety of one-class system, in which over two thirds of the agriculturists fall into the lower portion of the middle class, is found in Winn Parish, Louisiana. This area, which is the home of the state's famous Long family, contains large numbers of small subsistence farms owned by their operators. In Winn Parish, none of the farm people fall into the upper class and only one fifth belongs to the lower class, despite the fact that the typical farm is relatively small, not highly commercialized, and not always well adapted to the efficient use of machines or of modern practices and techniques, which would help to raise farm income. This pattern of rural stratification also is found throughout the "hill" sections of the South, in the "cut-over" areas near the Great Lakes, in some parts of New England, and in other sections where small subsistence farms predominate.

A third type of one-class system, that in which the bulk of the agriculturists fall into the center portion of the middle class, is exemplified by Meeker County, Minnesota. That unit contains many substantial family-sized dairy farms, enterprises that generate few if any upper-class families and comparatively few members of the lower class. This pattern is so widespread that more than a quarter of all farmers in the United States fall into the center portion of the middle class. They are engaged in a wide variety of enterprises, including dairying, general farming, the production of grains, truck farming, the corn, beef cattle, hog combination, and others.

FACTORS IN SOCIAL STRATIFICATION

As previously noted, even though the class and caste structure of the rural part of a nation taken as a whole may be exceedingly complex, in a given community it is usually fairly simple and relatively easy to comprehend. No single community embraces all the variations any more than a single county includes them all. Some of the more important factors associated with the principal divergences are as follows: (1) the size of the holdings or the extent to which the ownership of the land is concentrated in the hands of a few or is widely distributed among all the families of the community; (2) the importance of the industrial-agricultural combinations; (3) the forms of land tenure; (4) the amount of shifting from farm to farm; and (5) the racial composition of the population. Since the significant social strata are those embodied in an actual community taken as a single entity, no attempt will be made to evolve general classifications in which a given social stratum from one community is properly placed with respect to quite different strata from others. Instead, present purposes will be better served by an analysis that indicates how each of the above factors influences the social stratification of the various communities.

As is stressed in Chapter 8, the size of holdings and the distribution of rights to the land are basic in all considerations of rural social stratification. Only where there is great concentration of landownership is it possible to find a complete absence of the middle classes. Definitely a function of large estates and large-scale agriculture is the situation in which the social pyramid consists of a small number of the elite perched high on the social scale and the great mass of the population debased into a rural proletariat of landless agricultural workers. Under such circumstances, the social strata become petrified into a strong caste system, vertical social mobility becomes so unimportant as to be negligible, and there comes to be little relationship between a person's inherent native ability and his position on the social scale. Accident of birth and inheritance dominate in determining for all time the position a person shall occupy in such a society.

In sharp contrast are the results of widespread distribution of landownership. Such a system makes almost impossible the rise of gross inequalities. To be sure, a family-sized farm organization of agriculture involves some social stratification, but in any given area this is in a form and degree that more closely correlates ambition and inherent ability with social position. Vertical social mobility is not prohibited by the class structure; caste does not forever close the doors to ingress into or egress from the different social strata. A person's position in life is largely dependent upon his own efforts and does not depend mostly upon the status of his ancestors. This one-class variety of social stratification does differ, of course, from one section of the world to another, largely because of variations in the dimensions of family-sized farms. In areas where the units are large enough to elicit the maximum development of managerial capacities and to allow the most efficient use of agricultural machinery and implements, most of the farm families are likely to rank near the top of the middle class. Where the farms are small peasant holdings most of the agriculturists are apt to be found in the bottom layer of the middle class.

Social stratification also is greatly influenced by the extent to which a community combines agricultural and other occupational pursuits for its members, and especially the extent to which part-time farming is combined with fairly regular industrial or commercial employment. Where there is much industrial employment, or large-scale development of rural homes for urban workers, the population tends to be fluid. The process of selection attracts and repels the extremes; ordinarily the lowest social strata gravitate into the nearby purely industrial areas, especially in societies where effective welfare programs have been developed, and the highly successful move to residential areas more in keeping with their newly acquired social positions. Under such a system, the class differences in a community may be practically erased, and caste within the neighborhood can make but little headway. Moreover, agricultural-industrial combinations blur the lines of demarcation between occupational groups. People identify themselves with locality group-ings rather than with occupational and economic strata, and class conscious-ness tends to diminish. A great deal of such diminution is going on at present in sections of the world where family-sized farms are becoming increasingly significant parts of the overall agricultural situations. All is quite different in areas devoted almost exclusively to traditional agriculture of the plantation type. In such places, the lines between the classes and castes are rigidly drawn and generally cannot be crossed easily if at all. Social status tends to become "ossified" and to remain the same for the members of given families who succeed each other generation after generation. In many portions of the globe where large holdings predominate, the landowning elite resides in cities, so that the rural districts are populated almost exclusively by those who make up the lower class and by the few overseers and administrators who rank somewhat above them.

The forms of land tenure are closely allied with differences in social status. As indicated in Chapter 7, land tenure denotes a social relationship between the population and the land; it refers to a way of holding the land, to the property rights of the individual to the land. It is closely related to the patterns of social stratification, since these arise in part from the particular types of status which accrue to individuals because of the manner in which they are attached to the land. Whether a particular farm family is headed by a peon or other landless laborer, a sharecropper, a tenant, a renter, a manager, a part owner, or a full owner is highly significant in determining the social class into which its members will fall. Because the rural population is directly dependent for its sustenance upon the soil, and because the amount of pro-ductive land readily available to any sedentary group is definitely limited, the social regulations regarding the use of land, the manner in which control of the land sifts down to various levels of the class hierarchy, and the types of privileges or deprivations which the variations in control imply constitute an important part of the culture pattern of any agricultural group.

The frequency with which a farm family moves from one tract of land to another has much to do with its status in the community. Not infrequently this factor will far outweigh differences in tenure status. In some societies, farm laborers and farm tenants who are stable may attain much the same standing as their employers, whereas the tenant or renter who moves about frequently is considered on the same plane as casual laborers.

Where two or more sharply differentiated racial elements make up the population of a community, class division among the members of the one racial group are likely to be paralleled by those in the other, while between the two races caste differences are pronounced. The same may be true, of course, where different ethnic groups rather than races are involved. The rural communities of the southern United States serve as an example of the importance of racial differences in this respect. These locality groups have their upper-, middle-, and lower-class Negroes as well as similarly distinct statuses among the white population, but historical and cultural factors, including slavery and the plantation system, have generated and perpetuated a strong caste system between the races; this makes it difficult to scale the classes of the two racial groups properly in a single social pyramid. Generally, where the position of "master" is identified with one race and that of "man" with another, the pattern of stratification is characterized by elaborate social differences between the races. The "social distance" between white and Negro in the rural South, for example, was originally that between master and slave in the plantation complex, with the wide separation arising from the role each played in the total system. The status of slave unambiguously implied inferiority, and a black skin became the symbol of that inferiority. As a result, even now the identification between dark skin pigmentation and debased social status is extremely difficult to modify, although the position of slave and its successor, that of sharecropper, both have largely disappeared. Nor is the identification easily altered by the fact of migrating from the agricultural area in which it originated, as the problems faced by American Negroes in the nation's cities surely must attest. The net result of these factors working together, even at the moment, is a system of stratification that embodies some significant elements of caste *between* the races and many class distinctions *within* each racial group.

SOME EFFECTS OF SOCIAL STRATIFICATION

In Chapter 8, considerable effort is made to indicate and describe some of the principal features of the two great rural social systems. One of the major elements, which gives rise to many of the consequences discussed, is the prevailing pattern of social stratification. The principal contrast is, of course, that between the one-class system generally found in areas where the family-sized farm dominates the rural scene and the two-class pattern, which prevails where the large landed estate is the major feature of the agricultural situation. However, there are two additional results of the two-class system to which attention should be devoted. These are (1) the great deficiency among the rural population of the managerial skills and techniques necessary for successful agricultural operations; and (2) the oppressive, almost neurotic manner in which work with the hands and any other endeavors which resemble it are debased and degraded and the people who perform such work are accorded the lowest possible social position. Each of these effects will be treated separately.

The absence of managerial skills among those who actually till the soil is one of the most serious obstacles to efficient agricultural production and to the satisfactory organization of rural life that is to be found in the two-class system. In areas where plantations and other large estates overwhelm rural life, great emphasis is placed upon the use of traditional methods, no matter how antiquated and inefficient they may be. Usually they depend largely upon hand labor, although a few modern machines or implements may be used. A penalty also is placed upon innovation, whether introduced by the laborers, who are ordinarily discouraged from such behavior, the landowners, who disdain direct participation in the farming endeavors, or the various kinds of administrators, bailiffs, overseers, and drivers who are responsible for the actual management. But this malady is not the exclusive result of the two-class system, although it reaches its maximum in that situation. It also occurs widely in areas where the farms and holdings are privately owned but where they are so small and so greatly plagued by primitive systems of agriculture and other retarding factors that the operators and their families also must exist at comparatively low levels (see Fig. 59). This situation often is found in peasant societies, in which the bulk of the agriculturists are members of either the upper portion of the lower class or the lower segment of the middle class. In most of these cases, the people involved have never had the opportunity to learn more efficient ways of agricultural production or the various management techniques necessary to the successful operation of a farm or ranch. In addition, the farms ordinarily are so small that even if better methods were to become widely known among the farm people, it would be almost impossible for them to enlarge their holdings sufficiently to permit the use of the new knowledge, machines, and implements in an efficient, more productive manner. Virtually all of the agriculturists who live under these conditions at the moment have yet to ascend into the middle or upper portions of a genuine middle class, i.e., to attain a status comparable with that of the farmers in large parts of the United States and Canada. These relatively

FIGURE 59. The *minifundium* of a lower-class farm family in the state of São Paulo, Brazil. Photo courtesy of Carlos Borges Schmidt.

poor farm people include, of course, fairly large numbers of owner-operators in the southern United States.

The great disrepute in which manual labor is held in the two-class areas of the world is another of the principal barriers to the successful development of agriculture in those places. In the sections of the globe that are dominated by plantations and other large landholdings, work with the hands is the mark of those who fall into the lower class, and it is to be avoided at all costs by those who wish to keep from being identified as members of the lower class. It could hardly be otherwise where any substantial group of middle-class agriculturists is essentially lacking, for it is among the latter, wherever they are found in the world, that pride is taken in work and in the ability to produce as much as possible for the labor that is invested. The combination of these strongly positive attitudes toward work with the freedom and responsibility to manage the farming business as the individual farm family sees fit, has produced very high average levels of living for the agriculturists who inhabit the areas where the one-class family-sized farm system predominates.

Where the attitudes toward manual labor long have been negative, it is extremely difficult to change them and to eradicate their results, as witness the situations in much of Spanish America, Brazil, and the southern part of the United States. The plantation system of the latter, whether during the period of slavery or that of sharecropping, was distinctly a two-class system. Labor was disdained by those of the upper class and was the indelible brand of those of the lower class. Few social relationships linked the classes except that of master and man and all of the patterns of superordination and subordination that it involves. Even now that machines have replaced most sharecroppers and the lower class has dwindled in numbers as many of its members have migrated into urban slums, the values of Southern society still place a strong stigma upon manual labor. The opprobrium rests with all the oppressive weight of tradition upon those who are still part of the system as laborers, and lies especially heavily upon the Negro rural population. The landowner still often does not involve himself in the management of the plantation, leaving that to a hired manager, and the latter never condescends to perform any of the work involved. Thus, in many cases, although machines have forced much of the laboring class into other pursuits, the negative attitudes toward work and those who now perform it or who did so in the past have changed little. All of this, of course, is the more conspicuous because it exists within a society whose agricultural situation is largely dominated by the family-sized farm and the middle-class mentality it produces. In other parts of the world, where the two-class system is the rule rather than an exception, eradication of the unfavorable attitudes toward work with the hands is an infinitely more difficult task for those who would promote change and development in rural life.

TRENDS IN SOCIAL STRATIFICATION

Since the study of social stratification among agricultural people throughout the world is intimately associated with the two great rural social systems discussed above and in Chapter 8, it is necessary to examine the changes taking place in the relative importance of these two systems in order to comprehend the trends in stratification. Currently, there are operating throughout the world a number of factors which simultaneously are eroding the foundations of the traditional rural social system based on the large estate and its two-class pattern, while making for a social order in which family-sized farming units and a genuine middle class can play more significant roles. These forces certainly have not expended their energy, so that they may be expected to wax for some time. They are affecting different countries in different degrees; in many of the communist nations they are throttled by ideological forms that keep the large estates intact and under direct state control. It would, of course, be impossible to identify and describe all the factors which are bringing about significant modifications, but at least a few deserve mention.

First, there is a substantial decrease taking place in the extent to which landownership is the basis for the wealth, power, and social prestige of those in the so-called "best" families. Until recently, the large rural estates that these families owned and which they visited from time to time from their urban homes, were largely responsible for their wealth and status. This practice is on the wane for a number of reasons, of which some of the most important are directly related to the rapid pace of urbanization, currently taking place. In the last few decades, industry, transportation, communication, and other aspects of many national economies have offered lucrative opportunities for investment by those of wealth and position. This has divided the interests of even the most conservative landowning elites and has thus helped to undermine the monopolistic position of agricultural and pastoral estates as havens for capital. It has also brought into existence in no small number newly wealthy families, some of them of immigrant origin, who lack the traditional reliance upon landownership as the basis for power and influence. Furthermore, the rapid growth of cities and the high rates of reproduction of those in the upper classes of many societies have produced tens of thousands of individuals whose grandfathers or great-grandfathers were proprietors of huge estates. They personally, however, have had little or no contact with such familial properties or with any others. These and other forces are sharply weakening the foundation of the traditional two-class system of stratification based on the huge landholding. They already have erased its long-dominant role in many of the world's cities, and during the decades immediately ahead they will surely destroy its customary importance in most of the rural districts as well.

Second, in many societies, and especially in Latin America, suddenly everything to which the various designations of *latifundia* can be applied has come into disrepute. This term, of course, is most appropriate in connection with the world's traditional estates that are almost 100 per cent self-sufficient, in which the land is given over to pastoral activities of a rudimentary type or is not used at all, whose ownership serves as the visible manifestation of upper-class status. As late as 1940, throughout South America one seldom encountered an outcry against the perniciousness of this type of landholding or the system of social stratification generated by it. Today, it is difficult to find a single person of any standing who is willing to defend publicly this once universal and still dominant situation in which ownership and control of the land is highly concentrated in a few hands. There is, however, in some places, even among some of the communists, a tendency to exempt from the opprobrium attached to the *latifundia* those plantations in which the land is used intensively.

Third, it is clear that dozens of concomitants of urbanization are making a massive assault upon the long impregnable position of the large, poorly used, landed estate and the two-class system of social stratification for which it is responsible. For example, in Latin America one such factor is the highly speculative type of enterprise now being practiced widely by those who constitute one of the new urban types. Most of the people involved are of upper-class origins and pretensions, although they find it difficult to maintain the appearances of such a status, but the offspring of recent immigrants also figure to some extent. The activity itself is the renting of a few hundred acres of land, and, through the use of a highly mechanized system of farming, gambling upon a quick and large profit through the production of cotton, rice, or some other annual or semi-annual crop. Many such ventures have yielded fantastic profits, especially at first before the market was glutted, after which the new operators as well as the long established ones have felt the effects of plunging prices for the products involved. The most significant feature of this speculation is the powerful manner in which it is battering down the monopoly long exercised by the large landed estate.

Fourth, the mechanization of agriculture is an important component of the factor just described, but its general development and its disrupting effects upon traditional plantation systems and their societal patterns are so great that it deserves further specific consideration. This is especially true of its revolutionary impact upon such integral features of the established rural social system as the routine procedures used in cultivating the soil and the master-and-man or domination-subordination relationships between the persons involved. In the mechanized system of agriculture relatively few workers are needed, but those workers must have a large number of mechanical and agricultural skills that set them a world apart from the peons and other servile or semi-servile laborers. Indeed, on a mechanized farm the man responsible for the upkeep and operation of a tractor, combine, or other large and expensive piece of agricultural machinery frequently knows more about farming in general, including many features of farm management, than the owner of the land, the administrator left in charge, or the old style overseer. Such a situation presents many reasons for ignoring the centuries-old features of the traditional social system and for anticipating modifications of considerable proportions in the future. Not the least important of the possibilities is the one that would use a considerable number of skilled workers farming on their own as renters and even as owners of adequate family-sized units. The impact of all this upon the traditional class structure is tremendous.

Fifth, in connection with a few specific crops, such as sugar cane, the size and costliness of the machinery and equipment makes the ownership of the mill or factory into a juggernaut that crushes everything in the way of the further expansion of its gigantic landholdings. In many places this has meant the obliteration of the once proud masters of the plantations, either forcing them off the land completely or reducing them to a much lower status as tenants on land which once formed part of their own baronial estates. One of the most striking examples of the complete elimination of the small elite and the web of social and economic relationships integrating them with the huge mass of peons may be observed in Guyana, where, as the former British colony steps out on the stony pathway of a new and "underdeveloped" nation, all of the numerous sugar-cane plantations and mills are owned by just two companies. The change represented in such cases as this is, of course, the substitution for the patriarchal and often benign upper class of the cold, financially motivated company or corporation, or a form of organization that is only a step removed from the state farms of the communist parts of the world. In any case, though, the development helps to sound the death knell of the traditional two-class system of social stratification which was generated and perpetuated by the large landed estate.

Sixth, and finally, since the early 1950's, the peal of voices calling for agrarian reform has challenged to the utmost the long entrenched two-class system of social stratification that is the concomitant of the large landed estate. During the present decade, the slogan of agrarian reform in many parts of the globe has come to be thought of as a panacea, capable of materializing immediately the dreams of persons in all of the more humble stations of life and of solving the numerous chronic and acute problems found in many agricultural countries. For present purposes, however, the most important aspect of the outburst of enthusiasm for reforming man-land relationships is the almost universal extent to which this takes the form of increasing the importance and making for the well-being of a genuine middle social class composed of the owner-operators of family-sized farms. Under these conditions endless proposals are made to subdivide the large estates and to bring about the consolidation of many of the farm plots now recognized as being too small, into larger family-sized units in the hands of a true middle class.

There are, of course, many other agencies of change, such as the wholesale migration of rural workers to the cities, the shift from the mechanistic to the organic type of social solidarity, the gradual decline in importance of primary group relationships, the replacement to some extent of personalist directives by actual leadership, the ever-increasing gap or zone or exasperation that is opening between the soaring standard of living and the slowly increasing level of living, and the homogenization of society in general. But the trends in all of them point in the same direction: in the decades immediately ahead the two-class structure and the other basic components of traditional rural social systems are due to lose the roles and power they have had in the traditional social order. Either they will be incorporated into another system, in which the man who works the soil is a mere laborer (possibly on the "collective" or state farm of a communist nation), or something resembling a one-class system based on family-sized farms will emerge.

Where the family-sized farm is already the prevalent form of social organization there also are at work many forces making for changes in social stratification. Some, which tend to increase it, operate smoothly and steadily; a large number of social layers and greater differences between them come about in a gradual manner. Others, which make for leveling, work more spasmodically and convulsively. For example, before World War II trends in the rural areas of the United States seemed definitely to be in the direction of greater stratification. It appeared that a void was developing between the favored few at the top of the social scale and the less-privileged masses at the bottom. Life organized around the family-sized farm and the resulting middle-class mentality seemed doomed to extinction. Principally, this was coming about through the reduction of many members of the middle class to the lower-class category of farm laborers. Evidences of this tendency were the alarming increase of farm tenancy in the Midwest, the general increase in the size of farms, the mounting burdens of mortgage indebtedness, and the rapidly swelling army of displaced rural families who had turned to migratory agricultural labor as a way of life.

At present, however, there seems to be considerable reason for doubting that such a development is continuing. Temporarily, at least, the changes brought about by the national defense program, World War II, the boom times that accompanied reconversion, and the rearmament program precipitated by the wars in Korea and Vietnam seem to have reversed the trend toward greater stratification in rural America. Millions of agricultural workers, far more than the normal surplus of farm population, have been siphoned off to industrial and other employment in the urban areas. At the same time, by greater use of power and machinery, production on the farm has been raised substantially, greatly reducing the numerical importance of the lower agricultural classes, particularly in the South. In addition, in a period of rapid inflation, mortgage indebtedness has not been a way station on the road to bankruptcy as it frequently was a few decades ago, but it usually has worked greatly to the advantage of the borrower. During the last two decades, hundreds of thousands of farm operators have bought and paid for their farms in full; still others have completed paying for their farms purchased during the years preceding the outbreak of World War II at a fraction of their current money value. Under the circumstances prevailing from 1922 to 1940, a large part of them would have found it impossible to avoid slipping down into the category of farm laborers, but with the high prices of farm products and rapid inflation they have not merely paid for their farms but also have become thoroughly accustomed to the upper levels of middle-class living and deeply imbued with high standards of living as well. At no time since the outbreak of World War I have the relative number and importance of the middle classes in rural America ranked as high as at present.

Additional Readings

1. ANDERSON, C. ARNOLD, "Economic Status Differentials within Southern Agriculture," *Rural Sociology*, Vol. 19, No. 1 (March, 1954), pp. 50–67.

2. BAILEY, WILFRID C., "Social Stratification in Rural Society," in Alvin L. Bertrand (ed.), *Rural Sociology*, New York: McGraw-Hill Book Company, Inc., 1958, chapter 9.

3. FALS-BORDA, ORLANDO, *Peasant Society in the Colombian Andes*, Gainesville: University of Florida Press, 1955, chapter 10.

4. HIMES, JOSEPH S., *The Study of Sociology*, Glenview, Ill.: Scott, Foresman and Company, 1968, chapter 11.

5. HODGES, HAROLD M., *Social Stratification*, Cambridge, Mass.: Schenkman Publishing Company, Inc., 1964, chapters I–XI.

6. KAUFMAN, HAROLD F., *Prestige Classes in a New York Rural Community*, Cornell AES Memoir No. 260, Ithaca: Cornell University, 1944.

7. LOPREATO, JOSEPH, *Peasants No More*, San Francisco: Chandler Publishing Company, 1967.

8. NELSON, LOWRY, *Rural Cuba*, Minneapolis: University of Minnesota Press, 1950, chapters VIII and IX.

9. ROGERS, EVERETT M., *Social Change in Rural Society*, New York: Appleton-Century-Crofts, Inc., 1960, chapter 5.

10. SMITH, T. LYNN, *Colombia: Social Structure and the Process of Development*, Gainesville: University of Florida Press, 1967, chapter 9.

11. SMITH, T. LYNN, *Studies of Latin American Societies*, New York: Doubleday & Co., Inc., 1970, selection 10.

12. SMITH, T. LYNN, "A Study of Social Stratification in the Agricultural Sections of the United States: Nature, Data, Procedures, and Preliminary Results," *Rural Sociology*, Vol. 34, No. 4 (December, 1969).

13. SOROKIN, PITIRIM A., *Social Mobility*, New York: Harper & Brothers, 1927, chapters I–VI.

14. SOROKIN, PITIRIM A., *Society, Culture, and Personality: Their Structure and Dynamics*, New York: Harper & Brothers, 1947, chapters 14 and 15.

15. SOROKIN, PITIRIM A., CARLE C. ZIMMERMAN, and CHARLES J. GALPIN, *A Systematic Source Book in Rural Sociology*, Minneapolis: University of Minnesota Press, 1930, Vol. I, chapter VII; 1932, Vol. III, chapter XXI.

16. WAGLEY, CHARLES (ed.), *Race and Class in Rural Brazil*, Paris: UNESCO, 1952.

17. WARNER, W., LLOYD, MARCHIA MEEKER, and KENNETH EELLS, *Social Class in America*, Chicago: Science Research Associates, 1949.

12
MARRIAGE and THE FAMILY

Everywhere the family is the basic unit in the composition of society. As the most fundamental primary group, it is the arena in which the major part of the individual's personality is formed. Strongly unified through the operation of the most basic social ties, cemented by both the organic and the mechanistic types of solidarity, it is the most closely knit social group in existence. The great influence of this highly cohesive unit upon the individual, combined with the great number of such units, makes the family by far the most important form of social grouping known to mankind. Therefore, because much of rural life is familial in nature, the fundamental social institution of marriage and the family deserves careful analysis.

Historically, patterns of marriage and family living were features of the earliest civilizations of which we have records; they are to be observed among all societies of the present, no matter how isolated or slightly differentiated the latter may be. Throughout all history the rural family has played an especially significant role; and at the present time the family still is important, even in the most heavily urbanized societies. In the larger portion of the world it is the agency by which the bulk of future populations, both rural and urban, is produced and the crucible in which the majority of the citizens of the next generation are tested and molded. Even now, there are few societies in which the majority of the total population is born and reared in cities.

Although the family as a group is universally recognizable, its forms and even some of its functions are by no means always and everywhere the same. Strictly speaking, the term *family* is used to designate a relatively permanent, socially approved grouping of parents and children. It may also include relatives of the husband, the wife, or both. In the establishment of a given family are involved: (1) the institution of marriage; (2) reproduction of the species; and (3) socialization, or the training of new members of society. Because the human infant is helpless at birth and continues dependent upon others for a great many years, quite unlike the offspring of any animal species, the relationships within a given family extend over a long period of time. To assist in clarifying the concept, several other observations must be made. Technically, married pairs do not constitute families until offspring result from the marriage. In societies where polygamy is practiced, the functioning domestic unit may contain more than one husband or wife and still be styled a family. In some places, the unit that operates as a family and embodies all of its features is the "extended" form, including all persons who are related by bonds of kinship and embracing several "nuclear" families, each of which consists only of mates and children. If a marriage is terminated, by death, divorce, or separation, the term "broken family" is properly applied to the remaining members of the group. "Household," is a term closely related to the family, which sometimes may be used interchangeably with it but which has some specific connotations.

Since the foundation of a new family involves the institution of marriage, a brief consideration of the forms and conditions of matrimony well may precede other aspects of the subject. Added to this should be a consideration of some of the many possible variations of the human family.

MARRIAGE AND FAMILY TYPES

The institution of marriage is the central feature of all human societies, because it is more intimately related to social stability and cohesion, human happiness and satisfaction, and continuity of social organization and functioning than is any other social institution. As previously mentioned, marriage is indispensable in the family grouping, partly because it brings into being a socially approved matrix within which sexual expression is generally expected to take place. But marriage must not be thought of as identical with sex relations, or even regularized sex relations. Marriage is a genuine social bond: It is sanctioned by the group; it establishes family relations, particularly with respect to the offspring; and it provides a principal social system within which are found individual statuses and roles. In this last capacity, marriage has a certain socially accepted structure, it is expected to perform given functions for the society, and it generates particular processes or actions. In turn, the bases upon which it is founded generate types of families that vary from one society to another and between the rural and urban portions of each of them. It is these latter variations that are especially important for purposes of this volume.

Classifications of marriages and marriage forms are abundant, and each one has usefulness for special purposes. One who would understand his own society must be cognizant of the ways in which other people differ from his accepted patterns. Consideration of the various patterns of behavior with respect to marriage is one of the best ways of realizing how readily one accepts the cultural forms of his own particular group as "natural" and regards those of other groups as peculiar. Furthermore, even the marriage patterns that the members of one society take for granted generally include a few survivals of those customs considered odd when reported among strangers. The student of rural society must be familiar with cultural norms in many social groups in order that he not consider variation from the standards prevailing in one culture to be the mark of inferiority when they are found in another.

The first important variations in marriage forms arise out of differences in the manner of securing a mate. Economic considerations are usually involved in this, for only rarely in the history of the world has marriage been separated from pecuniary consideration. Furthermore, marriage has almost always and everywhere been regarded as a family and not an individual affair. Rare indeed is the case in which young people have been permitted to make their own matrimonial arrangements, although a view of the world which arises from the perspective of a North American might easily lead one to expect this condition to be universal. Far more prevalent has been the practice of considering marriage as an arrangement between family groups. Even now much of this prevails in rural areas throughout the world, including, in many cases, those in the United States. In some societies girls have been regarded as an economic asset, have been disposed of as property by the family, and have been received in a similar context by the respective groups into which they were married. So important have been the economic arrangements, that marriage by exchange or marriage by purchase has been almost universal. Child marriages, widespread throughout the world, are most frequently rational and often complicated negotiated exchanges between families.

Even where child marriages are lacking, the case is rare in which the family group relinquishes claim to an unmarried girl before adequate compensation has been received. Although varieties of bargaining are by no means the equivalent of one another, marriage by purchase has been much more widespread than marriage by exchange. An important variation of marriage by purchase is the case in which service has been substituted for an actual payment of goods; this is a marriage form known to all those who are familiar with the stories of the Old Testament. Other practices of the Hebrews that reveal the nature of their marriage forms are the *levirate,* a custom in which a brother was required to take as a wife the widow of his deceased brother and count as his brother's the first child of the marriage. Enlightening also is the feature of the Deuteronomic code which permitted only the husband to initiate a divorce.

Marriage by capture, another widely used method of securing a mate, also recognizes the economic value of women, but in this case prowess or cunning is used to avoid payment. In rural areas, including those of the western industrialized countries, marriage still remains more of a family affair than is true in cities; there are still survivals of the economic considerations in marriage, for in many cases changes in the distribution of ownership and control of given portions of land may be involved. But romantic love and its emphasis upon individualism have reduced group importance even in the most rural portions of such nations as the United States and are found increasingly in other parts of the world as components of courtship and the marriage relationship.

A second classification of marriages may be made upon the basis of the number of parties to the contract. Marriages involving only one man and one woman are *monogamous;* those in which three or more people are concerned, *polygamous.* Polygamous unions may be subdivided into those cases in which one husband is united with two or more wives (*polygyny*), and those in which one wife is associated in marriage with two or more husbands (*polyandry*). Group marriage (several husbands and several wives banded together indiscriminately), sexual communism, and complete promiscuity in sexual behavior are other possibilities in the way of marriage relationships, although actual cases are so rare as to make them virtually hypothetical. Monogamy as a marriage pattern is deeply embedded in the culture of rural America, and it is the principal form of marriage found throughout the world as a whole. It has its origins and justifications in several conditions. Monogamy is, for example, the most economically feasible arrangement for the bulk of the population in any society. Even those that permit plural marriages generally look upon polygamy as a privilege of the upper classes, either unavailable to the masses or involving far fewer spouses per union among that group. Monogamy is also consistent with the fact that the populations of most societies contain a roughly equal number of males and females in the marriageable ages; even though there might be as few as 85 or 90 persons of one sex for each 100 persons of the other, this would hardly constitute a sufficient imbalance to make widespread polygamy a very practical matter. Monogamy has also come to be rationalized as "proper" by many of the world's major religions; and evidence suggests that it may well be the best circumstance within which to rear children. Furthermore, the fact that all societies have established some division of labor along the lines of sex tends to make monogamy practical and convenient from this standpoint. Yet in urban America and other parts of the world with comparatively high rates of divorce, there seems to be developing a sort of progressive or "sequential" polygamy in which a woman has two or more husbands or a man two or more wives, although only one at a time in each case. Finally, Old Testament accounts and present-day practices in many important agricultural countries, especially in the Middle and Far East, indicate that monogamy is by no means an exclusive or even necessary rural trait. On the contrary, where economic advantage, the wish for higher status, and other considerations make it desirable to secure a large number of wives and to produce many children as symbols of sexual prowess and financial affluence, polygyny still occurs widely.

A third category of marriage types depends upon the locus of family authority. In most societies and particularly in rural areas, the power and authority enjoyed by the husband is greater than that wielded by his distaff counterpart. This is true even in societies, such as the United States, in which there are strong tendencies toward the equality of marriage partners, and it is most pronounced in those that are predominantly agricultural, including nearly all that are styled as "underdeveloped." Therefore, the rural family is frequently a *patriarchal* one in which the male head exercises his authority over a family that often consists of three or four generations having various kinship ties. In other places it is principally *patricentric,* in which case the authority also resides with the male head but in which the functioning family unit over which he presides is composed only of himself, his wife or wives, and children. This form is typical of the rural parts of the United States and Canada, and most of the societies of western Europe.

Matriarchal and *matricentric* rural families are not unknown. In places where agricultural laborers are found in their customary servile and semi-servile situations, the middle- and upper-class norms regarding the seriousness and stability of marriage often are less applicable. Under these conditions, found widely in Brazil, parts of Spanish America, and among Negroes of the lower class in all sections of the United States, matings are temporary and marriage is considered to be a casual matter. As a result, the typical functioning family unit comes to be composed of a woman and her dependent children and deserves the designation matricentric or "mother-centered." Sometimes the unit is composed of an elderly woman, her daughters, and their dependent youngsters; but in either case, adult males tend to be attached to the unit only nominally and to play partial and peripheral roles as family members. The matricentric family unit, characteristic of slaves, coloni, and other servile types, derives little of its support and stability from men and is unable to call forth the pressures of middle-class morality to alter this situation very greatly.

In the United States, among Negroes of the lower class, the relatively high proportion of households headed by women, the frequency of common-law marriages, and the comparatively high rates of divorce and desertion testify to the fact that this group commonly generates the matricentric family pattern. The structure originated in slavery, chiefly because individual African Negroes were torn from their families and from the cultures in which those families were given form and stability. Moreover, under slavery, adult males were bought and sold freely for either laboring or breeding purposes, without regard to family relationships. Because small dependent children were an economic liability, they were left with their mothers until they reached marketable age. Therefore, the only semblance of stable form which the Negro family under slavery could have was that which arose from the primary relationship between a woman and her relatively young children. The matricentric family that was created in this manner remained virtually unchanged in the rural South during the period following the Civil War. However, in the twentieth century large numbers of the products of this family type migrated to urban centers, where the restraints on behavior were fewer than they had been in the rural South; and the stability of the matricentric unit decreased still more among lower-class Negroes living in the cities. The experience of the last few decades does indicate, though, that as larger proportions of Negroes move into the middle class, the family units to which they customarily become attached take on much greater stability and lose the matricentric essence. In fact, the middle-class Negro family in the United States tends to be somewhat patricentric but to include an increasingly significant egalitarian dimension. (For the classic study of the matricentric feature and other aspects of the Negro domestic unit, see Ref. 129, *passim.*).

Marriages also may be classified according to several other criteria. From the standpoint of residence of the newly married pair, marriage may be *patrilocal,* in which the couple resides in the husband's community or even in the household of his parents, or *matrilocal,* where it establishes residence in close proximity to the wife's family. In rural America there seems to be some tendency toward patrilocal marriages, although the comparative lack of primogeniture makes them by no means the general rule. In this society there is a strong tendency toward a *neolocal* condition, or the establishment of a household removed from that of either set of parents, although economic needs, kinship considerations, and other factors sometimes make this difficult.

The matter of a family name is of great importance in the social world, and this, too, is intimately associated with marriage. Marriage forms in which the child takes the name of the father are properly called *patronymic;* those in which the child takes the mother's name, *matronymic.* Traditional American marriage patterns are patronymic, the wife and children taking the surname of the father. However, at present in certain urban groups there is a tendency to modify this traditional pattern by giving the child a new name formed by hyphenating the surnames of both parents. In other societies, such as many of those in Spanish America, the child is known by the surname of the father but generally also receives the maiden name of the mother, usually appended after that of his male parent.

The important questions of kinship and descent are also involved in the nature of the marriage relationship. A *bilateral* system, i.e., one considering the children to be kin to the families of both parents, is by no means universal, although it is the accepted one in the United States. In many groups, whose family type is called *matrilineal,* the child is considered a member of the mother's line of descent and is thought to bear no kinship to the father's relations. In other societies, whose family form is called *patrilineal,* children are kin only to the father's side of the house. Rural America has, of course, a bilateral system of identifying relationship, but in some communities the inheritance of property occasionally exhibits elements of the patrilineal system. Not always are daughters given an equal share with sons in the inheritance of family property, especially farm land. On the other hand, elements of the matrilineal system, are not entirely lacking in rural America. The Negro family, discussed above, exhibits many characteristics of a matrilineal condition, chiefly because the mother serves as the major integrating force.

Classification according to the principal constellation of roles that one plays in the family also deserves mention. When an individual marries, ordinarily he leaves his parental *family of orientation,* in which he learned many of the basic patterns of behavior expected by his society and many of the features of his culture, and establishes himself in the *family of procreation,* in which he becomes a parent and himself assumes the responsibility for socializing a few members of the next generation. Of course, in such places as the urban United States, this transition is rather abrupt and usually involves physical movement from one household to another, so that it produces a significant change in the individual's family milieu. In others, including the rural portions of many of the world's societies, the importance of the extended family as a functioning unit makes the transition a minor one and produces a minimum of physical mobility and change in the relationships of family members. In these cases, rather than encourage the establishment of a new and separate household, the larger family simply tends to absorb a person who marries one of its members. A classic example of this situation is the family in Japan prior to World War II.

MARITAL STATUS

A number of pertinent points need to be kept in mind in discussing marital status or condition. First, few persons under 15 years of age are married, so it is customary to confine discussions of this subject to the population aged 15 and over. Second, the most widely accepted classification used in discussing marital condition consists of four categories: (1) single, (2) married, (3) widowed, and (4) divorced. Since separation is an alternative to divorce that is taken commonly by members of the lower classes, persons who are married but separated should form a fifth category; but unfortunately it is impossible to secure satisfactory data about such people from the official statistics of most nations.

Farm people, particularly women, live in the married state to a much greater extent than does the urban population. Generally, this is true no matter which society is being examined, if the analysis is carried out in such a way as to control the distorting effects produced by variations in the age profiles of rural and urban people. Thus, among males of every age group the percentage married is generally higher in farming districts than in the urban populations. Furthermore, single persons and those who are divorced tend to be concentrated in the cities. These variations between rural and urban apply when different racial groups are involved, although the races themselves may exhibit quite different marital behavior if the class differences between them are sufficiently great. In the United States, for example, among the native white population of native parents and among Negroes, single persons of both sexes and practically every age group constitute larger proportions of the urban poulation than they do of the rural-farm group. A similar uniformity prevails among the females of the foreign elements in the population (native white of foreign or mixed parentage and foreign-born whites). But among males the foreign elements living in the United States exhibit a very interesting reversal of this uniformity: Among these groups at all ages there are higher proportions of single persons in the farm population than in the urban. It would appear that the foreign-born male or even the male of foreign parentage is considerably handicapped by his cultural heritage and by social barriers. Therefore, he is less able to secure a mate amid the keen rivalry created by the preponderance of men in rural districts than is his countryman in the city, where men are at a premium.

Divorced persons of both sexes, of all ages, and of all the various racial and nativity groups usually are much more prevalent, on a relative basis, in the cities than in the farming districts. This suggests that broken homes are not as prevalent in the country as in the urban centers, their suburbs, and the villages, partly because a larger portion of all families in rural areas remains stable and partly because many of the members of farm families that are broken up migrate to towns and cities. In societies in which there is considerable freedom of movement and people are inclined to migrate from place to place in relatively large numbers, there is also a strong tendency for widows to concentrate in cities. This situation is rather widespread in many nations, although in some places widows also show a strong tendency to gravitate to rural villages from the surrounding farms.

As previously suggested, in parts of the world where servile and semi-servile agricultural laborers are superabundant, quite different marriage patterns may prevail from those where the middle class predominates. For example, because Negroes have been disproportionately numerous in the most rural part of the United States—the South—it is important to indicate the principal ways in which the marital status of this group is distinctive. However, the sociocultural conditions of this group are similar in many ways to those of agricultural laborers throughout the world. Therefore, the rural southern Negro of the lower class, engaged in farm labor, exhibits marital patterns not unlike those found among persons of similar status in many other societies. Moreover, because of the slow rate at which such conditions change, it is not surprising that a substantial segment of the recent rural migrants to cities also exhibits marital characteristics which are quite similar to those of people who continue to live in the farming districts.

The data make it clear that even today the marital and family mores of lower-class American Negroes either are extremely ambiguous or at least diverge widely from those of the middle-class group, both white and Negro. Single persons are relatively fewer among the Negroes than the whites, a fact that is especially noticeable among the younger age groups. But although lower percentages of Negroes are single and although they marry at a younger age than whites on the average, the proportion of married among nonwhites is distinctively lower than among whites, a difference especially conspicuous for females, but prevailing for males as well. In this connection it should be remembered that a great many of the marriages of Negroes, especially in the rural South, are of the common-law type. The most distinctive difference between the races stems from the very high proportion of divorced and widowed persons to be found in the Negro group. In this case, in addition to the fact that some divorced and separated women report themselves as widowed, the death rate of Negro males is so much higher than that of Negro females and of white males as well, that the incidence of widowhood is relatively great.

In general, where the farm population is predominantly middle class, the proportion married is greater than among urban groups at a comparable level in the stratification system. Conversely, such farm areas contain smaller proportions of those who are single, widowed, and divorced than do the cities. But where agricultural laborers are abundant and the prevailing social status is that of the lower class, the norms regarding marital behavior often are quite different, with the result that while "marriage" is a common condition among the rural people, it is frequently of a nominal kind. Under these circumstances, the comparatively high incidence of divorce, separation, and widowhood, combined with the low percentage of single persons is not surprising.

SOME SALIENT FEATURES OF THE RURAL FAMILY

It is somewhat misleading to generalize about rural families as though those everywhere in the world had the same form and carried out their functions in the same way. Nevertheless there are some characteristics that tend to be more typical of rural than urban families wherever they are found. This is especially true when comparisons are made between rural and urban people who have roughly the same position in the stratification system.

Familism

One of the most significant and widespread features of the rural family is the condition of familism. It involves several things: (1) the subordination of personal goals to those of the family; (2) a high degree of control exerted over the individual by the family in such a way that it is actively imposed by the family and is also internalized by the person; (3) a deep sense of integration into the family structure so that a high degree of personal security develops; (4) a marked tendency for the family unit to be intergenerational, that is, to include members of several generations among the functioning group living under one roof or in close proximity; (5) a rather clear-cut definition of social roles for which behavior is prescribed and which depend upon a well-understood division of labor within the family; (6) a well-developed concept of family property, including land, capital, buildings, animals, and so on, which retards the development of extreme notions of individual property; (7) a high degree of continuity in the family, so that it does not come abruptly into existence when a new nuclear family is formed nor pass from the scene when the nuclear unit is dissolved; and (8) patterns of mutual aid in which family members are assisted when they remain within the confines of the original household and even when they venture outside it to establish separate households and operate their own farms. In part, this last condition is closely associated with the "agricultural ladder" in areas where family-sized farms prevail, for there a young adult member of the family frequently is assisted in the purchase or rental or his own farm. This step enables him to move upward from the position of unpaid family laborer or hired hand and into the position of farm operator.

Familism in its most fully developed form depends upon a comparatively low degree of physical movement of people from place to place within the society. Such a condition is more likely to exist in the rural portion than the urban segment of any society. Familism tends to break down when a substantial share of the members are mobile, when the society contains individuals with a large number of divergent values and attitudes, when housing and other physical conditions make it impossible for any but the members of nuclear units to live together, and when the occupations followed must be pursued outside of the family. Therefore, the agrarian way of life lends itself to the perpetuation of familism far more than does the urban way of life, which is geared to other kinds of occupations. It is possible, however, to generalize inaccurately that familism is the exclusive province of farm people. On the contrary, in many urban situations, particularly among the foreign born, there exists a viable family form, which embodies certain of the features of familism. This type generally involves several nuclear units, each confined physically to its own household, but all of which together provide for the welfare of all members, engage in frequent and highly personal interaction, create and enforce norms of behavior for all members, share certain mutual values and attitudes, and perhaps even hold and operate certain kinds of property. Yet the proportional incidence of such behavior is far greater in rural areas than it is in cities.

Given approximate similarities in class standing, as a union of husband and wife, parents and children, the rural family is much more closely integrated and more permanent than is the urban family. Statistics on divorce and desertion leave no room for doubt that marriage ties are more permanent in the country than in the city, largely as a result of the social control brought about under familism. In addition, the rural family retains its children under the parental eye and supervision to a much greater extent than is possible in the city; it also retains the children under the parental roof for a considerably longer time than can the urban family. Not only do rural children remain at home longer than urban children before marriage, but frequently rural families retain the children in the original homestead even after they have married. This practice is significantly less common in cities, although it is by no means unknown. The rural family fuses its members into one organic whole, obliterating the individual personalities to a much greater extent than does the urban family. This occurs because of the highly cumulative nature of the rural familial group, the interdependence engendered by the division of labor within the group, the long-continued and constant nature of the association, and the comparative weakness of competing institutions. In comparison with other social institutions, the family occupies a much more important place in the country than in the city.

Familism, of course, has advantages and disadvantages. Close daily contact between parents and children deepens their regard and affection for one another, subjects the youngsters perpetually to the traditional moral integrity of the farm family, and keeps constantly before the children's eyes the social ethics and acceptable behavior patterns of the family. Familism also provides youngsters with a thoroughgoing apprenticeship in the various agricultural endeavors of the family and equips them by experience for their own roles in the agrarian system. But on the negative side, the following must be recognized: (1) The family is somewhat of a closed corporation, altruistic with respect to members but selfish with regard to outsiders; (2) limited contacts make for narrow and inflexible views and practices; (3) the nature of the family association promotes clannishness; (4) the personalities of the individuals are kept near the same level; and (5) the apprenticeship in farming, which tends to be generated by familism, may become a highly cloistered type of existence, in which other occupational pursuits and other ways of life are not selected by rising generations simply because they know nothing about these alternatives. It is in such a way that, in tradition-oriented areas, many agricultural laborers who subsist close to the edge of survival perpetuate generation after generation of those who function within the same unchanging frame of reference.

Considerable disagreement would inevitably arise out of any attempt to evaluate the negative and positive results of a highly integrated family organization. There can be little doubt, however, that the development of a high degree of familism continues to be an outstanding feature of agricultural societies, that familism is more persistent in the farming districts than in the cities of any one nation, and that the family continues to be by far the most important group in rural society.

An Economic Producing and Consuming Unit

The farm family is a producing unit in the sense that all members are actively engaged in the operation of the farm, together comprising an active partnership. It is a consuming unit as well, in that it draws from the substance produced by its own members and by society at large. As a result, the individuals are tied to the landholding as the basis of a total way of life, not merely as a source of compartmentalized jobs. Furthermore, farming, even the form practiced by the lowest laborer, tends to have a higher degree of self-sufficiency and isolation about it than do practically any of the more segmented urban occupations. This condition is most pronounced, of course, in areas where subsistence is the key feature of the farm family, but it is also apparent where a relatively high percentage of the crops produced is sold for cash. In both kinds of situations, work is performed not merely by one or two family members outside of the family context, but by all members operating as a single unit. Even the child of five or six tends to have sufficient duties assigned to him that part of the role he learns to play is intimately involved with agricultural production. By the same token, the aged retain many responsibilities, even though their involvement in production tends to become less demanding and less vital as they advance in years. Therefore, at few points in his life does the member of a farm family play a role that is totally dependent economically; rather he comes to function in the domestic group in such a way that he is a genuine contributor to its economic substance. As a result, in large rural portions of the earth, children are considered to be economic assets rather than liabilities, even at very tender ages.

The farm family also consumes, of course, partly its own products and partly those that it purchases or for which it trades. It shares this economic function with the urban family to the degree that both make use of the labor of members in order to acquire the necessities of life as well as some of the luxuries. The production of a product which can be used directly or which can be sold for sufficient cash to help meet economic needs is generally the responsibility of all members of the farm family, whereas it usually falls to only one or two members of the urban family. Furthermore, the occupations of urban workers almost always remove them physically from the family group, whereas agricultural jobs rarely do so. Thus, for many farm families, production and consumption both can take place with little or no involvement in commercial trade, but for the urban family this is impossible. Urban occupations do not make for self-sufficiency. The very fact of urban heterogeneity in the jobs that must be done and the high degree of division of labor that results make urban occupations highly specialized and capable of providing directly for very few if any of the actual needs of the family. Rather, the wage earners in an urban family perform their highly specialized tasks, receive remuneration for these endeavors, and then are able to purchase needed goods and services. Other urbanites depend upon the tiny fraction of all of the city's goods and services produced by the wage earners of a single family, just as that single urban family relies upon the performance of vast numbers of other specialists in order to satisfy its wants. The key is interdependence, for at no point is there any appreciable sign of the self-sufficiency that either is or could be a characteristic feature of most of the world's rural families. Therefore, production by all of the members of the farm family and consumption by the farm household are inextricably interwoven, whereas wage earning by one or two members of the urban family and consumption by the urban household are much more clearly distinguishable as separate functions. As might be expected, the latter situation allows the urban worker to construe his occupational role as being almost completely isolated from the part he plays as a family member, whereas this is virtually impossible in farming districts.

The tendency toward self-sufficiency of the farm family is found at all levels of the class structure. In middle-class areas where the family-sized farm is found abundantly, the historical pattern has been one of almost exclusive self-sufficiency. This now is changing greatly, of course, in that such areas generally find themselves more interdependent with large urban communities and less able or compelled to rely strictly upon subsistence operations. In the case of the large landed property—the second of the two principal sizes of landholdings that dominate the world's agriculture—self-sufficiency of the estate as a whole is still generally the rule. Therefore, the needs of virtually all families residing on the holding are met through the producing and processing operations of the estate itself.

There are several other conditions that arise from the importance of the producing functions of the middle-class farm family. For example, when the successful operation of the farm is paramount in the minds of all members, there is a great tendency to place various living items in competition with those necessary for operation and enlargement of the farm. Furthermore, there is an extremely strong sense of the future among such farm families, leading to a philosophy of deferred gratification and the practice of investing high proportions of the available capital in land, buildings, equipment, breeding stock, and so on, rather than in typical "consumer" items. Under these conditions, there is much truth to the observation that in an area dominated by family-sized farms, one can start with little or nothing, lose money every year, and yet approach the end of life with a sizable investment in land, buildings, machinery, herds of livestock, and other long-term elements of agricultural or pastoral production. In addition, the fact that all family members participate in the operation of the farm makes it possible for the socialization of children to be carried out on a full-time basis by both mother and father. Male children are privileged to learn male roles, which include an occupational dimension, directly from their fathers rather than indirectly through their mothers or in a part-time fashion from their fathers. Finally, social status in the farming districts tends to be affected far more by the manner in which the family conducts the farm business than by conspicuous consumption, memberships in associations, constant upward mobility, and so on. In fact, in most small rural communities, the status of the family may be lowered by flagrant attempts to manifest affluence. Status, arising in large part from the way in which production is carried on, also tends to accrue to all members of the family to about the same degree rather than quite differently to each individual. The position of the family is a far more significant determinant of that of individuals in farm districts than it is in cities. By the same token, it is probably easier for farm youngsters to gain status locally than it is for urban children, since the former tend to be more involved in the farm business and to reflect the socioeconomic position of the parents. From the standpoint of the individual, this can provide security and protection from extreme pressure to struggle ruthlessly up the social ladder, but it also can impose unwanted restrictions on behavior.

Obviously, many of the conditions that result when the typical farm family is of the middle class either do not exist at all or are quite different when the customary domestic unit is of the lower class. The middle-class farm family is much concerned with perpetuating, enlarging, and operating the landholding efficiently; the lower-class laborer rarely can have any such interests. Therefore, among the latter, patterns of deferred gratification, the creation of social devices to preserve the integrity of the farm from one generation to another, the involvement of all family members in managerial activities, and the manipulation of budget items to ensure development of the farm are patent absurdities. All members of the farm family may be involved in production, either on their own minifundium or as laborers on some huge estate, but this is far more a matter of survival, habit, and resignation than of planning and rational intent. Consequently, the families of coloni, sharecroppers, migrant laborers, and other menial agricultural types well may constitute both producing and consuming units, but ordinarily at very low levels of living. In the case of lower-class agriculturists the inheritance of status generally renders rising generations incapable of improving greatly upon the social position of their parents. These conditions are a far cry from those described above in connection with the middle-class family operating a farm of adequate proportions.

Intergenerational Nature of the Farm Family

As a producing-consuming unit, the middle-class farm family needs to provide for continuity in carrying out the economic function and especially in preserving the ownership and control of the land upon which its economic position depends. Without such provision the death of those members whose age and vitality cause them to be charged with production and decision making about the operation of the farm could quickly destroy its productive ability and liquidate its holdings. One of the major features of the middle-class farm family which serves to prevent this breakup and to ensure continuity of operation and of landownership and control over many years is its intergenerational nature. That is, when the most productive members begin to age and to decline in their ability to manage the farm, a rising generation of young adults has already been trained and conditioned to assume the functions with a minimum of disturbance over the transition. In turn, these young adults expect their children to begin to play productive roles and this helps guarantee that the succession will continue smoothly. Under these conditions, found especially where the family-sized farm dominates agriculture, there is a strong tendency for the aged to retain control of the capital resources and to participate fully in managerial affairs after they have passed the peak of their laboring ability and sometimes even their managerial ability. Moreover, as cities expand and attract young adults from the farms, the rural districts come to contain even larger proportions of the elderly, which further enhances their relative importance. As a result, elderly people are likely to be found more frequently and the respect accorded them is likely to be greater in families living on farms than in those residing in cities.

The continuity between generations in rural sections contrasts sharply with that in urban-oriented areas in which the older person is separated by retirement from his occupation, which was already sharply separated from other family functions before retirement. The aging male especially finds himself in a circumstance in which his activity as a producer is virtually nonexistent. Moreover, this comes at a time in life when serious adjustments in roles are most difficult to make, thereby causing the lack of continuity between productive adulthood and unproductive old age to be even more debilitating psychologically. It is little wonder that in many cases the urban worker is subjected to confused role definitions and is relegated abruptly to a place of economic insignificance, largely because the urban occupational role fails to guarantee that he will be granted a position of importance in the family after retirement.

Various elements of form, certain patterns of inheritance, family involvement in the selection of marriage partners, and other features directly supporting the intergenerational nature of the rural family have come into being because of the wish to maintain intact a piece of agricultural or pastoral land. The practice of primogeniture, for example, whereby the eldest son inherits his father's property, leaving other children to seek their fortunes elsewhere, was generated largely by the wish to preserve the integrity of agricultural holdings. The "stem family," described by Le Play in France as a small father-centered unit practicing primogeniture, is one family form that was created for these reasons. It involves a group homestead; and the eldest son usually remains on the farm with the aging parents while other members go elsewhere to make a living. They continue, however, to maintain contacts with the central family unit and contribute to its support. In case of misfortune, the member from afar is entitled to return and receive assistance from the main "stem." This type of family fosters both the preservation of the past and the use of change. It seems especially fitted for situations in which overpopulated rural areas regularly contribute migrants to other areas, particularly to cities.

Interest in preserving the integrity of landholdings and in guaranteeing their transmission from generation to generation through certain of the family lines often has been involved in the various economic arrangements which have accompanied the selection of a marriage partner in many societies. Most frequently, bride price, forms of dowry, and other such arrangements have been emphasized in rural areas where concern over the long-term ownership and control of the land has been great. All these, of course, are factors which tend to enhance the intergenerational continuity of the rural family wherever it is found.

Other Features

The rural family generally possesses other salient features which distinguish it from the typical urban domestic unit. The rural family on the average is the larger of the two and it often contains persons who are not members of the nuclear unit of spouses and children. The range of functions that the farm family is expected to perform is greater than that demanded of the city family, even in societies that have become highly urbanized and whose rural people are influenced significantly by norms and patterns of behavior that emanate from urban centers. One farm family usually finds itself involved with others in interaction that is highly personal and informally structured, which involves a relatively small number of people seen on a regular basis. The social control to which the rural family and its individual members are subjected also tends to be informal and personal, but it is highly effective nonetheless. Control also tends to be based, to a much greater degree than is the case in urban centers, upon community consensus, consistency of values and norms, and relatively great rigidity. After all, the farming districts embody and perpetuate the traditional features of the society to a greater degree than do the cities, while the latter generate and incorporate the innovative aspects to a larger extent. As a result, social control in farming districts may produce for the individual high degrees of both restrictiveness and psychological security. Those aspects of life least subject to change are the most predictable and dependable, and for better or worse, this adds to the life of the farm family an element of security that the urban group may lack. There also tend to be substantial differences between rural and urban families in the patterns of childbearing and childrearing, in the ways in which family members participate in making decisions, and in the manner in which husbands and wives develop marital expectations and assess marital success or failure.

FAMILY FUNCTIONS

In all societies the family has been charged with the responsibility for performing certain necessary functions, essential for the well-being of society, which are carried on not at all or only partially by other agencies. In rural areas the range of these functions tends to be greater than it is in urban centers where many other institutions have assumed responsibility for some of the functions formerly carried out by the family. The most important of the societal functions usually performed by the family may be listed as follows: (1) the reproduction of the species; (2) the sustenance, care, and rearing of the offspring, especially during infancy and the several years of complete dependence; (3) the education and training of the young, including both the secular and the religious; (4) the induction of the new members of the human species into the larger society and the effort to help them establish their status in society's various groupings; (5) recreation; (6) the protection of members from enemies and dangers, including shielding them from psychosocial isolation through the development of affectional responses and of the mechanisms for contending with tension; (7) the care of aged and other incapacitated members and relatives; and (8) economic activities involving both production and consumption, although the proportions of these are combined quite differently and the forms they take are quite variable for farm and city families.

The rural family has performed and continues to perform all these functions in a more or less successful manner. In the all-important function of reproduction, the rural family in most societies has generated new members at a greater rate than has the urban domestic unit, although in some highly industrialized nations there is now a strong tendency for the rates of the two to converge. This is due in part to the predisposition for persons in the most fertile years to migrate from the farms to the cities and in part to a growing similarity in the birth norms of the two groups.

The rural family also has been highly successful in sustaining, caring for, and rearing the infants entrusted to it. In education and training, the apprenticeship system has operated in agriculture. In the case of middle-class groups in areas where the adequate family-sized farm prevails, the system has given the oncoming generation the intimate knowledge and practical skills necessary in the multiple operations and details of farm production and family living. Among disadvantaged laborers and other menial types this mechanism has inculcated within the rising generation the few modest skills, the accommodations to an unfavorable position in the class system, and often the fatalism, the hopelessness, and the other psychosocial features that characterize the agricultural laborer. Therefore, the elements that enter into the apprenticeship system by which the young are educated in considerable measure, vary greatly from one kind of agricultural situation to another. When rural and urban people of roughly the same class standing are compared, there can be little doubt that the rural family has been more influential both quantitatively and qualitatively than the urban in building into succeeding generations the psychosocial equipment of their ancestors.

Concerning the function of inducting members of the family group into the larger society, it seems necessary to distinguish between the effects upon members of the rural family who have taken their places in rural society and those who have migrated to urban centers. With respect to the former, it appears that the rural family has been highly efficient in determining the positions of its members in the larger groups, whether these positions be found in the upper, middle, or lower strata of society. So true has this been that rural society tends to have a distinctly observable caste nature, i.e., there is a strong tendency for the social position to be transmitted from one generation to another. But those members of rural families who have migrated to urban centers have been forced in large measure to shift for themselves. The rural family as a rule is able to wield little influence once the children have abandoned the rural community. This is one of the many factors, of course, that contribute to the experience that the rural migrant to an urban center often has with normative inconsistency, vague and poorly defined limits on behavior, psychosocial isolation, and similar conditions. For the recent migrant from a farm to a city, the family loses much of its protectiveness and its restrictiveness. In this respect, the migrant is much like one who has crossed national boundaries, essentially abandoning one sociocultural matrix for another that is quite different.

The rural family also has handled the recreational function almost exclusively. In middle-class areas large houses and abundant yard space have contributed to the maintenance of recreation as a family function, long after commercial entertainment began to supply specialized recreational services to the individuals from the urban home. Even with the coming of the automobile and the village movie, there still remained a great tendency for the rural family to engage as a unit in recreational activities. Family unions and picnics continue to be important elements in the rural life of most of the sections of a middle-class society. It need hardly be mentioned that the city is more greatly lacking in comparable activity. But even among slaves, coloni, sharecroppers, and other agricultural laborers at the bottom of the social scale, recreation is centered essentially in the single family, and that which does involve persons outside of the household tends to include simply a larger number of families in the same locality. It should be recalled, however, that the rigors of a marginal existence make it virtually impossible for much recreation to take place in any manner except in connection with the serious business of survival. Large blocks of leisure time and the creation of an elaborate institutional structure for its use are not likely to be characteristic of groups in such circumstances. Therefore, poverty essentially guarantees that the recreation in which people do engage will be highly localized, usually in the family.

Elaborate systems and large numbers of personnel for law enforcement are lacking in rural areas. In a way they are hardly necessary, since the family accepts much of the responsibility for the welfare of its members. Moreover, there still remains a considerable degree of collective community responsibility for informal social control in rural areas. There is a tendency for the members of one family to accept the need to regulate the actions of its own members, on the one hand, and to fasten accountability for the behavior of another individual upon all the members of the family to which he belongs, on the other. Families find it necessary to exercise a strong control over their members because of this; but they also protect individual members from encroachments by others, and they shield a member from the wrath of his opponents. The feuds carried on in the rural portions of most societies, discussed in Chapter 16, exemplify this condition. Family groupings also cooperate in protecting themselves from prowlers and strangers, both physically and psychologically. All in all, such an informal system continues to this day to maintain a considerable degree of safety for person and property in the rural areas. This familistic nature of mutual aid and protection is often especially pronounced among the upper-class owners of large landed estates, particularly when the family members reside on the large landholdings. This is found, for example, in Brazil, where the immediate family, which is usually a patriarchal one, often extends its protection to and exerts its control over all persons associated with the estate, not merely the members of the landholding clan. Yet, despite the familistic nature of protection among rural people generally, the fact remains that in such industrialized and urbanized societies as the United States, the rates of crime and delinquency in the rural districts are rising relatively rapidly. Therefore, the old forms of social control certainly operate less effectively than they once did, thereby creating a situation that calls for more formalized and more highly coercive social controls.

Today it is recognized that many of the dangers against which the individual needs protection are mental rather than physical. The growing frequency of mental disorders is one of the greatest crises facing modern civilization. Durkheim, in a penetrating analysis has shown the intimate association between mental strain, in the extreme form that results in suicide, and the degree of cohesion within the social group. Individuals with membership in strong and closely knit family groups avoid the dangers of suicide and other drastic forms of "escape" from life to a much greater extent than those lacking such a protective association (Ref. 108, p. 209). Undoubtedly, the strength of the rural family is the principal explanation of why rural people avoid such perils to so much greater an extent than urban persons. By its very nature the rural family creates a buffer between its members and the world outside of the neighborhood and small community, and even, to a great extent, that outside the family itself.

The rural family has performed faithfully in caring for the aged and otherwise incapacitated members and relatives, with the result that specialized institutions for the care of such people have been largely lacking in the rural areas of most countries. In considerable measure, this function of the family is generated as a by-product of those forces in rural society which give rise to the intergenerational family features mentioned above. Consequently, a much higher proportion of farm than city families has one or more grandparents living with the nuclear family. Maiden aunts, adopted children or those left temporarily with persons other than their parents, bachelor uncles, and persons incapacitated by one cause or another are met far more frequently in the rural than in the urban household.

This pattern of welfare provided by the family carries over to some extent when persons reared in a rural setting, even one of great poverty, move to an urban center. Individuals are sometimes disposed to send for a fairly large number of family members after they themselves become established in some kind of housing and acquire the financial resources with which to subsist. In many cases, there may be the strong feeling that even welfare and relief payments should be shared with other members of the family, largely because of the surviving attitude which places upon the person, responsibility to other relatives than those of the nuclear unit. Rural Puerto Ricans migrating to the mainland of the United States frequently exhibit this characteristic, as do Brazilians flocking from the arid Northeast to São Paulo and Rio de Janeiro, Indians moving to Bombay or Delhi from the rural villages, North Americans shifting from "Appalachia" or southern plantations to northern and western cities, and countless others. Generally, however, this feature, which is reminiscent of some elements of the stem family, does not long persist under urban conditions, and gives way rapidly to greater emphasis upon the isolated nuclear family and even upon the single individual.

Finally, the family carries out the economic functions of production and uses part or all of that which it produces. This imbues it with the production-consumption features discussed earlier.

THE LIFE CYCLE OF THE FARM FAMILY

As is the case with other social groups, the family too has a life history. But so intimately are the farm family and the farm business associated that the two often proceed together through the stages of a life cycle. Farm and family are especially closely related in societies that lay heavy emphasis upon the adequate family-sized holding and upon the social mobility which is associated with it, although they certainly mesh to a certain degree among upper- and lower-class rural people in societies dominated by other kinds of landholdings. With respect to the composition of the family in its relationship to the agricultural operations, the growth and decline of the farming enterprise, and the material well-being of the family group, four stages can be distinguished.

In the first phase, the young married couple is just starting as an independent or at least a separately identifiable group. Ordinarily, at first the landholding is limited in size, although in middle-class situations it is often sufficient for the two to maintain a reasonably high level of living. As a result, since both partners are capable of work and are not burdened by dependents, their overall economic well-being is comparatively great. In fact, in the lower-class agricultural family, considering the general deprivation to which it is subject at all points in time, its economic fortunes are likely to be the best in this first stage. In these early years, husband and wife have the opportunity, generally unobstructed by children or other family members, to develop the major features of their own relationship and usually to be in closer communication than is true at most other stages of the life cycle. However, this phase is ordinarily a short one.

The second stage begins when children are born to the couple, thereby increasing the financial strain upon the family. This is also a period during which there are likely to be very active efforts to enlarge the farm, improve the livestock and expand the herds, increase the amount and value of the machinery and equipment, and so on. Therefore, at this time the things necessary for farm-family living tend to compete most rigorously for budget priority with those necessary to achieve the family's business goals. But because it is necessary to feed more mouths, the interest in enlarging farm production may be even more intensified than that in adding increased amounts of land to the original holding. As a result this period is often one in which relatively large amounts of the available capital are invested in machinery, equipment, livestock, fertilizer, seed and so forth, and while the size of the farm may be increasing, these other factors of production frequently receive priority. All in all, the second stage is the most difficult period in the entire cycle. The couple is forced to exert much energy and to restrict consumption in order to care for and nourish young dependent children and to accomplish the difficult task of inducting them into the larger society, while at the same time they engage in the most demanding farming tasks.

In the third period, when the children move toward adulthood and self-sufficiency and comprise an abundant and efficient labor force, it becomes possible to place larger acreages under cultivation, and the farm is likely to be enlarged still more. This is the period in which the factors of land and labor can be combined most efficiently, for as reproduction ends and the children become adolescents and young adults, their usefulness approaches the maximum. Eventually, they are completely able to pay their own way. Some help on the farm; others work away from home for wages and send part of the proceeds back, at least for a time. All members are producers and none is wholly dependent. As a result, at least in the midwestern United States, Canada, and other areas of family-sized farms, the third stage of the life cycle of both the family and the farm tends to be the easiest, the most efficient, and the most prosperous. It is also the period during which the husband and wife tend to become absorbed more greatly in their specialized tasks among the total number to be carried out, despite the fact that familism and the producing-consuming functions in rural areas hold this separation at a minimum. This is also the period during which the farm reaches its maximum size. The acquisition of machines, equipment, farm animals, and the like is often emphasized less and receives a smaller share of the total financial resources than the addition of new land and finer buildings to the holding.

In the fourth and final stage, old age overtakes the original couple, while the children separate from the unit and establish families of their own. At the most, these young adults divide their loyalties between two households, and at the least they preserve only nominal ties with their parental family. This is true especially when rather wide territorial separation between the two groups is involved and when children have left farming areas for cities. The depletion of the labor force sometimes causes the landholding to be reduced in size, although the prevalence of intergenerational continuity often allows the entire holding to pass intact into the hands of one or more of the sons. This is possible, of course, only when at least one of the offspring is interested in operating the farm. But in many cases, no such condition exists and the parents, looking to retirement and financial security, may gradually reduce the size of the farm in order to subsidize their retirement. For many parents this is a period of increasing hardship. The lower productivity of the aged pair makes them more dependent for support upon the son or sons who have remained on the farm. The center of attention soon passes from the old group to one of its newer offshoots. However, before widowhood occurs and the original family unit disintegrates entirely, the relationship between the couple may come to include a higher level of communication and companionship. Less affected by the demands of farming and childrearing, the members are likely to develop more common and fewer specialized interests and pursuits. Sometimes these involve close communication with children and grandchildren; other times they occur in considerable isolation from the younger members.

In this last stage of the family life cycle there sometimes occurs a peculiar pattern of migration of one or both members of the elderly couple. Found especially in middle-class areas where the scattered-farmsteads pattern of settlement is the rule, it involves movement back and forth between the farm and a village or some other population center. It operates as follows: Elderly women show a considerable tendency to leave farms for villages and towns where they remain. If they are widows, the move generally is uncomplicated, but if they are married it also involves an elderly husband. For him a pattern of periodic shifts from the farm to the village and back again may then be set up. Elderly farm men, generally disposed to remain on the farm if left to their own devices, may be persuaded by their wives to move to town. Apparently, for the aged farmer life in the village lacks enough of the qualities of farm life, so that he may move periodically to the farm to join the son who is operating the unit, only to return after a time to join his wife in the village. This habit is sufficiently widespread in the United States, for example, to account annually for the short-distance migration of sizable numbers of men in the advanced years who have retired from active agriculture but who retain their interest in the farm.

The changes in the farm which are associated with the various stages of the family life cycle described above are most operable in places where the family-sized unit prevails. In plantation areas, among the upper class the tradition of preserving an original estate from generation to generation and the inflexibility of the social system that commonly results serve to modify many of the features connected with each of the phases of the family cycle. Generally, increases in production, enlargement of the holding, and improvements in efficiency are less involved in the case of the large estates than they are when family-sized farms are the paramount type of holding.

CURRENT CHANGES IN THE FARM FAMILY

The rural family, like any other social institution, is in the process of change almost constantly, although the rate of that change may range from extremely rapid to almost imperceptibly slow. At present in many societies the rate is far greater than it was a few generations ago. No factor is more significant in bringing about change in rural areas throughout the world than the influence exerted by cities over the lives of people both rural and urban. Moreover, urbanization exerts this widespread and highly pervasive effect over persons who are long-time residents of cities, those who have migrated recently from farms to urban centers, the ones who reside in areas immediately outside of the large centers, and even many who seem to carry on their lives in the most remote and isolated small rural communities of the world. The degree of influence varies, but almost nowhere are rural people and their social institutions completely insulated from changes brought about by the sociocultural phenomena associated with urbanization.

However, strong family organization is the way in which many of the changes engendered by urbanization are being met by the individual, and this has produced some factors that make for greater family stability. Although rarely noted in discussions on the subject, there are examples of cohesive family organization and continued stability despite the fact of long-term urban living. One of these is the Jewish population scattered throughout the world. Holding tenaciously to a patriarchal form of family organization, the Jews have nevertheless for centuries been city dwellers, except, of course, for the comparatively recent establishment of some of their number as farm people in the state of Israel. What is more important, they not only have survived but have multiplied in the city, a truly phenomenal experience for most societies whose urban groups have had to be replenished constantly by migrants from the farms. The strong organization of the Jewish family is the only factor readily at hand to explain why the Jewish people have been able to maintain their numbers and collective identity in an urban environment when practically all others have failed. The fact that urban residence is not necessarily inimical to a patriarchal type of family organization also is shown by the marked success of the upper-class Spanish American family. Almost always confined to the cities of the Latin American countries, this group has persisted for centuries. The success of the Jews and the Spanish Americans and also of many Japanese and Chinese living in various parts of the world, contrasted with the failure of modern families of many other religious and ethnic backgrounds even to maintain their members when faced with the exigencies of urban living, suggests that only the possession of strong family organization enables a society to cope successfully with the perplexing problems of urbanization.

In fairness, though, the North American family does seem now to be moving in the direction of greater stability and stronger organization in a large number of instances. This is occurring chiefly among middle-class Americans who seem to be gravitating into a type of family stability which involves several things: (1) The acceptance of urban employment as more or less completely isolated from the family and the apparent willingness to live comfortably with the fact that occupation is no longer a fundamental foundation for family cooperation, interaction, and stability; (2) the tendency to develop other bases upon which family organization can stand, which results partly in the growing emphasis upon suburban living and upon the importance of neighborhood units embodying primary social relations; and (3) the conscious reiteration of the value and importance of family living within this suburban matrix, a situation that is reinforced for individual families by the fact that a great many others seem to be taking similar positions.

Taking into account, then, the several outstanding exceptions to the assumption that urbanization necessarily brings about family disorganization, it is logical to examine some of the changes that the rural family is undergoing largely as a result of urban influences.

The first of these is the decline in the number of functions that the farm family is expected to perform. Economic functions have been especially affected as more farming has gone from subsistence to commercialized specialization. The farm family now consumes many more things than it produces or could produce even if it wished to do so. Metalworking, spinning and weaving, even the production of many food items are now in the hands of others. In part, this has come about because the needs of the modern rural family have become so numerous and varied that they could not possibly be met conveniently by family members. For example, animals as a source of power could be raised on the farm, tractors obviously cannot; irrigation that depends upon ditching and gravity could be carried out exclusively on the farm, but the manufacture of complex pumps and other parts of modern watering systems cannot; fertilization making use of various organic substances can be accomplished solely on the farm, but that involving commercial inorganic materials cannot; and so on. Other things that the farm family could produce, such as butter, cheese, wine, an endless array of canned goods, the intriguing contents of root cellars, meat, and others simply are not worth the trouble if the farm family has a cash income and can purchase these items from other sources. In addition, increasing numbers of farm people, especially women, are employed off the farm in nonagricultural occupations, thereby helping to enlarge the cash income available to the family and simultaneously absenting themselves from production as the function of the entire family. All of these developments are logical in any society that has gone from one composed of small communities whose economies were based upon subsistence agriculture to one made up predominantly of metropolitan centers geared to manufacturing, trade, and related activities, and whose agriculture is highly commercialized. Therefore, in heavily industrialized societies changes in the economic functions of the farm family have progressed much farther along the lines suggested than have those in countries whose national economies still are very much geared to agriculture, pastoral activities, or even the exploitation of natural resources.

Other functions, too, are now carried on far less extensively by the rural family in many societies. These include education, which is largely in the hands of schools; religious training, which has fallen increasingly to Sunday schools and churches; protection, which has become more the responsibility of formal law enforcement agencies; recreation, which grows more commercialized, especially for young people living in rural areas; welfare, which is handled much more frequently by agencies for the blind, the sick, and the aged; and so on. However, this so-called "defunctionalization" of the family must not be allowed to obscure the fact that there is a nearly irreducible number of tasks which both the rural and urban families continue to perform. These include reproduction, the physical care of children, responsibility for socialization, the development of a situation within which the emotional and affectional needs of family members are met, and even the ascription of social status or position for individual members, at least in their pre-adult years. The family also provides a structure through which property can be transferred, a factor which is likely to retain substantial significance for landowning rural families. The fact also remains that, relieved of some of the functions which it performed earlier, the rural family is free to concentrate a greater share of its energies and time on each of those that remain. Assuming that this concentration also provides a viable basis for unity, it is indeed misleading to assume, as many writers have done, that the strength of family organization and stability tends to diminish as the number of family functions becomes smaller. What is needed, of course, is a much more accurate evaluation of the quality of family interaction and cohesiveness that is generated as the unit goes about the business of performing those jobs that remain part of its responsibility.

It is fair to say that rural families lag considerably behind urban families in relinquishing certain tasks and modifying others. Therefore, if one wishes to ascertain some of the probable features of the future rural family in any society, he should look in part at those of the present urban family. On this basis it is likely that rural people in most societies eventually will be influenced strongly by urban conditions, as they now are in Australia, Canada, New Zealand, the United States, and much of Western Europe. Even at present other areas of the world are not without drastic changes occurring in the rural districts because of ideas, attitudes, values, behavior patterns, technology, and other sociocultural features that were created in urban centers and have emanated out into the open country. In many of these places, however, comparatively few of the many possible changes have actually taken place at this writing.

The second basic area in which change can be identified is that involving the personal relationships between individuals or social interaction, and family organization. Here many specific changes are underway. Patterns of familism show an increasing tendency to yield to greater emphasis upon the individual, especially the older adolescent and young adult. As a result interaction between family members comes to be based upon a greater divergence of goals and objectives, a decline in the feeling of integration into the family unit and subordination to its interests, a lesser tendency to extend mutual aid, a greater predisposition to define property as belonging to persons rather than to the entire family, and so on.

The locus of authority promises to change considerably, producing a situation in which the patriarchal features of the family decline and in which family interaction increasingly occurs on the basis of equality of members. To be expected is greater similarity in the statuses of husband and wife and of parents and children within the family. Where this change has occurred it usually has meant that aged parents are less likely to be included in family and farm decisions and may even be encouraged to leave the household for retired life in a nearby village or town. As these alterations go on and the relationships of members within the family become rearranged, their respective roles, too, are altered considerably. The appropriate behavioral expectations come to be defined differently by the various members so that

318

personal relations and family organization may be less clearly structured than before. The so-called "communication gap" between members of different generations reflects this greater tendency for the accepted conduct in a particular role to vary substantially from one generation to another. This comes about in part because the important groups in which the person interacts—the family, the peer group, the neighborhood, and the larger community —may disagree widely with each other as to the behavioral expectations and prohibitions that should accompany a given role. Inevitably, this conflict confronts the person with a larger number of moral choices for which he may have no single, clear precedent; and he may react on occasion in a manner that one or the other of these groups considers to be inappropriate. Thus the inconsistency of role behavior for the person becomes a factor making for a lower level of integration and cohesiveness of the family.

Additional changes in organization and in personal relationships in the rural family may be related to changes in sex behavior as a result of variations in the mores, to the tendency for informal social control to be replaced by a more formal sort, and to changes in patterns of decision making which come about as realignments occur in intrafamily status. Still others include redefinition of marriage and of the satisfactions that are expected from it, changes in the relationships with the larger extended family, decline in the size of the farm household, reductions in the average age at marriage and increases in the proportions married, a rise in the number and percentage of familes brought to the point of disorganization by divorce or separation, and so forth. In brief, as farm families throughout the world emerge from their isolation, reduce their self-sufficient features, and become more intimately involved with the world outside of the local community, they also become increasingly susceptible to changes that have already greatly affected urban families.

Despite the many changes just mentioned, there are likely to remain certain forms and a minimal intensity of interaction, which are almost guaranteed by rural living no matter how great the influence of urbanization. These can serve as a foundation for personal relationships and family organization. Most important is the fact that work and family life are far less easily separated in farming areas than they are in cities. Therefore, a certain amount of interaction and communality will be generated by the business of farming, whether on the adequate family-sized farm, the minifundium, or even the large estate. This collective feature may, of course, produce conflicts but it also forces accommodations and creates interaction of a sort that makes for family stability and preserves organization. In addition, the other functions that the family carries out and for whose performance most societies have found no adequate institutional substitute, guarantee both an intense level of family interaction and many of the forms which that interaction will take. Thus, although relationships among members may be weakened by the reduction in the number of functions performed by the family, they also may be strengthened as a greater share of time and effort is devoted to the smaller number of functions remaining. This new adjustment is simply the latest of many through which the human family has gone; and in the last analysis it is the viability of the institution and not the preservation of a particular form which has thus far been vital to human societies.

Finally, it seems probable that the constellation of functions in the farm family, even that most affected by urbanization, will continue to be larger than the collection of tasks in the urban group. This gives the rural domestic unit greater coherence and unity, and often a greater degree of affectional interaction than is exhibited by the urban family.

Additional Readings

1. BERTRAND, ALVIN L., "The Family: Characteristics and Trends," in Alvin L. Bertrand (ed.), *Rural Sociology*, New York: McGraw-Hill Book Company, Inc., 1958, chapter 14.

2. BURCHINAL, LEE G., "The Rural Family of the Future," in James H. Copp (ed.), *Our Changing Rural Society: Perspectives and Trends*, Ames: Iowa State University Press, 1964, chapter 5.

3. CLIFFORD, ROY A., "Levels of Living on Haciendas and Small Farms," in Charles P. Loomis and others (eds.), *Turrialba: Social Systems and the Introduction of Change*, Glencoe, Ill.: The Free Press, 1953, chapter XIII.

4. FRAZIER, E. FRANKLIN, *The Negro Family in the United States*, Chicago: University of Chicago Press, 1939.

5. LESLIE, GERALD R., *The Family in Social Context*, New York: Oxford University Press, 1967, chapters 2 and 3.

6. NELSON, LOWRY, *Rural Sociology* (second ed.), New York: American Book Company, 1955, chapters 15 and 16.

7. ROGERS, EVERETT M., *Social Change in Rural Society*, New York: Appleton-Century-Crofts, Inc., 1960, chapter 7.

8. SANDERS, IRWIN T., *Balkan Village*, Lexington: University of Kentucky Press, 1949, chapters V–VIII.

9. SLOCUM, WALTER L., *Agricultural Sociology*, New York: Harper & Brothers, 1962, chapters 14 and 18.

10. SMITH, T. LYNN, *Brazil: People and Institutions* (third ed.), Baton Rouge: Louisiana State University Press, 1963, chapter XVIII.

11. SMITH, T. LYNN, *Studies of Latin American Societies*, New York: Doubleday & Co., Inc., 1970, selection 12.

12. SOROKIN, PITIRIM A., CARLE C. ZIMMERMAN, and CHARLES J. GALPIN, *A Systematic Source Book in Rural Sociology*, Minneapolis: University of Minnesota Press, 1931, Vol. II, chapter X.

13. TAYLOR, LEE, and ARTHUR R. JONES, JR., *Rural Life and Urbanized Society*, New York: Oxford University Press, 1964, chapter 17.

14. WHETTEN, NATHAN L., *Guatemala: The Land and the People*, New Haven: Yale University Press, 1961, chapter 12.

15. ZIMMERMAN, CARLE C., *Family and Civilization*, New York: Harper & Brothers, 1947.

16. ZOPF, PAUL E., JR., *North Carolina: A Demographic Profile*, Chapel Hill: University of North Carolina Press, 1967, chapter VII.

13
RURAL EDUCATION *and* EDUCATIONAL INSTITUTIONS

Education ranks among the major tasks, and educational progress among the chief hopes of society. Moreover, this realization is no respecter of political systems, and it is not confined to any small segment of the world's societies; it is commonly found in nations that espouse various forms of democracy, it is a key feature of the programs of those that embrace the several varieties of communism, and it is fast becoming a basic element in the ones that seem to suffer from chronic chaos and the lack of clear direction in national policy. Education in its most significant form is the name applied to the process whereby the socially approved part of the cultural heritage is transmitted from one generation to the next, and the process whereby newly acquired knowledge is diffused among the members of society. For performing these functions, society has used a large number of institutions. Through the ages, the family has been by far the most important educational agency. In fact, in most societies and for most people it has been the only such agency, for the school ordinarily has been available chiefly to the children from the middle and upper classes. The family still retains many of its educational functions in the rural areas of all societies, especially the task of transmitting the activities, skills, and cultural elements that have to do with adjustment to the everyday routine of farm life and activities. In many places, however, reliance on the family as the sole educational institution is inadequate: The amount of knowledge generated by mankind, the rising aspirations of people throughout the world, and the levels of information required to meet the needs of life in contemporary society are such that considerable formal schooling is essential for both rural and urban people.

To a considerable extent in rural communities, there is a distinct division of labor between the family and the school in the educational sphere. Schools tend to give instruction in urban lore and activities, the family to instill in the children the knowledge and skills directed to everyday life on the farm. The school, however, is becoming more and more important as an educational agency, and it properly deserves a high place among the institutions of rural society. In addition to the family and the school, the educational process in rural areas goes on by means of the church, libraries, newspapers and magazines, the radio, television, and a host of other associations, organizations, agencies, and media. In societies such as Canada, the United States, and the Scandinavian countries, and some others, one of the most vital factors in the rural educational systems of the present day is an agricultural extension service that has its county, home-demonstration, and club agents distributed throughout practically all the counties and county-like subdivisions of these nations. With variations, these organizations, which are well known to the North American, have appeared in increasing numbers and with greater frequency throughout the world.

EDUCATIONAL STATUS

Because the rudiments of an education (and especially the ability to read, write, speak, and perform somewhat complicated calculations) are among the basic necessities of life, educational status is another important characteristic in the composition of a population. The illiterate person is shut off from many important current-day sources of information and advice, is unable to participate in many of the ordinary phases of everyday life, is limited in his contributions to the well-being of society, and is more at the mercy of unscrupulous associates than the individual who knows how to read and write. Often he also is easy prey to all sorts of movements and demagogues that promise to improve his position in life. Furthermore, underdevelopment and illiteracy tend to go hand in hand, although by no means can one safely assume that there is a direct relationship between the proportion of illiteracy and the degree of underdevelopment. Deficient education is now a far more serious problem than it was a few generations ago, for while farming in earlier ages required relatively little formal schooling, modern agriculture requires a well-educated rural population.

Analyses of available data on educational status reveal clearly that even in highly developed societies the benefits of the educational system have not been extended to people in rural communities to the same degree that they serve the residents of urban communities. In the United States, in

1960, for example, for those aged 25 and over, the median years of schooling completed by people in the urban population was 11.1; that for the rural-nonfarm group, 9.5; and that for the rural-farm category only 8.8. Similar disparities in the educational training of rural and urban people not only exist practically everywhere else in the world, but in most places the disadvantage of the rural population is even greater. Furthermore, though rates of illiteracy are low for all residence groups in the United States, Canada, Western Europe, and a few other places, in most of the world the proportion of those in the rural districts who cannot read or write is far above that in the cities.

Illiteracy also is far more prevalent among those of younger age in the rural-farm population than in the urban, which means that many rural youth are ill-equipped to move upward in the social scale. These young people, as they approach adulthood, constitute the bulk of those who migrate from the farming areas into cities throughout the world. The low levels of education that they obtain in the rural districts place them in a disadvantaged position in the cities, for while the practical experience they have gained in farming might be sufficient for them to carry on as farm laborers or as subsistence farmers, it in no way equips them to secure and hold "good jobs" in the cities. Industries that in an earlier age recruited large numbers of poorly educated rural youth to perform manual tasks of various kinds now require highly skilled workers. This pattern holds both in highly industrialized countries and in those where large-scale industrial development is just getting underway. Moreover, where rural youth do receive adequate educations, large proportions of them move to urban districts, with the result that the city is frequently the beneficiary of funds expended by rural people for education in their communities.

Disparities in levels of education between the inhabitants of rural and urban areas not only can be found in virtually every society in the world, but in the vast majority of countries they are even greater than in the United States. Well-educated farm populations are few indeed, for not only have those who work the land been ignored in most societies in the financing and development of schooling, but in many of them, the agriculturists have been deprived deliberately and systematically of educational facilities. This situation is especially common where the rural population is made up of a small landowning elite and a large landless proletariat. In many places, those who wield political power and dominate educational matters seem to be convinced that adequate education would convert a fatalistic and vegetating mass of farm laborers into a powerful group of malcontents, prepared to pull down the existing system of large landed estates and to revise drastically the established social order.

RURAL SCHOOLS

Rural schools are the formal institutions within which many essential skills and parts of the cultural heritage, especially those not directly related to agriculture and rural life, are conveyed to members of each new generation of those living in the rural areas. Despite recent improvements in country schools in some nations, in the majority of the world's agricultural communities, satisfactory systems of universal primary education are still to be devised, and the expansion of secondary educational facilities to rural areas remains a colossal task to be begun. Obviously, for the solution of this monumental problem, it is necessary to establish priorities for the use of scarce resources for educational facilities, based on a careful appraisal of what those facilities should make available to the rising generation.

What Should the Schools Provide?

From the formal statements of those experienced in the administration of educational programs and from the demands of rural people in many places, it seems that rural schools should provide the following:

1. A twofold program that can equip all children with the general education and understanding necessary for successful living in the modern world and that will enable them to acquire essential vocational training.

2. Instruction by well-trained teachers who possess not only the knowledge but also the qualities of temperament, speech, intellectual flexibility, and so on that will enable them to instruct successfully and significantly. Such teachers also should be interested in local community life. In rural areas, particular attention must be paid to this factor; in many places, rural teachers, almost always urban trained, have shown little understanding of or sympathy with the rural way of life.

3. Physical plants that are ample, safe, sanitary, and well equipped.

4. Suitable school equipment and instructional materials, including free, up-to-date textbooks and supplementary materials.

5. Ways and means for keeping children in school, at least up to the age of 18. This need presupposes that graduation from high school is a reasonable standard. Measures for minimizing the dropout rate include: rigorously enforced compulsory attendance laws; financial aid for those who are unable to bear even the costs of suitable clothes, writing instruments, and other items associated with "free" education; appeals to parents who are disposed to ask or to permit their children to leave school before graduation; and instruction in ways that give children maximum incentives to remain in school.

6. Substantial opportunities for adult and part-time education. Some of the vocational education for rural adults, especially those aged 18 to 25, should be adapted to the needs of those who will leave the farms for the cities. For such people, training

for work in industry, commerce, transportation, construction, or the services is imperative, and it is best given before the migrants leave the rural districts. Obviously, the bulk of the costs of such training should not be borne by the rural community.

Community facilities for education also should include: (1) adequate libraries for school and community use; (2) programs in cooperation with other community agencies to safeguard the physical and mental health of children and adults; (3) educational, therapeutic, and related services for handicapped children; and (4) guidance services in the areas of general education and vocational training.

The foregoing statements are intended to indicate that irrespective of the present stage of development of the educational systems of the various countries, as the minimum objectives for a modern rural educational program anywhere, the schools should provide the ways and means for transmitting the essential knowledge and developing the basic skills that are presupposed by modern systems of communication and transportation and that are vital to the attainment of reasonably adequate levels of living. Particular attention must be given to reading, writing, calculation, and speech. The school also should arouse and nurture in the student the aspirations and desires that will make for a full life and a well-rounded personality in the community of which he is or may become a part. It should be a major force in producing a rising tide of realistic aspirations. Especially if the family is settled into a routine existence and if the rural community is handicapped by low levels of living and the fatalistic acceptance of those levels, the school must instill new aspirations and desires in the developing child. Finally the school is obligated to instruct in the skills and techniques whereby the means to satisfy the new goals may be obtained. This reciprocal process is education in the truest sense of the word.

Magnitude of the Task

The relatively high birth rates in the rural areas and much rural-to-urban migration put a disproportionately large share of the burden of rearing and educating the oncoming generation upon the farm population. Whereas the school in urban areas may be considered to be performing its functions adequately if it prepares the members of each new generation for life in the cities, the rural school must actually do about all that is done to prepare other members of the same generation for life in the rural communities, and still others for urban life as well. Some societies have recognized this situation sufficiently to cause them to provide systems of equalization, whereby state or national funds are distributed to the counties or countylike units least able to support schools. Some of them also allocate funds for general education to the local units in proportion to the number of children of school age, a procedure that does much to equalize opportunities for education. More recently, in a few places, of which the United States is one, a fuller understanding of the magnitude, nature, and significance of rural-urban migration has brought about a considerable demand that educational opportunities also be equalized among states, departments, provinces, and so on. The seriousness of this matter is well illustrated by the relatively low levels of education of large numbers of rural people who are swarming into cities such as New York and Chicago, Rio de Janeiro and São Paulo, Bombay and Delhi, Rome and Milan, and practically every other metropolitan center in the world. In many countries, even the most elementary steps to prepare rural children for adult life in the cities are still to be taken.

The magnitude of the task confronting rural areas in the provision of educational services may be shown by the use of a few representative countries, data for which are reported in various issues of the *Demographic Yearbook* of the United Nations or in the censuses of the countries themselves. First, in South Africa, in 1960, 61.2 per cent of those aged 5 to 14, inclusive, resided in rural territory, although only 53.6 per cent of the total population was rural. For every 100 rural persons aged 20 to 44 (i.e., those who must carry the chief burden for the support of education) there were 160 children in the ages 5 to 14; the corresponding number in urban areas was only 84. Second, in the United States, where patterns of migration and a growing similarity between birth rates in the rural and urban areas have served to modify the situation, in 1960, 8.6 per cent of the children aged 5 to 14 resided in rural-farm areas, although only 7.5 per cent of the total population fell into this residence category. For every 100 persons aged 20 to 44, the numbers of children aged 5 to 14 were 89 and 57 in rural-farm and urban areas, respectively. Finally, even in Japan, where birth rates have been drastically reduced since World War II, in 1960, 40.6 per cent of the children aged 5 to 14 lived in rural areas, despite the fact that only 36.5 per cent of the nation's total population resided in such places. The disproportionately heavy burden for the support of rural education in Japan also is suggested by the fact that for every 100 men and women aged 20 to 44, there were 98 children aged 5 to 14 in the rural districts and only 71 in the cities.

The great rural-urban differences in educational opportunities frequently may not be attributed fairly to a lack of effort in the areas with the least adequate school facilities. In the United States, for example, the states that have the poorest facilities often are the ones putting forth the greatest effort, that is, the ones spending the largest shares of total state income for educational purposes. The levels of expenditure per student vary widely from state to state in this country, but not as greatly as does the financial ability to provide educational facilities. With few exceptions, those states with relatively low wealth and income are spending the highest proportions of the same for the support of education. This is greatly to their credit, of course, but it also means that the meager funds available are secured at the expense of other vital programs. The more affluent states are able to provide far more adequate schools, and other services, as well, with comparatively small proportions of their annual incomes. Except where funds for local expenditures are controlled rigidly by centralized national governments, this same situation tends to be repeated throughout the world. Even where such control does exist, relatively small proportions of the money trickle down to local areas for the support of schools and other local institutions and programs.

Problems of Rural Schools

Because of their small size and because they seem a particular, almost unique group in most societies, there are certain definite problems, in addition to those of finances, that are characteristic of rural schools. Some of them are as follows:

1. A low pupil-teacher ratio is typical of rural schools. The small size of many country schools reduces the average number of pupils in daily attendance per teacher in the rural areas to well below that found in the urban centers. While this may allow for greater attention to individual students, it also means that the teacher's efforts are expended for fewer children than could be taught just about as effectively. It raises the per-pupil expenditure without producing any significant increase in the quality of education.

2. School terms tend to be shorter in rural than in urban areas. As a result, despite the fact that the attendance record of the average rural child sometimes is better than that of his urban fellow, the former's exposure to learning is shorter than the latter's.

3. The average salaries of rural teachers are lower than those of urban teachers, and similar differences also prevail in the other expenditures per pupil.

4. The typical rural teacher must teach more subjects than the average urban teacher. This handicap, which is least acute for the lower grades, is more serious at the more advanced levels and especially in the high school. It is, of course, most serious where teacher-training programs are inadequate to begin with and in school systems where there is a tendency to assume that teacher proficiency in one area of study means only slightly less proficiency in various related areas. The athletic coach who is assigned to teach biology, the teacher trained to teach history who is given responsibility for classes in civics, and the high-school instructor with a bachelor's degree in chemistry who is expected also to handle the work in physics are a few typical examples of this problem.

5. The physical facilities in rural areas, much more often than those in cities, are characterized by small, inadequate buildings, poor lighting and heating, outdated and

deficient laboratory and demonstration equipment, poor sanitary facilities and water systems, and so on.

6. A rapid turnover of teachers plagues many country schools. Often the rate of replacement is so great that by the time a teacher in a rural school has become adjusted to her environment, she is ready to move on to a suburban or urban school, leaving the process to be repeated at the expense of the rural students. In many cases, the rural school is considered as a place in which one serves her teaching "apprenticeship" in anticipation of a more permanent and perhaps more lucrative and rewarding post in some town or city.

7. Curricula that are narrow, limited, and often ill suited to the needs of rural students, and that perpetuate formalism and traditionalism are common in the rural schools. Many such curricula contain little that is related to the environment of the pupils. In part, this problem exists because educators are by no means in agreement as to the fundamental objectives of the school, rural or urban. Some insist that the institution should supply to all children, in city and country, similar educational opportunities, assuming that rural children must have educational offerings as comprehensive as those available to urban children. This stance has some merits. Others place more stress on the values of vocational education, on the provision of training in the techniques of various occupations, including agriculture and stockraising. This position also has much to recommend it. In the past, in the United States, for example, the tendency has been to meet this dilemma by the development of curricula which emphasized a general classical educational offering, shaped partly by the pressure of college entrance requirements. However, relatively few of the farm children ever entered institutions of higher learning, and the position has been altered, that is, the "standardization" has been modified to some extent and some attention given to the vocational aspects of education. There seems to be little doubt that for rural children nearly everywhere, both kinds of offerings are necessary. This kind of differentiation, though, is most useful at the high school level, for few if any children in the lower grades are ready to decide either to remain on the farm or to migrate to a city.

8. Instruction in rural schools often suffers from the lack of supplementary materials and adequate libraries and tends to be limited largely to the information in the textbooks. Schoolroom situations in which teaching is limited to a "textbook" approach are apt to be plagued by the teacher's fear of the superior and inquisitive student. This, in turn, produces conformity to rigid norms of discipline and rote learning, a disposition to push students through the grades by "social promotion," obsessive adherence to the notion of teaching whole classes at the level of the "average" student, and failure to devote primary attention to the varying needs of all the children.

Many of these and other problems of the rural school are further aggravated where separate systems are maintained on the basis of race, ethnic origins, religion, socioeconomic class, or other divisions. Under these conditions, inequalities between the races or other groups are even greater in the rural districts than in the urban. For instance, when legally segregated school systems were maintained in the southern United States for whites and

Negroes, in many of the states the schools for white children fell well below the national average, and those for Negroes were only about half as well supported as those for whites. Even after segregated schools were declared to be unconstitutional (1954), because of the concentration of Negroes in rural areas, particularly in the plantation sections, the racial factor pulled the rural average down. The training of Negro teachers was, on the average, poorer than that of white instructors, terms were shorter in the schools for Negroes than in those for whites, and average attendance of black children was poorer than that of white children.

Some Approaches to the Problems of Rural Schools

As suggested by the foregoing discussion, the problems of the rural schools are many and varied; they call for a wide range of solutions. For present purposes, though, one basic endeavor, which is being used widely by some, and probably should be considered seriously by others who are interested in the development and improvement of rural education, deserves particular attention. This is the consolidation of schools within communities.

Consolidation of schools is the formula most frequently applied for solving the rural school's ills in some societies such as the United States. Unfortunately, critical examination and study of the results and the implications of consolidation are largely lacking. Neither have the advocates of consolidation always been careful to indicate the sense in which the phrase is used, and the connotations have been many and varied. Nevertheless, from the time of the National Education Association's *Report of the Committee of Twelve on Rural Schools,* in 1897, to the present, there has been at least general agreement among educators and social scientists that certain weaknesses are typical of rural schools. It is felt that many of the problems can be corrected through the consolidation of the smaller schools into larger units. Consolidation is asserted to be capable of bringing about a number of desirable conditions, among which are the following: (1) better trained teachers, more adequate supervision, and more effective administration; (2) more adequate school plants, placed in central locations and constructed so that educational purposes can be better served; (3) longer school terms; (4) the use of the consolidated school plant as a natural social center for its area; (5) a larger and more heterogeneous range of contacts for rural children; (6) increased school attendance; (7) an improved educational program, based on the nature of the social needs of rural children and dedicated to the improvement of their mental and physical growth; (8) enough students in each school to permit wholesome competition and stimulus in school work, adequate grading, development of group and project work, and the institution of satisfying extracurricular programs; (9) improvements in the programs for adults in the area served by the consolidated school; and (10) better attention to the health of rural children.

It is impossible to evaluate these asserted advantages of consolidation without rigidly defining just what that term includes in specific instances. Clearly, the maintenance of public schools for the children of one or a few families at high annual costs per pupil, as is reported from many isolated sections, calls for the elimination of some small schools in the interest of the general social welfare. Whether consolidation of schools is the ultimate solution is another question. Control of settlement may be a better way, especially where the agricultural population is in flux and patterns of residence are changing, or where new areas are opened up for settlement. On the other hand, few persons would wholeheartedly endorse a condition in which all the schools in a county or other relatively large and heterogeneous area are consolidated into a few units with almost complete disregard of community interests. Criticism of consolidation is especially justified if very young children must spend long hours, morning and night, on buses that transport them between their homes and distant towns.

Probably the soundest recommendation regarding the consolidation of schools is as follows: schools should be consolidated *within the community,* but they should not be consolidated away from the community. In other words, school consolidation should accompany, but not anticipate, the expansion of the community area; and the first few grades might well be handled on a different basis from the upper grades. In the consolidation of schools, the ignoring of community interests and boundaries and of the fact that the community is the locality grouping that embraces virtually all aspects of the lives of its people, might well result in a form of educational absenteeism fully as vicious as absentee landownership. Part of this difficulty arises, of course, from the fact that even among many of those charged with planning consolidation and evaluating its results, the natures of the rural and the rurban communities have been poorly understood. Indeed, rarely is an adequate definition of the term "community" employed. On the other hand, centralizing the rural schools of a given community may do much to erase undesirable neighborhood differences, to eliminate village-country friction, to integrate community activities, and to stimulate larger and more inclusive social groupings. If more than one village or community is included in the centralized school attendance district, however, and especially if the school district includes parts of two or more communities, the results may not be as promising.

In order that those defending and those opposing school consolidations may be discussing the same subject, the nature and extent of the unions referred to should always be stated explicitly. It is one thing to combine the schools of a given rural community, and quite another to consolidate the schools of several such locality groupings into the large units commonly found in the southern United States, where consolidation of schools is most advanced. We suggest the use of society's natural groups as the bases for drawing up school-attendance areas. This advocacy is based on the assumption that the hierarchy of social relationships, which pyramids from the person through the family and the neighborhood to communities of various sizes, is of great significance for rural education. These various groupings constitute the natural attendance areas; and their culmination, the community, is a logical unit for school administrative purposes. This point may be elaborated further. So far, society has thought it best to leave the child with the parents for the first six years, making the family the first educational attendance area. So efficient is the rural family in performing its educational functions, so many are the ideas, tasks, and skills involved in farm work and farm living, particularly in middle class areas, that it seems wise to continue this practice. From age six to nine or six to twelve, however, the child should begin in a gradual manner to participate in the larger society and to secure the elements of a formal education. In order that the transition may not be too abrupt and the child may continue to benefit most from family influences, his first school years should be spent in a small school in close proximity to the home. The neighborhood or the partial rural community is the natural unit best suited to serve as an attendance area for a school including the first three to six grades. As the child becomes more mature and advanced, as he becomes more sturdy physically, and as his social contacts increasingly occur outside the family circle, he may very well attend a school serving the entire rural community. Here he can continue, amid surroundings more removed from his home environment and more in contact with the larger world, with the completion of his elementary and the securing of his high school education. Eventually, many will seek junior college training in the small cities that form the nuclei of the various rurban or small urban communities before going on to even more distant centers for senior college or university work. Still others will, of course, go away to the universities and colleges immediately upon graduation from high school.

By proceeding in this manner, educational programs could capitalize on the natural social units in the rural districts. Beyond the elementary schools rooted in the smallest locality groups, the rural community can logically serve as a focal point for the educational activities of advanced elementary and high school levels, and the rurban community for the first two years of college instruction. Just as the community supplements and complements the neighborhoods and other very small locality groups in economic, political, and other social spheres, making life more complete by offering types of service that would be impractical on a neighborhood or hamlet basis, in the educational realm the rural and the rurban communities can contribute greatly as the focal points for more advanced educational activities. Furthermore, from the standpoint of social relationships in general, schools planned in such a manner that their boundaries of influence coincide with those of recognized locality groups will play a great part in increasing the elements of locality group solidarity in the rural areas. Properly organized, they can draw strength from the various rural groupings, and also feed back into these same locality groups the strength-giving elements of social interaction and the example of successful working together for the attainment of common purposes. In places where the development and improvement of rural life are to be accomplished fundamentally on the basis of community organization, the development of education in the manner described can become one of the most useful aspects of these efforts.

The school administration areas may very well be considerably larger than the school attendance districts. Whereas the latter probably best contribute to the achievement of educational goals if they are delineated as described previously, the former frequently can be created in such a way at the elementary, secondary, and higher levels that more than one rural community is involved.

OTHER EDUCATIONAL AGENCIES

By no means is education for rural people confined to that supplied by the family and the school. In fact, among adults who have completed their formal schooling and even those who have had little or no such training, other agencies and media may be the sole sources of information regarding improved farm practices, more efficient marketing and purchasing, new attitudes and values, and enlarged relationships with the urban portion of society and with the world at large.

Agricultural Extension Services

In societies where agriculture is technically advanced and where there is a tradition of seeking new and better ways of raising crops and livestock and of operating the farm business and the home, services of the extension type are important educational agents. The principal development of these organizations and of the agricultural research on which they are based has been in societies where the bulk of the agriculturists are middle-class operators of substantial family-sized farms, although once the services have been perfected, farm people elsewhere also benefit appreciably from the work of the agencies. The model of such efforts is the Agricultural Extension Service in the United States. This service, a truly twentieth-century phenomenon, owes its genesis largely to the fantastic career of one remarkable middle-class farmer, educator, and promoter, Seaman A. Knapp of New York, Iowa, and Louisiana. The story of his long and productive life should be studied in detail by everyone seriously interested in the problem of agricultural education in any part of the world (see Ref. 19). Indeed, the demonstration farms that he conceived and established in the late 1880's in order to convince farmers from Iowa and the neighboring states of the possibilities of farming on the prairies of southwestern Louisiana were the educational seeds from which the United States Agricultural Extension Service developed. As planned by Knapp himself, and under his close and well-informed supervision, these farms were operated by selected farmers in order to demonstrate to prospective purchasers of land in the area that Knapp was helping to develop that certain crop and livestock enterprises could be carried on successfully on prairie lands that were generally considered unfit for any other uses than primitive grazing. The intention was, of course, to make the Louisiana prairies so attractive to agriculturists from other parts of the country that they would migrate permanently to the region, buy the land that Knapp and his associates were promoting, and help to establish profitable agriculture there. He developed to a peak of efficiency never before known the technique of using actual plantings and careful management for the purpose of convincing agriculturists of the virtues of the land and the climate, and he freely employed various crop combinations in order to make them aware of the versatility of the area. Almost by accident, it was discovered that the advanced plow culture system of agriculture that the midwestern farmers had perfected in connection with wheat culture could be transplanted in its entirety for use in rice culture in Louisiana. This discovery brought about almost overnight the migration of tens of thousands of midwestern farm families to southwestern Louisiana and the transformation of hundreds of thousands of acres of waterlogged soils, which had been bypassed by settlers for about a century, into rich, productive farm lands.

Knapp's demonstration farm technique had barely been tested well in the unique setting where he developed it when, in response to pleas from friends in the United States Department of Agriculture, he tried it again in various parts of the South. The new problem was the havoc being wrought in the cotton fields of the region by the recent invader from Mexico, the boll weevil. In this way, Knapp's demonstration method became the basis for the establishment of the United States Agricultural Extension Service, which was fashioned out of the early efforts by Knapp in Louisiana and those he employed later when he went to Washington to help found the Service. The method also has come to include the use of such things as comparison plots to indicate the desirable results of employing various kinds of fertilizers, particular methods of weed control, and given types of insecticides and fungicides; model herds and flocks of animals to show the adaptability of a wide range of livestock breeds to forage and other conditions; certain crop and animal combinations to portray maximum use of land, labor, and management (e.g., the famous corn–beef-cattle–hog pattern of the Midwest); and a host of other demonstration techniques to emphasize to farmers the great improvements in agricultural and pastoral efficiency that can be obtained by applying the results of research in agriculture, animal husbandry, mechanics, and related fields.

Employing these procedures, the Agricultural Extension Service at present is outranked in importance as a rural educational agency only by the family and the school. This service now represents the cooperative efforts of the United States Department of Agriculture, the state agricultural colleges, county governments, and in some states, the local units of the national farmers' organizations. The program varies from state to state, depending to a considerable extent upon the breadth of view of the director and his chief advisers; but in every state, important work is being done, and in some states, the accomplishments are especially outstanding. Furthermore, to an increasing degree this service is acting as the model to be emulated in the agricultural extension activities in all parts of the world.

The organization of the Agricultural Extension Service is detailed and extensive. In Washington, it is an integral part of the United States Department of Agriculture and is headed by a director. Surrounding him are various deputies and associates, division chiefs, field agents, extension specialists, extension economists, home economists, administrative officers, editors, and others, comprising a considerable staff of persons in positions of responsibility. In each of the states, a division of agricultural extension is one of the important segments of the state college of agriculture. It is headed either by a dean (or provost or vice president) of the college of agriculture, with an assistant or associate dean actively in charge, or by a director of extension who is responsible to the dean. The agents in the various counties are responsible through district agents to the state director of extension. The agents in the counties are of several types: (1) agricultural agents and their assistants; (2) home demonstration agents; and (3) club agents or assistants in charge of club work.

The objectives and activities   are oriented around the goal of better living for rural people. To accomplish this an effort is made to increase farm incomes, promote better homes and higher planes of living, develop rural leadership, strengthen community life, increase appreciation of rural life among farm youth, disseminate knowledge among the general public concerning the place of agriculture in national life, and expand the mental and educational horizons of rural people. Increasingly, efforts also are being made to assist in the improvement of life for those who reside in the rural districts but who are not directly engaged in farming.

The accomplishments   are substantial. They include: the introduction of improved farm practices; stimulation of cooperation; promotion of diversified agriculture; assistance in the control of plagues and parasites; contributions to added consumption and security through improved practices in producing, preparing, and preserving home food supplies; improvement of nutritional practices and dietary habits; and stimulation of landscaping and home beautification. The Service also does much to foster social life and social contacts within the rural areas, to promote boys' and girls' club work, and to harmonize the interests of farm and nonfarm people.

The needs,   however, also are great, generated by the traditional features of farming and farm life and by new ones such as part-time farming, suburban expansion into the rural districts, and the tendency for rural and urban life to intermingle. Often the criticism is heard that only farmers who rank high on the social scale are reached through the regular extension channels. Whether or not this complaint is valid, the fact remains that there are millions of agriculturists, especially farm laborers, sharecroppers, and share tenants, who lack many of the basic skills and habits needed in efficient production, judicious consumption, and security-producing saving. If these people are to be reached at all, such agencies as the Agricultural Extension Service must do the work.

Rural Libraries

The library is the repository for the knowledge of the ages. However, most of these storehouses of information are located in cities and are practically inaccessible to the rural populations. This problem is especially prevalent in all parts of the world where a system of large landed estates and a two-class social system prevail. Books are lacking from private homes, community libraries are few and, as a rule, poorly equipped, and even some colleges and universities are without first-rate library facilities. For generations, such highly stratified rural societies have accumulated books, magazines, news-papers, and so on, not as public possessions housed in public buildings, cared for by well-trained public attendants, but in the private libraries of a few members of the landowning class. Some of these collections are magnificent; but it is not wise for any society to depend upon such an organization for storing the accumulated records of centuries. The libraries, being private possessions, are restricted in use to a few of the elite, and their fortunes depend upon the continued affluence of the few wealthy families. Adequate public library services must be institutionalized before this vital adjunct of education for rural people can be available to the great masses of the agri-culturists. Even at present, in many societies, rural library facilities are an almost unheard of luxury, either unavailable to farm people or useless to those large numbers who lack fundamental reading skills. In these places, the task of providing even basic reading for hundreds of millions of farm people who lack it is the greatest library problem.

Rural Newspapers and Farmers' Magazines

In societies where a relatively high proportion of the rural population is literate, the small-town weekly newspaper may be of considerable educational importance. In middle class farming areas, such as the midwestern portion of the United States, the small weekly newspaper has three basic functions: (1) it keeps people informed of happenings in the local community; (2) it wields important persuasive power in promoting or retarding community projects and activities; and (3) it constitutes an invaluable compendium of the history of the local community, often spanning several generations. On the other hand, the small-town weekly usually is not effective in informing its readers of occurrences in the greater society or the world at large. How-ever, in most parts of the societies where weeklies are of importance, rural people also have easy access to daily newspapers that supply information on these matters of national and international significance. The rural newspaper usually does little to disseminate new agricultural technology and practices. Perhaps its most significant function is to help generate community solidarity and cohesion, or the general feeling among the members that they are linked for better or worse with those who share the same locality and who also identify themselves as part of the particular community. In this capacity, by reporting seemingly insignificant items of local interest and color, by identifying the members of the community in wedding and birth announce-ments, obituaries, and other news items, by discussing problems of local con-cern, even if only occasionally, the weekly newspaper does much to promote community integration.

Farmers' magazines, usually circulated regionally or nationally, are significant in the agricultural education of rural people. They bring information regarding advances in agricultural technology, both in the articles they print and in the advertisements they run for farm machinery and equipment, pharmaceuticals and pesticides, seeds and plants, livestock, feed, fertilizer, home appliances, and so on. They also supply information about markets for various crops, data on farm credit, evaluations of recent and pending legislation of direct concern to farmers, and reports on production of various kinds. These publications also devote considerable space to articles and reports on various aspects of home management. In fact, insofar as the dissemination of new knowledge directly affecting farming is concerned, they are rivaled only by highly efficient extension types of service. Often, they are considerably more widespread than the latter. In any society where most of the rural people are highly literate and able to benefit from the publications, farmers' magazines have tremendous potential for adult education in the rural districts.

Radio and Television

Radio and television are other highly significant means of communication and education. They rank with the automobile, the telephone, and rural free delivery of mail in potency as agencies for overcoming the physical and psychosocial isolation of rural people. Rural dwellers, of course, have available the same programs as city people, and because of fewer competing attractions these offerings may be even more important for the former than for the latter. In the United States, these two media also do much to make the services of the Department of Agriculture and the agricultural colleges more readily available to farmers. Radio and television also are among the major means of disseminating urban traits in the rural areas and of exposing rural people to sociocultural features generated elsewhere in the world. They certainly do a great deal to promote the homogenization of society in the United States and other countries.

The distribution of radio and television sets varies widely, of course, from one rural area to another. Generally, they are found more often among farm people who are located relatively near to large urban centers and in societies where the complex changes associated with urbanization are well along in their course. However, even large numbers of the most disadvantaged agriculturists in all parts of the world are exposed to their influences. Already it is very difficult to find any inhabited place in the entire world where the transistor radio is not to be found. Therefore, the radio is one very effective instrument whereby the world's underprivileged rural masses are exposed daily to information and propaganda about other peoples and societies. Fictionalized or not, these accounts are highly influential in awakening new aspirations among many farm people; and in turn, the latter are increasingly disposed to migrate to cities in search of better opportunities, or to demand the reform of rural life so that their increased aspirations and desires may be satisfied. Furthermore, the spread of information and opinion by means of radio and television is not dependent upon literacy, so that the words and pictures they carry can be extended rapidly over far wider areas than are possible with "word pictures" of any other kind. Therefore, these two media are already of widespread importance in the broad process of education of rural people in the world's more affluent societies, and they are rapidly taking on this significance in many of those where rural life is of low quality.

Additional Readings

1. ARZE LOURIERA, EDUARDO, and ROY A. CLIFFORD, "Educational Systems," in Charles P. Loomis and others (eds.), *Turrialba: Social Systems and the Introduction of Change,* Glencoe, Ill.: The Free Press, 1953, chapter X.

2. BOHLEN, JOE M., "The Adoption and Diffusion of Ideas in Agriculture," in James H. Copp (ed.), *Our Changing Rural Society: Perspectives and Trends,* Ames: Iowa State University Press, 1964, chapter 8.

3. BRUNNER, EDMUND deS., IRWIN T. SANDERS, and DOUGLAS ENSMINGER (eds.), *Farmers of the World: The Story of Agricultural Extension,* New York: Columbia University Press, 1945.

4. ENSMINGER, DOUGLAS, "The Rural School and Education," in Carl C. Taylor and others, *Rural Life in the United States,* New York: Alfred A. Knopf, 1949, chapter VI.

5. FOLGER, JOHN K., and CHARLES B. NAM, *Education of the American Population* (A 1960 Census Monograph), Washington: Government Printing Office, 1967.

6. HATHAWAY, DALE E., J. ALLAN BEEGLE, and W. KEITH BRYANT, *People of Rural America* (A 1960 Census Monograph), Washington: Government Printing Office, 1968, chapter VI.

7. KOLB, JOHN H., and EDMUND deS. BRUNNER, *A Study of Rural Society* (fourth ed.), Boston: Houghton Mifflin Company, 1952, chapters 18 and 19.

8. LOOMIS, CHARLES P., and J. ALLAN BEEGLE, *Rural Sociology: The Strategy of Change,* Englewood Cliffs, N.J.: Prentice-Hall, Inc., 1957, chapters 8 and 13.

9. NELSON, LOWRY, *Rural Sociology* (second ed.), New York: American Book Company, 1955, chapters 19, 20, and 21.

10. ROGERS, EVERETT M., *Social Change in Rural Society,* New York: Appleton-Century-Crofts, Inc., 1960, chapters 9, 11, and 14.

11. SCHULMAN, SAM, "Intellectual and Technological Underdevelopment: A Case Study—Colombia," *Social Forces,* Vol. 46, No. 3 (March, 1968), pp. 309–317.

12. SMITH, T. LYNN, *Brazil: People and Institutions* (third ed.), Baton Rouge: Louisiana State University Press, 1963, chapter XIX.

13. SOROKIN, PITIRIM A., CARLE C. ZIMMERMAN, and CHARLES J. GALPIN, *A Systematic Source Book in Rural Sociology,* Minneapolis: University of Minnesota Press, 1931, Vol. II, chapter XII.

14. TAYLOR, LEE, *Rural-Urban Problems,* Belmont, Calif.: Dickenson Publishing Company, 1968, chapters 2 and 3.

15. TAYLOR, LEE, and ARTHUR R. JONES, JR., *Rural Life and Urbanized Society,* New York: Oxford University Press, 1964, chapters 18 and 19.

16. WAYLAND, SLOAN R., "Rural Education: Characteristics and Trends," in Alvin L. Bertrand (ed.), *Rural Sociology,* New York: McGraw-Hill Book Company, Inc., 1958, chapter 15.

17. ZOPF, PAUL E., JR., *North Carolina: A Demographic Profile,* Chapel Hill: University of North Carolina Population Center, 1967, chapter VIII.

14

RELIGION *and* THE RURAL CHURCH

Religion ranks as a major social force in rural society everywhere in the world. In a large number of places, the church has no serious contender as the most significant social institution in the rural community; in others, such as the United States, Canada, Western Europe, and Australia and New Zealand, as a farmers' institution it is rivaled only by the country school and sometimes by political and economic institutions. Religion frequently touches most other facets of life, and for this reason alone, the study of religion reveals the inadequacy of various unilateral interpretations of history and society. For example, Marx's monistic economic determinism can be criticized seriously by one who understands some of the pervasive influences of religious attitudes and beliefs. Even Marx's maxim "Religion is the opiate of the masses" is itself a clear acknowledgment of the fact that economic factors are not all-important in producing social forms and behavior. In explaining why economic forces do not work as anticipated, it admits the potency of the religious factor as a social determinant. (For the classic work on this influential role of religion, see Ref. 586).

Religion as such is a universal phenomenon, basically because it provides answers to questions that man is capable of asking but that he has not been able to resolve in any other meaningful or satisfying way; it enables man to contend with reality. No society lacks a complex set of nonempirical explanations for various human problems; as a motivating force, religion is always important, and in many situations it plays the dominant role. The study of religious culture and behavior and of the social and cultural results of religious beliefs deserves a primary place in the efforts of rural sociologists. If it is to be studied sociologically, however, religion as an institution and as a set of beliefs must not be confused with any of its particular brands. The products of various religious orientations are one thing, and are quite amenable to scientific study, but the validity of those orientations is quite another, and basically incapable of scientific demonstration. The sociologist is concerned with the forms, expressions, and results of religious activity, not with the truth or falsity of particular theological systems. For example, Puritan beliefs were a viable force in the organization of village life in early New England, and the comprehension of their influence forms a vital part of an overall understanding of rural life in America; but whether the beliefs and practices of the Puritans were "right" or "wrong" is a question that scientific inquiry cannot answer without leaving the scientific arena and calling upon the nonempirical. As such, speculation over this aspect of religion holds no proper place in the field of scientific investigation. Consequently, in the pages that follow, the nature of religion, the differentiating characteristics of rural religions in general, and the situations and prospects of the rural church in specific societies are examined subject to this necessary limitation.

RELIGION

Religion is a system within the larger society. As such it is composed of at least three basic parts, which make up the integrated whole. These are: (1) a form or structure; (2) a set of functions; and (3) a collection of processes. The structure of religion is perhaps its most obvious attribute, for it includes the particular ways in which religion has become institutionalized, the forms taken by the interaction between adherents, the specific hierarchy of statuses that religious organization generates, the relationships with other institutions in the larger society, and so on. The functions are those tasks for which religion has been created, chief among them being the initiation and legitimation of various nonempirical answers to questions about the meaning of man's existence and the human condition. The processes essentially are the dynamic features of the system, generated in the form of action as the designated functions are carried out within the institutional structural framework. The material features religion possesses, the various ceremonies and rituals to which it has given rise, and the pattern of basic values, beliefs, attitudes, and ideas upon which it founded are culturally important. Identifying religion as a system, however, does not set it apart distinctly from many other systems that are parts of human society. The question then becomes: What are the fundamental features of religion that distinguish it from other types of integrated human behavior and from other complex segments of the cultural environment?

The Concept

It is clear that the term "religion" refers to certain types of beliefs, practices, emotions, moods, attitudes, and values; but it is not easy to draw a line between what is religious and what is secular or nonreligious. To some, the idea of religion is inseparably connected with the idea of supernatural beings; Tylor (Ref. 542, Vol. 1, p. 424) suggested as a minimum definition of religion "the belief in spiritual beings." Frazer thought of religion as the conciliation or propitiation of supernatural powers that are believed to have power over nature and human life (cf. Ref. 128, Vol. 1, p. 222). Both of these eminent authorities make the idea of divinity the core of religion. There are many observances, however, that rank as religious phenomena even though no supernatural beings are involved. Furthermore, if the idea of deity is used as a criterion, the great religious system of Buddhism does not qualify as a religion! Other thinkers have stressed the element of mystery. Thus, Spencer thought (Ref. 480, p. 37) that religion consisted essentially of "the belief in the omnipresence of something which is inscrutable"; and Müller (Ref. 302, p. 18) defined it as "a struggle to conceive the inconceivable, to utter the inutterable, a longing after the infinite." But Durkheim (Ref. 107, pp. 28–29) correctly indicates that the element of mystery is not a primitive conception, that the idea of the supernatural is possible only after the concept of the natural has been evolved, and that associations or sequences that would seem miraculous to a person familiar with modern thought and science may be commonplace to the man of primitive culture.

Holiness, or *mana,* is the great concept of religion (see the articles on "Holiness" in Ref. 171), and awe is the chief religious attitude or emotion. The idea of holiness presupposes the division of the universe into two parts, the *sacred* and the *secular,* or profane. This way of dividing the universe into two domains and the attributing of holiness, or mana, to the persons, objects, rites, and so on making up the realm of the sacred seems to be the most distinguishing feature of all religious thinking.

Holiness, or mana, is not an easy concept to define. All groups have the same general idea, but specific connotations differ widely. Its expressions have been analyzed much more objectively among primitive groups than among the great religions of the present day, largely because anthropologists have contributed greatly to an understanding of the former. Since the Melanesian word *mana* has been widely used as a name for the general concept, it is of interest to consider the meaning that the Melanesians attach to it. Bishop Codrington has most clearly expressed its meaning in the following sentences:

There is a belief in a force altogether distinct from physical power which acts in all kinds of ways for good and evil, and which it is of the greatest advantage to possess or control. This is Mana. . . . I think I know what our people mean by it. . . . It is a power or influence, not physical, and in a way supernatural; but it shows itself in physical force, or in any kind of power or excellence which a man possesses. This mana is not fixed in anything, and it can be conveyed in almost anything. . . . All Melanesian religion consists, in fact, in getting this mana for one's self, or getting it used for one's benefit. (Ref. 77, p. 118, n. 1.)

Some of the more important connotations of the concept may be listed as follows: invisible, powerful, all-pervasive, mysterious, wonder working, supernatural, contagious, dangerous to those not accustomed to it or not specifically set apart to handle it, beneficial if properly used and detrimental if improperly handled, forbidden to the uninitiated (see the classic study in this field, Ref. 273). Taken together, these are quite sufficient to give rise to a condition or feeling of awe on the part of the individual. Clearly, the concept may contain the ideas of the supernatural and of mystery, but by no means is it confined to either or both of these elements; nor must they be present in order for religion to exist.

The realm of the sacred is extensive, and the variety of things that may be set apart as holy or possessing mana is very great. They include tangible objects, beliefs or states of opinion, and rites or modes of action. Among the ancient Hebrews, from whom a large part of modern rural religious culture has been derived, the realm of the sacred included, in addition to deities both true and false: places or locations, mountains, stones, springs, trees, the apparatus of worship, certain animals, times and seasons, numbers, many operations and processes (rites, prayers, vows, and even war), the name of deity, and persons (priests, kings, and an entire ethnic and cultural group).

Still another distinction must be made, however, for mysterious, wonder-working powers are attributed to states of action, objects, and beliefs that are not accepted as religious. The whole realm of the magical must somehow be set apart from the domain of the religious, although it sometimes is difficult to distinguish the two (see Ref. 614, p. 42). Durkheim made this differentiation on the basis of individual versus group participation and benefit. Magic is individual, although its distribution is universal. Especially in the rural areas, it does not serve as a unifying force among its adherents. "There is no Church of magic." Emphasizing the group and social aspects of religion as contrasted with the individualistic nature of magic, Durkheim arrived (Ref. 107, p. 47) at his famous definition, which holds that religion consists of "a unified system of beliefs and practices relative to sacred things," and that these beliefs and practices bind together all those who adhere to them into a single moral community (church). This definition combines two of the most widespread and accepted sociological theories of the origin of religion: the one that would derive religion solely from the idea of mana, and that which holds religion to be an expression of the social life of the community. It is this definition, then, that seems to hold the fundamental key to an understanding of the concept of religion in all of its full, rich connotations.

Rural Religious Culture

In the final analysis practically all great religions and most of the present-day denominations and sects have been developed in a rural environment, due to, if nothing else, the fact that these systems came into existence during a time when rurality characterized practically all of the world's people. Because of these rural antecedents, the chief differentiating characteristics of rural religious belief and practice are to be sought in the traditionalism of the country as opposed to the internationalism and cosmopolitanism of the city. Through what is known as cultural lag, many religious traits and practices persist in rural areas long after they have been abandoned or transformed in urban centers. As compared with other cultural elements, traits pertaining to religion usually change very slowly; and in the rural areas these changes are slowest of all.

History is filled with examples of this fact. So tenaciously did the peasants of the Roman Empire cling to their old religious beliefs and practices and so strenuously did they resist the spread of Christianity—a foreign introduction—that the name of their rural man, *paganus* (pagan), became synonymous with unbeliever. Similarly, the religious conservatism of English country folk, dwellers on the heath, added the word *heathen* to the English language. Moreover, many items still remain part of the unknown and inspire an attitude of awe in the country long after they have passed into the realm of the known among those acquainted with modern science and those who have acquired the sophistication of the cities. The belief that persons suffering from insanity are possessed of evil spirits still finds expression in hexing and voodoo practices that persist in some rural areas. Cases can still be found in which rural people drive the "devil" from the churn with a hot poker long after the relationship between temperature and successful butter-making is well known. Even with the present knowledge of meteorology readily available, persons who would not think of praying for or against an eclipse of the sun, who would have no fear of such an occurrence, devoutly offer prayers for rain quite naturally in the rural areas where the amount and distribution of rainfall is a matter of paramount concern.

Rural religion is filled with agricultural symbolism and imagery. It must be so if it is to be relevant to the farmer and to answer for him the basic questions that arise within an agrarian context. Sermons, songs, and even the sacred literature contain numerous examples, analogies, and references to words involving agricultural processes such as field, vineyard, sowing, reaping, sheaves, sickle, harvesting, shepherd, honey, fruit, tree, cow, lamb, and so forth. In fact, in many places, especially in earlier periods, the various gods, saints, and other religious beings were often the personifications of crops, animals, natural forces, and other factors that are highly important in agriculture and its related activities. As urban influences become dominant in any religious group, as persons tend to turn from an agrarian way of life to other pursuits and other ways of placating the forces with which they must deal, there is a tendency to slough off this agricultural coloration.

In rural religion there is a close association between the secular and the spiritual planes of life, or more properly, the religious element may be said to permeate almost all activities of rural life. Religious rites and ceremonies are associated with rising, retiring, meals, seasons such as harvest times, and often with preparing the ground and planting. Prayers contain invocations for assistance in the daily round of activities, providing favorable weather, safeguarding of family members, and many other aspects of daily living. In the formal, highly differentiated atmosphere of the city most of this association is lost, partly because the kinds of work and other activities to which it is related and the seasonal variations in occupational pursuits it suggests simple do not exist in the cities. Planting and harvesting times, which are carefully identified in the farming districts, are irrelevant to the city worker, and it is senseless for him to attach any special religious significance to these periods. Urban life also tends to be more segmented than that in the rural districts so that the religious and the secular usually are not as inseparably wedded as they tend to be in the country. In considerable measure, this segmentation arises from the fact that the typical urban occupation is not the core of a way of life for a whole family but is a detached activity that systematically removes one or two members from the family each day. Thus, the differences between religion in rural and urban areas arise in large degree from the fact that while rural life is heavily oriented to the natural or god-made environment, city life is more geared to the cultural or man-made surroundings. Religious orientations simply follow this lead, being related more to nature in the rural case and more to man, his material culture, and his technology, and other products of his works in the urban setting.

Faith in spiritual beings and in their power to aid and injure man is one important cornerstone of rural religion. In this respect, the rural man's faith is similar to that of many of his city fellows, but his belief is more universal and probably more intense. At a time when a literal acceptance and interpretation of the fundamental teachings of many religions is rapidly disappearing in cities throughout the world, the countryman's old-fashioned adherence to these traditional beliefs appears as a sharp contrast. In the United States, for example, the faithful, unvarying acceptance of the Bible as the word of God and its use as a handbook for guidance in everyday affairs continues widely in the rural areas; whereas the populations of urban centers have greatly modified both positions. The same is true of the farmer's greater adherence to the strict Puritanical moral code of the Old Testament. As a matter of fact, for this reason, the greatest modern stronghold of Puritanism seems to be in the rural South, although in the urban parts of that region, significant changes in attitudes toward religious doctrine certainly have occurred.

The traditional belief in an anthropomorphic personal God, who is constantly concerning himself with the details of life on earth, prevails in wide parts of the countryside long after the sophisticated urban classes have abandoned it in favor of a more impersonal, all-pervasive, noninterfering, unembodied force in the universe. In this case, the identification and definition of the deity becomes more vague and generally more difficult.

Finally, the uncompromising doctrine of salvation by one means only, a philosophic absolutism, prevails in rural areas long after more compromising "tolerant" doctrines are widespread in the city. In the farming districts, there is a greater rigidity of religious faith, a more ethnocentric conviction that one's own religion is the "right" one and that it alone can provide salvation. In the urban centers, there is a higher degree of skepticism and sophistication, a greater awareness that no single religious orientation provides all ultimate answers or is the single path to immortality. In part, this type of accommodation is forced upon the urban person by the fact that the city contains a large number of highly diverse, often diametrically opposed religions, each of which is completely plausible to its adherents. Thus, the farmer often is able to defend vigorously a type and degree of absolutism, founded in a general local consensus, which the city dweller no longer can accept.

These differences between religious culture in rural areas and that in the cities are most pronounced where the two segments of society are widely separated in other respects and where the rural population is comparatively immobile. Where representatives of the two residence groups communicate with each other frequently and significantly, the variations diminish, cultural blending occurs, and religious beliefs and practices become more alike. Ordinarily, those in the rural areas come to resemble more closely those found in the cities, although the process can occur in reverse. Of course, as with the diffusion of any aspects of culture, the rural areas accept certain of the features of religion that arise in the cities and reject others; and the same is true of the cities. The fact remains that, as the homogenization of society goes on, religious beliefs and practices are subject, albeit more slowly, to the process in much the same way as are other sociocultural features.

RELIGIOUS AFFILIATION

Church affiliation, i.e., the major religions, denominations, or sects to which people belong, is among the most important aspects of the sociological study of religion and the church. In view of this fact it is regrettable that so little actually is known about the proportions of various church memberships in many societies throughout the world. This is especially true in the United States, where the decennial census of population fails to give information concerning the religious affiliations of the people, data that would be as useful as those on residence, race, marital condition, age, sex, levels of education, and other characteristics, data that would be comparable to those obtained in the population censuses of most of the principal nations of the world. Before 1900, it was said that no United States census had called for information concerning religious affiliation because of three factors: (1) Census enumerators have a limited time in which to query the people; (2) the schedules were already long; and (3) the First Amendment to the Constitution restrains Congress from making any "law respecting an establishment of religion, or prohibiting the free exercise thereof," and this has been interpreted as forbidding the inclusion of questions about religion on the census schedules. Adding to the difficulty is the great diversity of religious bodies found in this country, both in the rural districts and in the cities, and the relatively high degree of autonomy that prevails among the individual congregations of many religions.

In the Permanent Census Act of 1902, Congress did provide for the regular collection, every 10 years, of data concerning the religious affiliations of the population. Unfortunately, however, this was not done as a part of the regular census of population, and was entirely divorced from the decennial enumeration. Moreover, the *1936 Census of Religious Bodies* was the last of these inventories to be published. At present some sample surveys conducted by the Bureau of the Census and some records kept and analyzed by various religious bodies provide the only sources of data on religious affiliations in this country. But not only are the procedures followed often clumsy, incomplete in results, much more expensive than they need be, and unable to secure comparability from denomination to denomination, but they fail to give a complete inventory of the religious affiliations or preferences of the population.

There is, however, one principle of universal applicability concerning the rural-urban distribution of religious affiliations not only in the United States but in virtually all societies. This is Livi's law, discussed in Chapter 3 in connection with the description of the racial and nativity characteristics of the world's rural populations. This law states that the traditional or "native" culture and practices of a society tend to be preserved among the rural folk; whereas the innovations, the new and the radical behavior introduced into a society, are most likely to be generated in or imported into the cities, with their diverse populations, and they are likely to remain concentrated there. Insofar as religious affiliation is concerned, this basic principle suggests that, typically, the "native" religions are disproportionately represented in the rural areas, whereas the "foreign" religions, those of more recent introduction into a society, are located predominantly in the urban centers (cf. Ref. 477, pp. 420–423). The validity of this generalization is borne out repeatedly by the available data on religious ties in many societies, including the United States. For example, in this country, the major Protestant denominations, which represent the long-term established religious orientations of the people, are heavily represented in the open country and in the small towns and villages. On the other hand, Roman Catholics, who were relatively few in the United States prior to the middle of the nineteenth century, are heavily represented in the cities; less than one fifth of their membership can be found in the rural areas. Where Catholics are the traditional, long-established group, however, as they are in south Louisiana, they are proportionately more numerous than Protestants in the rural areas, and the percentage of Protestants tends to rise in large cities such as New Orleans. Members of Jewish congregations, typically urban in most parts of the world, count less than one per cent of their total in the United States as belonging to rural populations.

The principle holds in other societies as well. For instance, in virtually all of Spanish America, Roman Catholics represent the "native" religion and they populate the countryside and villages to the almost complete exclusion of any other religious group. Protestants, Jews, and members of other major religious groups appear in increasing numbers in such metropolitan centers as Buenos Aires, Bogotá, Caracas, and Mexico City, but they are almost totally absent from the rural districts. Of course, where ancient Indian religious practices continue to be important, as they are in various sections of the Andes, the Yucatán Peninsula, parts of Central America, and some other sections of Spanish America, the rural areas are the strongholds of these traditional orientations. Roman Catholicism, although dominant for over 400 years in those places, still may be a cultural overlay on the Indian religious traditions. In some areas, especially the Caribbean, major features of African religions also are found, mixed frequently with those of Catholicism and of the ancient Indian groups. In these cases, too, the principle holds: the old, the traditional finds its greatest support and fullest expression in the farming areas; the more recent, the less familiar finds its greatest acceptance in the cities.

In Sweden, Scotland, and many other parts of Western Europe, various types of Protestantism dominate the rural countryside and other religions find their greatest proportions of adherents in the urban centers. In sub-Saharan Africa, the native religions are more apt to hold sway in the rural villages of the bush, whereas Protestantism, Catholicism, Judaism, Mohammedanism, and others introduced to the continent during various periods of conquest and colonial expansion are found to be much more important forces in the urban centers. Throughout most of Asia, the earliest native religions, whether Buddhism, Confucianism, Hinduism, or whatever, tend to dominate the rural districts; the later introductions, or Christianity, Judaism, and so on, are much more likely to be confined to the cities. Even in China, the ancient religions have persisted more stubbornly in the rural areas than they have in the cities, whereas the latter have adopted more readily the nonempirical or quasi-religious features of communism as promoted by the present government. Much the same is true in Cuba, parts of Eastern Europe, and other areas where doctrinal socialism has become a significant nonempirical force. The list could be continued indefinitely, but additional examples would simply illustrate Livi's basic principle as it relates to religious affiliation.

In the United States, despite the weaknesses in the data on this matter, there are some observations that can be made concerning religious affiliation, all of them consistent with the principle just discussed. The comparisons between religious groups in their relative importance in rural areas have more meaning if some of the denominational fragmentation is ignored and various kinds of Baptists are considered as one group, the many types of Lutherans as another, and so on. On this basis, and as indicated by the 1936 data, Baptists are highly important in the rural areas, especially those who belong to the Southern Baptist Convention, or to the Northern Baptist Convention (concentrated in the Middle Atlantic, East North Central, and West North Central states), and those who are members of the predominantly Negro groups. The latter are found in greatest numbers in Georgia, Alabama, Mississippi, and some other states of the deep South; but members of these black groups have increased tremendously in many of the nation's large cities to which Negroes have migrated. They are especially plentiful in the urban centers in Illinois, Ohio, and Pennsylvania. Extremely significant numerically among the rural people of the nation are Roman Catholics, who are widely scattered, forming an important group in nearly every state except a few of those in the deep South, but being most abundant in Pennsylvania, Louisiana, Wisconsin, Maine, Vermont, Massachusetts, Rhode Island, Connecticut, New

Mexico, Arizona, and California. The size of this group in the rural areas does not, of course, alter the fact that Roman Catholics are found in much higher proportions in the cities than they are in the farming districts. Methodists also are very significant numerically and relatively in the rural areas, particularly in Ohio, Pennsylvania, Illinois, Texas, North Carolina, and Virginia. Plentiful too are rural Lutherans, found in greatest abundance in the Northwest and in the states of Missouri, Ohio, Iowa, Minnesota, Wisconsin, Pennsylvania, Illinois, and the Dakotas. The rural strength of the Presbyterian Church in the United States lies in the northeastern part of the nation, with the numbers being particularly large in Pennsylvania, New York, and Ohio, although many members also live in North Carolina and Virginia. The rural adherents of the Disciples of Christ are most numerous in Indiana, Missouri, and Kentucky. Members of the Congregational and Christian Churches in the rural areas are found scattered mostly through the tier of states from New England westward to North Dakota. Most of the rural members of the Evangelical and Reformed Church live in Pennsylvania, although Ohio, Illinois, and Wisconsin contain sizable contingents. Most of the rural members of the Church of Jesus Christ of Latter-Day Saints (Mormons) are located in the Great Basin and the immediately surrounding states. Episcopalians, although largely urban, have some strength among rural folk in New York and Connecticut, with a substantial contingent scattered along the Atlantic coast from Massachusetts south to Virginia.

Smaller groups having a large proportion of their members located in rural America include descendants of Penn's Mennonite colonists, the United Brethren who stemmed from the Mennonites of Pennsylvania, some of the Dunker groups, members of the Religious Society of Friends (Quakers), and so on. In many cases, these smaller groups, usually fairly limited geographically, also are quite homogeneous ethnically, their respective members being almost exclusively German, Scandinavian, or English.

At the other end of the scale, where very small proportions of the members are rural, are the numerous Jewish groups, the various divisions of the Greek Orthodox Church, the Christian Scientist movement, the Salvation Army and its near relative, the Volunteers of America, the Old Catholic group, the Unitarians, and the Universalists. The Protestant Episcopal Church is a very interesting case in which a significant change in the composition of the membership occurred. Originally the established church in several of the southern colonies, this group found itself in such a disadvantageous position because of the Revolutionary War that it almost lost its rural following and was forced to make practically a new beginning in the young nation. In the rural areas one now sometimes finds it as a rallying point of planters in some of the fertile lowland sections of the South, but very rarely elsewhere. Such groups as the Plymouth Brethren first came to the United States late in the nineteenth century. On the whole, though, these situations support the hypothesis that the "non-native" religious bodies are concentrated in the cities, the native elements in the country.

THE RURAL CHURCH

In nearly all of man's history, because of the dominance of various rural ways of life, the rural church in its several forms has been highly important in all societies. In some of them, however, highly significant departures from this condition now are taking place; in others, they have been under way for a century or more. The case of the United States illustrates well the changing significance of the rural church as an all-pervasive social institution: it exhibits some of the typical factors that may bring about changes in religious organization, and it exemplifies some of the problems that may result when such changes occur.

Throughout the nineteenth century and well into the twentieth, the rural church was taken for granted as one of the chief bulwarks of rural society, and in fact, of the national society. People generally thought in terms of country life; figurative expressions and standards of thinking were largely those evolved in rural situations; and the expressions of rural faith followed closely the patterns of our rural culture. By the opening of the twentieth century, the forces of drastic rural change had undermined the foundations of the rural church in many parts of the country, especially in the older sections, such as New England and New York. In a forceful manner some of the nation's churchmen began calling attention to what was happening to the rural church, and to the forces underlying what they took to be its deterioration. The changes served to reduce the number and weaken the influence of the village and open-country churches of the nation, effects that were made even more pronounced when the automobile and good roads came to disrupt further the old patterns of rural organization and life. In fact, so serious did this decline of churches seem to be, that the entire field of the sociology of rural life came into being basically as a response to concern over the feared decadence of the rural church. Even at that, however, in many areas the church continues to have the widest distribution of membership of any voluntary organization in the rural community and it still funtcions as the strongest motivating force in a large number of rural districts.

Number and Distribution of Rural Churches

Accurate and reliable published data on the numbers of churches and church members in rural America are, as stated earlier, most difficult to acquire.

Moreover, since 1936, when Brunner (see Ref. 57, especially chap. 12) collected data on the church for his valuable resurvey of 140 rural villages, no comprehensive investigation has been made in this vital area. Nevertheless, there are sufficient studies on certain aspects of the topic to enable some general observations to be made.

Probably, the number of rural churches in the United States falls between 150,000 and 200,000, although it seems clear that the decline in numbers is continuing. For the most part, the rural churches are distributed over the nation in relation to population. Kolb and Brunner have observed (Ref. 230, p. 361) that density of population tends to be associated with the number of churches, the general rule being the greater the density of population the larger the number of churches per 1,000 population. A sparse population makes it difficult to establish a church, and large areas may be without church services under these conditions; but duplication of effort is eliminated and interdenominational strife is reduced. On the other hand, where density of population is high, division along denominational lines is facilitated, and the areas lacking church facilities are few. However, the reason for the number of churches to increase as the density of population increases may be that the Rocky Mountain region, where settlement is relatively recent, had only about one-fourth as many churches per 1,000 persons as did the South. Such a proposition receives support from the fact that there have been more churches in the Far West in the last few decades and fewer in all other sections.

Other important factors affecting the distribution of rural churches need to be taken into account. Among these may be listed the following:

(1) The balance between Protestants and Catholics in the rural population. For whites living in rural areas, Catholic churches average more than double the membership of Protestant churches. The more important the Catholic Church in rural areas, the larger the rural parish.

(2) The greater the rivalry among Protestant denominations in a rural area, the more churches per 1,000 population one is likely to find. In extreme cases, more than ten church congregations will be found in a single rural village of less than 2,500 inhabitants, creating a serious problem of "overchurching."

(3) Where society is still in the neighborhood stage, churches are relatively numerous. This situation does much to explain the large number of congregations to be found in the South relative to the population of the region.

(4) Where the traditional cultural pattern is deeply rooted and staunchly supported, as in the rural South, churches tend to be relatively numerous. As mentioned above, part of this situation is due to the retention of the neighborhood pattern of locality groupings.

(5) Biracial composition of population, where the races worship separately, as they still do in most of the South, and cultural diversity, where each foreign-language

group maintains services in its native tongue, as many do in the Northwest, have much to do with increasing the number of churches per 1,000 population.

Church Memberships

In the last century, increasing proportions of the American population have become members of churches. In 1850, about 20 per cent held memberships in recognized churches; whereas at present the proportion is over 60 per cent (Ref. 80, p. 20). However, this apparent increase seems due in part to the tendency of recent surveys of religious affiliation to cover the rural population more efficiently, to some duplicate counting, to the fact that strongly hierarchical religious organizations such as the Roman Catholic Church have become more significant and are likely to maintain more accurate and highly centralized lists of members, to the decline of the old autonomous and often isolated frontier church, and so forth. Furthermore, it is considerably easier at present to acquire church membership than it was in early America. The increase also is due in part to the fact that higher proportions of Americans, for whatever reasons, actually have become involved in the various aspects of organized religion and have seen fit to become official members of recognized religious bodies. Nevertheless, one should be most cautious about imputing greater religiousness to the population—rural or urban—on the basis of proportional increases in church memberships, although this factor may be involved to a limited extent.

The relatively small number of members per congregation is one of the most vexing problems of the rural church. Many of the smallest have closed their doors in the last few decades, thereby enabling some of their members to join other churches and to help increase somewhat the average number of members per church. All the members of a church that has gone out of existence rarely actually affiliate with some other body. As these closings have occurred, some consolidations or church unions have taken place, although that procedure seems to hold only limited promise for solution of the problem of the relatively small membership of the rural church (see the section on "Religious Cooperation" in Chapter 17). Consolidation is perhaps more necessary for the open-country churches than for those located in the rural villages, principally because the former are smaller on the average and less able to carry on their programs. Very few open-country congregations that have ceased to exist have done so because of consolidation, however; the proportion of mergers is larger in the villages, but even there, consolidation has been of limited significance up to the present time. The reluctance to unite with other church groups is greater where strong emphasis is placed upon congregational autonomy than where individual churches are parts of large and strongly hierarchical denominational organizations. As a result, church consolidation has proceeded further and more easily among Roman Catholics, Episcopalians, and Lutherans than it has among Baptists, Methodists, Quakers, and others to whom centralized control seems unnecessary and even obnoxious. Therefore, the denominations in the first group have been more successful in using church unions as a means of contending with the problems of small church memberships than have those in the latter. In turn, because of the distribution of the various denominations throughout rural America, church consolidation has taken place more fully in the Northeast, the Northwest, and in many of the Middle Atlantic states than it has in the South, the Midwest, and other areas where local autonomy is a principal feature of the prevailing denominations. No matter what the pattern of denomination distribution, the concept of consolidation finds considerable resistance in many of the rural areas simply because they are the strongholds of the traditional culture and thus tend to recoil from such serious innovations.

The memberships of many rural churches are growing, some of them rapidly; however, much of the increase comes from among people who live in rural areas but whose occupational and other interests lie outside of agriculture. For this reason, small-town and village churches have a much greater tendency to grow than do those of the open country, especially where a given village lies close to a large city and serves as a place of residence for an appreciable number of people who are more vitally interested in the affairs of the city than in those of farming. In such a case, some of the people who live in the farming portions of the open country also may attend churches in the small population center. Under these conditions, found increasingly in suburban areas, the membership of a given church usually becomes more heterogeneous and the range of services and programs that the members demand grows more diverse. The circumstances also may mean that the interest, the numerical base of financial support, and the varied talents necessary to carry on these programs successfully are more likely to be found within the congregation. Therefore, such churches tend to be the ones that are thriving and growing and that are responsible for the gradual increases in the average membership of churches throughout rural America.

The Program of the Rural Church

Practically every rural church is part of a denominational body. For this reason, its program is partially controlled by denominational policy. Some measure of direct supervision is given to the individual congregations by the denominational bodies; but the greater part of the responsibility for the local program is left in the hands of the minister. This state of affairs in itself often creates a severe problem in rural churches, for less than half of all village churches and less than one tenth of all open-country congregations have a full-time minister (Ref. 230, p. 370). In many places, especially in the South, this situation perpetuates the old, traditional phenomenon of the circuit rider who, equipped now with an automobile, may try to attend to the needs of the people in ten or twelve different congregations. Under these conditions, it is practically impossible for the minister to play successfully, in each of the churches, the role of an effective preacher, a trained counselor, a dedicated practitioner of the religious rites, an efficient administrator, a loyal servant of the people, and a conspicuously respectable family man.

Preaching constitutes the principal item in the program of the rural church. When the minister is nonresident, there may be little else. Every effort is made to hold one service a Sunday, but where the circuit system still persists, the minister may make his rounds only every two weeks or once a month. In many ways, the Sunday School is the most elemental part of the program of the rural church. Such an organization frequently is maintained for the children even in localities where there is no regular preaching service, for it can be conducted by interested laymen. The church program also may include various subsidiary organizations such as women's groups, those for young people, some for the men of the church, and so on. Generally, however, the success of these parts of the overall program depends on the presence of a well-trained minister with sufficient time to devote to his congregation. Where the circuit rider is the only minister available, neither these nor any other features of the program are likely to be highly successful or satisfying.

In the rural areas, a high proportion of those ministers who are available are inadequately trained; no small number is totally unqualified. Moreover, this problem tends to be most severe where congregational autonomy is the greatest, for there may be insufficient control exerted by any larger organization to insist effectively upon the adherence to certain minimal standards of education, training, and ability. It seems to plague the majority of the rural churches in the United States. As a result, programs are relatively poor and unrewarding, the institutions themselves are weak, and the activities and the leadership show little tendency to change (Ref. 230, p. 379).

Outlook for the Rural Church

For those who think nostalgically about the preservation of the open-country neighborhood church as a viable American institution, the outlook is poor. This type of congregation has been least able to adjust to social changes of most kinds; it has suffered the greatest depletion of its membership because of rural-to-urban migration; it generally lacks adequate finances; rarely can it recruit a well-trained minister, even on an effective part-time basis; and its program usually is inadequate and disappointing. Churches such as these continue to disappear throughout the rural parts of the nation, and they show every indication of vanishing almost completely in the future unless conditions change drastically. However, the prospects for survival and success of many village and small-town churches seem reasonably bright. Their average membership has increased substantially in some areas such as the Far West, and has remained stable in others such as the Middle Atlantic states and some of those in the South. Drawing members, ideas, talents, and support from nearby suburbs and even large cities as well as from the open country, these churches seem more able to adjust to other changes in the society, to attract reasonable amounts of money, and to accommodate to the needs for cooperation with other congregations, denominations, and even major religions.

RELIGIOUS VALUES AND CHANGE IN RURAL LIFE

One of the basic modern features of rural life throughout the world is the fact that, as never before, it is subject to the forces that precipitate social and cultural change. Chief among these is urbanization, which engenders vastly new patterns of culture, forms of interaction, and types of social behavior, many of which could not have arisen in a strictly rural setting. Moreover, because of the tremendous influence that cities generally exert over large portions of the societies in which they are located, rural people and their institutions have become increasingly involved in accommodation or adjustment to new and fundamentally different conditions. As a result, even though the process of change generally is slower and more strongly resisted in the rural areas than it is in the cities, it has tended to gain momentum and to bring about alterations in rural life at an unprecedented rate. One of the rural institutions most involved is the church; one of the elements of rural culture most affected is religious values.

In those societies where the family-sized farm has been a highly important way of organizing agriculture and where it has given rise to a large middle class, many forces already have had great impact on the nature of religious values. In particular, as discussed earlier, the composition of the membership of many churches has changed substantially with greater urbanization, and this change, in turn, has helped to alter and to modify many of the basic attitudes, beliefs, and values and many of the practices that are part of religion in the rural areas. To say that this alteration amounts to greater "secularization" is an oversimplification, for in many cases, one type of nonempirical or sacred orientation has been replaced or greatly modified by the introduction of another, preserving the fundamental features of religion despite the change in type. It does seem fair to observe that various social forces and processes have brought about greater heterogeneity within the memberships of individual churches and have introduced more diverse attitudes and values into them; simultaneously, some of the distinct and often bitter differences between various denominations and congregations have tended to diminish. This "ecumenism"—one element in the homogenization to which highly urbanized societies are especially subject—has reached into many of the world's rural areas and has made it difficult, if not impossible, for specific churches in particular communities to preserve the high degree of congregational and theologicial ethnocentrism they once possessed. Thus, the changes in these places have tended to produce greater tolerance, a serious questioning of religious beliefs and pronouncements once accepted as absolutes, and a modified core of basic values that represents more divergent sources. Similarly, the consolidation or union of many rural churches, discussed elsewhere, has produced greater differences within many individual congregations and has contributed to the growth of homogeneity across the whole spectrum of churches in the United States, Canada, Western Europe, and so on.

In many places where rural life is not yet so thoroughly affected by urbanization, where agriculture and related activities still form the core of existence for large proportions of people, other kinds of changes either are under way or are beginning to appear. Even though many of the probable basic alterations in social organization, and particularly in religious organization, have yet to take place, there is at least one fundamental change in religiously reinforced *values* occurring almost universally at present which holds great significance for nearly all forms of social organization. This change is the decline of fatalism, of the acceptance of a way of life or level of living near that of mere creature existence. We have suggested at several points in this volume that one of the most revolutionary changes occurring in rural areas throughout the "underdeveloped" world is the growing separation between levels and standards of living. These fundamental alterations in values are invading those sections of the globe where the large landed estate has dominated agriculture and where a rigid system of social stratification has created two widely separated classes. There may be no other idea in the annals of mankind that has been diffused more widely, more rapidly, or with greater impact than the dawning realization that the level of living need not be restricted indefinitely to that which exists at any given time. Even great religions, the enduring philosophical systems, and other major aspects of culture generally were disseminated in more limited areas and much more slowly.

These soaring aspirations, the increasing rejection of poverty and low social status as inevitable concomitants of human existence, are beginning to have great influence upon established religions in many parts of the world, forcing basic reappraisal and change upon them. Particularly challenged are those religions, such as Hinduism, that long have emphasized the fatalistic acceptance of the prevailing conditions of mortal existence and that have invoked the supernatural to this end. Precipitating the challenges in many cases have been other religions, notably Protestantism as it has developed in Western Europe and North America; for vital elements in the value systems of most of its denominations are the notions of individual worth, human dignity before God, the attainment of the "good life," and so on. Therefore, a number of social changes under way in many rural parts of the world revolve about these two diametrically opposed religious approaches, the one emphasizing the acceptance of disadvantaged material circumstances and enforcing social control within that framework, the other leading to faith in man's ability to bring about changes in these conditions. Where the latter comes to pervade men's thinking about their material condition, as it is doing throughout much of the present-day world, stress may be laid upon the use of institutionalized means to bring about change; but where those means are nonexistent or where they work slowly and for a small number, impatience for improvement frequently precipitates militant and even violent efforts to satisfy rising expectations.

A few examples should indicate the growing importance of these value orientations in various rural areas around the globe. In the southern United States, the religious views that began to gain acceptance by the Negro shortly after his arrival in the colonies, were partly conceived and largely sustained within a system of large landed estates using slave labor. Although the values and attitudes that the whites transmitted to the blacks were almost exclusively Christian and largely Protestant, they emphasized, for black people, resignation to the condition of slavery and, later, to that of sharecropping under highly deprived conditions; they fostered aspirations to an improved life only after death. However, the Negro was never immune to the various Christian teachings that stress freedom, dignity, and, at least as practiced, the "godliness" of material improvement and increases in social status. Eventually, these values became more meaningful to the Negro population of the United States, they brought fatalism and the institutions that it rationalized more into question, and they helped to increase the gap between reality and aspiration. The results of this change, and of others, such as urbanization, that occurred simultaneously, include the demand by much of the Negro population that its members be permitted full participation in American society, the wholesale migration of black people to urban centers in search of better socioeconomic opportunities, the great bundle of behavior called the civil-rights movement, the precipitation of considerable violence, and so forth. However, although large-scale agriculture is very much identified with many deprivations, it is curious that there has been little demand for the reform of rural life in the plantation areas, quite unlike the condition in many other societies, where "agrarian reform" is a commonly heard slogan.

Negro churches, once the places in which the Negro population sought solace in promises of a splendid life in the hereafter, and where it was taught to accept if not to like the mortal condition, eventually became the seats of organization, the focal points of opposition to the established patterns of accommodation between the races. Of course, consistent with Livi's law, much more of this change has taken place in the urban than in the rural churches, but even among the former it has occurred in the ranks of people who themselves have known plantation agriculture and the social system associated with it, and who are in communication with those remaining in the rural districts. As a result, the radically changed tenor of religious interpretations among vast numbers of American Negroes can be found both in the cities and in the plantation South.

A second example of serious opposition to the hoary religious value of fatalism may be found in the Mexican Revolution, a movement that began in violence in 1910 and whose sociocultural effects have extended up to the present time. Prior to the revolution, the vast majority of Mexicans were the hapless serfs of a few large landowners, supported in their powerful positions by the decades-long dictatorship of Porfirio Díaz. A major landowner in the country was the Roman Catholic Church; and the purposes of its more acquisitive clergy were best implemented by fostering attitudes of fatalism, servility, and resignation. To this end, the clergy used the mana of religion. In the incipient revolution, which eventually became an overt, bloody upheaval of far-reaching significance, there arose widespread discontent with the material conditions and with the preachments that helped to perpetuate them. With the military successes, the overthrow of Díaz, the Constitution of 1917, and the eventual rebuilding of Mexican society, there came stringent anticlerical provisions designed to strip the Church of its secular power, and the creation of a set of values reminiscent of various brands of Protestantism. Thus, for rural people, this syncretism of Mexican Catholic traditions with those from many other sources helped to create great interest in improving the lot of the peons through such measures as the subdivision of the old landed estates, the reestablishment of the *ejido,* or communal landholding, which was created in a somewhat different form in the ancient Aztec Empire, the development of family-sized farms, and other kinds of agrarian reform.

The Mexican case also illustrates a basic principle of cultural diffusion— that a cultural element, such as a value or attitude, has a reasonable chance of being adopted and incorporated successfully into a receiving culture only if it also adopts a broad complex of cultural features of which the element is an integral part and through which it acquires meaning. The mere idea that life can be improved, no matter how revolutionary, is a cultural fragment. In many cases, it has been spread from place to place unaccompanied by related cultural elements that would give it a reasonable chance of implementation. Rising expectations have spread broadly throughout some societies that have failed to provide effective means whereby higher standards of living could be transformed into higher levels of living. In these instances, the results occasionally have been a retreat into fatalism; more often they have been intensified frustration and a subsequent turn to various desperate efforts to precipitate change. In Mexico, the adoption of various values regarding progress and reform was accompanied by social realities that actually helped to implement the aspirations of the agriculturists. The revitalized place of the person in the social order, changes in social institutions, basic alterations in the patterns of social stratification, the restriction of some groups and the elevation of others, and so forth, did not merely sweep Mexico as a bundle of philosophical or theological statements of an ideal; but they actually were implanted as new realities for a large segment of the population. The religious response became in much larger measure than ever before, "a symbolic image of a social order." (On the matter of religion as an integral part of a *system* of organized human behavior, see Ref. 95, pp. 299–328. For an account of the Mexican Revolution and of the changes it has brought, see Ref. 18, chapters 28 and 29.)

A final case that illustrates the pervasiveness of changes in religious values and their relationship to rural life is that of sub-Saharan or "black" Africa. Christianity, largely Protestant, was introduced to large parts of the continent during the heyday of colonial expansion; but it was propagated and interpreted in such a way that it served to limit the behavior of the colored populations for the essential benefit of the white newcomers. Its use for this purpose probably was greatest among the Dutch Afrikaners in South Africa, where strict segregation or *apartheid* still is carefully supported by the teachings of the Dutch Reformed Church. As might be expected, these forms of Christianity were most thoroughly disseminated among the populations of the cities; although missionary zeal carried them into many of the rural villages of Africa, the various native religions remained much more significant there, resisting Christianity in some cases, blending with certain of its features in others. With the fading of colonialism, native Africans have come increasingly to emphasize those aspects of Christian dogma that teach equality and that have yielded the motivations to seek material improvement. Therefore, it is not surprising that the continent has produced a plethora of syncretistic and separatist religious movements. For the most part, they involve the selection of those portions of Christianity that are compatible with the rising aspirations of Africans, their combination with the underlying base of African belief systems, and the creation of a host of cults that might be described as fundamentally indigenous, but in which improvements of the level of living are vital parts of the value system. As a result, throughout Africa, first in the cities and later in the rural villages, people are abandoning those interpretations of Christian doctrine that helped to preserve the servile status of the black African, they are acquiring those features that emphasize equality and progressive change, and they are generating many new religious movements that are dedicated to the death of fatalism and to the reiteration of the worth of the African. The result is often fervent, abiding faith in the ability of Africans to improve the lot of the disadvantaged, both rural and urban, and in the supernatural forces and entities that are invoked to reinforce the new values. (For the case description upon which this analysis is based, see Ref. 95, pp. 351–355.)

Additional Readings

1. ENSMINGER, DOUGLAS, "The Rural Church and Religion," in Carl C. Taylor and others, *Rural Life in the United States,* New York: Alfred A. Knopf, 1949, chapter VII.

2. FALS-BORDO, ORLANDO, *Peasant Society in the Colombian Andes,* Gainesville: University of Florida Press, 1955, chapter 14.

3. HAYTER, EARL W., *The Troubled Farmer: 1850–1900,* Dekalb: Northern Illinois University Press, 1968, chapter I.

4. KAUFMAN, HAROLD F., *Religious Organizations in Kentucky,* Kentucky AES Bulletin No. 524, Lexington: University of Kentucky, 1948.

5. KOLB, JOHN H., and EDMUND deS. BRUNNER, *A Study of Rural Society* (fourth ed.), Boston: Houghton Mifflin Company, 1952, chapter 20.

6. LANDIS, BENSON Y., "Trends in Church Membership in the United States," *The Annals of the American Academy of Political and Social Science,* No. 332 (November, 1960), pp. 1–8.

7. LOOMIS, CHARLES P., and J. ALLAN BEEGLE, *Rural Sociology: The Strategy of Change,* Englewood Cliffs, N.J.: Prentice-Hall, Inc., 1957, chapter 7.

8. NELSON, LOWRY, *Rural Sociology* (second ed.), New York: American Book Company, 1955, chapters 17 and 18.

9. NORRIS, THOMAS L., "Religious Systems," in Charles P. Loomis and others (eds.), *Turrialba: Social Systems and the Introduction of Change,* Glencoe, Ill.: The Free Press, 1953, chapter IX.

10. ROGERS, EVERETT M., *Social Change in Rural Society,* New York: Appleton-Century-Crofts, Inc., 1960, chapter 8.

11. SKRABANEK, ROBERT L., "The Rural Church: Characteristics and Problems," in Alvin L. Bertrand (ed.), *Rural Sociology,* New York: McGraw-Hill Book Company, Inc., 1958, chapter 16.

12. SMITH, T. LYNN, *Brazil: People and Institutions* (third ed.), Baton Rouge: Louisiana State University Press, 1963, chapter XX.

13. SOROKIN, PITIRIM A., CARLE C. ZIMMERMAN, and CHARLES J. GALPIN, *A Systematic Source Book in Rural Sociology,* Minneapolis: University of Minnesota Press, 1931, Vol. II, chapter XIV.

14. TAYLOR, LEE, and ARTHUR R. JONES, JR., *Rural Life and Urbanized Society,* New York: Oxford University Press, 1964, chapter 20.

15. WHETTEN, NATHAN L., *Rural Mexico,* Chicago: University of Chicago Press, 1948, chapter XIX.

16. YINGER, J. MILTON, *Sociology Looks at Religion,* New York: The Macmillan Company, 1963.

15
POLITICAL INSTITUTIONS and LOCAL GOVERNMENT

There probably exists less systematized, scientific knowledge about the nature and processes of rural government, especially that at the local level, than about social institutions of other types. Nevertheless, it seems clear that the farmer, and rural folk generally, are concerned with two rather separate aspects of political activity and government. The first has to do with activities, services, functions, and controls at the local level, for in many respects "government" to rural people signifies primarily local government. The second pertains to the formal and functional relationships of the locality to the larger governmental units, such as the state, department, or province, and the nation. This has to do with the administrative, legislative, and judiciary machinery set up to relate the individual cells of the national structure to each other and with the effect of local political activity upon state and national life.

CHARACTERISTICS OF RURAL LOCAL GOVERNMENT

Local government, predominantly rural in most societies, is basic in national structure, and the importance of its processes and structure is due in part to the slowness with which they change. In no other part of social organization except that involving religion does institutionalization have more of an upper hand against its perpetual opponent, social change, than is the case with respect to rural government. In fact, great resistance to change is undoubtedly one factor that makes for the high degree of similarity to

367

be found in the local governmental activity and organization in various countries, in different sections of the same country, and in the same area at different times. The significance of local government is also due in part to the fact that this level is the one at which rural people actually contact political institutions and agencies, see them function, and participate directly in them. The small rural political entities generally are far more significant to rural people than are those at the national or state levels.

In identifying the features of rural local government, Sorokin, Zimmerman, and Galpin have stressed its highly familistic nature and have listed several of its chief characteristics (Ref. 478, pp. 540–545). They are as follows:

1. Local governmental units in many areas insist upon and generally enjoy a fairly high degree of autonomy, even though the central government may be a monarchy, an oligarchy, a republic, or a democracy. Moreover, this relatively great autonomy seems to exist whether the central government intends to encourage or restrict it, principally because detailed local affairs cannot be supervised closely by officials who are remote from the local scene. Obviously, these conditions applied more fully at times when transportation and communication were less adequate than they are now, although they still pervade many of the world's societies.

2. Local government is highly informal and is based largely upon local mores. Tradition, ancient practices, and personal relationships play vital parts in the operations of local political institutions.

3. Rule by discretion prevails in rural areas. Where the mores are major features of the political system, few are the formal laws and ordinances. Taxation, the execution of justice (often through extralegal associations, vigilante committees, and similar means), and the maintenance of roads, bridges, and schools are central functions of the local unit and are frequently carried out within the framework of a minimal formal structure. The authors of the *Systematic Source Book* also indicate that with the growing complexity of virtually all societies and the submersion of the local community in the larger political world, the informal type of government based on the mores is weakened, and that centralized government in which the state assumes control of rural affairs takes it place.

4. The stability of local government is very great and seems to remain fairly constant or to diminish only gradually, even where surrounded by rapid and significant change, including that which expands into local areas the programs of state and national agencies.

5. There is little or no specialized political leadership in rural areas. Political leaders are the same people as those who show the way in other fields of activity. After all, most frequently there is little in the way of material gain to be had through leadership in rural local governmental affairs; more commonly, the holding of office is an economic liability rather than an asset. In most of the county-like subdivisions of a Latin American country such as Colombia, for example, there seem to be few financial reasons why anyone should desire to be *alcalde*. Furthermore, leadership in rural

political affairs is most often vested in those who own and control the land—a class usually opposed to any changes likely to interfere with its continued monopolization of this fundamental resource. Thus landowners, other members of prominent families, and natural leaders of many types usually function as political leaders as well, or in other words a few aristocratic families almost automatically supply the bulk of the leaders (or better, the "directors" or "conductors") in all fields of activity, including the political. This is true in societies in which the ownership and control of the land is the privilege of a small elite, but it also prevails in those in which the ownership of the soil is fairly well divided among a group of middle-class agriculturists. Of course, the power base is much broader and more equitable in the latter case than in the former.

Furthermore, because of the concentration of landownership in many of the world's rural areas, "leadership" tends to follow a pattern of super-ordination-subordination, which flows logically from the two-class system of social stratification. In much of Latin America, for example, this is known as *caciquismo,* in which local political chiefs or landowners issue the orders which the masses must obey. Genuine political leadership which is based upon socioeconomic equality, exceptional vision, outstanding persuasive qualities, and the ability to muster consensus is virtually unknown in such situations. On the contrary, it finds its principal expression in areas of the world devoted to the family-sized farm and to the middle-class pattern of social stratification which is associated with that institution. Of course, in many sections of the globe where the two-class pattern prevails, the rigid stability of order-and-obey relationships and the political institutions based upon them are becoming increasingly intolerable to masses of dominated people. Under these revolutionary conditions, as docility and submissiveness give way to restless and often reckless discontent, an acute sense of injustice, and vocal demands for greater political freedom, the way is opened for demagogues of many kinds. The painful experiences in Latin America, Southeast Asia, Africa, and other areas with such figures—whether militarists, communists, or anarchists—illustrate the point.

RELATIONSHIP OF AGRICULTURISTS TO THE STATE AND NATION

In most countries of the world there is a definitely organized agrarian party having as its chief objective the promotion of the welfare of those who own and control the land. Immediately following the first world war many of these parties sprang into prominence in the "Green Rising" that swept Europe. Such organizations are especially likely to be found in those societies whose legislatures or parliaments are based upon proportional representation, principally because the fragmenting effect of such a situation allows at least a handful of "agrarians" to be elected. For example, if a legislative body were composed of 50 positions and the candidates for those offices represented seven different parties, a mere 2 per cent of the total vote would entitle a party to one representative; higher percentages would multiply the number. In societies where such "splintering" occurs, one of the parties which almost invariably is able to place a few representatives in the national or provincial legislative bodies is basically agrarian in its interests and policies. Moreover, the election laws of many countries allow candidates to seek office in districts where they feel their opportunities to be chosen are the best; candidates are not legally bound to stand for election in areas where they officially reside. Under these conditions, at least a few agrarians almost always are assured of ascendancy to the legistature or parliament, and often a sufficient number is elected to comprise a significant agrarian bloc within the body.

In nations such as Canada and the United States, where the majority rule prevails and where an individual may stand for election only in the district in which he legally resides, members of agrarian parties are far less likely to be elected to the various legislative bodies, let alone to be elected to high offices in the executive. The requirement that a candidate (or party in some cases) must receive a majority of the total vote cast in order to be elected is an effective barrier to the proliferation of splinter parties, and for this reason has usually been a deterrent to the rise of agrarian parties. Two-party systems are the rule where a candidate (or party) must obtain a majority and where this is the case the ends which farmers wish to attain generally must be realized through parties which are not basically agrarian in their orientations. Largely for these reasons the American farmer, for example, in his relations to his national government has lacked a national agrarian party. The nearest thing to one was the Democratic party of the South before the Civil War, although the post-war Democratic party in the region also has been largely agrarian in sympathy and objectives, in spite of its loss of strength because of the War and Reconstruction. The Republican party in the Midwest, too, has been geared in large part to the interests of farm people, but the two-party system of the United States rather effectively has set the farmers of one section of the country against those of other sections, and has prevented them from consolidating their interests and strength within a single party whose basic concern is the promotion of programs and policies that benefit rural people. Furthermore, at present it is clear that agrarians are finding themselves less and less powerful, even in such political strongholds as the Democratic party of the South and the Republican party of the Midwest, and their relative significance may be expected to wane even more as both parties become increasingly attuned to the needs of urban people.

However, although a national agrarian party is lacking in the United States, farmers have by no means failed to make their influence felt through organized political activity, part of which has been lobbying and part more direct action. Time after time, insurgency has spread like wildfire through the farm belts of the nation to make itself felt upon the policies of the administration in power (see Fig. 60). Almost from the first the substantial western farmer has been in opposition to the conservative classes along the eastern seaboard. Andrew Jackson owed his election in 1828, in no small measure, to the revolt of the western farmers against the political domination of the East. The Granger and the Greenback movements in the 1870's, the Farmers' Alliance and Populist movement in the 1880's, the Non-Partisan League (originally a farmers' movement) during the period of World War I, the Farm Bureau movement, the activities of the Farmer-Labor party in the Northwest, and Farmers' Holiday Movement in the Midwest during the depths of the great depression of the 1930's, and revived during the 1960's, are but a few of the activities of organized agriculturists that have marked our history. To the political efforts of the Grange, still one of the leading farm organizations, is due much of the railroad legislation, the establishment of state boards of agriculture, federal appropriations for agricultural colleges, compulsory education, federal development of water transportation, the establishment of the United States Department of Agri-

FIGURE 60. Revolt in the farm belt in the United States. From *Leslie's Illustrated Newspaper*, August 30, 1873.

culture, improvement of the services of the United States Weather Bureau, and national standardization of weights and measures.

Although other movements such as the Farmers' Alliance have not persisted and have not left many tangible results, in some ways they have created greater upheavals politically than the Grange. Formed by combining the Louisiana Farmers' Union, the Arkansas Agricultural Wheel, and the Texas Farmers' Alliance, and cooperating with the Northwestern Alliance, the total membership of the Alliance approximated two million farmers in the period around 1890. So strong was this group that it took over the control of the Democratic party in several southern states, dominated the legislatures of eight of them, elected governors of four, and sent more than 40 representatives to Congress. The Grange and the Farmers' Alliance together must be credited with placing the Secretary of Agriculture in the cabinet, effecting considerable railroad regulation, and bringing about the creation of the Interstate Commerce Commission. In addition their programs of activity had much to do with the creation of the rural free delivery service for farmers, and reform in the handling of the public domain.

Such tempestuous results of political interest among farmers are not confined to the United States. In fact, the rapidly rising aspirations of rural people throughout the world have already been manifested in a great variety of political activities. Many of the other efforts certain to appear will have a violent dimension, especially in societies where the level of living remains low while the standard, or aspiration, rises and where the existing social order is rigid and nearly incapable of allowing rural folk to translate their new needs and desires into reality. The appearance and the tenacity of the Viet Cong in Vietnam, the Mexican Revolution, and the countless demands for agrarian reform in many countries are merely three examples of the desperate ways in which rural people throughout the world may thrust themselves into political activities.

Effects of Urbanization

Burgeoning urbanization in most societies has brought many reductions in the legitimate political control exercised by rural people. This represents a basic change, for, whether or not agrarian parties have been able to elect many candidates to political offices, throughout much of the history of man, farming and other rural interests have controlled almost completely the governments of many nations and provinces. However, with the rapidly expanding importance of cities and towns in the twentieth century, especially its second half, this control already has been weakened considerably and promises to diminish even further. To be sure, in this increase of power among urbanites and the corresponding decline of that among farm people, substantial cultural lag exists; agricultural interests continue in many places to exercise greater political influence than might be expected from the numbers and proportions of people they represent. But this lag does not belie the fact that the rural-agricultural interests are losing by degrees much of the political control which they formerly enjoyed. In the United States, for example, this lessening of influence and power is manifested in such conditions as the grudging reapportionment of state legislatures, the re-arrangement of congressional districts, and the application by the courts of the one man, one vote rule to all legislative bodies except the Senate. Thus, the traditional political power structure, dominated by rural interests, long proportionately more influential than the numbers of people represented would suggest, is yielding relatively rapidly to one in which urban elements exercise the greater influence. This means, of course, that the welfare of rural people lies much less in the fact of control by their representatives and sympathizers over various political bodies and far more in the ability of their spokesmen to inform urban representatives of rural needs and to persuade them to take appropriate action. Such a condition makes it virtually impossible for rural interests to turn as much legislation to their advantage as once was the case or to ignore urban factions as they once did.

POLITICAL PROCESSES IN RURAL AREAS

The rural environment, both natural and man-made, should have tangible effects upon the political and governmental activities of rural people. Such is the case, for, although difficult to measure, many rural political campaigns have a distinctly recreational flavor. Political gatherings are one of the principal occasions for large assemblies of rural people, a situation which often helps to promote social solidarity among them, and those attending expect a good show. More objective data, however, can be secured concerning other important rural political phenomena. Consider as examples of these, rural participation in elections, voting for the candidates of one party versus ticket splitting, the popularity of nontraditional political doctrines and parties, and the nature of agrarian extremist or radical movements.

Participation in Voting

Does the farmer exercise the privilege of the ballot as frequently as does the city man, given a situation in which neither is prevented from doing so by threats of violence or other such drastic conditions which are directed against one group but not the other? Reasoning deductively and knowing the barriers of distance between the rural person and the polls, some writers have concluded that the farmer is less inclined to exercise the privilege of voting than is his urban counterpart. This is the basis for the claim that political interest and activity increase with urbanization. But studies in the United States, for example, far from supporting the idea that rural areas are deficient in voting, give rise to exactly the opposite conclusions. Thus, the fundamental work of Titus, who studied voting in the state of California (Ref. 532), points out that "the larger the city the smaller the vote relative to the voting population." This principle received further confirmation (Ref. 531, pp. 27, 41, 68) from other studies in California, Nevada, Wyoming, Montana, Minnesota, Ohio, New York, Washington, South Carolina, Tennessee, and Kansas. It was observed in the votes cast for presidential electors, Congressmen, governors, and state legislators. Manny's results in New England (Ref. 271, p. 7) agree that the rural population voted in as large proportions as the inhabitants of urban centers. Page's research demonstrated (Ref. 330, pp. 90–91) that, in Kansas, voters in rural areas and sparsely populated counties went to the polls in larger proportions than did those in the metropolitan centers and more densely populated counties. Burns and Peltason indicate (Ref. 62, p. 30) that, in general, city elections attract a relatively small share of the eligible voters.

The phenomenon under consideration is not confined to the United States. Sorokin, Zimmerman, and Galpin have summarized studies from all over the world to show that this tendency is also true elsewhere, and that in all probability the farmer is more likely to take advantage of his privilege to vote than is the average city man (Ref. 478, pp. 551–555). Probably fairly representative, the data indicate clearly that rural people, in spite of the disadvantage of physical isolation, vote in as large proportions as urbanites, who are much more accessible to the polls. In part, this occurs because in rural areas, men, who are likely to outnumber women, are the more inclined of the sexes to vote, and older people, who also are relatively abundant in rural areas, show a greater tendency than younger ones to appear at the polls.

Ticket Splitting

Farmers seem somewhat more likely to vote the straight ticket than do people in the cities. The indication is that farmers cling to traditional party platforms and creeds to a much greater extent than do urban residents. Moreover, greater sociocultural homogeneity tends to exist within rural communities than within those which are urban, and in many places one political party is likely to be far more accepted than the other by the members of the farm group. In the rural southern part of the United States, for instance, until recently entire slates of Democratic party candidates were elected by wide margins, with few voters splitting the ticket in favor of individual candidates of the Republican party. There is still some tendency in rural areas to preserve the one-party situation and to elect all of the candidates of the party in question. But there also are some factors that make for increased ticket splitting in many rural parts of the United States, as witness heavy proportional votes for national officials of one party and the election or very strong showing of local officials of the opposing party. Where the two-party system is at all operable, politicians can no longer be certain that a majority of votes cast by rural people for the presidential candidate of one party will sweep into office an entire slate of lesser candidates of the same party. In some measure, of course, this type of ticket splitting results from the highly personal nature of local rural politics, which prompts the voter to cast his ballot for or against specific individuals in the county or township no matter what their party affiliations. In all these cases, ticket splitting and voter desertion from parties that traditionally have dominated certain rural areas are on the increase. In this connection, recent elections are of great interest and deserve careful analysis because of the apparent changes in rural-urban differentiation in the balloting.

Radicalism and Revolution

The experience of the United States and that of many other nations amply demonstrates that the farmer is by no means always and everywhere staid and conservative. Probably over long periods of time he is less revolutionary than the city man, but at specific times and under particular conditions farmers have been radical in the extreme. There also seem to be some peculiar aspects about rural radicalism that differentiate it from that of the city. The most important of these is related to the ownership and control of the land. Whenever any large portion of the rural population lacks lands of its own to cultivate, or whenever any significant numbers of owner-operators are threatened with dispossession from their lands, desperation and revolt are likely to flare up in the farming districts. The "Farmers' Holiday Movement," which swept like wildfire through the midwestern United States and made its influence felt in the South during 1932 and 1933, is an excellent example of revolt among the farmers. Elemental in the extreme, without a clearly defined program and objectives, seeking by all possible means to prevent the dispossession of farm operators, the movement clearly typifies radicalism among farmers. Illustrative also are the desperate actions, often violent, among many of the world's agricultural masses as they confront conditions in which their rising aspirations for ownership and control of the land clash with rigid social systems that provide few or no workable mechanisms whereby that control may be achieved peacefully. The migratory rush of rural people toward cities in almost every nation, the demands of others for "agrarian reform," and the turn of many toward communism and anarchy all represent radical and revolutionary answers to this problem among large segments of the world's agriculturists.

Many of these conditions are fostered by the idea, itself a radical departure from the thought patterns that have characterized all but the last few hundred years of man's history, that the rural poor need no longer accept their lot as inevitable. The rapid spread of this concept seriously outdates, among elites and disadvantaged masses alike, any notion that traditional and conservative patterns of rural life can be preserved indefinitely. There are few contemporary changes in patterns of thought and behavior that rival this in significance, and it is little wonder that it inspires radical and revolutionary action on the part of agricultural people throughout the world.

Measures Favored by the Farming Classes

Farmers' interests do not coincide exactly with those of any one city class. As a result, farmers sometimes vote with one of the urban classes, sometimes with another; now with the laborers, at another time with the employers. In general, farmers in the United States have opposed such measures as minimum-wage laws and hour limitations, the softening of the criminal code, pensions for occupational groups such as teachers, increases in taxation, the modification of election laws to bring about greater popular rule, workmen's compensation, and civil-rights legislation. On the other hand, they have supported such things as the prohibition amendment, regulation of banks and corporations (especially railroads), imposition of tariffs, measures designed to promote honesty in governmental affairs, and, of course, price supports for various kinds of agricultural products. Thus, the agriculturists sometimes unite for political purposes with the urban laboring classes, sometimes with the middle classes, at other times with the upper, capitalistic classes of the cities, and occasionally with no particular stratum at all. In view of this, it is not strange that it has been impossible to organize farmer-laborer parties on a national scale. On the other hand, a strong agrarian bloc in all political parties seems most likely to advance the welfare of rural groups, and it is this condition that they tend to support, although in many cases the political power of such a bloc has already eroded seriously.

TYPES OF LOCAL GOVERNMENT

Local government among rural people throughout the world generally falls into two principal types, both historically and in contemporary societies. The first of these is the form in which the subdivisions of states, provinces, departments, and other units actually have considerable autonomy, are permitted the freedom to exercise *self-government* to a considerable extent, and are authorized to undertake on their own responsibility many important functions. In such cases, local governments are far more than the ultimate administrative extensions of the national government. This viable type of local government exists in relatively few societies, with the forms found in the United States and Canada probably representing the most highly developed and by far the most successful in existence. In fact, the claim to "democracy" in the United States rests fully as much upon the extent to which local governmental units are allowed to run their own affairs as upon any other basic factor. Traditionally in this country the people throughout the rural areas have been empowered and impelled to organize a great variety of their own "districts" for the organization and support of schools, the safeguarding of life and property, the development of irrigation and drainage, the construction and maintenance of levees, the implementation of health and welfare efforts, and so on. Moreover, even though many of these districts are more or less regimented to a county basis, the fact that they are created and made functional by local people for local purposes produces the essential nature of self-government. Within such a situation, of course, the qualities of genuine leadership, such as persuasion, rational programs and proposals, and the search for consensus find their greatest development, as distinct from situations in which the "leadership" is of a spurious sort involving little more than the implementation of orders that come from a higher level of government or the uncritical use of personalist tactics.

Genuine local self-government has taken many forms in the few areas where it is found to exist. In the United States, the county is its most widely employed and generally understood expression. The American farmers' local governmental institutions are a product of centuries of social evolution. For the most part their origins go back to the Old World, and especially to England, where the prototypes of American political organization were developing hundreds of years before the discovery of the Americas. Of course, similar antecedents once existed throughout other areas of the globe, especially in Europe where pre-Roman Latins established self-government in their small fortified agricultural villages, but many of these disappeared as the protracted age of kings came to dominate much of the world. In the colonization of North America a considerable variety of local governmental units was transplanted to the New World where, in the face of radically different conditions from those of the mother countries, they rapidly underwent fundamental changes. In the compact group settlements of New England, Old World patterns evolved into the township system of local self-government. In the southern colonies, however, a quite different system developed. Here, where large and widely separated plantations dominated the landscape, the county was developed as the basic unit of local government. In the middle colonies, somewhat of a compromise came into being, a form of local self-determination that used both the county and township. For example, in Pennsylvania, although towns were established as local governmental units, they were of little importance, their machinery and functions were vague and indefinite, and they cannot be said to have embodied the features of a viable system of self-government. In New York, however, where the system of local government also embraced both townships and counties, the townships had important functions and were definitely recognized as part of the county organization. New England left her imprint firmly upon the pattern of local self-government in New York.

As the fringes of settlement pushed westward across the continent, the local governmental and political institutions from the older states diffused with them, following to a considerable extent parallel lines of latitude. Even in the face of radically contrasting situations in the new settlements, the primary factor determining the nature of rural governmental units in the new states was the type of unit that the settlers had been accustomed to in the localities from which they came. In retrospect, then, the evolution of units of local self-government in the United States passed through a number of distinct phases: (1) the introduction of governmental patterns into the colonies from the mother countries, especially England; (2) radical changes to adapt them to the new environment, a remodeling that gave rise to the township system in New England, the county system in the South, and a mixed type in the middle colonies; and (3) the diffusion of these patterns with the settlement of the West, settlers from a given state establishing in their new surroundings the local governmental units to which they had been accustomed in the older sections. But in all of these cases, no matter what the structural form of local government, the units throughout the nation were marked primarily by self-determination under which local interests were served basically by programs, projects, taxing procedures, and other features which developed at the local level and which were in the hands of local people. In this respect, local rural government in the United States is almost unique as a means of meeting those needs that political institutions are generally designed to serve.

The second major type of local government, which is almost universal in the world at the present time, is the form in which the administration and government of a local district is merely the ultimate extension of the arm of the central, royal, imperial, or other form of national government. This type of political institution, in which local people do not participate so as to determine their own affairs, is of ancient origin. It is characteristic not only of such old despotisms as those of the Assyrians, the Medes and the Persians, the Egyptians, and others, but also of present-day kingdoms, sheikdoms, principalities, and others. Throughout the middle ages, the spread of feudalism and all the rigidity it entailed was especially significant in making this type of local government practically universal. Even now, where many "republics" and "people's democracies" have been established, the orders still flow from the central government to the smallest of the local units, by whatever name they may be called. Even in Latin America it is unthinkable that there could be a local election to decide for or against the issuance of bonds to be sold for the building of a school, the installation of a village water system, or the development of projects to drain or irrigate local lands.

THE GENERAL DEBILITY OF LOCAL GOVERNMENT

It is obvious from the preceding section that rare indeed is the case when local rural people are privileged to develop and maintain local self-government to the extent that is taken for granted in the United States and Canada. A very small share of the world's rural people actually are empowered to organize and support their own community schools, enforce law and order in their own localities, construct and maintain roads and bridges in their own communities, build public utilities systems that serve them, or engage in any of the multitude of activities that make local government vital and dynamic. Moreover, it is only this same small share that is privileged to assess, levy, and collect locally the taxes which are necessary to provide the many services that they need. From many points of view, it is the freedom, the responsibility, and the willingness of local people to impose upon themselves the necessary tariffs which entitles this form of local administration to be called "self-government."

On the other hand, large indeed is the proportion of the world's rural population that has little or no voice in whether or not the many services necessary to social life at the local level actually will be provided; and these rural people generally lack the power of taxation to bring about changes in this condition. The counties, municipios, villages, or other local political entities involved in this group often remain virtually immobilized as units of self-determination, and are merely the convenient administrative bodies through which the laws, policies, actions, and other endeavors of the central government are brought to bear directly upon the inhabitants of the rural districts. The officers of the law are responsible to state and national governments; the taxes are levied by the central government and the proceeds go into the national coffers, perhaps to be dispensed to local areas, but often to be diverted into other realms; the responsibility for local schools, such as they are, is mainly or even exclusively that of the national government, so much so that the simple requisition of a few supplies may involve endless entanglement in the red tape of the centralized government. In no sense may such units be said to possess genuine local self-government; in most respects they become the pawns of central government, administered and supplied or denied in such a way that in some countries they are almost completely powerless.

Large parts of Latin America, for example, contain local governmental units that suffer from many of the troubles mentioned above. Moreover, this problem is tied closely to others, especially those that arise from the inadequacy of various institutions, agencies, and services for local rural people. In part it is associated intimately with the large landed estate. Where this social institution and the system associated with it prevail, land, houses, churches, and other real property may belong to one large landowner and he and his representatives may constitute the only real law and government in the miniature barony over which he exercises his influence.

In many parts of the world, the local village may be assessed a certain amount of tax by the national government and may, occasionally, be allowed the "freedom" to apportion the taxpaying responsibility among the residents of the village and to collect these amounts as best it can. But in no way does this narrow latitude and meager initiative amount to popular self-government, nor does it even contain the rudiments of such a condition. It is merely a system of paying tribute in which the communities rather than the individuals are responsible for the payments. There is no thought that the amounts thus levied and collected will be used for the general betterment of the total local community, nor is there the slightest indication that the local people will have a voice in the uses to which the money is put or be allowed to design projects and programs which are financed by the anticipated revenues. The funds, of course, simply are not collected for use at the local level. Furthermore, the fact that the large landowner usually pays only a tiny fraction of his fair share means that the total amounts collected will be quite small in any event. This set of conditions was characteristic of Europe and Asia during most of their history and is still generally found in many parts of these two continents; and while it tends to appear less frequently as an official arrangement, it continues to operate in a *de facto* manner in wide areas.

Whether or not a system of weak local government in given rural areas is officially created or is simply an extralegal fact of life, where the large landed estate is the principal social feature, there tends to develop a morbid three-way association between the large holding, illiteracy, and the debility of local government. This is the situation where the large estates prevail in Latin America, Asia, Africa, the southern United States, and many other regions. The relationship between these three sociocultural conditions arises from the fact that the large landowners generally are in a position to enact or to secure the enactment of laws advantageous to their own social class and are able in this way to avoid the assessment of taxes which might then be used at the local level. Furthermore, not only do they fail to impose taxes upon themselves but they certainly do not allow local peasants, peons, share-croppers, coloni, or others of lower-class status to impose such taxes upon the large estates. Therefore, adequate educational facilities, one of the principal endeavors of local government in the United States and Canada, are virtually nonexistent in the local areas of societies where large holdings dominate rural life. The children of the privileged families, of course, are sent out of the local area to obtain educations, but those of the workers are forced to vegetate and are generally deprived of all but the most meager opportunities. In turn, they become adult agricultural laborers who transmit the same scanty culture to succeeding generations. Thus, where the large landed estate controls the local area, the accompanying weak governmental units lack the authority and tradition to use the general property tax for the support of schools, law enforcement, the construction of public facilities, and other services. The net result is a relatively high sustained percentage of illiteracy as well as serious deficiencies in many other aspects of rural life.

The weakness of local rural government has had ramifications in many areas. One of the increasingly important of these has to do with the creation and implementation of various kinds of "assistance" programs in "underdeveloped" countries where the proportion of rural people is high. Many such programs have failed simply because there is no workable system of local self-government in the societies involved. Obviously, aid programs which stand any chance of being successful must be carried out among the people who have the greatest need, and must, therefore, be conducted through some sort of institutional structure which operates among those who are the intended recipients of the programs. To a North American, the logical institutional framework through which aid programs might be carried out is government at the local level. However, where the local political units are weak and serve as nothing more than the outlying appendages of a vast centralized government, they are entirely unsuited to be the agencies through which programs are conceived and implemented locally, or even those through which projects created elsewhere can be carried on in a way that has significance and meaning for local people. Many persons engaged in assistance programs in immense sections of the world have already encountered the frustrations that arise from this inability of local government to devise, promote, and implement necessary programs and to meet certain needs of the residents. Many such efforts should never have been launched, principally because the weakness of local government had precluded any chance of success long before the efforts were actually begun.

Finally, in places where the local governmental unit is weak it also generally is relatively ineffective in helping to bring about community solidarity, which is mentioned elsewhere in this volume as a fundamental characteristic of community development and improvement of rural life. Local government in such places as Brazil, Colombia, and Venezuela, for example, does little in most cases to foster the unity of the village or other small population center, unless, of course, that solidarity arises among the subjects of a large landowner as a result of their common recognition and resentment of his control. Under these conditions, the development of a highly pervasive "consciousness of kind" may promote the strongest kind of solidarity. Even so, the mere existence of such a condition is not sufficient to bring about changes which would strengthen local government or transform it into a unit of popular self-determination within which many of the needs of local people could be met.

LOCAL RURAL SELF-GOVERNMENT IN THE UNITED STATES

Local political units in the United States, having avoided most of the weaknesses discussed above, are a stellar example of viable and functional self-determination among rural people and deserve consideration on this basis.

Functions

The rural population of the United States has always looked to state and local governmental units for the performance of a number of functions thought to be essential to the welfare of the people on the land. Many of these societal functions carried on by the government are of local significance only, and responsibility for them has been centered in the county or township unit. This is the ultimate in local self-government. Others, and probably the larger share of the governmental functions performed by local units, are actually state functions, which are delegated to the local divisions, but the administration of these, too, embodies many elements of self-government.

Throughout most of the United States, the principal unit of rural local government is the county. Other local governmental units, such as towns in New England and townships in the Midwest, do exist and are significant in meeting local needs in these places, but for the nation as a whole the county is the most important. The nature of the county is complex; it is at once an administrative agency and a quasi-corporation. Deriving its privileges from the state, the county possesses in general only those powers that have been expressly delegated to it by the state constitution or specifically granted to it by the state legislature.

The administrative functions usually performed by the county are concerned with such things as the following: (1) justice; (2) corrections and charities; (3) health measures and programs; (4) education; (5) highways and roads; (6) revenues; and (7) records. Recent developments have increased the importance of the county unit in agricultural extension work and other programs undertaken in cooperation with state and national governments. In fact, more and more federal activities are being organized on a county basis, although not always as county functions. Nevertheless, the functions mentioned above and others might well become principal activities of local government in those societies which are seeking to strengthen their local units and to infuse greater vitality into their entire political systems and into rural life in general.

The nature of the county's conventional governmental functions is fairly well known. The administration of justice involves the exercise of the police power, coroners' inquests in cases of sudden death or where foul play is suspected, and the provision of courts of justice. Activities in connection with corrections and charities on a county basis include the maintenance of county jails, provision of relief for the poor, and specialized welfare work. With the advent of state and national unemployment relief programs in 1932, and more recently of a host of related efforts, the welfare activities of the counties have assumed a role of great importance. Health administration involves taking proper precautions to insure sanitation and to provide hospitals, county nurses, and county physicians. In recent years the state, acting largely through the counties, has greatly broadened the public health facilities available to the rural population. Counties are also a basic unit in the provision of educational services, which are generally among their most important functions. Consolidation of schools and the provision of state aid to the counties have increased still more the importance of the county in educational administration. The local governmental unit was, for a long time, almost the only agency concerned with roads and highways, although state and national governments now have assumed a major share of the responsibility in this area. The county has performed an essential function in the administration of revenues. It is, on the one hand, the unit in which the state revenues are collected, and it may, with the proper authority, levy, collect, and disburse tax money for the performance of local governmental services. The keeping of deeds, mortgages, marriage registers, and other records is also a vital function of the county. Finally, many counties have performed essential services in connection with military organization, recreation, public service enterprises, and a host of miscellaneous activities. Throughout, the many functions change in importance; some increase and others diminish and many new ones are added constantly. But despite the specific activities involved the county in the United States has sufficient functions entrusted to it, either solely or in cooperation with larger governmental entities, to allow it to qualify easily as the local unit of genuine self-determination.

The organization of county governments follows no set pattern, conforms to no general principles; nearly every state has a system of its own. In each state there is provision for some elective county board that is responsible for the management of county affairs. Only rarely are the legislative, judicial, and executive functions clearly separated from one another. Neither is there any consistent practice of making executives responsible to a representative body. In county government there is no single officer who, unambiguously, is the chief official of the county, corresponding to the mayor of a town or city or the governor of a state. Furthermore, the county board or council, which levies taxes and determines administrative policy, has very limited legislative powers. Other officers, elective or appointive, perform various functions and are largely independent of the board, council, or commissioners. Sometimes one officer will carry out judicial as well as administrative functions.

Many in title and duties are the officials charged with performing the social functions that American rural society has vested in its county units. With great variation in responsibilities and name, each state except Rhode Island has provided some sort of county board. These are variously designated as the county commissioners, county court, fiscal court, board of supervisors, board of chosen freeholders, board of revenue, and police jury. Whatever the name, these boards are of two chief types: (1) those composed of representatives from local subordinate governmental divisions; and (2) those chosen on a county-wide basis. The powers of these boards vary widely but almost always include the right to levy taxes, borrow money, construct roads and bridges, build public buildings, grant relief to those who are disadvantaged, maintain public schools, spend money for public health and sanitation, and provide for the salaries and expenditures of other county officers. These powers, of course, relate directly to the many functions which the county is expected to carry out, the unencumbered performance of which we have suggested generates local self-determination. Thus it is these and other powers which disabled local units in other parts of the world might well come to hold and manipulate.

There is further variation in the county officers. Officials concerned with the judicial functions of the local unit of government include the county judge, the clerk of the court, the attorney, the sheriff, and the coroner. Finance officers usually consist of the assessor, the tax collector or treasurer, and the auditor. Important indeed are the clerical officers of the county, including the clerk and the recorder, and the surveyor. Other important county officers include the superintendent of education, the county health officers, and the directors of relief and public welfare.

Suggested Reforms

County government, model of self-determination or not, is frequently criticized. Students of rural government seem to be pretty thoroughly in accord concerning certain reforms of local government thought to be neccessary and desirable in order to strengthen further the usefulness of these units to local rural people, even in places where county government already works reasonably well. First, the elimination of many townships, small municipalities and other unnecessary local governmental units is urged. Second is recommended a reduction in the number of county units through consolidation, since frequently the country is only a fraction of the trading territory of a given city to which farmers go for commercial purposes. Included might be a serious effort to make county boundaries correspond more closely with those of "natural" communities. Third is suggested a reduction in the number of overlapping special districts which have been created for one purpose or another and a reworking of these to make their boundaries coincide as much as possible with those of the enlarged counties. Finally, it seems fairly well agreed that the small county board is superior to the large one, that it should be given more power, and that greater centralization of authority should be established in the county through the reduction of the number of county officials who would have to stand for election.

THE EXPANDING FUNCTIONS OF GOVERNMENT

Current trends in local governmental structure are definitely in the direction of greater centralization, and especially of more state control over local activities. This greater concentration of power in the state has accompanied the addition of new functions to the activities already performed by local governmental units, for increasingly the latter must serve in the capacity of intermediary between farm people and state and national governments. In the process, its functions expand but its independence tends to decrease. This affects all areas and is properly referred to, especially by its opponents, as a growing tendency toward state socialism. Yet, even persons who seem to oppose these changes on ideological grounds are frequently in the vanguard of those who seek various subventions for their own purposes and interests, be they concessions and privileges for transportation, banking, extraction and refinement of petroleum, or crop subsidies, higher tariffs on imports, and others. This occurs principally because, increasingly, whole societies appear to want the various programs conceived at the state and national levels and administered at the local level, even though the relative independence of the local governmental unit tends to decrease in the process.

Among national and state-national programs in the United States and other highly "developed" areas, several have been especially important in bringing about rapid expansion in the services which the local government must provide or administer for rural people. First is federal contribution to the establishment and maintenance of the land-grant colleges and universities and of the agricultural experiment stations which have been attached to the educational institutions. Decade after decade, the proportion of the necessary funds contributed by the national government has grown so that these operations are less and less exclusively in the hands of the various states. Second is agricultural extension work, which is an outstanding example of cooperation between state and local governments. Third is the program of vocational-agriculture work, which involves both training for teachers in agricultural colleges and support of vocational-agriculture departments in high schools. Fourth is the Farm Credit Administration, which embodies local lending agencies in each county as well as the farflung activities of the federal land banks, banks for farmer cooperatives, and a wide variety of other agencies. All of these and many other developments have helped to bring about participation in local rural affairs by the governments of much larger units. The twofold result is that many more programs are being conducted for the benefit of rural people, while their local governmental units, joining in these many ventures, become less autonomous and increasingly charged with the administration of programs developed at other levels of government. Local people may have little or no control over many of these latter efforts.

One of the most important developments impinging directly upon local rural government and affecting its independence as few other conditions could, was the assumption by the federal government of responsibility in the fields of relief and welfare. Federal involvement in these began in 1932, in the last months of the administration of Herbert Hoover, and was expanded and amplified greatly during the period of the New Deal generated under the presidency of Franklin Roosevelt. Until this development took place, one segment of farming was the principal marginal industry in the United States. That is, subsistence agriculture stood as the last refuge for those who were unable to earn their livings and sustain their families in manufacturing, commerce, transportation, or any other field of endeavor. As a result, on poor soil, in obscure and remote places, and under various other deprived conditions, millions of people living on farms existed at the creature level in this marginal economic position. Their ranks were swelled even more by the increasing numbers of offspring of sharecroppers and other agricultural laborers who were born on the large plantations but whose services were of little value there or in any other segment of the national economy. Of course, this condition was not confined to the United States; it existed widely in other parts of the world as well, and it continues to be the case in many countries.

Counties long had provided such "welfare" services as poor farms and almshouses, but these were hardly sufficiently attractive to draw significant numbers of people away from the farms and into the county seats. With the development of substantial relief and welfare programs by the federal government, however, administered at the local level through agencies located in county seats, the physical location of those who are marginal in the society changed. Subsistence farming declined as the borderline economic operation and welfare and relief took its place in this capacity. As a result of the great drawing power of the agencies created to administer the various programs, the rural poor poured in large numbers off the farms and into towns and cities of all sizes, from the smallest county seats to the largest metropolitan centers. In the United States, the program of Aid to Dependent Children became one of the major programs and the unmarried mother became one of its chief beneficiaries. As a result of this emphasis and because large numbers of those involved are Negroes, the program helped to foster the wholesale migration of members of that race into towns and cities of all sizes. Therefore, the program came to focus in considerable measure upon what the great Negro sociologist, E. Franklin

Frazier, called the "mother family," and played no small part in helping to perpetuate that unit. In turn, the fatherless children brought into the world and reared in this quasi-approved domestic unit frequently were the ones victimized in the 1960's by the emotional exhortations of the irresponsible exponents of "Black Power." The development of this relationship in any greater detail, however, is beyond the scope of the present volume. It is intended to stress, however, that, in the United States since 1932, the public welfare programs have replaced subsistence agriculture as what the economists style the "marginal industry."

At the present time, within the county budget a substantial portion of the funds raised from local tax sources is channeled into welfare programs. In earlier periods of time there were no collections made for this purpose, while at present the amounts used for welfare and relief stand second only to those employed in the construction, equipping, and staffing of schools. In any case, the development of welfare programs in the United States and elsewhere serves as an excellent example of the many kinds of forces that have come to affect the independence and the functions of local rural government, whether directly or indirectly. It is simply one of the multitude of comparatively new functions that local governments are expected to perform, sometimes on their own, but much more frequently in cooperation with state and national governments. The "cooperation," of course, does not always take place smoothly and there are a great many difficult adjustments which local governments are forced to make because of their changed roles. In the case of the serious involvement of the federal government in the welfare field in the 1930's and subsequent decades, for example, many serious clashes between traditional folkways and evolving stateways took place, producing group conflicts of considerable magnitude. Throughout, a principal area of disagreement has existed between those who wish to promote welfare services and those who consider them to be "dangerous" and capable of generating even more serious problems than they are designed to correct. There is little doubt that this argument will continue for decades to come.

The expansion in services which the local rural governments must provide also arises in part from the fact that more and more rural areas are subject to influxes of non-agriculturists who demand those services. Moreover, farm people consider many of the functions which they once performed for themselves to be the rightful responsibility of their local governments. Sanitation facilities, safe water, welfare services, and many more once were provided by individuals and families while others, such as law enforcement and marketing arangements, were handled informally through other parts of existing social organization. Many such endeavors involved little more than mutual assistance and the form of interpersonal cooperation which is often found in truly rural settings. However, partly because of the requirements and demands of those who now are establishing residences in rural areas, partly because of the much broader scope of services which long-term rural residents now define as "absolute necessities," and partly because the range of possible services that could be performed is infinitely broader than it once was, most rural local governments find themselves with rapidly expanding needs and burgeoning costs, which arise from the efforts to meet those needs. The local revenue situation, geared to amounts collected as property taxes under rural conditions where rates are low and populations small, generally is inadequate to support these efforts. Consequently, lacking the authority to impose the big "revenue-getting" sales and income taxes, local governments have had little choice but to plead for funds from larger governmental units and, therefore, to expand the number of things they do in cooperation with the larger units. Often the cooperation results in increased domination of the smaller units by the larger, and local rural government becomes increasingly remote from local rural people. It is doubtful that there are many realistic alternatives, however, or that an earlier stage of self-sufficiency of local government could be restored. Such a situation would probably necessitate the reversal of the rising standard of living (that to which people aspire), and the trends under way in the world at present indicate clearly that nothing is more unlikely. Therefore, it seems probable that while the functions of local government will continue to expand, its independence will be progressively curtailed.

Additional Readings

1. ADRIAN, C. R., *State and Local Governments,* New York: McGraw-Hill Book Company, Inc., 1960, chapter 12.

2. ANDERSON, WILLIAM, and EDWARD W. WEIDNER, *State and Local Government in the United States,* New York: Henry Holt and Company, Inc., 1951.

3. ENSMINGER, DOUGLAS, and WILSON T. LONGMORE, "Rural Local Government," in Carl C. Taylor and others, *Rural Life in the United States,* New York: Alfred A. Knopf, 1949, chapter VIII.

4. LANCASTER, LANE W., *Government in Rural America* (second ed.), Princeton: D. Van Nostrand Company, Inc., 1952.

5. NELSON, LOWRY, *Rural Sociology* (second ed.), New York: American Book Company, 1955, chapter 22.

6. Province of Saskatchewan, Royal Commission on Agriculture and Rural Life, W. B. Baker, Chairman, *Report No. 4: Rural Roads and Local Government,* Regina: Queen's Printer, 1955.

7. SMITH, T. LYNN, *Brazil: People and Institutions* (third ed.), Baton Rouge: Louisiana State University Press, 1963, chapter XXI.

8. SNIDER, CLYDE F., *Local Government in Rural America,* New York: Appleton-Century-Crofts, Inc., 1957.

9. SOROKIN, PITIRIM A., CARLE C. ZIMMERMAN, and CHARLES J. GALPIN, *A Systematic Source Book in Rural Sociology,* Minneapolis: University of Minnesota Press, 1931, Vol. II, chapter XVI.

10. TARVER, JAMES D., "Local Government: Characteristics and Problems," in Alvin L. Bertrand (ed.), *Rural Sociology,* New York: McGraw-Hill Book Company, Inc., 1958, chapter 17.

11. TAYLOR, LEE, and ARTHUR R. JONES, JR., *Rural Life and Urbanized Society,* New York: Oxford University Press, 1964, chapter 22.

12. WAGER, PAUL W. (ed.), *County Government Across the Nation,* Chapel Hill: University of North Carolina Press, 1950.

13. WILKENING, EUGENE A., and RALPH K. HUITT, "Political Participation among Farmers as Related to Socioeconomic Status and Perception of the Political Process," *Rural Sociology,* Vol. 26, No. 4 (December, 1961), pp. 395–408.

PART FOUR
SOCIAL PROCESSES IN RURAL SOCIETY

The study of social processes has not been given the attention due it in the field of rural sociology, despite the fact that these dynamic features are much involved in the rapid sociocultural change taking place in rural groups almost everywhere. *Competition* is a basic one of these social processes. It may be aggravated into open *conflict* of various kinds, or differences may be harmonized and efforts pooled through *cooperation,* either of the informal sort, which has always characterized rural society, or of the contractual kind, which has come to typify rural social organization and behavior to a greater degree in recent decades. The contacts of cultures and social groups may result in mutual adaptation or *accommodation,* one may *assimilate* or absorb the other, or a blending of the two (*acculturation*) may be the net result. *Homogenization* or the process of getting all of the components more uniformly distributed throughout the social body has been waxing in importance. Society and all the elements that go to make it up are never in a state of rest; and the cultural environment is ever-changing. *Social mobility* is one of the most important of all the social processes and is found to be increasingly operable in more and more rural districts throughout the world.

16
COMPETITION *and* CONFLICT

The basic social processes are opposition and cooperation. Out of these all the other processes operative in society seem to arise. Opposition in turn may be subdivided into two principal types: *competition* and *conflict*. Sociologists have long made the distinction between the two about as follows: Competition operates in a situation in which the individual expects to accomplish certain of his goals whether or not the persons with whom he is competing also achieve theirs; but in conflict the efforts of one individual are designed to prevent one or more others from realizing the ends toward which they are striving. Thus competition is simply the activities of two or more persons who are attempting to realize their own self interests by outdoing others, whereas conflict involves actions designed to prevent opponents from achieving their goals. Moreover, competition generally occurs within an institutional structure and is subject to various rules, whereas conflict is bound by few if any such regulations and may even be a distinct threat to the efficient operation or survival of institutions.

Opposition in general is rooted in scarcity, selfishness, egocentrism—all the elements that make for what Darwin called the "struggle for survival." If the struggle is indirect and impersonal it is termed competition; if it is direct and personal it is more properly called conflict. In competition, attention is concentrated on reaching the desired end and accomplishing the wished-for objective; there need be no thought of destroying or thwarting the rival. In conflict, on the other hand, the opponents are in one another's presence, each is aware that the other stands in his way, and each makes an effort to dispatch the other. Competition as a process is relatively continuous; conflict is intermittent—it may smolder for years and then break forth violently.

Opposition grows out of a clash of interests; it arises whenever one member thinks he can gain more from the other than he is forced to give. Through hatred, opposition may develop into chronic conflict and lose all the elements of calculated objectives. A case in point is the age-old struggle throughout the world between people whose way of life is based upon pastoral activities and those who live by cultivating the soil. Another example is the animosity between white laborers and the Orientals in California or between northern organized wage earners and the recent Negro migrants from the South. This form of conflict has become especially acute since automation and related processes have significantly reduced the number of unskilled and semiskilled jobs available to laborers of either race. A third illustration is the bitterness arising from the drive for Negroes to vote in the rural districts of the southern United States. A fourth and final case is the intermittent but extremely intense struggle in the United States between dairy farmers who produce milk and the distributors who sell it.

Opposition has its constructive aspects too. The right to oppose is essential to the preservation of a free society. Freedom of speech, freedom of press, and a sizable minority party are vital for the preservation of any social order. Frequently, strong opposition is a most important solidifying force; a foreign war is often resorted to by the nation that is torn by internal dissension with the result that unity may be strengthened within the society in question.

COMPETITION

Competition arises and finds expression in practically every field of social activity. Rare is the person who at some period in his life is not involved in intense competition for a job, for a mate, and for status and prestige. With many persons such striving is chronic. Most attention has been centered upon the materialistic struggle for existence, and there can be no doubt that economic competition is of primary importance. But there are many other interests that develop competitive relationships. Racial and cultural groups struggle to outdo one another, sometimes in the economic sphere, frequently along other lines. Practically every institution develops some competitive relationships with other institutions that are engaged in the fulfillment of similar needs. Probably in no situation is the solidarity of a small community more evident than where an athletic team from a local high school is engaging that of a neighboring community in competition. Children and adults alike identify with their team, enthusiasm and emotion run high, and both communities turn out en masse to witness the contest and to cheer their own representatives.

Within a community the most intense rivalry and competition may characterize the relationships between two or more church congregations of different denominations, and this may continue generation after generation. Or, as is widespread in northern Brazil, it may be that the competition is between two leading families or clans within the community or neighborhood. Between such kinship groups, the struggle for status goes on without end. Hardly any small community where primary-group relationships reign supreme is without a family or clan feud of a mild, bloodless nature. In some of the more isolated rural parts of the world these differences develop into violent conflicts and express themselves as full-grown blood feuds persisting from generation to generation. For purposes of classification, therefore, the major forms of competition may be designated as (1) economic; (2) racial, ethnic, and cultural; and (3) institutional. In addition, in the twentieth century, revolutionary changes in the methods of communication and transportation have created intense competition between rural trade centers, largely economic, partially institutional, which deserves separate analysis.

Economic Competition

In rural society economic competition lacks many of the essentials that make it "the life of trade" in commercial centers. The town or village merchant is forced into severe competition with his fellows for the patronage of the customers in the community trade area. But among farmers a comparable situation is almost entirely lacking. Only in the supplying of the limited local demand for vegetables, milk, wood, and other products is one farmer likely to see a danger or challenge in the marketing activities of any other individual farmer. After all, each agriculturist produces but an infinitesimal portion of any one of the major crops. What one's neighbor does is of small consequence in the total economic situation, for there is little chance of individual gain or loss through the variations in the production of his immediate neighbors. This is especially true, of course, in sections where subsistence farming rather than production for the market is the way of organizing the agricultural enterprises. Accordingly, rather than to engage in competitive practices designed to secure for himself the benefits that might go to his neighbors, the farmer is more strongly impelled to enter with them into mutual-aid activities for the purpose of increasing the welfare of all. However, if any part of the community's resources is common property, then intense competition and rivalry may result as individuals seek to exploit community resources for private ends.

When economic competition is to be found between farmers in agriculture, it is of a type that requires virtually no regulation. On the other hand, that found among urban industries involves a constant drive in the direction of creating monopolistic control, thereby making it subject to a detailed series of formal social restrictions intended to prevent the development of unfair advantage. Thus, the competition in present-day agriculture tends to resemble much more closely the form envisioned as ideal by the nineteenth-century exponents of *laissez-faire* economic philosophy than does that which now takes place between urban industries.

On the light side, competition adds much to the zest of farming, to the improvement of farm practices, and to the tone of social life in the agricultural community, especially where landownership is widespread and farming is typically a middle-class way of life. In mild forms it brings about much good-natured rivalry as to who will be first to finish haying, whose exhibits will place first at the county fair, whose cows will give the most milk, whose chickens will produce the most eggs, whose land will produce the most bushels of wheat or the largest number of pounds of cotton per acre, and numerous other contests of a similar nature. The question of whose horse can trot or run the fastest is the cause of keen competition in a large part of the farming communities of the United States and some other nations. Closely associated is intense rivalry among farmers in the rural art of "horse trading" of a great many varieties.

But economic competition among farmers has its more serious side also; this has to do mostly with the ownership and control of land. The old formula "To raise more wheat, to get more money, to buy more land, to raise more wheat," needs only to have the name of the commodity changed in order to make it applicable in every part of any nation whose agriculture is geared to landownership within the framework of the family-sized farm. Despite complaints of being "land poor," the ownership and control of land are still the major devices for securing social status in rural areas. In middle-class areas of the world, such as the midwestern section of the United States and Canada, the ownership is widely diffused among the farm families, whereas in two-class plantation areas, land monopoly by a few and the lack of ownership by the many make for the vast gulf between the two groups. In both cases, however, the key to social status is the ability to compete successfully for ownership and control of the land.

The struggle for land is, of course, as old as permanent settlement and sedentary agriculture. Recorded history is filled with episodes of "land-grabbing," sometimes resulting in scandal; probably equally important, although largely unrecorded, is the practice of squatting on unsettled lands. In parts of the United States, for example, lacking any systematic pattern of periodic subdivision of lands, such as that practiced by the Hebrews, those concerned with the aggregation and subdivision of estates have dealt with large units, as in the plantation sections of the South or in California. In other sections, such as the Middle West, where family-sized units have predominated, the stakes have been smaller. Until the 1930's and President Franklin D. Roosevelt's "New Deal," the local miser and moneylender had almost a monopoly on the business of granting loans to unsuspecting victims, lulling them into a sense of false security by leniency concerning the payments on principal and interest during prosperous times and relentlessly foreclosing and dispossessing them when times became hard and no succor was to be had. By the middle of the twentieth century, however, corporations, insurance companies, and the federal government had revolutionized the system of long-term farm credit.

Racial, Ethnic, and Cultural Competition

Racial, ethnic, and cultural competition in rural areas is usually rather local in character. Often it is community against community, with racial, ethnic, and cultural differences intensifying the rivalry. Frequently, too, this type of competition finds expression in the struggle for land. One finds, especially in the northern states of the United States, community after community from which the "old American" stock has been "crowded out" by more recent arrivals from Europe. In the South, where landownership is less widely distributed, the competition between whites and Negroes long assumed the form of rivalry for a limited number of places as sharecroppers on plantations. Although there were many exceptions, it seems that planters as a rule preferred Negroes to whites as croppers and that consequently the black man, in this respect at least, had an advantage over his white competitor. Frequently, whites of this economic class became embittered because the planters preferred Negroes to persons of their own race. This competition in the South between the races for some of the lowest status jobs to be had has played no small part in the problems of race relations which the region has faced for generations. On the Pacific coast competition for land has been a frequent cause of conflict between the Americans of Japanese descent and other residents of the area.

Institutional Competition

Competition may occur in the rural community between any two institutions of the same type or even between institutions of different types. Church competes with church, but the local religious organizations must also compete with the social club, the moving-picture theater, the school, and even the family radio, automobile, and television set. When hard pressed by a competitor the institution may resort to several tactics: (1) It may seek the destruction of the competitor. For example, many sermons attack the movies and other forms of recreation. Sometimes ancient "blue laws" have been dug up and invoked to prevent the operation of movies and other businesses from competing with churches for Sunday attendance. (2) It may withdraw from competition. A religious denomination may claim special protection from the state, a school may exploit the sentimental attachments of the alumni, a political party may exclude competitors from the ballot, and a business may resort to various subterfuges. (3) It may borrow from competitors, politely known as "constrained adaptation." And (4) the institution may elude competitors by developing a highly specialized program catering to particular tastes.

Competition Between Rural Trade Centers

Before widespread ownership of the automobile and before good roads came into existence, the trade centers catering to farmer transactions in the United States were in a stage of relative equilibrium. Lack of means of rapid communication and transportation made it essential that the retail outlets in close proximity to the farm should handle practically all the goods that the farmer's standard of living demanded; the farmer could not go great distances to trade. The coming of the rural free delivery program, followed after 1915 by the automobile, revolutionized the trading relationships of the farmer and the farm trade center. These new forces struck at one of the most limiting factors in farm life—the time it takes to go to town and back. The farmer's opportunities for choosing were greatly multiplied and the result was an intense competition between the existing trade centers for farmer business.

The competition between trade centers in the United States has been observed by many students and has played an important part in the thinking about rural life. In the twenties, the idea that rural villages, especially the smaller ones, were on their way to extinction gained widespread acceptance. It was felt that the small trade centers were disappearing because their functions were being seized and performed by the larger ones, principally because the advantages formerly held by the small center by virtue of its proximity to the farms, had been overcome by the influence of the automobile. As mentioned in Chapter 18, Galpin saw as the end product of this competition between trade centers the emergence of a new type of farmers' town, the rurban community. These units would be larger but fewer in number than the centers they were expected to replace. It was felt by many that, just as the consolidation of industry closed the small factories, the mail-order houses were closing village stores; and the farmer's automobile was passing through the village on the way to town. In fact, flour mills, and the shops of the carpenter, the wagon maker, the blacksmith, and the tailor actually are only a memory in rural districts. A new type of community did emerge as a result of the automobile; schools, churches, granges, lodges, and stores did relocate in the village. Out of the competition between villages the larger rurban community, including both the people of the town and those from the surrounding farms, was built up and much American farm life became reorganized about larger country towns as centers both economic and social. Many of the smaller villages also competed successfully for survival and became increasingly specialized parts of larger total communities in which the needs of farm people are met. These communities now frequently are composed of several differentiated population centers of different sizes and distances from their constituent farms. Thus competition between trade centers has been one of the most significant social forces at work in rural America in the twentieth century, although the outcome has taken some unexpected turns.

CONFLICT

Social conflict finds expression in practically all the avenues of social life. In rural areas, however, the following four types of conflict seem to outrank all others in significance: (1) pastoral-agricultural conflict, (2) town-country friction, (3) class struggle, and (4) interfamily and interclan strife. Religious and political dissensions and clashes are largely included within these four. Racial strife in rural areas has been of importance historically in some countries, especially in the southern United States in the period of reconstruction. Following this period relations between the races in the South were stabilized and took on a form of caste organization. As a result of this adaptation there was in the region relatively little racial struggle for the first half of the twentieth century. But in the years since 1954 and the "school desegregation" decision of the United States Supreme Court, the old accommodation has become unworkable. Imposition by whites and acceptance by Negroes of the stable, restrictive patterns of segregation are passing away slowly and painfully. In the process, bitter conflict flares frequently. The traditional restrictive southern pattern of white domination and Negro subordination has broken down and the condition in many ways has come to resemble that in the North, where no real mutual adjustment between the races ever has been reached and no predictable pattern of race relations has been developed. In both areas, the considerable amount of race conflict indicates the failure of an earlier form of accommodation and the absence of any clear-cut new form which would stabilize the situation. But the migration of Negroes to urban centers in the Northeast, the Great Lakes region, the Far West, and certainly the South has made this conflict far more an urban than a rural problem. As such it does not demand further discussion in the present volume.

Pastoral-Agricultural Conflict

Conflict between people who till the soil and those who raise and care for herds of cattle and horses, flocks of sheep, and other domesticated animals is found in many areas of the world. It arises in large part from the marked differences between the two groups in their relationships to the land. Year after year the farmer pursues intensively his cultivation of a comparatively small piece of land and is concerned with protecting and nurturing the crops which he expects to help him survive. His interests lie in the construction of permanent buildings, protective fences, extensive irrigation canals, terraces, and ditches. Quite contrary is the situation of the herdsman. His is the existence of a man on the move. His herds must find new pastures after a few weeks on old ones and must constantly seek fresh water supplies. In these endeavors, he finds the fences, irrigation lines, and other devices of the farmer to be intolerable obstacles, contrary to all of the demands of the pastoral way of life. This opposition of the agricultural and pastoral modes of existence has produced innumerable instances of the most acute and chronic conflict.

Examples of the struggle between rural social systems based upon the growing of crops and upon animal husbandry, respectively, may be found in man's earliest history. All people who have received their religious heritages largely from Hebrew sources are well acquainted with the one portrayed in the Old Testament in the story of Cain, a tiller of the soil, and his brother Abel, a keeper of sheep. Another of the many examples of pastoral and agrarian strife in the Near East and parts of the Mediterranean world is the age-old struggle between the two large segments of Arab societies, the nomadic bedouin of the deserts and the fellahin or peasants of the agricultural villages. Until very recently, at least, this conflict seems to have been a dominant feature of society throughout the Arab world. It was resolved in part when the two groups worked out a pattern of accommodation under which the agricultural villagers paid portions of their crops to the nomadic herdsmen for protection from the marauding animals and from other tribesmen.

Another account of the phenomenon under consideration deals with the Island of Cyprus. It is from the pen of Sir Hugh Foot, now Lord Caradon, at that time British colonial governor of the afflicted island, who succeeded in damping enough of the fires between the Greek and Turkish factions that it could be granted independence. The following paragraph contains a paradigm of what much of the world needs most.

We tackled the age-old problem of the devastation caused by the wandering herds of goats. These herds were owned and led by tough, ruthless mountain goat-herds, who terrorised the people of the settled villages and drove their goats through the cultivation of the plains, destroying trees and crops as they went and adding to the wide-spread damage caused by soil erosion. We hit on the plan of appealing to the Greek love of politics. We introduced a new law under which the people of any village area could hold a local plebiscite. If the popular vote was in favour of the tethered goat, then the wandering herds of goats from the mountains would be outlawed. For some time no village dared to vote for the tethered goat. They feared the wrath of their traditional enemies, the mountain goat-herds. But then one village at last voted for the tethered goat. Immediately the full force of the police went into the area to enforce the decision. Within a month or two the result of the elimination of the damage done by the herds of goats began to be seen. One village after another applied for a goat plebiscite. Overwhelming popular opinion backed by the authority of the Government triumphed. A scourge for centuries past was brought under control, and in wide areas eliminated altogether. (Ref. 123, pp. 145–146.)

Elsewhere in the Mediterranean area, the traditional practice of trans-humance, or the seasonal movement of flocks and herds between the cool mountain summer pastures and the less rigorous winter pastures at lower elevations, supplied the ingredients for almost ceaseless conflicts between the farmers and gardeners and the herdsmen of one type or another. In no coun-try, however, did transhumance become more thoroughly embodied in the economy and the privileges and immunities of the potentates who owned and controlled the herds of sheep become more pronounced than in Spain. In that country the institution of the Mesta, a special code which allowed the sheep of privileged persons and groups to range freely over pasture and farm alike, paralyzed agricultural development almost 200 years before the Spanish Empire was established in the New World. But the Mesta never attained any particular importance in the Americas, although its legal provisions were extended from Spain to her colonies. Two reasons for its failure to flourish in the extensive area from what is now the state of California to Cape Horn are rather self-evident: (1) Sheep husbandry was not a principal concern of the conquering Spaniards in most parts of America; and (2) the Iberian overlords and their descendants did not need the provisions of its unjust code in order to maintain their subjection of the Indian agriculturists. The latter were quickly forced into serfdom by other means. Nevertheless, the unceas-ing opposition between the indigenes, who lived by growing crops, and the landed proprietors of European origin, who carried on a rudimentary type of cattle ranching on their extensive domains, has characterized the entire period from the sixteenth century to the present. Actual conflict between the powerful pastoral masters and the weak agricultural masses, however, was most pronounced during two periods, namely, the epoch of the conquest itself and the era of the struggle for agrarian reform which surged forth in Mexico between 1917 and 1940 and which erupted throughout Latin America following World War II.

In many respects the Spanish conquest of America featured the uprooting of the Indian populations from their established fields, which then were converted into pastures for the cattle and horses of the conquistadores, fully as much as it did the search for gold. The droves of agile "razorback" hogs, which were the only breed known in Europe and America until well along in the nineteenth century, spearheaded the Spanish assaults upon the Indians and their possessions in the New World. Very quickly they made into dead letters the numerous decrees, orders, and laws prepared by the Council of the Indies and promulgated by Spain's sovereigns to protect the lives and lands of the natives from the encroachments of the Europeans. The natives quickly were driven from their ancestral possessions and crowded back into out-of-the-way places and up onto the slopes of the mountainsides, frequently onto terrains so steep that they should never have been cultivated, leaving the rich, fertile, and well-located valleys for use as pastures for the livestock of the Spaniards. These desirable lands then could be classed as "vacant" and available for legal Spanish ownership under the Laws of the Indies. In Colombia, for example, the seizure of the best-located and fertile valleys for use as pastures for the Spaniards' livestock forced the native Indians to resort to agriculture high on the slopes of the mountains and in other unsuitable places in order to grow patches of corn, potatoes, beans, and so on, with which they fed their families. This filled the level bottom lands best suited for farming with huge grazing estates and cluttered the foothills and mountainsides with tiny, underproductive subsistence farms. Such a situation was, perhaps, inevitable when a powerful pastoral people equipped with firearms and horses imposed their overlordship upon hosts of poorly equipped peasant cultivators.

No small part of the waves of discontent, agitation, rebellion, and revolution that have characterized the Latin American countries during the twentieth century, and especially since the close of World War II, is made up of direct and indirect expressions of the centuries-old conflict between the pastoral interests of the large landed proprietors and the pressing agricultural necessities of the humble rural masses of the population. Among the most striking examples of this are: (1) the Mexican Agrarian Revolution, which got under way about 1917 and proclaimed the objective of returning to the villages of peasants the lands that had been incorporated into the predominantly pastoral haciendas; (2) the "invasions" of thousands of Peruvian haciendas by country people, who claimed that portions of those estates had unjustly been taken from them, a wholesale series of direct actions that by 1950 had already filled Peru's courts with about 2,000 cases; (3) the forcible seizure by small farmers of the lands of thousands of Bolivian haciendas, which immediately preceded Bolivia's agrarian reform of 1953; (4) the all-out and to date successful efforts of Argentina's large landowners, especially in the province of Buenos Aires, to block all proposed programs for agrarian reform in that richly endowed and pastorally dominated country; and (5) the intense agitation for agrarian reform programs throughout Latin America, and the considerable advances made in this respect in some countries, such as Venezuela, Colombia, and Chile.[1]

In a large proportion of the world's societies in addition to those of Latin America, the conflict between farmers and herdsmen has worked strongly against those who till the soil, for the wealthy families who own large numbers of herding animals generally have had the advantage. In broad areas of the world generations of cattle, horses, sheep, goats, and other animals have trampled the farms and gardens of generations of peasants whose low social position and lack of political power have prevented them from taking measures to stop the onslaught. In many such instances their only recourse has been to seek the relative protection of poorer lands in which the graziers have had little interest. Often they have occupied such lands as illegal squatters. The situation has produced a great deal of acute conflict and it also has created the potential for a far more serious and widespread type of conflict. As standards of living rise and the zone of frustration between low levels of living and rising aspirations widens, this circumstance, wherever it is found in the world, is likely to be viewed by peasants as increasingly intolerable and requiring action. Some of that action is certain to take the form of violent conflict.

Pastoral-agricultural conflict in the United States has had two major expressions. In the first place, as population moved across the Appalachians following the close of the French and Indian Wars, or from the late 1760's, the hunters were in the vanguard. They later were accompanied and followed by herdsmen whose rangy cattle and razorback hogs roamed the woods on

---

[1] For further information about agrarian reform in many of the Latin American countries, see Ref. 442. There are some exceptions to the rule that agrarian reform endeavors in Latin America are part and parcel of the conflict between pastoral and agricultural interests. In Cuba and El Salvador the hopes of the peasants to acquire the ownership of the land had to be directed towards the subdivision of large sugarcane plantations and large coffee plantations, respectively.

about the same unrestricted basis as the deer and other game used by the Indians. The agriculture of these people at the cutting edge of the frontier was rudimentary, consisting almost exclusively of small patches of corn from which they made the bread and the spirits they consumed. Gradually, as the game was killed off or frightened away, the pastoral activity became dominant, and it expanded throughout the rugged terrain of the Appalachians, the Cumberland Plateau, and into the areas west of them. However, after the opening of the Erie Canal, the Wilderness Road, and the Cumberland Road, a flood of agricultural families moved into the fertile areas west of the mountains. According to Frank Owsley:

By 1840 the better agricultural lands in the older states and in many parts of the newer ones had been sufficiently settled by farmers to interfere with grazing upon the open range, and the herdsmen had largely disappeared from such lands. Those who had not desired to settle as planters and farmers, but preferred their occupation and the frontier with its plentiful game, fresh cattle ranges, and scarcity of neighbors, took up their abode in the pine forests and in the mountains where other graziers had already settled because they preferred such country. Here, protected by the sterile, sandy soils of the piney woods and the rugged surface of the highlands, the herdsmen and hunters found sanctuary from the pursuing agricultural settlers. Thus it was agriculture rather than slavery that pressed these settlers into the less fertile and more rugged lands. This was an old phenomenon. From ancient times an agricultural economy has driven the livestock grazier into the deserts and mountains, except in those states where the herdsmen control the government. (Ref. 329, p. 34.)

Thus those who tended livestock were forced back from one part of the rolling frontier to another and finally onto lands that were the most rugged, the least accessible, and generally the lowest in fertility. These were the mountains, the pine barrens, and even the deserts.

The second stage of pastoral-agricultural conflict in the United States began in the 1830's in the prairie sections of Indiana and Illinois as farming began to venture onto the unwooded areas which it had long avoided. John Deere's steel turning plow was highly significant in helping to bring about this expansion, for it would scour on the heavy soils of what is now the corn belt. No small part was played by barbed wire, which made it possible to exclude animals from more and more farms on the open grasslands of the Great Plains. The early opponents in the struggle were stockmen and farmers who raised wheat using McCormick's reaper to maximum advantage. But as the plow and the reaper became more readily available and as the railroads pushed to the Rocky Mountains and beyond, wheat production pushed farther west and the grain farmers of Indiana, Illinois, Iowa, and other parts of what is now the corn belt found it difficult to compete with those on the western plains.

Out of this crisis in the 1870's began the development of a new type of farming which eventually made up a significant form of accommodation in Illinois, Indiana, Iowa, and neighboring states—the corn, beef cattle, hog type of farming. This system blended pastoral and agricultural interests into one general way of life and came to characterize the broad area that is now the corn belt. Several factors were part of this development, including: (1) the large-scale production of corn; (2) the breeding of commercially valuable hogs of the "lard" type; (3) the use of the corn to fatten beef cattle, some of them raised on the farms themselves and others bought as "feeders"; and (4) the discovery that the better breeds of swine could derive maximum benefits from corn which had passed through the digestive tracts of cattle, thereby making the two animals inseparable parts of the complex and tying both to dependence upon the same crop. The net result was a highly successful type of enterprise involving the raising of corn and other forage crops, the feeder-lot fattening of beef cattle for the market, and the farrowing and fattening of large numbers of hogs per farm. In addition, substantial gardens were kept and flocks of poultry and a few milk cows were maintained for domestic purposes. Thus, the agrarian and pastoral interests were combined inextricably into one general enterprise, with the obvious result that conflict between the two factions was greatly minimized.

Yet, despite this effective form of accommodation, pastoral-agricultural conflict lingered long in the corn belt. In their analysis of an Iowa community, Moe and Taylor state that:

Agriculture on the frontier, before the coming of the railroad, was languishing for the want of a market. Grains, such as corn and wheat, were impossible as market crops because of their bulk. Cattle of high specific value were salable, and they provided their own transportation. Labor costs in caring for herds were small as was the capital investment under grazing conditions. These advantages of the cattle enterprise made Shelby County [Iowa] part of the cow country during the seventies, despite the railroads reaching Avoca in Pottawattamie County in 1869. The Shelby County papers took note of more than 800 head that were grazing in the county. Restraining laws, the spread of the practice of fencing, settlers using their enclosed land as wild-hay pasture, led to hostile encounters between farmers and graziers. Herders were warned about the trespassing of their herds. They were forced to seek open land farther West. There were few grazing areas in Shelby County after 1885. (Ref. 297, pp. 5–6.)

Settlement to the east and south of Shelby County proceeded at a more rapid pace than within the county, leaving a relatively larger amount of open prairie here than elsewhere. Graziers sent their herds in relatively large numbers to pasture on this prairie. Even before 1870 a few small herds were being grazed in the county and the practice increased through the 70's and into the 80's. By the middle of the latter decade farmers definitely held the upper hand over the graziers and were able, with the help of more stringent restraining laws, to drive the graziers from the county. (Ref. 297, p. 20.)

Town-Country Conflict

The fact that the social and economic environments of city and country people are vastly different is widely recognized. Also rather well understood is the proposition that these differences in the man-made environment or culture of the two groups have significant influences in molding the personalities of rural and urban people. That these personality differences and the differing folkways, mores, and cultural patterns in which they have their roots lead to a constant and often severe conflict between the rural and urban parts of societies throughout all ages everywhere is also rather generally understood. But that the village is the arena within which the ever-present latent antagonism between the farmers and the tradesmen of the village frequently flares up into open conflict has seldom if ever received any detailed analysis. The stress laid upon this point is not to overlook the fact that many rural-urban contacts result in ends highly satisfactory to both segments of society. It is merely to emphasize that the village serves as the focal point in which urban values, attitudes, and patterns of living clash head on with those from the country, and that a great deal of conflict is generated by this brusque contact.

This clash of interests arises in a great many aspects of life, but it may be illustrated with a few simple examples. Fundamental, of course, is the conflict of economic interests between the two factions as illustrated by the situation in the United States. Long after the city man has become so highly specialized that he is either a laborer, an entrepreneur, or engaged in managerial activities, the great bulk of the farmers continue to perform all three of these economic functions. For this reason and also because he deals largely with living growing things, lives in a sparsely-populated district, and has few but intimate and enduring social contacts, the farmer has a set of attitudes towards such things as wage rates, hours of work, and prices that is considerably different from that possessed by any one class of city men. Furthermore, the farmer's interests are those of both the primary producer of food and fiber and the ultimate consumer of other products; the villager and townsman are primarily interested in the middleman's profit. Yet the division of labor has made the village merchant and the open-country farmer mutually interdependent and out of the inevitable close contact which this situation produces comes the perpetual potential for open conflict. Moreover, the entire relationship is fraught with stereotyped conceptions which each group holds about the other. Many farmers think of townspeople as parasitic upon the country, and many villagers fail to appreciate how intimately their own welfare is related to that of people on the land. When open strife bursts forth, the farmer succeeds in making felt his importance in the village by going

406

elsewhere to trade, but at the same time has impressed upon himself through the medium of added costs and inconveniences the usefulness of the village.

In the field of educational theory and practice, the village is also the scene of conflict between the traditional rural attitudes and behavior and the innovations introduced by urban-trained teachers and curricula designed to meet the needs of city children. Sharp conflicts are engendered in respect to content, teaching methods, discipline, and school organization and administration. Not unusual are the cases in which the farm districts are hotbeds of discontent, containing people angered with the "frills" of a school curriculum, horrified by the "progressive methods" of instruction, disgusted with "lax" school discipline, and rebellious about actual or proposed delineation of school administration or attendance areas. Gerrymandering of school districts, which the farmer often thinks is for village advantage, and consolidations are frequently basic in all these disputes.

The village is also the place in which the modernistic religious practices and beliefs of the city collide with the traditional religious attitudes and expressions of the countrymen. The village is increasingly becoming the focal point for rural religious activities. But in the village church the farmer comes into contact with a trained minister who has been exposed to the facts and theories of modern biological and physical science, the current contributions of the social sciences relative to social and cultural change or the social functions of the church, and much of what may be considered critical or probing theology. The pulpit of the village church serves as the medium through which these ideas are disseminated in the countryside. Probably to the villager, and certainly to the farmer, much of the preaching of contemporary or unorthodox ministers is in fundamental conflict with many traditional beliefs that are deeply imbedded in cultural and emotional foundations. It is likely that the conflict between "modernism" and "fundamentalism" reaches its acme in the village church.

Although the village is the principal arena for the clash of rural and urban attitudes and patterns of living, these differences, as all others, must ultimately be resolved. Men cannot fight all the time. Some of the ways in which a *modus vivendi* is obtained are extremely interesting. *Sub rosa* a village business establishment may charge prices that represent a compromise between those thought to be fair by each of the rural and urban factions; public employees may keep longer working or office hours in the village which serves farm people than in the city; departures from traditional curricula or teaching methods may be less "progressive" than in the larger centers; and the minister's orthodoxy may be carefully examined before he is employed by the village church. In any event, the potential for conflict is accompanied by the potential for accommodation and while one may prevail at given times, over the long run the two tend to be found in a sufficiently workable balance so that life may proceed with a minimum of open violence.

Sharp cleavages between villagers and country people in the United States seem to be much more pronounced in the Midwest than in the South. In the former area they have exhibited themselves in such phenomena as the Granger Movement, the Non-Partisan League, and the Farmers' Holiday. Part of this cleavage is undoubtedly due to the fact that much of the farming land in the South is controlled, and its operations supervised, by a class of merchant-farmers residing in the village or town, who go regularly to the plantation to oversee the farming operations being carried on in the fields. There also seems to be a tendency for conflict to appear more frequently as the size of the village increases—the larger the village the more likely that there will be open hostility between its residents and the farmers in the surrounding area. Strife also seems to be more prevalent in those communities where the village residents are most hesitant about admitting farmers to membership in their social organizations.

The genesis, nature, and course of town and country conflicts are extremely diverse. Changes in facilities which villagers or farmers may view as existing for their greater respective benefit may precipitate conflict. Disagreements over schools and school policy and especially consolidation of small, rural schools into single, large units are a fruitful source of cleavage between people in the villages and those in the open country. Perhaps as old as the village itself, and a source of much disagreement, is the farmer's suspicion that the village merchant exploits while he serves. Not infrequently prices are compared item by item by farmers to prove that the village merchant charges prices exorbitant in comparison with those of some not far-distant town. To this the merchant answers that the farmer's insistence upon credit forces him to charge higher prices for goods. The distrust and latent conflict engendered by this situation then come to pervade most of the situations that bring farm and village people together to trade, resolve community problems, or make use of the services of various institutions.

The causes of town-country conflict deserve careful analysis because of the prevalence and the far-reaching consequences of this type of struggle. Village-open country friction may be generated by various unintended but antagonistic acts between village and farm people; by problems involving prices, credits, and banking; and by difficulties centering on school administration, cooperatives, industry, and politics. In various societies, these factors may be equally capable of fanning the smoldering town-country antagonism, but in the United States, the economic dimension has been particularly important.

408

Therefore, much of the struggle has centered on prices, markets, and credits and the farmer's increasing susceptibility to their fluctuations.

According to Taylor (Ref. 509, pp. 493–500), many struggles of American farmers arose as they acted either to protect themselves against the impact of an evolving commercialized and capitalized economy or to become successful parts of it. This, of course, occurred increasingly as farming passed from the subsistence stage to the commercial level and farmers found themselves caught up in the issues of an evolving social order and developing cultural environment to which they had not been accustomed before. This general movement has gone on for over three centuries and transcends any specific conflict situation or particular effort designed to resolve the conflict and enable the participants to seek a new accommodation. A considerable portion of it is town-country conflict, because the struggle to control prices, markets, and credits has taken the form of antagonism between those who farm the land and those who live in town, between the producer and the middleman, between the debtor and the creditor. Much of it involves suspicion by farmer and merchant or banker of each other. Moreover, in the process, government at various levels has frequently been suspected by farmers as the handmaiden of the "town" segment, basically manipulated by it, and out of the reach of farmer influence. Eventually, all of this became a general body of ideologies focused on the role of agriculture in a changing economy. This lent to the farmer corps a degree of unity and continuity, which has manifested itself in the formation of farmer pressure groups, farm blocs in Congress and state legislatures, and efforts to create favorable public opinion. In part, the movement has lacked solidarity, but the common social sentiments have been present anyway and the conflict no less real because of the partial unity.

In an earlier work (Ref. 511, pp. 612–616), Taylor gives an excellent account of the factors that make for town-country conflict. Condensed and modified somewhat in the light of his later findings, his analysis is as follows:

1. Differences in occupations create different modes of thinking. The farmer has acquired his skills and techniques rather unconsciously through a long period of apprenticeship under the tutelage of other members of the farm family. He fails to sense that his own skill depends to any degree upon training, much less to realize that skill and special aptitudes are necessary for the successful operation of a village business. The failure of some farmers' cooperatives as a result of poor management because of the farmer's unwillingness to secure the services of a highly skilled manager is all too well known. Furthermore, the farmer secures such a large portion of his living from the farm without direct money cost that he is unable to judge correctly the value of a dollar for the person residing in the village or town. The agriculturist thinks that the villager is growing rich at the expense of the farmer with whom he deals.

Neither does the villager understand the farmer and his psychology. Utterly dependent upon the exchange system, buying and selling on a profit-and-loss basis, the village merchant does not understand the farmer's suspicion of price dealings or the parsimonious element in his nature. Little realizing or appreciating the great multiplicity of aptitudes and skills called into play by the farmer's everyday work, the villager even underrates the mentality of the cultivator.

2. The apparent differences between rural and town levels of living are very real. The countryman observes the short working hours in town, sees the villager wearing "Sunday clothes" every day, passes by the fine homes, churches, and schools in the incorporated center. He realizes all too keenly that the townsman has the ready convenience of institutions and services which the farmer may lack or which he feels are controlled and operated basically by townspeople in their own interest. Idle town children at play attract his attention; his own children have no such freedom from toil. The farmer rebels mentally against his own living conditions and blames them upon the townsman, largely by imputing them to an inequitable economic situation in which the villager has the advantage. The townsman, in turn, knows that the farmer lives without some of the amenities of modern life, but often takes their absence as proof of the farmer's inferiority, and blames the countryman for his lack of urbanity, culture, and polished manners. This attitude of superiority is resented by the farmer even more than his own lack of facilities and gives rise to added suspicion, misunderstanding, and conflict.

3. Townspeople, even those in centers of no more than a few hundred, tend to identify themselves with the urban segment of the population and the graces of city life; they affect urban manners in their dealings with the people from the hinterland, consider themselves urbane, polished, and cosmopolitan, and display their accomplishments freely in the course of their contacts with farm people. Conversely, the farmer senses that after all the village is more similar to the open country than to the metropolitan center and resents what he considers to be affectations of urbanity by those in the nearby trade center.

4. The farmer must deal largely with the particular village and town classes in whose hands is concentrated the wealth of the centers, and he is likely to consider them as representatives of all villagers. Farmers have little reason to deal with section workers and other unskilled laboring groups of the town. Through his identification of all townsmen with the banking and merchant classes, the agriculturist is strengthened in his conviction that the country is being exploited to support the fine homes, the business establishments, and the relatively high levels of living of the townspeople. Moreover, the farmer often perceives that these members of the local elite possess greater polish than he, and he suffers from an uneasiness upon each contact with them. This unease is readily transformed into suspicion and dislike.

5. Industrial elements in the town, even though small, have only a remote connection with agriculture. Frequently, factory workers, railroad shop laborers, and other industrial personnel regard all farmers as potential competitors eagerly awaiting an opportunity to seize their jobs. This may be especially widespread if part-time farming is commonly combined with part-time industrial employment in the area. If the center is very large, such groups consider that the farmer has an easy time of it because his

food comes from the farm, his house rent is taken care of, and his fuel can be secured on his own land.

6. Although the institutional facilities of farmers often are deficient in material equipment, all the social institutions and the values they represent are strongly woven into the farmer's life. For this reason he is easily disgusted with the obvious commercialism of the tradesman, distrusts the merchant's ultimate interests and values, and rather vaguely is irritated at what he regards as the town's one-sided, superficial way of conducting personal relationships. He quickly becomes unhappy with the impersonal secondary contacts which may arise in his dealings with those even in the smallest towns.

7. In many ways the villager is merely a middleman between the farmer and the economic interests of far-distant centers of trade and industry. He is the local representative of detached economic interests of which the farmer is chronically distrustful. As the intermediary between the two, the townsman must use accepted business techniques in dealing with the city business establishments, and is also likely to put them into practice with his farmer customers. The farmer's bank notes are discounted at central banks, specified prices are relayed to him from the cities, and even city wage scales are charged when he seeks certain services such as car repairs. The farmer follows different practices in dealing with his neighbor on the farm, and resents the fact that he must adopt new ways in dealing with the villager. He may be especially outraged by charges for labor and by the fact that many small-town merchants and bankers have increased their own profits at the expense of the farmer who must negotiate with them largely on their terms for credits, loans, and other services.

8. Class consciousness and organization among farmers have resulted in their attempts to cooperate in supplying many of the necessary services. This kind of action strikes immediately at the villager's economic base of subsistence. Vested interests in the villages, towns, and cities have fought these attempts by the farmer to enter commercial and political arenas. Many of the farmer's political and business endeavors have failed, a fact he attributes in large measure to the opposition of the townsmen. Out of these attempts have come additional suspicion and hostility toward the town.

The antagonistic relationship between town and country has been a variable one in which a stable equilibrium has been difficult to achieve, chiefly because in the 300 years during which the town-country conflict has gone on in the United States, the change from a rural-dominated to an urban-dominated society has constantly produced new areas of conflict. Much of the conflict arises from the rapid rate of sociocultural change. The latter has taken many forms but chiefly it has brought increasing numbers and proportions of people under the influence of towns and cities and of ideas, values, and behavior patterns which emanate from them. Thus, the nation's social and economic organization has been greatly altered, with industrialization and commercialization producing new situations with which the American farmer has had to contend. Some results have been various farmers' movements, growing political identity of urban dwellers, efforts to reapportion rural-dominated state legislatures, and the tendency for town and city populations rather than farm people to decide political contests. Farmers have been part of a changing, overall social organization in which their relative numerical importance has decreased drastically and their political influence has diminished greatly. It is no wonder that the reaction to this situation often has taken the form of town-country conflict (see Ref. 626, pp. 117–120). In many cases, the conflict has been a symptom of the farmer's frustration and anxiety over his inability to remain abreast of these changes or to control them.

But various types of accommodation are not lacking. In a very real sense, the town and country forces have tended, in part, to come together in the rural-nonfarm segment of the population. Moreover, "rural-nonfarm" in the United States is not merely a residential category but is a new socioeconomic unit consisting of interdependent towns, rural residential areas, farms, and a variety of agricultural and nonagricultural industries. In some respects this development represents a partial adjustment of the long-time conflict between farm and town factions in the United States.

Class Conflict in Rural Society

Class conflict, while probably less intensive in the country than in the city, is nevertheless a fundamental form of rural social conflict. The bases of conflict in the country differ from those in the city. Urban class struggle in many parts of the world savors of socialism and communism in the sense that collective ownership or state control of the agencies of production is one of the goals. Farmers and peasants engaging in class struggle, on the other hand, very definitely have had the objective of decentralization of control. Class struggle among agriculturists is nearly always a struggle of the masses for land; growing out of the maldistribution of the ownership and control of the land, it can logically be designated as a function of large-scale agriculture in which the plantation is the dominant feature. The family-sized farm system of agriculture lacks the elements necessary for class struggle. Where this type of system prevails, farm laborers are few as compared with farm operators; the few laborers are mainly young men, sons of farm owners, themselves beginning to climb toward farm ownership. In family-farm areas the agricultural ladder is in operation, functioning as a social elevator to lift persons from the status of farm laborers, through the various grades of tenants, into the ownership and possession of the land they till. In such sections, there is little that resembles the closed-class system, little to array the social strata against one another. In fact, the middle class may account for virtually all of the population in these areas, allowing virtually no one to sift into the upper or lower extremes of the stratification system, and sparing such an area from potential conflict between a host of landless poor and a handful of landed elite.

The situation is very different where there is concentration of ownership in the hands of a few. In this case, the great mass of cultivators lacks the security that comes with ownership of the soil. Vertical mobility is practically impossible; only a few can ever hope for the ownership of land; virtually none is able even to expect equitable leasing arrangements; and the great masses are doomed to the permanent status of agricultural laborers. Inevitably this situation produces a closed-class system containing a tiny elite upper class, a huge disadvantaged lower class, and virtually no middle class. It contains all the elements necessary for class struggle. The present world-wide concern over agrarian reform and the thoroughgoing social changes it entails is a symptom of that struggle in which the landless not only demand access to landownership, but the basic rebuilding of entire social systems now centered on the rigid two-class pattern of stratification. Nowhere is this more evident than in "developing" nations in general and those of Latin America in particular. There, vast numbers of people are vitally involved in efforts to fill the great vacuum created by the centuries-long absence of a genuine middle class and to alter in a fundamental way the relationships between man and the land.

Perhaps the most intense and far-reaching twentieth-century class struggle among agriculturists is to be found in the Mexican Revolution, the battle of the masses for the lands once owned by their ancestors. As mentioned in Chapter 14, for centuries the large estate (*hacienda*) was the dominant institution in Mexico, as it still is in many other Latin American countries. In the Mexico of 1910, it was by far the most conspicuous feature of the land system. At the close of the Díaz regime, haciendas controlled the agriculture of the nation, set the pattern of social relations, and dominated the economic and political life of Mexico. Many of these haciendas were of unbelievable extent, some containing over a quarter of a million acres. Self-sufficiency was the all-important objective of their proprietors, and they were commercialized only to the slightest degree. But such excessive concentration of landownership in a dominantly rural nation necessarily meant that the bulk of the rural people would be landless. Most of them were almost entirely deprived of property rights in the land or even the rights to use land under any other conditions than those of serf. With such maldistribution of agricultural property, it is no accident that "land for the people" was the only slogan that awakened a ready response among the peons, that this cry became the watchword of the revolution, or that widespread agrarian reform followed the carnage.

Early successful revolutionary leaders were slow to sense the importance of the groundswell of agrarian discontent, to realize the intensity of the peasants' demands for land. In fact, a number of substantial efforts at revolution failed because this factor was not taken into account sufficiently by those who attempted to foment the several rebellions. The famous agrarian leader who was well acquainted with the acute desire of the peasants for greater freedom and for control of the land was Emiliano Zapata. Generally rebellious over abuses long imposed upon the landless peasants even before Madero led the successful uprising against Díaz, Zapata was fired with only two ideas— liberty and return of the land to the cultivators. In the Madero revolution his power was great; but when Madero refused the immediate restoration of lands to the peasants, he turned against that popular chief, returned to his native mountains, and again took up arms with the vow that he would not lay them down until he and his peasant following were once more in possession of their village lands. Only a month after the election of Madero as president, Zapata, uncompromising in his ideals, put forth the famous Plan of Ayala, ordering his followers to use armed might in seizing and holding lands. His efforts had only mixed success in his lifetime, but, although Zapata never became president, and died fighting for his ideals, his influence has been of the highest significance in the Mexican Revolution. *Agrarismo* and *Zapatismo* became almost synonymous, and everywhere in Mexico the name of the reformer is linked closely with the efforts to reapportion land on an equitable basis and to rebuild Mexican society around an entirely different set of relationships than those that surround the large landed estate. Today he has already gone far on the road to deification, is considered a superman, a symbol of agrarianism in its highest forms. Many of his principles of reform have become integral parts of modern Mexican society and have helped to make the country one of the most advanced in Latin America.

All in all, the Mexican Revolution is one of the most significant agrarian movements of the twentieth century. It was preceded by centuries of land monopoly, first under the control of the elite of the Aztec civilization, and later of the Spaniards and their descendants. Antithetical to the *ejido,* a communal landholding found in pre-Columbian Mexico, the huge estate became the basic core of social organization in the nation. Despite periodic efforts by the landless serfs to change the pattern of ownership and the restrictive two-class system it generated, not until 1910 to 1920 was it possible for them to overthrow the system, reestablish the *ejido,* and initiate limited use of a very small variety of the family-sized farm. The class conflict represented in these events was of the most violent sort, producing several decades of upheaval and chaos and resulting not merely in a superficial coup but in a genuine social revolution of wide proportions.

Concerted mass efforts to obtain decentralization of landholdings have not developed to any great extent in the United States. The widespread distribution of family-sized farms and the predominant middle-class mentality of the rural population are, of course, the factors responsible. However, in areas where large estates are the rule, such as parts of California and the plantation sections of the South, most of the elements needed for violent and vicious struggle have been present, and sporadic outbursts of aggravated conflict have seized the headlines. Labor strikes in California's "factories in the field" may be expected to recur from time to time, and the same is likely in Florida's citrus districts and in other parts of the nation where landless workers supply the lion's share of the labor used in agricultural production. However, with the rapid mechanization of agriculture in these and the cotton plantation areas there would seem to be less danger of a repetition of the serious disorders that plagued some of the latter in the 1930's. Then the activities of the Sharecroppers' Union of Alabama, and the work of the Southern Tenant Farmers' Union in Arkansas and other southern states were widely publicized. Class conflict was a feature of all of these. But mechanization has virtually eliminated sharecropping in the South and it promises to reduce drastically other forms of agricultural labor in other types of farming elsewhere in the country. Therefore, it seems that large-scale agriculture in the United States will depend decreasingly upon laborers and that serious conflict between the two classes generally represented in such a system will become less likely.

In many other parts of the world the class situation oriented to the large landed estate and its ills well may generate large amounts of turbulence and violence. It has already produced great waves of discontent and frustration. Wherever rising aspirations of the landless are confronted by inflexible systems of stratification, which preserve and enforce privilege and poverty, the potential for violence between the masses and the aristocracy is great. It may center around the issue of landownership, but no matter what its core issue, is almost certain to bring about chaos and eventual basic rebuilding of social systems, destruction of traditional privileged classes, and desperate efforts by the masses to ascend the social ladder. In its most tragic form, the violence may become chronic, devastating a society decade after decade, and pitting embittered class factions against each other in such a way that workable accommodations may loom distant indeed. Nowhere is this condition better illustrated than today in Vietnam.

Family and Clan Conflict

The strength of the individual family unit and its cohesion or clannishness with other units related by blood remain as major social assets of the rural community. But the strength of the individual units or combination of units also leads to rivalry, strife, and conflict with other family groups. Familism cements the relationships among all members of the in-group, but it also fans the flames of antagonism, for rival clans and extended families are especially likely to conflict with each other if they preserve a high degree of in-group solidarity and ethnocentrism and maintain a minimum of cooperative relationships with other such groups. Common residence helps to propagate this internal unity. The solidarity itself provides tinder for full-scale conflict, for an affront to one member is likely to be taken as an insufferable insult to the entire group and to call forth a general assault upon all members of the offending family or clan. Moreover, where family and clan solidarity is strong and the unifying bonds are numerous, there may be only a nominal devotion to the total community, the nation, or the larger society. Under these conditions, unity, consensus, social participation, and interdependence in the larger units may be considerably less than that in localized kinship groups and may be ineffective in unifying the latter into one integrated and functioning whole. In such a situation conflict between the component parts flares easily and often, making it largely impossible to create social efficiency. Sharply divided communities are scattered throughout the world, and one can hardly find such a locality group situation in which the lines of cleavage fail to follow family lines closely. Thus family and clan conflicts tend to continue generation after generation in rural areas where life is tradition-oriented, relatively undifferentiated, and comparatively slow to change.

Where clans have been an important form of social organization, conflict between them has been perpetuated in part by the fact that the clan tends to endure over a relatively long period of time, transcending any one set of individuals and preserving the traditions of several generations. In many cases, one of these traditions may be a feud which flares periodically into open violence but which is rarely abandoned as the generations follow each other. Under these conditions, the specific incident which sparked the feud and even those which rekindle it periodically may be completely forgotten while the atmosphere of conflict, latent or overt, remains. For example, only the resounding defeat in 1746 of the Scottish clans ended the many feuds between them, and even then struggles flared periodically between their descendants. However, with the essential unity and pride of these groups reduced, the feuds eventually dwindled to various petty confrontations.

The blood feuds among the Appalachian mountaineers in the United States are, of course, universally known. But a feud is merely an extreme form of conflict between families, and interfamily conflicts of milder forms are omnipresent. In the feud, arms are employed by each group in an effort to exterminate the other or drive its members from the territory. Feuds spread like wildfire to all blood relatives, to those related by marriage, and even to the friends of the families concerned. But the fact that feuds also linger in areas far removed from the Appalachians is not so well publicized. And the fact that such feuds in rural areas are, after all, closely related to the rivalry between the best families in towns and villages throughout the world rarely receives the recognition it deserves. In fact, interfamily conflict in these two types of communities often differs only in degree.

Additional Readings

1. BEERS, HOWARD W., "Rural-Urban Differences: Some Evidence from Public Opinion Polls," *Rural Sociology*, Vol. 18, No. 1 (March, 1953), pp. 1–11.

2. BERNARD, JESSIE, *American Community Behavior* (revised ed.), New York: Holt, Rinehart and Winston, 1962, chapters 5 and 6.

3. BERTRAND, ALVIN L., "The Emerging Rural South: A Region under Confrontation by Mass Society," *Rural Sociology*, Vol. 31, No. 4 (December, 1966), pp. 449–457.

4. HEADY, EARL O., and JOSEPH ACKERMAN, "Farm Adjustment Problems and Their Importance to Sociologists," *Rural Sociology*, Vol. 24, No. 4 (December, 1959), pp. 315–325.

5. NELSON, LOWRY, *Rural Sociology* (second ed.), New York: American Book Company, 1955, chapter 8.

6. SANDERS, IRWIN T., *The Community: An Introduction to a Social System* (second ed.), New York: The Ronald Press Company, 1966, chapter 8.

7. SANDERSON, DWIGHT, *Rural Social and Economic Areas in Central New York*, Cornell AES Bulletin No. 614, Ithaca: Cornell University, 1934.

8. SLOCUM, WALTER L., *Agricultural Sociology*, New York: Harper & Brothers, 1962, chapter 11.

9. SMITH, T. LYNN, "Agricultural-Pastoral Conflict: A Major Obstacle in the Process of Rural Development," *Journal of Inter-American Studies*, Vol. XI, No. 1 (January, 1969), pp. 16–43.

10. TAYLOR, CARL C., *The Farmers' Movement, 1620–1920*, New York: American Book Company, 1953.

17
COOPERATION

Strictly speaking, to cooperate means to operate or manage jointly, essentially under the implicit assumption that all participants in any particular endeavor are involved equally and that none is dominant over any other. More commonly, however, cooperation is defined as working together for the attainment of common or similar objectives. Like competition, it is a form of striving, but cooperation is striving with others, whereas competition is striving against others. All large permanent groups, other than those resulting from conquest and held together by force, are forms of cooperation. Society itself is the example *par excellence* of cooperation. Among the social processes cooperation is entitled to a position in the front rank. Therefore, it should be made clear that when we speak of cooperation, we view it as a very broad, dynamic, and highly significant feature of most social groups and not merely as joint purchasing and marketing arrangements made by farmers on the basis of the Rochdale principles. These latter "farmer cooperatives" are merely one relatively recent form of the general process of cooperation in the rural areas.

The motivations that bring about cooperation are not well understood, but it does seem clear that the stimuli that result in two or more persons or groups working together are many and varied. For example, the pooling of men's efforts for the purpose of fighting a common enemy is universal both geographically and historically. People everywhere also seem to have found it necessary to unite in the establishment of tribunals for the purpose of hearing and settling disputes within the group. As ancient as the earliest traditions of the Hebrews is the construction of public works as an incentive to cooperation. Concrete evidences of cooperative effort in other early civilizations are the irrigation ditches and reservoirs for controlling the waters of the Nile, the Euphrates, and the Ganges rivers. In the western half of the world, the magnificent terraces and the structures of stone built by the Incas of Peru and the pyramids of the Mayas and the Aztecs, demonstrate that cooperative activities of a high order long prevailed in this section. In all periods, the need to maintain social control has resulted in cooperation through various types of government, involving as cooperating participants either all who are governed or at least those who do the governing. Perhaps the most universal motivation that generates cooperation is the need to train new members of the wider society. The mutual effort that arises from this endeavor takes the long-term, intense, and highly personal form that occurs in families. Finally, the drive to meet economic needs also impels people into joint efforts of a great many kinds. Thus, the needs and motivations that produce cooperation may be reflected in extremely personal joint endeavors in small groups or highly impersonal ones in large groups. They may precipitate common efforts among persons and groups who generally like and respect one another and who are motivated by those feelings, or among those who are highly antagonistic but who recognize that their respective interests are best met by cooperation. Often in contemporary urban societies, cooperation is a necessity and the motivations that bring it about are highly rational. In any case, the stimuli are so many and varied that cooperation manifests itself at all periods of time and among all peoples in their economic and other social activities.

TYPES OF RURAL COOPERATION

Cooperation may be divided into a variety of types depending upon the purposes of the investigator. The careful student of human society cannot afford to neglect the phenomenon of *symbiosis* or *commensalism*. These are the terms used by the naturalist in referring to situations in which plants and animals of different species live together in harmony and mutual helpfulness, directing their energies not so much against one another as against an unfriendly environment. This is certainly one form of cooperation, although obviously not purposive; and it has a human counterpart in the mutual aid that members of pioneering settlements in frontier areas or of other small neighborhood groups give to one another.

Among human beings, however, cooperative activities range through all degrees, from rather spontaneous reactions such as the pioneering practices of neighboring and mutual aid, to the calculated contractual form of united effort typified by the farmers' cooperative marketing associations, purchasing associations, and credit unions. In primary groups, such as the rural neighborhood, informal mutual aid is widespread, but as social differentiation proceeds and human contacts grow less personal and more formal, mutual aid tends to be replaced by cooperative activities based more on deliberate conscious efforts. Finally, in highly differentiated and heterogeneous societies, typified by urbanized and industrialized states, organized governmental police powers evolve and enforce all sorts of activities for the public good. In the process, a highly formalized type of cooperation is generated in which large numbers of people literally are compelled by necessity to participate. Large bureaucratic organizations of a great many kinds represent this most remarkable type of cooperation, which is carried on by multitudes of self-seeking persons who operate jointly in an extremely structured way. In this case, complex formalized cooperation is brought about in such a manner that the very different ends of those who staff the organization, of those who have dealings with it, and of the larger society all are met reasonably adequately.

Perhaps, for purposes of analysis, cooperative effort may best be classified as being contractual or non-contractual. With competitive cooperation, which grows out of social differentiation, the development of impersonal relations, and self-centered necessity, the many varieties of these two types of cooperation make up the principal modes of working together in human society.

Non-Contractual Cooperation

This term refers to all those mutual-aid practices whereby neighbor assists neighbor in the accomplishment of desired ends without any specific contractual agreement concerning the mode, method, time, or amount of payment. There usually exists, though, sufficient consensus on the matter so that any given person fully expects to contribute his services when the need arises, and he learns to anticipate a certain level of mutual effort from his neighbors when particular kinds of tasks are to be done. Thus, mutual aid, while informal, certainly is not indiscriminate and is neither expected nor given unless specific kinds of situations come into being. Aid almost certainly would be extended, for example, when illness prevented the harvesting of a crop by a farm family but it would be withheld if laziness had caused the inability to take the harvest.

Rooted in primary-group relationships, cooperation of the non-contractual type enjoyed widespread favor in the United States and Canada from the establishment of the colonies until early in the twentieth century, basically because people in general accepted favors only with the tacit understanding that they would return them. Such cooperation was actually an institutionalized, though informal, mutual helpfulness and assistance practiced by people who knew each other well and who shared the same geographically limited locality and most of the same values and attitudes. It included in these countries, all of the pioneer practices of barn-raisings, house-raisings, husking bees, distribution of game and other foodstuffs to neighbors, quilting parties, and so forth. Under this heading are also classed community or neighborhood cultivation of the fields of a widow or disabled neighbor, donations of feed to the farmer whose haystacks had burned, assisting a neighbor to cut his grain before the first frost, and so on. It certainly was not unique that when the early settler in the piney woods of Mississippi had cut and squared enough trees for the construction of a cabin, "there came to him men out of the pathless depths of the woods, summoned by some mysterious telegraphy, and they 'raise' " (Ref. 352, p. 80). This cooperation of a very efficient type, found commonly in rural America during the time when the agrarian way of life was the fundamental feature of social existence and the cultural environment, was pronounced in areas where the family-sized farm prevailed. In those places, neighbor helped neighbor in order to accomplish certain tasks that could not be carried out efficiently or at all by the members of one farm family. This kind of cooperation, of course, is also important in other parts of the world, such as Western Europe, where family-sized farms are rather widespread.

Monette wrote as follows concerning mutual aid in the pioneer primary groups of the United States:

Did a neighbor wish to erect a cabin, or to roll his logs, or to gather his harvest, each man was a willing hand, and in turn received aid from others. At such places an idler or an indifferent spectator dared not approach, or the contempt of the hardy pioneers settled upon him. Did any contract a debt, it was paid in labor or by the exchange of commodities; and the force of the moral sense, sustained by public sentiment, was a stronger guarantee than all the forms of law, which often serves as a protection against honest demands. Did a man want a bushel of salt, he received it in exchange for a cow and a calf. So equal was the distribution of their scanty wealth, that no one envied that of his neighbor; if any were in want, they freely received from those who could give. (Ref. 298, Vol. 2, p. 16.)

Despite the recent commercialization of agriculture in the United States, many of these practices of mutual aid and neighboring remain deeply graven in the patterns of rural culture. Even today, the average farmer can count upon a considerable amount of help from his fellows in time of sickness, death, ravages of fire to his house or barn, and similar catastrophies. But the onslaught of urban mores and the disintegration of the cumulative community make it ever more difficult to maintain these informal mutual-aid patterns of cooperation. Where secondary contacts prevail, favors are not returned and mutual-aid advances are accepted as donations or charity;

sometimes the recipient may construe the extension of aid as having gained the advantage over a gullible donor. This, of course, changes the entire character of cooperation and tends to render obsolete the earlier non-contractual forms. When an individual's neighbor becomes only the one living nearby and has no other significance to him, cooperation must be of a contractual nature in order to be successful.

Non-contractual cooperation also occurs in other areas than those in which the family-sized farm is the dominant type of agricultural holding. This type of cooperation is often used by the agricultural villagers who operate their own small subsistence farms or *minifundia* in the eastern half of the world and in Latin America. Specifically in the latter case, it is not an unusual phenomenon among foreign-born farm people who have come recently to such places as southern Brazil. This way of working together occurs among the laborers on large plantations throughout the world, although this often takes the passive form of mutual encouragement in the minimal performance of work rather than that of joint participation in the accomplishment of certain difficult and ambitious tasks. Non-contractual cooperation may even be found among the owners of the large landholdings, but it is greatly limited by the fact that large estates almost everywhere in the world operate as self-contained units, engaging in the routine production of crops and animals by traditional methods. Moreover, when many hands are needed on a given plantation, they are almost always found among the laborers already in residence. Rarely are the laborers on one plantation sent temporarily to another to assist in the various farm tasks that create peak needs for workers, and never do the landowners themselves offer their own labor for the benefit of their neighbors. Such a concept, commonplace in the areas of family-sized farms, is completely foreign where work with the hands or any other kind of behavior that might be construed as manual labor is held in great disrepute.

Contractual Cooperation

This type of cooperation occurs through a formally constituted organization, by means of definitely specified rules, and upon a strict give-and-take basis. As noted before, there is some tendency today to restrict the use of the word "cooperation" to this formally organized type of association. Contractual cooperation may be highly impersonal; it tends also to be highly rationalized and directed toward ends that are pursued within a complex framework of rules and regulations. Cooperation of this kind has doubtless arisen among many peoples as their societies became differentiated and complex and as the old primary-group relationships became engulfed by those of a secondary or special-interest nature. However, the pattern that prevails throughout the Western World today goes back largely to Robert Owen and his associates in Europe, a group active in the first half of the nineteenth century. They sought an order that would differ radically from the system of laissez faire, in which the profit motive might be harnessed to the promotion of the general welfare, and they undertook one venture after another designed to bring about such a new type of society. Interestingly enough, their labors were concentrated in the urban centers and among the working classes, rather than in the rural districts, and it was Owen and his followers who set the stage on which were evolved the principles now generally accepted as distinguishing cooperative associations from other forms of business organization. These are the so-called Rochdale principles developed by a group of workers in one of England's small industrial cities. Although these principles have by no means changed the whole basis of economic organization throughout the Western World, they constitute a considerable force in both Europe and America. In the latter, for example, several cooperative communities were established under the direct personal sponsorship of Owen, and many others have a definite relationship to his projects.

Curiously, European cooperative associations organized along Rochdale lines probably enjoy their greatest influence in the cities among industrial workers, whereas the American cooperatives are used to a greater extent by the nation's farmers. Nevertheless credit unions, cooperative purchasing organizations, and other formally structured associations have spread to some extent from the farming areas to the cities in the United States.

Competitive Cooperation

This kind of cooperation arises out of the impersonal relations that develop as society differentiates and turns from a mechanistic to an organic basis for its cohesion. As this transition takes place, social unity comes to be based upon the interdependence of the highly dissimilar groups and individuals who make up the society. Under these circumstances, an extremely formalized type of cooperation comes into being, simply because it is a functional necessity if the many components of society are to attain their respective ends at the same time that they are engaged in intense competition with each other. This competition and the large numbers of people and high degree of heterogeneity involved help to add the impersonal dimension to the relationships between groups and individuals, and enable them psychologically to use each other as instruments for achieving their own ends. As this goes on, any one person also becomes a specialized contributor to the well-being of his fellows, although his contribution is essentially an inadvertent by-product of his own self-seeking. Ultimately, the survival of this kind of cooperation depends in large measure upon two things: (1) a highly institutionalized framework of rules and regulations, expectations and prohibitions, which are enforced by the police power; and (2) a reasonable level of success among those who make up the society in actually achieving their respective goals without abridging unduly each other's rights to follow his pursuits. Inevitably, such complex competitive cooperation as this precipitates formality, contractuality, and even a type of brittleness in interaction, not to mention constant watchfulness on the part of the individual to make certain that the social confines within which he is free to operate are not violated or restricted by others.

COOPERATION IN THE ECONOMIC FIELD

The economic contacts of the farmer with nonfarm groups arise out of problems of credit, the purchasing of equipment and supplies, and the marketing of farm produce. Accordingly, where the farmer has been concerned, economic contractual cooperation has been confined largely to these three areas. But even when these efforts are found to be reasonably well-developed and the benefits are available to a substantial share of the farm population, they tend to be limited to those sections where the family-sized farm predominates. Some such arrangements have appeared in other places, but any significant impact upon the bulk of the agriculturists in those areas is yet to be felt. Therefore, the kinds of contractual cooperation to be examined in this section are best illustrated with examples from the United States and Canada.

Cooperative Associations

The development of cooperative associations for performing the economic functions of marketing, purchasing, and credit extension makes an interesting chapter in the history of rural America, Canada, Scandinavia, and some other parts of Western Europe. It has begun to occur significantly in several additional areas, such as India, Japan, and Korea. Such associations have given the farmers in many of these places tremendous leverage in dealing with other groups. Indeed, so important have they been that there is, as was mentioned before, a definite tendency to restrict the term "cooperation" to this specialized contractual form, instead of allowing it its full, rich connotations. In general, cooperative associations differ from the corporation or stock company in four respects: (1) Such associations usually adhere to the rural precept of "one man, one vote," irrespective of the amount of funds invested; (2) the fundamental purpose is more efficient service rather than the securing of profits; (3) earnings or savings are prorated to members and patrons according to the amount of business transacted with the association; and (4) all ledgers are open to all members. These four, of course, are the famous Rochdale principles, which have found wide application in the countries mentioned above.

Among farmers in the United States, economic cooperation of the contractual type had its beginnings before the Civil War. The local association was the first to appear, since neighbors have always found it advantageous to work together in the rural districts. For example, a cooperative cheese factory existed in Wisconsin as early as 1841. Cooperative ventures for the irrigation of arid lands began among the Mormons as soon as the first members of that group arrived in the Great Basin (1847). The Mormons used the principle that labor should constitute the basis of stock in each of their cooperative ventures in irrigation. Local cooperative livestock shipping associations (driving associations at first), cooperative grain elevators, wool pools, ginning associations, and assembling plants for fruits, vegetables, poultry, and so on, were early developments. For a time they were confined largely to a neighborhood basis—a handful of neighbors here and there, who united their efforts in the establishment of a cheese factory, the operation of a wheat elevator, the erection and operation of a creamery, and so forth. Some of these cooperative associations were little more than the old informal mutual-aid practices placed upon a contractual basis. These early ventures in contractual economic cooperation received great impetus in the disturbed conditions and deflation that followed the Civil War. During the 1870's, a wave of cooperative agitation swept the country. It was diffused among the laboring classes in the cities through the efforts of the Knights of Labor. Among farmers, joint undertakings of the contractual type were enthusiastically sponsored by the Patrons of Husbandry, better known as Grangers. The efforts of both these groups were largely unsuccessful, at least from the immediate point of view, and interest in cooperatives lagged during the closing years of the nineteenth century. In no small measure, these failures might be attributed to the laissez faire economic attitudes that prevailed at that time and to the high degree of independence of the American farmer and his great reluctance to yield any of his autonomy for potential advantages, which might arise from collective action.

Following the turn of the twentieth century and a number of fairly serious economic reverses in American agriculture, the cooperative movement took on new life, gained momentum, underwent fundamental changes in outlook and objectives, and developed into a large-scale undertaking. In part this was one phase of a revitalized outlook on rural life fostered by Theodore Roosevelt, and especially by the report of the Country Life Commission, which he appointed. Among rural people, much of the development was due to the activities of two great farmers' organizations—the Farmers Educational and Co-operative Union and the American Society of Equity. Still later the American Farm Bureau became one of the most important of the large farm organizations to encourage formal cooperation. All these groups set about the establishment of local cooperatives, consumer's societies, and selling agencies. The Equity, which later gave way to the Equity Union, went into the broader field of developing central plants for the processing of farm products. Its creameries eventually came to manufacture as much as three million pounds of butter in a single year. The Farmers Union and the Equity Union also set up local livestock shipping associations, later combining them with central exchanges for livestock. Both also ventured into the field of the cooperative purchase of farm equipment and supplies.

The cooperative movement, which took on new life in the early years of the twentieth century, attained its most rapid expansion in 1920, for more than 1,800 farmers' cooperative marketing associations were formed in that single year; it crested in 1929 to 1930, when 10,546 associations were in operation. Thereafter, the number fell steadily, although by no means does this decrease demonstrate that the cooperative has become less important in American agriculture. Some of these associations have grown to large proportions and have become very powerful in the areas where their members are located. In the main, the decline in numbers of these organizations is a phenomenon similar to that which has been occurring in American agriculture generally, i.e., farms have grown fewer but larger on the average in recent years. Similarly, among cooperatives the decrease in numbers is mainly the result of greater coordination and consolidation of their efforts. Clearly, the more powerful positions of the cooperatives that remain in operation and their tendency to be composed of several smaller, formerly independent associations is evidence of their growing strength in many areas, and of their tendency to become increasingly complex. Thus, in recent years, individual cooperatives have grown larger on the average insofar as numbers of members are concerned; they account for an increasing share of the purchasing and marketing done by American farmers; their total membership continues to rise despite the fact that the rural-farm population continues to decrease; and they tend to become involved in a greater diversity of fields. The cooperative association, then, remains an important part of American agriculture and shows every indication of becoming even more significant in its various far-flung enterprises (see Ref. 382, pp. 350–364).

The cooperative is consistent with certain of the attitudes of the American farmer and is a logical response to a number of socioeconomic problems by which he has been plagued. Being principally though not solely an economic venture, the cooperative holds out the promise of relieving to some degree the fact that the farmer is more or less helpless in the marketplace. Alone, he has no influence on the prices he must pay for the goods he purchases nor can he affect in any manner the returns he receives for his products; but joined with others he can enjoy a considerable degree of bargaining power in both areas. Yet the cooperative, while it extends his own farming endeavors and affords him certain economic advantages, is unlikely to curtail in any significant way the freedom and independence he prizes so highly. Furthermore, the cooperative is a logical development in areas where the family-sized farm prevails and where each operator prides himself on being a small investor, a manager, and a laborer in the farm business. These conditions allow farms to grow to adequate size but they seldom permit the ostentatious largesse that is common where the plantation is the dominant agricultural unit. As a result, cooperation in the family-sized farm areas is a major method whereby the farmer can extend his influence; but in places where the large landed estate is the dominant unit, such associations are uncommon. For example, cooperatives in the United States have sprung up in considerable number in the Midwest but are quite scarce in the South. Of course, because of its size and the attitudes that generally surround it, the plantation can afford to purchase, produce, and market with a considerable amount of waste; even under the worst conditions it can return to its upper-class owner sufficient income to preserve his high place in the social scale. The great bulk of the agriculturists associated with the large estate—the laborers—are not allowed and do not expect to have any vital interest in the net return to the plantation. Conversely, the owner-operator of the family-sized farm, given the dimensions of his holding and the attitudes of success and vertical mobility that have penetrated the whole system of which he is a part, can and will tolerate little in the way of excessive costs, inefficient production, and depressed prices. His social position usually depends upon the intensive use of a few hundred acres, whereas that of the large landowner frequently rests upon the indifferent, often haphazard and ineffective use of many thousands of acres. Thus such conditions render the use of various kinds of cooperatives highly logical in the family-sized farm areas but rather illogical in those places where the large landed estate holds sway.

In some cases in the United States, there is a growing alienation between the cooperative and its members. This has occurred in very recent years, chiefly because some associations have grown so large that individual farmers no longer feel themselves to be significant parts of the cooperative or to have any real voice in its operations. Such a condition is a far cry from the original form of contractual cooperation among comparatively small groups of rural neighbors, usually for a few specific purposes. In fact, the early cooperative was partly a reaction of farmers against "big business," of which American agriculturists generally have been suspicious; and it is likely that the individual farmer will continue to express considerable suspicion of his own cooperative should it take on many of the features of the large, impersonal, and poorly understood industrial corporation. The farmer who lacks what he considers to be a significant part in the marketing cooperative to which he belongs may come to view it as no more advantageous to him than the old-style middleman by whom he once felt victimized. Part of this disenchantment flows from the fact that as cooperatives have grown, they have had to use managers and other nonfarmer personnel in order to carry out the complex tasks of the association; often, the farmer feels that these people do not understand his problems, that they do not speak his language, and that they are marginal to the whole field of farming and farm problems. The situation is not helped, of course, by the fact that cooperatives have grown to the extent that their interests have expanded out of the confines of the local community across states, regions, and even the nation.

In part, the approach to a solution of these problems of human relations within the large cooperatives has included painstaking efforts to publicize the activities of the cooperatives among the members, to constitute boards of directors in such a way that they are truly representative of the farmer constituency, even if the board members are not necessarily typical of the membership at large, and to leave policy decisions as much in the hands of the general membership as is possible. Yet, the fact remains that many members of more than one cooperative feel uninformed about the activities of their association, fear that their individual contributions and criticisms go unrecognized, and are convinced that the ideals under which the association was established are far from the realities. Part of this inheres in the growing size of cooperatives, as already mentioned, and part in the breakdown of interaction between the membership and the managerial personnel. Not the least important factor is the failure of many farmers to become involved actively in the affairs of the associations or to seek information regarding them. But ultimately, perhaps the single most significant element is the fact that while farmers generally operate within a constellation of primary groups, most cooperatives have become large secondary groups and have, therefore, also become nearly as uncomfortable to the farmer members as large urban centers, great industrial corporations, or other secondary groups.

In the history of American agriculture, real successes in large-scale cooperative ventures have not been numerous and have been confined largely to a few crops, particularly fruit, dairy products, and grain. Cooperative marketing of cotton, the crop on which such a large percentage of the farm population long has been dependent, has been beset by all manner of pitfalls and can hardly be said to have enjoyed any significant measure of success. Perhaps the outstanding cooperatives are those of the California citrus growers. In spite of the general rule that cooperatives handling fruits and vegetables have had a high mortality rate, the California association, by federating small locals into a powerful state organization, growing a special crop, and spreading over a large enough area to control the bulk of the supply, has attained a high degree of success. Across the nation, the situation at present leaves little doubt that the cooperative associations are among the most important of farmers' organizations. Regionally, they have been and remain highly concentrated in the Midwest, especially in Minnesota, Wisconsin, and Iowa. They have enjoyed considerable development in Washington, especially in the Puget Sound area, in Oregon, and, of course, in California. Others are found in the Northeast and some are scattered widely across the various grain belts of the nation. As noted before, they are particularly scarce in the South.

Credit for productive purposes, including the purchase of land, the construction and repair of buildings, the raising of crops and livestock, and the purchasing of supplies and equipment, is one of the farmer's most pressing needs. Generally speaking, though, until recently, cooperatives in the United States had made little progress in this field, although agricultural credit unions have been among the most successful types of cooperation among the farmers in other nations, particularly France, Italy, and Russia. In the 1930's, under the supervision of the Farm Credit Administration, there was established a comprehensive system, with governmental assistance, for extending credit to farmers. This changed the farm credit situation completely. Since that time there have sprung into existence thousands of farm-loan associations, all with farmers as members and officers and all forming an integral part of the Farm Credit Administration. From these units, agriculturists have been able to borrow for uses in connection with the acquisition and improvement of lands and buildings, the production of crops and livestock, and even the financing and operation of cooperatives.

Finally, there are several disadvantages of cooperative associations which need to be noted. In addition to the problems that have arisen in connection with the expanding size and complexity of cooperatives, already discussed, there are certain other disadvantages to cooperative undertakings of the contractual nature. (1) The formation of cooperatives fosters specialization in agriculture. This simplifies the life of the farmer in many respects, but it also eliminates many of the activities in which he formerly engaged,

430

decreases many of his skills and aptitudes, and in general makes life more dull and monotonous. In many cases, it deprives him of the autonomy and self-sufficiency that accompanied his former role as unrestricted entrepreneur and manager. (2) When specialization is highly developed, many by-products go to waste, a situation that is practically impossible on the general farm. (3) Cooperative associations have a tendency to drain the best food and produce out of the community through their grading procedures and their insistence that only the most superior represent the association, and to leave the unsalable portions for local consumption. And (4) every advance in specialization makes the farmer more dependent upon the fluctuations of the business cycle, reduces his ability to provide for his own future, and diminishes the security that comes from producing a considerable part of his living on the farm. Even though these problems may not outweigh the advantages derived from cooperative associations, they are the unanticipated negative results that must be considered in evaluating the benefits of these associations.

Conditions and Factors in Cooperation

A number of conditions led to the formation of farmers' cooperatives, both in the United States and in other countries. Interest in these conditions led to a number of studies during the time when cooperatives were just beginning to gain prominence, and the conclusions of two of these early works comprise an excellent summary of the conditions that prevailed in the period of formation.

For New York State, Williams analyzed in some detail the conditions that were essential for the organization of the Dairymen's League, a rather typical farmers' cooperative of the early twentieth century. Most of the same factors were instrumental in the formation of farmers' cooperatives elsewhere. According to Williams, five general conditions that resulted in the formation of the League were as follows: (1) The growth of cities brought about the concentration in limited areas of millions of consumers, who were not themselves producers of milk and who were absolutely dependent upon the surrounding territory for supplies of dairy products; (2) New York farmers by the early part of the twentieth century had become a highly homogeneous group; (3) about three fourths of all New York farmers owned their farms; (4) important improvements took place in the means of transportation and communication, and the greatest of these was the development of the motor truck; and (5) isolation had diminished with the development of communication and transportation and especially the diffusion of the automobile into rural areas. This made possible interaction between farmers living miles apart, and the like-mindedness achieved by more intimate association greatly strengthened the solidarity of the group.

In addition to these general conditions, several psychosocial effects were of considerable importance. (1) Farmers were keen to sense the need for some collective action; (2) behind them was a long historic struggle in cooperative action; (3) previous attempts, even though they had ended in failure, had done much to develop in the rising generation persons much more skilled than their predecessors in such arts of leadership as were necessitated by organizations like the League; (4) important changes in the farmer's attitude toward custom had taken place, for the technological changes in the methods of production, which had been truly revolutionary, had created a different attitude toward other heritages; (5) other groups, both laborers in the cities and farm groups elsewhere, apparently were making a success of cooperation; (6) the principle of collective bargaining had gained acceptance and was no longer regarded as something foreign, unbecoming, and to be shunned; and (7) there was a long series of grievances against middlemen in general and the dealer in farm produce in particular.

With these conditions existing in the early years, the farmer came to realize that each by himself was powerless. He joined the cooperative to benefit himself, realizing that his interests were opposed to those of the produce dealer, identical with those of other farmers. He believed, too, that the other farmers were being exploited by the middlemen. This sense of injustice about his own condition and that of others whom he construed as kindred was one of the great factors in inducing farmers to join the cooperative (Ref. 607, pp. 172–181).

It is interesting to compare Williams' analysis of the conditions making for cooperation in New York State with Branson's analysis of the factors underlying cooperation among farmers in Denmark. The latter concluded that cooperation among Danish farmers was successful because of: (1) extreme poverty and an initial consciousness of kind in that poverty; (2) the eradication of illiteracy and the widespread diffusion of knowledge; (2) a high density of population achieved through the village form of settlement; (4) a geographic location convenient to one-hundred million consumers; (5) nearly 100 per cent of farm ownership; (6) "organization from the bottom up"; (7) modest beginnings by small groups with meager capital; (8) reliance upon self-help, asking nothing from the state that the farmers through cooperative efforts could do for themselves; and (9) the assistance of the state in the provision of transportation and terminal facilities (Ref. 47, pp. 209–219; cf. Ref. 205, pp. 45–49).

The needs that first generated contractual cooperative associations are still present in agriculture. Basic among them is the farmer's wish to be able to deal from a position of strength with those who buy his product, those from whom he must purchase supplies, equipment, and so on, and those to whom he must turn for credit. Periodically, cooperative movements assume new forms and directions, which represent changes in the efforts to meet these needs. For example, substantial numbers of American farmers now are interested in developing more aggressive bargaining associations, possessing several of the characteristics of industrial labor unions, in order to contend more successfully with processors and other buyers of their produce. This interest extends to the passage of laws that would facilitate bargaining, the imposition of penalties on buyers who favor unorganized farmers, the systematic withholding of farm produce from the market in order to command higher prices, and even the forcible exclusion of nonmembers from participation in the price benefits that may arise from the activities of the bargaining associations. If implemented, these conditions would create a "closed-shop" type of situation on the assumption that benefits won by those who are organized should not be shared by those who are not. Important portions of the people who belong to such groups as the Farm Bureau, the Farmers Union, the Grange, and especially the National Farmers Organization, support these and other elements of cooperation, which is developed to a high point of formality and characterized by rational contractual arrangements (see Ref. 144, pp. 24–25, 42–44).

Yet, along with the calculated interest in this intensified type of cooperative bargaining, there appear certain attitudes toward formal cooperation that have existed for a long time among American farmers: (1) Farmers prefer to establish the bargaining associations with little or no involvement of other groups in the society; (2) they wish to retain within the bargaining associations the illusion if not the reality of certain primary-group features, reminiscent of the old type of informal mutual aid; (3) they still manifest the perennial attitudes, often correct, that they are being exploited by produce buyers and that the nonfarm population has no real understanding of their problems; (4) they wish to have the bargaining associations controlled if not operated by persons chosen from their own ranks; (5) they are most jealous of their independence, intending to yield as little individual freedom as possible while they realize the benefits which would come from collective bargaining; and (6) they cling to ambivalent attitudes about government by demanding that the latter create a "favorable climate" for the associations but that it refrain from any serious regulation of them (Ref. 144, p. 70). Therefore, while these attitudes and values seem to drive farmers to a greater degree of competition with other groups in the society, they also help to preserve their "consciousness of kind" and to bring about the extension of formal cooperative efforts to meet new challenges in the economy.

COOPERATION AS A CULTURE PATTERN

Despite the long history of mutual-aid activities in rural communities, in most places contractual cooperation represents a sharp break with traditional culture patterns. Basically, of course, the departure involves the adoption of a formal type of cooperation by farmers whose mutual assistance once was almost exclusively of the informal type. The emergence and growth of the cooperative movement, then, suggests a close relationship between the appearance of new opportunities and the genesis of new types of social relationships. Furthermore, once the early cooperatives began to flourish and to become widely known, they provided the model and the rationale for an increasingly wide variety of other types of cooperative activity. Like a chemical reaction, in many places the pattern spread from one activity to another, eventually embracing many variations of the three basic forms of formal cooperation, i.e., purchasing, marketing, and the extension of credit, but so great has been the proliferation of such activities that the cooperative configuration has overspread the economic field and reached out in other areas. In fact, in some communities, formal cooperation has become so pervasive that it has resulted in the operation of hospitals and libraries, the establishment of various kinds of specialized educational programs, and the creation of insurance companies and other nonagricultural business pursuits; it even has affected the relations between town and country. And each time cooperation succeeds in one area of endeavor, the way is paved for its use in others.

A relatively early example of the development and diffusion of a cultural pattern built around the central core of contractual cooperation was the Xavierian movement in eastern Nova Scotia. There, in the 1930's, nearly a quarter of a million farmers, fishermen, and other rural folk of Scottish, French, Irish, and English ancestry initiated the use of cooperative associations in practically every aspect of life. Their business enterprises included about 70 savings banks, a parent store and a number of branches, a bakery, a milk pasteurizing plant, and a tailoring establishment. They included also cooperative lobster canning factories, sawmills, and a wide variety of community industries. In a very real sense, all of these were the direct outgrowth of the study clubs sponsored by the diocesan college, St. Francis Xavier, and led by men with a religious zeal that encouraged the maximum use of all legitimate means in order to bring about greater material wellbeing (see Ref. 304, pp. 76–77). Furthermore, the cooperative activities were not confined to economic questions but included libraries and educational activities in the most real sense of the word. The college study clubs, in which the whole movement was rooted, were the training fields for democratic citizenship of the higest type (cf. Ref. 44, pp. 140–144).

The experience in Nova Scotia and thousands of other communities throughout the world amply demonstrates the keenness of perception, the validity of generalization shown by Sir Horace Plunkett in 1910 when he wrote:

Gradually the [cooperative] Society becomes the most important institution in the district, the most important in a social as well as an economic sense. The members feel a pride in its material expansion. They accumulate larger profits, which in time become sort of a communal fund. In some cases this is used for the erection of village halls where social entertainments, concerts and dances are held, lectures delivered and libraries stored. Finally, the Association assumes the character of a rural commune, where, instead of the old basis of commune, the joint ownership of land, a new basis for union is found in the voluntary communism of effort. (Ref. 345, pp. 128–129).

It is clear from many examples that because farmers have such a deep-seated tradition of assisting one another by mutual-aid activities, contractual cooperative ventures, once they demonstrate their practicability, are likely to spread rapidly from one enterprise to another until they form the warp and woof of community structure. Therefore, much of what sociologists have learned about primary- and secondary-group relationships and the diffusion of cultural features can be employed to understand the development, expansion, and spread of contractual cooperative associations. As a culture pattern, formal cooperation among rural people has been diffused, adopted, and altered according to a number of principles characteristic of the dissemination of culture generally. In the first place, those farmers who have been involved most successfully in cooperative ventures tend to be highly rational and progressive and to be motivated strongly by the search for greater efficiency, especially in the manipulation of various segments of the economy. (For an appraisal of rationality in this connection, see Ref. 92.) Usually, they are the farm people who also find attractive such things as more efficient mechanization, improved cropping practices, better pest controls, and other innovations. Therefore, the attitudes toward the farming enterprise are extremely important in persuading farmers to create or to join cooperative organizations. In fact, so important in this respect are the drive to succeed and other motivations that make up a high standard of living, that when this factor is held constant, age, marital status, race, religion, and other characteristics are relatively unimportant in determining which farmers will become involved successfully in efforts designed to promote efficiency. This applies in general to the adoption of innovations, a major one of which is certainly the contractual cooperative association. It should be no surprise, then, that part-owners and full-owners are likely to work more actively in cooperatives than are persons in other tenure categories or that the proportion of satisfying memberships in cooperatives declines as one descends the hierarchy of tenure positions.

In the second place, as a consequence of the conditions just mentioned, the major cooperative movements have occurred among the dynamic middle-class operators of family-sized farms. They have been far less prevalent among the agriculturists in the areas of the world where the large landed estate dominates rural life and also where the *minifundium* is the principal type of agricultural holding. Those who are highly conservative, who produce little more than is essential for existence, who favor security over all else, who cling to the traditional ways of farming, or who are marginal in their operations are generally not to be found involved in thriving cooperative endeavors of the contractual sort. Thus, in the areas of the family-sized farm, the participants in formal cooperative associations tend to rank rather high in the class system of the local community by virtue of their incomes, levels of living, years of education, prestige in the local area, and so on.

In the third place, the most successful participants in cooperatives are those who also are involved widely in other types of community affairs. Frequently, it is these people who have learned to combine the relatively great individualism of the family-sized farm operator with various well-defined formalized cooperative activities so that neither the individualism nor the cooperation seriously jeopardizes the other. Moreover, the members who are most likely to remain loyal to given cooperatives and who both give and receive support, are those who join under no coercion and who remain part of the organization on a strictly voluntary basis. Members who are forced or cajoled into joining such organizations are very likely to drop out. (On the matter of loyalty to cooperatives, see Ref. 81.) Furthermore, the persons who remain in cooperatives and who derive maximum benefits from them consider that their particular associations are useful and believe participation to be profitable. Thus, the meanings that people attach to the associations and to their participation in them are far more vital in bringing about diffusion of the cooperative movement and in generating loyalty of members than are the actual experiences themselves (Ref. 81, p. 168).

In the fourth place, the members who remain with the cooperative and who find it useful ordinarily view it as an integral part of a network or pattern of culture complexes that comprise a total rural way of life. The cooperative association, or any other part of culture that is presented to rural people as an isolated element having no meaningful sociocultural context, is generally not adopted at all or has a poor chance of success if it is established under these conditions, no matter how successful it might have been in its place of origin. Of course, in the case of the formal cooperative association, the way is partially paved for its adoption by the universality of informal cooperation among rural folk, but even so, unless this new way of organizing certain aspects of farming fits harmoniously into the pattern of life in rural areas, it is not likely to have much value for local people. For example, any cooperative association designed to manipulate the market in a money economy that is introduced into a subsistence agricultural economy, cannot have much relevance for the local people and it is almost sure to fail. The activities of those who would help to reform rural life throughout the world have shown all too often that efforts to introduce single agricultural implements or practices into new areas are usually doomed to failure unless a whole complex of other material items, ideas, attitudes, concepts, and so on accompanies them to provide meaning. Thus, successful diffusion of the formal cooperative association is subject to the transplantation of a whole plethora of logically related sociocultural features to provide a context within which such an association makes sense.

Finally, because the farm community is a primary group itself, or at least possesses many primary characteristics, the personal influences exerted by farmers upon each other are highly significant in bringing about success or failure of cooperative associations. Favorable attitudes toward such organizations often are sufficiently contagious in a strictly personal way so that serious and profitable involvement of a large proportion of local people results. But by the same token, unfavorable attitudes can spread just as rapidly with the opposite effect. Attitudes are conditioned by many other things too, of course, but the personal element remains highly significant in the rural districts. In fact, as discussed earlier, so significant are primary contacts to rural people, that when a given cooperative comes to be characterized chiefly by impersonal secondary contacts, feelings of noninvolvement, anonymity, and powerlessness may become serious handicaps to the operation of the organization. Indeed, for individual members, there may occur considerable ambivalence between rationality and the success orientation on the one hand, and such things as personal ties, responsibility to neighbors, favoritism, familism, and old-style mutual-aid on the other hand. (For a study of situations such as these, see Ref. 121.) More than one cooperative has found that its problems in interpersonal relations, born of declining primary contacts, have been more serious than the difficulties it originally was created to solve.

RELIGIOUS COOPERATION

The church, one of the principal nuclei of rural social groupings, has always played an important role in cooperation of all types. Furthermore, religious motives, centered about the church, have been the moving force in many forms of cooperation. With the disintegration of the cumulative community in many societies and the substitution of organic solidarity for cohesion based upon similarities, there occurs a great change in the entire pattern of social relationships. Especially subject to alteration are the relationships or associations with nonmembers of the intimate group. Mingling with and coming to know persons with widely differing cultural heritages, sharply contrasting social characteristics, and diametrically opposed mores is one of the most effective ways of developing tolerance and broad-mindedness. As a rule, however, none of the traits of a traditional culture pattern is clung to more tenaciously than the customs and traditions associated with the church. In those parts of the world where nearly all the members of a given rural community belong to one particular denomination or sect, cooperation in religious matters is relatively simple. But where the community contains a variety of religious congregations, cooperation in this area may be extremely difficult. In the United States, for instance, because of the heterogeneity of religious memberships, leaders of the various Protestant denominations long have lamented the serious "overchurching" of the rural community as evidenced by the presence of six to ten small struggling congregations in a single rural village, and have deplored the lack of more cooperative relations between them. For this reason the emergence of various cooperative tendencies among divergent church groups in rural areas is a matter of no slight consequence. Cooperative efforts are in evidence along many lines, including the following: (1) In many communities the local pastors of all denominations have formed a council for the purpose of discussing common aims and problems; (2) pastors on invitation exchange pulpits on stated occasions; (3) union meetings are held periodically in many communities, with leaders and lay members of several denominations cooperating; and (4) there has been a definite tendency toward the development of union churches in rural areas. The latter phenomenon, because of its prevalence in the rural parts of the United States, deserves additional discussion.

The movement for the consolidation, merger, or union of local churches in this country had made little headway before 1890. At that time the depopulation of many rural areas and the decline of the village in some sections of the country created many pressing problems for the rural institutions, including the church, which served the population of these sections. The earliest federated church reported was in a declining Massachusetts community, the union having occurred in 1887 (Ref. 201, p. 25). But for 25 years the movement made little progress and overchurching continued as a vexing problem in many rural communities. After 1912, however, consolidation made rapid headway as the migration of rural people to cities went on apace and the concern over the viability of rural institutions intensified; by 1924, the surveys of the Institute of Social and Religious Research discovered almost 1,000 united churches in the villages and open-country areas of the North and West, but they found not a single one in the South. The united churches discovered by the Institute were of four types: (1) federated churches, in which each congregation kept its affiliation with the denominational body; (2) undenominational churches, where the congregations uniting severed all denominational ties; (3) denominational united churches, a category designed to fit those cases in which one of the congregations retained denominational ties and the members of the other congregations accepted them; and (4) affiliated churches, so called because loose and vague ties were retained with one or more of the parent denominations. That these various kinds of unions were prompted by overchurching is evidenced by the fact that they were largely confined to the smaller villages, the number in towns being almost insignificant. More than 85 per cent of the congregations entering formal unions with those of other denominations were either Northern Baptist, Congregational, Methodist Episcopal, or Presbyterian of the U.S.A. Scattered congregations from 12 other denominations also entered the unions, but this number included no foreign-language denominations, nor any Catholic, Jewish, or Christian Science congregations. However, individual members of the united churches represented at least 50 different faiths (Ref. 54, pp. 76–79; cf. Ref. 230, pp. 375–378).

At present, complete or partial consolidation of rural churches includes the federated, undenominational, denominational united, and affiliated forms mentioned above. In addition, other efforts to bring about cooperation between churches, while avoiding consolidation, allow them to retain maximum theological and practical autonomy and to expand their services to members. For example, in given cases joint programs may be created for the youth of several churches; one minister may serve several congregations, much as did the old circuit riders; two or more groups may share the same physical plant and hold their services at different times; several local churches may work out a single budget in order to generate maximum economies. Yet, important as the movement toward united churches and other forms of close cooperation has been in specific communities, recent trends do not seem to justify the belief that it will solve the problems of the rural church in America. It is conspicuously absent in many places, and only a small portion of the rural churches that close their doors even now do so because their congregations have merged with one or more others. Even where consolidation has saved some churches from bankruptcy, many serious internal divisions remain, born essentially of the fact that union almost invariably creates greater dissimilarities within the membership. The rural church in many places now has to accommodate nonfarm inhabitants who use the villages and even the open country as residences, but who have little association with farming or with local traditions. As this goes on, the local area may come to include people with a variety of religious affiliations, those with few or no religious interests, and even some who are actively anti-religious. Thus, the new heterogeneity and the persistence of the older congregational autonomy tend to act in concert to retard church unions. Furthermore, people who are recent arrivals in local rural communities and who have little to do with an agrarian way of life, often find that their differences from the farm folk place them in the category of "strangers." Thus, schisms are introduced into rural churches whose memberships become diversified by this means, making cooperation even more difficult. In any case, in the United States, and in many other places where substantial sociocultural changes are taking place, tradition, continuity with the past, local autonomy and integrity, the fundamental base of nonempiricism, and other features common to the overall religious institution, especially in the rural districts, make it difficult to bring about effective cooperation between its various segments and representatives.

TECHNICAL COOPERATION

One additional area of joint endeavor, which differs from the other forms discussed in this chapter but still deserves the name, is technical cooperation. The term includes the plethora of programs generated by the United Nations, the Alliance for Progress, various governments, and other formal organizations to assist in the improvement of rural life in the so-called underdeveloped nations. Since World War II, this form of cooperation has assumed more significant proportions, has become widely known, and has produced some notable successes and some disappointing failures.

The results of these action-oriented programs have been affected greatly by existing patterns of culture, including the attitudes, beliefs, ideas, and values of the people in the societies involved. Many of the efforts have been conceived within the middle-class frame of reference, which is characteristic of most North Americans and which may or may not be significant or even comprehensible to rural people in other parts of the world. In particular, this viewpoint emphasizes the three economic functions typical of the operator of the adequate family-sized farm, namely those of the capitalist on a small scale, the independent manager, and the willing laborer. It assumes that the farmer, if given the opportunity, can and will invest capital wisely, manage the farm efficiently, and hold labor to be dignified and worthy of the best use possible. The middle-class mentality, then, constitutes a particular pair of spectacles through which many of the participants in technical cooperation view rural life and labor elsewhere in the world.

In the various sections of the earth for which technical cooperation has been intended, there is tremendous variation in the values encountered and in the receptivity to such cooperative ventures. For example, wide indeed are the differences one encounters between the European immigrants in southern Brazil and the Indians in the Andes; between the peasants in Southeast Asia and the small herders in the African bush; between the Negro sharecroppers in the delta of the Mississippi and the migrant agricultural laborers in California; between the owners of large plantations and the laborers who work for them. Therefore, there are many basic departures from the middle-class network of values, and these differences affect efforts to bring about technical cooperation. Several of the variations follow:

In the first place, prevailing class systems generate particular patterns of values. Where small landowning elites and great masses of lower-class laborers make up the agricultural population, the resistance to technical improvement is often great. It may flow both from the upper-class families who will tolerate few changes of any kind, least of all those that seem to jeopardize their exalted status, and from the lower-class laborers to whom the slightest departure from tradition may loom as a potential threat to their creature-like way of life. On the coffee *fazendas* of Brazil, the cotton plantations of the southern United States, the rubber plantations of Malaya, the cattle *estancias* of Argentina, and in other places where the large land-holding and a rigid two-class system of stratification go hand in hand, technical cooperation may be resisted as a foreign intrusion designed to disorganize a highly institutionalized and stolidly supported mode of existence. When new technology is not entirely rejected, it often is accepted by those who hold power in the rural areas only as a way to increase their own wealth. Almost never does it cause landowners and laborers to operate the agricultural enterprise jointly in order to increase the returns to both groups.

In the second place, class systems of this kind are usually associated with the great disrepute of human toil. Labor is defined as the sole province of the lowly and is steadfastly avoided by those who are somewhat above them in the social scale. The fundamental problem that such ideas about manual labor pose in relation to technical cooperation is, of course, how the performance of the ordinary tasks on the farm can be made socially acceptable to others than the people definitely known and admitted to be of lower-class status. If this basic hurdle could be surmounted, the solution of other problems related to technical cooperation could be effected comparatively easily.

In the third place, where labor is performed exclusively by members of the lower social class, it is likely to be used with extravagant abandon. In much of Latin America, for example, there is expressed almost constantly the need for more hands to perform the work; but by no reasonable standard can laborers be said to be scarce. Rather, capital is expended so sparingly and managerial activities are reduced so close to the minimum that the amount that any one worker can produce is infinitesimally small. Even the simplest tools, not to mention work stock or other sources of power, are largely lacking. Men and women work for the most part with their bare hands, and the amount of human toil that goes into the production of a ton of sugar, a bag of coffee, a sack of beans, a bushel of wheat or corn, or a unit of any other product is almost beyond belief. Thus, prevailing ideas and practices relating to labor and its role in the productive process ensure that the volume of the product can never be large enough to divide into any substantial shares for all those who have a hand in producing it. Ultimately, of course, these ideas determine that the level of living for all except a few members of the elite must be very near the mere creature level of existence. Here, too, is a basic value of utmost importance in connection with technical cooperation.

In the fourth place, closely related to the nature of the class structure throughout much of the underdeveloped world, is what might be styled a mindset of resignation, a deep-seated pessimistic outlook on life, a fatalistic acceptance of the idea that the things which work perfectly well in the agriculture of the midwestern United States, Canada, or Western Europe are bound to fail in the world's underdeveloped societies. In part, this negative view arises from the fact that upward vertical mobility is difficult if not impossible, while downward movement in the social scale is all too common, even for many of the abundant offspring of upper-class parents. Many who find themselves sinking to lower levels in the class structure become convinced that in spite of all they might do, the descent is largely inevitable. As a result, there persists the widespread feeling that it is hopeless to accept agricultural innovations or to try new undertakings, and the successful promotion of technical cooperation under these conditions becomes more difficult. In turn, of course, many of the old ways lead only to further failure and to the reinforcement of the belief that long-range plans in agriculture or any other sector of society are futile.

Finally, in many of those places under consideration, education has been largely the exclusive privilege of the elite. Rarely are there any high schools to be found outside the principal cities and towns; frequently elementary schools are lacking as well. Furthermore, the education received often has been that of the "gentleman," encompassing a superficial approach to a wide variety of subjects, often esoteric, but devoid of the concentration in one or a few areas necessary to produce technical specialists. Under these conditions,

442

the educated members of a society are basically unable, even if they are willing, to call upon the intensive, highly focused training necessary to generate technological advancements. Moreover, not a few specialists from the "developed" nations, which attempt to encourage technical cooperation, have found themselves called upon in the "emerging" nations to be generalists, to solve all manner of problems outside of their realms of competence. Some of them are unwilling to attend to the hosts of elementary matters involved, and many are unprepared by training and experience to deal with the practical problems of farming in the areas in which they are working. Consequently, neither local people nor foreign "experts" have been able in many cases to produce substantial technical cooperation.

In general, then, some basic values must be examined critically and many of them changed drastically before technical cooperation can proceed in those vast portions of the world where it is most needed.

Additional Readings

1. BEAL, GEORGE M., *The Roots of Participation in Farmers' Cooperatives*, Ames: Iowa State College, 1954.

2. BEAL, GEORGE M., DONALD R. FESSLER, and RAY E. WAKELEY, *Agricultural Cooperatives in Iowa: Farmers' Opinions and Community Relations*, Iowa AES Research Bulletin No. 379, Ames: Iowa State College, 1951.

3. CRAMPTON, JOHN A., *The National Farmers Union*, Lincoln: University of Nebraska Press, 1965.

4. FOLKMAN, WILLIAM S., "Board Members as Decision Makers in Farmers' Cooperatives," *Rural Sociology*, Vol. 23, No. 3 (September, 1958), pp. 239–252.

5. FOLKMAN, WILLIAM S., "Cooperation and Opposition in Rural Society," in Alvin L. Bertrand (ed.), *Rural Sociology*, New York: McGraw-Hill Book Company, Inc., 1958, chapter 20.

6. FOLKMAN, WILLIAM S., *Membership Relations in Farmers' Purchasing Cooperatives*, Arkansas AES Bulletin No. 556, Fayetteville: University of Arkansas, 1955.

7. KIMBALL, SOLON T., "Rural Social Organization and Coöperative Labor," *American Journal of Sociology*, Vol. 55, No. 1 (July, 1949), pp. 38–49.

8. MAYO, SELZ C., "Age Profiles of Social Participation in Rural Areas of Wake County, North Carolina," *Rural Sociology*, Vol. 15, No. 3 (September, 1950), pp. 242–251.

9. NELSON, LOWRY, *Rural Sociology* (second ed.), New York: American Book Company, 1955, chapter 9.

10. ROGERS, EVERETT M., *Social Change in Rural Society*, New York: Appleton-Century-Crofts, Inc., 1960, chapters 10 and 16.

11. ROHWER, ROBERT A., "Organized Farmers in Oklahoma," *Rural Sociology*, Vol. 17, No. 1 (March, 1952), pp. 39–47.

12. SLOCUM, WALTER L., *Agricultural Sociology*, New York: Harper & Brothers, 1962, chapter 20.

13. SMITH, T. LYNN, *Studies of Latin American Societies*, New York: Doubleday & Co., Inc., 1970, selection 15.

18
HOMOGENIZATION, ACCOMMODATION, ASSIMILATION, and ACCULTURATION

All life is a process of intermingling, adaptation, and adjustment. Society itself is a large system in a vast arena in which individuals and groups are constantly moving about, intermingling, and adjusting themselves to one another, to the physical environment, and to the man-made environment or culture. Sociologists employ a considerable variety of terms in reference to the processes of producing heterogeneity in the makeup of populations and societies, and of bringing about adaptation and adjustment on the part of the dissimilar components of various social bodies. Many of these are not always precisely defined and appropriately used, and some are highly ambiguous. It is no easy task to determine the exact meaning of some of the most generally used terms. Nevertheless at least four concepts seem essential in the analytical study of the processes of intermingling, adaptation, and adjustment. These are: (1) homogenization of society; (2) accommodation; (3) assimilation; and (4) acculturation.

Homogenization is probably the least difficult of the four to understand and define. The term should be used with reference to society in a sense exactly analogous to that it acquired in connection with milk and other liquids. This is to say that the homogenization of society is the process by which such factors as migrations, diffusion, borrowing, and others bring about an intermingling of populations, societal patterns, and cultural traits and thereby create a greater heterogeneity in the composition of society in each given locality while at the same time they are reducing the differences between any two segments of the general society. In other words it is the bringing about of a situation in which all of the societal components are more equally distributed throughout the entire social body.

Adjustment is of two types: one brought about by biological variation and selection, called *adaptation;* and the second due to social adjustments, called *accommodation.* The latter must be defined broadly enough to include social adjustment or accommodation between the man-made and the natural environments. Conflict and accommodation are closely related, the latter either growing out of the former or being the social adjustment between groups who otherwise might come into active conflict. Accommodation groups are many and varied, some of the principal varieties being castes and classes, denominations, clubs, and nations. In contrast are the conflict groups, including such organizations as gangs, sects, and nationalities. The process of accommodation refers to the manner by which a group achieves adjustment with its social milieu and is typified by the transition from gang to club, sect to denomination, nationality to nation. The ultimate result of accommodation is social organization, whereas out of conflict comes political order, and from competition comes a state of equilibrium. Stages in the process of accommodation are domination, toleration, compromise, conciliation, and conversion. A special form of accommodation, *modus vivendi,* occurs when groups in conflict agree to disagree on certain fundamental questions but to carry on together other certain undisputed functions.

The nature of the process of accommodation may also be stated in a slightly different way. If competition becomes immediate, direct, and personal, or if radically different cultures and races come into intimate contact with one another, conflicts are almost sure to arise. But such conflicts often are of necessity short-lived or intermittent. Individuals, groups, and cultures, even though antagonistic to one another, must discover some means of compromise, if only for short breathing spells. Accommodation is properly used to refer to the process by which such differences are resolved. Therefore, it is a rather conscious organization of social relationships to the end of reducing conflict, disciplining competition, and establishing a working agreement that will enable divergent personalities, groups, and cultures to go about their varied activities. Each person or group retains its own characteristic traits, and each adjusts to a situation in which others are permitted the same privilege.

Conflict is not inevitable in the contact of one group, race, or culture with another; some contacts are extremely fleeting, and accommodation is not the only process of adjustment that arises from social and cultural contact. Not infrequently contacts are peaceable; members intermarry, groups fuse, and cultures blend with each other. To these many processes are given the names *assimilation* and *amalgamation*. The distinction between the two is seldom if ever clear. As used by social scientists, assimilation is usually restricted rather rigidly to social aspects, whereas biological crossing or intermarriage is referred to as amalgamation. Nevertheless, assimilation, in the popular mind, and even among some scholars, seems to carry the connotation of biological mixing, so much so that many scholars have prefixed the term with *social* or *cultural* to ensure the sense in which it was used. Assimilation may be thought of more as a political than a cultural concept. Thus, it is the gradual process by which peoples of diverse racial stocks and heterogeneous cultural heritages, when circumtsances place them in a common territory, achieve enough social solidarity to maintain a national existence. We speak of an immigrant as being assimilated when he has lost the marks of the alien and has acquired enough of the language and ritual of his new home to enable him to get along.

But even if assimilation were expanded to include both biological fusing, or amalgamation, and psychosocial processes, all the difficulties with the term would not disappear. Miscegenation coupled with complete acceptance of the cultural heritage still does not guarantee assimilation. For example, although the American Negro's culture is almost exclusively derived from his white fellows, the Negro is not assimilated. There are today in the United States millions of persons more white than black who have completely, both individually and as a group, accepted the cultural heritage of the white Americans. Racially, they stand close to the members of the white group; culturally they are practically identical; nevertheless, socially they stand with the Negroes. It is for this reason that desegregation may be said to be occurring widely in the United States, while true integration remains a relatively uncommon phenomenon. Moreover, a rather complete acceptance of the cultural heritage may occur without miscegenation or intermarriage—many persons of Chinese or Japanese descent, born in the United States, have acquired the American cultural heritage and completely lost that of Asia, without in any sense undergoing a racial change. But in spite of these difficulties, assimilation, viewed as a complete fusion of personalities and physical features, is more thoroughgoing when it is accomplished in the primary group, and particularly in the family where the child's cultural and physical environment is a fusion of those of both parents.

Acculturation is a fourth term used in referring to adaptation or adjustment at the social or cultural level. Anthropologists have applied the term *assimilation* to the process by which cultural synthesis is achieved, and *acculturation* to the results of cultural contact. Sociologists, in general, use the latter term to designate the acquisition by persons or groups of new culture traits and the incorporation of them into their accustomed pattern of living. Unlike assimilation, acculturation thus used includes the acquisition by the individual of the cultural heritage of the group. It is not synonymous with education, because one may know about things or practices in great detail and never adopt them as his own, and may also be unaware of many of the behavior patterns that are most characteristic of his particular group. Not until one adopts as his own and incorporates into his daily pattern of life the new culture traits is he acculturated. Following this line of analysis further, some sociologists have used the term to designate the process of adjusting to culture, and have introduced the compound, *reacculturation,* to refer to the process that occurs when a person who is acculturated into one cultural heritage moves to an area in which another prevails and adjusts himself to the man-made environment of the group residing there. It should be evident from the above that, although the term "acculturation" overlaps in many respects the concept of assimilation, the two are by no means identical. Acculturation has the decided advantage of lacking biological connotations. It also fills a distinct need for a term to designate the process by which the person acquires the cultural heritage of the group into which he is born.

HOMOGENIZATION OF SOCIETY

Most of the dynamic forces at work in society at the present time make greater homogenization nearly inevitable. The net result of their operation, of course, is to bring about a more equal distribution throughout the total society of the various elements of which it is composed. Among these forces are increased movement of people from one part of the nation to another; more social mobility whereby members of the society change their respective social positions with greater ease; and vast improvement in systems of communication, especially the mass media, enabling persons in every corner of the land to be exposed to ideas, attitudes, and patterns of behavior previously unknown to them in their respective segments of the society. Included also are the big-business nature of most industry, which keeps large numbers of workers shifting from place to place; the standardization of education, relieving it in many cases of its sectional characteristics and imbuing it with significantly more cosmopolitan interpretations of subject matter and techniques of teaching; and the tendency for large rural areas to come more under the standardizing influence of ideas engendered in large urban centers. These and other forces impel increasingly in the direction of specific communities that are more heterogeneous internally, whether they are large urban groupings or small rural clusters, and of a total society that is more homogeneous. For example, while the characteristics of people living in a specific hamlet, town, city, or metropolis become increasingly diverse, at the same time they come to resemble more closely those of people living in other such places throughout the length and breadth of the land, until the tendency for the various social elements to be distributed throughout the entire social body becomes a genuine homogenization of society.

Homogenization of society in the United States has progressed relatively far. Therefore, if this society is taken as an example of the phenomenon of homogenization, it is possible to examine several reliable demographic indicators of the form the process has taken and the extent to which it has progressed. In the first place, since 1910, the redistribution of the Negro population has been a significant factor helping to produce homogenization. Before World War I, this large group of people was confined almost exclusively to the rural South, but the war precipitated the migration of large numbers of them to cities of the North and the East. The 1920 to 1930 period of agricultural hardship and great industrial growth then accelerated this rural-to-urban movement to the cities that had been earlier recipients; and a significant number began to flow into the cities of the South during this period as well. The latter movement continued during the depression years of the 1930's when the migration to northern cities slowed. World War II again encouraged the movement of Negroes to cities throughout the nation, and especially to the West Coast, where few had lived previously. Finally, the 1950 to 1960 decade, the most recent one for which data are available, witnessed an acceleration of the movement of Negroes to urban centers. The effect of this overall migration has been to reduce heavy proportional concentrations of Negroes in some parts of the nation while infusing them into the populations of areas that previously had contained practically no members of that race, thereby contributing importantly to the total pattern of homogenization of American society.

Second, the aged population is now far more evenly distributed throughout the nation than it was in 1910; the proportions of persons aged 65 and over in the 50 states are much closer to the national average than they were in the decade following the turn of the century. In that early period, inordinately large numbers of the elderly were found living in New England, the Great Lakes region, and some parts of the Midwest, whereas relatively small numbers could be found in most of the South, the West South Central region, and all of the Mountain and Pacific states, except California. Fifty years later, not only had the proportion of those 65 and over in the total population grown, but the great disparities between the several regions of the United States had been reduced considerably with the accompanying result that the more even distribution of the elderly had become an important factor making for the homogenization of American society.

Third, the historic imbalance between males and females in various parts of the nation has been reduced substantially, helping to produce greater homogenization of American society. Typically, large areas of the West, which once was the great frontier of the continent, contained as many as two thirds more men than women, but at present, even where super-abundances of men are to be found, these seldom exceed the female population by more than 10 per cent. In the same manner, the states of the South, which long has had proportional excesses of women, no longer exhibit substantial imbalances between the sexes. In the case of this demographic factor, too, the fact that few areas of the nation now function under the heavy numerical dominance of either the male or female population has helped to make for substantial homogenization throughout the society.

Fourth, the distinctions between basically rural and fundamentally urban portions of the nation have become far less clear. No longer is it accurate to identify whole states or groups of states as agrarian, generally lacking in cities of any size and in the characteristics that accompany urban living. The very rapid growth in the twentieth century of towns and cities in all parts of the society has been instrumental in precipitating its homogenization, for in no state has the proportion of urban people failed to grow significantly since 1910. Morever, much of the homogenization has occurred because the ideas, attitudes, values, behavior patterns, and other aspects of social organization and the cultural environment that were created in the nation's cities have been diffused throughout the total society. Therefore, the tendency for urbanization to become the way of life for larger and larger proportions of people in all sections of the country is instrumental in effecting the more uniform distribution of the various ethnic, demographic, and social and cultural elements, which we have called "homogenization of society."

Fifth, the religious elements of which society is composed also seem to have become more evenly scattered throughout the entire society. The data necessary to demonstrate this proposition conclusively are incomplete because religious affiliation is not included in the decennial census of population. However, those compiled by the Roman Catholic Church concerning the baptism of children into the membership of the Church are reasonably complete and do indicate that the Roman Catholic population of the United States has become more evenly disseminated throughout the nation. The concentrations have become heavier in some areas and lighter in others, but the general tendency has been for this segment of the population to appear more uniformly throughout the total social body.

Sixth, marital status no longer exhibits wide variations from one area to another. No more do some sections contain large relative scarcities of married people and others great proportional deficiencies of the unmarried; no longer do the social and cultural values that are closely associated with marital status tend to vary as widely from place to place as was the case a half century ago. Even when the factors of age and sex are held constant, the greater evenness with which the various marital categories are distributed offers strong evidence that the homogenization of society in the United States has gone on apace.

Finally, the rate of reproduction now shows greater similarities from one area of the nation to another and from one segment of the society to another. The trend is one of convergence, whereby the levels of reproduction have become more similar between rural and urban populations and among the states of the nation, the various racial and ethnic groups, and even the several socioeconomic strata of which the society is composed. No longer is it accurate to speak of farm areas as the cradle of the nation, nor to stress the prospect of endless fertility differentials between the poor and the affluent. Rather, reproduction rates and the highly significant social values to which they are related, show a strong tendency to join the highly inclusive process of homogenization under whose influence sectional distinctions diminish while local variations become greater.

The foregoing general conclusions concern the United States and are based on observations for that country. However, many of the same forces that have produced homogenization in the nation are at work throughout the present-day world. Urbanization, increasing levels of education and exposure to improved means of communication, reliable transportation, rising aspirations, physical and social mobility, the large-scale commercialization of production of goods and services, and others, contribute in most societies to homogenization. In some places, the increase in uniformity is rudimentary; in others it is as well developed as it is in the United States; but practically everywhere it is going on to some extent. When it becomes possible to depend upon the demographic indicators discussed above for every society, and to collect reliable materials that deal with values, attitudes, customs and habits, basic ideas of right and wrong, and so forth, these can be expected to indicate the growing momentum of this fundamental social process in large areas of the modern world.

ACCOMMODATION

The forms of accommodation or mutual adjustment of groups of people are many and varied. If one were to analyze them in detail, he would have a minute description of the social processes that have crystallized to form a large part of the social organization or structure of any particular society. Only a few of the principal forms that are especially significant in the study of rural society are included in the following pages.

Subordination and superordination seem almost inevitable concomitants of accommodation. Social interaction on terms of absolute equality is inconceivable, especially if a large number of persons is concerned. The result would be not society, but babel. When human beings mingle with one another, the phenomena of subordination and superordination always appear as parts of the overall process of accommodation.

Although adequate analyses of the forms of accommodation in the family, the neighborhood, and the community are lacking, it would seem that these would provide a most fruitful field for study of this important social process. In large numbers of rural families throughout the world, the pattern of subordination and superordination often is as follows: In situations in which all members of the family participate, the function of authority and the responsibility for directing, stimulating, and disciplining the other members of the group rest with the father. In his absence, both the authority and the responsibility reside with the mother. When the children are left by themselves to care for the farm work, the oldest child or the oldest boy receives the mantle of authority to direct the activities of the younger children and is charged with the responsibility of carrying forward the work of the farmstead. In the absence of the oldest son, the responsibility and authority move down the scale to the second oldest child, and so on through the entire membership, until only the youngest member is relieved of the responsibility of directing the work of brothers and sisters. Even he, however, may be charged with the obligation of directing the hired help in the absence of other members of the family group.

Slavery and the system of sharecropping that succeeded it represent some of the most significant forms of accommodation in the rural southern part of the United States. Moreover, the post-slavery period of a century and its various abuses have been examined by many observers of human behavior and thus provide well-studied examples of types of accommodation and adjustment that have occurred in many other parts of the globe. In the beginning, of course, the accommodation between slave and master in the southern United States was imposed by force. The slave had three distinguishing characteristics, slavery three indispensable elements. The slave was the physical property of another person, at the base of the pyramid socially and politically, and a compulsory laborer. Slavery operated to accommodate whites and Negroes of the ante-bellum South to one another; when the established patterns of paternalistic relationships were disturbed by emancipation, great confusion arose. The elimination of slavery did not destroy the customary forms of accommodation between the Negro farm laborers and the white planters of the rural South, however. The system of sharecropping long perpetuated many of the essential features of the old pattern of accommodation.

Viewed from the standpoint of the number of rural persons affected, or of the persistence of the structural pattern, the sharecropping wage system that was in vogue until recently in the cotton states long was one of the most important of all the processes of accommodation to be found in rural America. Moreover, while it has virtually disappeared from the cotton areas of the United States, it remains in wide use in other portions of the globe. Year after year, from immediately after the Civil War and the freeing of the slaves until a decade or so ago, the system provided a working arrangement between the planters and the laborers of the southern states. In the truest sense of the word it provided a general basis upon which the planter and the laboring classes accommodated themselves to each other's efforts. Through the process of accommodation provided by sharecropping, millions of laborers, white and Negro, together with the southern landlords, annually produced the nation's most important commercial crop. At the same time, of course, the system was a rigid one, which often relied on coercion and violence, and which eventually helped to produce both revolts and endemic nonviolent resistance.

The origin of the channels through which the accommodative processes flowed goes back to the years immediately following the Civil War. When the slaves received their freedom, the change spelled, of course, the disruption of the previous form of accommodation characteristic of the system of slavery. Immediately, at the close of the war, great problems of accommodation faced the landowners of the dismantled South and the Negroes who drifted back to their accustomed haunts after their first brief experience of freedom and individual self-responsibility. The first working arrangement attempted was well known in other sections of the country, namely, the payment of cash wages for labor. Money was scarce, however, and for this and other reasons the attempt proved unsatisfactory and was abandoned after a brief period of trial. It was soon replaced by sharecropping, the evolution of which is well analyzed by Robert Preston Brooks. He outlines the developments as follows: (1) At first among the Negroes the belief was widespread that the plantations would be carved up into parcels and presented to the ex-slaves as Christmas gifts in December, 1865. (2) To cope with the Negroes' newly secured liberty to move from place to place, strict vagrancy laws were passed—the county court was empowered to bind out the vagrant for a twelve-month period. (3) The plantation organization, then as now, required close supervision of all the details of operation; those engaged in cotton planting never had the slightest idea of abandoning this feature. (4) As early as 1865 the cash-wage system was under fire: wages fixed by the Freedmen's Bureau were relatively high, money was practically nonexistent, the planter could not demand steady work from his hands, and the evidence concerning the general unreliability of the wage hands was overwhelming. (5) By 1867 labor was extremely scarce and the planters were forced to make terms with the Negroes; however, even in 1869 a convention of planters agreed that the old wage system was superior to the newer sharecropping system that was being adopted. (6) Brought into the arena at the same time were the Negro's dislike of close supervision, the great demand for labor, and the scarcity of cash. (7) The crop lien, which at first was a device whereby the planter received advances from the merchant by pledging his crop as security, came into being; later it was adopted between the planter and the cropper also. (8) Some merchants attempted to combine planting with their mercantile enterprises, and there arose a tendency for the Negroes to abandon the strict planter-regulated plantations for the looser merchant-regulated farming arrangements; here the phenomenon of absenteeism came into full play. (9) The lien laws, however, proved to be effective agencies in transforming the system; the planters refused to assign their liens to merchants, and instead procured supplies, "furnished" their laborers, and deferred settlement until the end of the year; the laborer or cropper received the value of the crop he produced less the advances he had secured; both were willing to give up money payments, the planter because he was alarmed at the fall in the price of cotton and the laborer because he was dismayed at the drop in wages; the planter did not give up his right of supervision, but it was relaxed. (10) The workers on the plantation were all placed under supervision; the others became renters (Ref. 49, pp. 13–63).

Thus, slavery was simply replaced by another form of accommodation sometimes as abusive of the Negro population as the previous bondage had been. Under slavery, Negroes themselves were bought and sold as laborers, and economic prudence required that the plantation owner maintain them in a manner that at least preserved life and health in order to gain the maximum return from his substantial investment in human bodies. The plantation required a high level of agricultural, business, and other skills, and it necessitated adequate physical treatment of slaves. With emancipation, human beings no longer were traded but their labor continued to be bargained for under what finally emerged as the sharecropping system. The "free" Negro found himself trading his labor for crop wages, not merely to the owners of large plantations, but also to those marginal operators whose planning involved nothing more than accumulating sufficient Negro laborers to produce a crop in a given year, often on rented land. Under these conditions, of course, maximum work for minimum wages and subsistence allowances, trickery and cajolery by those who hired them, and an abiding low level of existence became the lot of a large proportion of free Negroes (see Ref. 486, pp. 13–14).

Generally, under a sharecropping system, the worker makes available only his labor whereas the landlord supplies all other means of production. Such a situation obviously places virtually all the risk on the latter, and as a result, he usually expects to exercise complete control over the activities of the laborer. The pattern of accommodation represented in sharecropping is a fairly complex one, in that the details of the arrangement usually are worked out in such a way that the respective contributions of the landlord and laborer amount to a partnership between them; but it is not an efficient partnership, for each contributes an absolute minimum of the means of production necessary to produce what often amounts to a meager crop. At most points in the relationship, each is concerned primarily with extracting the maximum advantage from the other while contributing as little as possible to the arrangement. However, in this case the laborer is usually far less able to manipulate the situation to his advantage than is the landowner; and the worker frequently falls back upon the only weapon at his command—resistance to performing efficiently the job that he has contracted to do. Furthermore, in the United States, the landlord frequently supplied the laborer with living quarters, food, and small amounts of money and kept a running account of this indebtedness. When the crop was harvested and divided, the amount of the debt was deducted from the worker's share; and while croppers benefited in a few cases from this arrangement, more often it served to keep them economically, socially, and psychologically dependent upon the landlord. In effect, this dependence made the system very little different from the earlier condition of slavery. Even when sharecropping passed into oblivion in the United States not many years ago, it was plagued by disproportionately great advantages gained by landlords over laborers, general lack of incentive among workers to produce efficiently, and the notion, lingering from the days of emancipation from slavery, that liberty was tantamount to idleness.

As early as 1869, there was much discussion of the relative merits of cash wages and sharecropping as forms of accommodative relationships between the planters and their work hands. One of the most interesting studies is that conducted by Loring & Atkinson, Cotton Brokers and Agents of Boston, Massachusetts (Ref. 263). This firm circulated widely throughout the South a questionnaire asking for information concerning these conditions and practices in the hope of being able to use the information to encourage people and capital to move into the cotton belt. The materials secured are of the highest interest and the conclusions of great significance. Loring and Atkinson reported the existence of share and wage laboring systems and concluded that both systems had advantages and disadvantages. For the share system these advantages are listed as follows:

1. It stimulates industry by giving the laborer an interest and pride in the crop. It has been found by experience that comparatively a small part of the laborers are influenced by these stimulants, but with this small class they certainly have a positive existence.

2. It is regarded by the laborer as a higher form of contract, and is, therefore, more likely to secure labor, especially in undesirable localities.

3. It gives the laborer a motive to protect the crop.

4. It does not subject the farmer to loss from a failure of, or a decline in, value of his crop.

5. It secures laborers for the year, with less likelihood of his breaking the contract, a thing he sometimes likes to do when the hard work begins.

Some of the disadvantages of the share system are—

1. The difficulty of discharging hands when they become inefficient or refractory.

2. The great difficulty of carrying on the general work of the farm, the tendency being to drift into a mere system of cropping, the most pernicious of all systems under which the laborer of a country has ever been employed—a system that leads to idleness on the part of the laborer for a large part of the year, to indolence and indifference on the part of the farm owner, to decay and ruin in the farm, and general decline in the productive resources of the country.

3. The annoyance and perplexity of harvesting and dividing the crop, requiring the gin-house to be subdivided, and leading to a great loss of time in ginning and packing the crop. Also, settlements are often unsatisfactory at present on account of the ignorance of the negro, and his tendency to suspect unfair dealing.

4. The disadvantage of having the laborers dictate methods of cultivation according to their own notions, which are seldom the right ones. (Ref. 263, pp. 28–30).

They likewise indicated the following advantages of the wage system:

1. It gives the farmer control over the labor, he having the power to discharge.

2. It stimulates industry and enterprise in the farmer. Profits go into his pockets, losses come on his shoulders.

456

3. It leads to economy in labor, causing the farmer to reduce the laborers to the smallest number consistent with the execution of the work, substituting mule labor and labor-saving machines for hand labor, both tending to *make labor more abundant*.

4. It enables the farmer to carry out a general system of improvement on his farm; to keep the fences, ditches, roads and buildings all in proper repair, and to pay due attention to other crops than cotton, all of which is impossible under the present share system.

5. It necessitates close personal attention from the farmer, *forcing* thriftiness upon him and preventing indolence, for the very essence of the system lies in constant and active supervision (Ref. 263, p. 30).

Probably biased in favor of the wage system and ignorant of the psycho-social equipment of the ex-slave, Loring and Atkinson were unable to find any noteworthy disadvantages to cash wages except that "the wage system labors under the *temporary* disadvantage that the freedman prefers a share, and having complete control, he prevents its use" (Ref. 263, emphasis supplied). Temporary disadvantage or not, sharecropping remained in most general use in the South until the rapid mechanization of cotton production after World War II disrupted these arrangements, which had been in vogue for more than three quarters of a century. This mechanization ended the great dependence on human labor that pervaded cotton production for over two centuries and brought to an end in the United States the widespread use of the debilitating sharecropping system. Of course, few students of society, acquainted as they are with the gradualness of social and cultural evolution, are surprised that the cropper system, which resembled more closely the old slave system than it did the cash-wage system, should be the pattern of accommodation that persisted so long in the cotton belt.

One of the principal elements in sharecropping as an accommodative process in the South was that of supervision; neglect of this element probably leads to more misunderstanding of the plantation complex in various parts of the world than does any other single thing. The amount of supervision that the management of the plantation would exercise was usually understood in advance, and it often was so complete that all the cropper's agricultural endeavors were directly supervised by the landlord or his manager. On closely supervised plantations throughout the South, the landlord usually determined the holidays, and these amounted to two or three days a year; Saturday afternoons and Sundays were rest periods; funerals also were an occasion for holidays. The management controlled the work stock, although frequently the hands were allowed to use them for going to town and even for work off the plantation. As a rule, each cropper was assigned a work animal for the year, although some plantations pooled the livestock and distributed it weekly. Implements, too, were usually allotted for the season, but several families may have had to share a common piece of equipment such as a farm wagon. The assignment of plots to croppers was largely in the hands of the landlord, although at certain seasons of the year all the laborers may have been concentrated into a gang and worked as a single unit. Often this was done at planting and harvesting times. Daily rounds were made by the plantation manager for the purpose of instructing the workers in the details of the cultivation process and inspecting the lands and crops; but these tours had the important effect of reiterating constantly the lack of autonomy and freedom of operation available to the cropper in the performance of his farming tasks.

Another of the most interesting and significant processes of accommodation now under way in rural America is that going on between farmers' trade centers of various types. There was a time when every trade center, from the general store at the crossroads to the large wholesale and retail center, was striving to be a complete service center for all the farmers associated with it. Every village and hamlet, from those that grew around essential services to those artificially propagated by the coming of the railroad, had visions of growing and developing into a large metropolis. Many village policies were framed with this as the basic consideration rather than the question of most efficiently and satisfactorily filling the immediate needs of the farmers in its trade basin. The merchants in a given village, instead of concerning themselves with the type of service they were best fitted to render, frequently banded together and subsidized highly uneconomical specialized retail units, such as shoe stores, to persuade them to locate in the village. Before the coming of the automobile and hard-surfaced roads, the internal structure of farm trade centers showed little tendency toward specialization; every trading place from the open-country store up was in serious competition with every other.

Galpin early observed the intense competition between existing trade centers, sensed the importance of the automobile and good roads in the competitive process, and reflected upon the changes that were to occur. According to him, when the crossroads post office was replaced by the rural free delivery route, a decline occurred in the hamlet; farmers began to relate themselves to larger and larger towns; hamlets and villages were started on an endurance test for their lives. The coming of the automobile made it still more difficult for the small and inefficient centers to survive. These developments led Galpin to conclude that eventually each farm family would be related to a single, large, and complete retail center (Ref. 138, p. 91). Thus he conceived the competition between trade centers as a bitter struggle that would end only when large numbers of them had been eliminated, leaving a much smaller number of large farmers' towns or rurban communities. However, since Galpin wrote, the process of accommodation has actually given rise to a quite different situation, preserved the great mass of the small trade centers, created new ones, and in general is making rural trading facilities a much more differentiated system, rather than simplifying them as Galpin predicted.

Since 1900 there has been a tendency in the United States for centers of various sizes to become distributed far more evenly throughout the nation. This movement has had the effect of increasing the efficiency of rural organization by placing each farm family in contact with several centers of varying sizes and has freed them from the situation in which their loyalties and interests were tied only to one. It has also had the homogenizing influence of reducing the differences between locality groups throughout the nation, and, of course, has simultaneously increased the internal heterogeneity of more localized clusters of centers. Furthermore, the internal structure of American trade centers has changed greatly. Principally, centers of various sizes have become increasingly specialized, dividing among them the various services, agencies, institutions, and other means of meeting needs required by farm families. Thus, small centers tend to specialize in caring for the most immediate requirements of farm people; medium-sized centers tend to see to a larger number of less pressing needs; and the largest, most heterogeneous towns tend to fulfill those that are the least urgent, which often can be met on the relatively infrequent occasions when the farm family is able to travel the distance involved and to expend the time required to seek the services of the largest centers. This division of labor among trade centers of various sizes has become increasingly pronounced since the turn of the century. One result, of course, is to preserve large numbers of small centers, not because they are capable of meeting all the needs of given farm families, but because they are specialists engaged in attending to a fraction of the total requirements of those families. Some small trade centers, especially those that are poorly situated with respect to arteries of transportation, will certainly disappear, but a great many others will avoid the fate that Galpin predicted for them.

These general conclusions concerning the persistence of many small trade centers meeting certain specialized needs rather than the general requirements of farm people are supported by an early study by Sanderson (Fig. 61).

An investigation of the settlement of the Great Plains of the United States and of the subsequent cultural evolution in the area also gives a great deal of insight into the process of accommodation. In this case the more important aspects of the adjustment are those involved in the accommodation of social institutions to physiographic features that are radically different from those

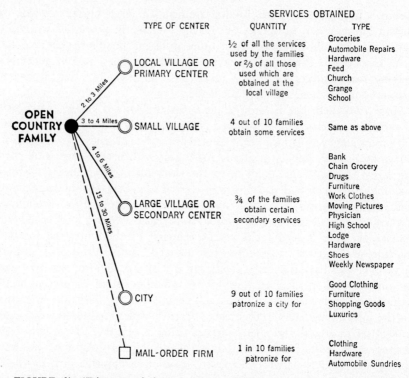

FIGURE 61. "Diagram of the relations to service centers of an average open-country family living within the service areas of a medium-sized village." Reproduced from Dwight Sanderson, *Rural Social and Economic Areas in Central New York*, Cornell Agricultural Experiment Station Bulletin 614, Ithaca, 1934, p. 95.

in which the institutions were generated and by which they were conditioned. No aspect of cultural evolution is more interesting, and few cases of accommodation have been more important to social welfare than that involved in the most satisfactory use of the resources of the plains states.

Before the settlement of the Great Plains in the latter half of the nineteenth century, American institutions had evolved in a natural environment whose predominant features were (1) a humid climate, (2) forested lands, and (3) gently rolling to hilly terrain. As the frontier edged forward through the semihumid fringe of the plains and onto the plains proper, these natural features gave way to a world that was semiarid, treeless, and relatively flat. Although a foresighted few recognized that existing institutions were inadequate to cope with the problems of settlement and successful living in this radically different milieu, their alarms went unheeded. The process of settlement proceeded rapidly along the lines previously deeply graved in the cultural patterns of the American frontier. Few examples of cultural lag are more clear cut than this one.

Let us examine a little more closely the problems that arose at the time of settlement of this vast area. First, settlement was approaching the geographical limits of the subhumid region, within which average annual rainfall varied from 20 to 28 inches. West of the isohyetal line of 20 inches of rainfall, roughly delineated by the 100th meridian (which forms the eastern boundary of the Texas Panhandle and divides the Dakotas into nearly equal parts) successful agriculture is possible only by means of irrigation. However, adequate water being unavailable throughout most of the vast area, the land should have been devoted almost exclusively to grazing, not on holdings the size of the 160-acre homesteads, but on those of least 2,000 or 3,000 acres. Included within each should have been small irrigated tracts to supply necessary foodstuffs. Moreover, strict controls on ownership of water rights and use of the line village as a settlement pattern should have been logical ways of organizing the opening up of the plains.

As is well known, no such desirable modifications in our land policy were ever put into general effect. Land policies generated in and adapted to humid regions were continued when settlement overspread the plains. The wide expanses of the arid, treeless plains were homesteaded in small tracts, and a large part of them put under the plow.

Experience in the years following early settlement has thoroughly substantiated the conclusion that most of these lands are better suited for grazing than for the cultivation of crops and that basic changes in land policies were essential. There was a rapid influx of settlers into the plains, especially in the decade 1880 to 1890, when population gains took place amounting to 299 per cent in the Dakotas, 265 per cent in Montana, 201 per cent in Wyoming, 135 per cent in Nebraska, and 113 per cent in Colorado. In the next decade, however, drought was intense, and the area staged a dress rehearsal of the tragic "dust bowl" era that was to come in the 1930's. As a result, many homesteads were abandoned, and large numbers of people left the stricken area. Depopulation and bitter experience promoted the process of accommodation; but as the effects of the first disaster became more remote, people again flocked onto the lands west of the 100th meridian. World War I and the high prices for wheat brought tremendous acreages of the arid lands under the plow, and with the destruction of the buffalo grass, the stage was rapidly set again for the dust bowl disaster of the Thirties.

These data should not be interpreted to mean that the process of accommodation was not working. Fundamental changes were operating to bring about a more satisfactory adjustment of people and institutions to the natural environment. Indeed, it is unlikely that the process of accommodation has ever moved more rapidly than it did in the plains states during the last century. Some of the widely diffused inventions that made adjustment possible were the six-shooter, which enabled the newcomers to wrest the plains from the Indians and to modify the legal patterns inherited from the East; barbed wire, which enabled the shift from an open-range grazing economy to one that involved the destruction of the sod cover and the cultivation of moisture-depleting crops; and the windmill, which freed people from settlement near surface water supplies and allowed them to establish their residences broadly across the entire plains. Desirable aspects of the necessary adjustment included the enlarging of the homestead unit and the revision of land and water laws. To be sure, lawmakers reversed the trend toward smaller homesteads and revised the land laws to recognize the value and necessity of timber culture and of grazing; there were also changes in water laws and riparian rights. More recent planning of soil and water use has produced such practices as alternate-year cropping to preserve soil moisture, the use of cover crops, and others. However, these efforts to improve the adjustment between people and the land were not sufficient, for the accommodation process must still make much headway before the inhabitants of the Great Plains will have a culture adjusted to the environment. After World War II, a succession of relatively wet years and high prices for wheat seemed to cause many people to forget the hardships and depopulation of 1930 to 1940; but in more recent years, renewed threats of serious drought and the accelerated flow of people away from agriculture generally have helped to bring about sufficient depopulation in the area under consideration to improve the balance between people and the land. Agriculture in the area seems to be coming to adapt better to the natural conditions of the plains, and the process of accommodation has now produced a more logical and responsible relationship between men and the land than has existed throughout the period of nonindigenous settlement.

ASSIMILATION

Not only does the late and unlamented southern system of sharecropping represent one of the most important examples of the process of accommodation that has operated in rural America, but the incorporation of hundreds of thousands of whites into that pattern offers one of the significant instances of assimilation. This incorporation appears to have reached its maximum around 1930 or 1935, when the number of croppers was the largest on record and the geographic dispersion of the sharecropping system the greatest. According to data in the *1935 Census of Agriculture,* nonwhite sharecroppers in the southern states totaled 368,408, and the number of whites was only slightly less, 347,848. Proportionately, of course, Negroes were in excess, but geographically whites disseminated the cropping pattern much more widely than did Negroes.

The evidence also seems to indicate that the whites were so thoroughly incorporated into the system that in many respects the outlook and status of the white sharecropper were not very different from those of his Negro fellow. Of course, the positions of members of both races were uniformly quite low. During the heyday of the system, a given plantation might shift suddenly from Negro to white labor, or vice versa; families of one race would move into cabins recently vacated by those of the other, and on the same terms; women and children of the white race worked in the fields as did the Negroes. In fact, many plantations depended entirely upon white people for labor. The paternalistic landlords believed it to be their obligation to take care of the sharecroppers, and the croppers expected aid from the planters whenever they fell into financial difficulty; and this attitude of dependence was found no less often among whites than among Negroes. In the rural South, tenure status was often quite alike for members of both races so that the one found itself victimized and restricted by the sharecropping system to about the same degree as the other. So thoroughly were the whites assimilated into the sharecropping monolith that the stereotype of the "childlike" cropper, improvident and laboring regularly only because of hunger, and sustained by the benevolent paternalism of the landlord, finally fitted them as well as it did the Negroes. Likewise, the cropper's basic assumption that there was "nothin' but a livin' in it" for him found as ready acceptance by the white man as by the Negro. Thus the parallel status and consistency of behavior patterns, attitudes, expectations, and outlooks reflected a high degree of assimilation of whites and Negroes in the sharecropping complex of a decade or two ago.

ACCULTURATION

Studies on the blendings of culture are only in their beginning stages. In the analysis of culture contacts between primitive groups the cultural anthropologists have made a creditable beginning, but much less is known concerning the nature of the cultural fusions occurring among more advanced civilizations. Despite the fact that rural America long has been a great crucible in which the most heterogeneous cultural elements have been combined into something of a cultural unity, the details of the process are still unknown. In this field, as in so many others, the questions that can be asked are of much greater significance than are those that can be answered.

In all having to do with acculturation and the other members of the "culture" family that has proliferated to such an extent since about 1930, the student needs to exercise the utmost in the way of insight and critical discrimination. The fact is that looseness is much more prevalent than exactness in the general usages of the fundamental terms and concepts. Most confusing of all is the frequency with which culture or one of its derivatives is used when social or societal obviously is the meaning involved. It may be helpful to keep in mind that culture is man-made environment; whereas society is structures and actions or activities. For example, the reasons for which, in the contemporary United States, John Doe marries Mary Roe in a civil or religious ceremony to form a monogamous union are cultural; but all the activities connected with the arrangements, possible rehearsals, and the nuptial rites themselves are social or societal. Culture provides the forms and regulations that are involved; and society the interactions among all of the persons who take part in any way.

Several beginnings have been made in the kind of analysis essential before the workings of the process of acculturation among rural social groupings throughout the world can be understood. Fundamental to all is a study of social origins, and fortunately, this has not been entirely neglected. In tracing the history of American agriculture, for example, the contributions of the American Indian have been noted. It is well known that the cultivation of maize, "Irish" potatoes, sweet potatoes, beans, squash, tomatoes, pineapples, tobacco, peanuts, several varieties of cotton, and many other plants was among the cultural practices of the aborigines of this hemisphere. It has also been pointed out that the Indian's agricultural methods were made part and parcel of the farm practices of the colonists. From the Indians also came the methods of preparing many foods for consumption. An important field for research would be a thorough analysis of the elements found in contemporary agricultural systems, indicating both material and nonmaterial elements borrowed from indigenous populations, those brought by the first arrivals from other parts of the world, those derived from various ethnic and cultural groups migrating in more recent years, and those invented or discovered in specific societies since the arrival of the first nonindigenous or foreign elements. Until this analysis has been made, little understanding of the basic features in agricultural progress and change can be secured. Similar investigations are needed with respect to food habits and many other phases of culture. In the absence of such thoroughgoing studies it is doubtful that even the cultural differences between the various regions of a society can be properly evaluated. For instance, to what extent are the agricultural practices of the midwestern United States the product of a cultural blending of the best ideas, skills, and techniques of Europe grafted onto the old Indian and colonial stocks? Do those of the South represent primarily an evolution of the cross between Indian and colonial sources? Had immigration been lacking, would the agricultural techniques of the United States be as far advanced as they are? What is the correct role of agricultural experimentation in the growth and diffusion of agricultural skills? Or, taking a different society, to what degree are the farming practices and agrarian way of life in southern Brazil a result of the combination of recent elements brought from Portugal, Germany, Poland, Japan and other nations with those that were developed by the early Portuguese colonists, their Negro slaves, and the indigenous predecessors?

The great variety and wealth of ideas and skills brought to such countries as these by immigrants have seldom received much attention; yet some work now being done indicates clearly that it is naive to consider as one sided the process by which the immigrant stock—with all its material objects, customs, social organization, and so on—becomes merged with the larger society. Actually, it is many faceted; and because all the phases of culture are affected, as well as individual persons, the process is more properly referred to as acculturation that as assimilation. For example, the process of acculturation, operating in the United States, has involved Norwegians, Poles, Welsh, and other ethnic groups in the Great Lakes region. It has encompassed the cultures of many Indian tribes and those of the French, Spanish, Anglo-Americans, and Negroes in Oklahoma, where the New South converges with the West. Acculturation has taken place widely in the Southwest where various ethnic strains have come together to produce a blending of Spanish-American and Anglo-American cultures. Finally, it has gone on freely in Louisiana where persons of Anglo-Saxon, African, Spanish, and French cultural heritages have come together to a sufficient extent to produce a culture blend unlike that to be found anywhere else in the society.

The work of diffusing or introducing agricultural technology illustrates the process of acculturation in many parts of the earth. It involves the blending of farming practices that long have prevailed in given societies as part of the cultural heritage with those that are introduced from outside the communities or societies involved. Therefore, the receipt of new agricultural technology and practices, the adoption of certain aspects of these, and the adaptation and general rebuilding of the new technology and the receiving culture to fit each other all represent the acculturative process. Acculturation of this kind may result in changes in social organization and the cultural environment that are far-reaching in their influence on the people involved, and may precipitate sequential chains of still other changes. For example, the development and widespread adoption of sophisticated agricultural technology early in the twentieth century in the United States freed large numbers of workers from farm employment at the same time that the maturing Industrial Revolution created great demands for industrial workers. In turn, this change helped to bring about a massive stream of migration from the farms to the cities. Eventually, the great migration and tendency to congregate in huge metropolitan areas brought into being a form of American society that is fundamentally urban in major respects. Finally, the pervasive nature of urbanization in the United States has been very significant in making for the homogenization of the total society and for greater heterogeneity in local communities or groups of communities.

The studies of the diffusion and adoption of new agricultural practices is a major line of work among the current generation of rural sociologists, and the body of knowledge already available relative to this aspect of the process of acculturation is considerable. More remains to be done to integrate this work with what is known about the sociocultural entities designated as the systems of agriculture (Chapter 9), and with our understanding of the great transplantations of agricultural knowledge prior to the flourishing of the agricultural experiment stations and the agricultural extension services in the United States since 1925. Agriculture and rural life in this country, for example, owe much to great purposeful introduction of specific crops and cropping systems, such as the rice culture for which Thomas Jefferson was largely responsible, and the cane-sugar industry that was transplanted from Hispaniola to Louisiana by the planters who were successful in escaping to the mainland during the great agrarian reform that took place in Haiti as part of the French Revolution. They also are based in no small part on the mass transfer of the production techniques from one crop to another. Consider, for example, the application of farming techniques that had been perfected for wheat growing to the raising of rice in Louisiana by farmers who migrated from the midwestern states to the prairies of that state late in the nineteenth century. In addition, there are at least a few cases in which an entire type of farming was transplanted from one nation to another.

Such examples as these could be examined in detail in many other parts of the world such as Brazil, broad realms of the Caribbean area, Africa, wide sections of Europe, Southeast Asia, and others; but much more study and research are necessary before these specific examples are properly known and before the operation and results of the process of acculturation will be thoroughly understood. (For one example of careful research on the adoption of agricultural practices and its relationship to other sociocultural factors, see Ref. 366. See also the issue devoted to this topic, *Rural Sociology*, Vol. 23, No. 2 [June, 1958]; and Ref. 382.)

Additional Readings

1. BERTRAND, ALVIN L., *Basic Sociology: An Introduction to Theory and Method,* New York: Appleton-Century-Crofts, Inc., 1967, chapters 4–7 and 12.

2. FUJII, YUKIO, and T. LYNN SMITH, *The Acculturation of Japanese Immigrants in Brazil,* Gainesville: University of Florida Press, 1959.

3. HALPERN, JOEL M., *The Changing Village Community,* Englewood Cliffs, N. J.: Prentice-Hall, Inc., 1967.

4. HOSTETLER, JOHN A., "Old World Extinction and New World Survival of the Amish: A Study of Group Maintenance and Dissolution," *Rural Sociology,* Vol. 20, Nos. 3–4 (September-December, 1955), pp. 212–219.

5. MOORE, WILBERT, *Social Change,* Englewood Cliffs, N. J.: Prentice-Hall, Inc., 1963, chapters 4–6.

6. NELSON, LOWRY, *Rural Sociology* (second ed.,), New York: American Book Company, 1955, chapter 10.

7. PARENTON, VERNON J., "Socio-Psychological Integration in a Rural French-Speaking Section of Louisiana," *Southwestern Social Science Quarterly,* Vol. XXX, No. 3 (1950), pp. 188–195.

8. PRICE, PAUL H., and GEORGE A. HILLERY, JR., *The Rural-Urban Fringe and Louisiana's Agriculture,* Louisiana AES Bulletin No. 526, Baton Rouge: Louisiana State University, 1959.

9. SANDERSON, DWIGHT, *Rural Social and Economic Areas in Central New York,* Cornell AES Bulletin No. 614, Ithaca: Cornell University, 1934.

10. SLOCUM, WALTER L., *Agricultural Sociology,* New York: Harper & Brothers, 1962, chapter 12.

11. SMITH, T. LYNN, "The Homogenization of Society in the United States," *Memoire du XIX Congress International de Sociologie,* Vol. 2 (1960), pp. 245–275.

12. SMITH, T. LYNN, *Studies of Latin American Societies,* New York: Doubleday & Co., Inc., 1970, selection 16.

13. VANDIVER, JOSEPH S., "Accommodation, Assimilation, and Acculturation," in Alvin L. Bertrand (ed.), *Rural Sociology,* New York: McGraw-Hill Book Company, Inc., 1958, chapter 21.

19

SOCIAL MOBILITY

The shifting of persons or culture traits in social space, i.e., from one social group or class to another, is properly referred to as social mobility. Movement from group to group without respect to vertical or class differences is known as *horizontal* mobility; and the shifting of traits or persons up or down in the social scale, as *vertical* mobility. Social climbing or sinking may occur within the group on the part of the individual member, or it may take place as the whole group gains or loses status in the general society. A given change may include mobility of both types, and frequently the breaking of old group ties and the establishment of new ones are associated with changes of both a horizontal and a vertical nature. Migration, the movement of persons or traits in physical space, is associated but is not synonymous with social mobility. Nomadic tribes constantly on the move may exhibit little or no social mobility, and that which does exist is not a function of migration. As mentioned in Chapter 4, individuals may move from farm to farm, from the farms to the cities, and so on, and yet experience no change in social position. Certainly, migratory agricultural laborers, physically among the most mobile groups in a society, tend to find that their lowly social positions readily become ossified and that the channels of vertical social mobility are almost completely closed to them. Whether or not measurable changes in status occur, in sedentary societies the movement of a person from one territory to another is nearly always accompanied by the disruption of old group relationships and the establishment of new ones. In the case of the migrant laborers, though, few of these relationships and ties ever come into being, and consequently, there are few to be broken up and altered.

GENERAL CHARACTERISTICS AND EFFECTS OF SOCIAL MOBILITY

Social mobility may occur in connection with any of the wide variety of social groups that become differentiated from one another in the course of social evolution. (For the early classic work on the subject, see Ref. 473.) Particularly significant are those forms of mobility involving the increase or decrease of wealth and income; the gain or loss of prestige, power, privilege, and authority; the shifting from one occupational group to another; and the significant changes that may occur in the level of education.

Some societies are highly mobile, others quite immobile; but no society, including those with rigid caste systems, is known in which the various social strata have been entirely closed to members from the other layers, nor is any society known in which there have been absolutely no obstacles connected with shifts from one class or group to another. Moreover, there is no record of the long-time existence of a truly classless society of any appreciable size, in which vertical mobility, hypothetically, would be totally absent. Vertical social movement is present to some degree in every society because there is everywhere the one condition that is fundamental to its existence—a system of stratification. This universal structural condition exists because a pattern of social layers, each composed of persons with certain common elements of status, is a functional necessity; it enables a society to offer to its members the differential rewards of status, prestige, power and authority, and so on necessary to recruit personnel to perform the multitude of tasks that the society wishes to have carried out. Furthermore, unless those who comprise the various strata of society reproduce themselves in numbers precisely commensurate with the numbers of positions to be filled and jobs to be done at each level, there will be some kind of movement up or down as certain individuals are recruited to function at higher levels and others, less capable or constituting a surplus, are relegated to lesser positions. For example, in many of the countries of Latin America, the fertility rates among the members of small landowning elites are sufficiently high to produce more people than there are old and new positions in this exalted stratum of society. Thus some unavoidably find themselves forced in a downward direction, often into an amorphous intermediate stratum between the top and bottom extremes of the stratification system, sometimes into a genuine middle class, and occasionally into the lower class. (For an analysis of this phenomenon in one Latin American country, see Ref. 445, pp. 339–342.) In this manner, relatively high fertility sets the stage for a certain amount of vertical mobility, even in an area where societies long have been rigidly stratified and where the class system often is spoken of as being closed.

There seems to be no evidence of a perpetual, uninterrupted and irreversible trend of increase or decrease in mobility of the vertical type. Rather, this process varies in magnitude and in the proportions of people involved from place to place, group to group, and time to time, even in the same society. In a given society there appears to be a rhythmic variation from mobile periods to immobile periods. Mobility seems to be greater in the so-called democracies than in the autocracies, but there are many exceptions to the rule. In the case of vertical mobility, or the shifting up or down the social pyramid, a wide variety of social institutions serve as channels of circulation; many agencies play the role of staircase or elevator. Important among these are the army, the church, the school, governmental hierarchies or bureaucracies, political parties, professional societies, economic organizations such as corporations, and the family. Their importance as channels of vertical social circulation, as agencies for lifting some persons up the social scale and debasing others, varies in time and space; but everywhere and always some of them are functioning to shift persons from one social class to another. However, the rising and sinking of persons in the social scale is not a matter of chance; there is a certain selectivity involved. The same social institutions that serve as channels of vertical circulation also serve as agencies of testing and selection; these agencies sort and grade the persons in the population and tend to place them in a social class commensurate with their abilities, at least in societies where there can be relatively free movement from class to class. It is a fact of fundamental importance that the church, the school, the family, and the occupational institutions are not only agencies for passing on the cultural heritage from one generation to another, but also are instruments of selection and distribution, testing grounds that are largely responsible for sorting out the types of persons who rise or sink in a given society. If the institutions perform their functions well, the distribution of persons within the social classes is equitable and in accordance with the capacities of the individuals; if they fail to perform efficiently the tasks of testing, selecting, and distributing the members of society throughout the social classes in an equitable manner, men located in positions for which they are not fitted or in which they are not interested can weaken or even destroy society itself.

The factors that bring about vertical mobility are many, but three seem to be primary. (1) In many places, differential fertility of people in the social classes has the net result of creating a vacuum in the higher social layers and bringing about the rise of persons from the middle and lower classes to fill the vacancies created by the failure of the upper classes to reproduce themselves. There are exceptions, though, such as that in parts of Latin America noted above. (2) Biological variation continually endows some children with more ability than their parents, some children with less, so that the offspring are not always suited for positions in society that correspond exactly with those occupied by their parents. These discrepancies cause some sinking and some rising on the social scale. (3) Every change of the cultural base, or man-made environment, affects the populations of various social strata. In times of disorder—strikes, revolution, war, or racial conflict—a particular type of personality may rise rapidly to prominence, that in times of peace and order might remain undisturbed in an inferior position. Some military leaders, for example, may be relatively unsuccessful as private citizens, possessed of little potential to rise in the social scale, until conditions of war materialize and boost them into prominence through the military channel of mobility. Or skilled artisans enjoying relatively high status in the handicraft stage of social evolution may degenerate into the less respected category of the "jack-of-all-trades" when the factory system comes to dominate society. Religious personnel of many types may enjoy exalted positions in the prescientific times of a given society, only to lose much of this esteem when science and rationality come to pervade social life, but to rise again when the group generates crises and questions that seem to have satisfactory explanations and answers only in the realms of the nonempirical or supernatural. The history of man is replete with examples of secularization and religious resurgence of which this kind of mobility is a vital part.

Effects of Social Mobility

The process of social mobility has significant and far-reaching effects upon the general nature of the larger society, the personalities of the individuals making it up, the system of social organization, and the nature of the other social processes. The general effects of social mobility are discussed immediately; those more peculiar to rural society are given near the end of the chapter.

Intense vertical mobility that is generated through a progressive wasting of the upper class of society, if long continued, might ultimately lead to the disintegration of society itself. It could be that under such circumstances the city would progressively drain from the country those who ranked high in the social pyramid and the upper classes would draw off the most capable elements from the middle and lower classes. Ultimately, such a trend could mean the diminution of the most highly endowed ethnic elements, the derivation of a larger share of the population from its least fit portions, the exhaustion of the elite, and the decay of the nation. The effects of mobility on the personalities of society's members are more immediate. With a significant increase in mobility follow: (1) more plastic and versatile individual behavior and a lesser tendency toward conformity; (2) less narrow-mindedness, intolerance, and provincialism; (3) more intellectuality, more superficiality, more mental strain, and more mental disease; (4) increased skepticism, misoneism, cynicism, psychosocial isolation and loneliness, and hedonism; and (5) the distintegration of the traditional mores. The effects of mobility upon the other social processes and upon social organization are also pronounced. Where an open-class system exists and vertical mobility is able to operate rather freely, it facilitates the distribution of individuals in an equitable manner among the social classes. This contributes to economic prosperity and rapid social change and to the disintegration of an established cultural pattern. In fact, in areas of the world where levels of living rise sharply in a short period of time, this disruptive effect may be one of the most important unintended consequences. Social mobility makes for complexity in social relationships and generally alters the lines of social cleavage among the various groups and classes. Finally, it makes for an increase in individualism, usually followed by intensive efforts to develop contractual forms of collectivism of a cosmopolitan type and a social cohesion that is founded upon the interdependence of the dissimilar factions which make up the society.

SOCIAL MOBILITY IN RURAL SOCIETY

Significant variations in social mobility are indicated in Chapter 2 among the important factors differentiating the rural world from the urban. Quantitatively the differences are pronounced, mobility in rural areas being considerably less than it is in cities. Less divorce and separation, the tendency for the rural family to retain children within the parental home for longer periods than the urban family, and many other elements are evidences of less interfamily mobility in the country than in the city. Occupationally, farm classes are recruited almost entirely from children of farmers; but at most times and in most places the city receives newcomers from the rural areas. Urban people shift occupations readily; and in general, occupational mobility is far greater in urban areas than in the open country.

Some of the mobility in the rural areas is of the vertical type, and substantial improvements in status do take place for individuals; but a good deal of it is of the horizontal sort, whereby persons change the social settings within which they function without changing in any significant way their positions in the social scale. Migration, of course, is often involved. The constant treks of migratory agricultural workers, the movements of farm laborers into cities where many become low-paid urban laborers, the shifts of various groups from region to region, the annual migrations of many agricultural families from farm to farm, and so forth, all illustrate the kind of movement that transports people into a new social milieu but leaves them at approxi-

473

mately the same level in the stratification system. Inherent in much of this physical mobility, however, is the individual desire to rise in the social scale, for few farm people leave one plantation for another, one region for another, or the rural districts for the cities without the hope of improving their positions on the social ladder. The fact that many of these aspirations come to naught indicates that involvement in significant vertical mobility is a much more difficult matter for many rural people than is participation in various types of migration.

Some of the factors contributing to the lower vertical mobility of farming populations are noted in Chapter 2. Other factors making for less mobility, both vertical and horizontal, in rural areas are as follows: (1) The caste element is still prevalent in rural society, especially where the large landed estate is a dominant feature, and this fact creates serious difficulties in the way of moving from one social stratum to another; (2) rural groups are comparatively few, with the result that there is little opportunity for changing from one group to another; (3) rural groups also are relatively small, with the consequence that they contain relatively few high-level positions; (4) primary-group controls still continue as important factors in rural society, and these serve to hamper the individual in his movement from group to group, if not class to class; (5) the patriarchal element continues strong in rural societies, and the vesting of control in the hands of the elders makes for less experimentation with the new, and consequently less shifting from group to group than is the case where the opposition to change is not so great; and (6) familism is still important in rural areas so that the personality of the rural person is submerged in the group and the tempo of changes on the part of individuals is considerably slower than it is where family considerations are of less importance.

From the qualitative standpoint, too, there are important differences between social mobility in the country and in the city. It seems fairly certain that a change from group to group or from class to class represents a greater break with custom in the country than in the city. Thus mobility in the rural districts is more disruptive of relationships between people, it calls for a greater degree of accommodation to the new circumstances, and it tends to touch a larger number of facets of the individual's life than is the case in the urban centers.

It also should be indicated that there are wide variations in mobility among the various social classes of the rural districts. The planters of the upper class and the family-sized-farm operators of the middle class are relatively stable territorially in their respective regions; and they have large investments of time and other resources in particular holdings. Hence they are strongly attached to local institutions and shift but little from one social group to another. This is not the case among the farm laborers, who are near the bottom of the social pyramid in every society of which they form a part. Great territorial mobility is always mentioned as one of the outstanding characteristics of this group; it needs only to be noted that movement in space inevitably means the severing of ties with local institutions as often as the moves occur. For example, when sharecropping was common in the southern United States, the laborers generally moved about the first of January, creating in some plantation areas a turnover of enrollment in the rural schools of 50 per cent or more in the very middle of the school year. Corresponding changes occurred in all the groups to which the croppers belonged. Yet despite all of their thrashing about, these unprivileged and uneducated people were held within certain narrow limits on the social scale by the nature of the whole system of which they formed an integral part.

There are interesting shifts of other kinds that have occurred among rural people. In the United States, for instance, there have been wholesale transferrals of membership from one political party to another. Traditionally, farmers above the Mason-Dixon line have been towers of strength in the Republican party and those below it have been stalwarts in the Democratic party; but in recent decades, these customary allegiances have been violated time after time as farm people of one party have supported the candidates of the other. Generally, of course, these switches occurred when particular aspirants to political office seemed to advance programs and policies attractive to the rural folk and to manipulate prejudices and biases that often were those of the rural people. Not infrequently, the changes have occurred in such a way that the votes of the farm people have gone to the candidate who seemed to be the most conservative, and who tended to nurture this same quality among those in the rural districts. There also have been forms of horizontal mobility with an economic dimension. Important among these is the tendency for many farm people to seek part-time and even full-time work off the farms, which brings about changes in occupation and in the patterns of life that may be associated with various occupations. There even has been some horizontal movement in the area of religion, particularly as rural churches either have consolidated or have closed their doors, thereby forcing many members to transfer their allegiance to churches outside their own neighborhoods and sometimes even communities. Occasionally, the failure of churches of one denomination has brought about the transfer of memberships of some farm people to churches of others. In this case, though, rarely have changes been so drastic as to convert Protestants into Catholics, Buddhists into Moslems, Christians into Jews, and so on. In the United States, many of the changes have been from one Protestant denomination to another.

VERTICAL MOBILITY

Vertical mobility, its nature and extent, the channels that make it possible, its variations from one society to another and from place to place within the same society, and other features are of paramount interest to one who would examine the entire phenomenon of social mobility. Sociologists, while greatly interested in the vertical social movement of rural people in a large number of societies, have been able to study the matter in the United States, especially in the South and the Midwest, to a greater degree than elsewhere. In this connection, there has been particular interest in mobility as it is related to farm tenancy and farm ownership. Therefore, mobility conditions in this country can be used to illustrate the general observations in the present section. Moreover, while some discussion of the matter is given in Chapter 8, in the section "Two Great Rural Social Systems," the topic is so important for social organization and change, and is of so much concern to contemporary societies, that additional treatment and even some reiteration are in order. In the main, of course, so fundamental are the differences in the patterns of social mobility in areas devoted to family-sized farms and those given over to large plantations, that the two conditions may best be considered separately.

Family-Sized Farms and the Agricultural Ladder

In areas given over largely to the family-sized farm system of agriculture, vertical mobility generally is of a distinctive type. This is present in Canada, portions of northwestern Europe, much of the United States, and a few other places. Particularly significant for study are such areas when there are no rapidly fluctuating land values to endanger the operator's equity in the land and to bring about corporation farming, chain farming, and various other types of absentee ownership. In family-sized farm areas the socioeconomic scale is limited largely to the intermediate levels of the nation's general social pyramid. Social classes are few, caste is unimportant, and sizable numbers of farmers occupy successively the various social strata that are found in the area.

For analytical purposes, it is important to seek the time and region within which this type of mobility may be observed in its purest form. Such was the situation in the midwestern portion of the United States during the closing years of the nineteenth century and the opening decades of the twentieth. Students of land tenure early referred to the vertical mobility present in the system as "climbing the agricultural ladder." Generally speaking, the young farmer on his way to ownership began work as an unpaid laborer on the home farm and remained there until about the age of nineteen; then he probably hired out to neighboring farmers for a cash wage; after a brief interval in this category, or the second rung of the agricultural ladder, the youth amassed sufficient savings to purchase a team and equipment and advanced to the third rung of the ladder, the stage of the tenant or independent renter. Eventually, the top rung or farm ownership was attained by all but a small proportion of those who had started at the bottom. For example, in 1900, the agricultural ladder was functioning freely in the United States for large numbers of farm people whose tireless efforts in farming propelled them through the successive stages of this particular form of vertical mobility. Spillman's early study in Illinois, Iowa, Kansas, Minnesota, and Nebraska showed that at the turn of the century, vertical mobility was occurring so widely that although 39 per cent of all farm operators interviewed were tenants, only 10 per cent of those who had attained the age of 65 years remained in the tenant category (Ref. 481, pp. 170–179). Moreover, one fifth of all the farm owners studied had occupied all four rungs of the agricultural ladder: they had started as unpaid laborers on the home farm, and had been successively hired men on the farms of others, tenants, and owners. Thirteen per cent of all had skipped the tenant stage but passed through the other three; 32 per cent had missed the hired-man stage, going directly from the home farm to the tenant category; and 34 per cent had passed directly to ownership from the category of unpaid laborers on the home farm. This group, of course, contained that large number of farmers who had acquired their land by inheritance.

Of considerable significance in substantiating the existence of widespread vertical mobility among the farm population of the United States is the decreasing proportion of tenants and the increasing percentage of owners as the age of operators increases. There are, however, wide variations by race. Small indeed is the relative share of the white farm operators who remain in the category of tenants after age 65 is reached. For example, in recent decades the figure has been under 15 per cent. Even in the South, where tenancy is more common than it is in the other farming regions, the proportion is very little higher. Among Negroes the situation is different, owing in part to their close association with the plantation system, but also in part to the fact that the same government that forced the freedom of the slaves abandoned practically all responsibility for inculcating in them and their descendants the habits, skills, techniques, and so on essential to climbing the agricultural ladder or, indeed, to decent independent living at any level. Such training in the arts of advancement as they received was largely at the hands of the very communities that were economically strangled by their emancipation, the Civil War, and the reconstruction period. It is little wonder, then, that Negroes who remained in southern agriculture had only minimal opportunities to climb the agricultural ladder and to aspire to eventual ownership of a parcel of land of any size. It is clear, of course, that Negroes in large numbers eventually responded to this virtual absence of significant vertical mobility in agriculture by migrating to cities, where they were led to believe the chances for improvements in status were somewhat better. In this respect, the experience of the Negro has much in common with that of agricultural laborers and low-status farm tenants throughout the world, for vast numbers of these people, too, are deserting agriculture in search of opportunities in the cities.

The agricultural ladder, which operated as described above for vast numbers in the family-sized farming areas of the United States as recently as the opening decades of the twentieth century, was not given only to one-way traffic. Many reverses of direction occurred; and it is likely that slipping back into lower-status positions was accentuated in times of severe financial depression. As one might expect, there tended to be a direct relationship between the propensity to move upward and the degree to which the three basic functions of the family-sized farm operator were carried out successfully. That is, if a particular farm family was able to acquire and invest financial resources wisely in the farm business, was capable of honing to a fine edge its managerial skills and techniques, and was willing and able to labor efficiently and diligently at the farm tasks, movement up the agricultural ladder was virtually assured, both for the family as a whole and for individual members who departed from it to pass through the successive stages described above. If, however, a given family was inept at investment, unequal to the demands of responsible management, and unwilling or unable to carry out the many manual tasks of farming, there was little to prevent it from suffering severe reverses in vertical mobility or to hold it at any particular level far above the bottom. The young man reared in such a situation also might find himself poorly equipped to move upward in the social ranks. Thus the agricultural ladder involved the movement of farm people both up and down, although the success of the family-sized farm in broad areas of the United States clearly suggests that the magnitude of upward traffic far outstripped that of the downward flow. Moreover, the rapid growth of urban industry after the turn of the century allowed those who failed in agriculture, as well as many who were successful, to move to the cities, and thereby prevented the buildup of a large rural proletariat in almost all except the plantation sections of the nation.

In recent decades, the nature of the agricultural ladder in family-sized farming areas has changed markedly although it still continues to operate and to produce a degree of vertical mobility that is approximately the same as that which has existed in these farming areas for generations. The ladder as it is found at present seems to have lost some rungs and to have acquired others. The young, unpaid family worker is less available than he once was because of the greater demands exerted on his time by formal education. There is a substantial degree of participation in the affairs of the family farm, however, often in the form of 4–H Club or other projects that are rather highly individualized. Farm youngsters, of course, still devote a considerable share of their summer days and nonschool hours to farm tasks. Also, a young man may be less likely to hire out as a wage hand to a neighbor in order to accumulate sufficient capital to become a farm operator in his own right; but he is more likely to enter into a partnership with his father on the family farm. Finally, eventual ownership and operatorship of the farm may come not through the purchase of a separate unit, but through the gradual acquisition of control and ultimate inheritance of the family's farm. Sometimes it comes about through marriage. In a sense, then, the vertical mobility of the young aspiring farmer is less a matter of individual achievement and is less likely to involve the establishment of a new farm than was the case in 1900. More involved than ever before, though, are the close partnership of father and son in the operation of one farm and the gradual passing of the ownership of that unit from the former to the latter. Meanwhile, the earlier type of full-time apprenticeship, through which the youthful, unpaid family worker and young hired man was introduced to farming, has been replaced to a degree by more years of formal schooling and by a part-time apprenticeship within the confines of one farm. Mobility still is present, of course, for the young man's status gradually rises as he assumes more responsibility and eventual control. In many cases, it is further enhanced as both father and son improve the farm, add to its size and value, and augment its productivity. Certainly, there is less dispersion of their efforts than was true under the conditions of the older agricultural ladder. (For a discussion of a number of these changes, see Ref. 169, pp. 258–262.)

The reasons for the changes mentioned above are several. Family-sized farms that are sufficiently large to be profitable in an era of mechanized farming are very expensive; their cost is far beyond the amount that most young men could hope to accumulate as hired hands and renters. The supply of good land that either is free for the taking or to be had at nominal prices is exhausted in most places where the institution in question predominates. Furthermore, on the average, owners of farms live longer and remain active longer than did those of earlier generations. Consequently, a young man who hopes eventually to inherit his father's farm may indeed be middle aged before that transfer takes place. As a result, necessity may force him into the kind of partnership with his father described above so that his most productive years can yield him a reasonable rate of return. Finally, the relatively high degree of emphasis that farm and nonfarm people place upon education generally precludes children, adolescents, and even many young adults from entering farming fully at any level until those educations have been completed. This factor commits to education most of the years that the members of earlier generations invested in farming as unpaid family workers and as hired hands on neighboring places. Moreover, few young men who have been educated in high-school and college programs of agriculture are willing to step onto the lowest rungs of the agricultural ladder. Their training and attitudes generally equip them for much fuller participation in farming, often as partners with their fathers. These same orientations also are almost certain to be shared by the young women whom they marry. (For a review of some of these reasons, see Ref. 382, p. 119.) Thus, because of several changes in the nature of agriculture in the family-sized farm areas of the United States, vertical mobility has assumed a somewhat different form from that of earlier generations. There is little evidence, however, to suggest that it goes on any less briskly or that it involves a smaller share of the farm population in those places than was the case in 1900.

Large-Scale Agriculture and Vertical Mobility

In the plantation areas of the world the patterns of vertical social mobility are considerably different from those of the midwestern part of the United States and other regions where the family-sized farm is predominant. The very existence of large-scale agriculture, as exemplified in the plantation system, or the large fruit and vegetable farms of Florida and California, is evidence that the agricultural ladder is not functioning to any great degree. Were this type of vertical mobility to operate extensively, it would in a short time destroy the large landholdings. Furthermore, the patterns of mobility found in the deltas, river bottoms, upland valleys, and other stretches of fine land where plantations reign supreme, have a considerable influence in the areas of small holdings that often spring up on the slopes of the nearby hills and mountains. Again, because it has been studied thoroughly, the plantation system in the southern United States will serve as an example of the type of social mobility found in the places where large landed estates of various kinds dominate rural life. The conditions are repeated in large truck-crop holdings in southern California and south Florida, bonanza farms in Montana, coffee *fazendas* and sugar *usinas* in Brazil, cattle *estancias* in Argentina, sugar and cotton *haciendas* in Peru, rubber plantations in Ceylon, and so forth.

The failure of the agricultural ladder to function fully in areas where large landholdings predominate does not, however, demonstrate that vertical social mobility is completely lacking in these places. Climbing and sinking on the social scale go on in the rural areas of such regions just as they do elsewhere, but the nature of the general pattern is different. Contrary to popular opinion, in some countries many laborers manage to accumulate enough capital to make a start as independent renters and even to begin the purchase of farms. In the southern United States, for example, at various times white and nonwhite laborers, wage hands and share-croppers, and even occasional migrant workers have been able to embark upon the independent operation of farms and thereby to begin a move up the agricultural ladder. In Brazil, too, Germans, Italians, Japanese, and others brought into the country early in the twentieth century to serve as laborers on the large estates shortly were able to accumulate sufficient capital to acquire their own small farms, largely in the southern part of the country. In both of these cases and in others, however, such a movement even part of the way up the social scale almost invariably means migration away from the immediate areas of the large estates. There is, of course, much land in plantation areas for sale; sometimes it may be had at extremely low prices; but it is not available in small tracts and, therefore, is rarely converted into family-sized farms. As the traveler Charles Nordhoff wrote of the southern United States in 1875: "Nobody, except a land-speculator, likes to sell land; especially where it has been his home. And these people are not land-speculators" (Ref. 319, p. 71). The planter would have to possess the skills and techniques of the real-estate dealer to subdivide and sell his lands to small holders successfully. Furthermore, even if he were willing to attempt this, the task of getting sufficient purchasers for his entire acreages at one time would be far beyond his capacities. To sell off parts of the landholding year after year would mean a continual readjustment of plantation operations. Moreover, in many plantation areas, there is a non-empirical value of considerable strength connected with preserving a large estate intact, even if it is to pass into other hands. Most planters, wisely from their standpoint, either sell the plantation in its entirety or keep it all, sometimes as land used inefficiently or in no way whatsoever. Governmental agencies such as the Federal Land Bank pursue the same course. The net result is, with the plantation system monopolizing the best land in the South as it does, that it is practically impossible for those ascending the agricultural ladder to attain the status of either independent renter or owner in the good land areas. Therefore, renters and owner-operators, both white and Negro, appear in the piney woods sections, the isolated niches, and other parts of the region where land is relatively poor and the individual's chances for success as an independent operator are extremely low.

In connection with the endeavors of some laborers to become farm operators as early as 1883, Frances Butler Leigh reported:

Notwithstanding their dissatisfaction at the settlement, six thousand dollars was paid out among them, many getting as much as two or three hundred apiece. The result was that a number of them left me and bought land of their own, and at one time it seemed doubtful if I should have hands at all left to work. The land they bought, and paid forty, fifty dollars and even more for an acre, was either within the town limits, for which they got no titles, and from which they were soon turned off, or out in the pine woods, where the land was so poor they could not raise a peck of corn to the acre. These lands were sold to them by a common class of men . . . and most frightfully cheated the poor people were. But they had got their land, and were building their little log cabins on it, fully believing that they were to live on their property and incomes the rest of their lives, like gentlemen. (Ref. 242, pp. 78–78.)

Since Mrs. Leigh wrote, the situation has changed but little. The plantation has continued to blanket the most productive soils; the independent renter and the owner-operator of a family-sized farm have no part in such a system; and persons ascending the social ladder have to abandon the districts in which the plantation continues to operate for the poor piney-woods areas or those where the large holdings are disintegrating if they are to set themselves up as farm operators. Between 1900 and 1950, many families that had acquired a little livestock and capital while working under close supervision as plantation laborers or sharecroppers moved to the nearby piney woods and bargained to purchase a farm or to rent one under reasonably equitable and unsupervised conditions. Some of them stayed, eking out a meager existence on the poor soils of such hilly areas for the remainder of their days. Probably a larger number, however, soon dissipated their few resources, lost their livestock, equipment, and even the payments they had put into the land, and made their way back to the plantations to begin again as laborers or as closely watched tenants. A considerable degree of social mobility of the vertical type is exhibited in these cases, but unfortunately, positions on the top rung of the agricultural ladder, i.e., farm ownership, were almost impossible to achieve and retain.

With variations, this same situation may be found in a number of the plantation areas of the world. Some exhibit a slightly higher degree of vertical movement than others, but the maximum net result is only limited social mobility in all of them. In Brazil, for example, some movement up the agricultural ladder is found among agricultural workers in western São

Paulo and four other southern states. Part of this movement has gone on in association with the migration of people to these areas, as discussed in Chapter 4. The great bulk of Brazilian peasants and agricultural laborers, however, are essentially socially immobile elements in the system of large landed estates, bound on the one hand by the virtual nonexistence of customs and provisions that would allow them to acquire land in the plantation areas, and on the other hand, at least until very recently, by their failure to entertain any notion of vertical mobility or aspiration to landownership as a realistic possibility. Moreover, even if land were to become easily available and fatalistic attitudes were to change rapidly, the Brazilian farm laborer still would be ill equipped to engage in the managerial and entrepreneurial functions that would generate for him success as an autonomous farm operator (Ref. 444, pp. 232–233). In this kind of situation, the elements of caste remain highly significant and the chances of overcoming them are slight, even though some of those at the lower levels may possess degrees of intelligence and other attributes which, if developed, would allow them to rise rapidly in a less rigid system of stratification. As it is, though, the positions in the social scale of the great mass of Brazilian agriculturists are fixed within rather narrow limits by the accident of birth, especially if they remain on the land; and so it is in plantation areas virtually everywhere else in the contemporary world.

There is, however, a considerable amount of one type of limited vertical mobility in many of the areas where the large landed estate predominates. It involves the movement of people up and down on the lower rungs of the agricultural ladder, generally somewhere beneath the level of long-term, stable cash renters.

In the plantation South, the agricultural ladder has never been the simple affair found by the studies in the Midwest, where vertical mobility is institutionalized for the mass of farm people, where it is looked upon as a positive value intimately associated with participation in agriculture, and where the means to achieve higher status are almost universally recognized, respected, and available. One highly significant endeavor to generate vertical mobility on the southern cotton plantation, conducted around the turn of the century when the large estates dominated rural life, is Alfred Stone's "A Plantation Experiment." This ambitious project, which brings out the inevitable tendency of large-scale agriculture to promote endless rising and falling on lower rungs of the agricultural ladder, deserves extensive quotation:

[It was to] the desire and hope of building up some such "assured tenentry" that our experiment largely owed its inception. Its salient features were: uniformity of tenant system, all land being rented at a fixed cash rental; the sale of stock, implements, and wagons to tenants upon exceptionally favorable terms; the exercise of proper super-vision over the crop; the use of a contract defining in detail the undertakings of each party; the handling and disposition of the gathered crop by the plantation manage-ment. Let there be no misunderstanding of the motives behind all this. There was nothing philanthropic about it. It was a business proposition, pure and simple, but certainly one with two sides to it. The plan was to select a number of negro families, offer them the best terms and most advantageous tenant relation, and so handle them and their affairs as to make them reach a condition approaching as nearly as possible that of independence. The hope was that, having accomplished this purpose, we would thereby also have in large measure solved the labor problem, having attached to the plantation by ties of self-interest a sufficient number of these independent renters to make us in turn measurably independent of the general labor situation. The problem before us was to place in the hands of these people the means of acquiring something for themselves, and then, in every instance of deficient individual initiative, by proper supervision to make them acquire it. (Ref. 487, pp. 271–272.)

After six years of operation the following results were detailed:

. . . We brought to the plantation, at the close of the season of 1898, 30 new families, and began the first year, 1899, with a total of 58. On 1064 acres of cotton land we made but 459 bales of 500 pounds average, a family average of 7.9 bales. The average price received was 7.50 cents per pound; and the entire crop, cotton and seed, brought $21,633.88, or a family average of $373.51. Of the families on the place, 26, or 44.8 percent., left at the end of the year. We moved in 27 families, and, with the 59 which the addition gave us, cultivated 1048 acres of cotton in 1900. The crop was 817 bales, or 13.8 per family. It sold at an average price of 9.94 cents, and with its seed brought $47,541.66. This was an average cash product value of $805.79 per family. The number of families who left the place at the close of the year was 13, or 22 percent. of the total. We secured 15 new ones, and had on the place 61 families in 1901. We had this year in cotton 1348 acres, and raised 1270 bales, 20.8 to the family. At an average price of 7.90 cents for the cotton this crop, including seed, realized $60,724.04, being $995.77 per family. We lost 16 families this year, 26.2 percent. of the whole force, and moved in 24 new squads, which gave us 69 for 1902. The latter year we raised 1131 bales of cotton on 1341 acres. Seed and cotton brought $54,593.26, the average price for the latter being 8.08 cents per pound. The average product of cotton was 16.4 bales per family, the average value of cotton and seed $791.20. At the end of the year we lost 17 families, 24.6 percent. of the total, and moved in 23 for the following year. This gave us 75 squads for 1903. We cultivated 1392 acres of cotton, and raised 741 bales, 9.8 to the family. This brought 11.77 cents per pound, the cotton and seed selling for $53,527.73, or an average of $713.70 per family. At the close of the season 31 families, 41.3 percent. of our working force, left the plantation. (Ref. 487, pp. 272–273.)

The single planter was helpless in the face of the cultural pattern of habitual migration established as slavery's aftermath, for Stone reports:

. . . From 1899 to 1903, leaving out of consideration the 30 new families brought in at the beginning of the former year, we moved in 124 families. In the same period we lost 103. Of the 79 families on the place in 1904 but 8 were with us in 1899. Of the

103 who have left, some with little, some with much, not one has become an owner of land. Most have simply continued as tenants elsewhere. Many have lost what they carried away, and have become share-hands on other plantations. Some have dropped into the ranks of day laborers. A few have drifted into towns. Let me illustrate one of these removals. In December, 1900, we moved in a crew of 7 people. They all represented themselves as working hands, though one of the men was over sixty-five, with a wife past sixty. Their entire outfit consisted of a horse, worth a liberal valuation of $50, and $58 worth of miscellaneous and indescribable household effects. In December, 1903, while riding over the place one day, my attention was arrested by a procession slowly approaching me. It consisted partly of two wagons, one buggy, two mules, one horse, three cows, two calves, and five dogs—the property of this same crew of seven. In addition they had with them outside wagons enough to assist them in hauling away 285 bushels of corn, $190 worth of household effects (including a sewing-machine for each woman and a gun for each man), and a half-dozen crates of hogs and several of poultry. During the three years they had paid rents and accounts amounting to $4168.96, had received in cash $747.85, and had cash paid for help in their crops to the amount of $393.90. Their accounts, of course, included a variety of purchases in addition to their living expenses. They carried away $1100 worth of personal property. They left to get rid of the supervision incident to plantation management, and removed a short distance to the property of a nonresident, and secured their advances from a merchant. In November last I learned that the head of the squad had applied to a neighboring planter for a location for 1905, and wanted the latter to lift a debt of $1000 for him. (Since the above was put in print this squad has returned to us to make a crop the present year. It surrendered all it had, save household effects, to its merchant, and in addition we advanced $75 to cover a balance. It begins where it started before, with nothing, and this time will work on shares.) (Ref. 487, pp. 275–276.)

Stone's experiment throws a great deal of light upon the process of vertical mobility in both its ascending and descending aspects. In addition it reveals much concerning the territorial mobility of the cotton laborers. At the end of six years the experiment was abandoned. Says Stone:

. . . We demonstrated our ability to make independent, property owning families out of poverty-stricken material. These families in turn demonstrated the fact of their independence by severing relations with us almost as promptly as we put them on their feet. After the termination of three years we had begun to feel reasonably certain that even the most practical appeal we could make to radically improve material welfare would be generally overcome by an apparently instinctive desire to "move." After the experience of five years we were quite satisfied of our entire incapacity to make the average plantation negro realize the remotest causal relation between stability and prosperity. (Ref. 487, p. 274).

The situation Stone described was found commonly in the plantation South and in other areas of large holdings, especially during periods when sharecropping was of paramount importance. At present, the kind of vertical mobility that it represented, the circulation up and down on the bottom few rungs of the agricultural ladder, still may be found in many parts of the world in forms not very different from that described by Stone. Such conditions are ample evidence, of course, that the plantation system does not equip laborers with the capabilities necessary to function independently as farm operators over long periods of time. They also demonstrate that the tendency to migrate from farm to farm is closely allied with vertical mobility in the lower levels of the rural stratification system and is, therefore, much more common among laborers than among operators. Finally, they suggest strongly that movement toward high rungs of the agricultural ladder is most likely to take place if farm folk establish themselves relatively permanently on given farms as owners or as renters holding long-term leases, and continue year after year to invest their resources and efforts in the enlargement and the improvement of those particular farms. In most cases, the annual drift from farm to farm is about as futile in creating substantial and sustained increases in social position as is the frequent shift of urban laborers from job to job or from city to city. In neither instance do the conditions intervene that would make for a significantly higher level of success. Basically, then, while a certain amount of vertical mobility may be present in plantation areas, as described above, a very high proportion of the social movement is of the horizontal sort. That is, it brings about changes in the social situation without producing any significant, long-lasting changes in the position in the social scale.

In the final analysis, though, the severe limitations on vertical mobility in areas dominated by large holdings arise mainly from the nature of the two-class system it generates. The gap between the laboring class at the bottom of the social scale and the landowning class at the apex is so broad, that any upward mobility except that limited amount that occurs *within* each stratum is virtually unthinkable. It is totally unrealistic to conceive of coloni as moving into the elite layer of society, although if a genuine middle class existed, the step from the lower level to the middle might be attained by some of the laborers. Thus vertical mobility is able to take place in the areas of the family-sized farm partly because there are comparatively small intervals between the various steps on the agricultural ladder, making status aspirations realistic. After all, such places frequently are dominated almost totally by the middle class. It can take place so slightly in plantation areas partly because the intervals between the existing social levels are so fantastically wide that serious aspirations for higher status are most unrealistic.

Effects of Rural Social Mobility

Among agriculturists, as with others, every change in social or physical space has a double aspect. On the one hand it shatters existing social bonds, and on the other it means the establishment of new ones. Vertical and horizontal mobility, as well as territorial, disintegrates the social relationships and social structure in the old groups and causes significant modifications in the arrangements of the new. In these ways, mobility exerts important influences upon the nature and structure of rural society. Some of its more important results for rural society are as follows: (1) Mobility tends to mix thoroughly all the ethnic and cultural elements in a society. Accordingly, the more mobile a society, the greater is the admixture, and the more heterogeneous it will be in racial stocks, nationalities, mores, religious beliefs, attitudes and values, and cultural traits generally. (2) Mobility tends to eliminate unique and distinctive features from any particular group. Previous local patterns tend to be replaced by those of a more general nature. Within the community, social differences are increased, but the community itself comes to resemble more closely such locality groups in the larger society. This pattern, of course, is the essence of homogenization of society, discussed elsewhere in this book. (3) The more mobile the population, the more plastic is its behavior, the larger the social vista, the less the prevalence of narrow-mindedness, and the slighter the dependence upon tradition. Also, the more mobile is the population, the greater is the disintegration of the traditional mores and the higher the incidence of deviance and antisocial behavior. (4) As mobility increases, rural social institutions lose their traditional character and force, become less stable or more flexible, and are likely to lose much of their hold upon the people. A mobile population is likely to be less concerned about the maintenance and support of schools, churches, and other institutions, unless they recognize that the continued strength of those institutions is vital to the process of vertical mobility in which they may wish to continue to participate. As a result of the lower degree of interest, they are likely to be less intense in their attachment to the local community, more broadminded or cosmopolitan. (5) As mobility increases in the rural community, social contacts become less intimate, more formal and more superficial, psychosocial isolation increases, and social relationships take on a higher degree of anonymity. The pattern of social interaction approaches that of the city; contractual relationships are more common. (6) The shifting of individuals from group to group and class to class is accompanied by a confusion in the patterns of solidarity and antagonism. Lines of cleavage become confused and blurred; the social world becomes much more intricate; behavior expectations and the definitions of social roles grow more vague; the stability generated by the localized and nearly complete consensus of an earlier age diminishes.

Additional Readings

1. BERTRAND, ALVIN L., *Basic Sociology: An Introduction to Theory and Method,* New York: Appleton-Century-Crofts, Inc., 1967, chapter 10.

2. LIPSET, SEYMOUR M., "Social Mobility and Urbanization," *Rural Sociology,* Vol. 20, Nos. 3–4 (September-December, 1955), pp. 220–227.

3. NELSON, LOWRY, *Rural Sociology* (second ed.), New York: American Book Company, 1955, chapter 12.

4. ROHWER, ROBERT A., "Social Relations in Beginning as a Farm Operator in an Area of Prosperous, Commercial Farming," *Rural Sociology,* Vol. 14, No. 4 (December, 1949), pp. 325–335.

5. SCHWARZWELLER, HARRY K., and JAMES S. BROWN, "Social Class Origins, Rural-Urban Migration, and Economic Life Chances: A Case Study," *Rural Sociology,* Vol. 32, No. 1 (March, 1967), pp. 5–19.

6. SOROKIN, PITIRIM A., *Society, Culture, and Personality: Their Structure and Dynamics,* New York: Harper & Brothers, 1947, chapters 23–26.

7. SOROKIN, PITIRIM A., *Social Mobility,* New York: Harper & Brothers, 1927, chapters VII–IX.

8. SOROKIN, PITIRIM A., CARLE C. ZIMMERMAN, and CHARLES J. GALPIN, *A Systematic Source Book in Rural Sociology,* Minneapolis: University of Minnesota Press, 1930, Vol. I, chapter VIII.

PART FIVE

CONCLUSION

The factors in human behavior, the magnitude and direction of sociocultural change, and some observations about the future of the agricultural classes throughout the world are treated in a brief conclusion.

20
CONCLUSION

It is neither necessary nor desirable to conclude a volume such as this with an elaborate summary, for the various points are best understood in the contexts in which they appear in the several sections of the text. It is in order, however, to examine again what is perhaps the single most important feature of rural areas everywhere—sociocultural change. Whether one is talking of societies in which many basic changes have occurred, those in which they are now going on, or the ones in which they have yet to take place, change must be taken into account repeatedly in any study of rural life. Moreover, in viewing sociocultural change in rural areas, it is well to keep in mind two general principles. First, because about five generations of people help constitute a society at any given time, irrespective of what else it may be, sociocultural change always amounts to a change in the rules of a game while that game is in progress. Second, sociocultural change is the antithesis of institutionalization. Hence there are always likely to be differences of opinion and even conflict between the members of a society who stress the values of change and progress and those who wish to institutionalize sociocultural features of one kind or another. Persons and groups resist, especially, proposed changes in the things they themselves have sought to institutionalize. In the last analysis, of course, all social forms, functions, and processes, and all change as one of those processes, are simply products of human behavior and of the factors that underlie and influence that behavior.

THE FACTORS IN HUMAN BEHAVIOR

Sociology and all social science is an attempt to explain human behavior, to get at the fundamental bases of personality, to determine and account for the social relationships that prevail among men. All the conditions or factors underlying and influencing human behavior may be reduced to four large categories: (1) innate or biological factors, including the psychological; (2) geographic factors; (3) cultural factors; and (4) social factors. The first set includes everything with which man is equipped at birth, the original nature of man, and only that; the second embraces all the multifarious elements of the natural environment, with which rural people especially must deal; the third pertains to that portion of the environment that man himself has produced and that he passes on from one generation to another; and the fourth involves action or behavior of people in groups.

Formerly, writers endowed the human being with a long list of instincts or complex patterns of biologically inherited behavior. Since about 1925, psychologists have greatly reduced the number of inherited behavior traits and patterns attributed to man. They also have abandoned the hypothesis of instincts, or the biological transmission of complicated patterns of behavior, in favor of less differentiated original tendencies or impulses. Few, if any, of these instinctive tendencies, drives, organic desires, biological needs, or preponderant reflexes are peculiar to man. This is certainly the case with respect to those most frequently mentioned, i.e., the ones involved in feeding, drinking, vocalization, bodily elimination, rest and sleep, muscular activity, sexual activity, the avoidance of stimuli that result in pain, and the tendency to seek repetition of pleasurable sensations. Because these tendencies are not limited to man, they should be used only with great caution as the differentiating characteristics of human nature and group action. Even upright posture and the opposition of thumb and forefinger, and perhaps even the ability to communicate symbolically are not peculiar to the human species. Indeed, except for a more complex and more plastic nervous system, it is difficult to find any distinctively human features that might be used for establishing the specific biological basis of human behavior. A biological basis there must be, but it is broad and scarcely deterministic. The range of potential behavior patterns is tremendous; the behaviors specifically determined by biological structures are few, and they are not unique with man.

Neither are geographic influences of much worth in explaining human nature and the activities of groups. Certainly they have played a role in the remote past, but as man ascended the scale of civilization, the influences of geography on his behavior became less and less determinative. Even in earliest times, however, although geography and the natural environment limited the types of social systems and the various kinds of cultural environments man could create, rarely did these natural elements rigidly determine what he actually would create. Even where geographic elements are most unfavorable to human habitation and limit the freedom to act, man has always had potentially available to him a wide range of sociocultural means whereby he could meet his needs in conjunction with his fellows.

Many of the most fundamental determinants of human nature are cultural. It appears to be true that man alone possesses the unique biological constitution that enables him to develop and transmit cultural phenomena; but even this ability may be only a slight variation, merely a matter of degree, from the biological equipment of other animal species. The actual *possession* and *use* of culture, on the other hand, are a difference of kind; they create a tremendous chasm between man and the remainder of the animal kingdom. He alone is a culture-making, culture-preserving, and culture-transmitting animal. Because of the material and nonmaterial cultural environment with which he has surrounded himself, man lives in a very different world from that inhabited by the other animals. Even where he adopts other species through domestication so that they become adapted to and even dependent upon man's cultural world, they never come to have a share in it or to develop a minimal understanding of it. Were it not for man, who serves as a carrier of culture, it would all perish in short order.

Implicit throughout this book are the propositions that the cultural factors are primary determinants of what man is (human nature) and of group behavior, that the cultural heritage can be modified and changed, and that what is called human nature will change along with modifications in the cultural framework or structure. To a considerable degree farmers differ from urban people because of the differences in the cultural influences impinging upon them. Even granting that man does not as yet completely understand his biological base, the possession of culture is the primary thing that makes man human; and the differences in the cultural heritages of various groups are the primary determinants of the diversity in mankind. Human nature changes as the institutional pattern and other cultural elements are changed. More detailed and specific knowledge concerning the particular manner in which cultural forces operate offers the chief hope for a more complete predictability of human behavior.

Finally, the activities of men as members of groups and societies themselves are powerful factors in determining the human nature of individuals, the differences between personalities, and the course of sociocultural change and development. Among the strictly social or societal determinants of human nature and group activities are such factors as size, density, distribution, and characteristics of the population; the varieties and intensity of social interaction; the nature and degree of social differentiation; the extent and types of social stratification; and the different kinds of domestic, religious, educational, administrative, recreational, and welfare activities. Specific societal forms such as the way in which the population is arranged on the land, the nature and distribution of property rights in land, the group bonds, the class and caste structure, the nature and strength of domestic, educational, religious, and governmental institutions—all these are the molds in which human nature is cast. Analysis within this societal framework and of the activities taking place within it is the essence of sociology, whether directed toward the understanding of rural life or any other set of human phenomena.

SOCIOCULTURAL CHANGE IN RURAL AREAS

The cultural heritage, the social organization, and the social processes of a group or society are constantly changing in magnitude, content, and structure. New traits and activities are being added, old ones sloughed off, and new combinations are being made of existent components and patterns of integration. Only a small part of the change is due to the loss of arts or traits or to the conscious abandonment of knowledge once obtained. Fundamentally, sociocultural phenomena are cumulative. The persistence of many old forms, the modification of some, and the addition of new ones make the process largely one of growth and differentiation of the social and cultural bases; and the development of more intricate types of social activity leads to almost infinitely greater complexity. Through resistance to change or pure sociocultural inertia, many old forms and ways persist long after their usefulness seems past; by and large, however, culture traits and action patterns persist because they possess utility. Even though a material feature in which a culture trait is objectified may wear out, be lost, or be destroyed, the knowledge of how to duplicate the object remains, and utility calls forth new copies of the old. Furthermore, as the horizons of knowledge become wider, many cultural traits and social activities that seem to have lost all usefulness actually prove to possess some utility for some people, even though that utility was hitherto obscured to those who study and attempt to comprehend human behavior and the cultural environment.

The possession of a large and complex cultural heritage and an intricate social organization by itself is no proof of the genius of a people; nor is the absence of such a heritage and type of organization evidence of biological inferiority. Who is to say, for example, that the vastly differentiated cultural equipment and the infinitely varied types of social activities of a highly urbanized society are superior to the less complicated social and cultural attributes of a small rural society? The size and complexity of the social organization and cultural heritage are largely a function of the system of social contacts; limits in the bulk and the rate of growth of these socio-cultural features are chiefly the results of isolation, be it physical, psychological, political, or ideological. A given group or society may add some traits and activities to its sociocultural base through invention and discovery; it generally adds many more by borrowing and transplantation. Invention is the successful combination of two or more previously existing traits (or complexes) or activities into a new, functioning unity. The larger the base and the more complex its structure, the greater the opportunities for new combinations or inventions. When man through science develops a systematic method of interrogating nature, inventions are greatly multiplied. Discovery refers to the obtaining of a bit of knowledge in the first place. It is largely a fortuitous procedure, the result of fortunate coincidences or accidents. Discovery, for example, added to the cultural heritage the knowledge of edible plants and animals upon which agriculture and stockraising are based. Borrowing of culture traits refers to the conscious adoption of the traits of another group or culture. Transplantation of sociocultural features denotes the tendency of people to transfer traits and activities from one group to another.

The mechanics and the dynamics of sociocultural change in rural areas have been almost completely remade during recent years. Most important of all is the fact that in the present century, the system of communication and transportation has been thoroughly revolutionized. With these developments has come a complete change in the patterns of interaction within the community, as well as in the nature and frequency of contacts between communities. These innovations mean that sociocultural change in rural areas is radically different from what it was 50 or even 20 years ago. Under the pattern that prevailed until recently, rural people necessarily had to depend for additions to their culture and their activities almost entirely upon their own personal ingenuity and skill. Even if new devices and ideas were discovered, practically all the social and economic channels that would facilitate their rapid transplantation were lacking; the resistance that would prevent their spread was great. The result was a static type of rural society. Changes were so slow, innovations so rare as to be strange and often to be regarded with suspicion. Stagnation was the inevitable result of lack of social contacts and social interaction.

Today rural people in a society such as the United States are in frequent communication with one another and with townspeople and city dwellers. They even have some dealings with the members of other societies. The telephone, the telegraph, the radio, television, the automobile and better roads, the airplane, differentiation of contacts with social and service centers, the decline of the cumulative and the rise of special-interest groups, agricultural extension services, agencies and groups who would help to reform and improve rural life—all of these and many other forces contribute to the increased tempo of sociocultural change in rural areas. The typical farm family no longer is attached largely to a given locality group, but divides its interest, loyalty, patronage, and other attachments among a number of such groups, including in many cases a specific neighborhood, one or more partial or incomplete rural communities, a given rural or rurban community, one of the smaller urban communities, and one of the great metropolitan communities. In other words, it is integrated into a variety of locality groups at several rather distinct levels. Under such circumstances it can more quickly use the invention of another farmer, even though it is made in a distant part of a nation; and farmers everywhere can learn with relative ease of attitudes and values that exist throughout the world and that may be radically different from their own. In brief, the modern systems of social interaction and communication make possible a much more rapid dissemination of useful inventions and discoveries among farm people, a process that has been greatly retarded in the past by the lack of contact between the many small parts of a highly segmented rural society. They also make readily available to rural poeple all urban social and cultural phenomena; and in many ways this factor has produced the most drastic changes in rural life.

The net result of all this is to reduce greatly the rural-urban sociocultural differences. As suggested above, the most important factor in this change is, of course, the rapid dissemination of urban traits and activities to rural areas. However, with improved methods of communication between farm families, sociocultural transplantations within strictly rural territory of traits and activities germane to rural life are likely to increase. Furthermore, future developments may mean a greater ruralization of the city and a lesser urbanization of the country. Certainly, the growth of suburbs and the strong tendency of nonfarm people to establish residences in the open country serves as a bridge between the farm and urban portions of many societies. The generalization that the city is the innovator, the country the preserver of culture traits and ways of acting may be less true in the future than it has been in the past, because present trends represent a progressive erasure of differences between city and country, a greater standardization, and far more homogenization of society in general. The country itself is becoming less a balance wheel and more a dynamo.

In this interchange of values, ideas, and behavior patterns between the rural and urban segments, the rural people are experiencing many more deeply significant changes than the urban. Moreover, because the standardizing influences of cities have been felt during a relatively short time, many of the changes in rural areas have occurred rather quickly, some of them spectacularly. However, though increasing proportions of people in many societies have come under the influence of urban ideas, values, and behavior patterns, urban-oriented society has not replaced rural-oriented society, but is growing out of it; and this new combination of rural and urban features has produced a large number of other specific changes. Among the more important are the following: (1) a substantial decline in the extended-family system and in the diverse subsistence economy associated with it, in which the family was a self-sufficient producing unit and farming an inclusive way of life; (2) a simultaneous rise in importance of the nuclear family as a consumer unit and of an occupational situation in which one or two wage earners supply necessary income for the family; often a substantial part of the rural family's income is derived from nonagricultural sources; (3) a decrease in the strength of traditional behavior norms and an increase in the importance of individualism, and egoism in social life; (4) a modification of social and economic organization, with extreme division of labor and specialization by tasks having great impact upon both; (5) a series of changes in political organization manifested in the growing political domination by urban dwellers, tremendous reductions in the political power of rural populations, decline in the importance of landownership as a means of political power, and a tendency for high position in the rural areas of most societies to become less significant in national politics; (6) a set of pervasive social movements, including efforts to organize farm labor, demands for agrarian reform, and civil-rights movements designed to elevate the positions of various racial, ethnic, and religious groups; (7) the development of a more heterogeneous sociocultural matrix within which the individual's personality is formed and within which he must work out for himself some reasonably comfortable pattern of accommodation: Inevitably, such a situation is less restricted and less predictable than the older more rural one in which homogeneity characterizes the social and cultural framework within which the members of each new generation acquire their human personalities; (8) a decrease in the tendency for various groups within society to rear and train children in mutually exclusive ways of life, particularly in rural and urban populations, members of various racial and ethnic groups, and people of different religious faiths: When the persons pertaining to these distinctive portions of society mingle, resultant personalities reflect the influences of all of them; (9) a vast growth in the number of elements that comprise the sociocultural system and in the intricacy of the same.

The rural base of social organization has changed least, of course, in the more remote and isolated sections of the world and in those where various factors have preserved traditional types of agriculture as a way of life for the masses of the population. Furthermore, a majority of the world's people still are tradition-oriented members of strictly agricultural communities. Even in the huge peasant societies of the world, however, influences that disrupt the traditional ways of life are being felt; and as urbanization proceeds, the pace of sociocultural change is sure to quicken.

THE FUTURE OF THE AGRICULTURAL CLASSES

The welfare of the farmer in many societies is now fully as dependent upon the nature of state and national policies for agriculture as it is upon the individual efforts of the farm family itself. Where this condition does not yet apply, it certainly promises to do so in the future. The tariff, the general property tax, the commercialization and mechanization of agriculture, specialization by tasks and enterprises, the operation of various regulatory agencies, the endeavors of groups that provide credit, the activities of national and international organizations that seek to improve farm life, and many other factors all have had a part in bringing this situation about in some societies. In others they promise to become increasingly common and influential features affecting rural life, for, as never before, the plight of agricultural people everywhere is the focus of endeavors to bring about fundamental changes. The well-being of the people on the land demands that national and state or provincial policies should not discriminate against them, and that they share somewhat equally in opportunity, income, and participation in the use of modern goods and services. In the last analysis, only comprehensive development of sociological fact and theory, including the increase of knowledge concerning all of the subjects discussed in this volume, can form the basis upon which adequate state and national policies can be established.

Additional Readings

1. BEAL, GEORGE M., "Social Action: Instigated Social Change in Large Social Systems," in James H. Copp (ed.), *Our Changing Rural Society: Perspectives and Trends*, Ames: Iowa State University Press, 1964, chapter 7.

2. BERTRAND, ALVIN L., "Agricultural Technology and Rural Social Change," in Alvin L. Bertrand (ed.), *Rural Sociology*, New York: McGraw-Hill Book Company, 1958, chapter 26.

3. BERTRAND, ALVIN L., "The Emerging Rural South: Under Confrontation by 'Mass' Society," *Rural Sociology*, Vol. 31, No. 4 (December, 1966), pp. 449–457.

4. LARSON, OLAF F., and EVERETT M. ROGERS, "Rural Society in Transition: The American Setting," in James H. Copp (ed.), *Our Changing Rural Society: Perspectives and Trends*, Ames: Iowa State University Press, 1964, chapter 2.

5. LOOMIS, CHARLES P., and J. ALLAN BEEGLE, *Rural Sociology: The Strategy of Change*, Englewood Cliffs, N. J.: Prentice-Hall, Inc., 1957, chapters 1 and 14.

6. NELSON, LOWRY, *American Farm Life*, Cambridge, Mass.: Harvard University Press, 1954.

7. OGBURN, WILLIAM F., *Social Change*, New York: The Viking Press, 1927.

8. ROGERS, EVERETT M., *Social Change in Rural Society*, New York: Appleton-Century-Crofts, Inc., 1960, chapters 1, 15, and 17.

9. SLOCUM, WALTER L., *Agricultural Sociology*, New York: Harper & Brothers, 1962, chapters 9 and 10.

10. SMITH, T. LYNN, *Colombia: Social Structure and the Process of Development*, Gainesville: University of Florida Press, 1967, chapters 6 and 10.

11. SMITH, T. LYNN, "Some Major Current Rural Social Trends in the United States of America," *International Social Science Journal*, Vol. XXI, No. 2 (1969), pp. 272–285.

12. WILKENING, EUGENE A., "Some Perspectives on Change in Rural Societies," *Rural Sociology*, Vol. 29, No. 1 (March, 1964), pp. 1–17.

BIBLIOGRAPHY

1. ACKERMAN, JOSEPH, and MARSHALL HARRIS, *Family Farm Policy*, Chicago: The University of Chicago Press, 1947.

2. ADRIAN, C. R., *State and Local Governments*, New York: McGraw-Hill Book Company, 1960.

3. AKTAN, RESAT, "Mechanization of Agriculture in Turkey," *Land Economics*, Vol. XXX, No. 4 (1957), pp. 273–285.

4. ALEXANDER, FRANK D., "The Problem of Locality-Group Classification," *Rural Sociology*, Vol. 17, No. 3 (September, 1952), pp. 236–244.

5. ALEXANDER, ROBERT J., "Agrarian Reform in Latin America," *Foreign Affairs*, Vol. 41, No. 1 (October, 1962), pp. 191–207.

6. ALLEGER, DANIEL E., "The Role of Agriculture in Retirement Adjustment: A Study of Five Florida Counties," *Rural Sociology*, Vol. 20, No. 2 (June, 1955), pp. 124–131.

7. ALLEN, HAROLD B., *Rural Reconstruction in Action: Experience in the Near and Middle East*, Ithaca: Cornell University Press, 1953.

8. American Friends Service Committee, *Social and Technical Assistance in India: An Interim Report*, Philadelphia: American Friends Service Committee, 1956.

9. ANDERSON, A. H., and C. J. MILLER, *The Changing Role of the Small Town in Farm Areas*, Nebraska AES Bulletin No. 419, Lincoln: University of Nebraska, 1953.

10. ANDERSON, C. ARNOLD, "Economic Status Differentials within Southern Agriculture," *Rural Sociology*, Vol. 19, No. 1 (March, 1954), pp. 50–67.

11. ANDERSON, C. ARNOLD, and T. LYNN SMITH, *Research in the Social Psychology of Rural Life*, New York: Social Science Research Council, 1933.

12. ANDERSON, WILLIAM, and EDWARD W. WEIDNER, *State and Local Government in the United States*, New York: Henry Holt and Company, Inc., 1951.

13. ARENSBERG, CONRAD M., and SOLON T. KIMBALL, *Culture and Community*, New York: Harcourt, Brace & World, Inc., 1965.

14. BAALI, FUAD, *Relations of the People to the Land in Southern Iraq*, Gainesville: University of Florida Press, 1966.

15. BAALI, FUAD, "Relationships of Man to the Land in Iraq," *Rural Sociology*, Vol. 31, No. 2 (June, 1966), pp. 171–182.

16. BAALI, FUAD, "Social Factors in Iraqi Rural-Urban Migration," *American Journal of Economics and Sociology*, Vol. XXVI, No. 6 (1966), pp. 359–364.

17. BAER, GABRIEL, *Population and Society in the Arab East*, London: Routledge and Kegan Paul, 1964.

18. BAILEY, HELEN M., and ABRAHAM P. NASATIR, *Latin America: The Development of Its Civilization* (second ed.), Englewood Cliffs, N.J.: Prentice-Hall, Inc., 1968.

19. BAILEY, JOSEPH C., *Seaman A. Knapp*, New York: Columbia University Press, 1945.

20. BAILEY, LIBERTY H., *The State and the Farmer*, New York: The Macmillan Company, 1908.

21. BAKER, GORDON E., *Rural versus Urban Political Power*, New York: Random House, Inc., 1955.

22. BANKS, VERA J., CALVIN L. BEALE, and GLADYS K. BOWLES, *Farm Population—Estimates for 1910-62*, Economic Research Service, Washington: Government Printing Office, 1963.

23. BEAL, GEORGE M., *The Roots of Participation in Farmers' Cooperatives*, Ames: Iowa State University Press, 1954.

24. BEAL, GEORGE M., DONALD R. FESSLER, and RAY E. WAKELEY, *Agricultural Cooperatives in Iowa: Farmers' Opinions and Community Relations*, Iowa AES Research Bulletin No. 379, Ames: Iowa State College, 1951.

25. BEALE, CALVIN L., "Rural Depopulation in the United States: Some Demographic Consequences of Agricultural Adjustments," *Demography*, Vol. 1, No. 1 (1964), pp. 264–272.

26. BEERS, HOWARD W., "Rural-Urban Differences: Some Evidence from Public Opinion Polls," *Rural Sociology*, Vol. 18, No. 1 (March, 1953), pp. 1–11.

27. BELCHER, JOHN C., "The Nonresident Farmer in the New Rural Society," *Rural Sociology*, Vol. 19, No. 2 (June, 1954), pp. 121–136.

28. BENVENUTI, BRUNO, *Farming in Cultural Change*, Assen, Netherlands: van Gorkum, 1961.

29. BERNARD, JESSIE, *American Community Behavior* (revised ed.), New York: Holt, Rinehart and Winston, Inc., 1962.

30. BERTRAND, ALVIN L., *Agricultural Mechanization and Social Change in Rural Louisiana*, Louisiana AES Bulletin No. 458, Baton Rouge: Louisiana State University, 1951.

31. BERTRAND, ALVIN L., *Basic Sociology: An Introduction to Theory and Method*, New York: Appleton-Century-Crofts, Inc., 1967.

32. BERTRAND, ALVIN L., "The Emerging Rural South: A Region under Confrontation by Mass Society," *Rural Sociology*, Vol. 31, No. 4 (December, 1966), pp. 449–457.

33. BERTRAND, ALVIN L., *The Many Louisianas: Rural Social Areas and Cultural Islands*, Louisiana AES Bulletin No. 496, Baton Rouge: Louisiana State University, 1955.

34. BERTRAND, ALVIN L., "Rural Locality Groups: Changing Patterns, Change Factors, and Implications," *Rural Sociology,* Vol. 19, No. 2 (June, 1954), pp. 174–179.

35. BERTRAND, ALVIN L. (ed.), *Rural Sociology,* New York: McGraw-Hill Book Company, 1958.

36. BERTRAND, ALVIN L., and FLOYD L. CORTY (eds.), *Rural Land Tenure in the United States,* Baton Rouge: Louisiana State University Press, 1962.

37. BERTRAND, ALVIN L., and HAROLD W. OSBORNE, *Rural Industrialization in a Louisiana Community,* Louisiana AES Bulletin No. 524, Baton Rouge: Louisiana State University, 1959.

38. BINNS, BERNARD O., *The Consolidation of Fragmented Agricultural Holdings,* Washington: Food and Agricultural Organization of the United Nations, 1950.

39. BIZZELL, WILLIAM B., *The Green Rising,* New York: The Macmillan Company, 1926.

40. BLAISDELL, D. C., *Government and Agriculture,* New York: Farrar and Rinehart, 1940.

41. BOGUE, DONALD J., *The Population of the United States,* Glencoe, Ill.: The Free Press, 1959.

42. BOGUE, DONALD J., and CALVIN L. BEALE, *Economic Areas of the United States,* Glencoe, Ill.: The Free Press, 1961.

43. BONILLA, FRANK, "Rural Reform in Brazil," *Dissent,* Vol. IX, No. 4 (1962), pp. 373–382.

44. BOYLE, GEORGE M., "Nova Scotia: An Experiment in Education," *Yearbook of Agricultural Cooperation,* London: Horace Plunkett Foundation, 1935.

45. BRACEY, H. E., *English Rural Life,* London: Routledge and Kegan Paul, 1959.

46. BRANNEN, C. O., *The Relation of Land Tenure to Plantation Organization,* U.S. Department of Agriculture Bulletin No. 1269, Washington: Government Printing Office, 1924.

47. BRANSON, E. C., *Farm Life Abroad,* Chapel Hill: University of North Carolina Press, 1924.

48. BREMER, FREDRIKA, *The Homes of the New World; Impressions of America,* New York: Harper & Brothers, 1854.

49. BROOKS, ROBERT P., *The Agrarian Revolution in Georgia, 1865–1912,* University of Wisconsin Historical Series, Vol. III, No. 1, Madison: University of Wisconsin, 1914.

50. BRUCHER, FELIX, *Vocational Agriculture Education in Developing Countries, General Remarks and the Program in the Syrian Arab Republic,* Damascus: Ford Foundation, 1962.

51. BRUNNER, EDMUND deS., *The Growth of a Science,* New York: Harper & Brothers, 1957.

52. BRUNNER, EDMUND deS., *Radio and the Farmer*, New York: The Radio Institute of the Audible Arts, 1935.

53. BRUNNER, EDMUND deS., "The Small Village, 1940–1950," *Rural Sociology*, Vol. 17, No. 2 (June, 1952), pp. 127–131.

54. BRUNNER, EDMUND deS., *Village Communities*, New York: Doubleday, Doran & Company, 1928.

55. BRUNNER, EDMUND deS., GWENDOLYN S. HUGHES, and MARJORIE PATTEN, *American Agricultural Villages*, New York: Doubleday, Doran & Company, 1927.

56. BRUNNER, EDMUND deS., and JOHN H. KOLB, *Rural Social Trends*, New York: McGraw-Hill Book Company, Inc., 1933.

57. BRUNNER, EDMUND deS., and IRVING LORGE, *Rural Trends in Depression Years*, New York: Columbia University Press, 1937.

58. BRUNNER, EDMUND deS., IRWIN T. SANDERS, and DOUGLAS ENSMINGER (eds.), *Farmers of the World: The Story of Agricultural Extension*, New York: Columbia University Press, 1945.

59. BUCK, SOLON J., *The Granger Movement*, Cambridge, Mass.: Harvard University Press, 1913.

60. BURCHINAL, LEE G., "Correlates of Marital Satisfaction for Rural Married Couples," *Rural Sociology*, Vol. 26, No. 3 (September, 1961), pp. 282–289.

61. BURGESS, ERNEST W., HARVEY J. LOCKE, and MARY M. THOMES, *The Family: From Institution to Companionship* (third ed.), New York: American Book Company, 1963.

62. BURNS, JAMES M., and JACK W. PELTASON, *Government by the People*, Englewood Cliffs, N. J.: Prentice-Hall, Inc., 1957.

63. BURRUS, JOHN N., *Life Opportunities*, Oxford: University of Mississippi, 1951.

64. BUTTERFIELD, KENYON L., *Chapters in Rural Progress*, Chicago: The University of Chicago Press, 1908.

65. BUTTERFIELD, KENYON L., *The Farmer and the New Day*, New York: The Macmillan Company, 1919.

66. BUTZ, EARL L., "Agribusiness in the Machine Age," in *Power to Produce, Yearbook of Agriculture, 1960*, Washington: Government Printing Office, 1960, pp. 380–384.

67. CARRIER, LYMAN, *The Beginnings of Agriculture in America*, New York: McGraw-Hill Book Company, 1923.

68. CARROLL, H. K., *The Religious Forces of the United States*, New York: The Christian Literature Company, 1893.

69. Center for Agricultural and Economic Development, *Problems and Policies of American Agriculture*, Ames: Iowa State University Press, 1959.

70. CHANG, PEI-KANG, *Agriculture and Industrialization,* Cambridge, Mass.: Harvard University Press, 1949.

71. CHANNING, EDWARD, *Town and Country Government in the English Colonies of North America,* Baltimore: Johns Hopkins University, 1884.

72. CHAPARRO, ALVARO, and RALPH H. ALLEE, "Higher Agricultural Education and Social Change in Latin America," *Rural Sociology,* Vol. 25, No. 1 (March, 1960), pp. 9–25.

73. CHRISTIANSEN, JOHN R., and others, *Industrialization and Rural Life in Two Central Utah Counties,* Utah AES Bulletin No. 416, Logan: Utah State University, 1959.

74. CLARK, ROBERT C., and NOEL P. RALSTON (eds.), *Directing the Cooperative Extension Service,* Madison: University of Wisconsin, 1962.

75. CLAWSON, MARION, *The Land System of the United States: An Introduction to the History and Practice of Land Use and Land Tenure,* Lincoln: University of Nebraska Press, 1968.

76. CLAWSON, MARION, *The Public Domain in 1953,* Department of the Interior, Bureau of Land Management, Washington: Government Printing Office, 1953.

77. CODRINGTON, ROBERT H., *The Melanesians,* Oxford: The Clarendon Press, 1891.

78. COLEMAN, LEE, "Differential Contact with Extension Work in a New York Rural Community," *Rural Sociology,* Vol. 16, No. 3 (September, 1951), pp. 207–216.

79. COOLEY, CHARLES H., *Social Organization,* New York: Charles Scribner's Sons, 1925.

80. COPP, JAMES H. (ed.), *Our Changing Rural Society: Perspectives and Trends,* Ames: Iowa State University Press, 1964.

81. COPP, JAMES H., "Perceptual Influences on Loyalty in a Farmer Cooperative," *Rural Sociology,* Vol. 29, No. 2 (June, 1964), pp. 168–180.

82. COPP, JAMES H., "Toward Generalization in Farm Practice Research," *Rural Sociology,* Vol. 23, No. 2 (June, 1958), pp. 106–107.

83. COUGHENHOUR, C. MILTON, "An Application of Scale Analysis to the Study of Religious Groups," *Rural Sociology,* Vol. 20, Nos. 3–4 (September-December, 1955), pp. 197–207.

84. COWHIG, JAMES D., *Age-Grade School Progress of Farm and Nonfarm Youth, 1960,* Economic Research Service, Agricultural Economic Report No. 42, Washington: Government Printing Office, 1963.

85. CRAMPTON, JOHN A., *The National Farmers Union,* Lincoln: University of Nebraska Press, 1965.

86. CRANE, VERNER W., *The Southern Frontier, 1670–1732,* Durham: Duke University Press, 1928.

87. CRIST, RAYMOND E., *The Cauca Valley, Colombia: Land Tenure and Land Use,* Baltimore: Waverly Press, 1952.

88. CRIST, RAYMOND E., *Land for the Fellahin: Land Tenure and Land Use in the Near East,* New York: Robert Schalkenbach Foundation, 1961.

89. DAVIS, JOHN H., "From Agriculture to Agribusiness," *Harvard Business Review,* Vol. 34 (1956), pp. 107–115.

90. DAVIS, JOHN H., and RAY A. GOLDBERG, *A Concept of Agribusiness,* Boston: Harvard Business School, 1957.

91. DAVIS, KINGSLEY, and WILBERT E. MOORE, "Some Principles of Stratification," *American Sociological Review,* Vol. 10, No. 2 (April, 1945), pp. 242–249.

92. DEAN, ALFRED, HERBERT A. AURBACH, and C. PAUL MARSH, "Some Factors Related to Rationality in Decision Making Among Farm Operators," *Rural Sociology,* Vol. 23, No. 2 (June, 1958), pp. 121–135.

93. DEBOW, J. D. B., *Statistical View of the United States: A Compendium of the Seventh Census,* Washington: A. O. P. Nicholson, 1854.

94. DERBER, MILTON (ed.), *The Aged and Society,* Champaign, Ill.: Industrial Research Association, 1950.

95. de WAAL MALEFIJT, ANNEMARIE, *Religion and Culture,* New York: The Macmillan Company, 1968.

96. de YOUNG, MAURICE, *Man and Land in the Haitian Economy,* Gainesville: University of Florida Press, 1958.

97. DIES, EDWARD J., *Titans of the Soils,* Chapel Hill: University of North Carolina Press, 1949.

98. DITCHFIELD, P. H., *Old Village Life, or Glimpses of Village Life through the Ages,* New York: E. P. Dutton & Company, 1920.

99. DONALDSON, THOMAS, *The Public Domain,* House Miscellaneous Document No. 45, Washington: Government Printing Office, 1884.

100. DUBOIS, W. E. BURGHARDT, *Economic Co-operation Among Negro Americans,* Atlanta University Publication No. 6, Atlanta: Atlanta University, 1907.

101. DUCOFF, LOUIS J., "Classification of the Agricultural Population in the United States," *Journal of Farm Economics,* Vol. 37 (1955), pp. 511–523.

102. DUNCAN, OTIS DUDLEY, "Gradients of Urban Influence on the Rural Population," *Midwest Sociologist,* Vol. 18 (1956), pp. 27–30.

103. DUNCAN, OTIS DUDLEY, and ALBERT J. REISS, JR., *Social Characteristics of Urban and Rural Communities, 1950,* New York: John Wiley & Sons, Inc., 1956.

104. DUNCAN, OTIS DURANT, *Factors Related to Levels of Living of Oklahoma Farm Families,* Oklahoma AES Bulletin No. B 429, Stillwater: Oklahoma State University, 1954.

105. DUNCAN, OTIS DURANT, "Rural Sociology Coming of Age," *Rural Sociology,* Vol. 19, No. 1 (March, 1954), pp. 1–12.

106. DUNCAN, OTIS DURANT, and others, *Social Research on Health,* New York: Social Science Research Council, 1946.

107. DURKHEIM, EMILE, *Elementary Forms of Religious Life,* London: Macmillan & Co., Ltd., 1915.

108. DURKHEIM, EMILE, *Suicide: A Study in Sociology* (trans. by John A. Spaulding and George Simpson), Glencoe, Ill.: The Free Press, 1951.

109. DWIGHT, TIMOTHY, *Travels in New England and New York,* London: W. Baynes and Son, 1823, 4 vols.

110. DYER, WILLIAM G., "Development of a Mormon Line Community," *Rural Sociology,* Vol. 21, No. 2 (June, 1956), pp. 181–182.

111. EDDY, EDWARD D., JR., *Colleges for Our Land and Time,* New York: Harper & Brothers, 1957.

112. ELLIS, L. W., and EDWARD A. RUMLEY, *Power and the Plow,* New York: Doubleday, Page & Co., 1911.

113. ERASMUS, CHARLES, *Man Takes Control,* Minneapolis: University of Minnesota Press, 1961.

114. FAIRLIE, JOHN A., *Local Government in Counties, Towns, and Villages,* New York: D. Appleton-Century Company, 1906.

115. FALS-BORDA, ORLANDO, *Facts and Theory of Sociocultural Change in a Rural Social System,* Monografías Sociológicas No. 2 Bis. Bogotá: Departamento de Sociología, Universidad Nacional de Colombia, 1960.

116. FALS-BORDA, ORLANDO, "Fragmentation of Holdings in Boyacá, Colombia," *Rural Sociology,* Vol. 21, No. 2 (June, 1956), pp. 158–163.

117. FALS-BORDA, ORLANDO, *Peasant Life in the Colombian Andes,* Gainesville: University of Florida Press, 1955.

118. FINLEY, JAMES R., "Farm Practice Adoption: A Predictive Model," *Rural Sociology,* Vol. 33, No. 1 (March, 1968), pp. 5–18.

119. FIRTH, RAYMOND, *Elements of Social Organization,* London: Watts and Co., 1951.

120. FLORES, EDMUNDO, "Land Reform in Bolivia," *Land Economics,* Vol. XXX, No. 2 (May, 1954), pp. 112–124.

121. FOLKMAN, WILLIAM S., "Board Members as Decision Makers in Farmers' Co-operatives," *Rural Sociology,* Vol. 23, No. 3 (September, 1958), pp. 239–252.

122. FOLKMAN, WILLIAM S., *Membership Relations in Farmers' Purchasing Cooperatives,* Arkansas AES Bulletin No. 556, Fayetteville: University of Arkansas, 1955.

123. FOOT, SIR HUGH, *A Start in Freedom,* London: Hodder and Stoughton, 1964.

124. FORD, AMELIA CLEWLEY, *Colonial Precedents of Our National Land System as It Existed in 1800,* Bulletin of the University of Wisconsin No. 352, Madison: University of Wisconsin, 1910.

125. FORD, EDMUND A., *Rural Renaissance: Revitalizing Small Schools,* Department of Health, Education, and Welfare Bulletin No. 11, Washington: Government Printing Office, 1961.

126. FORD, THOMAS R., *Man and Land in Peru,* Gainesville: University of Florida Press, 1955.

127. FORD, THOMAS R. (ed.), *The Southern Appalachian Region: A Survey,* Lexington: University of Kentucky Press, 1962.

128. FRAZER, J. G., *The Golden Bough,* London: Macmillan & Co., Ltd., 1925–1926, 12 vols.

129. FRAZIER, E. FRANKLIN, *The Negro Family in the United States,* Chicago: The University of Chicago Press, 1939.

130. FREEDMAN, RONALD, and DEBORAH FREEDMAN, "Farm-Reared Elements in the Non-farm Population," *Rural Sociology,* Vol. 21, No. 1 (March, 1956), pp. 50–61.

131. FUGUITT, GLENN V., "The City and the Countryside," *Rural Sociology,* Vol. 28, No. 3 (September, 1963), pp. 246–261.

132. FUGUITT, GLENN V., "Urban Influences and the Extent of Part-time Farming," *Rural Sociology,* Vol. 23, No. 4 (December, 1958), pp. 392–397.

133. FUJII, YUKIO, and T. LYNN SMITH, *The Acculturation of Japanese Immigrants in Brazil,* Gainesville: University of Florida Press, 1959.

134. FULLER, VARDERN, *Labor Relations in Agriculture,* Berkeley: University of California Press, 1955.

135. FULMER, JOHN L., *Agricultural Progress in the Cotton Belt Since 1920,* Chapel Hill: University of North Carolina Press, 1950.

136. GALLAHER, ART, JR., *Plainville Fifteen Years Later,* New York: Columbia University Press, 1961.

137. GALPIN, CHARLES J., *My Drift into Rural Sociology,* Baton Rouge: Louisiana State University Press, 1938.

138. GALPIN, CHARLES J., *Rural Life,* New York: D. Appleton-Century Company, 1920.

139. GALPIN, CHARLES J., *Rural Social Problems,* New York: D. Appleton-Century Company, 1924.

140. GALPIN, CHARLES J., *The Social Anatomy of an Agricultural Community,* Wisconsin AES Bulletin No. 34, Madison: University of Wisconsin, 1915.

141. GALPIN, CHARLES J., and T. B. MANNY, *Interstate Migrations Among the Native White Population as Indicated by Differences Between State of Birth and State of Residence,* Washington: Government Printing Office, 1934.

142. GARCÍA, LUIS ROBERTO, "Notes on Land Tenure in Colombia," *Rural Sociology*, Vol. 10, No. 4 (December, 1945), pp. 416–418.

143. GEE, WILSON, *The Social Economics of Agriculture* (third ed.), New York: The Macmillan Company, 1954.

144. GIFFORD, CLAUDE W., "How Farmers Vote to Use Bargaining Power," *Farm Journal*, Vol. 92, No. 5 (May, 1968), pp. 24–25 and 42–44.

145. GILLETTE, JOHN M., *Constructive Rural Sociology*, New York: Sturgis and Walton Company, 1913.

146. GILLETTE, JOHN M., *Rural Sociology* (third ed.), New York: The Macmillan Company, 1936.

147. GIST, NOEL P., "Ecological Decentralization and Rural-Urban Relationships," *Rural Sociology*, Vol. 17, No. 4 (December, 1952), pp. 328–335.

148. GITTINGER, J. PRICE, *Planning for Agricultural Development: The Iranian Experience*, Washington: Center for Development Planning, National Planning Association, 1965.

149. GODKIN, JAMES, *The Land-War in Ireland*, London: Macmillan & Co., 1870.

150. GOLDSCHMIDT, WALTER, *As Your Sow*, New York: Harcourt, Brace and Co., 1947.

151. GOMME, GEORGE L., *The Village Community, with Special Reference to the Origin and Form of Its Survivals in Britain*, London: Walter Scott, Ltd., 1890.

152. GOSSE, A. BOTHWELL, *The Civilization of the Ancient Egyptians*, London: T. C. and E. Jack, 1915.

153. GRADY, HENRY, "Cotton and the South," *Harper's Magazine*, Vol. LXIII (1881).

154. GRANOTT, A., *The Land System in Palestine*, London: Eyre and Spottiswoode, 1952.

155. GRAY, L. C., *History of Agriculture in the Southern United States to 1860*, Washington: The Carnegie Institution of Washington, 1933, 2 vols.

156. GREEN, JAMES W., and SELZ C. MAYO, "A Framework for Research in the Actions of Community Groups," *Social Forces*, Vol. 31, No. 4 (May, 1953), pp. 320–327.

157. GRISWOLD, A. WHITNEY, *Farming and Democracy*, New York: Harcourt, Brace and Co., 1948.

158. GROSS, EDWARD, *Work and Society*, New York: Thomas Y. Crowell Co., 1958.

159. GROSS, NEAL, and MARVIN J. TAVES, "Characteristics Associated with Acceptance of Recommended Farm Practices," *Rural Sociology*, Vol. 17, No. 4 (December, 1952), pp. 321–327.

160. GULICK, JOHN, *Social Structure and Cultural Change in a Lebanese Village,* New York: Wenner-Gren Foundation for Anthropological Research, 1955.

161. HAGOOD, MARGARET J., *Farm-Operator Family Level-of-Living Indexes for Counties of the United States, 1930, 1940, 1945, and 1950,* Department of Agriculture, Washington: Government Printing Office, 1952 (mimeographed).

162. HALLER, ARCHIBALD O., "Planning to Farm: A Social Psychological Interpretation," *Social Forces,* Vol. 37, No. 3 (March, 1959), pp. 264–268.

163. HALLER, ARCHIBALD O., and EDGAR F. BORGATTA, "Rural Sociology in 1967," *The American Sociologist,* Vol. 3, No. 4 (November, 1969), pp. 289–290.

164. HALPERN, JOEL M., *The Changing Village Community,* Englewood Cliffs, N.J.: Prentice-Hall, Inc., 1967.

165. HAMILTON, C. HORACE, "Population Pressure and other Factors Affecting Net Rural-Urban Migration," *Social Forces,* Vol. 30, No. 2 (December, 1951), pp. 209–215.

166. HAMILTON, C. HORACE, "Some Current Problems in the Development of Rural Sociology," *Rural Sociology,* Vol. 15, No. 4 (December, 1950), pp. 315–321.

167. HARDEN, WARREN R., "Social and Economic Effects of Community Size," *Rural Sociology,* Vol. 25, No. 2 (June, 1960), pp. 204–211.

168. HARDIN, CHARLES M., *The Politics of Agriculture: Soil Conservation and the Struggle for Power in Rural America,* Glencoe, Ill.: The Free Press, 1952.

169. HARRIS, MARSHALL, "A New Agricultural Ladder," *Land Economics,* Vol. 25 (1950), pp. 258–262.

170. HARRIS, MARSHALL, *Origin of the Land Tenure System in the United States,* Ames: Iowa State University Press, 1953.

171. HASTINGS, JAMES, *Encyclopedia of Religion and Ethics,* New York: Charles Scribner's Sons, 1925.

172. HATCH, EARL, *Rebuilding Rural America,* New York: Harper & Brothers, 1950.

173. HATHAWAY, DALE E., *Government and Agriculture,* New York: The Macmillan Company, 1963.

174. HATHAWAY, DALE E., J. ALLAN BEEGLE, and W. KEITH BRYANT, *People of Rural America* (A 1960 Census Monograph), Washington: Government Printing Office, 1968.

175. HATHAWAY, DALE E., and ARLEY D. WALDO, *Multiple Jobholding by Farm Operators,* Michigan AES Research Bulletin No. 5, East Lansing: Michigan State University, 1964.

176. HAWLEY, AMOS H., *Human Ecology: A Theory of Community Structure,* New York: The Ronald Press Company, 1950.

177. HAYTER, EARL W., *The Troubled Farmer: 1850–1900,* Dekalb: Northern Illinois University Press, 1968.

178. HEADY, EARL O., and JOSEPH ACKERMAN, "Farm Adjustment Problems and Their Importance to Sociologists," *Rural Sociology,* Vol. 24, No. 4 (December, 1959), pp. 315–325.

179. HEADY, EARL O., and others, *Interdependence Between the Farm Business and the Farm Household with Implications of Economic Efficiency,* Iowa AES Research Bulletin No. 398, Ames: Iowa State University, 1953.

180. HEATH, DWIGHT B., "Land Tenure and Social Organization: An Ethnohistorical Study from the Bolivian Oriente," *Inter-American Affairs,* Vol. XIII, No. 4 (Spring, 1960), pp. 46–66.

181. HEIN, CLARENCE J., "Rural Local Government in Sparsely Populated Areas," *Journal of Farm Economics,* Vol. XLII, No. 4 (November, 1960), pp. 827–841.

182. HERO, ALFRED O., JR., *The Southerner and World Affairs,* Baton Rouge: Louisiana State University Press, 1965.

183. HERSKOVITS, MELVILLE J., *Acculturation,* New York: J. J. Augustin, 1938.

184. HILL, GEORGE W., and MARION T. LOFTIN, *Characteristics of Rural Life and the Agrarian Reform in Honduras,* Tegucigalpa: OEA Mision de Asistencia Tecnica, 1961.

185. HILLERY, GEORGE A., *Communal Organizations: A Study of Local Societies,* Chicago: The University of Chicago Press, 1968.

186. HILLERY, GEORGE A., "Definitions of Community: Areas of Agreement," *Rural Sociology,* Vol. 20, No. 2 (June, 1955), pp. 111–123.

187. HIMES, JOSEPH S., *The Study of Sociology,* Glenview, Ill.: Scott, Foresman and Company, 1968.

188. HIRSCHMAN, ALBERT O., *Journeys Toward Progress: Studies of Economic Policy-Making in Latin America,* New York: The Twentieth Century Fund, 1963.

189. HIRSCHMAN, ALBERT O. (ed.), *Latin American Issues,* New York: The Twentieth Century Fund, 1961.

190. HITT, HOMER L., J. ALLAN BEEGLE, and JOHN N. BURRUS, "Levels and Trends in Rural Mortality," *Rural Sociology,* Vol. 19, No. 1 (March, 1954), pp. 75–78.

191. HITT, HOMER L., and ALVIN L. BERTRAND, *Social Aspects of Hospital Planning in Louisiana: Mortality, Facilities, Personnel, Population, Education, Living Conveniences, Purchasing Power,* Louisiana Study Series No. 1, Baton Rouge: Louisiana Agricultural Experiment Station and Health and Hospital Division of the Office of the Governor, 1947.

192. HITT, HOMER L., and PAUL H. PRICE, *Health in Rural Louisiana at Mid-Century,* Louisiana AES Bulletin No. 492, Baton Rouge: Louisiana State University, 1954.

511

193. HO, PING-TI, *Studies on the Population of China, 1368–1953,* Cambridge, Mass.: Harvard University Press, 1959.

194. HODGES, HAROLD M., *Social Stratification,* Cambridge, Mass.: Schenkman Publishing Co., Inc., 1964.

195. HOFFER, CHARLES R., "The Development of Rural Sociology," *Rural Sociology,* Vol. 26, No. 1 (March, 1961), pp. 1–14.

196. HOFFSOMMER, HAROLD (ed.), *The Social and Economic Significance of Land Tenure in the Southwestern States: A Report on the Regional Tenure Research Project,* Chapel Hill: University of North Carolina Press, 1950 .

197. HOFSTADTER, RICHARD, *The American Political Tradition,* New York: Alfred A. Knopf, Inc., 1948.

198. HOFSTEE, E. W., "Rural Sociology in Europe," *Rural Sociology,* Vol. 28, No. 4 (December, 1963), pp. 329–341.

199. HOIBERG, OTTO G., *Exploring the Small Community,* Lincoln: University of Nebraska Press, 1955.

200. HOLT, JOHN B., *German Agricultural Policy, 1918–1934,* Chapel Hill: University of North Carolina Press, 1936.

201. HOOKER, ELIZABETH R., *United Churches,* New York: Doubleday, Doran & Company, 1926.

202. HOSELITZ, BERT F., *Sociological Aspects of Economic Growth,* Glencoe, Ill.: The Free Press, 1960.

203. HOSTETLER, JOHN A., "Old World Extinction and New World Survival of the Amish: A Study of Group Maintenance and Dissolution," *Rural Sociology,* Vol. 20, Nos. 3–4 (September-December, 1955), pp. 212–219.

204. *How Farm People Accept New Ideas,* North Central Regional Publication No. 1 of the AES, Special Report No. 15, Ames: Iowa State College, 1955.

205. HOWE, FREDERIC C., *Denmark: The Cooperative Way,* New York: Coward-McCann, Inc., 1936.

206. HUNTER, FLOYD, *Community Power Structure,* Chapel Hill: University of North Carolina Press, 1953.

207. *International Encyclopedia of the Social Sciences,* New York and Glencoe, Ill.: The Macmillan Company and The Free Press, 1968, 17 vols.

208. JAMESON, J. FRANKLIN, *Johnson's Wonder-Working Providence, 1628–1651,* New York: Charles Scribner's Sons, 1910.

209. JEHLIK, PAUL J., and RAY E. WAKELEY, *Population Change and Net Migration in the North Central States, 1940–50,* Iowa AES Research Bulletin No. 432, Ames: Iowa State College, 1955.

210. JOHNSON, CHARLES S., *Shadow of the Plantation,* Chicago: The University of Chicago Press, 1934.

211. JOHNSON, CHARLES S., EDWIN R. EMBREE, and W. W. ALEXANDER, *The Collapse of Cotton Tenancy*, Chapel Hill: University of North Carolina Press, 1935.

212. KAHL, JOSEPH A., *Comparative Perspectives on Stratification: Mexico, Great Britain, Japan*, Boston: Little, Brown and Company, 1968.

213. KAMPE, RONALD E., *The Agricultural Economy of Lebanon*, Department of Agriculture, Washington: Government Printing Office, 1965.

214. KANTOR, MILDRED B. (ed.), *Mobility and Mental Health*, New York: Charles C Thomas, 1965.

215. KAUFMAN, HAROLD F., *Prestige Classes in a New York Rural Community*, Cornell AES Memoir No. 260, Ithaca: Cornell University, 1944.

216. KAUFMAN, HAROLD F., *Religious Organizations in Kentucky*, Kentucky AES Bulletin No. 524, Lexington: University of Kentucky, 1948.

217. KAUFMAN, HAROLD F., *Rural Families with Low Incomes: Problems in Adjustment*, Mississippi AES Sociology and Rural Life Series No. 9, State College: Mississippi State University, 1957.

218. KAUFMAN, HAROLD F., "Toward an Interactional Conception of Community," *Social Forces*, Vol. 38, No. 1 (October, 1959), pp. 8–17.

219. KAUFMAN, HAROLD F., and WILFRID C. BAILEY, *Rural Sociology and Rural Development Programs*, Mississippi AES Sociology and Rural Life Series No. 7, State College: Mississippi State University, 1956.

220. KAUFMAN, HAROLD F., and KENNETH P. WILKINSON, *Community Structure and Leadership: An Interactional Perspective in the Study of Community*, Mississippi State University Social Science Research Center Bulletin No. 13, State College: Mississippi State University, 1967.

221. KAUFMAN, HAROLD F., and others, "Problems of Theory and Method in the Study of Social Stratification in Rural Society," *Rural Sociology*, Vol. 18, No. 1 (March, 1953), pp. 12–24.

222. KENKEL, WILLIAM F., *The Family in Perspective*, New York: Appleton-Century-Crofts, 1960.

223. KESTER, HOWARD, *Revolt Among the Sharecroppers*, New York: Covici Friede, Inc., 1936.

224. KILE, O. M., *The Farm Bureau Through Three Decades*, Baltimore: Waverly Press, 1948.

225. KIMBALL, SOLON T., "Rural Social Organization and Cooperative Labor," *American Journal of Sociology*, Vol. 55, No. 1 (July, 1949), pp. 38–49.

226. KIVLIN, JOSEPH E., and FREDERICK C. FLIEGEL, "Orientations to Agriculture: A Factor Analysis of Farmers' Perceptions of New Practices," *Rural Sociology*, Vol. 33, No. 2 (June, 1968), pp. 127–140.

227. KOLB, JOHN H., "Dr. Galpin at Wisconsin," *Rural Sociology*, Vol. 13, No. 2 (June, 1948), pp. 130–145.

228. KOLB, JOHN H., *Emerging Rural Communities*, Madison: University of Wisconsin Press, 1959.

229. KOLB, JOHN H., and EDMUND S. BRUNNER, *A Study of Rural Society*, Boston: Houghton Mifflin Company, 1935.

230. KOLB, JOHN H., and EDMUND deS. BRUNNER, *A Study of Rural Society* (fourth ed.), Boston: Houghton Mifflin Company, 1952.

231. KOLB, JOHN H., and LeROY J. DAY, *Interdependence in Town and Country Relations in Rural Society*, Wisconsin AES Bulletin No. 172, Madison: University of Wisconsin, 1950.

232. KOLB, JOHN H., and DOUGLAS G. MARSHALL, *Neighborhood-Community Relationships in Rural Society*, Wisconsin AES Research Bulletin No. 154, Madison: University of Wisconsin, 1944.

233. KOLB, JOHN H., and ROBERT A. POLSON, *Trends in Town-Country Relations*, Wisconsin AES Research Bulletin No. 117, Madison: University of Wisconsin, 1933.

234. KREITLOW, BURTON W., *Rural Education*, New York: Harper & Brothers, 1954.

235. KROPOTKIN, PETER, *Mutual Aid: A Factor in Evolution*, New York: McClure, Phillips & Co., 1902.

236. KURTZ, RICHARD, and JOEL SMITH, "Social Life in the Rural-Urban Fringe," *Rural Sociology*, Vol. 26, No. 3 (September, 1963), pp. 24–38.

237. LANCASTER, LANE W., *Government in Rural America* (second ed.), Princeton: D. Van Nostrand Co., Inc., 1952.

238. LANDIS, BENSON Y., "Trends in Church Membership in the United States," *Annals of the American Academy of Political and Social Science*, No. 332 (November, 1960), pp. 1–8.

239. LANDIS, PAUL H., *Rural Life in Process* (second ed.), New York: McGraw-Hill Book Company, 1948.

240. LARSON, OLAF F., "Income and Welfare of Rural People—Agricultural Research Significant to Public Policy, Public Welfare, and Community Improvement," *Rural Sociology*, Vol. 30, No. 4 (December, 1965), pp. 452–461.

241. LARSON, OLAF F., "Sociological Aspects of the Low-Income Farm Problem," *Journal of Farm Economics*, Vol. 37 (1955), pp. 1417–1427.

242. LEIGH, FRANCES B., *Ten Years on a Georgia Plantation Since the War*, London: R. Bentley & Sons, 1883.

243. LEONARD, OLEN E., *Bolivia: Land, People, and Institutions*, Washington: Scarecrow Press, 1952.

244. LEONARD, OLEN E., *Canton Chullpas: A Socioeconomic Study in the Cochabamba Valley of Bolivia,* Office of Foreign Agricultural Relations, Washington: Government Printing Office, 1948.

245. LEONARD, OLEN E., *Pichilingue: A Study of Rural Life in Coastal Ecuador,* Office of Foreign Agricultural Relations, Washington: Government Printing Office, 1947.

246. LEONARD, OLEN E., *The Role of the Land Grant in the Social Organization and Social Processes of a Spanish-American Village in New Mexico,* Ann Arbor: Edwards Brothers, Inc., 1948.

247. LEONARD, OLEN E., *Santa Cruz: A Socioeconomic Study of an Area in Bolivia,* Office of Foreign Agricultural Relations, Washington: Government Printing Office, 1948.

248. LERAY, NELSON L., and others, *Plantation Organization and the Resident Labor Force, Delta Area of Mississippi,* Mississippi AES Bulletin No. 606, State College: Mississippi State University, 1960.

249. LERNER, DANIEL, *The Passing of Traditional Society: Modernizing the Middle East,* Glencoe, Ill.: The Free Press, 1958.

250. LESLIE, GERALD R., *The Family in Social Context,* New York: Oxford University Press, 1967.

251. LIONBERGER, HERBERT F., *Adoption of New Ideas and Practices,* Ames: Iowa State University Press, 1960.

252. LIONBERGER, HERBERT F., "The Diffusion of Farm and Home Information as an Area of Sociological Research," *Rural Sociology,* Vol. 17, No. 2 (June, 1952), pp. 132–140.

253. LIONBERGER, HERBERT F., and EDWARD HASSINGER, "Neighborhoods as a Factor in the Diffusion of Farm Information in a Northeast Missouri Farming Community," *Rural Sociology,* Vol. 19, No. 4 (December, 1954), pp. 337–384.

254. LIPPITT, RONALD, and others, *The Dynamics of Planned Change,* New York: Harcourt, Brace & World, Inc., 1958.

255. LIPSET, SEYMOUR M., "Social Mobility and Urbanization," *Rural Sociology,* Vol. 20, Nos. 3–4 (September-December, 1955), pp. 220–227.

256. LONGMORE, WILSON T., and CARL C. TAYLOR, "Elasticity of Expenditures for Farm Family Living, Farm Production, and Savings, United States, 1946," *Journal of Farm Economics,* Vol. XXXIII, No. 1 (February, 1951), pp. 1–19.

257. LOOMIS, CHARLES P., *Studies in Rural Social Organization,* East Lansing: Michigan State College Bookstore, 1945.

258. LOOMIS, CHARLES P., and J. ALLAN BEEGLE, *Rural Social Systems: A Textbook in Rural Sociology and Anthropology,* New York: Prentice-Hall, Inc., 1950.

259. LOOMIS, CHARLES P., and J. ALLAN BEEGLE, *Rural Sociology: The Strategy of Change,* Englewood Cliffs, N.J.: Prentice-Hall, Inc., 1957.

260. LOOMIS, CHARLES P., and others, *Rural Social Systems and Adult Education,* East Lansing: Michigan State University Press, 1953.

261. LOOMIS, CHARLES P., and others (eds.), *Turrialba: Social Systems and the Introduction of Change,* Glencoe, Ill.: The Free Press, 1953.

262. LOPREATO, JOSEPH, *Peasants No More,* San Francisco: Chandler Publishing Co., 1967.

263. LORING, F. W., and C. F. ATKINSON, *Cotton Culture and the South Considered with Reference to Emigration,* Boston: A. Williams & Co., 1869.

264. MACIVER, ROBERT M., *Community: A Sociological Study,* London: Macmillan and Company, Ltd., 1920.

265. MACIVER, ROBERT M., *Society: Its Structure and Changes,* New York: R. Long and R. R. Smith, Inc., 1931.

266. MACIVER, ROBERT M., *Society: A Textbook of Sociology,* New York: R. Long and R. R. Smith, Inc., 1937.

267. MADDEN, J. PATRICK, *Economies of Size in Farming,* Department of Agriculture, Agricultural Economic Report No. 107, Washington: Government Printing Office, 1967.

268. MADDOX, JAMES S., *Land Reform in Mexico,* New York: American Universities Field Staff, 1958.

269. MAINE, SIR HENRY S., *Village Communities in the East and West,* New York: Henry Holt & Company, 1889.

270. MAITLAND, F. W., *Domesday Book and Beyond,* Cambridge: University Press, 1897.

271. MANNY, THEODORE B., *Attitudes Toward Rural Government,* Department of Agriculture, Washington: Government Printing Office, 1929.

272. MANNY, THEODORE B., BUSHROD W. ALLIN, and CLIFTON J. BRADLEY, *Farm Taxes and Local Government in Crittenden and Livingston Counties, Kentucky,* Kentucky AES Bulletin No. 355, Lexington: University of Kentucky, 1934.

273. MARETT, R. R., *The Threshold of Religion,* London: Methuen & Co., 1909.

274. MARSH, C. PAUL, and A. LEE COLEMAN, "The Relation of Farmer Characteristics to the Adoption of Recommended Farm Practices," *Rural Sociology,* Vol. 20, Nos. 3–4 (September-December, 1955), pp. 289–296.

275. MARTIN, WALTER T., *The Rural-Urban Fringe: A Study of Adjustment to Residence Location,* Eugene: University of Oregon Press, 1953.

276. MARTINSON, FLOYD M., "Personal Adjustment and Rural-Urban Migration," *Rural Sociology,* Vol. 20, No. 2 (June, 1955), pp. 102–110.

277. MASPERO, GASTON, *The Dawn of Civilization, Egypt and Chaldea,* London: Society for Promoting Christian Knowledge, 1910.

278. MAVROMMATIS, A., *The Development of Cooperatives in Lebanon,* Rome: Food and Agricultural Organization of the United Nations, 1963.

279. MAYO, SELZ C., "Age Profiles of Social Participation in Rural Areas of Wake County, North Carolina," *Rural Sociology,* Vol. 15, No. 3 (September, 1950), pp. 242–251.

280. MAYO, SELZ C., "An Approach to the Understanding of Rural Community Development," *Social Forces,* Vol. 37, No. 2 (December, 1958), pp. 95–101.

281. MAYO, SELZ C., *Organized Rural Communities: A Series of Case Studies from Western North Carolina,* North Carolina State College AES Progress Report No. Rs-20, Raleigh: North Carolina State College, 1954.

282. MAYO, SELZ C., and ROBERT McD. BOBBITT, *Rural Organizations: A Restudy of Locality Groups in Wake County, North Carolina,* North Carolina AES Technical Bulletin No. 95, Raleigh: North Carolina State College, 1951.

283. McBRIDE, GEORGE M., *Chile: Land and Society,* New York: American Geographical Society, 1936.

284. McBRIDE, GEORGE M., *The Land Systems of Mexico,* New York: American Geographical Society, 1923.

285. McCONNELL, GRANT, *The Decline of Agrarian Democracy,* Berkeley: University of California Press, 1953.

286. McCUNE, WESLEY, *The Farm Bloc,* New York: Doubleday, Doran, 1943.

287. McKINNEY, JOHN C., and EDGAR T. THOMPSON (eds.), *The South in Continuity and Change,* Durham: Duke University Press, 1965.

288. McVEY, FRANK L., *The Populist Movement,* New York: American Economic Association, 1896, Vol. I.

289. McVOY, E. C., and LOWRY NELSON, *Satisfaction in Living: Farm Versus Village,* Minnesota AES Bulletin No. 37, Minneapolis: University of Minnesota, 1943.

290. MEAD, MARGARET, *Cooperation and Competition Among Primitive Peoples,* New York: McGraw-Hill Book Company, Inc., 1937.

291. MELVIN, BRUCE L., "The Rural Neighborhood Concept," *Rural Sociology,* Vol. 19, No. 4 (December, 1953), pp. 344–358.

292. MERTON, ROBERT K., *Social Theory and Social Structure* (third ed.), New York: The Free Press, 1968.

293. MERTON, ROBERT K., LEONARD BROOM, and LEONARD S. COTTRELL, JR., (eds.), *Sociology Today,* New York: Harper & Row, Publishers, 1959.

294. METZLER, WILLIAM H., *Migratory Farm Workers in the Atlantic Coast Stream: A Study in the Belle Glade Area of Florida,* Department of Agriculture, Washington: Government Printing Office, 1955.

295. MIGHELL, RONALD L., *American Agriculture: Its Structure and Place in the Economy*, New York: John Wiley and Sons, Inc., 1955.

296. MOE, EDWARD O., *New York Farmers' Opinions on Agricultural Programs*, Cornell Agricultural Extension Bulletin No. 864, Ithaca: Cornell University, 1952.

297. MOE, EDWARD O., and CARL C. TAYLOR, *Culture of a Contemporary Community: Irwin, Iowa*, Department of Agriculture Rural Life Studies No. 5, Washington: Government Printing Office, 1942.

298. MONETTE, JOHN W., *History of the Discovery and Settlement of the Valley of the Mississippi*, New York: Harper & Brothers, 1846, 2 vols.

299. MOORE, E. HOWARD, and RALEIGH BARLOWE, *Effects of Suburbanization Upon Rural Land Use*, Michigan AES Technical Bulletin No. 253, East Lansing: Michigan State University, 1955.

300. MOORE, WILBERT, *Social Change*, Englewood Cliffs, N. J.: Prentice-Hall, Inc., 1963.

301. MORRILL, JUSTIN S., *State Aid to the U.S. Land-Grant Colleges*, Burlington, Vt.: Free Press Association, 1888.

302. MÜLLER, F. MAX, *Introduction to the Science of Religion*, London: Longmans, Green & Co., Ltd., 1873.

303. NATIONAL RESOURCES COMMITTEE, *Our Cities: Their Role in the National Economy*, Washington: Government Printing Office, 1937.

304. NEARING, PETER A., "The Xavierian Movement," *Rural Sociology*, Vol. 2, No. 1 (March, 1937), pp. 76–77.

305. NELSON, LOWRY, *American Farm Life*, Cambridge, Mass.: Harvard University Press, 1954.

306. NELSON, LOWRY, "George Edgar Vincent: Rural Social Scientist," *Rural Sociology*, Vol. 31, No. 4 (December, 1966), pp. 478–482.

307. NELSON, LOWRY, *The Mormon Village: A Pattern and Technique of Land Settlement*, Salt Lake City: University of Utah Press, 1952.

308. NELSON, LOWRY, *The Mormon Village: A Study in Social Origins*, Brigham Young University Studies No. 3, Provo: Brigham Young University, 1930.

309. NELSON, LOWRY, "The Rise of Rural Sociology Abroad: The Pre-Purnell Period." *Rural Sociology*, Vol. 30, No. 4 (December, 1965), pp. 407–427.

310. NELSON, LOWRY, *Rural Cuba*, Minneapolis: University of Minnesota Press, 1950.

311. NELSON, LOWRY, "Rural Life in a Mass-Industrial Society," *Rural Sociology*, Vol. 22, No. 1 (March, 1957), pp. 20–30.

312. NELSON, LOWRY, *Rural Sociology* (second ed.), New York: American Book Company, 1955.

313. NELSON, LOWRY, *Some Social and Economic Features of American Fork, Utah,* Brigham Young University Studies No. 4, Provo: Brigham Young University, 1933.

314. NELSON, LOWRY, *The Utah Farm Village of Ephraim,* Brigham Young University Studies No. 2, Provo: Brigham Young University, 1928.

315. NELSON, LOWRY, CHARLES E. RAMSEY, and COOLIE VERNER, *Community Structure and Change,* New York: The Macmillan Company, 1960.

316. NIELSON, N., *Medieval Agrarian Economy,* New York: Henry Holt & Company, 1936.

317. NIKOLITCH, RADOJE, "The Adequate Family Farm—Mainstay of the Farm Economy," *Agricultural Economics Research,* Vol. XVII, No. 3 (July, 1965).

318. NORDHOFF, CHARLES, *The Communistic Societies of the United States,* New York: Harper & Brothers, 1875.

319. NORDHOFF, CHARLES, *The Cotton States in the Spring and the Summer of 1875,* New York: D. Appleton and Company, 1876.

320. OGBURN, WILLIAM F., *Social Change,* New York: The Viking Press, Inc., 1950.

321. OGBURN, WILLIAM F., and MEYER F. NIMKOFF, *Technology and the Changing Family,* Boston: Houghton Mifflin Company, 1955.

322. OLMSTEAD, F. L., *A Journey in the Back Country,* New York: Mason Brothers, 1863.

323. OLMSTEAD, F. L., *A Journey in the Seaboard Slave States,* New York: G. P. Putnam's Sons, 1904.

324. OLMSTEAD, F. L., *A Journey in the Seaboard Slave States, with Remarks on Their Economy,* New York: Dix & Edwards, 1856.

325. ORGANIZATION OF AMERICAN STATES, *Plantation Systems of the New World,* Washington: Pan American Union, 1959.

326. ORGANIZATION FOR EUROPEAN ECONOMIC CO-OPERATION, *Community Development: Some Achievements in the United States and Europe,* Paris: Organization for European Economic Co-operation, 1960.

327. OSGOOD, HERBERT L., *The American Colonies in the Seventeenth Century,* New York: The Macmillan Company, 1904.

328. OWEN, ROBERT, *A New View of Society* (fourth ed.), London: Longman, Hurst, Rees, Orme and Brown, 1818.

329. OWSLEY, FRANK L., *Plain Folk of the Old South,* Baton Rouge: Louisiana State University Press, 1949.

330. PAGE, THOMAS, *Legislative Apportionment in Kansas,* Lawrence: University of Kansas, 1952.

331. PARENTON, VERNON J., "Socio-Psychological Integration in a Rural French-Speaking Section of Louisiana," *Southwestern Social Science Quarterly*, Vol. XXX, No. 3 (1950), pp. 188–195.

332. PARK, ROBERT E., and ERNEST W. BURGESS, *Introduction to the Science of Sociology*, Chicago: The University of Chicago Press, 1921.

333. PARKS, W. ROBERT, *Soil Conservation Districts in Action*, Ames: Iowa State University Press, 1952.

334. PARSONS, KENNETH H., RAYMOND J. PENN, and PHILIP M. RAUP (eds.), *Land Tenure: Proceedings of the International Conference on Land Tenure and Related Problems in World Agriculture Held at Madison, Wisconsin, 1951*, Madison: University of Wisconsin Press, 1956.

335. PAYNE, RAYMOND, "Developments of Occupational and Migration Expectations and Choices Among Urban, Small Town, and Rural Adolescent Boys," *Rural Sociology*, Vol. 21, No. 2 (June, 1956), pp. 117–125.

336. PEDERSEN, HARALD A., "Cultural Differences in the Acceptance of Recommended Practices," *Rural Sociology*, Vol. 16, No. 1 (March, 1951), pp. 37–49.

337. PEDERSEN, HARALD A., "Mechanized Agriculture and the Farm Laborer," *Rural Sociology*, Vol. 19, No. 2 (June, 1954), pp. 143–151.

338. PEDERSEN, HARALD A., and ARTHUR F. RAPER, *The Cotton Plantation in Transition*, Mississippi AES Bulletin No. 508, State College: Mississippi State University, 1954.

339. PENN, WILLIAM, "A Further Account of the Province of Pennsylvania, 1685," in Albert Cook Myers (ed.), *Narratives of Early Pennsylvania, West New Jersey and Delaware, 1630–1707*, New York: Charles Scribner's Sons, 1912.

340. PETERS, W. E., *Ohio Lands and Their Subdivision*, Athens, Ohio, Privately Printed, 1918.

341. PHELPS, HAROLD A., and DAVID HENDERSON, *Population in Its Human Aspects*, New York: Appleton-Century-Crofts, 1958.

342. PHILLIPS, U. B., *American Negro Slavery*, New York: D. Appleton-Century Company, 1918.

343. PHILLIPS, U. B., *A History of Transportation in the Eastern Cotton Belt to 1860*, New York: Columbia University Press, 1908.

344. PIKE, FREDERIC B. (ed.), *Freedom and Reform in Latin America*, Notre Dame, Ind.: University of Notre Dame Press, 1959.

345. PLUNKETT, SIR HORACE, *The Country Life Movement in The United States*, New York: The Macmillan Company, 1910.

346. POE, CLARENCE, *How Farmers Co-operate and Double Profits*, New York: Orange Judd Co., 1915.

347. POLK, WILLIAM R. (ed.), *The Developmental Revolution: North Africa, Middle East, South Asia,* Washington: Middle East Institute, 1963.

348. PORTES, ALEJANDRO, ARCHIBALD O. HALLER, and WILLIAM H. SEWELL, "Professional-Executive vs. Farming as Unique Occupational Choices," *Rural Sociology,* Vol. 33, No. 2 (June, 1968), pp. 153–159.

349. POTTER, JACK M., MAY N. DIAZ, and GEORGE M. FOSTER (eds.), *Peasant Society: A Reader,* Boston: Little, Brown and Company, 1967.

350. POWELL, GEORGE H., *Cooperation in Agriculture,* New York: The Macmillan Company, 1913.

351. POWER, EILEEN, *Medieval People,* New York: Doubleday Anchor Books, 1954.

352. POWERS, STEPHEN, *Afoot and Alone: A Walk from Sea to Sea by the Southern Route,* Hartford: Columbia Book Co., 1872.

353. President's National Advisory Commission on Rural Poverty, *The People Left Behind,* Washington: Government Printing Office, 1967.

354. PRICE, PAUL H., and GEORGE A. HILLERY, *The Rural-Urban Fringe and Louisiana's Agriculture,* Louisiana AES Bulletin No. 526, Baton Rouge: Louisiana State University, 1959.

355. PRIESTLEY, HERBERT I., *The Coming of the White Man, 1492-1848,* New York: The Macmillan Company, 1929.

356. "Problems of the Cotton Economy," *Proceedings of the Southern Social Science Research Conference,* New Orleans, 1935, Dallas: Southern Methodist University, 1936.

357. PROTHERO, ROWLAND E., *English Farming Past and Present,* London: Longmans, Green and Company, 1912.

358. PROUDFIT, S. V., *The Public Land System of the United States,* Department of the Interior, Washington: Government Printing Office, 1923.

359. Province of Saskatchewan, Royal Commission on Agriculture and Rural Life, W. B. Baker, Chairman, *Report No. 4: Rural Roads and Local Government,* Regina: Queen's Printer, 1955.

360. Province of Saskatchewan, Royal Commission on Agriculture and Rural Life, W. B. Baker, Chairman, *Report No. 5: Land Tenure,* Regina: Queen's Printer, 1955.

361. Province of Saskatchewan, Royal Commission on Agriculture and Rural Life, W. B. Baker, Chairman, *Report No. 6: Rural Education,* Regina: Queen's Printer, 1956.

362. Province of Saskatchewan, Royal Commission on Agriculture and Rural Life, W. B. Baker, Chairman, *Report No. 7: Movement of Farm People,* Regina: Queen's Printer, 1956.

363. RAMSEY, CHARLES E., and WALFRED A. ANDERSON, *Some Problems in the Regional Study of Migration,* Cornell Department of Rural Sociology Bulletin No. 53, Ithaca: Cornell University, 1959.

364. RAMSEY, CHARLES E., and JENARO COLLAZO, "Some Problems of Cross-cultural Measurement," *Rural Sociology,* Vol. 25, No. 1 (March, 1960), pp. 91–106.

365. RAMSEY, CHARLES E., ALLAN D. ORMAN, and LOWRY NELSON, *Migration in Minnesota, 1940–50,* Minnesota AES Bulletin No. 422, St. Paul: University of Minnesota, 1954.

366. RAMSEY, CHARLES E., ROBERT A. POLSON, and GEORGE E. SPENCER, "Values and the Adoption of Practices," *Rural Sociology,* Vol. 24, No. 1 (March, 1959), pp. 35–47.

367. RAPER, ARTHUR F., *The Japanese Village in Transition,* Tokyo: General Headquarters, Supreme Commander for the Allied Powers, Natural Resources Section Report No. 136, 1950.

368. RAPER, ARTHUR F., *Preface to Peasantry,* Chapel Hill: University of North Carolina Press, 1936.

369. RAPER, ARTHUR, F., "The Role of Agricultural Technology in Southern Social Change," *Social Forces,* Vol. 25, No. 1 (October, 1946), pp. 21–30.

370. RAPER, ARTHUR F., *Tenants of the Almighty,* New York: The Macmillan Company, 1943.

371. RAPER, ARTHUR F., and IRA deA. REID, *Sharecroppers All,* Chapel Hill: University of North Carolina Press, 1941.

372. RASMUSSEN, WAYNE D. (ed.), *Readings in the History of American Agriculture,* Urbana: University of Illinois Press, 1960.

373. RAVENSTEIN, E. G., "On the Laws of Migration," *Journal of the Royal Statistical Society,* Vol. XLVIII (1885), pp. 167–235.

374. REDFIELD, ROBERT, *The Folk Culture of Yucatán,* Chicago: The University of Chicago Press, 1941.

375. REDFIELD, ROBERT, "The Folk Society and Culture," *American Journal of Sociology,* Vol. 45, No. 5 (March, 1940), pp. 731–742.

376. *Report of the Country Life Commission,* Sixtieth Congress, Second Session, Senate Document No. 705, Washington: Government Printing Office, 1909.

377. RICH, MARK, *The Rural Church Movement,* Columbia, Mo.: Juniper Knoll Press, 1957.

378. RICHTER, H., "Consolidation of Scattered Farm Holdings in Germany," *Foreign Agriculture,* Vol. II (1938).

379. RIDGWAY, HELEN, *County and Regional Libraries,* Chicago: American Library Association, 1949.

380. ROBOCK, STEFAN H., "Rural Industries and Agricultural Development," *Journal of Farm Economics,* Vol. 34 (August, 1952), pp. 346–360.

381. ROGERS, EVERETT M., *Diffusion of Innovations,* Glencoe, Ill.: The Free Press, 1962.

382. ROGERS, EVERETT M., *Social Change in Rural Society,* New York: Appleton-Century-Crofts, 1960.

383. ROGERS, EVERETT M., and HAROLD H. CAPENER, *The County Extension Agent and His Constituents,* Ohio AES Research Bulletin No. 858, Columbus: Ohio State University, 1960.

384. ROHWER, ROBERT A., "Organized Farmers in Oklahoma," *Rural Sociology,* Vol. 17, No. 1 (March, 1952), pp. 39–47.

385. ROHWER, ROBERT A., "Social Relations in Beginning as a Farm Operator in an Area of Prosperous Commercial Farming," *Rural Sociology,* Vol. 14, No. 4 (December, 1949), pp. 325–335.

386. ROOSEVELT, THEODORE, *The Winning of the West,* New York: The Current Literature Publishing Company, 1905, Vol. I.

387. ROSS, EDWARD A., *The Outlines of Sociology* (second ed.), New York: D. Appleton-Century Company, 1933.

388. ROSS, MURRAY G., *Community Organization: Theory and Principles,* New York: Harper & Brothers, 1955.

389. ROZMAN, DAVID, and RUTH E. SHERBURNE, *Population in Massachusetts: Trends, Distribution, Characteristics, 1900–1950,* Massachusetts AES Bulletin No. 496, Amherst: University of Massachusetts, 1957.

390. RUSHING, WILLIAM A., "Objective and Subjective Aspects of Deprivation in a Rural Poverty Class," *Rural Sociology,* Vol. 33, No. 3 (September, 1968), pp. 269–284.

391. RYAN, BRYCE, "The Agricultural Systems of Ceylon," *Rural Sociology,* Vol. 20, No. 1 (March, 1955), pp. 16–24.

392. RYAN, BRYCE, *Social and Ecological Patterns in the Farm Leadership of Four Iowa Townships,* Iowa AES Research Bulletin No. 306, Ames: Iowa State College, 1942.

393. RYAN, BRYCE, "A Study in Technological Diffusion," *Rural Sociology,* Vol. 13, No. 3 (September, 1948), pp. 273–285.

394. SAKOLSKI, AARON M., *Land Tenure and Land Taxation in America,* New York: Robert Schalkenbach Foundation, 1957.

395. SANDERS, IRWIN T., *Balkan Village,* Lexington: University of Kentucky Press, 1949.

396. SANDERS, IRWIN T., *The Community: An Introduction to a Social System* (second ed.), New York: The Ronald Press Company, 1966.

397. SANDERS, IRWIN T., "Rural Sociology: Its Unfinished Business," in *Papers for the Fiftieth Anniversary of Rural Sociology at Cornell University, 1915–1965,* Ithaca: Cornell University, 1968, pp. 15–24.

398. SANDERS, IRWIN T., "Theories of Community Development," *Rural Sociology,* Vol. 23, No. 1 (March, 1958), pp. 1–12.

399. SANDERSON, DWIGHT, *The Farmer and His Community*, New York: Harcourt, Brace & Company, 1922.

400. SANDERSON, DWIGHT, *Locating the Rural Community*, Cornell Country Life Series, Ithaca: Cornell University, 1920.

401. SANDERSON, DWIGHT, *The Rural Community: The Natural History of a Sociological Group*, Boston: Ginn and Company, 1932.

402. SANDERSON, DWIGHT, *Rural Social and Economic Areas in Central New York*, Cornell AES Bulletin No. 614, Ithaca: Cornell University, 1934.

403. SANDERSON, DWIGHT, *Rural Sociology and Rural Social Organization*, New York: John Wiley & Sons, Inc., 1942.

404. SANDERSON, DWIGHT, and ROBERT A. POLSON, *Rural Community Organization*, New York: John Wiley & Sons, Inc., 1939.

405. SATO, SHOSUKE, *History of the Land Question in the United States*, Johns Hopkins University Studies in Historical and Political Science, Fourth Series, Vols. VII-IX, Baltimore: Johns Hopkins University, 1886.

406. SAUER, CARL O., *Agricultural Origins and Dispersals*, New York: American Geographical Society, 1952.

407. SAUNDERS, JOHN V. D., "Man-Land Relations in Ecuador," *Rural Sociology*, Vol. 26, No. 1 (March, 1961), pp. 57–69.

408. SAUNDERS, JOHN V. D., *The People of Ecuador: A Demographic Analysis*, Gainesville: University of Florida Press, 1961.

409. SAUNDERS, JOHN V. D., *Social Factors in Latin American Modernization*, Graduate Center for Latin American Studies, Vanderbilt University, Occasional Paper No. 5, Nashville: Vanderbilt University, 1965.

410. SAUNDERS, LYLE, and OLEN E. LEONARD, *The Wetback in the Lower Rio Grande Valley of Texas*, Inter-American Education Occasional Papers No. VII, Austin: University of Texas, 1951.

411. SAVILLE, JOHN, *Rural Depopulation in England and Wales, 1851–1951*, London: Routledge and Kegan Paul, 1957.

412. SCHAFFER, ALBERT, "A Rural Community at the Urban Fringe," *Rural Sociology*, Vol. 23, No. 3 (September, 1958), pp. 277–285.

413. SCHULER, EDGAR A., "The Present Social Status of American Farm Tenants," *Rural Sociology*, Vol. 3, No. 1 (March, 1938), pp. 20–33.

414. SCHULER, EDGAR A., *Social Status and Farm Tenure: Attitudes and Social Conditions of Corn Belt and Cotton Belt Farmers*, Department of Agriculture, Washington: Government Printing Office, 1938.

415. SCHULER, EDGAR A., and GUS TURBEVILLE, "The Relation of Rural Reading and Library Use to Some Ecological Factors," *The Library Quarterly*, Vol. XVIII, No. 3 (July, 1948), pp. 171–184.

416. SCHULMAN, SAM, "The Colono System in Latin America," *Rural Sociology,* Vol. 20, No. 1 (March, 1955), pp. 34–40.

417. SCHULMAN, SAM, "Intellectual and Technological Underdevelopment: A Case Study—Colombia," *Social Forces,* Vol. 46, No. 3 (March, 1968), pp. 309–317.

418. SCHWARZWELLER, HARRY K., and JAMES S. BROWN, "Social Class Origins, Rural-Urban Migration, and Economic Life Chances: A Case Study," *Rural Sociology,* Vol. 32, No. 1 (March, 1967), pp. 5–19.

419. SEEBOHM, FREDERIC, *Customary Acres and Their Historical Importance,* New York: Longmans, Green & Company, 1914.

420. SEEBOHM, FREDERIC, *The English Village Community,* New York: Longmans, Green & Company, 1926.

421. SEEBOHM, M. E., *Evolution of the English Farm,* Cambridge, Mass.: Harvard University Press. 1927.

422. SELZNICK, PHILIP, *TVA and the Grass Roots,* Berkeley: University of California Press, 1953.

423. SENIOR, CLARENCE, *Land Reform and Democracy,* Gainesville: University of Florida Press, 1958.

424. SEWELL, WILLIAM H., CHARLES E. RAMSEY, and LOUIS J. DUCOFF, *Farmers' Conceptions and Plans for Economic Security in Old Age,* Wisconsin AES Bulletin No. 182, Madison: University of Wisconsin, 1953.

425. SHANNON, LYLE W. (ed.), *Underdeveloped Areas,* New York: Harper & Row, Publishers, 1957.

426. SHARP, EMMIT K., and CHARLES E. RAMSEY, "Criteria of Item Selection in Level of Living Scales," *Rural Sociology,* Vol. 28, No. 2 (June, 1963), pp. 146–164.

427. SHELDON, WILLIAM DuB., *Populism in the Old Dominion: Virginia Farm Politics, 1885–1900,* Princeton: Princeton University Press, 1935.

428. SHRYOCK, HENRY S., JR., *Population Mobility Within the United States,* Chicago: University of Chicago Community and Family Study Center, 1967.

429. SIMPSON, EYLER N., *The Ejido: Mexico's Way Out,* Chapel Hill: University of North Carolina Press, 1937.

430. SIMPSON, GEORGE, *Emile Durkheim on the Division of Labor in Society,* New York: The Macmillan Company, 1933.

431. SIMS, NEWELL L., *Elements of Rural Sociology* (third ed.), New York: Thomas Y. Crowell Company, 1940.

432. SIMS, NEWELL L., *A Hoosier Village,* New York: Longmans, Green & Company, 1912.

433. SIMS, NEWELL L., *The Rural Community: Ancient and Modern,* New York: Charles Scribner's Sons, 1920.

434. SKRABANEK, ROBERT L., "Commercial Farming in the United States," *Rural Sociology*, Vol. 19, No. 2 (June, 1954), pp. 136–142.

435. SKRABANEK, ROBERT L., and VERNON J. PARENTON, "Social Life in a Czech-American Rural Community," *Southwestern Social Science Quarterly*, Vol. XXXI (1950).

436. SLOCUM, WALTER L., *Agricultural Sociology*, New York: Harper & Brothers, 1962.

437. SMALL, ALBION W., and GEORGE E. VINCENT, *An Introduction to the Study of Society*, New York: American Book Company, 1894.

438. SMITH, HANNIS S., *Library Service for Rural People*, Department of Agriculture Farmer's Bulletin No. 2142, Washington: Government Printing Office, 1959.

439. SMITH, J. M. POWIS, *The Origin and History of Hebrew Law*, Chicago: The University of Chicago Press, 1931.

440. SMITH, MERVIN G., and CARLTON F. CHRISTIAN (eds.), *Adjustments in Agriculture: A National Basebook*, Ames: Iowa State University Press, 1961.

441. SMITH, ROBERT S., *Transferring the Farm to the Next Generation*, Cornell AES Bulletin No. 901, Ithaca: Cornell University, 1953.

442. SMITH, T. LYNN (ed.), *Agrarian Reform in Latin America*, New York: Alfred A. Knopf, 1965.

443. SMITH, T. LYNN, "Agricultural Systems and Standards of Living," *Inter-American Economic Affairs*, Vol. III (1949), pp. 15–28.

444. SMITH, T. LYNN, *Brazil: People and Institutions* (third ed.), Baton Rouge: Louisiana State University Press, 1963.

445. SMITH, T. LYNN, *Colombia: Social Structure and the Process of Development*, Gainesville: University of Florida Press, 1967.

446. SMITH, T. LYNN, "Colonization and Settlement in Colombia," *Rural Sociology*, Vol. 12, No. 2 (June, 1947), pp. 128–139.

447. SMITH, T. LYNN, *Current Social Trends and Problems in Latin America*, Gainesville: University of Florida Press, 1957.

448. SMITH, T LYNN, "Fragmentation of Agricultural Holdings in Spain," *Rural Sociology*, Vol. 24, No. 2 (June, 1959), pp. 140–149.

449. SMITH, T. LYNN, *Fundamentals of Population Study*, Philadelphia: J. B. Lippincott Co., 1960.

450. SMITH, T. LYNN, "The Homogenization of Society in the United States," *Memoire du XIX Congress International de Sociologie*, Vol. 2 (1960), pp. 245–275.

451. SMITH, T. LYNN, "Land Tenure and Soil Erosion in Colombia," *Proceedings of the Inter-American Conference on Conservation of Renewable Resources*, Denver, September, 1948, Washington: Government Printing Office, 1949, pp. 155–160.

452. SMITH, T. LYNN, *Latin American Population Studies,* Gainesville: University of Florida Press, 1960.

453. SMITH, T. LYNN, "Next Steps in Rural Sociological Research in the South," *Rural Sociology,* Vol. 16, No. 2 (June, 1951), pp. 118–126.

454. SMITH, T. LYNN, "Notes on Population and Rural Social Organization in El Salvador," *Rural Sociology,* Vol. 10, No. 4 (December, 1945), pp. 359–379.

455. SMITH, T. LYNN, *The Process of Rural Development in Latin America,* Gainesville: University of Florida Press, 1967.

456. SMITH, T. LYNN, "The Racial Composition of the Population of Colombia," *Journal of Inter-American Studies,* Vol. VIII, No. 2 (April, 1966), pp. 213–235.

457. SMITH, T. LYNN, "The Redistribution of the Negro Population of the United States, 1910–1960," *The Journal of Negro History,* Vol. LI, No. 3 (July, 1966), pp. 155–173.

458. SMITH, T. LYNN, *Rural Sociology: A Trend Report and Bibliography,* published as *Current Sociology,* Vol. VI, No. 1, Paris: UNESCO, 1957.

459. SMITH, T. LYNN, "The Social Relationships of Man to the Land in Portugal," *Sociologia,* Vol. XXV, No. 4 (December, 1963), pp. 319–343.

460. SMITH, T. LYNN, *The Sociology of Rural Life* (third ed.), New York: Harper & Brothers, 1953.

461. SMITH, T. LYNN, "Some Observations on Land Tenure in Colombia," *Foreign Agriculture,* Vol. XVI (June, 1952), pp. 119–124.

462. SMITH, T. LYNN, *Studies of Latin American Societies,* New York: Doubleday & Company, Inc., 1969.

463. SMITH, T. LYNN, "A Study of Social Stratification in the Agricultural Sections of the United States: Nature, Data, Procedures, and Preliminary Results," *Rural Sociology,* Vol. 34, No. 4 (December, 1969).

464. SMITH, T. LYNN, JUSTO DÍAZ RODRÍGUEZ, and LUIS ROBERTO GARCÍA, *Tabio: A Study in Rural Social Organization,* Department of Agriculture, Office of Foreign Agricultural Relations, Washington: Government Printing Office, 1945.

465. SMITH, T. LYNN, and HOMER L. HITT, *The People of Louisiana,* Baton Rouge: Louisiana State University Press, 1952.

466. SMITH, T. LYNN, and DOUGLAS G. MARSHALL, *Our Aging Population— The United States and Wisconsin,* Wisconsin's Population Series No. 5, Madison: University of Wisconsin, 1963.

467. SMITH, T. LYNN, and PAUL E. ZOPF, JR., *Fundamentals of Population Study* (second ed.), Philadelphia: F. A. Davis Co., 1970.

468. SMITH, W. H., *Canada: Past, Present, and Future,* Toronto: Thomas Maclear, 1851, Vol. I.

469. SNIDER, CLYDE F., *Local Government in Rural America,* New York: Appleton-Century-Crofts, 1957.

470. SOHN, RUDOLF, *The Institutes: A Textbook of the History and System of Roman Private Law* (trans. by J. C. Ledlie), Oxford: The Clarendon Press, 1907.

471. SOROKIN, PITIRIM A., *Contemporary Sociological Theories,* New York: Harper & Brothers, 1928.

472. SOROKIN, PITIRIM A., *Social and Cultural Dynamics,* New York: American Book Company, 1937, 4 vols.

473. SOROKIN, PITIRIM A., *Social Mobility,* New York: Harper & Brothers, 1927.

474. SOROKIN, PITIRIM A., *Society, Culture, and Personality: Their Structure and Dynamics,* New York: Harper & Brothers, 1947.

475. SOROKIN, PITIRIM A., *Sociological Theories of Today,* New York: Harper & Row, Publishers, 1966.

476. SOROKIN, PITIRIM A., *The Sociology of Revolution,* Philadelphia: J. B. Lippincott Co., 1925.

477. SOROKIN, PITIRIM A., and CARLE C. ZIMMERMAN, *Principles of Rural-Urban Sociology,* New York: Henry Holt & Company, 1929.

478. SOROKIN, PITIRIM A., CARLE C. ZIMMERMAN, and CHARLES J. GALPIN, *A Systematic Source Book in Rural Sociology,* Minneapolis: University of Minnesota Press, 1930–1932, 3 vols.

479. SOUTHWORTH, H. M., and B. F. JOHNSTON (eds.), *Agricultural Development and Economic Growth,* Ithaca: Cornell University Press, 1967.

480. SPENCER, HERBERT, *First Principles,* New York: D. Appleton & Company, 1899.

481. SPILLMAN, W. J., "The Agricultural Ladder," *American Economic Review Supplement,* Vol. IX (1919), pp. 170–179.

482. SRINIVAS, M. N., *Caste in Modern India and Other Essays,* Bombay: Asia Publishing House, 1962.

483. STAMP, L. DUDLEY, *Man and the Land,* London: Collins, 1955.

484. STEWARD, JULIAN H. (ed.), *Handbook of South American Indians,* Bureau of American Ethnology Bulletin No. 143, Washington: Government Printing Office, 1948.

485. STIRLING, PAUL, *Turkish Village,* London: Weidenfeld and Nicholson, 1965.

486. STONE, ALFRED H., "The Negro and Agricultural Development," *Annals of the American Academy of Political Science,* Vol. XXXV (1910).

487. STONE, ALFRED H., "A Plantation Experiment," *Quarterly Journal of Economics,* Vol. XIX (1904).

488. STRAUS, MURRAY A., "Family Role Differentiation and Technological Change in Farming," *Rural Sociology,* Vol. 25, No. 2 (June, 1960), pp. 219–228.

489. STRAUS, MURRAY A., "Personal Characteristics and Functional Needs in the Choice of Farming as an Occupation," *Rural Sociology,* Vol. 21, Nos. 3–4 (September-December, 1956), pp. 257–266.

490. STREET, JAMES H., *The New Revolution in the Cotton Economy,* Chapel Hill: University of North Carolina Press, 1957.

491. Subcommittee on the Diffusion and Adoption of Farm Practices, Rural Sociological Society, *Sociological Research on the Diffusion and Adoption of New Farm Practices,* Lexington: University of Kentucky, 1952.

492. SUMNER, WILLIAM G., *Folkways,* Boston: Ginn and Company, 1907.

493. SUSSMAN, MARVIN B. (ed.), *Community Structure and Analysis,* New York: Thomas Y. Crowell Company, 1959.

494. SUTHERLAND, STELLA H., *Population Distribution in Colonial America,* New York: Columbia University Press, 1936.

495. SUTTON, WILLIS A., JR., and JIRI KOLAJA, "The Concept of Community," *Rural Sociology,* Vol. 25, No. 2 (June, 1960), pp. 197–203.

496. SUTTON, WILLIS A., JR., and JIRI KOLAJA, "Elements of Community Action," *Social Forces,* Vol. 38, No. 4 (May, 1960), pp. 325–331.

497. SUZUKI, PETER, "Village Solidarity Among Peasants Undergoing Urbanization," *Science,* Vol. CXXXII, No. 3431 (1960), p. 891.

498. TAEUBER, CONRAD, and IRENE B. TAEUBER, *The Changing Population of the United States,* New York: John Wiley & Sons, Inc., 1958.

499. TAEUBER, CONRAD, and CARL C. TAYLOR, *The People of the Drought States,* Works Progress Administration, Washington: Government Printing Office, 1937.

500. TAIETZ, PHILIP, and others, *Adjustment to Retirement in Rural New York,* Cornell AES Bulletin No. 919, Ithaca: Cornell University, 1956.

501. TANG, ANTHONY M., *Economic Development in the Southern Piedmont, 1860–1950: Its Impact on Agriculture,* Chapel Hill: University of North Carolina Press, 1958.

502. TANNENBAUM, FRANK, *The Mexican Agrarian Revolution,* New York: The Macmillan Company, 1929.

503. TARVER, JAMES D., "Ecological Patterns of Land Tenure, Farm Land Use, and Farm Population Characteristics," *Rural Sociology,* Vol. 28, No. 2 (June, 1963), pp. 128–145.

504. TARVER, JAMES D., and CALVIN L. BEALE, "Population Trends of Southern Non-metropolitan Towns, 1950 to 1960," *Rural Sociology,* Vol. 33, No. 1 (March, 1968), pp. 19–29.

505. TAVES, MARVIN J., and NEAL GROSS, "A Critique of Rural Sociology Research, 1950," *Rural Sociology*, Vol. 17, No. 2 (June, 1952), pp. 109–118.

506. TAYLOR, CARL C., "The Development of Rural Sociology Abroad," *Rural Sociology*, Vol. 30, No. 4 (December, 1965), pp. 462–473.

507. TAYLOR, CARL C., "Dr. Galpin at Washington," *Rural Sociology*, Vol. 13, No. 2 (June, 1948), pp. 145–155.

508. TAYLOR, CARL C., "Early Rural Sociological Research in Latin America," *Rural Sociology*, Vol. 25, No. 1 (March, 1960), pp. 1–8.

509. TAYLOR, CARL C., *The Farmers' Movement, 1620–1920,* New York: American Book Company, 1953.

510. TAYLOR, CARL C., *Rural Life in Argentina,* Baton Rouge: Louisiana State University Press, 1948.

511. TAYLOR, CARL C., *Rural Sociology* (second ed.), New York: Harper & Brothers, 1933.

512. TAYLOR, CARL C., and others, *Columbia Basin: Pattern of Rural Settlement,* Problem 10, Department of the Interior, Bureau of Reclamation, Washington: Government Printing Office, 1947.

513. TAYLOR, CARL C., and others, *India's Roots of Democracy: A Sociological Analysis of Rural India's Experience in Planned Development Since Independence,* New Delhi: Orient Longmans, 1965.

514. TAYLOR, CARL C., and others, *Rural Life in the United States,* New York: Alfred A. Knopf, 1949.

515. TAYLOR, HENRY C., *Agricultural Economics,* New York: The Macmillan Company, 1923.

516. TAYLOR, HENRY C., *The Decline of Landowning Farmers in England,* Madison: University of Wisconsin, 1904.

517. TAYLOR, HENRY C., "Galpin Undertakes the Study of Rural Life," *Rural Sociology*, Vol. 13, No. 2 (June, 1948), pp. 119–129.

518. TAYLOR, LEE, *Rural-Urban Problems,* Belmont, Calif.: Dickenson Pub. Co., Inc., 1968.

519. TAYLOR, LEE, and ARTHUR R. JONES, JR., *Louisiana's Human Resources,* Part II, *Agribusiness and the Labor Force,* Louisiana AES Bulletin No. 562, Baton Rogue: Louisiana State University, 1962.

520. TAYLOR, LEE, and ARTHUR R. JONES, JR., *Rural Life and Urbanized Society,* New York: Oxford University Press, 1964.

521. TAYLOR, LEE, and GLENN NELSON, *Minnesota's People and Farms 1950–1960,* Minnesota AES Miscellaneous Report No. 45, Minneapolis: University of Minnesota, 1961.

522. TAYLOR, PAUL C., *Venezuela: A Case Study of Relationships between Community Development and Agrarian Reform,* Caracas: Bureau of Social Affairs of the United Nations, 1961.

523. TAYLOR, PAUL S., "Can We Export 'The New Rural Society'?" *Rural Sociology,* Vol. 19, No. 1 (March, 1954), pp. 13–20.

524. TERPENNING, WALTER A., *Village and Open-Country Neighborhoods,* New York: D. Appleton-Century Company, 1931.

525. THOMLINSON, RALPH, *Demographic Problems,* Belmont, Calif.: Dickenson Pub. Co., Inc., 1967.

526. THOMPSON, EDGAR, T., "The Climatic Theory of the Plantation," *Agricultural History,* Vol. XV (1941).

527. THOMPSON, JAMES W., "East German Colonization in the Middle Ages," *Annual Report of the American Historical Association, 1915,* Washington: Government Printing Office, 1917.

528. THOMPSON, WARREN S., "Differentials in Fertility and Levels of Living in the Rural Population of the United States," *American Sociological Review,* Vol. XIII, No. 5 (October, 1948), pp. 516–534.

529. THOMPSON, WARREN S., *Ratio of Children to Women, 1920,* Census Monograph No. XI, Washington: Government Printing Office, 1931.

530. THOMPSON, WARREN S., and DAVID T. LEWIS, *Population Problems* (fifth ed.), New York: McGraw-Hill Book Company, 1965.

531. TITUS, CHARLES H., *Voting Behavior in the United States,* Publications of the University of California at Los Angeles in the Social Sciences No. V, 1935.

532. TITUS, CHARLES H., "Voting in California," *Southwestern Political and Social Science Quarterly,* Vols. VIII, IX, and X (1928–1929).

533. TÖNNIES, FERDINAND, *Gemeinschaft und Gesellschaft* (third ed.), Leipzig: Hans Bushe, 1935; translated as *Community and Society* by Charles P. Loomis, East Lansing: Michigan State University Press, 1957.

534. TREAT, PAYSON, J., *The National Land System, 1785–1820,* New York: E. B. Treat and Company, 1910.

535. TREAT, PAYSON, J., "Surveys of Land," *Cyclopedia of American Government,* New York: D. Appleton-Century Company, 1914.

536. TRUE, A. C., *A History of Agricultural Education in the United States— 1785–1925,* Department of Agriculture, Washington: Government Printing Office, 1929.

537. TRUESDELL, LEON E., *The Development of the Rural-Urban Classification in the United States: 1874–1949,* Bureau of the Census, Series P-23, No. 1, Washington: Government Printing Office, 1949.

538. TUMIN, MELVIN M., *Social Class and Social Change in Puerto Rico,* Princeton: Princeton University Press, 1961.

539. TUMIN, MELVIN, M., *Social Stratification*, Englewood Cliffs, N.J.: Prentice-Hall, Inc., 1967.

540. TURNER, FREDERICK J., *The Frontier in American History*, New York: Henry Holt & Company, 1921.

541. TYLOR, EDWARD B., "On the Origin of the Plough and Wheel-Carriage," *Journal of the Anthropological Institute of Great Britain and Ireland*, Vol. X (1881).

542. TYLOR, EDWARD B., *Primitive Culture*, London: Henry Holt & Company, 1871, 2 vols.

543. United Nations, Bureau of Social Affairs, *Social Progress through Community Development*, New York: United Nations, 1955.

544. United Nations, *Demographic Yearbook*, years 1948–1967, New York: United Nations, 1949–1968.

545. United Nations, Food and Agricultural Organization, *Agriculture in the Near East: Development and Outlook*, Rome: Food and Agricultural Organization, 1953.

546. United Nations, Food and Agricultural Organization, *Indicative World Plan for Agricultural Development, 1965–1985: Near East*, Rome: Food and Agricultural Organization, 1966.

547. United Nations, Food and Agricultural Organization and the International Labour Organization, *Progress in Land Reform: Third Report*, New York: United Nations, 1962.

548. United Nations, *Social Implications of Industrialization and Urbanization in Africa South of the Sahara*, Paris: UNESCO, 1956.

549. United Nations, *Studies of Selected Development Problems in Various Countries in the Middle East*, Beirut: United Nations Economic and Social Office, 1967.

550. United States Bureau of the Census, *Historical Statistics of the United States, Colonial Times to 1957*, Washington: Government Printing Office, 1960.

551. United States Bureau of the Census, *U.S. Census of Population: 1960, General Population Characteristics, United States Summary*, Final Report PC(1)-1B, Washington: Government Printing Office, 1961.

552. United States Bureau of the Census, *U.S. Census of Population: 1960, General Social and Economic Characteristics, United States Summary*, Final Report PC(1)-1C, Washington: Government Printing Office, 1962.

553. United States Bureau of the Census and the Agricultural Marketing Service, *Effect of Definition Changes on Size and Composition of the Rural-Farm Population, April 1960 and 1959*, Census-AMS Series P-27, No. 28, Washington: Government Printing Office, 1961.

554. United States Department of Agriculture, *After a Hundred Years, Yearbook of Agriculture, 1962*, Washington: Government Printing Office, 1962.

555. United States Department of Agriculture, *Changes in Agriculture in 26 Developing Nations, 1948–1963,* Washington: Government Printing Office, 1965.

556. United States Department of Agriculture, *Consumers All, Yearbook of Agriculture, 1965,* Washington: Government Printing Office, 1965.

557. United States Department of Agriculture, *Contract Farming and Vertical Integration in Agriculture,* Agricultural Information Bulletin No. 198, Washington: Government Printing Office, 1958.

558. United States Department of Agriculture, *Development of Agriculture's Human Resources: A Report on Low-Income Farmers,* Washington: Government Printing Office, 1955.

559. United States Department of Agriculture, *Farmers in a Changing World,* Yearbook of Agriculture, 1940, Washington: Government Printing Office, 1940.

560. United States Department of Agriculture, *Farmer's World, Yearbook of Agriculture, 1964,* Washington: Government Printing Office, 1964.

561. United States Department of Agriculture, *Land, Yearbook of Agriculture, 1958,* Washington: Government Printing Office, 1958.

562. United States Department of Agriculture, *Power to Produce, Yearbook of Agriculture, 1960,* Washington: Government Printing Office, 1960.

563. United States Department of Agriculture, *Rural Industrialization,* Agricultural Information Bulletin No. 252, Washington: Government Printing Office, 1961.

564. United States Department of Agriculture, *Science for Better Living, Yearbook of Agriculture, 1968,* Washington: Government Printing Office, 1968.

565. United States Department of Agriculture, *Science in Farming, Yearbook of Agriculture, 1943–47,* Washington: Government Printing Office, 1947.

566. United States Department of Health, Education and Welfare, *Vital Statistics of the United States: 1960,* Vol. II, *Mortality,* Part B, Section 9, Washington: Government Printing Office, 1961.

567. United States Department of Labor, *Negro Migration in 1916–17,* Washington: Government Printing Office, 1919.

568. VANCE, RUPERT B., *Farmers Without Land,* New York: Public Affairs Committee, 1937.

569. VANCE, RUPERT B., *How the Other Half is Housed,* Chapel Hill: University of North Carolina Press, 1936.

570. VANCE, RUPERT B., *Human Factors in Cotton Culture,* Chapel Hill: University of North Carolina Press, 1929.

571. VANCE, RUPERT B., *Human Factors of the South,* Chapel Hill: University of North Carolina Press, 1932.

572. VANCE, RUPERT B., and NADIA DANILEVSKY, *All These People,* Chapel Hill: University of North Carolina Press, 1945.

573. VANCE, RUPERT B., and NICHOLAS J. DEMERATH (eds.), *The Urban South*, Chapel Hill: University of North Carolina Press, 1954.

574. VIDICH, ARTHUR J., and JOSEPH BENSMAN, *Small Town in Mass Society*, Princeton: Princeton University Press, 1958.

575. VOGT, EVON Z., *Modern Homesteaders: The Life of a Twentieth Century Frontier Community*, Cambridge, Mass.: Harvard University Press, 1955.

576. WAGER, PAUL W. (ed.), *County Government Across the Nation*, Chapel Hill: University of North Carolina Press, 1950.

577. WAGLEY, CHARLES (ed.), *Race and Class in Rural Brazil*, Paris: UNESCO, 1952.

578. WALLACE, ALFRED R., *Travels on the Amazon*, London: Ward Lock & Co., 1911.

579. WARNE, FRANK J., *The Tide of Immigration*, New York: D. Appleton-Century Company, 1916.

580. WARNER, W. LLOYD, and PAUL S. LUNT, *The Status System of a Modern Community*, New Haven: Yale University Press, 1942.

581. WARNER, W. LLOYD, MARCHIA MEEKER, and KENNETH EELLS, *Social Class in America*, Chicago: Science Research Associates, 1949.

582. WARREN, G. HENRY, *Adam Was a Ploughman*, London: Eyre and Spottiswoode, 1947.

583. WARREN, ROLAND L., "The 'Common Land' in Southwest Germany: The Behavior of a Prefeudal Institution under the Strains of Industrialization," *Rural Sociology*, Vol. 22, No. 3 (September, 1957), pp. 271–273.

584. WAYLAND, SLOAN R., *Social Patterns of Farming*, New York: Columbia University Seminar on Rural Life, 1956.

585. WAYLAND, SLOAN R., EDMUND deS. BRUNNER, and FRANK W. CYR (eds.), *Farmers of the Future: Prospects and Policies for Establishing a New Generation on the Land*, New York: Columbia University Press, 1953.

586. WEBER, MAX, *The Protestant Ethic and the Spirit of Capitalism* (trans. by Talcott Parsons), New York: Charles Scribner's Sons, 1958.

587. WEEDEN, WILLIAM B., *Economic and Social History of New England, 1620–1789*, Boston: Houghton Mifflin Company, 1891.

588. WEITZ, RAANAN (ed.), *Rural Planning in Developing Countries*, London: Routledge and Kegan Paul, 1965.

589. WEST, JAMES, *Plainville, U.S.A.*, New York: Columbia University Press, 1945.

590. WESTON, GEORGE M., *Progress of Slavery in the United States*, Washington, Privately Printed, 1857.

591. WHARTON, CLIFTON, R., JR., "The Green Revolution: Cornucopia or Pandora's Box?" *Foreign Affairs,* Vol. 47, No. 3 (1960), pp. 464–476.

592. WHARTON, CLIFTON R., JR. (ed.), *Subsistence Agriculture and Economic Development,* Chicago: Aldine Publishing Company, 1969.

593. WHETTEN, NATHAN L., *Guatemala: The Land and the People,* New Haven: Yale University Press, 1961.

594. WHETTEN, NATHAN L., *Rural Mexico,* Chicago: The University of Chicago Press, 1948.

595. WHETTEN, NATHAN L., *Studies of Suburbanization in Connecticut, Three: Wilton: A Rural Town in Metropolitan New York,* Connecticut AES Bulletin No. 230, Storrs: University of Connecticut, 1939.

596. WHETTEN, NATHAN, L., "Suburbanization as a Field for Sociological Research," *Rural Sociology,* Vol. 14, No. 4 (December, 1951), pp. 319–330.

597. WHETTEN, NATHAN L., and ROBERT G. BURNIGHT, "Internal Migration in Mexico," *Rural Sociology,* Vol. 21, No. 2 (June, 1956), pp. 140–151.

598. WHETTEN, NATHAN L., and E. C. DEVEREAUX, JR., *Studies of Suburbanization in Connecticut, One: Windsor: A Highly Developed Agricultural Area,* Connecticut AES Bulletin No. 212, Storrs: University of Connecticut, 1936.

599. WHETTEN, NATHAN L., and R. F. FIELD, *Studies of Suburbanization in Connecticut, Two: Norwich: An Industrial Part-Time Farming Area,* Connecticut AES Bulletin No. 226, Storrs: University of Connecticut, 1938.

600. WHITE, MAX R., DOUGLAS ENSMINGER, and CECIL L. GREGORY, *Rich Land—Poor People,* Farm Security Administration Report No. I, Indianapolis: Farm Security Administration, 1938.

601. WILKENING, EUGENE A., "Some Perspectives on Change in Rural Societies," *Rural Sociology,* Vol. 29, No. 1 (March, 1964), pp. 1–17.

602. WILKENING, EUGENE A., "Techniques of Assessing Farm Family Values," *Rural Sociology,* Vol. 19, No. 1 (March, 1954), pp. 39–49.

603. WILKENING, EUGENE A., and RALPH K. HUITT, "Political Participation among Farmers as Related to Socioeconomic Status and Perception of the Political Process," *Rural Sociology,* Vol. 26, No. 4 (December, 1961), pp. 395–408.

604. WILLCOX, WALTER F., *Introduction to the Vital Statistics of the United States, 1900 to 1930,* Washington: Government Printing Office, 1933.

605. WILLCOX, WALTER F. (ed.), *Natural and Political Observations Made upon the Bills of Mortality by John Graunt,* Baltimore: Johns Hopkins University Press, 1939.

606. WILLIAMS, B. O., "Mobility and Farm Tenancy," *Journal of Land and Public Utility Economics,* Vol. XIV (1938).

607. WILLIAMS, JAMES M., *The Expansion of Rural Life,* New York: Alfred A. Knopf, 1926.

608. WILLIAMS, JAMES M., *Our Rural Heritage,* New York: Alfred A. Knopf, 1925.

609. WILLIAMSON, ROBERT C., "Social Class and Orientation to Change: Some Relevant Variables in a Bogotá Sample," *Social Forces,* Vol. 46, No. 3 (March, 1968), pp. 317–328.

610. WILLIS, J. C., *Agriculture in the Tropics,* Cambridge: The University Press, 1909.

611. WILSON, WARREN H., *The Farmer's Church,* New York: D. Appleton-Century Company, 1925.

612. WOOD, WILLIAM, *A Sussex Farmer,* London: Jonathan Cape, 1938.

613. WOOFTER, T. J., JR., and others, *Landlord and Tenant on the Cotton Plantation,* Works Progress Administration, Washington: Government Printing Office, 1936.

614. YINGER, J. MILTON, *Religion, Society, and the Individual,* New York: The Macmillan Company, 1957.

615. YINGER, J. MILTON, *Sociology Looks at Religion,* New York: The Macmillan Company, 1963.

616. YOUMANS, E. GRANT, *The Educational Attainment and Future Plans of Rural Youths,* Kentucky AES Bulletin No. 664, Lexington: University of Kentucky, 1959.

617. YOUNG, JAMES N., and SELZ C. MAYO, "Manifest and Latent Participators in a Rural Community Action Program," *Social Forces,* Vol. 38, No. 2 (December, 1959), pp. 140–145.

618. ZETTERBERG, HANS L. (ed.), *Sociology in the United States of America,* Paris: UNESCO, 1955.

619. ZIMMERMAN, CARLE C., *The Changing Community,* New York: Harper & Brothers, 1938.

620. ZIMMERMAN, CARLE C., *Consumption and Standards of Living,* New York: D. Van Nostrand Company, 1936.

621. ZIMMERMAN, CARLE C., *Family and Civilization,* New York: Harper & Brothers, 1947.

622. ZIMMERMAN, CARLE C., *Patterns of Social Change,* Washington: Public Affairs Press, 1956.

623. ZIMMERMAN, CARLE C., and SETH RUSSELL (eds.), *Symposium on the Great Plains of North America,* Fargo: North Dakota State University Institute for Regional Studies, 1968.

624. ZIMMERMAN, CARLE C., and CARL C. TAYLOR, *Rural Organization: A Study of Primary Groups in Wake County, North Carolina,* North Carolina AES Bulletin No. 245, Raleigh: North Carolina State College, 1922.

625. ZNANIECKI, FLORIAN, *Cultural Sciences,* Urbana: University of Illinois Press, 1953.

626. ZOPF, PAUL E., JR., *North Carolina: A Demographic Profile,* Chapel Hill: University of North Carolina Population Center, 1967.

LIST of FIGURES

FIGURE

FIGURE

LIST of TABLES

AUTHOR and SOURCE INDEX

SUBJECT INDEX